PROPHETS & SAGES

AN ILLUSTRATED GUIDE TO UNDERGROUND AND PROGRESSIVE ROCK 1967-1975

MARK POWELL

First published in Great Britain in 2010 by Cherry Red Books
(a division of Cherry Red Records Ltd.), Power Road Studios, 114 Power Road, Chiswick, London W4 5PY

Copyright Mark Powell © 2010

ISBN: 978 1 901447 76 7

Design by: Becky Stewart
Cover Design: Phil Smee
Edited by: Michael Heatley

Produced for Cherry Red Books by Richard Anderson

Printed in the UK by Ashford Colour Press

Becky Stewart would like to thank Phil Smee, Jon Richards, Jon Hiseman, Barry Plummer and Chris Hewitt for their help with picture contribution and extra special thanks to Phil Chamberlain who scoured his NME and Record Mirror collection for the featured artists providing many of the visuals herein.

CONTENTS

1971

1972

1973

1974

TWENTY ADDITIONAL LESSER-KNOWN GREATS FOR YOUR COLLECTION

A FURTHER TEN UK ALBUM-CHARTING GREATS THAT NEED LITTLE INTRODUCTION

TEN GREAT PROGRESSIVE AND UNDERGROUND ROCK SINGLES

PREFACE

The rise of 'progressive' and 'underground' music in the late Sixties and Seventies was a phenomenon that saw record companies shift millions of LPs to an eager audience for whom the album sleeve was almost as important as the music. Artwork was designed to reflect the atmosphere created by the music and was, more often than not, presented in gatefold sleeves with lyrics printed for the enlightenment of thousands of long-haired males in bedrooms and student bedsits up and down the land.

The idea that rock music could be taken and presented seriously began with the Beatles' experiments on their albums 'Revolver' in August 1966 and continued with the cycle of songs that was 'Sgt Pepper's Lonely Hearts Club Band' in June the following year. With many talented musicians tiring of playing music steeped in American culture, a uniquely British, and latterly European, art form was born.

Justin Hayward of the Moody Blues summed up the shift: 'I was from a lower middle-class household in Swindon. Although I was exposed to music by American artists and the blues, I felt that it was dishonest to try and play music that spoke of a culture and a condition of living that I hadn't experienced. I hadn't worked in the cotton fields of the South and felt I should write songs that reflected my thoughts of an English way of life.' It was this desire by musicians to create a statement that was uniquely European, as opposed to American, in influence that was one of the catalysts in the birth of progressive rock.

When describing the impetus behind the formation of King Crimson, Greg Lake told me: 'Looking back I think we set out to make original music. We set out to be different. Our musical roots were European rather than American. I think a lot of the rock music up until then had roots in American culture and our music stood out as a result.' It was this desire to be different that spurred on those musicians who fronted the underground and progressive movement in the UK and in Europe. Indeed, it is the results that feature in the pages of this book.

At first glance, the stylistic difference between groups as Barclay James Harvest and rock experimentalists Can is vast. A deeper look would reveal that both acts often sat (and continue to sit) alongside each other in a large number of record collections. Progressive groups drew upon many diverse sources of inspiration; jazz, blues, classical music, folk, rock and avant-garde electronic music. It is the broad church that makes of the music of the progressive and underground era so fascinating and enduring. It was also this sense of pushing boundaries and viewing progressive rock albums as works of art that was attractive to the sizeable audience of hippies, students and followers of the emerging counterculture of the late Sixties and early Seventies.

More surprisingly, and much to the chagrin of certain music critics, the music of the era as set out in these pages continues to have a sizeable following throughout the world and continues to have a major impact.

In my travels to Europe, the United States, Japan and South America, I have encountered many aficionados of the music this book celebrates, a significant number of whom are too young to have witnessed many of the artists listed perform. Despite the critical derision of decades past, it seems that this music will always have its followers, defenders and champions.

Finally, the selections made in this book are purely my own choice, in part inspired as an answer to a question I am frequently asked: 'What are your favourite albums of the genre?' I offer this selection as my answer. My choices deliberately omit some of the most widely known albums by artists such as Pink Floyd, Genesis and Yes because much has been written about them already. Most followers of psychedelic, underground and progressive music are aware of key albums such as 'Dark Side Of The Moon', 'The Lamb Lies Down On Broadway' or 'Tales From Topographic Oceans'.

Where I have included material by these artists, it is to draw attention to their aspects of their work that the casual observer may overlook. Indeed, every album by Genesis, King Crimson, Yes, and Pink Floyd issued during the years covered by this book is essential listening. It is also arguable that Beatles albums such as 'Revolver', 'Sgt Pepper's Lonely Hearts Club Band', 'Magical Mystery Tour' (albeit originally issued as an album in the US only), 'The Beatles' (aka the 'White Album') and 'Abbey Road' count as 'proto-progressive'. While it is doubtful that any of the music discussed in this book would have existed without the Beatles' groundbreaking work, they could hardly be described as 'underground', even though their albums were championed by the UK underground press.

Readers may note that the music featured in the book is of a European (mainly British) origin. During the period covered in these pages, the progressive movement was almost entirely of European origin, a fact this publication reflects. There were, of course, exceptions to this rule. Both Todd Rundgren and Frank Zappa were inventive American artists whose music remains awe-inspiring and inspirational in its originality. I strongly urge the curious to explore both artists' incredibly diverse repertoire without delay.

While many readers will debate the albums listed here, this book is intended to be an overview of albums that will always remain special to me. I hope that if something is unfamiliar to you, you will find much worthy of further investigation.

I would like to thank all at Cherry Red Books for making this publication possible, in particular Adam Velasco and Richard Anderson. Phil Smee and Becky Stewart offered assistance beyond the call of duty, and Jon Wright and Keith and Monika Domone assisted with providing facts and information on a few entries. I am also hugely indebted to my wife Vicky for her proofreading talents and patience. This book is also a 'thank you' to the team at Plastic Wax 25 years ago, particularly Alasdair, without whom I would never have been exposed to such wonderful music which became such a part of my life. What a journey it started!

MARK POWELL 2010

PROPHETS & SAGES

AN ILLUSTRATED GUIDE TO UNDERGROUND AND PROGRESSIVE ROCK 1967-1975

MARK POWELL

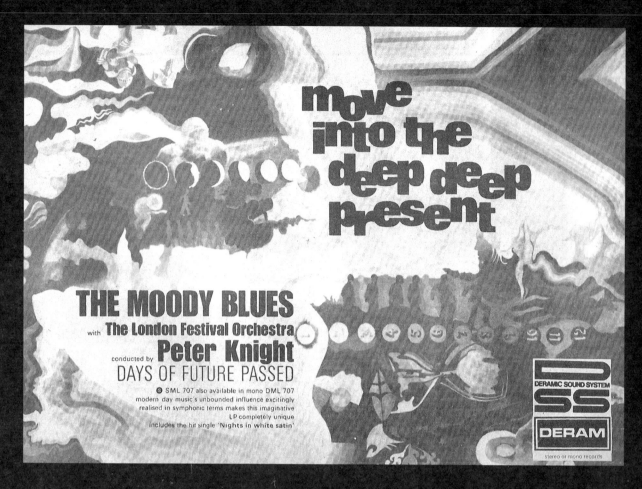

"A very ambitious record. Since "Sgt. Pepper", groups have realised what **CAN** be done and the Moody's have been lucky enough to be involved in an LP which could give them the reputation for which they have long been searching. Musically magnificent, and very interesting... it may well be over the heads of some pop buyers, but this is not through any pretentiousness. It could be a big chart LP soon. ★★★★

Record Mirror 2/12/67

'I'm just beginning to see. Now I'm on my way...'

THE MOODY BLUES 'Days Of Future Passed'

First released as Deram SML707 in November 1967
Available on CD as Deram 983215-0
(2CD deluxe edition with 19 bonus tracks and 5.1 Surround Sound Mix)
and Deram 530663-1 (single CD edition with 10 bonus tracks)
Highest UK chart position: Number 27

The Day Begins
Dawn: Dawn Is A Feeling
The Morning: Another Morning
Lunch Break: Peak Hour
The Afternoon: Forever Afternoon (Tuesday?)
Evening: The Sun Set/Twilight Time
The Night: Nights in White Satin

Graeme Edge	**Drums, Vocals**
Justin Hayward	**Guitars, Vocals**
John Lodge	**Bass, Vocals**
Mike Pinder	**Mellotron, Keyboards, Guitar, Vocals**
Ray Thomas	**Flute, Harmonica, Vocals**

With the London Festival Orchestra conducted by Peter Knight
Recorded at Decca Studios, West Hampstead, London
Produced by Tony Clarke
Engineered by Derek Varnals

Executive producer Hugh Mendl

In August 1966 British popular music changed forever. The Beatles, whose music had spearheaded a momentous explosion of creativity by other groups following in their wake, had completed their masterpiece 'Revolver' which heralded a new era of studio experimentation, as evidenced on supremely creative works such as 'Eleanor Rigby', 'She Said, She Said', 'Love You To' and 'Tomorrow Never Knows'. 'Revolver' also saw the Beatles' career as a live act draw to a close with a concert at Candlestick Park in San Francisco, leaving them free to concentrate on pushing the boundaries of recording still further with the single 'Penny Lane' b/w 'Strawberry Fields Forever' and culminating in the groundbreaking 'Sgt Pepper's Lonely Hearts Club Band' album.

These exceptional achievements and the general musical sea change did not go unnoticed within the British music industry, with many other artists eager to push the boundaries of popular music into previously uncharted territory. Artists with a background of rhythm and blues and beat music soon began to undergo a rapid stylistic change. The Moody Blues were no exception and, like the Beatles, their music would be a huge influence on a generation of musicians who would pioneer early progressive rock.

The band evolved out of the healthy Birmingham R&B scene of the early Sixties where the line-up of Ray Thomas (harmonica, percussion, vocals), Mike Pinder (keyboards, vocals), Graeme Edge (drums), Denny Laine (guitar, vocals) and Clint Warwick (bass, vocals) evolved into one of the most popular local attractions. Formed in March 1964, the group had signed to Decca Records and had scored a British Number 1 hit with their cover of Bessie Banks' 'Go Now'. With the single having such a high-profile champion as Paul McCartney (who enthusiastically sang its praises on the Beatles' 1965 tour), the record scaled the charts throughout the world, including the US where it reached Number 10 on the Billboard chart.

Despite such an auspicious start to their career, by the late summer of 1966 the group were at a crossroads. Follow up singles failed to match the success of 'Go Now' in Britain, and although the Moody Blues were still a popular live attraction in Europe, their fortunes were at a low ebb. Denny Laine and Clint Warwick had both departed the group and new members Justin Hayward (guitar, vocals) and John Lodge (bass, vocals) were recruited.

Lodge had performed with Ray Thomas in the band El Riot and the Rebels prior to forsaking a career in music to study metallurgy. Upon qualifying, he resumed his musical acquaintance with Thomas and accepted a role in the Moody Blues. Swindon-born Justin Hayward had previously performed with British rock'n'roll pioneer Marty Wilde and recorded two solo singles for EMI's Parlophone label. His application to join Eric Burdon and the Animals had arrived too late for consideration, but Burdon passed his details on to Mike Pinder with an enthusiastic recommendation.

Obliged to fulfil a series of cabaret dates, the Moody Blues embarked on a potentially soul-destroying short tour of clubs in England, still performing their R&B-based set. The tour had the effect of inspiring the band to abandon their R&B material and to strive to create an unique sound of their own. 'We had been playing music that wasn't suited to our characters,' Justin Hayward later recalled. 'We were lower middle-class English boys singing about life in the deep south of the US and it just wasn't honest. As soon as we began to express our own feelings and to create our own music our fortunes changed.'

The most dramatic change in the sound and musical fortunes of the Moody Blues came with the purchase of a Mellotron. This keyboard had been developed by a West Midlands based company, Streetly Electronics, in the early Sixties and was based on a similar instrument, the Chamberlin. Both were unique in that under each key was a loop of tape featuring a recording of a real instrument such as a violin or flute. Tapes could be pre-selected to provide orchestral or choral sounds and each time a key was depressed a playback head would engage with a tape loop to provide the desired sound. While plying his trade as a semi-professional musician, Mike Pinder had worked at Streetly Electronics and, aware of the Mellotron's potential, was keen to acquire one.

Following the UK club shows Mike received a phone call that would change the sound of the Moody Blues. 'Les Bradley of Streetly Electronics gave me a call and told me that he had found me a suitable instrument at the Dunlop tyre factory social club. I went to see it and just had to have it. At three hundred pounds, instead of the usual three thousand pounds, the instrument was a steal.' It can be argued that Pinder's experimental use of the Mellotron would be responsible for the instrument becoming a staple ingredient of progressive rock over the next decade.

With a new line-up established, a series of concerts in Belgium were arranged and, in October 1966, the band relocated themselves in the town of Mucron, which served as a base while they wrote a host of new material (which utilised the Mellotron to great effect) and embarked on a series of concerts. The band's shows time generally consisted of two 45-minute sets. The first was the band's old act, including 'Go Now', while the second incorporated newly written material that featured the Mellotron and the flute-playing of Ray Thomas. A series of concerts in Paris at the end of 1966 supporting Tom Jones was the first indication that the Moody Blues were on the right path when the self-penned compositions won greater ovations than the older covers.

Upon returning to England, the Moody Blues had contractual obligations to fulfil with Decca Records, being £5,000 in debt to the record company. Decca appointed staff producer Tony Clarke to supervise recording a new single and, on 30 March 1967, they entered Decca Studios in West Hampstead to record their first session with a new line-up. The resulting single 'Fly Me High' b/w 'Really Haven't Got The Time' was released in May. Although the single failed to chart, it did gain much airplay and, sufficiently enthused, Decca urged a series of follow-up recording sessions in late May and June, although the symphonic leanings of the band were still to surface.

On 17 July 1967 the Moody Blues recorded 'Love And Beauty', their first use of a Mellotron on a session. The band had left their old R&B influences behind them and were now producing music of a truly unique and original style. 'Love And Beauty' b/w 'Leave This Man Alone' was released as Decca F12670 in September 1967. To promote its release, a BBC session recorded for the Easybeat programme also included a John Lodge composition, 'Peak Hour', taken from a song cycle the band had been performing and developing in concert for some months. It was a taste of things to come.

In September 1966, Decca had established the Deram label with the intention of establishing an imprint for the release of innovative popular music. The company were also eager to promote a new method of stereo recording with greater channel separation known as the 'Deramic Sound System'. Decca A&R boss Hugh Mendl approached the Moody Blues in September 1967 with the idea of recording a rock version of Dvorak's Ninth Symphony with an orchestra, as a means to promote the new system. The band agreed on the condition that they would be given the freedom to record with producer Tony Clarke and engineer Derek Varnals without interference from Decca executives. Thus, in October 1967, the Moody Blues returned to West Hampstead.

Once ensconced behind the closed doors of the recording studio, they lost no time in persuading Clarke and orchestral arranger Peter Knight to abandon the idea of reworking Dvorak and to record their carefully crafted cycle of songs instead. Knight had been particularly keen to orchestrate the Moodies' recent compositions and it took him just three weeks to write orchestral arrangements for the album. This was recorded and mixed at a frantic pace utilising two studios as band and orchestra recorded

their parts separately. All the material on the album that would become known as 'Days Of Future Passed' (a title conceived by Decca and not the band themselves) had been extensively performed on the road. As a result, the standard of performance was consistently high and the band exuded a confidence gained by familiarity with the music.

The songs accumulated were arranged to form the loose concept of a working day. The album began with an opening orchestral arrangement by Peter Knight, 'The Day Begins', which made melodic references to all the songs and included a Graeme Edge poem. This led into the first song, 'Dawn Is A Feeling', composed by Mike Pinder and featuring the magical combination of lead vocals from Mike and Justin Hayward.

'Another Morning' was a whimsical Ray Thomas piece in keeping with the mood of the summer of 1967, reflecting on the world as perceived by a child. John Lodge's strident 'Peak Hour' had been an early stage favourite in the band's revised live set and had first been recorded as part of a September 1967 session for BBC radio. Justin Hayward's 'Tuesday Afternoon' opened the 'Afternoon' section of the album's second side. Credited as 'Forever Afternoon (Tuesday?)', the song was considered a potential single before being set aside in favour of 'Nights In White Satin'. In America, the situation was later reversed when 'Tuesday Afternoon' was released with 'Another Morning' in July 1968, reaching Number 24 on the Billboard chart. This segued into John Lodge's powerful '(Evening) Time To Get Away' which demonstrated the Moody Blues' splendid use of harmony perfected in their days as an R&B-influenced group.

Mike Pinder's 'The Sun Set', an Indian-influenced piece that demonstrated his ability at manipulating a Mellotron, began the 'Evening' section and led into the urgent Ray Thomas' psychedelic opus 'Twilight Time', another powerful on-stage number. The album's closing section was its tour de force. The superb 'Nights In White Satin', an evocative and melancholic song which demonstrated the band's grasp of dynamics, had been written at the beginning of 1967 by Justin Hayward.

First recorded for a BBC radio session in April that year, the song became regarded as one of the crowning moments of the Moody Blues' career and that of its writer. Graeme Edge later recalled: 'I think the first indication that "Nights" was something extraordinary was when we recorded the song for the BBC. After recording a version of the song for Decca we all felt we had created something marvellous. It was quite an emotional experience to hear the finished mix for the first time.' Indeed, the innovative use of double-tracked Mellotron plus a memorable flute solo and orchestral arrangement resulted in a fusion of rock, folk and classical music that had previously been unheard of. The influence of 'Nights In White Satin' on other musicians would prove to be far-reaching over the ensuing years.

The 'Evening' section closed with the Graeme Edge poem 'Late Lament'. 'I'd written both those pieces of verse because the "Morning" section appeared rather empty when we first heard it,' reflected Edge. 'The latter part of the poem seemed a perfect end to the record. I'd originally written the words as lyrics for someone else to put some music to, but poetry has a rhythmic structure that makes it difficult to turn into a song so Tony Clarke suggested recording it as a spoken-word piece.'

A playback session was arranged at the recording centre for Decca executives to hear the results of much time, effort and money. The assembled Decca executives, band members, wives and associates listened to the album in a dimly lit recording studio. John Lodge later recalled: 'After that playback session finished and the studio lights came on once more the smiles on our faces said it all. We knew we had been right to stick to our principles and record our own music.' However, faced with something that bore no resemblance to a rock-influenced recording of a Dvorak symphony, reaction among the executives was mixed. Decca's managing director was less than impressed, declaring that 'You can't dance to it; you can't play this at a party.' However, thanks to the championing of Hugh Mendl and the head of London Records in the US, Walt McGuire, 'Days Of Future Passed' was released in Britain on 11 November 1967 as Deram SML707. It was preceded a day earlier by the release of 'Nights In White Satin' b/w 'Cities' as Deram DM161.

The evocative mixture of symphonic rock music, orchestral arrangements and spoken word struck an immediate chord with the music-buying public in Britain, the album gaining extensive airplay on the newly established BBC Radio 1. Both album and single entered the UK chart on 27 December 1967, the former reaching Number 27. 'Nights In White Satin' reached a peak of Number 19, although this classic song would return to the UK Top 20 on two further occasions over the next dozen years. Both album and single made a huge commercial impact throughout Europe.

In the US the album's impact would prove even greater, although over a longer period of time. 'Days of Future Passed' entered the Billboard chart on 4 May 1968 and spent an incredible 103 weeks on the listings over the next five years, eventually attaining a peak of Number 3 in 1972. In August that year, 'Nights In White Satin' was belatedly released as a single in the US and became a Number 2 hit. The impact of 'Days Of Future Passed' was to prove both immense and long-lasting. Its influence on musicians destined to take their place in rock's hierarchy such as Genesis and King Crimson is undeniable, while its impact on the world's listening public is incalculable. Viewed over 35 years later, the album is a remarkable achievement and can be seen as the blueprint for the progressive and symphonic rock revolution that was to follow.

THE NICE
'The Thoughts Of Emerlist Davjack'

First released as Immediate Records
IMLP016 (mono)/IMPS016 (stereo) in December 1967
Available on CD as Sanctuary Records CMQDD790
(2CD deluxe edition with 18 bonus tracks)
Highest UK chart position: N/A

Flower King Of Flies
The Thoughts Of Emerlist Davjack
Bonnie K
Rondo
War And Peace
Tantalising Maggie
Dawn
The Cry Of Eugene

Keith Emerson	**Organ, Piano, Harpsichord, Vocals**
Lee Jackson	**Bass Guitar, Vocals, Tympani**
David O'List	**Guitar, Trumpet, Flute, Vocals**
Brian Davison	**Drums, Tubular Bells, Tympani**

Recorded at Olympic Studios, Barnes, London
Arranged and Produced by Emerlist Davjack (the Nice)
Engineered by Glyn Johns

In May 1967 a group exploded onto the British music scene that would play a significant part in pioneering a new genre of rock music while creating some of the most original and exciting works of the ensuing three years. The Nice would go down in history as one of the most exciting live acts of their age and as the creators of a series of excellent albums that would fuse the worlds of rock and classical music, taking in elements of jazz, psychedelia and rhythm and blues on the way, effectively spawning the genre of progressive rock in their wake with the release of their debut album 'The Thoughts Of Emerlist Davjack' in December 1967. In Keith Emerson, the Nice had one of the most gifted keyboard players of their generation, whose talent combined with a rhythm section of Lee Jackson (bass, vocals) and Brian 'Blinky' Davison (drums) to make a music powerhouse par excellence. Guitarist Davy O'List's innovative playing would also grace their music for the first year of their existence.

Like many of their contemporaries, the Nice was born out of a series of groups that emerged during the British rhythm and blues boom of the mid-Sixties and the musical activities and ambitions of Keith Emerson. 'I began my life as a musician in the town of Worthing in Sussex,' he would later recall. 'Firstly I was a member of the Worthing Youth Swing Orchestra, then I had a jazz group, the Keith Emerson Trio, which led to me joining a blues band called John Brown's Bodies.

'I used to jam a lot in Brighton with a very good drummer called Brian Walkley who played in a blues band that were starting to make waves in London called Gary Farr and the T-Bones. Brian encouraged me to join the T-Bones and that became my first full-time professional band. It was very much blues-based as they backed people such as Muddy Waters and Sonny Boy Williamson when they came to the UK.' It was while a member of the T-Bones that Emerson first used the Hammond organ, a keyboard with which he would forever be associated.

Frustrated by the limitations of the T-Bones, Emerson departed to join the VIPs, but his time with the outfit was short-lived. 'I'd worked with Lee Jackson, who was a bass guitarist, in the T-Bones and we both loved the same music, both jazz and classical. I'd always said to Lee that if I ever had the opportunity I would like to work with him again. That opportunity arose when the VIPs weren't doing too well and a friend of mine who was a road manager approached me and mentioned that he was working for an American artist who had been a member of the Ikettes and had signed to Immediate Records, a label which had been set up by Andrew Loog Oldham, who was then the manager of the Rolling Stones.'

The singer in question was PP Arnold who had recently recorded a cover version of Cat Stevens' 'The First Cut Is The Deepest' for Immediate. Oldham told Emerson to assemble a band to enable her to tour, and he recruited Jackson on bass and vocals, Davy O'List (previously with the Attack) on guitar and Ian Hague on drums. With little time for rehearsals this new band set off on tour with Arnold.

The singer suggested changing the name of the band from the Naz to the Nice and also proved to be an unwitting catalyst in shaping their future success and identity. 'She suggested we ought to warm up the audience at her shows by playing for half an hour before she came on to perform her own set,' recalled Keith. 'I asked her what she wanted us to play during our part of the show and she replied, "Whatever you want." At that point it gave us the opportunity to try some original material in front of an audience.'

The opening sets by the Nice began to attract them a loyal following in their own right and also gained column inches in the UK music press. The big break came at the Windsor Jazz and Blues Festival in August when the Nice were allotted their own set and were hailed as one of the best bands of the event. By this time Ian Hague had been replaced on drums by Brian 'Blinky' Davison.

' During the afternoon some bands played in a large marquee that had been set up,' Keith Emerson later reflected. 'Our road manager decided to set off a smoke bomb outside the marquee which attracted a lot of people to the entrance to see what was going on. When they heard us play they all came into the tent and it soon filled up. We went to town during our set and as a result of this we were offered a residency at the Marquee Club in London…gold dust in those days.'

The Windsor Festival also led to a contract with Immediate Records and, within weeks, the Nice were starting work on their debut album at Olympic Studios. The material recorded was drawn from pieces devised during their opening sets for PP Arnold. Pieces such as 'Flower King Of Flies' and 'The Thoughts Of Emerlist Davjack' were psychedelic in approach, but the epics 'Dawn' (with its sinister Keith Emerson recital) and 'War And Peace' fused psychedelic influences with classical music. The album closer, 'The Cry Of Eugene', was another creative advance, with Davy O'List's guitar playing proving to be particularly imaginative. The first fruits of these recording sessions appeared in November 1967 with the release of the single 'The Thoughts Of Emerlist Davjack' b/w 'Azrael (Angel Of Death)'.

In hindsight, the musical style of the Nice was considerably ahead of many of their contemporaries, and the failure of the single to chart in the UK was due to it being unfriendly to daytime radio. At this point the band embarked on a package tour of

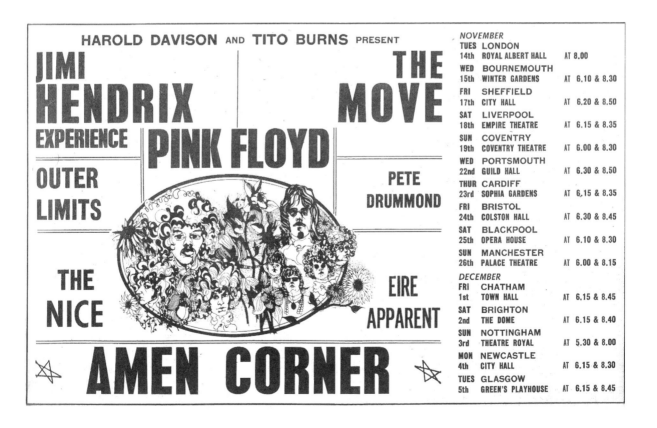

HAROLD DAVISON AND TITO BURNS PRESENT

JIMI HENDRIX EXPERIENCE

THE MOVE

PINK FLOYD

OUTER LIMITS

PETE DRUMMOND

THE NICE

EIRE APPARENT

AMEN CORNER

NOVEMBER		
TUES 14th	LONDON ROYAL ALBERT HALL	AT 8.00
WED 15th	BOURNEMOUTH WINTER GARDENS	AT 6.10 & 8.30
FRI 17th	SHEFFIELD CITY HALL	AT 6.20 & 8.50
SAT 18th	LIVERPOOL EMPIRE THEATRE	AT 6.15 & 8.35
SUN 19th	COVENTRY COVENTRY THEATRE	AT 6.00 & 8.30
WED 22nd	PORTSMOUTH GUILD HALL	AT 6.30 & 8.50
THUR 23rd	CARDIFF SOPHIA GARDENS	AT 6.15 & 8.35
FRI 24th	BRISTOL COLSTON HALL	AT 6.30 & 8.45
SAT 25th	BLACKPOOL OPERA HOUSE	AT 6.10 & 8.30
SUN 26th	MANCHESTER PALACE THEATRE	AT 6.00 & 8.15
DECEMBER		
FRI 1st	CHATHAM TOWN HALL	AT 6.15 & 8.45
SAT 2nd	BRIGHTON THE DOME	AT 6.15 & 8.40
SUN 3rd	NOTTINGHAM THEATRE ROYAL	AT 5.30 & 8.00
MON 4th	NEWCASTLE CITY HALL	AT 6.15 & 8.30
TUES 5th	GLASGOW GREEN'S PLAYHOUSE	AT 6.15 & 8.45

the UK playing alongside the Move, the Jimi Hendrix Experience and Pink Floyd. The tour brought the Nice even wider exposure (thanks in part to Davy O'List deputising for an ailing Syd Barrett in Pink Floyd's set on more than one show). The album 'The Thoughts Of Emerlist Davjack' appeared in December 1967, and although it failed to chart, enjoyed much praise from the emerging UK underground press.

A US tour in January and February 1968 saw the band enjoy an enthusiastic reaction from American audiences, but the tour also led to Davy O'List sampling LSD for the first time, leading to the guitarist flirting with the drug and increasingly erratic performances on stage. By the time the Nice returned to England and were ensconced in the confines of the recording studio once more, the trio of Emerson, Jackson and Davison had resolved to dismiss O'List.

The Nice entered a new phase of their career which would see them delve further into the world of classical music, enjoy both singles chart success (with 'America' b/w 'Diamond Hard Blue Apples Of The Moon' in July 1968) and a string of chart albums, beginning with 'Ars Longa Vita Brevis' in November 1968, that would influence a host of new progressive groups in their wake. Although rudimentary in places, 'The Thoughts Of Emerlist Davjack' remains the blueprint the Nice laid down for others to follow and it remains a delight over four decades from its release.

THE NICE

THE NICE—a possible hit with their first solo release.

Pat Arnold's backing group with a deep-thinking number, framed in a startling backing of organ, celeste, clavioline, strings, walloping beat and incredible tempo changes. Who's Emerlist Davjack? Well, he (she or it) wrote it – and it's good!

NME 22/11/67

'Heaven's rain falls upon the faces of the children who look skywards'

THE CRAZY WORLD OF ARTHUR BROWN
'The Crazy World Of Arthur Brown'

First released as Track Records 612005 (mono)/613005 (stereo) in June 1968
Highest UK chart position: Number 2
Available on CD as Esoteric Recordings ECLEC22178

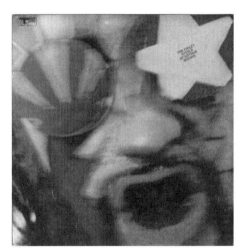

Prelude – Nightmare
Fanfare – Fire Poem
Fire
Come and Buy
Time/Confusion
I Put a Spell On You
Spontaneous Apple Creation
Rest Cure
I've Got Money
Child of My Kingdom

Arthur Brown	**Lead Vocals**
Vincent Crane	**Organ, Piano**
Drachen Theaker	**Drums, Percussion**
Nick Greenwood	**Bass Guitar**
With	
Pete Townshend	**Bass Guitar**

Orchestral arrangements by Vincent Crane
Recorded at IBC Studios, London
Produced by Kit Lambert
Associate producer Pete Townshend

Arthur Brown remains one of the most charismatic and colourful artists to emerge on the psychedelic rock scene of the late Sixties. With his first band, the Crazy World of Arthur Brown, he found himself at the forefront of music that was groundbreaking, entertaining and bizarre, with his live performances likened by serious music critics as being the psychedelic equivalent of the medieval English mummer's plays.

Born in Whitby, Yorkshire in 1944, Brown relocated to South Wales when he was 11 years old, performing in local choirs throughout his teenage years. Arthur's first steps on the road to rock infamy came in 1965 with his recording debut with the Black Diamonds, a Reading-based student R&B group who recorded a flexidisc single in aid of the local university rag week. Brown's first serious outfit was the Arthur Brown Set, another rhythm and blues-influenced group who performed in the London area.

In early 1966 Arthur moved to Paris, spending nearly a year in the city performing on the club circuit and developing both his amazing vocal technique and theatrical performing style.

While in Paris he also contributed, albeit without credit, to the soundtrack of Roger Vadim's film La Curée. Released in the US and Britain under the title The Game Is Over, the film starred Jane Fonda and Peter McEnery and spawned a rare soundtrack album released by Atco Records in the US. Soon after this Brown returned to England, later recalling: 'I had to leave France rather quickly, because my band had set fire to a club owned by the Mafia – not a sensible move. So I found myself in West Kensington. As luck would have it, the landlady of my lodgings had a daughter who, at the time, was going out with a certain keyboard player called Vincent Crane. He used to rehearse upstairs, and I got to know him.'

Brown teamed up with Crane in a group he had already established, but it became obvious that Brown's ambitious ideas were beyond the scope of the musicians Crane was working with. 'Vincent and I decided to get rid of everyone else, starting from scratch. We advertised in the Melody Maker for a drummer, and Drachen Theaker answered. He had been on his way to the final auditions for a place in the Jimi Hendrix Experience, but got stuck in a traffic jam and lost out to Mitch Mitchell. So it was our gain. Vincent was classically trained and Drachen was very much into the avant-garde and also had a huge collection of African records, so we really developed an exciting musical approach. I was writing the sort of lyrics that nobody could get a handle on back then; later on, Bowie would do something similar, but at the time I was out on my own. In order to illustrate the lyrics I began to wear costumes on stage to bring it all to life. In every respect, we were not a normal band.'

By now the underground scene in London was growing into a major creative force and the Crazy World of Arthur Brown soon became darlings of the crowds who flocked to the UFO Club on London's Tottenham Court Road along with Soft Machine and Pink Floyd. Brown's outrageous stage performances began to attract column inches. 'We were called decadent and disgusting by some elements of the tabloid press, and this attracted the attention of the big record labels. We were wined, dined and courted by everyone. However, I never felt the major companies knew what we were about. So, instead we signed to Track Records, which was run by the Who's management company.'

Who guitarist Pete Townshend was instrumental in getting Brown's band signed to Kit Lambert and Chris Stamp's recently established imprint. In September 1967 Track Records released the debut single by the Crazy World of Arthur Brown, 'Devil's Grip' b/w 'Give Him A Flower,' and thoughts turned to recording an album. After Joe Boyd declined to work on the record, Lambert, with Townshend acting as an associate producer, would supervise the recording sessions.

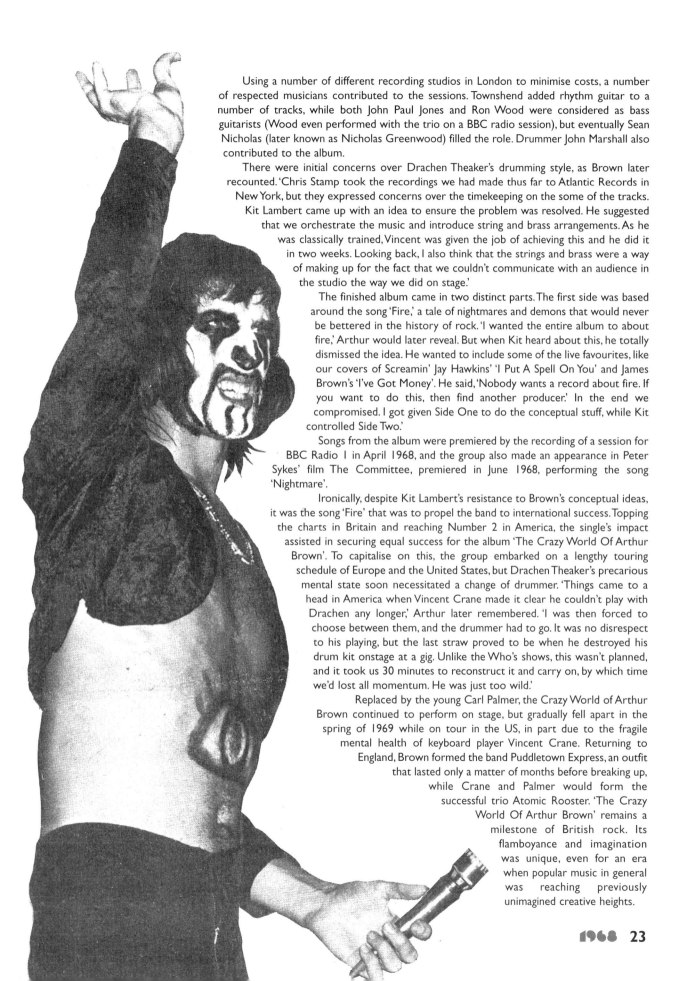

Using a number of different recording studios in London to minimise costs, a number of respected musicians contributed to the sessions. Townshend added rhythm guitar to a number of tracks, while both John Paul Jones and Ron Wood were considered as bass guitarists (Wood even performed with the trio on a BBC radio session), but eventually Sean Nicholas (later known as Nicholas Greenwood) filled the role. Drummer John Marshall also contributed to the album.

There were initial concerns over Drachen Theaker's drumming style, as Brown later recounted. 'Chris Stamp took the recordings we had made thus far to Atlantic Records in New York, but they expressed concerns over the timekeeping on the some of the tracks. Kit Lambert came up with an idea to ensure the problem was resolved. He suggested that we orchestrate the music and introduce string and brass arrangements. As he was classically trained, Vincent was given the job of achieving this and he did it in two weeks. Looking back, I also think that the strings and brass were a way of making up for the fact that we couldn't communicate with an audience in the studio the way we did on stage.'

The finished album came in two distinct parts. The first side was based around the song 'Fire,' a tale of nightmares and demons that would never be bettered in the history of rock. 'I wanted the entire album to about fire,' Arthur would later reveal. But when Kit heard about this, he totally dismissed the idea. He wanted to include some of the live favourites, like our covers of Screamin' Jay Hawkins' 'I Put A Spell On You' and James Brown's 'I've Got Money'. He said, 'Nobody wants a record about fire. If you want to do this, then find another producer.' In the end we compromised. I got given Side One to do the conceptual stuff, while Kit controlled Side Two.'

Songs from the album were premiered by the recording of a session for BBC Radio 1 in April 1968, and the group also made an appearance in Peter Sykes' film The Committee, premiered in June 1968, performing the song 'Nightmare'.

Ironically, despite Kit Lambert's resistance to Brown's conceptual ideas, it was the song 'Fire' that was to propel the band to international success. Topping the charts in Britain and reaching Number 2 in America, the single's impact assisted in securing equal success for the album 'The Crazy World Of Arthur Brown'. To capitalise on this, the group embarked on a lengthy touring schedule of Europe and the United States, but Drachen Theaker's precarious mental state soon necessitated a change of drummer. 'Things came to a head in America when Vincent Crane made it clear he couldn't play with Drachen any longer,' Arthur later remembered. 'I was then forced to choose between them, and the drummer had to go. It was no disrespect to his playing, but the last straw proved to be when he destroyed his drum kit onstage at a gig. Unlike the Who's shows, this wasn't planned, and it took us 30 minutes to reconstruct it and carry on, by which time we'd lost all momentum. He was just too wild.'

Replaced by the young Carl Palmer, the Crazy World of Arthur Brown continued to perform on stage, but gradually fell apart in the spring of 1969 while on tour in the US, in part due to the fragile mental health of keyboard player Vincent Crane. Returning to England, Brown formed the band Puddletown Express, an outfit that lasted only a matter of months before breaking up, while Crane and Palmer would form the successful trio Atomic Rooster. 'The Crazy World Of Arthur Brown' remains a milestone of British rock. Its flamboyance and imagination was unique, even for an era when popular music in general was reaching previously unimagined creative heights.

CARAVAN 'Caravan'

First released as Verve Forecast SVLP6011 in October 1968
Highest UK chart position: N/A
Available on CD as Verve 882 9522

Place of My Own
Ride
Policeman
Love Song With Flute
Cecil Rons
Magic Man
Grandma's Lawn
Where But For Caravan Would I?

Pye Hastings	**Guitar, Bass Guitar, Singing**
Richard Coughlan	**Drums**
David Sinclair	**Organ, Singing**
Richard Sinclair	**Bass Guitar, Singing**

Recorded at Advision Studios, London
Produced by Tony Cox
Engineered by Gerald Chevin

The English city of Canterbury is home to two highly respected universities and is at the very heart of English history thanks to its Cathedral and its status as the seat of the Church of England. In the mid Sixties it was arguably even more conservative than today, and it seemed highly unlikely that a musical style would be named after the city. The 'Canterbury Sound' first came to prominence with the arrival of Soft Machine on the underground scene in 1967, but they would soon be joined by a band from the same roots whose music would be almost as original.

Caravan was born out of local soul-influenced band the Wilde Flowers, a group subject to many line-up changes and featuring, at various times, Kevin Ayers (guitar), Richard Sinclair (guitar), Robert Wyatt (drums), Hugh Hopper (bass) and Brian Hopper (saxophone). The band was augmented in 1965 when Hugh Hopper recruited trainee dental technician and drummer Richard Coughlan when Robert Wyatt decided he would rather sing than play drums. Shortly afterwards a new guitarist arrived. Pye Hastings was born in Banffshire, Scotland and moved to Canterbury at the age of 12. He knew members of the Wilde Flowers through his friendship with Kevin Ayers, who taught him his first guitar chords while both were living abroad. 'I came back to England and the rhythm guitar spot was vacant in the band. Richard Sinclair had gone to art college, so I filled the vacancy. The Wilde Flowers were just changing from an R&B-based band to becoming a soul band, which I was really into. Dave Sinclair joined at that point. He was originally our bass player, but after a week he said he wasn't happy in that role and turned up with a keyboard, a Vox Continental organ I think. Kevin then left to go to Spain and that left Dave Sinclair, Brian and Hugh Hopper, Richard Coughlan, myself and Robert Wyatt. Then Robert left and later on appeared back on the scene with Kevin in Soft Machine.'

With Wyatt and Ayers enjoying some notoriety with Soft Machine, the remaining musicians in Wilde Flowers soldiered on, settling by January 1968 on a line-up of Pye Hastings on guitar and vocals, Richard Sinclair on bass guitar and vocals, Dave Sinclair on keyboards and Richard Coughlan on drums. Discovering that musical tastes were beginning to change in favour of psychedelia, the band decided to rethink their musical direction. 'We found that all the gigs were running out as no-one wanted a soul band any more,' reflected Hastings, 'so we decided to write our own material and Caravan was born.'

By now Soft Machine had found themselves darlings of the hippies who frequented London's Middle Earth and UFO clubs, emerging alongside Pink Floyd as icons of the newly emerging underground scene. As a result of Soft Machine's initial success, the newly formed Caravan soon had thoughts of playing in London in the hope of securing a record contract. In May 1968 this was realised when they performed at legendary underground club Middle Earth. 'We made a demo using one microphone and a little Philips reel to reel tape recorder, which wasn't really that good,' Pye Hastings later explained.

'I decided that Island Records were a good company to target first and so I went to their offices in Oxford Street and dropped the tape into their receptionist. I'd originally wanted to see Chris Blackwell, but he was busy. A week later I got a call from a chap called Tony Cox. He was a songwriter who wanted to get into production and was linked up with a chap called Ian Ralfini at Robbins Music. Tony had seen us at the Middle Earth Club in London and liked what he had heard. He asked me if I had a demo tape and I told him that the only one in existence was with Chris Blackwell.'

Tony Cox promptly called Island Records to obtain the tape. This sudden interest in Caravan from a music business rival caused Island to reappraise the situation. 'Island decided not to release the tape to Tony and so I went around to their offices the

Caravan makes a really gripping debut

CARAVAN: †Place Of My Own (Verve).

A NEW group for whom great things have been predicted. And I must say that Caravan's debut disc has a gripping compulsion. I like the sound these boys make.

This track features a philosophic soloed lyric, palpitating drums, rattling tambourine and, above all, some scintillating organ work—not just blues chords, but some genuine jazz improvisations.

Holds the interest with its constant tempo and mood changes, but you need to hear it a few times before the full impact hits home.

next week to get it back myself. Chris Blackwell saw me and said that he had heard the tape. He told me that he liked the band but asked, "Who is the crap singer?" to which I replied, "It's me, actually." Blackwell proposed that we record as an instrumental band instead. The Nice were very popular at the time and he thought that we could go down the same road as them, but I wasn't interested in doing that at all so he gave the tape back to me.'

With the demo now back in his possession Hastings duly delivered it to Tony Cox, who persuaded Ian Ralfini and Martin Wyatt of Robbins Music to journey down to Canterbury to hear the band perform at the Beehive Club. Both Wyatt and Ralfini were especially impressed with Hastings' song 'Place Of My Own', and a contract was signed in the back of Ralfini's car. A recording deal was struck with MGM offshoot Verve Records who had recently established a London office and boasted American acts such as Frank Zappa and the Mothers of Invention, the Velvet Underground and Janis Ian on their roster. Caravan were one of the first signings to Verve's newly established London office, but the publishing and recording deals did not bring forth riches to Messrs Hastings, Coughlan, Sinclair and Sinclair.

'We were paid seven pounds a week each by Robbins Music as a retainer,' Hastings would later explain, 'and in addition they offered to pay for a place to rehearse. At the time we were looking for a place to live and couldn't find anywhere to rent at all. We'd just left a house in Whitstable, where we'd lived and rehearsed, and discovered that nobody wanted to let a property to a group of long-haired musicians. We did find somewhere to rehearse, a hall in a village called Graveney in Kent. Both Dave and

Richard Sinclair were keen campers, so they turned up with a couple of tents and pitched them outside. We managed to get two more from somewhere else and we all lived there. When it got a bit colder we pitched our tents inside the hall and turned the heating on. We were in there for three months before it got too cold to stay.'

Caravan entered Advision Studios in Bond Street at the end of the summer of 1968 with Tony Cox as producer to record their debut album. Pye Hastings later looked back on those sessions with fondness. 'Most of the material had been performed live and was all rehearsed before we got to the studio. The songs weren't written specifically for the album; "Ride" was a possible exception. Tony Cox wouldn't let us attend the mixing on the grounds that if there were five people in the control room it would take five times as long to mix, which isn't strictly true. I think he wanted total control.'

The album sessions saw the guest performance of Pye's flute-playing brother Jimmy on the song 'Love Song With Flute'. Richard Sinclair handled vocals on 'Grandma's Lawn' and 'Policeman,' both his own compositions, with Pye switching to bass for these songs and Sinclair handling lead guitar. The psychedelic influence was very much present on 'Magic Man', 'Grandma's Lawn' and 'Cecil Rons' while 'Place Of My Own', one of the first songs Pye had written, showed the whimsical direction the band's music would take.

The album's epic closing track, 'Where But For Caravan Would I?' was Caravan's first attempt at a longer, more complex piece and was co-written with an ex-Wilde Flowers colleague. 'I based the melody for that song on a tune that Brian Hopper had written in the Wilde Flowers days,' Hastings remembered. 'We extended it and re-worked it, but the basic tune was Brian's, hence his credit on the album.'

Released in October 1968 on the Verve Forecast label, 'Caravan' was an impressive debut with a sound very much of its time. It deserves to be considered alongside Pink Floyd's 'The Piper At The Gates Of Dawn,' the Pretty Things' 'SF Sorrow,' Traffic's 'Mr Fantasy' or Family's 'Music In A Doll's House' as being an early landmark in British psychedelic/progressive music. The striking album cover was devised by Richard Zeff, who photographed the band at this studio in Notting Hill Gate, and Miles, editor of underground newspaper International Times, provided liner notes very much in keeping with the progressive underground scene of the day.

'The album had quite a distinctive sound,' commented Hastings, 'but it wasn't representative of Caravan at the time because Tony Cox gave the album a big echoing sound which wasn't how we sounded on stage.' In January 1969 'Place Of My Own' and 'Ride' were chosen as the A and B-side of the band's first UK single, leading to appearances on the German TV show Beat Club and BBC2's Colour Me Pop.

Despite such a promising start 'Caravan' was only in the shops or a matter of months before MGM/Verve ceased their operations in the UK and the band found themselves without a record label. Fortunes improved when, in 1970, they signed to Decca Records for whom they recorded a series of fine albums with ever increasing success. Although Caravan's debut stands out as being slightly different to the rest of the band's catalogue, its charm and psychedelic whimsy makes it a true classic.

CREAM 'Wheels Of Fire'

First released as Polydor 582 031/2 (mono)/58 3031/2 (stereo) in August 1968
Highest UK chart position: 3
Available on CD as Polydor 531 812-2

IN THE STUDIO:

White Room
Sitting on Top of the World
Passing The Time
As You Said
Pressed Rat and Warthog
Politician
Those Were The Days
Born Under A Bad Sign
Deserted Cities Of The Heart

LIVE AT THE FILLMORE:

Crossroads
Spoonful
Traintime
Toad

Ginger Baker	**Drums, Percussion, Vocals**
Jack Bruce	**Bass Guitar, Acoustic Guitar, Cello, Piano, Calliope, Vocals**
Eric Clapton	**Lead Guitar**
with	
Felix Pappalardi	**Viola, Organ Pedals, Swiss Hand Bells**

Recorded at IBC Studios, London in July and August 1967 and at Atlantic Studios, New York in September and October 1967 and January and February 1968 and June 1968

Produced by Felix Pappalardi by arrangement with Robert Stigwood

Cited by many as defining the concept of the 'power trio' and writing the blueprint for heavy rock which others like Led Zeppelin quickly developed, there can be few acts who were so influential and commercially successful in such a short time as Cream. The group brought together the talents of three of the finest British musicians of their generation. Ginger Baker (drums) and Jack Bruce (vocals, bass) had served a long apprenticeship on the British jazz and blues scene of the early Sixties. London-born Baker had begun playing traditional jazz, while Jack Bruce had received a formal musical education in Glasgow before moving south to London.

Baker and Bruce had first performed together in Alexis Korner's Blues Incorporated before leaving to join the Graham Bond Quartet; this soon became the Graham Bond Organisation, a group that performed some 300 dates a year. The strain of life on the road led to a rift developing between Bruce and Ginger Baker which eventually saw Bruce quit the Graham Bond Organisation. Never the most stable of personalities, Bond's erratic behaviour eventually led Baker to think about forming a new band. In effect, he had been organising the business of the Organisation for some months and had begun to tire of his role. He had been impressed by the playing of a gifted guitarist from Ripley in Surrey, and Eric Clapton was Baker's choice for guitarist in a new outfit.

Clapton had been a major figure on the British blues scene for the past three years, coming to prominence as a member of the Yardbirds. Raised by his grandparents, the slightly introverted Clapton developed a love of American rhythm and blues and traditional blues in his early teens and took up the guitar, an instrument for which he demonstrated an early aptitude. He attended Kingston-Upon-Thames College of Art upon leaving school, but was expelled for playing his guitar during lectures.

While working as a manual labourer on building sites Clapton also performed in fledgling R&B groups such as the Roosters and Casey Jones and the Engineers. His considerable prowess did not remain un-noticed and in the autumn of 1963 he replaced Anthony 'Top' Topham as lead guitarist in the Yardbirds, a group about to succeed the Rolling Stones as resident band at the leading

London R&B Club the Crawdaddy, run by their manager Giorgio Gomelsky.

Gomelsky soon secured a recording contract for the group with EMI's Columbia label and the album 'Five Live Yardbirds' was recorded at the Marquee Club, proving to be a showcase for Eric Clapton's ever-increasing confidence and ability. Being a self-confessed purist, Clapton soon departed the Yardbirds following the release of the single 'For Your Love', citing the record as being too far removed from the blues.

He joined John Mayall's Bluesbreakers in April 1965 and made such an impact on the London music scene that graffiti soon began to appear on walls stating 'Clapton is God'. He left Mayall's band to travel around Europe some months later, but by November 1965 had returned to England and was back with the Bluesbreakers. By now Jack Bruce had also been recruited, but left within a matter of weeks to join Manfred Mann.

At a Bluesbreakers concert in Oxford in April 1966 Ginger Baker, attending as a member of the audience, asked to sit in for a few numbers. Struck by his rapport with Clapton, Baker immediately asked the guitarist to be part of his new band. At Clapton's insistence, Jack Bruce was also approached by Baker and, putting previous differences aside, accepted. Cream was born.

A strong songwriting partnership was soon established between Jack and London-based beat poet Pete Brown. Brown was initially invited to early Cream writing sessions by Baker, who had known Brown when he performed with Graham Bond's Organisation at various jazz and poetry readings. Following abortive attempts at writing with Baker, Brown collaborated with Bruce on the song 'Wrapping Paper' beginning a partnership that continued for many years. The release of the single 'I Feel Free' and album 'Fresh Cream' later that year put Cream on the map, and the band's concert debut in America the following year brought them a massive following in the US.

The album 'Disraeli Gears' saw Cream produce a record of psychedelic blues-rock that was unique for its time and became a huge hit on both sides of the Atlantic and. Recorded at Atlantic Studios in New York in May 1967 under the supervision of producer Felix Pappalardi, the album was a stunning musical statement filled with lyrically surreal images.

'There was never any restriction on what I could or couldn't write for Cream,' Jack Bruce would later comment. 'I wrote things like "We're Going Wrong" on my own, but I was mainly writing with Pete Brown at that time and we would come up with inventive things like '"Dance The Night Away'. The only issue I had was communicating my musical ideas to Eric and Ginger. Because I could read and write music I could put my ideas on paper, but as Eric

CREAM — GINGER BAKER, JACK BRUCE and ERIC CLAPTON — were this week awarded a Gold Disc for a million U.S. sales of " Sunshine Of Your Love," a track from their " Disraeli Gears " album and also their current single here. The group started its farewell tour of the United States today (Friday).

NEW MUSICAL EXPRESS

A get-together for the BEE GEES, CREAM and their manager ROBERT STIGWOOD—but it happened more or less by accident in an airport lounge ; Copenhagen's. The BEE GEES had just completed two sell-out concerts in the City and were waiting for a plane to take them on to Stockholm. The CREAM had been equally successful in Copenhagen and were waiting for a plane back to London. The line-up (l to r standing) ROBIN GIBB, JACK BRUCE, ROBERT STIGWOOD, COLIN PETERSON, VINCE MELOUNEY and GINGER BAKER ; (seated) BARRY GIBB, MAURICE GIBB and ERIC CLAPTON.

**** CREAM: WHEELS ON FIRE
(Polydor, 583031/2)

A double-album which American fans of Britain's fantastic trio have gone mad about. On the first LP are nine studio-made tracks and on the second are four long sessions recorded live at the Fillmore. **Jack Bruce** gets five composing credits and **Ginger Baker** four. **Felix Pappalardi**, who produced, augments the trio on various instruments. Jack takes most of the vocals, **Eric Clapton** making his guitar sing for him, while Ginger keeps up a rock-steady drum beat, adding marimba, tubular bells, glockenspeil and even a recitation on Pressed Rat And Warthog. The numbers are varied in the extreme, from briskly paced songs to slow, morbid ones. Everything sounds good.

Jack Bruce sounds so wistful in Passing The Time, and shows his ability almost on his own in As You Said, in which he sings, plays acoustic guitar, cellos, having a little help from Ginger but Eric is not on this at all. Jack turns on a blues vocal sound in Born Under A Bad Sign and Willie Dixon's Spoonful, which is given over 16 minutes at the Fillmore. I liked the playing on the " live " LP better than the studio one, and throughout Eric Clapton's guitar offerings are extra exciting. Jack's harmonica work specially on Traintime, is another big asset, and Ginger's drumming on the near-16 minute Toad track is exceptional.

Other titles: White Room, Sitting On Top Of The World, Politician, Those Were The Days, Deserted Cities Of The Heart, Crossroads.

couldn't read music I found it quite hard to put my ideas across as I'm not a guitarist. I would sit at the piano and play what I'd written and we usually managed to get that down on tape.'

Due to the Stateside success of their second album Cream faced a treadmill of a seemingly endless stream of concerts, the only respite being time off to cut their third album. The double vinyl 'Wheels Of Fire', released in August 1968, was recorded in gaps between live concerts. Sessions began at IBC Studios in London in July and August 1967, sessions continuing at Atlantic in September and October that year and into January and February 1968, with final mixes being completed in June of that year. If anything, the studio material on 'Wheels Of Fire' was even more adventurous than that on 'Disraeli Gears,' particularly on outstanding Bruce-Brown compositions such as 'White Room,' 'Politician', 'Deserted Cities Of The Heart' and 'As You Said', each different in style.

'White Room' was arguably the finest rock composition recorded by the band, while 'Politician' hung upon a bluesy riff set to splendidly satirical Pete Brown lyrics. 'As You Said' featured Bruce on acoustic guitar and cello with Baker on percussion and was virtually a Bruce solo track, influenced in part by the guitar playing of Richie Havens. 'Deserted Cities Of The Heart' was an elaborate rock track featuring Bruce's excellent cello-playing along with contributions from producer Felix Pappalardi.

Ginger Baker also offered three compositions to the sessions, written in collaboration with jazz musician Mike Taylor. 'Passing The Time' was another highlight featuring a whimsical opening and closing section bisected with a splendid example of Cream's ability as a rock power trio. 'Pressed Rat And Warthog' was a surreal piece featuring Ginger reciting lyrics to an elegant musical arrangement, while 'Those Were the Days' was a psychedelic masterpiece with highly visual lyrics.

Meanwhile, Cream's respect for the blues was demonstrated in their cover version of 'Howlin' Wolf's 'Sitting On Top Of The World' and in a fine cover of Booker T Jones' 'Born Under A Bad Sign'.

The decision was made to make Cream's third album a double set, comprising highlights from shows at the Fillmore West in San Francisco on 7 March 1968 and a three-night residency at Winterland in the same city. Stunning covers of Robert Johnson's 'Crossroads' and Willie Dixon's 'Spoonful' were joined by a powerful version of 'Traintime' (a live high spot of Graham Bond Organisation concerts) featuring Bruce on harmonica and vocals, and the lengthy drum solo of 'Toad'.

Released in August 1968, 'Wheels Of Fire' reached Number 3 in the UK chart and topped the US Billboard listings. Despite some critical indifference, the album became the first double album to earn platinum sales status. It also successfully presented the different facets of the trio, the studio sides including classic material such as 'White Room' and 'Politician' and the live album serving as an example of the improvisational side of the group.

By the time 'Wheels Of Fire' appeared it was apparent that the relentless schedule of work would eventually take its toll. 'A lot of hard work went into making Cream as successful as it was,' Jack Bruce later reflected. 'There was a tremendous amount of gigging and effort involved. When you're in the middle of all that you just work every day and don't think too much about what you're doing. You're not aware that one song or the other might go on to be important and something you'd forever be associated with.

'When you look at the number of gigs Cream did in such a short time it's astounding. When we weren't on the road we were in the recording studio and I look back now and think, "God, how did we ever do that?" But we were young and we did manage to keep up with the pace until in the end the relentless cycle of touring and recording led to exhaustion, which in turn led to a lack of new material from all the members of the band. I suppose that combined with the feeling that we'd said all we could musically and it was clear to us that it was time for us to go our separate ways.'

Cream bowed out on stage at the Royal Albert Hall in London on 26 November 1968. With each member enjoying solo careers, neither Baker nor Bruce achieved the commercial success of Clapton. In 2005 the musical world was surprised by the announcement that Jack Bruce, Ginger Baker and Eric Clapton would reunite as Cream to perform a series of concerts at the Royal Albert Hall. Those reunion performances led to a series of appearances at Madison Square Garden in New York some months later.

Forty two years on from the release of 'Wheels Of Fire', the music and influence of Cream remains as vital as ever and was never finer than the material gathered on the four sides of this record.

FAREWELL SHOW SADDENED THE CREAM

CREAM, pictured at rehearsals for their farewell concerts (l to r) JACK BRUCE, GINGER BAKER and ERIC CLAPTON.

THE deification of the Cream was completed at the Royal Albert Hall around 11 o'clock on Tuesday of last week when the pulse of the last of their two encores melted into the tumult and applause and when the last clap and the final heartfelt plea of " God Save The Cream " had faded away into an atmosphere of high emotion.

Five thousand united voices hit a cry of rapture and a shower of confetti launched from the front row cascaded over Eric Clapton's bowed head.

An ecstatic fan who had prepared himself all evening for this chance charged across the side of the stage and ran off in jubilation and triumph, brandishing his "spoils " — Ginger's drumsticks — in the air. The Cream was all over.

Jack, Eric and Ginger will rise again in different guises, in different spheres, but Tuesday night's farewell performance put the Cream as a unit in its place in pop history alongside Haley, the Beatles, Presley and others.

On Monday afternoon this week, Jack and Eric were to be found at the IBC Studios near Radio One-derland in Portland Place where, I was told, they were recording.

Ginger was notable for his absence and so too was any semblance of work when I arrived — to find Jack, Eric and their American record producer Felic Pappa-lardi chatting together in a small circle at one end of the deserted studio.

"We were just discussing our breakfast," offered Eric as a welcome.

We talked about the concerts, which had been a sad occasion for them also, and Jack confessed: "I was really depressed for two or three days afterwards. It was quite moving; I just didn't expect it."

Eric, who was wearing a magnificent crochet coat of many colours made by a loving fan, agreed. "We didn't really expect anything like that. It was a great reception, as good as any we have had anywhere. I don't want to knock American audiences but quality wise it was as good and we didn't play many encores over there."

There was a summons from above for Jack to take a phone call and Eric continued: "The first show was sad because we knew it would have to be kept short and that inhibits you.

"But otherwise the other groups would have to have been cut down to about three minutes each."

Jack, Eric and Ginger have each written a new song for what will be their last LP and those will be recorded in the studio. The remainder will be made up from "live" recordings taken from four of their concerts in the American farewell tour.

As even now there is considerable bewilderment as 'to why a split is necessary, I asked Eric to put the reason in as concise a form as possible.

His answer, I think, sums it up: "It is like the Cream was a concensus of what we thought we could do as individuals within a group but — because of the nature of the line up, the different backgrounds, the different points of reference — the conglomeration that resulted was such a vast compromise to what we would all have liked to do as individuals.

"Maybe we will all get together to play again some time in the future and there is no reason why we should not appear on each other's records, though it wouldn't be a big publicised thing if we did so."

And what of the future, which has also been the subject of much speculation and very little fact.

"I don't think any of us are sure what we are going to do from this. There are just certain ideas we have, just idealistic things we want to do," said Eric.

"But there are so many pressures that maybe it has made all this seem more exaggerated than it is. In essence, perhaps all we really need is a break.

"This business devours so much of your time. You don't know if you are doing the right thing or the wrong thing — or even who you are!"

Apart from studio work, which is not so demanding, Eric feels that he wants to have a rest for as long as he can, particularly from working on the road.

"This time I have no idea of what I will do as far as line-up and playing is concerned. I've got the sound; that is in my head. And I will work as close to that as I can.

"Maybe in January or February I will go into a studio and get some people there and try some things out. It will be very much a trial and error thing."

What of the widely-held belief that Eric wants to return to the blues?

"The Cream never really played that much blues," he answered.

"I think we aimed to start a revolution in musical thought. We set out to change the world, to upset people and to shock them. At the start we were going to play Elvis Presley numbers — but what happened was that we fell into doing these long instrumental pieces. Really the Cream was just an instrumental group.

"When I play on my own it includes various blues figures, twelve bar things, Chuck Berry and loosely around that.

"The sound will be bluesy, but I am not going to start playing 'Dust My Broom' or things like that."

How does he feel about the intellectualising of the Cream?

"It doesn't matter how you dig it as long as you like it. Some of the lyrics we write might not mean anything to anyone else . . . because I never thought we were as good as they thought we were.

"The public appreciation always surprised me because I never thought we really got it together to deserve that much acclaim," he concluded with remarkable honesty.

Last time I saw Jack he told me that the Cream had really reached its peak while on their last but one tour of the States and it was sad that the British audiences had not had a chance to see them at their height.

At the two Albert Hall concerts, 10,000 were witness to the peak they have reached while thousands more were unable to get in — and ironically it was their last performance.

"Yes I do feel rather guilty about that — I must admit," said Eric, whose breakfast arrived at that minute. And I left him eating his cornflakes.

God Save The Cream.

They're surprised and a little guilty now that it's all over

By NICK LOGAN

DEEP PURPLE 'Shades Of Deep Purple'

First released as Parlophone PMC7055 (mono)/PCS7055 (stereo)
in September 1968
Highest UK chart position: N/A
Available on CD as EMI Records 4 98336 2

And The Address
Hush
One More Rainy Day
Prelude: Happiness
I'm So Glad
Mandrake Root
Help
Love Help Me
Hey Joe

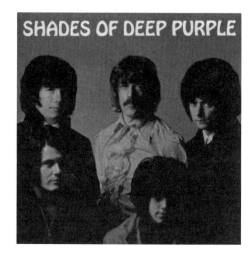

Rod Evans	**Lead Vocals**
Jon Lord	**Organ, Vocals**
Ritchie Blackmore	**Lead Guitar**
Nick Simper	**Bass Guitar, Vocals**
Ian Paice	**Drums**

Recorded at Pye Studios, Marble Arch, London
Produced by Derek Lawrence
Engineered by Barry Ainsworth

Although they would become true giants of hard rock alongside Led Zeppelin and Black Sabbath, the rise to global fame by Deep Purple was destined to take longer than their counterparts and would see the group endure a significant line-up change. At the same time, they would enjoy almost immediate success in the United States while remaining relative unknowns in their homeland for the first 18 months of their existence.

Deep Purple first came together at the end of 1967 when former Searchers drummer Chris Curtis sought to form a new outfit to go under the name of Roundabout. The idea behind the concept was that of a revolving line-up, with musicians coming in and out of the band as required and Curtis as the central figure. With London based businessman Tony Edwards as manager, Curtis first contacted keyboard-player Jon Lord (previously with British R&B group the Artwoods) to join him. Curtis had also made contact with Ritchie Blackmore, an innovative guitarist that he had met on the club scene in Hamburg.

Before any serious music had been made, Lord tired of Chris Curtis' dictatorial attitude and had declared himself 'out' of the Roundabout project. With Lord's departure, manager Tony Edwards felt that the idea of assembling a group of talented musicians was still viable. Contacting Lord and Blackmore, Edwards brought the pair of musicians together at Lord's flat to work on some basic ideas for new music.

To make ends meet Lord had been playing live shows with the Flowerpot Men, a group who had enjoyed a one-off hit with their single 'Let's Go to San Francisco'. While on a soul-destroying tour of British clubs Lord had met bass guitarist Nick Simper and he was soon drafted into the new band. Blackmore suggested drummer Bobby Woodman as a suitable candidate and by February 1968 the musicians had gathered in a farmhouse in rural Hertfordshire to rehearse and write. During these sessions Woodman was replaced by Ian Paice, then playing with Maze, who brought with him vocalist Rod Evans. Within weeks the band had engaged the services of former Joe Meek associate Derek Lawrence who had now established a production company.

Lawrence recorded a series of demos with the band at London's Trident Studios in March 1968 which led to a contract with newly formed American label Tetragrammaton. Roundabout undertook a Scandinavian tour in late April, during which time they changed their name to Deep Purple. With a weekend of studio time booked at Pye Records' studio in Marble Arch, Deep Purple cut their debut album. Such was the rushed booking of the studio and the limited time available that the band essentially recorded their current stage act live in the studio. The exciting Blackmore and Lord instrumental 'And The Address' opened the band's act at the time and was a suitable first track for the album.

With influences being drawn from acts such as Cream, Jimi Hendrix, the Beatles and Vanilla Fudge, the material recorded incorporated imaginative cover versions of 'Help', 'I'm So Glad' and 'Hey Joe', all reworked to include lengthy classical music inspired musical introductions; 'Hey Joe', for instance, drew on Ravel's Bolero. The outstanding original composition was arguably Blackmore and Evans' 'Mandrake Root' which dominated the second side of the record and would remain in the band's set after Evans' departure. Perhaps the finest track on the album was a reworking of 'Hush', a song by American singer-songwriter Joe South which was given a drastic overhaul by the band. With sessions complete, Derek Lawrence added excerpts from BBC sound-effects albums at the mixing stage to link the tracks.

No sooner had sessions been completed than Deep Purple's American label demanded masters be shipped immediately to the US for release. Released in July 1968 'Shades Of Deep Purple' was accompanied by a flurry of American press publicity. Vetoing the band's suggestion of releasing 'Help' as their first single, Tetragrammaton wisely selected 'Hush' instead. The single soon reached a peak of Number 4 on the Billboard chart which, in turn, helped propel the album to Number 24.

In the UK 'Hush' was released as a single by EMI's Parlophone label but failed to enjoy chart success. 'Shades Of Deep Purple' appeared in Britain in September 1968 with little or no publicity on EMI's part. While still on the club circuit in the UK, the band's situation in America could not have been more of a contrast; Deep Purple were engaged to play an eight-week tour of the US in October of that year, along with a booking on the TV show Playboy After Dark.

Although considerably different from the harder-edged rock music that would grace such successors as 'In Rock' and 'Machine Head', 'Shades Of Deep Purple' remains a remarkable album that has been unfairly criticised when compared to the work of later line-ups. As if to emphasise the timelessness of the music, British band Kula Shaker enjoyed a huge European hit single nearly 30 years later with their version of 'Hush', a virtual carbon copy of Deep Purple's arrangement.

Originally the five boys who make up Deep Purple were with other groups, but they had mutual admiration for each other as musicians. Recently in Denmark, they nicked a lot of the honours in competition with the likes of J. Hendrix and the Cream. They now live in a country house in Sussex. And they live in hopes that their fine debut disc "Hush" (Parlophone) is the hit it deserves to be. What's more, I understand they are all proficient darts players and we'll look to them to bring a deep purple glow to our team . . . as opposed to the black depression we felt about our last humiliating defeat!

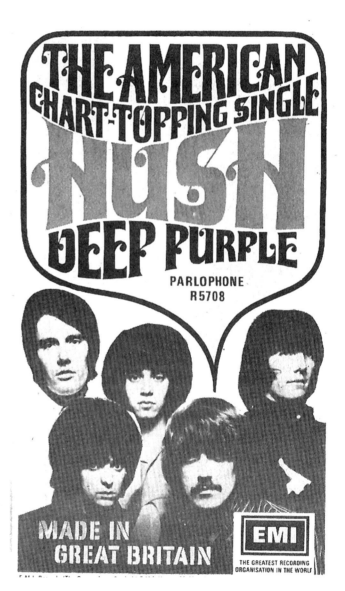

FAMILY 'Music In A Doll's House'

First released as Reprise RLP6312 (mono)/R(S)LP6312 (stereo) in September 1968
Highest UK chart position: Number 35
Not currently available on CD

The Chase
Mellowing Grey
Never Like This
Me My Friend
Variation On A Theme Of 'Hey Mr Policeman'
Winter
Old Songs New Songs
Variation On A Theme Of 'The Breeze'
Hey Mr Policeman
See Through Windows
Variation On A Theme Of 'Me My Friend'
Peace Of Mind
Voyage
The Breeze
3 X Time

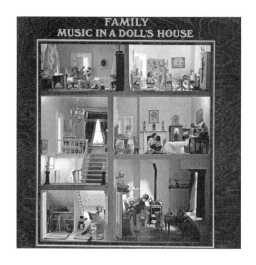

Roger Chapman Lead Vocals
John Whitney   **Lead Guitar, Steel Guitar**
Jim King   **Tenor and Soprano Saxophones, Harmonica, Vocals**
Ric Grech   **Bass Guitar, Violin, Cello, Vocals**
Rob Townsend   **Drums**

Recorded at Olympic Studios, Barnes, London
Produced by Dave Mason
Engineered by Eddie Kramer

In 1967, a group from Leicester made a significant impression on the London-based music scene with the release of their first single, 'Scene Through The Eye Of A Lens'. A party to launch the record saw such significant figures as John Lennon, George Harrison and Brian Jones attend a performance by Family.

Fronted by powerhouse vocalist Roger Chapman, Family were to become one of the most commercially successful bands in the early progressive era and were certainly one of the most gifted.

Family's roots could be traced back to 1962 with the formation of the Farinas by four students at Leicester Art College: John 'Charlie' Whitney (guitar and vocals), Jim King (saxophone and vocals), Tim Kirchen (bass) and Harry Overnall (drums). With the failure of their only record, a single for Fontana, to chart, Tim Kirchen departed and was replaced by Ric Grech on bass. Also recruited was singer Roger Chapman. With Chapman's arrival the band branched out from their soul and blues-based sound and began to write their own material. By the end of 1966 they had evolved still further with Grech also playing violin, giving them a most unique style.

A NEW ALBUM FROM
THE HAPPENING
FAMILY
MUSIC IN A DOLL'S HOUSE

RLP 6312 (M)   RSLP 6312 (S)

FAMILY

Millions have cried
For millions that died
For things that they strived
But more millions just sighed
Made excuses and lied
Stood numb, stupefied
With mouths open wide
Wondering which side
Of the fence they should ride.
While I'm swept by the tide
Thinking I've tried
But still mystified
By the rules I abide.
Apart from the colour
Which slowly gets duller
We're all,
Just so much confetti.

Roger Chapman
Dukeslodge Music Ltd

All songs written
by Roger Chapman
John Whitney and the Family

"Me My Friend"
"Hey Mr. Policeman"
Released on Reprise July 5

The first Family album
"Music In A Doll's House"
Produced by Dave Mason   released July 19
Executive producer John Gilbert

Publicity Leslie Perrin 68 Oxford Street
London W1 01-636 7122
Agency Paragon Representation
A Dukeslodge Enterprises production

Family Happenings
Tour of the Year with Tim Hardin
Tuesday July 16-Royal Albert Hall-London
Thursday July 18-De Montfort Hall-Leicester
Friday July 19-Sophia Gardens Pavillion-Cardiff
Saturday July 20-Victoria Hall-Leeds
Friday July 26-Free Trade Hall-Manchester
Sunday July 28-Empire-Sunderland
Woburn Fest. with Hendrix. Family et al. on Saturday July 6
Traffic & Family concert at Guild Hall Portsmouth July 17

Changing their name to the Roaring Sixties they came to the attention of American producer and legendary counter-culture figure Kim Fowley, who offered to record and produce a series of demos. Fowley had recently become involved with another leading British underground outfit, Soft Machine, and felt he could propel the Roaring Sixties to the next level of success. Upon discovering the existence of another group who had already registered the name Fowley suggested they should become the Family.

With demos recorded (and a series of dubious photos with the band dressed in gangster suits), Family began to perform extensively on the UK club scene, soon ditching both the suits and Fowley. Appearances at such leading psychedelic clubs as UFO brought them a full-time management and production deal with aspiring manager John Gilbert, son of film director Lewis Gilbert. Entering Olympic Studios in Barnes, Family recorded their first single which was licensed to Liberty Records in September 1967. Produced by Jimmy Miller, 'Scene Through The Eye Of A Lens' featured contributions from Traffic members Jim Capaldi, Dave Mason and Steve Winwood. A stunning record, the single surprisingly failed to chart and Liberty declined an option to sign Family to an album deal. At this point Harry Overnall was replaced on drums by another Leicester veteran, Rob Townsend. Frustrated by the lack of record company interest, John Gilbert funded the recording of Family's first album, deciding to license the record once it was completed. Venturing back to Olympic, Dave Mason, then on a brief sabbatical from Traffic, was engaged as producer. The album that resulted would utilise current studio technology to its fullest and would be regarded as a stunning and confident debut. The Chapman-Whitney writing partnership was blossoming into a special creative force which verged from the power of tracks such as 'Peace Of Mind', 'Winter', 'Me My Friend' and 'See Through Windows' to the considered psychedelic calm of 'The Breeze', 'Mellowing Grey' and 'Hey Mister Policeman' and the jazz-influenced 'Old Songs New Songs'. Dave Mason offered his song 'Never Like This' to the sessions, with Family backing him on the B-side of his first solo single, 'Little Woman' to return the favour. The finished album was arguably one of the most imaginative productions of the year. It was effectively a continuing cycle of songs interspersed with various instrumental pieces that took the listener on a musical trip that was the creative equal of contemporaries such as Traffic and Pink Floyd. With work completed on the record, the UK office of American label Reprise offered Family a long-term record deal and the album 'Music In A Dolls House' was released in July 1968 to great acclaim, reaching Number 35 on the UK chart.

In hindsight the album was light-years ahead of its time, which may have prevented it gaining a higher chart placing, but Family were now firmly placed among the ranks of rising British bands. Of all the many enjoyable albums they were to record until their demise in 1973, 'Music In A Dolls House' remains their most rewarding.

PARAGON

AGENCY AND ARTISTES REPRESENTATION 17·18·19 STRATFORD PLACE LONDON W1
TELEPHONES 01-499 7651/2/3 TELEX 27133 TELEGRAMS & CABLES PEEKABOO LONDON W1

Brian Auger and Julie Driscoll
Blossom Toes
Family
Ottilie Patterson

EVE HOLROYD
CAROLANN NICHOLLS

Family
a side **Second Generation Woman**
b side **Hometown** RS 23315 Released November 8th

A Duke-Slade Enterprises production personal management John Gilbert Tel 01-362-7326/5834 Agency Paragon Representation
Publicity Leslie Perrin 68 Oxford Street London W1 The 2nd Family Album will be released in January

PINK FLOYD 'A Saucerful Of Secrets'

First released as Columbia SX 6258 (mono)/SCX 6258 (stereo) in June 1968
Highest UK chart position: Number 9
Available on CD as EMI Records 8 29751 2

Let There Be More Light
Remember A Day
Set the Controls For The Heart Of The Sun
Corporal Clegg
A Saucerful Of Secrets
See-Saw
Jugband Blues

David Gilmour	**Guitar, Vocals**
Nick Mason	**Drums, Percussion**
Roger Waters	**Bass Guitar, Vocals**
Richard Wright	**Keyboards, Vocals**
with	
Syd Barrett	**Guitar, Vocals on 'Jugband Blues' and 'Remember A Day'**

Recorded at EMI Studios, Abbey Road, London
Produced by Norman Smith

THE PINK FLOYD

THE PINK FLOYD have become a five-man group with the addition of 21-year-old singer-guitarist David Gilmur. His joining them will allow the Pink Floyd to maintain their basic four-piece unit at the same time as freeing one of the group to explore new instruments and add further experimental dimensions to their already distinctive sound.

Gilmur, a close friend of Syd Barretts and Roger Waters from Cambridge, has been rehearsing with the rest of the Floyd for several weeks and is now working with them on both live appearances and their currently heavy recording schedule.

The new five-member Floyd embark on their first European tour on February 18th, which includes a performance at the First European International Pop Festival in Rome.

Of all the acts to emerge from the UK underground scene of late 1966 and early 1967, few would disagree that Pink Floyd were the most influential and successful. Although no longer active, their catalogue sales reach numbers few active artists ever attain, but throughout their career they consistently refused to bow to commercial pressures or compromise their musical integrity.

It was very different in December 1967. At this time the fortunes of Pink Floyd were at a crossroads due to the failing mental health of their chief muse, Roger 'Syd' Barrett. It was Barrett who had brought together Roger Waters (bass, vocals), Richard Wright (keyboards, vocals) and Nick Mason (drums) and it was Barrett who named the band, taking the name from two blues artists, Pink Anderson and Floyd Council. Beginning life as an R&B-influenced outfit, the group soon incorporated long experimental instrumental pieces in their set alongside cover versions.

With Barrett revealing himself to be a songwriter of startling originality, the group dropped the covers and evolved into London's first and most accomplished psychedelic outfit. A residency at the Marquee Club (during which they first experimented with a mind-expanding light show) ensured they attracted a wider audience, with new managers Peter Jenner and Andrew King taking every opportunity to present the band to the emerging underground audience. A live appearance at the launch of International Times at the Roundhouse greatly enhanced their reputation.

The single 'Arnold Layne,' recorded at Sound Techniques studios in London and financed by Jenner and King, was subsequently leased to EMI's Columbia label and gave the band their first UK hit single in March 1967. A full contract was negotiated with EMI and follow-up 'See Emily Play', proved to be even more successful, rising to a peak of Number 6 in the UK. Work then began with producer Norman Smith on the band's debut album, 'The Piper At The Gates Of Dawn'. The record featured sonic experimentation on pieces such as 'Astronomy Domine' and 'Interstellar Overdrive' alongside Barrett's child-like slices of pop whimsy on pieces such as 'The Scarecrow', 'Bike', 'Matilda Mother', 'Lucifer Sam' and 'The Gnome'.

The album, a psychedelic masterpiece, reached the UK Top 10 later that year. By the time of its release, in August 1967 Barrett was showing the first signs of mental instability due to his increased intake of LSD.

By the band's first American tour in October 1967 he was barely capable of performing and on an important TV appearance he stood still, refusing to mime to 'See Emily Play'. The tour was cut short and Pink Floyd returned home. Faced with the reality that Syd Barrett was incapable of performing live Waters, Wright and Mason recruited an old Cambridge friend of Syd, David Gilmour on guitar with the idea that he could fill Barrett's shoes on stage while Syd could still write and record with the group.

Within weeks it became apparent that this was an unworkable situation and main songwriter Barrett was soon dismissed.

Viewing their actions as career suicide, Peter Jenner and Andrew King dropped Pink Floyd from their management roster, opting to manage Barrett instead. With the odds stacked against them, Pink Floyd signed with their agent Brian Morrison for management carried on regardless and set about completing their next album for EMI. Sessions for a second album had begun in October 1967, but had stalled because of Barrett's deteriorating health.

PINK FLOYD

A Saucerful of Secrets, Columbia SX6258(m) SCX6258(s)

y d pinkfloyd

Sole Agency & Management:- BRIAN MORRISON AGENCY
164 CHARING CROSS ROAD, LONDON W.C.2

E.M.I. Records (The Gramophone Co. Ltd.) E.M.I. House, 20 Manchester Sq. London W.1

Taking 'Let There Be...' as a sampler, this instantly impacts itself as a truly inventive barrier-breaking group performance. The avant-garde writers have already raved about it – and certainly it's way ahead of the singles style of this somewhat under-rated outfit. Particularly on the instrumental side, they launch often-savage waves of sound – mostly beautifully constructed and of splendid power. This is music to listen to, dig deep into... forget it as background sounds for a party.
Very highly commended. ★★★★★

RECORD MIRROR 3/8/68

1968

These sessions at De Lane Lea Studios saw the Barrett composition 'Vegetable Man' and Richard Wright's 'Remember A Day'. While the latter would be retained, 'Vegetable Man' was deemed unusable by the rest of the band and unsuitable for release as the next single. Also recorded was another Barrett track, 'Jugband Blues', on which Syd wanted to use a Salvation Army band for the middle section of the track. Producer Norman Smith had argued with Barrett that the band parts should be scored, while Syd asked the band members to 'Play whatever you want'. The final mix saw Smith get his way, with parts of the cacophony Barrett preferred added at the end.

With the band occupied on the road and faced with the problem of replacing Syd, sessions resumed without Barrett in earnest at Abbey Road studios in January 1968. The first songs recorded were Richard Wright's 'It Would Be So Nice' and the Roger Waters composition 'Julia Dream,' both of which were selected for release as a single in March 1968. The whimsical nature of the A-side would later lead Nick Mason to describe the song as 'fucking awful' and lead to speculation that Pink Floyd were finished as a commercial force without Barrett within their ranks.

Determined to prove detractors wrong, Pink Floyd set about creating a piece of music that would define their sound for the next four years. 'A Saucerful Of Secrets' was a glorious blend of avant garde experimentation involving a microphone stand being rolled up and down a guitar fretboard, while the strings of a grand piano were scraped and plucked, all underpinned by a solid percussive pattern. This crescendo of sound gave way to a glorious coda of vocals and organ to create a stunning soundscape. Richard Wright would later declare 'We all thought it was one of the finest things we'd put on record, but Norman Smith objected to us recording it saying "It's too long. You can't put that on record." Thankfully we got our way.' Equally impressive was the epic space rock of 'Set the Controls for the Heart of the Sun,' (a staple of Pink Floyd live shows well in to the Seventies and also performed by Roger Waters in his solo concerts) which also defined the sound of the new Pink Floyd.

Of the song-based material, 'Let There Be More Light' was influenced by science fiction, while 'Corporal Clegg' was Roger Waters' first lyrical foray into the futility of war, a subject that would dominate his later work. Richard Wright's 'See Saw' was a piece of whimsical psychedelia that reflected earlier work.

Released in June 1968, 'A Saucerful Of Secrets' turning point in Pink Floyd's fortunes. Critic Derek Jewell declared: 'Much of the album reflects a concern with the science fiction other-world. The very long title track is typical, with menacing organ chords overlaid by rustling glass and metal and creature noises. But super-imposed in yet another dimension throughout the record are susurrant voices and hypnotic snatches of melodies, often Arabic in flavour, so that the effect is both worldly and otherworldly. Though there is some monotony, this is experimentalism within a structure.'

For a record borne out of such uncertain times, 'A Saucerful Of Secrets' was a confident declaration of an assertion of a new musical direction for the band. As David Gilmour correctly stated some years later, 'We knew that we had to start the ball rolling again. "A Saucerful Of Secrets" was the start back on the road to some kind of return. It was the album we began building from.'

PRETTY THINGS 'SF Sorrow'

First released as Columbia SX6306 (mono)/SCX6306 (stereo) in December 1968
Highest UK chart position: N/A
Available on CD as Snapper SMMCD565

SF Sorrow Is Born
Bracelets Of Fingers
She Says Good Morning
Private Sorrow
Balloon Burning
Death
Baron Saturday
The Journey
I See You
Well Of Destiny
Trust
Old Man Going
Loneliest Person

Phil May	**Vocals**
Wally Allen	**Bass Guitar, Guitar, Vocals, Wind Instruments and Piano**
Dick Taylor	**Lead Guitar and Vocals**
John Povey	**Organ, Sitar, Percussion and Vocals**
Twink	**Drums and Vocals**

Recorded at EMI Studios, Abbey Road, London
Produced by Norman Smith
Engineered by Peter Mew

By the beginning of 1967 the Pretty Things, like their contemporaries, had made a dramatic stylistic change from being one of Britain's greatest R&B bands into pioneers of the burgeoning psychedelic scene.

The band had formed in 1963 when guitarist Dick Taylor, who had been an early member of the Rolling Stones, and fellow art student and vocalist Phil May recruited John Stax on bass, Brian Pendleton on rhythm guitar and drummer Viv Andrews. By May 1964 the band had secured a residency at the 100 Club on London's Oxford Street and were managed by Jimmy Duncan and Bryan Morrison.

The Pretties' raw R&B sound and unkempt image led to offers by various labels who saw them as a potential rival to the Rolling Stones. On signing to Fontana Records later that year, Viv Andrews was replaced by Vivian Prince. The release of the single 'Rosalyn' led to an appearance on influential TV show Ready Steady Go!, while a string of singles promised much but failed to enjoy the success they deserved. By early 1967 the band had undergone a series of line-up changes and had begun to absorb the influence of psychedelia.

Keen to broaden their musical horizons, they recorded a final album for Fontana, 'Emotions', which saw them try to free themselves from their R&B past. It was a mixed affair, with strings and brass added after the band had assumed they had finished. Soon after, the Pretty Things signed to EMI's Columbia label, having evolved into a fully-fledged psychedelic rock band with Taylor and May joined by Wally Allen (bass, vocals), John Povey (keyboards, vocals) and Skip Alan (drums). Phil May had expressed a desire to bring to fruition a conceptual story in song he had been working on. 'When we signed to EMI we all felt we had to move on and take things to the next level musically. It slowly came to me that, if we didn't have to be bound by the limits of a four-minute single, we should make our next album a continuous cycle of songs joined together by a theme. It had been done in classical music for many years, so we thought we should do that in a rock context.'

Teaming up with former Beatles engineer Norman Smith, also the producer of Pink Floyd, the first Pretty Things record released by EMI's Columbia label was the impressive 'Defecting Grey'. 'That song began life as a seven-minute track we'd put together with Norman Smith. He showed us what could be achieved in the studio. He really inspired us to use new sounds in our music such as the Mellotron and embraced the idea of using Indian instruments like the sitar.' 'Defecting Grey' was actually several themes interwoven to produce a continuous piece of music. Edited into a more manageable four minutes, the track was a brave choice for a single release but failed to chart.

However, it spawned the idea for the Pretty Things' major creative statement. 'Looking back, I think "'Defecting Grey'" was a model for what became "SF Sorrow". That single was when we really began work on the album.' The 'SF Sorrow' concept was based upon Phil May's abstract tale of a man who had grown up in an English town, married, fought in a war and set off to a new land, tragically losing his wife. May's lyrical imagination knew no bounds and the music, written by the band, was their finest to date. Wonderful material such as 'SF Sorrow Is Born', 'Private Sorrow', 'Balloon Burning', 'Baron Saturday', 'The Journey', 'I See You', 'Trust', 'Old Man Going' and 'Loneliest Person' were psychedelic masterpieces equal to anything being recorded by Pink Floyd or the Beatles at that time.

Completion of the album was not an easy task as EMI demanded another single, duly delivered in the form of the superb 'Talking About The Good Times'. Work was also interrupted by the unexpected departure of drummer Skip Alan. Faced with the task of finding a replacement quickly, John Alder (known as Twink) from the band Tomorrow was drafted in as a replacement. 'We'd demoed the album with Skip in the band,' Phil May would later reflect, 'and had written the material and recorded about half of the album. But when he left us suddenly we had to bring in Twink. We had no money to pay him so we offered him a share of the publishing on the tracks he played on instead. It grated that he ended up getting credited on material on which he'd had no share of writing, but that was all we could do.'

'SF Sorrow' was finally released in December 1968, the product of over a year's work with producer Norman Smith. A marvellous work, it failed to enjoy the commercial success it deserved, in part due to a lack of promotion. One ardent admirer was Pete Townshend of the Who, who would cite 'SF Sorrow' as inspiration for him writing 'Tommy' some months later. 'SF Sorrow' suffered a delayed release in America, surfacing several months after 'Tommy' and leading journalists to assume it was an imitation of Townshend's work. Fortunately history has set the record straight and 'SF Sorrow' is now seen for what it was – the first 'rock opera' and one of the finest albums of the late Sixties by a British band.

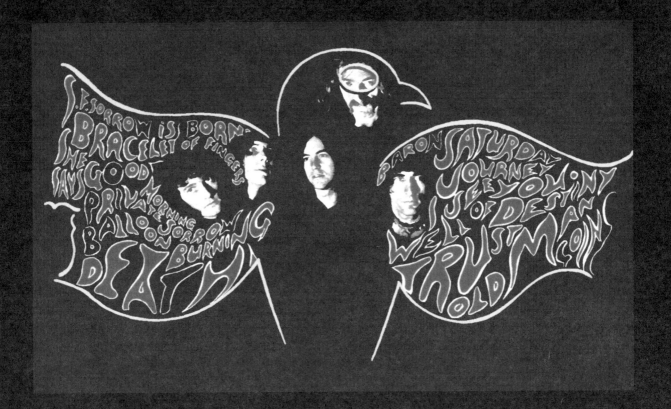

★ ★ ★ ★ As soon as I heard the opening track, S.F. Sorrow Is Born, I had to have a quick look at the cover to convince myself that this group was the old Pretty Things. Yes, there they all were: Phil May, Wally Allan, Dick Taylor, John Povey and Twink. Music written by the group, sleeve design and story by Phil May, photography by Dick Taylor. The Pretty Things take over the record industry!

They have improved out of all recognition and have produced an album which should rate as one of the best of 1968. A theme runs through the record concerning S.F. Sorrow, the tracks linking with the sleeve story, and they are all very good. Private Sorrow, Balloon Burning and Death are outstanding tracks. So if you're tired of being told how good the new Beatles and Stones LPs are, this could be for you.

NME 21/12/68

SOFT MACHINE 'The Soft Machine'

First released in the US as ABC Probe CRLP4500 in November 1968
Highest UK chart position: N/A
Available on CD as Polydor 532 050-5

Hope For Happiness
Joy Of A Toy
Hope For Happiness (Reprise)
Why Am I So Short?
So Boot If At All
A Certain Kind
Save Yourself
Priscilla
Lullabye Letter
We Did It Again
Plus Belle Qu'une Poubelle
Why Are We Sleeping?
Box 25/4 Lid

Kevin Ayers   **Bass Guitar, Vocals**
Mike Ratledge   **Keyboards**
Robert Wyatt   **Drums, Percussion, Vocals**

Recorded at Record Plant Studios, New York City
Produced by Chas Chandler and Tom Wilson

Of all the artists featured in the pages of this book, few underwent such a stylistic musical transformation as Soft Machine. Starting life as a band that absorbed soul and jazz influences, the group were one of the first to embrace psychedelia before heading off on a jazz-influenced tangent. In the course of their history Soft Machine would undergo a series of bewildering line-up changes that would eventually see no original members left within their ranks. In hindsight Soft Machine's evolution could have only taken place in the musical free-thinking environment that was the music scene of the late Sixties/early Seventies. It was an evolution that would produce some of the most startlingly brilliant and innovative music of the period.

The roots of Soft Machine lay in the city of Canterbury in Kent and the circle of bohemian friends with Robert Wyatt at their core. Gathering at the large Georgian house owned by Robert's mother, Honor, Wyatt shared the company of Kevin Ayers, Hugh and Brian Hopper, Mike Ratledge and drifting Australian beatnik Daevid Allen, spending many hours listening to modern jazz and being exposed to the world of beat poetry and Dadaist art. By June 1963 this circle of friends had formed the band the Wilde Flowers featuring Robert Wyatt on drums, Hugh Hopper on bass, Brian Hopper on guitar and saxophone, Richard Sinclair on rhythm guitar and Herne Bay resident Kevin Ayers as vocalist. The Wilde Flowers would go through many changes with musicians such as Richard Coughlan and Pye Hastings joining the fold.

In 1965 Ayers and Wyatt travelled to Deya in Mallorca with Robert Wyatt to stay with the poet Robert Graves; lured by the prospect of good weather, blue sea and a relaxed lifestyle. This trip established Ayers' love of the Balearics and subsequently prompted another visit to the island with Daevid Allen. It was on this visit that Ayers and Allen were introduced to Wes

Brunson, an American heir to a fortune, who urged the two travellers to start a serious band, lavishing sums of money on them in the process.

In June 1966 Ayers and Allen, along with Robert Wyatt and Larry Nowlan, had formed the band Mister Head and undertaken a few local concert appearances. (The remnants of the Wilde Flowers, Pye Hastings, Richard Coughlan and Richard Sinclair, eventually formed Caravan with keyboard-player Dave Sinclair.) By August 1966, spurred on by Wes Brunson, Mike Ratledge had joined their ranks and a series of demos had been recorded with the intention of securing a recording contract. The name Bishops of Canterbury only lasted a solitary performance before the group adopted Soft Machine, taking the name from a William Burroughs novel with Allen securing the permission of the author.

The earliest recorded appearances of Soft Machine took place in September 1966 at the infamous Star Club in Hamburg where a scheduled three-night booking became less than one night when the band was reportedly forced off-stage by a hostile audience. Returning to London, Soft Machine performed at one of the earliest Spontaneous Underground 'happenings' at the Marquee Club and at the All Saints Hall in Ladbroke Grove supporting Pink Floyd. Like them, Soft Machine began to incorporate long improvisations in their jazz-influenced music and were soon darlings of the emerging underground scene in London with regular performers at UFO, psychedelic club nights held at the Blarney Ballroom on Tottenham Court Road. By the end of 1966, Soft Machine and Pink Floyd were London's most talked-about groups.

In December 1966 Soft Machine undertook their first serious recording session at CBS Studios in London with American producer Kim Fowley. Aside from the taping of an aborted track 'Fred The Fish' (since lost), the session would produce the excellent Kevin Ayers track 'Feelin' Reelin' Squealin''. A session at Advision Studios the following month with former Animals' bassist Chas Chandler acting as producer would lay down the basis of the track 'Love Makes Sweet Music' which would be completed in early February 1967 at Olympic. Soft Machine's debut vinyl outing, 'Love Makes Sweet Music' b/w 'Feelin' Reelin' Squealin'' was released as Polydor BM56151 in at the end of February. A remarkable record, it gained considerable airplay on pirate radio stations, particularly John Peel's Perfumed Garden show on Radio London, and ensured Soft Machine were in demand as a live attraction.

In April recording sessions with producer Giorgio Gomelski took place at De Lane Lea with the view that this material would form the band's first album. Deemed unsatisfactory, these recordings would remain unreleased until 1971 when French label BYG Records added the tracks to two compilation albums. They would later gain notoriety when released as the album 'Jet Propelled Photographs'. The same month saw Soft Machine participate in the biggest psychedelic gathering in London, the 14-Hour Technicolor Dream, which took place at Alexandra Palace on 29 April and also featured Pink Floyd, the Move, the Pretty Things, the Crazy World of Arthur Brown, Graham Bond and the Social Deviants. The event gained much media coverage and resulted in a great deal of publicity for Soft Machine who, despite having only released one single, now enjoyed a loyal following.

The summer of 1967 was spent performing in France where the band performed various concerts in and around St. Tropez. Returning to the UK on 24 August, Daevid Allen was refused re-entry to the UK on the grounds that his visa had expired. Returning to France, Allen settled in Paris and would eventually form Gong. Back in England, Ayers, Ratledge and Wyatt resolved to continue as a trio and secured increasing work in Belgium and France. The band ended the year with an appearance at 'Christmas On Earth Revisited' at London's Olympia where they joined Pink Floyd, Jimi Hendrix Experience, the Who, Eric Burdon and the Animals, Tomorrow et al in one of London's last major psychedelic events.

Soft Machine soon became more formally involved with Jimi Hendrix Experience managers Chas Chandler and Mike Jeffery, and the band secured the support slot on Hendrix's US tour that took place in February and March 1968. Accompanied by roadie Hugh Hopper, the tour was to prove highly eventful, with Mike Jeffery securing Soft Machine a recording contract with ABC/Probe Records. Recording took place at Record Plant studios in New York City in April 1968 with Mothers of Invention, Velvet Underground and Eric Burdon and Animals producer Tom Wilson and manger Chas Chandler supervising proceedings.

The music written and performed by Soft Machine is arguably some of the finest produced during the latter days of psychedelia and represents the first throes of progressive rock. Compositions such as 'We Did It Again', 'Why Are We Sleeping', 'Hope For Happiness' and 'Joy Of A Toy' had all been tried and tested in concert, and on record Soft Machine revealed the extent of their considerable musicianship and creativity. The experimental editing techniques used in the recording process would serve as an inspiration for legions of aspiring musicians over the following decades and resulted in a seamless and perfect work.

As is true of most great art, the music contained within the grooves of Soft Machine's first album was to appeal to the select number of music buyers who were 'in tune' with the new direction in which popular music was heading. Even more frustrating was the delay in releasing the album in the US and failure to gain a British release at all, although it did appear in France and Holland in November 1968 where it was enthusiastically received.

Despite producing such a fine work, all was not harmonious within the ranks. Briefly returning to London in May, Ayers, Ratledge and Wyatt recruited former Dantalion's Chariot guitarist Andy Summers for further US dates. By mid-July, Summers had departed, Soft Machine now operating as a three-piece. The next two months were spent touring with Jimi Hendrix once more, finishing in Los Angeles where musical disagreements began to arise between Kevin Ayers and the duo of Wyatt and Ratledge. While his fellow band members flew back to England, Robert Wyatt remained in Los Angeles for a few more weeks to work with Hendrix.

The sheer exhaustion of performing night after night over a two-month period, combined with recording sessions, proved to be too much for Kevin Ayers. Fatigued and amicably at odds with Wyatt and Ratledge's desire to take the musical direction of the band more towards jazz and away from song-based material, he announced his intention to pursue a solo career. He was to be replaced in Soft Machine by the band's roadie and friend Hugh Hopper. Ayers spent time in Deya writing songs and, returning to England, secured a solo recording contract with EMI's Harvest label.

In December 1968 the new line-up of Soft Machine began rehearsals for their next album, destined to be another masterpiece. However, the musical pastures explored on the band's first album would forever hold a special place in the hearts of many followers.

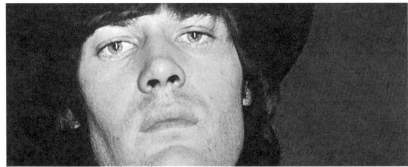

The Soft Machine

'THE WALL ON WHICH THE PROPHETS WROTE IS CRACKING AT THE SEAMS'

KEVIN AYERS: 'Joy Of A Toy'

First released as Harvest SHVL768 in December 1969
Highest UK chart position: N/A
Available on CD as EMI Harvest 07243-582776-2-3

Joy of a Toy Continued
Town Feeling
The Clarietta Rag
Girl On A Swing
Song For Insane Times
Stop This Train (Again Doing It)
Eleanor's Cake (Which Ate Her)
The Lady Rachel
Oleh Oleh Bandu Bandong
All This Crazy Gift Of Time

Kevin Ayers	Vocals, Guitar, Bass, Keyboards, Piccolo, Recorder, Mouth Organ, Kazoo

GUEST MUSICIANS:

Robert Wyatt	Drums
Mike Ratledge	Organ
Hugh Hopper	Bass
Rob Tait	Drums
David Bedford	Keyboards and arrangements

Recorded at EMI Studios, Abbey Road, London
Produced by Peter Jenner and Malcolm Jones
Engineered by Peter Mew

When Kevin Ayers departed Soft Machine in December 1968, few would have guessed that a career as one of Britain's finest and most influential musical talents would lie ahead of him. Like his peer and fellow Harvest label pioneer Syd Barrett, he was always profoundly uneasy with the self-promotion the music business demanded, a feeling which led to him departing Soft Machine after a gruelling American tour.

Ayers retreated to Mallorca and spent time in Deya writing songs with an acoustic guitar. He returned to England and recorded a series of demos on a Bayercord four-track tape recorder in Herne Bay. These caught the attention of Peter Jenner and Andrew King, original managers of Pink Floyd and now proprietors of Blackhill Enterprises, organisers of the Hyde Park free concerts and managers of Syd Barrett, Roy Harper and the Edgar Broughton Band among others. Signing to Blackhill led to Ayers becoming one of the first artists to secure a contract with EMI's newly established Harvest label. In July 1969 he entered Abbey Road studios with Jenner as producer and with a group of musicians that included Robert Wyatt, Mike Ratledge, Hugh Hopper and arranger David Bedford.

The music that would be recorded over the next eight weeks would comprise one of the most enduring and original albums to appear on Harvest, and would be much more whimsical in feel than Ayers' work with Soft Machine. Bedford's arranging skills came to the fore on pieces such as 'Joy Of A Toy' and 'Town Feeling', which featured a beautiful oboe part by Paul Minns. Other highlights destined to achieve legendary status in the Ayers canon were the evocative 'Girl On A Swing' and 'Song For Insane Times' which featured Ayers' old bandmates Mike Ratledge and Robert Wyatt.

Ratledge also contributed his distinctive organ sound to the gloriously psychedelic 'Stop This Train (Again Doing It),' a track which began with the innovative use of a gradually sped-up tape recorder to simulate the sound of a steam train gathering momentum. Equally enduring would be 'Eleanor's Cake (Which Ate Her)', a vignette featuring a charming Bedford arrangement.

Perhaps the definitive Ayers track recorded in those summer months of 1969 was 'The Lady Rachel', a song that immediately became a live favourite. Such was its appeal that in February 1972 the song was re-recorded at Abbey Road studios with a full and dramatic orchestral arrangement written by David Bedford.

A final session took place in September 1969 to record the superb 'Soon Soon Soon', a song sharing the refrain of Ayers' composition 'We Know What You Mean', recorded by Soft Machine in April 1967. 'Joy Of A Toy' was released in December 1969 and, although failing to make the UK chart, made a significant impact on the ever-growing underground audience. Melody Maker declared; 'Joy, beauty and mystery abound in this album by the former Soft Machine guitarist. His songs are simple but fascinating, with the warm, hazy and sometimes sinister feel of songs half-remembered from distant childhood. The arrangements, featuring members of Soft Machine on some tracks, capture the spirit of the thing perfectly: subtle, mysterious, richly textured and delicately funky.'

With no regular backing group for live concerts, Ayers would address this situation by forming the Whole World in 1970, featuring David Bedford on keyboards, Lol Coxhill on saxophone, Mick Fincher on drums and young guitarist/bass player Mike Oldfield, and record 'Shooting At The Moon'. He would go on to record some of the most interesting music released by Harvest and make a lasting impression on British music, continuing to record on and off to this day. Of all his recorded work, however, nothing sums up the musical approach of Kevin Ayers better than 'Joy Of A Toy', his most satisfying listening experience.

JACK BRUCE 'Songs For A Tailor'

First released as Polydor Records 583058 in September 1969
Highest UK chart position: 6
Currently available on CD as Polydor 065 603-2

Never Tell Your Mother She's Out Of Tune
Theme For An Imaginary Western
Tickets To Water Falls
Weird Of Hermiston
Rope Ladder To The Moon
The Ministry Of Bag
He The Richmond
Boston Ball Game 1967
To Isengard
The Clearout

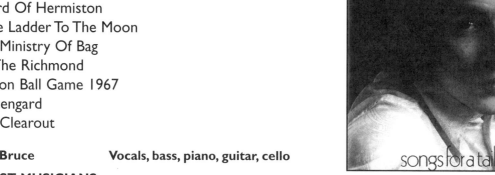

Jack Bruce	**Vocals, bass, piano, guitar, cello**

GUEST MUSICIANS:

Jon Hiseman	**Drums**
Dick Heckstall-Smith	**Tenor and Soprano Saxophones**
Chris Spedding	**Guitar**
Harry Beckett	**Trumpet**
Henry Lowther	**Trumpet**
Art Themen	**Tenor saxophone**
Felix Pappalardi	**Guitar, Vocals**

Recorded at Morgan Studios, Willesden, London
Produced by Felix Pappalardi for the Robert Stigwood Organisation
Engineered by Andrew Johns

With the demise of Cream in November 1968, Jack Bruce, the bass player, vocalist and multi-instrumentalist who wrote the majority of the band's material with lyricist Pete Brown, pondered his future. In just two and a half years Cream released four albums ('Fresh Cream', 'Disraeli Gears', 'Wheels of Fire' and 'Goodbye') and notched up sales of over 35,000,000 albums and were awarded the first ever platinum disc for sales for the double album 'Wheels Of Fire'. The Jack Bruce and Pete Brown partnership was responsible for writing most of the group's material including 'I Feel Free', 'White Room', 'Politician' and 'Sunshine Of Your Love'.

But the extensive and endless cycle of touring and recording took its toll and a mutual decision was made to split the band. Prior to Cream undertaking a farewell series of concerts Bruce had gathered together musical friends Dick Heckstall-Smith (who had played with him in the Graham Bond Organisation), drummer Jon Hiseman (who had replaced Ginger Baker in Bond's group before joining John Mayall for his 'Bare Wires' album) and virtuoso guitarist John McLaughlin to record the jazz album 'Things We Like' in August 1968. Although completed in only four days, the recordings were to remain unreleased until 1970.

'Although I had recorded "Things We Like" in August 1968,' Jack would later recall, 'I wanted an album of songs to be my first solo release and felt an album of jazz material wouldn't be right as my first solo statement.' With a number of unrecorded songs written for Cream with collaborator Pete Brown and a further selection of new material, Bruce gathered a circle of musicians around him which would include Hiseman, Heckstall-Smith, guitarist Chris Spedding, drummer John Marshall and special guest George Harrison. Enlisting the services of Cream producer Felix Pappalardi, he entered Morgan Studios in Willesden, London at the beginning of April 1969 to begin work on his first post-Cream album.

Bruce later explained; 'I had wanted to make a true solo album some time before Cream split up but wanted the feel of the record to be very different to Cream, as I had so much more instrumentation to play with. Part of my frustration with Cream was that it was such a limited band in the studio and on stage. I think by using people like Chris Spedding on guitar, who was the total antithesis to Eric in terms of playing, helped make a different sound. Chris was a very understated player. John Marshall was also a very different drummer to Ginger. He had a bit of the "Ringo Starr" about him in the way that he played a great backbeat. I suppose it was a conscious effort on my part to make a record that sounded very different from Cream.

'At the time people like Ahmet Ertegun, boss of Atlantic Records, told me that I should look for a couple of young musicians and form another trio. Being me I decided to do exactly the opposite of course.' One of the earliest songs to be taped was a jazz-rock tour de force, 'Never Tell Your Mother She's Out Of Tune', featuring Jack on piano and bass guitar, Henry Lowther and Harry Beckett on trumpet, Dick Heckstall-Smith and Art Themen on saxophone and Jon Hiseman on drums. The song also boasted a special guest. 'George Harrison played rhythm guitar on the last Cream session when we recorded "Badge", which he co-wrote with Eric, and I was really impressed by his playing because he added a lot to the song. When it came to recording "Never Tell Your Mother She's Out Of Tune" I thought of him straight away and called him up. Luckily he agreed to do it and his contribution was really valuable.'

Another early track to be attempted was 'Ministry Of Bag', a jazzier demo having been recorded earlier. The experimental 'Boston Ball Game 1967', with its 'doubled' lyrical structure, was originally known as 'Plastic Eye', the music being conceived by Jack in 1967. 'I was staying in Boston while I was playing there with Cream,' he later remembered. 'We had a pretty hard time in the city. It was the final of the baseball World Series and we were staying in a hotel where we were virtually prisoners due to the fact that Boston was such a rednecked city and we were dressed in our hippy clothes. It was a horrible time with all sorts of personal things going down and our only form of release was to play at a place called the Psychedelic Supermarket, which was a parking garage that had been vaguely done up and turned in a venue. We would go there and there would be about 10 or 12 people waiting to see us play. It was a depressing time and I got really fed up so Pete and I wrote this song which was basically a kind of yell against the redneck attitude. The double lead thing was something I had tried with "'I Feel Free" and "Sunshine Of Your Love" and I decided to take it one step further with this track.'

'Boston Ball Game' wasn't the only song to have its origins in the days of Cream, as Pete Brown would later recount. 'Songs like "Weird Of Hermiston" and "The Clearout" were demoed for Cream. The band was on the road all the time and there was very little time available to write, so everyone looked to whoever had the most material available and it was usually Jack and myself. There was opposition to some of the material that Jack and I wrote for the band from Atlantic Records and Ahmet Ertegun dismissed much of it as psychedelic rubbish.'

Bruce would later comment: 'The rejected song that surprises me now is "Theme From An Imaginary Western". I think that would have made a great Cream number. I remember playing it to Eric who said that it sounded like a rip-off of the Band. As I'd written the music around 1962 I knew it wasn't. In a way I think it was good that it ended up on my album as it's one of the songs I'm most proud of.'

'"Theme From An Imaginary Western" is a song with a powerful resonance,' Pete Brown agreed some years later. 'Jack and I hit something there, which was a natural fusion of words and music. When music is as strong as that Jack had written and is so full of images, it makes it easier to get the words. The song was about the early British R&B bands seen as cowboys and pioneers. We'd all grown up with Western movies and in a way I think the musicians on the British R&B, jazz and blues scene of the Sixties all thought of themselves in that way! Musically the Graham Bond Organisation were pioneers and it was a mythologisation of that band really.'

The song 'Weird Of Hermiston' was another album highlight, with roots in literary history, as Pete Brown would later state. 'I think "Weird Of Hermiston" has a very Scottish feel. Robert Louis Stevenson's last novel was called Weir Of Hermiston and he never finished it. That novel has a feeling of doom, which is enhanced even more by the fact that the novel remained unfinished. Jack is a great reader and we both looked to literature for inspiration; it was reflected in this song.'

The album was completed in the first week of June 1969 and released under the title 'Songs For A Tailor' in September 1969. 'I dedicated the title to a good friend of mine, Jeannie Franklin,' Bruce explained. 'She used to make clothes for me and had a shop on Santa Monica Boulevard which was the epitome of LA chic in 1967 and '68. She originally made clothes for Motown bands like the Four Tops and then for Cream and other British bands. We became good friends and on the day that I began work on the album I got a letter from her which finished with the words "Sing some high notes for me," which is something she used to say. She was the girlfriend of Richard Thompson of Fairport Convention and was unfortunately killed the day I received the letter when Fairport's van crashed on the motorway and also killed their drummer Martin Lamble. That's the reason the album got its title.'

'Songs For A Tailor' has gone on to become one of Jack Bruce's most highly regarded works. Its material remains timeless, a fact borne out by its nomination as one of the 500 most important albums of all time in a poll of music journalists in 2000. The breadth of music included on the record is breathtaking and a testament to the musicianship of Jack Bruce and his writing partnership with Pete Brown.

'The great thing about "Songs For A Tailor",' Brown would add, 'is that Jack continued his relationship with Felix Pappalardi as producer. Felix put a lot into that record. The atmosphere and form of the songs are unique and I don't think anyone else wrote in that way at the time. Jack's knowledge of jazz and classical music came to the fore and it gave me a wide canvas upon which to paint words. There are very few musicians who are able to provide such variety in their writing.' 'Songs For A Tailor' is indeed a masterwork.

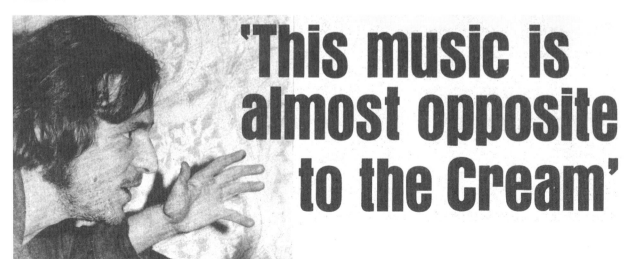

'This music is almost opposite to the Cream'

Now Jack Bruce to star in his own TV showcase

FORMER Cream bassist Jack Bruce is to star in his own one-hour colour-TV special to be directed and produced by Tony Palmer, famed for his pop documentary, "All My Loving." Bruce's first solo LP " Songs For A Tailor " is issued by Polydor on August 29, and the TV show will be based on this album.

The film is being made by Robert Stigwood's own company—which is also filming the Bee Gees' special " Cucumber Castle." Bruce is also writing the script for the film, which revolves around his own life story, and much of the action will be shot on location in his native Scotland.

Tony Palmer — who also directed the TV coverage of the Cream's farewell concert — is expected to include filmed sequences of the Cream in action. It is not yet known whether the other ex-members of Cream, Eric Clapton and Ginger Baker, will participate in the Bruce special — although it is considered probable they will do so if they are in Britain at the time of shooting.

BRUCE: MASTER MUSICIAN

JACK BRUCE: SONGS FOR A TAILOR (Polydor, 583058; 37s 6d)

THE strength of the Cream's exciting appeal was, to quite an extent, the vocals of bass player Jack Bruce. Now Jack has had the freedom of playing not only bass, but piano, cello and organ on this, his first solo LP. He did all the arrangements, composed all the music and sings all the Pete Brown lyrics.

He picked the musicians from his friends — Harry Beckett and Henry Lowther, trumpets; Dick Heckstall-Smith and Art Theman, soprano and tenor saxes; Jon Hiseman and John Marshall, drums; Chris Spedding, guitar; LP producer Felix Pappalardi, vocals, percussion, guitar. Only engineer Andrew Johns kept silent at the mikes.

So what does it add up to? A very interesting and varied bunch of tunes, all with plenty of powerful beat and drive to them, specially the fast opener, Never Tell Your Mother She's Out Of Tune. This is followed by a folksy number, Theme For An Imaginary Western. But best on side one is the slightly wierdo Rope Ladder To The Moon, with a compelling tune to it.

On the three tracks trumpets and saxes are used, there is a full jazzy sound, which urges Jack's voice along to greater efforts, as in The Ministry Of Bag. Jack sings in a high, monotone voice for Boston Ball Game 1969, making it an eerie sounding experience. He also gets some far-off beauty into the music of He The Richmond, and a driving bass uniqueness about To Isengard.

The entire album proves one thing we've had an inkling about for a long time — that Jack Bruce is a very talented contemporary all-round musician. **AE.**

Other titles: **Tickets To Waterfalls, Weird Of Hermiston, The Clear Out.**

JERRY LEE LEWIS: I'M ON FIRE (Mercury mono and stereo 134 204 MCY; 38s 7d).

After a spate of country and western albums, Jerry Lee returns to rock. Most of the tracks are already well-known, but it's nice to have them all on one album. Memphis Beat typifies his style — plenty of pounding piano, guitar riffs and a bawling vocal, just the way his fans like to hear him. Pen and Paper is in the country style and is about a man who's got to write and tell his girl he's found someone new — all very sad.

I'm On Fire is one of the out-and-out rockers that has people on their feet and in the aisles all over the world and This Must Be The Place which has lots of piano pumping. Other recommended tracks include If I Had It All To Do Over, country again, and Baby (You've Got What It Takes) on which Jerry Lee duets with his sister **Gail Lewis. RG.**

Other tracks: **She Was My Baby (He Was My Friend), This Must Be The Place, What A Heck Of A Mess, Rockin' Pneumonia and Boogie-Woogie Flu, Hit The Road Jack, The Hole He Said He'd Dig For Me, Bread and Butter Man.**

Jack Bruce U.S. tour, new band

JACK BRUCE will tour America in January.

He confirmed this week his plans to form a new 10-piece band for the tour. He has also invited Jon Hiseman and Dick Heckstall-Smith of the Colosseum to feature with him on the coast-to-coast dates.

Bruce also plans a concert at London's Festival Hall some time in December.

CAN 'Monster Movie'

First released in Germany as Music Factory SRS1 in January 1969
First issued in the UK as United Artists UAS29094 in July 1969
Highest UK chart position: N/A
Currently available on CD as Spoon Records SPOONCD004

Father Cannot Yell
Mary, Mary So Contrary
Outside My Door
Yoo Doo Right

Holger Czukay	**Bass**
Michael Karoli	**Guitar**
Jaki Liebezeit	**Drums**
Malcolm Mooney	**Vocals**
Irmin Schmidt	**Keyboards**

Recorded in 1968 and 1969 at the Schloss Norvenich, near Cologne
Produced by Can
Engineering and editing by Holger Czukay

For all the innovative rock music to come from the shores of the British Isles in the late Sixties, it would be difficult to find much which compared to the sounds that emerged from a castle near Cologne in Germany, committed to tape in the closing months of 1968 and the beginning of 1969. Can's stunning debut album 'Monster Movie' caused a stir in the musical world, the repercussions of which are still felt over 40 years later.

Can hailed from a dark and sinister place, a place where 'father could not yell' because he 'hadn't been born yet' and where 'any colour was bad'. Such foreboding lyrical musings sprung liberally from the mind of American sculptor Malcolm Mooney, who would improvise his disturbing visions to repetitive rhythms via Can's human drum machine, Jaki Liebezeit.

When these stark elements were added to keyboard-player Irmin Schmidt's spacey effects, the unique guitar work of 19-year-old Michael Karoli and Holger Czukay's solid bass, the result was progressive music in the literal sense. Derided by some at the time as self-indulgent noodling, Can's music went far deeper than that. They viewed their art in the same context as the great experimental 20th-century painters. Just as Picasso or Dali were exceptional painters in a conventional manner but chose the path of experimentation, the members of Can were capable musicians who eschewed the conventional rules of music-making. They worked by one rule: there were to be no rules.

Can's modus operandi was to let both musical and environmental influences flow through each member to create music of a truly spontaneous nature. Indeed, the expressionist metaphor is appropriate as their original vocalist, Malcolm Mooney, was a painter and sculptor, while Irmin Schmidt and wife (and future Can manager) Hildegard were very involved in Cologne's fertile modern art scene.

The roots of Can lay in the so-called 'new music' school of thought that emerged in the late Fifties and early Sixties, pioneered by American composer John Cage and German experimentalist Karlheinz Stockhausen. Stockhausen pioneered electronic music on works such as Hymnen, and was a major influence on the emerging rock/avant garde movement, including notable German disciples Tangerine Dream, recently formed in Berlin.

Two of Can's guiding lights met at the Stockhausen classes of the mid Sixties, both eager to change what they saw as stagnant musical thinking. Irmin Schmidt was a classically trained pianist and conductor in the process of forsaking a promising career as an orchestral conductor to explore his own musical visions. In early 1966 he travelled to New York to enter a conducting contest. While there, to use his own words, he 'got corrupted.' The emerging New York music and arts scene fascinated Schmidt, who met John Cage and spent many nights with minimalist composer Terry Riley. Absorbing the influences of Steve Reich, LaMonte Young and artist Andy Warhol, Schmidt returned to Cologne with new and adventurous musical ideas. Meeting Holger Czukay at the Stockhausen classes encouraged Schmidt to suggest the two of them form a band that would encompass the 'new music' influences, free-form jazz and rock.

After sharing his ideas with an American, David Johnson, who rented a room at his house, Schmidt was introduced to Michael Karoli, a young Swiss guitarist firmly schooled in rock and beat music of the day. Through his admiration for Manfred Schoof's free-jazz group, Schmidt met drummer Jaki Liebezeit. The improbable union of three musicians all aged over 30 and a teenager, all with diverse and apparently unrelated musical backgrounds, became a reality and Can was born.

Michael Karoli - guitar

Holger Czukay - bass

'The idea of forming a band was mine,' Irmin Schmidt would later reflect. 'I wanted to found a group because I came from the so-called 'new music' school. Rock wasn't the only "new music". Rock was as new as Stockhausen in this century. Let's call it pop music, as it's easier to put it into a category. In this whole wide world of popular music, which encompasses rock, jungle, techno, jazz or whatever, there exists artistic elements and artful musicianship, as there is within so-called "new music". In all these fields you find a lot of art and also a lot of shit too!

'Being pretentious and calling what you do art doesn't make you artistic. The quality of the artist makes music art. At the time we formed I was very influenced by John Cage. He was not such a musical influence in the sense of saying that you should play in this way or that – it was more the way you thought about music. It freed you from any kind of old thinking, and you started back at zero again.

"I wanted to gather musicians from all of the modern musical phenomena. Jaki came from a jazz background and played music from all styles of jazz history. At the time we formed Can he was playing free jazz. Holger was playing a little jazz and was studying in the same class as me on the Stockhausen courses. I had been conductor at the opera house and had given piano recitals. I'd played piano concertos and conducted symphony orchestras and I performed a lot of new music. It led me to perform Cage's music. In fact, I was one of the first in Germany to perform Cage's music. I met Cage when I was in the States, although I never worked with him. Even just meeting him from time to time and spending an evening with him influenced me a lot.

'Strangely enough, now I realise, when I look back, how much he did for me. I wasn't aware of it so much at the time, as there were so many other influences around. My idea was to bring the most unfitting musical elements together and create a totally new musical phenomenon, which I did. I brought together jazz, new music, and someone who was 10 years younger than the rest of us, who was just innocent and hadn't studied music much, but who wanted to make really big music.

'Michael was extremely clever and was a really great musician without any formal education. He helped prove that this new way of taking to playing the guitar, without 10 or 20 years' experience, could result in giving birth to something passionate and nurture a great musician, which is what Micky definitely is. Since we didn't know each other well and weren't friends, it meant that we all had to fight for our own corners. Everybody had their own individual ideas about music, but we all wanted to get away from the old ideas and start again. What we had in common was a dream. We wanted no hierarchy, with no individual composer. We would do everything together, creating spontaneous common compositions. No individual would be the author. The group would be the author, which meant the group would grow together until it became an organism. The basic idea was a vary Cage-ian one. The idea was that everything around you, every sound – trams, cars, etc – everything is music if you are the medium through which it can flow. You structure those things and turn them into music. That was what we did and we finally succeeded.' Shortly after their formation, Can was offered a large room in which to rehearse and record at the Schloss Norvenich, a castle just outside Cologne. It was here, while working long into the night with flautist David Johnson briefly aboard, that American vocalist Malcolm Mooney became involved with the group. 'Malcolm was a friend of Serge Tcherepnin, a composer in the Stockhausen class,' Schmidt would later explain. 'Serge and I worked a lot together at the time we were in the same class. His father was a famous composer and Hildegard went to visit Serge in Paris. While there she met Malcolm. Malcolm was travelling around the world and she suggested that he come stay with us in Cologne. He was an extremely interesting guy and Hildegard liked him a lot.

'Malcolm was a painter and sculptor. Since Cologne has a very rich art scene with a lot of galleries and I was very involved with the art scene – I knew more painters and sculptors than musicians – Hildegard suggested he come to visit us. The notion was to see if he could break into that scene. Malcolm came to stay and I took him to our studio, which was where I spent my day. I say studio, but it was just a room where we played. He turned up and just started singing. Immediately, Malcolm and Jaki became one sort of huge rhythm machine. Malcolm had a great sense of rhythm and immediately those two became a unit. At that point we asked him to stay.'

David Johnson departed the band shortly afterward, leaving the quintet to embark on a series of recording sessions. Some tracks from those sessions appeared on the posthumously released 'Delay' album in the early Eighties, and others became their first album. Can's approach was based on long, spontaneous recorded improvisations. These were consolidated by bassist Holger Czukay, who quickly became an astoundingly adept and imaginative editor of recording tape, able to create new compositions out of improvised recording sessions. The sounds achieved by this quintet were stunning examples of the embryonic Can's creativity. The energy on these early recordings is a kind of fusion between Jimi Hendrix and Stockhausen. Certainly, nothing like it had ever been heard before in either the field of rock or 'new music'.

It quickly became apparent that Can should take the important step of recording material for an album. This caused a dilemma among band members, as Schmidt later explained; 'Since we had embarked on this form of spontaneous composition, you couldn't suddenly prepare music for making a record. You couldn't rehearse pieces, go into a studio, produce it and make a record. We had a totally different kind of plan. It didn't make much sense to go into professional studios, because it either wouldn't be our music or we would have to spend a hell of a lot of money. At that time studios were very expensive. We decided that we would record with very basic equipment, just two stereo Revox tape recorders, a couple of microphones and our instruments and amplifiers. It worked!'

The album 'Monster Movie' worked and continues to work. With such daring music as 'Father Cannot Yell', 'Outside My Door' and the side long 'Yoo Doo Right', the production on the album was truly unique. However, this adventurous approach was met with indifference from German record labels when master tapes were presented to them for consideration by Hildegard

Schmidt. The band decided to release the album themselves on the Music Factory label, pressing a limited run of 600. As fortune had it, one of those copies landed on the desk of the boss of the newly opened German office of Liberty/United Artists in Munich. Irmin Schmidt later explained; 'Siggi Loch, who was head of Liberty/UA in Germany, heard "Monster Movie" one day and really freaked out about it.'

Loch offered the band a contact and United Artists re-released 'Monster Movie' straight away. 'Siggi was very helpful in the first years of Can. We had a very good time with him in Germany, and he passed our album on to United Artists in England, who were also very helpful.' 'Monster Movie' proved very popular with a German audience that favoured the avant-garde experiments by acts such as Pink Floyd. In Britain, radio DJ John Peel was one of the first people to pick up on 'Monster Movie,' playing it frequently on his influential BBC Radio 1 show.

The influence of Can's debut album cannot be overstated. It launched the group on a decade of musical innovation and notoriety, during which their music would visit musical plains that others, lacking their stomach for avant-garde adventurism, dared not tread. In the late Seventies, musicians embarking on rock's new wave movement would cite their music as a major influence. Their influence and legacy that began with 'Monster Movie' continues to loom large over serious rock music.

Malcolm Mooney - vocals

Irmin Schmidt - keyboards

Jaki Liebezeit - drums

COLOSSEUM 'Valentyne Suite'

First released as Vertigo Records VO1 in November 1969
Highest UK chart position: Number 15
Currently available on CD as Sanctuary SMBCD386

The Kettle
Elegy
Butty's Blues
The Machine Demands A Sacrifice
The Valentyne Suite:
a. January's Search
b. February's Valentyne
c. The Grass Is Always Greener

Dave Greenslade	Keyboards, Vibraphone
Dick Heckstall-Smith	Saxophones
Jon Hiseman	Drums and Percussion
James Litherland	Guitars and Vocals
Tony Reeves	Bass

With the New Jazz Orchestra arranged by Neil Ardley
Recorded at Morgan Studios, Willesden, London
Produced by Tony Reeves and Gerry Bron

Colosseum were formed at the end of 1968 by former Graham Bond Organisation and John Mayall's Bluesbreakers members Jon Hiseman (drums), Dick Heckstall Smith (saxophone) and Tony Reeves (bass), who joined keyboard player Dave Greenslade and guitarist James Litherland to form this ambitious progressive jazz-rock group. In truth, all members of the band had already earned considerable reputations for their musical abilities. Hiseman, Reeves and Greenslade had played together as teenagers in a local band in Eltham, South London as far back as 1960. Dave Greenslade spent tenures with both Chris Farlowe and the Thunderbirds and Geno Washington's Ram Jam Band, while Hiseman and Reeves were members of the New Jazz Orchestra, a 19-piece ensemble that pushed the perceived boundaries of the genre.

In 1966 Hiseman joined the Graham Bond Organisation, a band that had just suffered the loss of drummer Ginger Baker who had departed to form Cream with Jack Bruce (also an earlier member of Bond's band) and Eric Clapton. It was here that he teamed up with Heckstall-Smith, one of the finest saxophonists of his generation. The pair struck up an immediate musical rapport and by the middle of 1967 both musicians had begun to tire of Bond's erratic behaviour.

Hiseman accepted an offer to join Georgie Fame's group and Heckstall-Smith joined John Mayall's Bluesbreakers. In 1968 Mayall expressed a desire to head in a more jazz-based direction for his next album, and, in keeping with his philosophy of having a revolving line-up in his backing group, recruited Hiseman on drums and Reeves on bass as the suggestion of Heckstall-Smith. This new line-up of the Bluesbreakers recorded the excellent 'Bare Wires' for Decca later that year.

The experience of playing together as a live unit inspired Hiseman, Reeves and Heckstall-Smith to think about forming their own group. Inspired by the transformation taking place in popular music, particularly the success of Cream, Colosseum came together in the autumn of 1968. Managed by impresario Gerry

FESTIVAL INTERNATIONAL DE 14 ORCHESTRES EUROPÉENS (EUROPEAN BANDS) JAZZ TRUMPET WORKSHOP DRUM CLINIC MONTREUX SUISSE SWITZERLAND 18-22 JUIN 1969 6 CONCERTS: KENNY BURRELL QUARTET KENNY CLARKE COLOSSEUM FENTON HIGH SCHOOL BIG BAND ELLA FITZGERALD TOMMY FLANNAGAN TRIO EDDIE HARRIS QUARTET LES McCANN TRIO JOHN SURMAN HOFFMANN COMBE VOUMARD TENTET TEN YEARS AFTER CLARK TERRY & ERNIE WILKINS FESTIVAL BIG BAND PHIL WOODS QUARTET

Bron, who signed the band to his stable of artists, Colosseum recorded their first album in the closing months of 1968 and early 1969. 'Those About To Die Salute You' was leased by Bron to Philips' Fontana label and reached a height of Number 15 in the UK charts, partly as a result of the stunning live shows the band were performing.

By now Philips had devised the concept of a new progressive imprint, Vertigo and it was decided that Colosseum's next album should launch the new imprint. The centrepiece of this new record was to be a Jon Hiseman/Dave Greenslade epic in three 'movements' known as 'The Valentyne Suite'. Originally performed on stage with the piece 'Beware The Ides Of March' as its closing section, for the recording sessions the first two sections 'Theme One – January's Search' and 'Theme Two – February's Valentyne' were joined by Dick Heckstall-Smith's 'The Grass Is Always Greener'. 'The Valentyne Suite' would come to dominate the second side of the album.

The first side contained more song-based material, opening with the strident and powerful 'The Kettle', which had begun life as a jazz piece written by Heckstall-Smith and Hiseman. By the time it ended up on record it was a stunning power-trio track featuring Hiseman, Reeves and Litherland, evoking comparisons with Cream. 'Elegy' was an excellent James Litherland work featuring a string section and superb soprano sax playing from Heckstall-Smith, while 'Butty's Blues' featured an imaginative arrangement by Neil Ardley performed by the New Jazz Orchestra. The side closer, 'The Machine Demands A Sacrifice' was an excellent band composition set to lyrics by Pete Brown.

Released in the late summer of 1969, 'Valentyne Suite' was adventurous in style, being a true fusion of jazz and rock. The album also firmly established the Vertigo label, securing another Top 20 chart placing in the UK and reaching the same heights as its predecessor. Its creative and commercial success led to Colosseum drawing large audiences, particularly in German, where they had a large loyal following. By the time 1970's 'Daughter of Time' was recorded, the band had undergone a line-up shift with Mark Clarke replacing Tony Reeves, and Dave 'Clem' Clempson replacing James Litherland (who formed the band Mogul Thrash with John Wetton). Chris Farlowe's recruitment on vocals completed the changes.

'Valentyne Suite' remains Colosseum's most essential album. It defined a new style of rock music and, in the album's title track, ploughed a new pathway in a style of rock that was termed progressive by the British music press of the time.

Thanks to Jon Hiseman for the use of these images

HIGH TIDE 'Sea Shanties'

First released as Liberty Records LBG83264 in October 1969
Highest chart position: N/A
Not currently available on CD

Futilist's Lament
Death Warmed Up
Pushed, But Not Forgotten
Walking Down Their Outlook
Missing Out
Nowhere

Tony Hill   **Guitar, Vocals**
Simon House   **Violin**
Peter Pavli   **Bass, Vocals**
Roger Hadden **Drums**

Recorded at Olympic Studios, Barnes, London in June and July 1969
Produced by Denver Gerrard
Engineered by George Chkiantz

In the late Sixties, with countless groups of aspiring and idealistic musicians coming together to seek their own musical Nirvana, few were as original and awe-inspiring as High Tide. In their all too brief career, Tony Hill (guitar, vocals, keyboards), Simon House (violin, viola, keyboards), Peter Pavli (bass) and Roger Hadden (drums, organ) recorded two albums of power, originality and beauty. Their fusion of hard rock and the Gothic violin playing of Simon House in turn gave birth to a stylistic hybrid that, four decades later, defies classification. High Tide was the vision of one of Britain's most original and creative guitarists, Tony Hill. Hill had first come to the attention of a wider public as rhythm guitarist with the highly talented American group the Misunderstood. Formed in California in 1965, the band had come to the attention of young British DJ John Pee, who, while working in California, had attended an early performance. Acting in a managerial capacity, Peel suggested the band follow him to England to pursue a career in Europe.

Soon after their arrival in Britain the Misunderstood recruited a former member of Newcastle-based group the Answers, Tony Hill. Signed to Fontana in the autumn of 1966, the band cut the outstanding single 'I Can Take You To The Sun' co-written by Hill

and vocalist Rick Brown. Further sessions resulted in the single 'Children Of The Sun', the group enjoying a series of high-profile shows at London's Marquee Club.

Just as the Misunderstood began to enjoy success, influencing British bands such as the Move and Pink Floyd in the process, the American members of the band were deported from the UK following a brief trip to France in the early months of 1967. This left Tony Hill seeking further session work on the London scene which included a six-month spell as part of the trio Turquoise with David Bowie and his partner Hermione Farthingale. A series of concerts followed at such important venues as the Roundhouse, Middle Earth and the Wigmore Hall in London and a series of demos recorded before Hill set his sights on new musical pastures. His ambitions were realised when High Tide were formed in the early months of 1969. Their highly imaginative blend of folk, psychedelia, and hard rock with a dark edge was unique for its time and the band soon came to the attention of the Beatles' Apple Corps, signing a publishing deal in the spring of 1969. They cut several demos in March of that year with the specific intention of securing a recording contract. High Tide's connection with Apple meant that they were soon approached by several labels, eventually negotiating a contract with the British office of Liberty/United Artists at the end of April.

Liberty was changing its focus as a label, with 23 year-old A&R head Andrew Lauder keen to steer the label towards the newly emerging underground album market. 'I'd just begun to dabble in A&R at that time,' Lauder would later recall, 'the Groundhogs being the first band that I signed directly. Their first album for Liberty sold well and the signs were very encouraging for signing other album-orientated bands. I actively began to look for other suitable acts for the label and High Tide came along via Clearwater Productions, an underground management and agency company based in Acton.' Clearwater Productions was set up by Doug Smith, Richard Thomas and Max Taylor to promote the underground acts they managed who included High Tide, Skin Alley and Trees and would become a major force in the Ladbroke Grove hippie scene. High Tide were the first of Clearwater's acts to reach the attention of a major label, and within weeks of signing, the band had recorded a BBC Radio 1 session for John Peel's Night Ride show and were soon ensconced at Olympic Studios in Barnes to begin work on their first album. Sessions were supervised by Denver 'Denny' Gerrard previously a member of the outfit Warm Sounds who had recorded singles for Immediate and Decca's Deram label. Gerrard was in the throes of recording a solo album and sessions for High Tide's debut offering commenced alongside those for his own LP, on which High Tide would act as backing group. Sessions were conducted at a rapid pace with the band recording the essence of their live act at that time. The magnificent 'Futilist's Lament' was one of the first recordings attempted. A work of brutal power, it would prove to be an effective opening track to the first High Tide album. This would soon be joined by the excellent 'Death Warmed Up', 'Pushed But Not Forgotten', 'Walking Down Their Outlook', 'Missing Out' and 'Nowhere,' all examples of dark, doom-laden progressive rock.

Following the recording sessions High Tide undertook regular concert appearances throughout the UK, receiving their first notable music press coverage in an early edition of ZigZag magazine in September 1969. The article stated that; 'High Tide's forthcoming album lacks some of their on-stage onslaught, but is worth buying to be numbed by the beauty of Simon House's violin and Tony Hill's slicing guitar. Onstage, their volume sometimes causes trouble with balance, but they produce the most spaced-out sound I've ever heard. Try and hear them straight, it's a trip in itself.'

The enthusiastic write-up followed a series of appearances at concerts staged over three consecutive weekends at All Saints Hall in Ladbroke Grove in August 1969 by Clearwater Productions, who used the events to showcase their acts. The final August concert proved to be particularly memorable, with High Tide and Skin Alley being joined by the unknown Group X. Doug Smith later recalled; 'High Tide had just been signed by Apple Publishing and Liberty and had all this brand new equipment. This band, Group X, turned up and said "Can we play? Can we use your gear, man? It's nice and new." We agreed to let them open the show. That was the first appearance by Hawkwind.'

The fruits of the recordings of the early summer were released in October 1969 as 'Sea Shanties', adorned in a striking Paul Whitehead-designed gatefold sleeve and receiving universal praise in the British underground press. Despite failing to chart, it notched up healthy enough sales to secure commitment from Liberty to release a follow-up. Although High Tide would record a second album prior to disbanding, it is the dark, sometimes brutal, sometimes delicate 'Sea Shanties' which stands out as their finest hour.

JETHRO TULL 'Stand Up'

First released as Island Records ILPS 9103 in August 1969
Highest UK chart position: Number 1
Currently available on CD as Chrysalis 7243 5 35458 2 6

A New Day Yesterday
Jeffrey Goes To Leicester Square
Bourée
Back To The Family
Look Into The Sun
Nothing Is Easy
Fat Man
We Used To Know
Reasons For Waiting
For A Thousand Mothers

Ian Anderson	Vocals, Flute, Acoustic Guitar, Mandolin, Balalaika, Bouzouki, Mouth Organ
Martin Lancelot Barre	Electric Guitar, Flute on 'Jeffrey Goes To Leicester Square' and 'Reasons For Waiting'
Glenn Cornick	Bass
Clive Bunker	Drums
David Palmer	String arrangement and conducting on 'Reasons For Waiting'

Recorded at Morgan Studios, Willesden, London
Produced by Ian Anderson and Terry Ellis

Jethro Tull began life in the northern English seaside town of Blackpool, with the formation of blues group the Blades with Ian Anderson (vocals), Jeffrey Hammond-Hammond (bass) and John Evan (drums). This line-up soon changed with the addition of Barriemore Barlow on drums and the movement of John Evan to keyboards. By December 1967 the Blades had become John Evan Smash with Glen Cornick replacing Hammond-Hammond on bass. Opting to try their luck in London, the band relocated there.

Finding life as a struggling blues band too much to bear, both Evan and Barlow decided to move back to Blackpool, leaving Anderson and Cornick to assemble a new band with Mick Abrahams on guitar and Clive Bunker on drums. After a series of concerts under the name Bag of Blues they became Jethro Tull, named after an 18th-century agriculturalist who had invented the seed drill. The band's first single appeared in early 1968 on MGM, but 'Sunshine Day' b/w 'Aeroplane' was bizarrely credited to Jethro Toe and failed to make any chart impression. It did however lead to a residency at the Marquee Club in London in June 1968 which brought them to the attention of Chris Wright and Terry Ellis who had just founded the Chrysalis Agency.

Ellis and Wright began to get Jethro Tull high-profile support slots, including one supporting Pink Floyd at the Hyde Park

Free concert on 29 June that year and a storming set at the Sunbury Jazz and Blues Festival in August. Inevitably, Chrysalis opted to fund Tull's first album soon after. The impressive results were released as 'This Was' later that year on the Island label, with whom Wright and Ellis had negotiated a production and marketing deal. An excellent debut, it soon entered the UK charts and peaked at Number 10. Extensive touring followed the release and a non-album single, 'Love Story' b/w 'Christmas Song', appeared in November 1968 and charted at Number 29.

By this time a rift had grown between Ian Anderson and Mick Abrahams which led to the guitarist's departure to form Blodwyn Pig. He was initially replaced by Birmingham-based guitarist Tony Iommi (later to form Black Sabbath), who appeared with the band on the aborted Rolling Stones Rock And Roll Circus TV show, recorded on 11 December 1968 but eventually released in 1995. Iommi was permanently replaced by Martin Barre prior to Tull's first US tour, which assisted in 'This Was' reaching Number 62 on the US chart.

The first studio sessions for Tull's second album began at Morgan Studios in Willesden in April 1969. The music was to be a cohesive blueprint for the future direction of the band, with the music featuring folk, classical, jazz and blues influences. Of the material recorded, songs like 'Bourée', 'Nothing Is Easy', 'Fat Man', 'Look Into The Sun', 'We Used To Know', 'Reasons For Waiting'

and 'Back To The Family' were all a radical departure from their early material. With the exception of 'A New Day Yesterday', the band had abandoned their earlier blues influences and instead headed into the world of jazz (on 'Bourée') and folk ('Fat Man'). Indeed, early live performances of these songs were greeted with derision in some quarters of the UK music press, with accusations that the band had in some way sold out their early followers.

However, any fans Jethro Tull were to lose by this change of direction would be made up for by the vast numbers who found this new sound appealing. To demonstrate this, the single 'Living In The Past' b/w 'Driving Song' was to give Tull their first UK Top 10 hit single and assisted in propelling the band to stardom prior to their second album. Released in August 1969, 'Stand Up' topped the UK charts while the band were touring America and would reach Number 20 on the Billboard chart, a wonderful achievement by any standards.

Jethro Tull would embark on a career as one of Britain's most enduring bands, recording a string of hugely successful albums. Ian Anderson still refers to 'Stand Up' as one of his favourites. With every track outstanding, it remains the bands most fully realised effort.

JETHRO ARE BACK

NOT
WISHING TO
DISAPPOINT
ANYONE
WHO SAID
AMERICA
WOULD
CHANGE
THEM!

JETHRO TULL / LIVING IN THE PAST

C.W. DRIVING SONG WIP 6056 *RELEASED* 25th APRIL

 PRODUCED BY TERRY ELLIS AND IAN ANDERSON FOR CHRYSALIS PRODUCTIONS LTD

island

ISLAND RECORDS LIMITED 155-157 OXFORD STREET LONDON W1

JETHRO TULL "Stand Up" —
A New Day Yesterday; Jeffrey
Goes To Leicester Square;
Bourée; Back To The Family;
Look Into The Sun; Nothing Is
Easy; Fat Man; We Used To
Know; Reason For Waiting; For
A Thousand Mothers (Island ILPS
9103).

ALREADY a massive hit, this
is perhaps one of the
finest LP's of its kind to be
produced in Britain. The hard
intelligent sounds, the depth of
some of the lyrics and the overall complexity of the instrumentals makes it into a must LP
for those interested in white progressive blues. The cover is
good and original, but not to my
personal taste.
★ ★ ★ ★

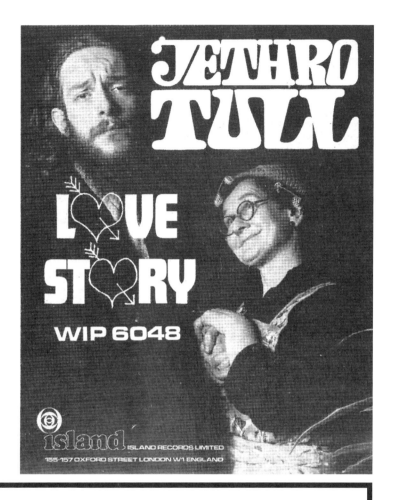

We are proud of

'SWEET DREAM'
cw '17'
by
JETHRO TULL

The first on Chrysalis released October 17

manufactured and distributed by island records

KING CRIMSON 'In The Court Of The Crimson King'

First released as Island ILPS9111 in October 1969
Highest UK chart position: Number 5
Currently available on CD as Panegyric KCSP1

21st Century Schizoid Man *(including 'Mirrors')*
I Talk To The Wind *(including 'March For No Reason'*
and 'Tomorrow And Tomorrow')
Epitaph
Moonchild *(including 'The Dream' and 'The Illusion')*
The Court Of The Crimson King *(including 'The Return*
Of The Fire Witch'
and 'The Dance Of The Puppets')

Robert Fripp   **Guitar**
Ian McDonald   **Reeds, Woodwinds, Vibes, Keyboards, Mellotron, Vocals**
Greg Lake   **Bass Guitar, Lead Vocals**
Michael Giles   **Drums, Percussion, Vocals**
Peter Sinfield   **Words and Illumination**

Recorded at Wessex Sound Studios, London
Produced by King Crimson for EG Productions, 'David and John'
Engineered by Robin Thompson
Assistant engineer Tony Page

King Crimson were arguably one of the main protagonists of the stylistic approach to music termed progressive by the music press. This stunning group was, and remains, one of the most innovative bands to burst forth on the rock music scene at the end of the Sixties, guided by visionary leader Robert Fripp.

Crimson came together from the ashes of the band Giles, Giles and Fripp, a trio comprising Bournemouth musicians Robert Fripp on guitar, Peter Giles on bass and vocals and Mike Giles on drums. After recording an eponymous album for Decca's Deram label, Peter Giles departed leaving Fripp and Mike Giles to assemble a new group. In came Greg Lake on bass guitar and lead vocals and Ian McDonald on woodwind instruments and keyboards. This ensemble was joined by lyricist extraordinaire Pete Sinfield who would also act as lighting technician for the group's live performances. The idea for the band was initially conceived at the end of November 1968 when it became apparent to Fripp that the trio he was then part of was coming to a creative crossroads.

Rehearsals began in the basement of the Fulham Palace Café in London in January 1969. During an intensive three months of rehearsals, King Crimson fused influences ranging from jazz and folk through classical music to the avant garde in a musical style that was unique, emotive and powerful and was to impress every listener lucky enough to witness the band performing. Their formal debut concert performance at the Speakeasy Club in London, a regular haunt of both musicians and record-company A&R staff, in April took the audience by storm and they soon found themselves with a host of

MICHAEL GILES

IAN McDONALD

King Crimson

ROBERT FRIPP

GREGG LAKE

PETE SINFIELD

influential admirers. Still minus a record contract, however, King Crimson were invited to record a session for BBC Radio 1 DJ John Peel in May 1969.

Having signed to David Enthoven and John Gaydon's EG Management, Crimson secured a 12-week residency at the Marquee Club. By this time their innovative music and experimentation with the Mellotron had gained the interest of several labels, including the Moody Blues' newly established Threshold imprint. In an attempt to secure creative freedom, Crimson's management decided to fund the recording of the band's debut album themselves, preferring to license on the finished work to a record company in preference to having creative pressures applied while sessions took place. Following a triumphant appearance supporting the Rolling Stones at their legendary Hyde Park concert on 5 July 1969, they entered Wessex Studios in London to begin work on their masterpiece. Initial sessions with Moody Blues producer Tony Clarke proved unsatisfactory, so the band made the decision to produce themselves.

With sessions taking place throughout the remainder of July and August, interspersed with a busy concert schedule, King Crimson's debut album began to take shape. There can be few aficionados of progressive rock who are unfamiliar with the excellence of the material recorded. Opening with the superb hard-edged jazz fusion of '21st Century Schizoid Man' and following with the delicate 'I Talk to The Wind,' the epic Mellotron-soaked 'Epitaph,' the

Crimson fire

Immediately after King Crimson's performance at Chicago's Kinetic Playground on Saturday, gangsters burnt the club to the ground. Iron Butterfly, the group who were playing with King Crimson, lost all their equipment in the fire, while Crimson themselves lost a mellotron.

gorgeous 'Moonchild' and the stunning climax of 'The Court Of The Crimson King,' the album was a breathtaking debut, laced with the lyrical magnificence of Peter Sinfield, that took the world of British popular music by the scruff of the neck and woke it up to the creative possibilities of rock music.

Released by Island Records in October 1969, 'In The Court Of The Crimson King' received tremendous critical acclaim, (with Pete Townshend of the Who declaring the album 'an uncanny masterpiece'). Adorned in an equally dramatic sleeve design, painted by Sinfield's friend Barry Godber, who was to tragically succumb to a heart attack in 1970 at the age of 24, the record reached Number 5 in the UK and was to be instrumental in giving birth to a new wave of pale imitators.

'This is the ultimate album,' Underground paper International Times declared. 'There is little one can fault with it; the arrangements make masterful use of multi-tracking, compressing and reducing, the standard of playing almost defies belief at times, the vocals are merely excellent and the numbers are brilliantly and exactly written. A gassy, jazzy, heavy, complex, smooth and totally magnificent album: written, arranged, played and produced by the most original band since… (fill in and send your answers to Apple Ltd, Savile Row, London, for instance).'

The following month King Crimson undertook an intensive US tour which assisted the album in reaching Number 28 on the Billboard charts. The toll of delivering a series of wonderful performances on tour had its consequences. Internal strains within the group began to come to fore while in America, with Ian McDonald announcing both his and Michael Giles' departure as the US tour drew to a close. Soon after returning to England, Greg Lake also announced his intention to form Emerson Lake and Palmer with Keith Emerson and Carl Palmer, although he did contribute to sessions for Crimson's next album, 'In The Wake Of Poseidon'.

King Crimson would be steered through a series of line-up changes until Robert Fripp's decision to end the group in 1974, delivering inspired music with each successive album. He would reactivate King Crimson in the early Eighties, putting the group on sabbatical and resuscitating it as he saw fit into the new millennium. Of all the incredible work recorded by various line-ups of the band, the jaw-dropping impact of the music, and indeed the artwork, of 'In The Court Of The Crimson King' remains enduring.

WHAT PETE TOWNSHEND THINKS
ABOUT KING CRIMSON

An uncanny masterpiece. An uncanny masterpiece. Title? Song titles? You might know more than I, but I've got the ace card cos I've the album weeks before release to review no less. What depths one has to stoop to to hear new albums before everyone else. How marvellous is the feeling when I walk in a room and say, "you haven't heard it? More's the pity!" Cos I've heard it and its incredible.

But its also over careful, cautiously rampant guitar solos scream all over you but never miss a note. Silent drums drum and a million bloody mellotrons whine and soar like sirens down a canyon. Endless, or at least seemingly endless passages through extemporised classic non-effervessant secret-keeping become boring. Drums click and sniff, mellotrons breathe, unidentifiable woodwind multiplies, a voice reminiscent of a Zombie ungs. Its time consuming and expensive but somehow, even if you don't get into their complex musical fantasies and indulgences you have to stand and straighten your back when out of all that comes THE COURT OF A CINSONGKRIM ("The Ultimation" says Plum) Bob the roadie comes round. he is already a fan of KING CRIMSON and is extra eager to listen. He doesn't leave his seat until the album is finished, then, after having hung around for about two hours decides to leave. I know when he's had enough.

You must have gathered its good. Undeniably. But in some ways too good too soon if thats possible. You will only know what I'm getting at when you hear it for yourself, its akin to being a ritual it really isn't. The ritual is future worship. The adulation of unnecessary perfection. I hear it, and I know it had to cost at least ten thousand pounds to make. If they chucked out as much as I think they did in order to embrace the remainder it could have cost twenty thousand. I can't tell if its worth it.

A friend listening to the album from a room below says, "Is that a new WHO album?" Deeply I'm ashamed that it isn't, but I'm also glad some how. That kind of intensity is music not Rock.
Twenty first century schizoid man is everything multitracked a billion times, and when you listen you get a billion times the impact. Has to be the heaviest riff that has been middle frequencied onto that black vinyl disc since Mahlers' 8th.
An American chick comes round with a friend and tells me, "They're all real musicians." I don't know where to look. I was never more aware of any other single fact.

Oh well. YINGYANGYINGYANGYINGYANGYINGYANGYINGYANGYINGYANGYINGYANGYINGYANGMYGGGGGGGGENERATION OOH and by the way, THUNDERCLAP NEWMAN. Same to you.

SD 8245/TP 8245

On Atlantic Records and 8 Track Cartridges

CRIMSON KING - PARTS I AND II

One of the most advanced and far sighted groups on the underground scene. King Crimson has come up with a musical montage that defies description on a few lines. It's a pop epic, embracing all manner of styles and ideas with a lyric that's sheer fantasy. Not commercial? Well not altogether perhaps, though it does have a catchy chorus. But please do try to hear this pop extravaganza... it's great!

NME 25/10/69

SUCCESS STAGGERS CRIMSON!

FASHIONS are pleasant but can be dangerously short-lived. In roaring out from nowhere in a matter of half a dozen months to become the fashionable Underground attraction of the day King Crimson have a problem.

"It's very worrying," agreed drummer Mike Giles, speaking from their manager's Kensington mews house before the group left for its debut tour of America. "But I cannot see what on earth we can do about it.

BY NICK LOGAN

"How much are we responsible for what has happened? We started off doing our thing and after that it was not up to us at all. People either go to see you or they don't. If they do then word gets passed

"But there must be some value around"

behind the fashionability. People seem to like the group and we can only hope that they genuinely like the music."

King Crimson's success — their first album "In The Court Of The Crimson King" is at No. 4 in this week's NME LP Chart — really has been staggering. Too staggering for some, notably the groups who had been slogging round the circuit only to discover King Crimson racing past them to become the biggest potential success the Underground has produced this year.

So while the majority of critics, Underground connoisseurs and musicians have been showering lavish praise in their direction — "original," "sensational," "the new Beatles" — there has also existed a small but vociferous band of detractors.

"I think we have had our success a little too fast for some of the people who've been trying to make it for ages," says Mike Giles.

But although the band could be called an overnight success, its members certainly couldn't.

Giles, a 27-year-old who speaks with deliberation and much forethought, has been playing drums for 12 years, first in Bournemouth alongside people like Zoot Money, Peddler Roy Philips and Shadow John Rostill and then in London from 1967. Session work and various unsuccessful groups came before he formed Giles, Giles and Fripp with Robert Fripp.

Fripp himself, King Crimson's lead guitarist, had spent three somewhat soul-destroying years playing in a resident hotel band, backing cabaret artists like Bob Monkhouse and Norman Vaughan before the "forgettable" group with Mike Giles, about which they don't like to talk.

Ian McDonald, 23 and on alto sax, clarinet, flute and mellotron for King Crimson, is a former army bandsman who has played in all kinds of outfits from classical orchestras to wind ensembles.

Former draughtsman and member of The Gods, where he switched from lead to bass guitar, Greg Lake is now the lead vocalist while fifth member Pete Sinfield doesn't actually play in the group but writes their lyrics and operates the famed King Crimson light show.

The group came together in January this year; first Robert and Mike, closely followed by Ian and then Greg.

Pete, a one time computer executive, drifted in later: "I thought how bad the lights were in some clubs and I said I would build them some to give colour on stage. At the beginning I was just changing the lighting for each song but eventually I started 'playing' the lights with the music."

Different

All five brought different influences. Says Mike Giles: "You have got jazz from me, classics from Bob, Beatles and Dylan from Pete and Ian and heavy rock music from Greg. But the divisions aren't really that satisfactory because we all like jazz, we all like Beatles and Dylan etcetera . . ."

The group rehearsed for three months in a room beneath a cafe in London's Fulham Palace Road and made its first public appearance in April.

"There was a very hard core of people who gave us support early on," said Mike Giles. "They spread the good word for us around the clubs and when we went out and did our first gigs we found a lot of people already knew about us."

Their biggest stroke of luck was a booking on the Rolling Stones' Hyde Park extravaganza. It is no meagre tribute that more than a quarter of a million Stones fans who had sat for hours on the hard ground raised howls of delight and surprise for the aggressive music of King Crimson.

Like many of their Underground contemporaries, the group has a loathing of "hype," although Pete and Mike say it has been somewhat exaggerated.

KING CRIMSON (l. to r.), IAN McDONALD, MIKE GILES, PETE SINFIELD, GREG LAKE AND ROBERT FRIPP.

"It was because everybody had been messed around by managers and agents," explained Pete. "Particularly Bob, Mike and Greg who have been through every bad scene in the pop machine."

And Mike's definition of "hype": "Helping one's self without helping others at the same time. Our sort of protest about 'hype' is aimed at the 'hypers,' the ones who are still doing it."

"What does the word pretentious mean to you?" asked Pete suddenly.

"Pretending to be something you're not," I replied.

"Because we've been called pretentious," Pete continued, "and I can't see it.

"I think most people are not quite sure what to make of us actually. Audiences aren't quite sure what bits they should applaud. We may be a little bit ahead of our time. They can see there is something worthwhile but they are not sure what."

Mike: "What do we do? Stop pushing ahead, cash in on what is simple for people to understand, or go by our own standards.

Simplicity

"I hope this doesn't sound pretentious but another group could come along and simplify what we play and they would be away.

"There are strong feelings in the band to get into more involved music. If we did this straight away I don't think we would have an audience for it.

"Nevertheless we enjoy what we do at the moment and believe in it, and it earns us enough money to set up the machinery to get into the music we want to in time."

The group made its debut album three times; more through their own inability to be their own producers than for musical reasons.

Pete: "We were trying so hard. And we were rushed at the end to get it finished. It could have been much better."

Mike: "It could have been 50 per cent better. When we started we were going to be a recording group more than a live group and it appears to have turned out the other way.

"There is a definite lack of feel on the album in some places and only about 30 per cent of the sound everybody wanted. What is missing is the presence, the harshness, the attack.

"We ideally need a sixth member of the band in the shape of a producer."

As is so often the case when a group makes it breakthrough, King Crimson is now in America. They left last week for a two-month tour, complete with three tons of equipment including Pete Sinfield's lights. "It will cost a fortune to send," said Mike.

*

T.I.M.E.: SMOOTH BALL (Liberty, LBS/LBL 83232; 38s 7d)

T.I.M.E. stands for Trust In Men Everywhere, but what that is supposed to mean in connection with this LP, I don't know. I don't know who's got all the goodies this week, but it certainly isn't me. This one is competent, enough but there I run out of praise. It's unoriginal, boring, and really is a waste of the wax it's cut on. Sorry, T.I.M.E., but Take It From Me, you've wasted your T.I.M.E. with this one. **GC.**

More Led on this LP

LED ZEPPELIN II (Atlantic stereo 588 198; 37s 6d)

MUSIC for the paranoic 20th Century city man — another brilliant album from the remarkable Led Zeppelin and the first in transit, so to speak, as "Led Zeppelin 1" was recorded when the group was in an embryionic state and was based largely round the ideas of Jimmy Page.

by Nick Logan

This brings out more of the group, particularly **Robert Plant,** and also shows that the Zeppelin isn't confined to one groove. It can make full use of the subtle shading between the harsher, heavier doses of rock and blues.

Perhaps the most remarkable thing about "Led Zeppelin II" is that the group manages to maintain the element of surprise so obvious when you first hear them.

Thank You and Ramble On, both written by Page and Plant, are softer examples of the Zeppelin style than we've heard on record before. The first is gentle with a Christmassy organ towards the end; the second was inspired by "Lord Of The Rings" and features acoustic and electric guitar and some soft drumwork.

Whole Lotta Love, What Is And What Should Never Be, both among the best tracks, and Heartbreaker and Livin' Lovin' Wreck are typical pieces of hard rock Zeppelin.

Moby Dick is a showcase for some excellent drumming from **John Bonham** and The Lemon Song, with lines like "Squeeze my lemon till the juice runs down my leg," is the most interesting in the set. The Page guitar and some really throbbing bass work from **John Paul Jones** are among its notable features, but, with distortion and the Zeppelin veering between its heaviest and softest, it really has the lot.

Bring It On Home, featuring Plant on harmonica and in a softer vocal key, is the closer — erupting into a schizophrenic ending.

Led Zeppelin have been one of the success stories of 1969 and this extremely good album will serve to quicken their stride towards a place among the world's top groups.

MORE SINGLES reviewed by Derek Johnson

Harmonic CSN blend

CROSBY, STILLS & NASH: † Suite: Judy Blue Eyes (Atlantic).

THE thing that impresses me most of all about the Crosby, Stills and Nash team is its harmonic blend — flowing, golden and really gorgeous. And it's in evidence again on this Stephen Stills composition.

With an ear-catching backing of jangling guitars, tambourine and a snappy beat, the trio displays its jazz-based artistry to even greater advantage than in "Marrakesh Express," specially the delightful scat passage at the end.

Taken at the same pace as "Express," but rather more involved and complex in its interpretation, it's a fascinating and lyrical piece which dresses straight-forward pop in a cloak of quality. Hear it!

Nancy Sinatra, Young & Most

NANCY SINATRA: † The Highway Song (Reprise).

WRITTEN by Kenny Young (to whom Clodagh Rodgers has cause to be grateful) and produced in London by Mickie Most, this is a commercial item which enables Nancy Sinatra to purvey her sultry personality to full advantage.

And Messrs Young and Most have thrown in every possible sales gimmick—a catchy la-la chorus with a group lustily joining in, an infectious toe-tapping beat with a Mexican flavour, a party atmosphere, a simple and quick-to-register tune, and even a touch of Nancy's famous "walking" bass. If it's not lost in the rush, it could catch on.

NME 8/11/69

AMERICA CALLING

BURDON SCREAMS AT KING CRIMSON

KING CRIMSON held court at the Whiskey A Go Go this week, playing to a receptive and appreciative audience. Except for Eric Burdon's screaming interruptions during their second show opening night, King Crimson should take back memories of satisfying and impressing their L.A. audiences.

Before their first show, I talked with bass guitarist and lead singer, **Greg Lake.** Since the group is relatively unknown as yet here in America, their early shows at the Fillmore East met with a general lack of response. But Greg was happy to report that coinciding with their album release, things have gotten better along each step of their tour.

"At the Miami Pop Festival they responded to us incredibly. It was beautiful to see all the people standing up after we played . . . a standing ovation — it was great. The Festival itself was badly organised and a washout. It was a pity all those kids had to sit in three inches of mud for three days."

ANN MOSES in Hollywood

Hesitant

Like so many British groups, **King Crimson** seem hesitant about releasing singles on the American market. "If we find a single which we think is valid as a single, not one released purely for the purpose of promotion, we'll release a single. Otherwise no.

"We won't create a single. Most of our album tracks are eight or nine minutes and that's how they will stay. We won't cut them down for singles because they are total works. Chop a piece out of it and it's like chopping a corner out of a painting."

I wondered how the group reacted when the early shows produced little audience appreciation. Did it make the group do any less of a show when the crowd was unenthused?

"If there is a lack of reaction," Greg commented, "it's just something one has to accept and do as much as he can to create a reaction, which we try to do anyway. We try and play at maximum all the time. I don't think we ever go on the stage and do half a job. You put your maximum in and if you don't get reaction, then you don't.

"It's just hard luck if they don't dig it. It's a pity for them because they have paid money to see something they are not enjoying, which is a pity. There is nothing I can do about that. I can only play and sing and hope they dig it. That's it."

RITCHIE YORKE'S EAST COAST COLUMN

AN important happening in North American music this year has been the popularity decline of soul records. Last year, the Top Ten was swamped with soul music — some of it really first class, but much pretty mediocre.

The decline is because of two factors — the over-commercialisation of soul and the entire Negro sub-culture, plus the recent unwillingness of radio stations who are against the emergence of a black identity to play so-called "coloured records."

There are about 2,500 pop music stations here, with 99.9 per cent of them owned by white people.

A few years back, station owners watched as pop fans turned their dials off the top 40 stations and started listening to the r-and-b stations, programmed by and featuring only Negroes. There was a tremendous boom in

NME 8/11/69

MAN '2 Ozs Plastic With A Hole In The Middle'

First released as Dawn Records DNLS3003 in September 1969
Highest UK chart position: N/A
Available on CD as Esoteric Recordings ECLEC2128

Prelude/The Storm
It Is As It Must Be
Spunk Box
My Name Is Jesus Smith
Parchment And Candles
Brother Arnold's Red And White Striped Tent

Micky Jones	**Guitar, Vocals**
Roger 'Deke' Leonard	**Guitar, Vocals, Harpsichord, Harp, Piano, Percussion**
Clive John	**Organ, Piano, Vocals**
Ray Williams	**Bass**
Jeff Jones	**Drums**

Recorded at Pye Studios, Marble Arch, London
Produced by John Schroeder
Engineered by Alan Florence, Brian Humphries and Howard Barrow

The Man band was born in 1968 when Welsh pop band the Bystanders (who had had a brief flirtation with the UK singles chart with '98.6') fell under the influence of the music emerging from the US West Coast by bands such as Quicksilver Messenger Service, the Grateful Dead and Jefferson Airplane. Dispensing with the services of singer Vic Oakley, Mickey Jones (guitar), Clive John (keyboards, guitar), Jeff Jones (drums) and Ray Williams (bass) recruited singer-guitarist Roger 'Deke' Leonard, then playing in Welsh band the Dream, into their ranks and changed their name to Man.

In the closing months of 1968, Man recorded their first album for Pye Records (the Bystanders' former label), working with ex-Bystanders producer John Schroeder. Schroeder was a champion of the band's work and fought for them to be allowed time to create their debut work, a record which had a loose concept. 'Revelation' was released in January 1969 and was met with critical interest in the UK, but failed to make a lasting commercial impression.

'The band held a post mortem, looking for reasons for the album's failure,' Deke Leonard would later comment with characteristic wit. 'We all agreed it couldn't possibly be the music, so it had to be organisational. We took a quick inventory of our current position. There were no gigs in the book. We didn't have an agent, a manager or a publicist. We had absolutely nobody working on our behalf. There was a clue in there somewhere.'

Despite the lack of manager or agent, Pye consented to allow Man back into their studios in London's Marble Arch to record a follow-up album with John Schroeder producing once more. Relocating to a flat in Streatham, South London, the members of Man began to write new material. 'The weather was spectacular that summer, but we were entombed in the permanent gloom of our ground-floor flat in Tierney Road, where the heavy curtains were never drawn and the lights were always dimmed. We'd often rehearse through the night, playing at full volume. Surprisingly, given that the flat was in a built-up, terraced road, we didn't receive a single complaint from the neighbours.'

One of the earliest pieces written was 'The Storm', an extended instrumental piece that featured a rolling chord-sequence with seagull noises provided by Leonard. The piece was destined one of the highlights of early Man shows, along with the classic 'Spunk Rock'.

TOO MUCH . . . MAN!

AT one time producer John Shroeder had a group which made records but did not have hits. One night he went to see them on a gig to say he was dropping their contract. But what he heard made him really listen.

The group was playing what they **wanted** to play and it was something completely different to what they had done before. So instead of cancelling the contract, John renewed it. So a new group was born called simply . . . Man.

REACTIVE

Their music has been referred to by some as "reactive". This comes from the words creative and reactionary. What it really amounts to is a mixture of hard rock and poetical gentleness. Shroeder has done a good producing job on Man's first album using studio tricks and techniques to fine effect. The album is titled "Revelation" and is available on Pye NSPL 18275. Individual tracks are:

And In The Beginning . . .; Sudden Life; Empty Room; Puella! Puella! (Woman! Woman!); Love; Erotica; Blind Man; And Castles Rise In Children's Eyes; Don't Just Stand There (Come In Out Of The Rain); The Missing Pieces; The Future Hides Its Face.

STORY OF MAN

Basically the LP tells the story of man from the beginning up to the space age in musical terms. The musician's involved are: Roger Leonard, guitar, piano, harp, percussion and vocals. Clive John—organ, piano guitar and vocals. Mike Jones—lead guitar and vocals. Ray Williams—bass guitar and vocals. Jeff Jones on drums and percussion.

The opening track is aptly titled "Sudden Life" is a hard rock number. The side ends with "Erotica" which definitely won't get

MAN—One track won't be heard on radio.

any plays on the Radio! I have been assured that it was not included for sensational effect. "Blind Man" starts off as hard rock but tails off to a gentler end. A classical influence is apparent at the beginning of "And Castles Rise In Children's Eyes". "The Missing Pieces" includes such well-known catch phrases as "sock it to me" and "here comes the judge" ending with war effects and the sound of a woman crying at the futility of it all. "The Future Hides Its Face" tells how far man has come. The album closes with the conversation between an astronaut and ground control, thus taking you up to the present day.

An interesting LP, but it does tend to be a bit gimmicky at times.

★ ★ ★ ★   I.M.

Another fine number was the Clive John acerbic rocker 'Shit On The World'. Entering Pye Studios, the band laid down the tracks for their second album in a series of three-hour sessions. Both 'Spunk Rock' and 'Shit On The World' brought Man into conflict with Pye executives who took issue with the titles of both songs.

'Pye informed us that we couldn't have "Spunk" or "Shit" in the song titles,' Deke Leonard later reflected wryly. 'Clive, who bore the brunt of the argument, told them to call the songs whatever they liked, but what, they said, if we didn't like their choices? "Well, it is as it must be," said Clive. It wasn't until we saw the final album cover that we saw "Spunk Rock" had become "Spunk Box" (the dull bastards had changed the wrong word) and "Shit On The World" had become "It Is As It Must Be".'

Further conflict occurred when the band's desire to experiment with different instrumentation during recording sessions for the piece 'Parchment And Candles' met the disapproval of noted arranger, songwriter and Pye staff producer Tony Hatch as Deke Leonard would later recall. 'Quite often we would follow Tony Hatch in the studio. On one occasion we found a harpsichord still set up. I started picking out a tune on it and when Schroeder heard it he liked it and suggested that we put it down on tape. As we finished, Tony Hatch came back into the studio and when he saw what was going on he erupted. He got on the Tannoy and boomed, "If you haven't paid for the hire of an instrument you should not use it. It's rude. Get off it, now." Although he was morally correct, I thought he was being very petty minded. "How does 'Fuck off!' sound?" I retorted.'

Despite this degree of conflict, the resulting album '2 Ozs Plastic With A Hole In The Middle' was one of the first releases on Pye's progressive Dawn imprint when it appeared in September 1969. It failed to make much of an impact in the UK, but brought Man to a wider audience in Europe, particularly Germany, where the group honed their craft via an intense gigging schedule. 'We recorded the album in Pye's cavernous Studio One, where they did all the orchestral stuff and film music, and set up in a tight circle in the middle of the floor,' Deke Leonard would later reflect. 'We were lit by a solitary beam from a spotlight located high above our heads. It was like being in a time capsule, hermetically sealed off from the outside world and its irritations. We were in the right place at the right time. We all felt that if we couldn't do it here, we couldn't do it anywhere.

'All the people involved in the recording will tell you that this is the best album Man ever recorded. We were playing like demons. Everybody was firing on all cylinders and sparking off each other and we filled each unforgiving minute with 60 seconds of our finest work. It was exhilarating. It is the single, most satisfying studio experience I've ever had. If you don't like this Man album, then you'll never like a Man album.' There is no finer endorsement...

MOODY BLUES 'To Our Children's Children's Children'

First released as Threshold THS1 in November 1969
Highest UK chart position: Number 2
Available on CD as Threshold 983215-6

Higher And Higher
The Eyes Of A Child – Part One
Floating
The Eyes Of A Child – Part Two
I Never Thought I'd Live To Be A Hundred
Beyond
Out And In
Gypsy
Eternity Road
Candle Of Life
Sun Is Still Shining
I Never Thought I'd Live To Be A Million
Watching And Waiting

Graeme Edge   **Drums, Vocals**
Justin Hayward **Guitars, Sitar, Vocals**
John Lodge   **Bass, Sitar, Cello, Vocals**
Mike Pinder   **Mellotron, Keyboards, Guitar, Vocals**
Ray Thomas   **Flute, Vocals**

Recorded at Decca studios, West Hampstead, London
Produced by Tony Clarke
Engineered by Derek Varnals, Adrian Martins and Robin Thompson

By the middle of 1969 the Moody Blues had every reason to feel proud of their achievements over the past eighteen months. They had successfully made the transition from a British R&B-influenced beat group regarded as having little future prospects despite having a Number 1 single under their belt two years previously into a confident rock band. Since the recording of the successful 'Days Of Future Passed' in 1967, the Moody Blues had recorded the albums 'In Search Of The Lost Chord' and 'On The Threshold Of A Dream', each more commercially and creatively successful than the last. Although not as overtly experimental as their previous effort, 'On The Threshold Of A Dream' sailed to Number 1 in the UK, remaining on the listings for an unprecedented 73 weeks.

The Moody Blues were a world-beating act, securing worldwide adoration from legions of followers, but their relationship with Decca Records was the source of increasing frustration. As John Lodge later recalled, 'We had grown tired of having to fight to get our ideas for album covers and artwork approved. We wanted to have our own label, where we didn't have to argue about having gatefold sleeves or inserts with our albums. We saw both music and artwork as a complete package and felt that advertising and promotion should also become part of this.'

After negotiations with Decca chairman Sir Edward Lewis, the Moody Blues were given exclusive use of Studio One at the Decca recording centre in West Hampstead. Limited by the technical facilities available, the band set about rebuilding the facilities, installing state-of-the-art Westlake audio equipment at their own expense. Importantly, inspired by the Beatles' formation of their own label, Apple, while remaining within EMI Records, the Moody Blues established Threshold Records under the auspices of Decca, eventually signing their own roster of artists.

In later years, the responsibility of Threshold would prove to be something of a noose around the necks of the band. 'Threshold had an office to look after us, a sound and lighting system for touring and a recording studio at our disposal,' remembered Graeme Edge. 'Our other intention was to sign other artists to the label, giving them artistic freedom and the use of our studio when we weren't using it.'

Indeed, Threshold were soon rumoured to be interested in signing new British band King Crimson who, although different musically, had been inspired by the Moody Blues' use of the Mellotron. Although Threshold failed to secure Crimson, the label did

MOODY BLUE MIKE PINDER WRITES

We're working well in U.S.

THE man who is doing for the meletron what Hendrix did for the electric guitar — Mike Pinder of the Moody Blues — phoned the NME on Thursday with the news that the Moodies are now well and truly through the sound barrier on their second American tour.

"MY meletron was really in an experimental stage on our first tour and it kept letting us down but this time it's been working to perfection and so have we," said Mike happily.

"A geat many people still seem to think that our orchestral effects were being produced by studio musicians but this time we've been able to prove that all our albums since 'Days Of Future Passed' are all our own work and we have had standing ovations at every venue.

"We started out on a sour note when we missed our first booking at the Los Angeles' Forum due to a hang-up over work permits but Ray and I managed to get there ahead of the others and apologised.

"We volunteered to do a free concert the following day and that was a storm. We've played two dates now with Humble Pie and they too have been getting a good reaction.

"The really great thing for us has been to learn that all our albums are still selling in the States. I saw the sales on 'Days Of Future' for example and they are now over 300,000.

"We are selling as much as 50,000 copies a month in America of our previously released LPs and that is especially pleasing to us because we have always placed a special emphasis on trying to record material that would not date.

"Our new album 'To Our Children's Children' is being released here next week.

"There was a time when the Moody Blues were considering giving up live performances and becoming strictly a studio group but we soon realised how much we would miss and tours like this one really bring it home.

"There is nothing like physically playing in front of an audience to give you inspiration — unless you've played to crowds of 300,000 people you can't really explain what it does for a musician. Believe me session musicians really miss that live form of communication.

"I can't tell you how much we are looking forward to our British tour!"

MOODY BLUES (Mike Pinder is top left).

NME 6/12/69

sign a number of musicians, including hard-rock act Trapeze who achieved success in the US. 'Eventually we all found ourselves on the wrong side of a desk, saying things to artists that had been said to us!' said Graeme Edge. 'Eventually it all got too much, and so the phase of Threshold as a label didn't last.'

As 'On The Threshold Of A Dream' was scaling the UK album charts, sessions began on the Moodies' next project. After three May weeks the band took a month-long sabbatical, reconvening at the beginning of July and continuing until the first week of September. The imminent landing of the first man on the moon proved a major source of inspiration, and an underlying theme of exploration, space travel and discovery permeated the music.

The album began with the epic Graeme Edge poem 'Higher And Higher,' which featured sound effects created to sound like a Saturn V rocket taking off. 'We actually got NASA to send over a recording of a real rocket taking off, but when we listened to the tape it sounded like a damp squib!' recalled John Lodge. 'We had to set about creating our own rocket sound which ended up sounding more authentic.' This epic introduction faded into the thoughtful Lodge composition 'The Eyes Of A Child.'

Ray Thomas' whimsical 'Floating' would bisect the piece on the final album and Justin Hayward's introspective 'I Never Thought I'd Live To Be A Hundred' was also destined to be divided into two parts on the finished album. The last verse was credited as 'I Never Thought I'd Live To Be A Million' and served as the album's penultimate track. 'Beyond' was an ambitious and effective Graeme Edge-composed instrumental that featured Mike Pinder pushing a Mark II Mellotron to its limits. This gave way to Pinder's beautiful cosmic ballad 'Out And In' which closed the album's first side.

Justin Hayward's strident 'Gypsy', one of his most powerful songs written to date, featured both evocative guitar-playing and an outstanding vocal delivery while Ray Thomas' self-seeking 'Eternity Road' (with its wonderful Hayward guitar solo) ranks as one of his most fully realised works. 'Candle Of Life' was a John Lodge composition featuring a vocal contribution from Justin that urged a greater compassion throughout the world, while Mike Pinder's 'Sun Is Still Shining' was a lighter piece of cosmic whimsy that climaxed in a sitar crescendo. The album closed with Hayward's 'Watching And Waiting'. 'People were always telling me that I needed to write another song to equal "Nights In White Satin",' he later recalled. 'When I came up with "Watching And Waiting" I thought that it was one of my best songs and we all felt sure it would be a certain hit.'

Bizarrely, upon its release as a single in October 1969, 'Watching And Waiting' made no impact on the charts on either side of the Atlantic. Justin added 'When the single failed to sell we were all mystified, although with the benefit of hindsight I do see why it didn't capture the public's imagination in the way "Nights In White Satin" did.'
With recording completed, the Moody Blues undertook a series of concerts in Europe before making a major impact at the Isle of Wight Festival on 30 August. One week later, on 5 September, the band organised the now traditional album playback to friends, family and record-company executives.

'To Our Children's Children's Children' was released as Threshold THS1 in November 1969, adorned in a striking Phil Travers-designed sleeve. 'The idea behind the album was to imagine that the record had been placed under a foundation stone that wouldn't be removed for a couple of hundred years,' recalled Graeme Edge. Justin Hayward would also later add: 'It was the inside of the sleeve that really said something. We were depicted gathered around a fire in a cave with just musical instruments and a tape machine and outside there was nothing. I don't know where we were, but we were trying to project the thought that we were on a planet that wasn't earth, somewhere that was Utopia for us.'

The album was another huge seller, reaching Number 2 in the UK and Number 14 in the US. To coincide with the release, the Moody Blues embarked on yet another US tour which climaxed with an appearance at a festival in Palm Beach, Florida on 30 November where the band shared a bill with such rock heavyweights as the Rolling Stones, Ten Years After, the Band, King Crimson, Janis Joplin, Iron Butterfly and Steppenwolf. 'To Our Children's Children's Children' firmly established the Moody Blues in rock's major league and is perhaps their most finely balanced work, treading a path between studio experimentation and a grasp of melody.

MOODIES WRITE FOR YOU

IT is rarely that a group comes along in which all the members have a definite point of view to express. One such group is the Moody Blues and to enable all five members to have a fair crack of the whip, I asked them to write whatever they felt strongly about (reports Richard Green).

The result: a deep insight into the group's "togetherness," an attack on supergroups and, as a special bonus for NME readers, a poem by pianist Mike Pinder. Here is what each have to say.

doesn't spotlight any big names in particular. There are so many people making good sounds it's difficult choosing what to listen to. I think Jethro Tull said a lot with "Living In The Past."

I know I rely on the past and personal experience for writing, not necessarily about things that have happened to be but things I would have liked to have happened. I enjoy sadness in music even more than joy because it seems to get to the soul quicker. Nat King Cole really had that sad happy thing sussed and I admired him so much.

I'm looking forward to the release of the album we've just finished. There are several more varied styles

GRAEME

JUSTIN

of music than we've ever tried before. That's the beautiful thing about being in a group where all five members write material. You get so many different ideas and opinions verbally as well as musically, there's never a dull moment.

Actually, that's probably why the album has taken longer than usual to record this time. We all got completely hung up making it. Life is pretty good just at the moment and it's changing and getting better all the time.

RAY THOMAS: To explain what the Moodies mean to me without sounding melodramatic is very difficult. To me the Moodies are family. I remember my parents saying "You can't pick your family, but you can always pick your friends" and they're cool. This is obviously true to a point, but after a time I found myself in the beautiful

tions of skilled musical technicians so "pop, progressive" or whatever the current superlative is, is heading down this dangerous path.

Following an attempt by Crosby, Stills and Nash to produce an act of genuine musical empathy we have the various highly skilled twelve bar manipulators forming themselves into bands with the idea of them being short-term transient entities hammering out the same worn old cliche with the idea of a quick conversion of their abilities into cash.

Music — along with the other arts — is an expression of the soul, it is the only thing that man has that no other animal has and to present it in its best form, the musicians play-

ing it must have a deeper understanding of each other and the music than merely what chord comes next.

Cliche bashers — learn from modern jazz, you can only fool some of the people some of the time.

MIKE

MIKE PINDER: Sitting in my garden
I see everything's a game.
Butterflies are mating
And the blackbird's tune's the same,
All the world is humming
In a never ending hive,
Shouldn't everyone of us
Be glad to be alive.
But you and Me.
—And nothing is changing—

RAY

position of having four brothers of my own choosing all on exactly the same scene, and that's really too much.

Over the past couple of years we've had quite a few additions, what with marriages and births, bringing the family total up to twenty. Only a small family you may think, until you make places like the Isle of Wight. Then you realise it's so very much bigger. So many brothers and so many sisters all on exactly the same scene . . . too much. Brothers like Richard Green who drinks too much sometimes, but I suppose every family has it's black sheep!

Me? I'm like every family man, I love my family.

GRAEME EDGE: Supergroups! With my tin hat firmly placed on my head and ready to repel boarders I welcome the chance to expose the hype of the century. Just as modern jazz was ruined by solo egos relying on past reputations and triumphs to throw together meaningless combina-

82

Top left: Finished inner gatefold sleeve
Top right: Original photo used
Below left: Outtake from album photo sessions

The sun is still shining, look at the view;
The moon is still dining, with me and you.
Now that we're out here, open your heart
To the universe, of which we're apart...

The Moody Blues "Sun is Still Shining"
from the album 'To Our Children's Children's Children'

QUINTESSENCE 'In Blissful Company'

First released as ILPS9111 in September 1969
Highest UK chart position: N/A
Not currently available on CD

Giants
Manco Capac
Body
Gunga Mai
Chant
Pearl And Bird
Notting Hill Gate
Midnight Mode

Phil 'Shiva' Jones	**Vocals and Keyboards**
Alan Mostert	**Lead Guitar**
Ron 'Raja Ram' Rothfield	**Flute, Bells, Percussion**
Dave 'Maha Dev' Codling	**Rhythm Guitar**
Richard 'Shambu Babaji' Vaughn	**Bass**
Jake Milton	**Drums, Percussion**
With	
Mike **Sitar**	
Surya **Tamboura**	

Recorded at Island Studios, Basing Street, London
Produced by John Barham

Quintessence was a band that could have really only been born in the heady climate of London's Notting Hill Gate area in the late Sixties. By 1968 the area had become the home of London's hippie community, attracting musicians, artists, writers, poets, preachers of radical politics and of the underground press such as Oz and International Times. It was no surprise as the word of London's new 'freak friendly' enclave spread that newly arrived travellers and radicals from Europe, America and the Antipodes would be attracted to the area.

One such person was Ron Rothfield, an Australian flautist who had graduated from Melbourne Conservatory before travelling to New York in the early Sixties and absorbing the modern jazz scene of the city. He drifted to Greece in 1966 and stayed there until the military junta took control in 1968. Leaving for London, Rothfield soon settled in Ladbroke Grove and, inspired by the explosion of underground music, decided to form a jazz-rock band in an attempt to ride this wave of creativity. An ad was placed in Melody Maker stating that potential band members should be resident within the Ladbroke Grove area.

As a result of this advertisement, the musicians who would form Quintessence came together. The multi-cultural influences of the Ladbroke Grove area, also home to London's West Indian population, was reflected in the ethnic diversity of those musicians who formed the band. Indeed, only guitarist Dave Codling hailed from England. Of the remaining musicians both Ron Rothfield and vocalist Phil Jones were Australian, drummer Jake Milton (formerly with Junior's Eyes) Canadian, bass guitarist Richard Vaughn American and lead guitarist Allan Mostert Mauritian.

QUINTESSENCE (Island): Allan, Raja Ram, Jake, Maha Dev, Shambhu, Shiva.

concert:
Rock 'n' raga

It was a strange date for a rock group. The programme to Sunday's concert at St. Pancras Town Hall, London, said it was a "Night Of Indian Delights" - yet the final part of the evening was given to Quintessence.

The reputation of Quintessence has travelled, like that of King Crimson, virtually through word of mouth. And like King Crimson, Quintessence have a new album released which looks as if it might establish their reputation nationwide.

Sunday's concert confirmed their talent. Perhaps it wasn't such a strange billing after all. Quintessence have an electric approach to rock - mixing Indian rhythms with blues and rock orientated basics.

It is an extraordinary mixture which shouldn't work. So many groups during the great hippie days of 1967 tried the same approach and failed. Quintessence succeed.

The concert began with classical Indian music, with sitars, tablas and flutes. There were some Indian folk dancing and singing. This set the mood of the evening and prepared the way for Quintessence.

Their forty minute spot was sensational. After the two hours of gentle Indian music, the rock music of Quintessence, with its Eastern undertones, came as a release.

The set ended with their version of the Hare Krishna Mantra which they threaten to perform next month with the Rahda Krishna Temple. It should be good music.

Quintessence are a very promising group indeed.   **R.P.**

With influences as diverse as jazz, blues and rock, it was inevitable that the music the members created would be a reflection of all of these styles. The common thread within the band was an interest in Indian music and culture. This was demonstrated in the band's earliest material which fused both Western jazz and blues scales with more modal Indian ragas. The abundance of Indian influences within the band's music led to them making the acquaintance of the Hindu religious teacher Swami Ambikananda.

While many western rock musicians flirted with things Indian, the members of Quintessence were completely sincere in their desire to study Hindu teachings and, under the tutorage of Ambikananda, they adopted new identities. Ron Rothfield became Raja Ram, Phil Jones became Shiva, Richard Vaughn became Shambu Babaji and Dave Codling became Maha Dev. Swami Ambikananda had established an ashram community in Ladbroke Grove which is still in existence today and Quintessence became an integral part of this community, a spiritual element reflected prominently in the band's music.

Making their live debut at the Arts Lab in Covent Garden, Quintessence soon became regulars on the underground music circuit, along with fellow Ladbroke Grove residents Hawkwind and Skin Alley. They also appeared at one of the Hyde Park free concerts of that summer of 1969. With reviews of Quintessence concerts appearing in the pages of the London underground press, it didn't take long for the group to attract the interest of record labels.

It was Island who eventually offered the band a contract as Maha Dev later recalled. 'We were rehearsing under a fish and chip shop in Ladbroke Grove one night when who should walk in but Muff Winwood and Chris Blackwell of Island Records. At that point we had no serious ambitions. We were just having a blast, jamming in the Haight Ashbury of London. We'd had a couple of offers from other labels, but for us Island was the local friendly neighbourhood record label and we decided to take them up on their offer of a record contract.'

Joining a label that had recently focused on the emerging British underground scene, Quintessence entered Island Studios to record their debut album. Splendid material such as 'Giants', 'Gunga Mai', 'Manco Capac' and the lengthy 'Midnight Mode' were successful fusions of Indian music and acid rock, a particular highlight being the autobiographical 'Notting Hill Gate'. This, the band's theme song, was re-recorded for release as a single with a much harder-edged feel and superb guitar work from Alan Mostert. 'In Blissful Company' appeared in September 1969, adorned in a lavish gatefold sleeve with a booklet of photographs and prose written by the band. The release of the album led to an increase in live activity, with Quintessence concerts notable for their atmosphere of incense, energy and improvisation.

The following year would see Quintessence rise to new heights of success with the release of their second, self-titled album in May 1970 which reached Number 22 in the UK. It attempted to capture the feeling of the band's live performances on record, but much of the material lacked the sheer freshness of their first album. In the ensuing two years Quintessence would record a final album for Island before moving to RCA, recording the albums 'Indweller' and 'Self' before splitting up.

Of all the music recorded by this musically unique group, 'In Blissful Company' was their finest album, eschewing much of the preaching of their later work and focusing more on the musical fusion of jazz, rock and traditional Indian music. It caught Quintessence at the peak of their powers.

QUINTESSENCE IS BANNED

QUINTESSENCE has been banned from future appearances at Bristol Colston Hall, as a result of a concert the group played there last Friday. The venue's management told the NME that the group " would not be welcome again " because it was felt that joss-sticks, which are handed out to the audience as a regular feature of the band's act, constitute a fire risk. A spokesman for the group argued that smoking, which the hall allows, is more of a fire hazard than joss-sticks.

SPOOKY TOOTH 'Spooky Two'

First released as ILPS9098 in March 1969
Highest UK chart position: N/A
Available on CD as Island UICY93502 (Japanese import)

Waitin' For The Wind
Feelin' Bad
I've Got Enough Heartache
Evil Woman
Lost In My Dream
That Was Only Yesterday
Better By You, Better Than Me
Hangman, Hang My Shell On A Tree

Mike Harrison	**Vocals**
Gary Wright	**Keyboards, Vocals**
Luther Grosvenor	**Guitar, Vocals**
Greg Ridley	**Bass**
Mike Kellie	**Drums**

Recorded at Morgan Studios, Willesden, London
Produced by Jimmy Miller
Engineered by Andrew Johns

By 1969, Island Records was arguably one of the most hip and happening of all the British record companies, with the A&R vision of founder Chris Blackwell and his team of Guy Stevens and Muff Winwood paying dividends with success from acts such as Traffic, Jethro Tull, Fairport Convention and Spooky Tooth.

One of Island's most inspired signings, Spooky Tooth had a long association with label from an earlier incarnation known as the VIPs. The band had begun life in Carlisle in 1963 as an R&B influenced outfit with a line-up featuring Mike Harrison on vocals, Jimmy Henshaw on guitar and keyboards, Frank Kenyan on guitar and Walter Johnstone on drums. They were joined by former Dakotas member Greg Ridley on bass and embarked upon touring the UK circuit. The VIPs' recording debut came with the release of the single 'Don't Keep Shouting At Me' b/w 'She's So Good,' in 1964. It failed to make an impression on the UK charts, but did lead to increased live work both in Britain and Germany, where the group soon won a cult following.

In early 1966, under the slightly revised moniker of the Vipps, the band recorded the single 'Wintertime' b/w 'Anyone' for CBS before being approached by Guy Stevens, now an A&R man for Island Records, who had long been an admirer of the group. Signing to Island, two singles were released in relatively quick succession, 'I Wanna Be Free' b/w 'Don't Let It Go' in late 1966, and

'Straight Down To The Bottom' b/w 'In A Dream' in January 1967. By the time of the release of the second single, the original line-up of the band had fractured with Luther Grosvenor (previously with the Hellions, a group that also included future Traffic members Jim Capaldi and Dave Mason in their ranks) replacing Frank Kenyan and Mike Kellie (previously with Birmingham band Locomotive) replacing Walter Johnstone. To fill the shoes of Jimmy Henshaw came Keith Emerson of Gary Farr and the T-Bones. This line-up lasted only a few months, recording material released in Europe only and performing on the live circuit, before Emerson departed to form the Nice.

At this point the remaining members of the VIPs were swept along by the emerging underground British psychedelic scene, changing both musical direction and their name to Art. Absorbing the influences of the emerging rock movement from the US and Britain, Art recorded the album 'Supernatural Fairy Tales' in the late spring of 1967, which, in hindsight, can

SPOOKY'S 'CEREMONY'.. A CATHOLIC MASS WITH ELECTRONIC ADDITIONS!

MUSICAL TRANSPLANTATION has become a vogue art. The latest practitioneers, Spooky Tooth, unveiled their new brainchild last week.

"Ceremony" is the result of the grafting of one style of music on to another. Spooky Tooth recorded a Catholic Mass and Pierre Henry, the French avant-garde composer, completed the music by adding his electronic sounds. The result is the new album on Island Records.

Explaining Gary Wright of Spooky Tooth: "Pierre Henry called us one day – he's just heard our second album and I suppose he liked us – and he suggested that we do an album together. That was really the first time anyone of us had heard of him.

"It was a bit weird really because he couldn't speak a word of English. We

recorded our bit and sent the tapes to him. And that's the last we've heard from him. Our bit was very good, I thought, but we haven't heard what he's going to do with it.

"It was his idea entirely. It's the first time he's worked with a rock group though. Hope it'll be O.K." The album comes out at a time when Spooky are making their second American tour. "We'll be playing at the Kinetic Playground in Chicago, the Tea Party in Boston, and a few other places.

"Last time we were in America we got a good reception. Audiences are larger in the States. Over here you get the universities and Middle Earth to play at – but over there, there are so many more places to play at."

Spooky Tooth also played with the Rolling Stones in Florida. "It was great," said Gary, "There were no hassles over who should top the bill."

now be viewed as a seminal British psychedelic/ progressive album and also as a marked shift in Island Records' musical direction. Along with Traffic, Art defined the sound of Island in 1967.

The band's superb version of Buffalo Springfield's 'For What It's Worth', renamed 'What's That Sound' was released as a single, failing to chart but receiving much attention from pirate radio stations such as Radio London and Radio Caroline. By the end of October 1967, prior to the release of 'Supernatural Fairy Tales', Art had recruited American keyboard-player Gary Wright and changed their name to Spooky Tooth, under which moniker they would continue to enjoy a relationship with Island and find greater commercial success.

Wright was an American who had travelled to Europe as a psychology student. He was also a fine musician who had come to Chris Blackwell's attention supporting Traffic in an earlier ban. His addition to a line-up of Mike Harrison, Luther Grosvenor, Greg Ridley and Mike Kellie was to prove fortuitous in terms of musical creativity and direction. Spooky Tooth entered the studio in November 1967 with producer Jimmy Miller, who was scoring success with labelmates Traffic, to record the single 'Sunshine Help Me' b/w 'Weird'. The A-side was a strong Gary Wright composition that would gain much airplay on underground radio shows upon its release in January 1968. The band's real impact came with the release of their first album, 'It's All About', in July 1968. A superb collection of songs impeccably produced by Jimmy Miller, it was a particular success in Europe.

In an attempt to secure a singles-chart placing, an imaginative cover version of the Band's 'The Weight' was issued in September 1968; this also enjoyed success in Europe but failed to chart in the UK. In November the band entered Morgan Studios in London to begin recording 'Spooky Two'. Sessions continued into the following year, interrupted by European touring commitments, but by the time sessions were completed in January 1969 it was apparent that the band had delivered a masterwork. Featuring such wonderful material as the psychedelic 'Lost In My Dream', the majestic 'Feeling Bad', the hard rock of 'Evil Woman', the introspection of 'Hangman, Hang My Shell On A Tree' and 'Waiting For The Wind', the music demonstrated a band at the peak of their creative powers. Jimmy Miller's production gave the material an added dimension, focusing more on the live sound than the studio trickery employed on the first album.

Issued in March 1969, 'Spooky Two' became the band's first American release, leading to a demand for live appearances in the country. Despite this breakthrough, Greg Ridley announced his departure in September 1969 to join with Steve Marriott and Peter Frampton in the newly formed Humble Pie. Andy Leigh joined the band on bass guitar and Spooky Tooth would team up with French electronic music pioneer Pierre Henry to record the ambitious 'Ceremony', a record that divides opinion among fans to this day. Spooky Tooth would record into the next decade (albeit with a hiatus), but 'Spooky Two' remains a triumph and was voted one of the Top 10 greatest albums issued by Island Records by a poll of writers in Mojo magazine.

Spooky Tooth

WHITE NOISE 'An Electric Storm'

First released as ILPS9099 in June 1969
Highest UK chart position: N/A
Available on CD as Island 984319-7

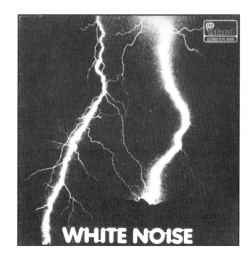

Love Without Sound
My Game Of Loving
Here Come The Fleas
Firebird
Your Hidden Dreams
The Visitation
Black Mass – An Electric Storm In Hell

David Vorhaus	**Production co-ordination and special stereo sound effects**
Delia Derbyshire and Brian Hodgson	**Electronic Sound Realisation**
Paul Litton	**Percussion**
John Whitman, Annie Bird, Val Shaw	**Vocals**

A Kaleidophon Production
Recorded at Kaleidophon Studios, London

1969 was a year in which independent record labels such as Elektra, Immediate and Island began to make their commercial mark in Britain. Of these companies, Island was undoubtedly the major player.

Of the all the albums they released that year, 'An Electric Storm' by White Noise was the most experimental and groundbreaking. The album was equally surprising for the fact that two of the three members of White Noise were not long-haired rock musicians but respected pioneers of electronic music who worked at the BBC's legendary Radiophonic Workshop.

Delia Derbyshire had graduated from Cambridge University in 1959 where she had read mathematics and music. Long attracted to the possibilities afforded by electronic sound recording, she attempted to secure a position as a recording engineer for Decca Records but was informed that the company did not employ female sound engineers. She briefly worked for the United Nations in Geneva before returning to England, initially working for music publishers Boosey and Hawkes before joining the BBC in 1960 as a trainee studio manager.

She soon applied for a position at the newly founded BBC Radiophonic Workshop, a unit established to create sound effects and electronic music for its programmes on radio and television. It was while working here that she met fellow experimentalist Brian Hodgson in 1962. In the Radiophonic Workshop Derbyshire created one of her most famous works, namely the electronic version of Ron Grainer's 'Doctor Who' theme for the cult television series, while Hodgson created the legendary sound effects of the Tardis and developed the distorted vocal effects of Doctor Who's mortal enemies the Daleks.

In 1966 Derbyshire and Hodgson teamed up with fellow electronic music pioneer Peter Zinovieff to form Unit Delta Plus, a collective designed to create electronic music and promote its use in film, television, advertising and the arts. The collective achieved notoriety by performing at the legendary Million Volt Light and Sound Rave at the Roundhouse in London's Chalk Farm in February 1967. The event featured a live performance by Unit Delta Plus and the playback of 'Carnival Of Light', a 14-minute music and sound collage edited and created by Paul McCartney.

However, White Noise was the brainchild of American-born student David Vorhaus, the son of a film director who was blacklisted during the McCarthy communist witch hunts of the late Forties and early Fifties. Vorhaus took a postgraduate course at North London Polytechnic while studying classical music and the double bass and was obsessed with the idea of fusing the worlds of music and electronics to create a new musical form.

The White Noise concept began while Vorhaus was still a student. 'I was playing in an amateur orchestra at college one night I was doing my postgraduate degree,' he later explained. 'The conductor mentioned that there was a lecture on electronic music in the adjacent hall to where I was rehearsing. Electronic music was like a fantasy to me as electronics and music were my passions. I never thought I could possibly earn a living making electronic music. I saw myself having a career in the London Symphony orchestra as a bass player, although I wasn't overly thrilled at the thought of doing that for the rest of my life. The lecture I attended was being given by Delia Derbyshire and Brian Hodgson and I was utterly enthralled to learn that others had succeeded in establishing a career for themselves by combining an interest in electronics and music.

'After the lecture I approached them and began chatting; we immediately got on like a house on fire and within about a week of this we had resolved to set up an experimental studio, Kaleidophon. I suppose my initial attraction to them was that I could actually make devices they were dependent upon the BBC Radiophonic Workshop for. The attraction for me was obvious in the fact that Delia and Brian were true pioneers and had access to the tools of the Radiophonic Workshop.'

Initial recording work was undertaken by Vorhaus, Derbyshire and Hodgson at night after staff had finished work for the day. 'It was all very unofficial and the BBC was unaware of us using the studio and equipment for our own ends,' added David. The idea of recording an album in those early months of 1968 was far from the minds of the trio. 'I had the idea to record a couple of electronic music tracks for fun with the intention of trying to secure their release as a single,' explained Vorhaus. 'I contacted an old school friend, John Whitman, and asked him to sing two songs I had written, "Love Without Sound" and "Firebird". I played some double bass parts and these were then the recordings were sped up and manipulated to sound like other instruments. Both of these pieces were recorded at the BBC Radiophonic Workshop.

'I initially took the finished results to Decca Records who said they would like to release it, but I thought I would see what other opportunities existed and so I met with Chris Blackwell, the boss of Island. Chris also loved what we had done; however, he told me that the music would be lost if it was released as a single. He thought that an album of this music could become a cult hit and become more successful. Being very green, I thought the idea of a single might be more appealing as a hit single might change the face of music by turning a wider public onto electronic music. Chris enlightened me by pointing out that at that time most of the singles-buying population had an average age of 12 old. He said that hit singles didn't make as much money as albums and grossed on average £3,000. He then wrote a cheque for £3,000 and gave it to me saying, "Here, you've just had your first hit single. Now, will you do an album?" I just couldn't refuse an offer like that.'

Armed with the cheque, Vorhaus, Derbyshire and Hodgson were then faced with the dilemma of where to record. 'As soon as we got the money,' Vorhaus would later explain, 'we had to immediately build a studio and make a lot of the outboard equipment. It was obvious that we couldn't record a whole album by sneaking into the Radiophonic Workshop in the evenings when no-one was looking. The only route open to us was to build our own studio, although we never told Island that of course! At the time I was living in a large bedsit in Fellows Road in Camden and we decided to adapt the place into a studio. We put up some screens; got together some microphones and Revox tape recorders and we were away.

'This set-up wasn't destined to last very long as two people in the house died within a week of us beginning to make strange electronic sounds in my bed-sit and the landlord blamed us for it. In reality one person who died was an old man well into his eighties and the other had been terminally ill, so their deaths were nothing to do with us, but it didn't look good and we were given 24 hours' notice to vacate the bedsit! We then found a place on Camden High Street and that's really where our Kaleidophon studio started. It was intended that the studio would last for just a year while we made the White Noise album. That year somehow stretched out to 20 as we couldn't be bothered to move once we had established ourselves in the building.'

The recording sessions were time consuming and exacting affairs, with the construction of each piece taking weeks. Vorhaus explained the techniques used thus: 'In those very early days nearly everything we achieved was done by tape manipulation, cutting up fragments of tape and the use of audio oscillators that were used for electronic tests that were manipulated to enable us to tune sine waves to particular frequencies by the use of a tuning fork. Every electronic note was tuned in this way, recorded and then they were edited together in particular sequences to form a tune. It was easier to achieve the effect of echo by the use of tape machines and we created reverb by running two tape machines out of phase to achieve the desired effect.

We had to make almost every piece of equipment as things like a mixing desk cost an absolute fortune in those days. The idea of purchasing a multi-track machine was ridiculous, so we overcame this by having a bank of six Revox tape machines that were all locked together by a simple mains switch. It was only as we began the "White Noise" album that Robert Moog had developed the huge modular synthesiser in the US, which came onto the market as the album was completed, but there were no British synthesisers at that time; the first was the VCS3 which was made by Peter Zinovieff.'

Such innovation came at a price. Nearly a year had elapsed since the deal with Island records had been finalised and as yet the album was still incomplete, with the highly ambitious 'The Visitation' taking nearly three months to complete. To make matters worse, Chris Blackwell had passed responsibility for the project on to Guy Stevens, a trusted cohort who was very uneasy about the viability of such an adventurous project so outside of the usual music released by 'conventional' Island artists such as Traffic, Jethro Tull or Mott the Hoople.

'Eventually we received a letter from Island stating that unless they received masters of the album within seven days they would take legal action against us to recoup the advance,' David Vorhaus remembered. 'We had only completed about three-quarters of the album and had half a side's worth of music to finish. Faced with the prospect of a potential lawsuit we decided to finish the album in one night. I got a friend of mine, Paul Lytton, to play drums to a tape loop for 15 minutes and we improvised by throwing all sorts of sounds to make this horrific soundscape. After a brief Satanic introduction which was edited on to the beginning, we had the closing track for the album.'

The resulting 'Black Mass: An Electric Storm In Hell' was perhaps the most interesting track on the album, clearly owing a debt to Pink Floyd's 'A Saucerful Of Secrets' but taking experimental music to further extremes than even Pink Floyd would dare go. Masters of the album, now entitled 'An Electric Storm', were duly delivered to Island and met with a muted response.

'Guy Stevens was managing Island in Chris' absence and he told us that he didn't think it was very commercial and wouldn't give us any significant promotional budget for the album. We were told to give a pep talk to the Island sales reps and I think that

was as far as "promotion" went,' reflected David. 'When the album first appeared I think it sold about 200 copies in the first year. It was well received by underground DJs though. Kenny Everett actually used parts of the album such as "Here Come The Fleas" as jingles on his radio show and slowly more people became aware of it. Gradually it grew in stature and sold quite healthily, notching up thousands of sales and with an underground audience treating the record as a great trippy experience. It remained on catalogue well into the Seventies.'

In hindsight, the influence of 'An Electric Storm' was significant on musicians such as Hawkwind, Brian Eno and German experimentalists Kraftwerk and Tangerine Dream and other early purveyors of a genre that became known as space rock. However, influence did not bring great riches. 'The year after the album's release was incredibly impoverished,' Vorhaus explained much later. 'The combined income from Kaleidophon studio and White Noise was £280 for the year and things began to break up at that point.

'Delia and Brian concentrated on working on other projects. I went into all sorts of directions and recorded the "White Noise II" album for Virgin in 1974. I wanted to do a concerto for synthesiser and I think the sounds that I made on the album soon became clichéd, unlike the first album which featured sounds that were created by tape manipulation and were unique. I also turned Kaleidophon into a 16-track studio and began to record conventional bands and worked on albums.' The influence of 'An Electric Storm' on a whole new generation in the Nineties and into the millennium has led to musicians such as Aphex Twin and the Chemical Brothers citing the album as an inspiration. It remains a truly unique audio experience.

Pete Brown & Piblokto

LIVING LIFE BACKWARDS: HIGH FLYING ELECTRIC BIRD (Harvest 5008)
A Record of The Week - some high talent here on a pacey hard-driver.
Really gets going and keeps going

★ ★ ★ ★ ★

Record Mirror 11/10/69

'THIS MAGICAL SOUND THAT I LONG TO EXPRESS...'

PETE BROWN & PIBLOKTO!
'Things May Come And Things May Go, But The Art School Dance Goes On Forever'

First released as Harvest SHVL768 in April 1970
Highest UK chart position: N/A
Currently available on CD as BGO Records BGOCD522

Things May Come And Things May Go, But The
Art School Dance Goes On Forever
High Flying Electric Bird
Someone Like You
Walk For Charity, Run For Money
Then I Must Go And Can I Keep
My Love's Gone Far Away
Golden Country Kingdom
Firesong
Country Morning

Pete Brown	Vocals, Talking Drum, Whistle, Tambourine, Cornish Slide
Jim Mullen	Guitars
Roger Bunn	Bass
Dave Thompson	Keyboards, Saxophone
Rob Tait	Drums and Percussion

With guest on 'Things May Come And Things May Go,
But The Art School Dance Goes On Forever'

John Mumford	Trombone
Ray Crane	Trumpet

Recorded at EMI Studios, Abbey Road, London
Produced by Pete Brown

'Hours of fun and digestable parody on the cover plus down home cartoon strips inside depicting fab exploits of Piblokto. As for Pete Brown since the Battered Ornaments days, he seems to have Piblokto pretty well in hand. Not much individuality in the outlook, but a credible performance of jazz/blues/free verse splintered by very weird macaroni voices. Sometimes sounds like early Tull. 'Piblokto skids in LP wheely bout!' Nice sax arrangements.' **L.G.**

RECORD MIRROR 28/3/70

Although best known for his role as lyricist in his songwriting partnership with Jack Bruce both in the context of Cream and Jack's solo work, by 1969 Pete Brown had begun to make an impression as a singer and musician in his own right. His career as poet had been established for some years, beginning as far back as 1960 when he became a professional performance poet. In 1961 he joined the New Departures group with Michael Horowitz, successfully combining the worlds of poetry and jazz and coming to a wider audience at the Paris Biennale festival in 1961. By the mid-Sixties Brown was a major figure on the British poetry scene, making legendary performances at the Royal Albert Hall in 1965 and 1966 alongside such literary figures as William Burroughs, Allen Ginsberg and Robert Creeley.

Brown had also been a well-known figure on the British jazz and blues circuit through his friendship with saxophonist Dick Heckstall-Smith (who had performed with the New Departures group) and Graham Bond, an equally innovative musician whose band the Graham Bond Organisation was to feature Heckstall-Smith, Jack Bruce and Ginger Baker. It was through his association with the members of the Bond Organisation that Brown was asked to contribute lyrics to music by Baker's newly formed trio, Cream.

After initial failed attempts at collaboration with Baker, Brown teamed up with bassist Jack Bruce, beginning a fruitful partnership that would produce such classic works as 'I Feel Free', 'Sunshine Of Your Love', 'White Room' and 'Politician.' With

Cream's career taking off in a phenomenal way, Brown's thoughts came to performing music in his own right and he soon formed the First Real Poetry Band featuring John McLaughlin and Danny Thomson among others. After recording a series of demos for Polydor which failed to secure a contract, the group fell apart.

Brown contacted an old friend, saxophonist George Khan, and they formed the Battered Ornaments around the nucleus of Rob Tait on drums, Chris Spedding on guitar and Butch Potter on bass. The Ornaments soon came under the wing of Blackhill Enterprises, and through Blackhill a contract was soon forthcoming with EMI. A single, 'The Week Looked Good On Paper' b/w 'Morning Call', duly appeared on EMI's Parlophone label in early 1969. With the formation of Harvest in June that year, the Battered Ornaments album 'A Meal You Can Shake Hands With In The Dark' was the second release on the label. The album featured a line-up of Brown, Spedding, Tait and Potter alongside Charlie Hart on organ and violin, Pete Bailey on percussion and Dick Heckstall-Smith on saxophone, and was a heady mixture of jazz, blues, rock and avant-garde experimentation.

Work on a follow-up began in March 1969 at Abbey Road studios and had neared completion when, in July, the Battered Ornaments were booked to support the Rolling Stones at their legendary free concert in London's Hyde Park. The night before the performance Brown was fired from the group by the other musicians. With his departure, all his contributions to the forthcoming album were erased, Chris Spedding replacing Pete's vocal work.

By the time the second Battered Ornaments album, 'Mantle-Piece', was released in November 1969, Brown had formed a new and more adventurous group, Piblokto!, featuring Jim Mullen on guitar, Roger Bunn on bass, Dave Thompson on organ and Laurie Allan on drums. Within weeks Allen had been replaced by Rob Tait and the band had secured the agency services of Gerry Bron (joining a roster including Colosseum and Juicy Lucy) and had signed to Harvest.

Piblokto!'s first vinyl offering was the single 'Living Life Backwards' b/w 'High Flying Electric Bird' released in October 1969. With the A-side a stunning rock tour de force in 7/8 time (later covered, but not released, by Jeff Beck's band Beck, Bogert and Appice), the single failed to make any UK chart impression, but did lead to increased live work and also to acclaim in France, thanks to the efforts and support of Harvest' local label manager Philippe Constantin.

Brown had written the excellent 'My Love's Gone Far Away' and 'Then I Must Go But Can I Keep', with guitarist Chris Spedding and originally intended them for the Battered Ornaments. But it was material written with Jim Mullen that would be a revelation. 'High Flying Electric Bird', 'Walk for Charity, Run for Money' and 'Golden Country Kingdom' were all diverse in style but featured music of an imaginative nature even by the standard of those heady times. The incredibly named 'Things May Come and Things May Go, But the Art School Dance Goes On Forever' was another highpoint, demonstrating Brown's lyrical dexterity and adept arranging skills. Brown also collaborated with bass guitarist Roger Bunn on the splendid 'Country Morning'.

The album 'was released in April 1970 and was a real leap forward in terms of Pete Brown's standing as a solo artist, and was all the more remarkable given the limited recording time made available to the band by EMI. It was particularly enthusiastically received in continental Europe, but failed to make any chart impression in Britain. In an attempt to boost the commercial fortunes of Piblokto!, another excellent single, 'Can't Get Off The Planet' b/w 'Broken Magic' was released by Harvest as in July 1970, once more evading commercial success.

Piblokto!'s second album, 'Thousands On A Raft' appeared in October 1970 and was almost as impressive as its predecessor, but by the time it had appeared a series of line-up changes had occurred that would eventually prove fatal. Rob Tait and Dave Thompson were the first to depart the fold to join the newly formed Vinegar Joe, followed soon after by Jim Mullen who left to join Brian Auger's Oblivion Express. Replacements were found from former members of the South Wales band the Eyes of Blue, namely keyboard-player Phil Ryan (with whom Brown continues to enjoy a fruitful working partnership) and drummer John 'Pugwash' Weathers. A new guitarist was found in fellow Welshman Brian Breeze. The single 'Flying Hero Sandwich' b/w 'My Last Band' was recorded and released prior to the appearance of 'Thousands On A Raft' but suffered the same fate, and soon after Brown decided to terminate his association with Harvest.

Despite this, the group continued to work a near continuous schedule in Europe, which eventually resulted in the departure of Breeze and Weathers, respectively replaced by another ex-Eyes of Blue member Taff Williams and drummer Ed Spevock, Piblokto! were destined to last only a few more months and performed their final concert at a club in Montpelier, France in October 1971, according to Brown 'to an audience of gangsters'. Although their legacy was brief, the recordings the band made for Harvest are essential listening for connoisseurs of the British underground scene. 'Things May Come And Things May Go, But The Art School Dance Goes On Forever' is their finest moment.

94

EGG 'Egg'

First released as Deram Nova SDN14 in March 1970
Highest UK chart position: N/A
Available on CD as Esoteric Recordings ECLEC2035

Bulb
While Growing My Hair
I Will Be Absorbed
Fugue In D Minor
They Laughed When I Sat Down At The Piano
The Song Of McGillicudie the Pusillanimous
*(or Don't Worry, Your Socks Are Hanging in the
Coal Cellar With Thomas)*
Boilk
Symphony No 2:
First Movement
Second Movement
Blane
Third Movement *(on initial test pressings and on CD release only)*
Fourth Movement

Dave Stewart	**Keyboards**
Hugo 'Mont' Campbell	**Bass, Vocals**
Clive Brooks	**Drums and Percussion**

Produced by Egg
Recorded at Lansdowne Studios, London
Engineers – Peter Gallen and Les Cunningham
'While Growing My Hair' recorded at Trident Studios, London
Engineered by Roy Thomas Baker

By the autumn of 1969 the so-called progressive or underground rock boom was taking hold of Britain's long-haired youth. Three-minute 'pop' material was out and long, complex compositions, drawing their inspiration from jazz, blues, psychedelia and classical music, were the order of the day. Album sales had overtaken single sales and, anxious to capitalise on this new trend, the major UK record companies established imprints (inspired by the success of independents such as Island and Elektra) with an underground credibility and scouted for acts to sign.

EMI established Harvest with great success while Philips developed Vertigo and Decca set up the short-lived Nova label as companion to their Deram imprint. Nova releases were sold at a lower price of 28 shillings and sixpence, a ploy by Decca to entice the underground record-buying public to purchase albums by new, unknown acts. The experiment had mixed results both commercially and creatively, but few of the initial releases on Nova had the quality or enjoyed the subsequent legendary status of the debut album by a young trio from London who had assumed the identity of Egg.

Egg had evolved from the band Uriel, formed while three of the members were pupils at the City of London School. Uriel featured guitarist turned keyboard-player Dave Stewart, guitarist Steve Hillage and bass guitarist Hugo 'Mont' Campbell. Drummer Clive Brooks was recruited via an ad in Melody Maker. With an average age of just 17, Uriel's first concert took place at a youth club in Sheen, Surrey in early 1968. Inspired by acts such as the Nice (particularly Keith Emerson's pyrotechnic organ-playing), Jimi Hendrix, Cream, Pink Floyd and Fleetwood Mac, Uriel played a handful of local concerts.

In the summer of 1968 Uriel secured a residency at the Ryde Castle Hotel on the Isle of Wight and also opened concerts on the island for both Fairport Convention and the Crazy World of Arthur Brown. When Hillage departed the fold to attend university in Canterbury to study history and philosophy, Stewart, Campbell and Brooks decided to dispense with a guitarist and continue as a trio. A series of concerts at the underground Middle Earth club night, (by this time held at the Roundhouse in Chalk Farm, north London) led to the band securing management with Middle Earth's promoters Dave Howson and Paul Waldman, who suggested the band change their name to Egg.

The new year of 1969 began with a series of high-profile support slots for Love Sculpture, Family, the Pretty Things and Soft Machine. By now the management team of Howson and Waldman were beginning to get record-company interest in their new signing. Egg began to drop cover versions from their set and experiment with writing more complex material, Mont Campbell's lyrics displaying a distinctly English sense of humour. This change of musical direction paid off when Egg secured a contract with Decca Records in June 1969.

The single 'Seven Is A Jolly Good Time' b/w 'You Are All Princes' was released in August on the Deram label. As the single's A-side proclaimed, its chorus was

indeed in 7/4 time, not the most common of time signatures for a hit single and a clear indication of the band's future musical direction. Underground press reaction was favourable with comparisons being made with Soft Machine, a declared influence.

Although the single failed to chart, Egg were offered the chance to record their first album for Nova. Prior to recording sessions commencing Stewart, Campbell and Brooks reunited with ex-colleague Steve Hillage (then on summer break from university) to record an album for the obscure Zel label under the pseudonym Arzachel. Hillage subsequently returned to his studies in Canterbury and Egg entered Lansdowne Studios in Holland Park in October 1969 to record their eponymous debut album for Decca.

The material recorded revealed a surprising musical maturity for a group with members not yet 20 years old. Remarkably, Decca gave Stewart, Campbell and Brooks the unprecedented freedom of being able to produce their first album themselves. Working with engineers Peter Gallen and Roy Thomas Baker, compositions such as the excellent 'I Will Be Absorbed', 'The Song of McGillicudie The Pusillanimous (Or Don't Worry James, Your Socks Are Hanging In The Coal Cellar With Thomas)' and 'While Growing My Hair' were all penned by Mont Campbell and displayed complexity and originality unique to the band.

The album's second side comprised a lengthy suite by Campbell and Dave Stewart. 'Symphony No 2' initially comprised four movements, along with the avant-garde track 'Blane'. Prior to the release of the album, however, the third movement, an adaptation of Stravinsky's Rite Of Spring, was removed due to a threatened lawsuit by the composer's estate. With some copies of the album already pressed with this track, albums were hastily recalled and new artwork pasted over the original rear sleeve.

'Egg' was released on 13 March 1970 with a striking cover photograph devised by David Wedgbury. A liner note on the rear of the sleeve declared: 'The music on this LP is not dancing music, but is basically music for listening to,' which essentially summed

up the contents.

Egg's debut was released to coincide with other Nova albums such as 'Expansions On Life' by the Elastic Band, 'Places And Faces' by Harvey Andrews, 'Barbed Wire Sandwich' by Black Cat Bones and 'Feeling Free' by Pacific Drift. Unfortunately 'the Nova catalogue Egg' was promoted as a whole, which meant that the possibility of attention being lavished on an individual album was slim. Although 'Egg' was one of the two biggest-selling releases on the short-lived label, (the other being the debut by rock duo Clark-Hutchinson), the album failed to reach the wider audience it deserved.

Despite sales being less encouraging than expected, critical response was extremely positive. The band had gained a small but loyal following thanks to sporadic concert appearances supporting the likes of Taste, Procol Harum and Family and the enthusiastic support from Richard Williams of Melody Maker (later an early presenter of BBC TV's Old Grey Whistle Test) who referred to Egg as 'super-efficient rock musicians with the kind of enquiring minds which make the current scene so exciting.'

With Decca staff producer Neil Slaven seeing Egg as potential competitors to Soft Machine, he persuaded Decca to give the band the chance to record a follow-up album for the prestigious Deram label. Soon after its release, Egg would cease to exist, with Dave Stewart becoming a key member of Hatfield and the North. In 1974 Egg were briefly reunited in the studio to record their last long-playing opus, 'The Civil Surface', for Virgin's Caroline label. In the Eighties Stewart would find single chart success with former Zombies vocalist Colin Blunstone and his partner Barbara Gaskin with respective cover versions of 'What Becomes Of the Broken Hearted' and 'It's My Party'.

Although Egg's second album 'The Polite Force' and 'The Civil Surface' are often lavished with critical attention, their charming self-titled debut LP has much to commend it. Forty years on it still has the ability to excite.

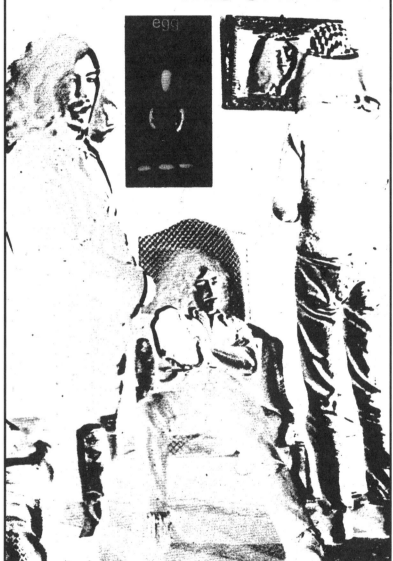

really unusual LPs don't turn up very often...
this one does

EGG

ⓢ SDN 14   Ⓜ DN 14

EMERSON LAKE AND PALMER 'Emerson Lake And Palmer'

First released as Island Records ILPS9132 in November 1970
Highest UK chart position: Number 4
Available on CD as Sanctuary Music SMRCD055

The Barbarian
Take A Pebble
Knife Edge
The Three Fates
a. Clotho
b. Lachesis
c. Atropos
Tank
Lucky Man

Keith Emerson   **Organ, Piano, Moog Synthesiser**
Greg Lake   **Vocals, Bass Guitar, Acoustic Guitar**
Carl Palmer   **Drums, Percussion**

Produced by Greg Lake
Engineered by Eddy Offord
Recorded at Advision studios, London

The formation of Emerson, Lake and Palmer in May 1970 was regarded at the time as sensational by the European music press. Keith Emerson, Greg Lake and Carl Palmer had seemingly thrown away hard-won success in their respective previous bands the Nice, King Crimson and Atomic Rooster to form a group to satisfy their musical and creative ambitions.

'With the Nice I had explored a lot of musical avenues that interested me,' Keith Emerson later remembered, 'and I really enjoyed playing with Lee Jackson and Brian Davison, but by the end of the Sixties the whole psychedelic scene was coming to an end and I realised that it was time to look at doing something new. My writing had improved a lot and I was keen to experiment with things like electronics in music, particularly with the Moog synthesiser which had just been invented. I also wanted to remain within the trio format and felt that I should seek some new musicians to work with who could bring something fresh into a band.

'When I told Brian and Lee I wanted to disband the group they were both astonished and very upset. I really felt strongly that I should move on, but I was sad that Brian and Lee were unhappy. I'm glad to say that we remained the best of friends. I'd actually spoken with quite a few bass players about forming a new band before I settled on Greg Lake. The first person was Chris Squire who I tried to steal from Yes. He said that he'd love to do it but felt that he wasn't really a lead singer but was more of a harmony/backing vocalist. Then I spoke to Jack Bruce. Cream had split recently and we met up. He played me a lot of his solo material which I thought was great, but then he said "If I do play with you we'd have to play all my material, I don't really want to play any of yours," so it was obvious to me that it wouldn't work out with Jack.'

Greg Lake would later add: 'In December 1969 King Crimson and the Nice were playing at the Fillmore West in San Francisco. Both of our bands were supporting the Chambers Brothers for three nights in succession. It was on the first night we were there that King Crimson made the decision to disband. That night after the show I met with Keith Emerson in the hotel bar. Keith and I had struck up a rapport and would get together. We began talking about what each other's plans were. I told Keith that Crimson was breaking up and Keith told me that he thought he'd taken the Nice as far as it could go and was looking to do something new; that's where we decided to form a band together.'

Returning to England, Emerson and Lake fulfilled their remaining commitments before coming together to search for a suitable drummer to complete their planned new outfit. 'I got a call from Robert Stigwood who asked me if it was true that I was looking for a drummer,' Greg Lake later remembered. 'I told him it was and he said "I've got a guy who would be just right for you. His name is Carl Palmer and he's played with the Crazy World of Arthur Brown and Atomic Rooster. Would you be interested in having a talk with him?" Carl came to the rehearsal room, we played together and that was it. We realised we had found the drummer we had been looking for.'

Emerson remembers viewing the young Carl Palmer with some cynicism when he arrived at the arranged audition. 'We organised a rehearsal to audition Carl in a room in Soho. Greg and I set up our equipment and then in came Carl. He set up his drum kit and I remember that the first thing I noticed was that he had a picture of the children's storybook character Noddy on the front of his bass drum skin. I said "How old are you?" and he replied that he was 20. I then asked him how long he had been playing and he replied, "I don't know. My dad took me to my first gig." Greg and I looked at each other and thought, "Mmm, we've got a kid here." I asked Carl to play a shuffle and he got into a groove immediately. I then began to jam along and then Greg joined in before Carl just took off. I thought, "Okay. He's the guy for us."

'Carl still had some obligations to sort out with the Robert Stigwood Organisation, but he sorted that out. What I was struck with was the fact that Carl was so bright and bubbly. We pretty soon fell into our own roles within the group. I was always trying to push the musical envelope further and further, while Greg was more into musical simplicity and basic melody. Carl seemed to take on the role of musical referee, so there was a real sense of balance within the group from the beginning.'

Carl Palmer recalled the early weeks of ELP's existence as being a time in search of new material and the definition of the trio's own musical identity. 'There wasn't really a huge abundance of material around when it came to getting together our first live set or material for our first album. The band jammed together really well, and some of those ideas were later transformed into new material, but the pressure on to perform live and to record an album was on us almost straight away.'

Through Greg Lake being managed by EG Management, Emerson Lake and Palmer signed a production deal with the company who, at that time, were distributed by Island Records. Entering Advision Studios in July 1970, Greg Lake took on the role of producer, with Eddy Offord as engineer.

'I don't think making our first album came together that easily,' Lake later remembered. 'There was no writing period as such. We were just booked into a recording studio and expected to make an album. In those days I think record companies thought that musicians were clever bastards who just went into a studio, plugged in a guitar and magically came up with an album in a couple of weeks. We came into the studio with the pieces we had at that time and we had to make something out of that.'

Keith Emerson concurred. 'Greg and I didn't find it easy when it came to working on new music for us to play and record. Greg had some ideas that evolved, such as '"Take A Pebble", but my ideas were approached very cautiously by him, so I thought the best way to get things rolling might be to work on an adaptation of an existing piece of music. I'd already proved that that sort of thing could work in the Nice with our approach on things such as "The Karelia Suite" or '"The Brandenburg Concerto".' It was by accident that I attended a classical concert at the Royal Festival Hall in London where one piece performed was Ravel's arrangement of Mussorgsky's "Pictures At An Exhibition". I was really taken by the piece and so the next day I went to Chappell's music store in London and asked for the score of work.

'The piece originally been composed for piano by Mussorgsky, but it was new to me, so I took the sheet music around to Greg and played it to him. He thought it sounded great and thought that we really could do something with an arrangement of it. We worked on the piece, but decided we still had some work to do with our interpretation and so it was left off the sessions for our first album.

'Carl had rather a radical approach...wanted to experiment with time signatures and was keen to try out adaptations of work by composers such as Bartok. So I dug out a work he had composed called "Allegro Barbaro" and we did a lot of rearranging until it became "The Barbarian". That was the first track that we recorded during those sessions. We did pretty much the same thing with a piece by Janacek called "Sinfonietta" which after some reworking became "Knife Edge". Greg's "Take A Pebble" began life as an acoustic song but we added an extended musical interlude in the middle which worked very well.'

Palmer's impressive percussion tour de force 'Tank' and Emerson's 'Three Fates' made up the material recorded. However, the song which would establish ELP in America and turn the album into something special was devised at the eleventh hour of the allotted studio time as Lake would later recall. 'We had a day of recording time left and had realised that we were still one song short from delivering and album's worth of material. It was a bit disconcerting and we all looked at each other in the studio control room and asked each other if anyone had any other material they could offer. I said "Well I've got this folk tune that we could have a go at." We all thought it might be better than nothing so I began to record it, but Keith really couldn't find his way into the song at all.

ELP PLAY TO 50,000

EMERSON, Lake and Palmer closed their five-week European tour with a concert on Friday at Milan, where 50,000 people attended the Velodromo Vigorelli stadium. The concert, which had twice been held off because of bad weather and Greg Lake's tonsilitis, was filmed by a 30-man TV / film crew who accompanied the band on the second half of their tour.

A TV spectacular from the tour will be screened world-wide in the autumn.

The group are currently in Paris, where they are spending a week recording a new album.

KEITH EMERSON at Lyceum.

Emerson, Lake & Palmer live show for TV

EMERSON, Lake & Palmer's concert at London Lyceum on December 9 — which, as previously reported, was filmed by Visual & Musical Entertainments — is likely to be screened by BBC-2 early in the New Year, and discussions are currently taking place with producer Stanley Dorfman with this in view. The event proved to be only the second occasion on which a Lyceum concert has been sold out in advance — the first being the Stones' appearance there a year ago. There was a power cut during the concert, but electricity was provided by the TV generators.

'He couldn't find a part that was right and so he went out to the pub for a drink. While he was gone Carl and I decided to put a take down with just guitar and drums and it sounded terrible, but when the bass track was added it began to take shape and sound like a band. Then I tracked the harmony vocals. Keith came back from the pub, heard it and then suggested that he could do a Moog solo at the end. We were just beginning our experiments with synthesisers at that time and thought it would be a good idea. Of course the solo became a famous part of that song.

'The interesting thing about it is that when we recorded the last part of the solo on the track Keith was adjusting the synthesiser as the track was being played back and was really just practising. He didn't realise that I was recording it. When I listened to the playback I called Keith to come back into the control room to listen to the take he initially refused to as he said he had just been rehearsing. He eventually relented and realised that it fitted and that became the great finishing touch to "Lucky Man".'

With recording completed, Emerson, Lake and Palmer performed their first live concert at Plymouth Guildhall on 26 August 1970. The following day they appeared at the huge Isle of Wight Festival. Carl 'Things really did move at a breathtaking pace,' Palmer would later comment. 'One minute we were in a Soho rehearsal room and the next we had recorded our first album and were on stage at the Isle of Wight festival playing to 500,000 people. It was quite a mindblowing step to perform to so many people on your second gig as a band.

'It was really the luck of the draw that it became our second ever gig. It was mainly because the brother of Ricky Farr, one of the promoters, was the singer Gary Farr who had previously fronted a band called the T-Bones. They were quite an attraction in the mid Sixties and Keith had played with them. My band the King Bees had supported them in Birmingham and they were quite a draw on the club circuit. When Gary Farr found out Keith was in a new band he pulled some strings and we got on the bill at the last minute. We only played for 45 minutes. We were literally flown in and flown right out again, so I never got to see any of the other acts on the bill. We had time to do "Rondo" and "Pictures At An Exhibition" and we were gone. We went to that festival as an unknown band and left as an internationally recognised act. It was quite something.'

The album 'Emerson Lake And Palmer' was released in the UK in November 1970 and reached a chart height of Number 4, adorned in a striking sleeve designed by artist Nic Darnell. When released in America in January 1971, the album reached Number 18 on the Billboard chart thanks to the release of 'Lucky Man' as a single. Greg Lake later commented; 'Atlantic Records edited the track and released it as a single which got heavy rotation on American radio, and "Lucky Man" became the track that really opened up America for ELP. It wasn't until we actually got to perform in America for the first time that most people really became aware of the other side of the band. The combination of both the hit single and then the impact of the band were enough to ensure that ELP enjoyed the later huge success it had in the States.'

Although often critically derided, Emerson Lake and Palmer became one of the most successful and important progressive rock bands of the Seventies. Their debut album was the point when the band's fusion of classical music, folk and electronic experimentation came together to produce something special.

On sale Friday, week ending November 21, 1970   NEW

LEFT TO RIGHT KEITH EMERSON, GREG LAKE AND CARL PALMER

KNOCKING KNOCKERS!

E.L.P.

EMERSON, Lake and Palmer should work. On paper, the group have one of the world's best rock organists, a competent drummer and a good bass player/vocalist. So what went wrong at their London debut at the Royal Festival Hall last week?

Well, for a start the whole premise of transfering Mussorgsky's 'Pictures At An Exhibition' to a rock context. The 40 minute piece said very little, but appeared merely as a vehicle for Emerson's extraordinary showmanship.

There was very little for the group to gain by the piece, yet they insisted in carrying it on to the bitter end.

The second half of the programme proved to be better — if only because it was more varied. EL And P included their own tribute to Jimi Hendrix, 'Barbarian', a Greg Lake song — which was lovely if only they'd stuck to the vocal parts and missed out the long instrumental bit in the middle — and finally 'Rondo'.

Now that really did seem a cop-out. Like Delaney And Bonnie and Led Zeppelin who give the kids 'something heavy' with a closing rock 'n' roll medley, so EL and P revert back to Emerson's Nice days.

Throughout the whole show Emerson jived between organs, piano, and Moog Synthesiser creating some of the weirdest noises since 'Journey Into Space'. But as John Peel said: "a tragic waste of electricity and talent."

KEITH EMERSON

IT'S OFFICIAL. One of the new bands from the ashes of the Nice are 'Emerson, Lake And Palmer' with Keith Emerson, Greg Lake from King Crimson and Carl Palmer from Atomic Rooster. Carl will be working with Atomic Rooster until June. Said Greg: "Until then we're rehearsing whenever Carl's not working". At the beginning of June we get solidly into rehearsals and we hope to be on the road at the beginning of July." Meanwhile Lee Jackson's new band, the Jackson Heights will be debuting at Record Mirror's Extravaganza '70 on June 6.

GROUNDHOGS 'Thank Christ For The Bomb'

Originally released as Liberty LBS83295 in June 1970
Highest UK chart position: Number 9
Currently available on CD as Liberty 07243 584823 2 4

Strange Town
Darkness Is No Friend
Soldier
Thank Christ for the Bomb
Ship On The Ocean
Garden
Status People
Rich Man, Poor Man
Eccentric Man

Tony McPhee	**Guitars and Vocals**
Pete Cruickshank	**Bass**
Ken Pustelnik	**Drums**

Recorded at De Lane Lea studios, Holborn, London in February 1970
Produced by Tony (TS) McPhee for Zak Productions
Engineered by Martin Birch

As the Sixties drew to a close, one of Britain's most talented blues outfits was undergoing a major musical transformation that would see them propelled into the upper reaches of the British charts with several classic, powerful rock albums with conceptual themes ranging from the folly of war to madness to environmental concern.

The Groundhogs were formed in 1963 by guitarist Tony McPhee and found initial fame on the UK blues scene as backing band for visiting US blues musician John Lee Hooker. Known as John Lee's Groundhogs, the band broke up in 1965. McPhee was briefly in the beat group Truth before forming Herbal Mixture in 1966 with former Groundhogs bassist Pete Cruickshank. Releasing two singles for EMI's Columbia imprint, Herbal Mixture developed into a psychedelic group, but failed to record further singles or an album.

McPhee continued to pursue work as a session musician until the early months of 1968 when Andrew Lauder, A&R head of the newly established London office of Liberty Records, suggested he put together another version of Groundhogs. The so-called 'second wave' of the British blues boom was in full swing with acts such as Chicken Shack, Fleetwood Mac, Savoy Brown and Ten Years After all enjoying success, and Lauder felt a reformed Groundhogs could be equally successful. McPhee retained the services

of bass-player Pete Cruickshank and added newcomers Ken Pustelnik on drums and singer Steve Rye.

This incarnation recorded 'Scratching the Surface' in 1968, a traditional blues album. By the time 1969's 'Blues Obituary' had been recorded, Rye had left and British blues was losing its momentum. Inspired by musicians such as Jimi Hendrix, McPhee was keen to expand the focus of the band and to develop his writing to cover weightier subjects. To this end he was encouraged by his manager Roy Fisher to write a controversial concept for the Groundhogs' third album that would get the band noticed in the UK press and widen their audience.

'Roy suggested that we should write an album called '"Thank Christ for the Bomb"',' McPhee later recalled. 'His reasoning was that we needed to be controversial to get noticed. Taking into account the press furore following John Lennon's statement that the Beatles were more popular than Jesus Christ, Roy thought coupling the figure of Christ with the subject of the atomic bomb would get us noticed. I was very unsure of this initially, but after thinking about it I began to see the idea had some potential.'

The first composition McPhee wrote for this new theme was the song that would become the title track. 'It began life as a story about a soldier from the First World War who had been injured by a bomb blast in the trenches and was sent back home, never to fight again. As I began to develop the idea in the other songs on the album, the subject-matter began to take on the subject of alienation. The world has different levels of alienation, from communities that can't accept individuality to countries or cultures that can't communicate with each other.'

The superb 'Strange Town' was a tale of alienation inspired by an altercation the guitarist had on a London bus. 'I overheard two women complaining about the colour of the bus conductor, so I remonstrated with them,' McPhee would recall. 'As I left the bus one of them shouted out "Get the lice out of your hair" as a reference to my long hair. That quip gave me the inspiration for "Strange Town" and one of the most effective lines in the lyrics.'

The Groundhogs began work at De Lane Lea studios in Holborn, London in February 1970 with engineer Martin Birch. 'From the moment we met Martin,' McPhee revealed, 'things came together in the studio. Even mistakes worked. For instance, Martin accidentally erased the acoustic guitar track on the first part of "Soldier", but when we played it back it worked much better with the acoustic guitar coming in after the second verse. It seemed that we were on a roll.'

The material recorded was a far cry from the preceding Groundhogs albums, with songs such as 'Ship On The Ocean', 'Garden' and 'Eccentric Man' all powerful, intelligent rock workouts. Arguably the finest moment came in the form of the seven-minute title track. Beginning with an acoustic guitar-and-vocal tale of impending Armageddon, it climaxed with a stunning hard-rock cacophony cut dramatically short by a distant siren and the thunder of an explosion that died away in the album's runout groove.

'Thank Christ for the Bomb' was championed by BBC Radio 1 DJ John Peel, who declared the record to be one of the finest of the year. 'Thanks to Peel playing the album,' McPhee reflected, 'we found ourselves in the album charts the following week.' Breaking into the UK Top 10, 'Thank Christ For The Bomb' launched a new phase in the career of the Groundhogs and gained the trio many new followers on the live circuit. 'I'm still very proud of the album,' McPhee later declared. 'It was the first record to feature all of my own compositions. From the moment we had finished mixing the album we all felt that we had come up with something special.'

The testament to how special 'Thank Christ For The Bomb' remains for many is the fact that many tracks can still be heard at Groundhogs concerts 40 years later. It is an album no collection of rock music should be without.

BO HANSSON 'Music inspired By Lord Of The Rings'

First released in Sweden as Silence Records SRS4600 in September 1970
Released in the UK as Charisma CAS1059 in October 1972
Highest UK chart position: Number 34
Available on CD as Virgin CDV2960

Leaving The Shire
The Old Forest And Tom Bombadil
Fog On The Barrow Downs
The Black Riders And Flight To The Ford
At the House of Elrond And The Ring Goes South
A Journey in The Dark
Lothlorien
ShadowFax
The Horns Of Rohan And The Battle Of
The Pelennor Fields
Dreams In The House Of Healing
Homeward Bound And The Scouring Of The Shire
The Grey Havens

Bo Hansson	**Organ, Guitar, Moog Synthesiser, Bass**
Rune Carlsson	**Drums**
Gunnar Bergsten	**Saxophone**
Sten Bergman	**Flute**

Recorded at a summer house near Stockholm and at Studio Decibel, Stockholm in the winter of 1969
Produced by Anders Lind and Bo Hansson
Recorded by Anders Lind

In 1972, a talented Swedish multi-instrumentalist became known to a wider audience throughout Europe and the US by the release of an unique album of music inspired by JRR Tolkien's Lord Of The Rings.

Bo Hansson was born on 10 April 1943 in Gothenberg. As a young child he was brought up in the north of Sweden, but by the mid-Fifties his parents were forced to move to Stockholm, leaving the young Bo in the care of family friends who lived in a remote cottage in dense woodland. When his parents' circumstances changed, Hansson was able to follow them to Stockholm where he soon eagerly absorbed the new rock music from America and, latterly, Britain. Bo taught himself to play the guitar and joined one of Sweden's first rock bands, Rock-Olga.

Soon, Sweden became gripped by the blues explosion and Hansson joined pianist Slim Notini, a Swedish equivalent of John Mayall who nurtured many aspiring musician, in Slim's Blues Gang. After a short stint with Notini, Bo became a founder member of blues-rock outfit the Merrymen, and achieved some prominence in Scandinavia when they supported the Rolling Stones and secured a recording contract with Polydor.

At the point the group's success seemed assured, Hansson left, expressing his desire to explore a wider musical palate. Always a keen admirer of modern jazz, Bo witnessed a performance by American jazz organist Brother Jack McDuff at Stockholm's Gyllene Cirkeln Club in 1966 that was to have a permanent effect on his musical outlook. Inspired by McDuff's mastery of the Hammond organ, he set aside his guitar and resolved to hone his talents on this keyboard instrument.

After much encouragement from friends including former Merrymen bandmate Bill Ohrstrom (who acted as guarantor for the hire-purchase instalments), Hansson finally acquired his own Hammond. Ohrstrom secured a position as a producer and A&R man at Polydor's Swedish office and introduced Bo to other musicians with a view to forming a new musical partnership. One of them was jazz drummer Janne Karlsson. The musical chemistry was instant and the duo Hansson and Karlsson soon signed to Polydor, recording the highly innovative instrumental album 'Monument' in 1967.

Over the next two years Hansson and Karlsson toured Scandinavia constantly, supporting such acts as Cream and the Jimi Hendrix Experience. Following a night-long jam with Hendrix in Stockholm's Klub Filipis, Hendrix became a devotee of the duo's work, later recording their composition 'Tax Free'. By 1969, Hansson and Karlsson had recorded three albums, but after the release of 'Man At Moon' the same year Bo announced his intention to plough his own musical furrow. The music scene in Sweden had changed radically, thanks in part to the wave of progressive bands that had emerged in Britain, and bands now began to write their own material and sing lyrics in Swedish. A burgeoning musical underground was born in Sweden, something the local offices of the major international labels were slow to appreciate.

Amid all this activity, Bo Hansson began to write music inspired by Lord Of The Rings, a book he had borrowed from a girlfriend, and ensconced himself in friend's vacant apartment to record demos of his ideas. The friend would later return from his travels to discover that Hansson had managed to get him evicted due to the volume of his playing! With the basis of a musical idea, Bo approached friend and recording engineer Anders Lind, who had worked on the Hansson and Karlsson albums, with a view to recording his new work. Lind had recently established Sweden's first independent rock label, Silence, and saw this as its first release.

With finances in short supply, Lind and Hansson rented a house on an island off Stockholm in the summer of 1969 and began work, recording on a borrowed four-track tape machine with Rune Carlsson contributing drum parts. To finish the record, Anders Lind managed to secure some time in the studios of Swedish National Radio and make use of the only 8-track tape machine in the country on the pretext that he wanted to evaluate a machine before purchasing one. These sessions featured contributions from Gunnar Bergsten on saxophone and Sten Bergman on flute.

'Music Inspired By Lord Of The Rings' was released on Silence Records in the autumn of 1970 and immediately became a best-selling album in Sweden. Copies began to make their way to Britain via import and came to the attention of Tony Stratton-Smith, owner of the recently founded Charisma Records. Hansson's masterpiece had waited nearly two years to gain a release outside Sweden, but Stratton-Smith's efforts not only secured it a UK release but also an American release on Sire. '...Lord Of The Rings' revealed Hansson to be a highly original talent, with music encompassing a variety of styles from rock through jazz to classical evoking the imagery of Tolkien's books. With a redesign of the sleeve, 'Music Inspired By Lord Of The Rings' appeared in Britain in October 1972 and became Hansson's only UK chart album.

While his career had only begun to take off in Britain, Bo had busied himself writing more music and within a short time had accumulated enough material to record a second solo album. For these recordings, once again begun in the same summer house as '...Lord Of The Rings', Hansson began to work on a broader musical canvas and, after committing basic ideas to tape, entered Studio Decibel in Stockholm to put 'Magician's Hat' together. He recorded two further albums in the Seventies, 'Attic Thoughts' and 'Watership Down', before retiring from a solo career soon after.

He continued to guest with various musician friends on many projects, and his four solo albums began to acquire cult status. In 1985 he resurfaced with the atypical 'Mitt I Livit' (translated as 'The Middle Of Life'), released on Silence in Sweden only, which featured a selection of songs in Swedish written by Hansson and featuring several vocalists. Unfortunately critical response was lukewarm and, aside from a brief reunion of Hansson and Karlsson in 1999, this proved to be his last recorded work. In 2008 he returned to the concert stage, performing several shows in Sweden to great acclaim, but passed away in Stockholm in April 2010 aged 67.

Nearly four decades on from the release of '...Lord Of The Rings', Hansson's debut solo work still commands a loyal following. It is the finest tribute to his musical inventiveness, containing some of the most original instrumental music to emerge from Europe in the early Seventies.

HIGH TIDE 'High Tide'

First released as Liberty LBS83294 in July 1970
Highest UK chart position: N/A
Not currently available on CD

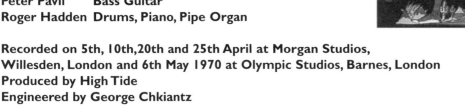

Blankman Cries Again
The Joke
Saneonymous

Tony Hill	**Guitar, Vocals, Acoustic Guitar, Organ**
Simon House	**Electric Violin, Organ, Piano**
Peter Pavli	**Bass Guitar**
Roger Hadden	**Drums, Piano, Pipe Organ**

**Recorded on 5th, 10th, 20th and 25th April at Morgan Studios,
Willesden, London and 6th May 1970 at Olympic Studios, Barnes, London
Produced by High Tide
Engineered by George Chkiantz**

In October 1969 High Tide's debut album 'Sea Shanties' was released to universal praise in the British underground press and, despite failing to chart, notched up enough sales to secure commitment from Liberty to release a follow-up. This highly original outfit's small but loyal fan base included DJ John Peel who supported the band's music on his BBC Radio 1 show. High Tide received further attention when 'Sinister Morning' by Denny Gerrard was released by Decca's Deram Nova imprint in January 1970. The album had been recorded at the Olympic sessions in 1969 at which Gerrard had produced 'Sea Shanties'.

At the beginning of April 1970 the group convened at Morgan Studios to begin work on their second opus. The material recorded was more sophisticated in nature than their debut, although equally powerful and innovative. Confident in their abilities in the studio, High Tide undertook production duties themselves, retaining engineer George Chkiantz. Sessions spanned a mere five days, four in April at Morgan and a final session and mixing at Olympic on 6 May. Sessions were dominated by two lengthy tracks, the epic 'Saneonymous' (recorded in several parts over three sessions), and a newly rearranged 'Great Universal Protection Racket', an earlier version of which failed to make the final running order of 'Sea Shanties'.

'At that time life for us was nothing except making blissful music.' Tony Hill would later recall. 'We set about recording our second album in the newly installed 16-track studio and began to explore further musical possibilities in terms of guitar and violin

duets, cannon fast and slow, diminished and augmented chords and scales, interwoven with familiar majors and minor chords for stability. We were on fire as a band.'

With the complexity of 'Saneonymous' dominating the Morgan sessions it is surprising that two stunning tracks would be completed and mixed in the space of a short final session at Olympic on 6 May. 'Blankman Cries Again' and 'The Joke' were among the finest songs ever recorded by High Tide, featuring dark lyrics and superb gothic musical backing, both committed to tape with speed and efficiency. With two lengthy works in the can, the decision was made to consign 'The Great Universal Protection Racket' to the vaults in favour of the more complex 'Saneonymous'.

'High Tide' was released in July 1970 in a textured sleeve designed by Joanna Enderby-Smith and, despite favourable reviews, failed to sell in greater quantities than its predecessor in the UK, although sales increased significantly in European countries such as Italy. High Tide continued to undertake an extensive gigging schedule, recording a further demo session for Liberty later in the year which produced the track 'Ice Age'. Although the band still pushed musical boundaries, their association with Liberty ceased within months.

Simon House departed the fold to join the Third Ear Band, signed to EMI's Harvest label. He contributed to their outstanding soundtrack to Roman Polanski's film Macbeth and continued to perform with the group until lured away to join Hawkwind in 1973. Tony Hill, Peter Pavli and Roger Hadden became involved with the group Rustic Hinge. By 1972 Hadden had sadly developed mental health problems, eventually being hospitalised. Former Arthur Brown drummer Drachen Theaker began to collaborate with Hill, recording a series of demos which later appeared on the 1990 release 'The Flood'.

Following the demise of High Tide Pavli would become a member of Hawkwind collaborator and science-fiction author Michael Moorcock's band Deep Fix. He would also perform with Hawkwind frontman Robert Calvert. The early Nineties saw a revitalised High Tide record the album 'Ancient Gates' on which Tony Hill was joined by Peter Pavli, Drachen Theaker, violinist Dave Tomlin and vocalist Sushi Krishnamurthi. Sadly, following Drachen Theaker's untimely death, future projects were shelved.
In their brief existence, High Tide retained a musical excellence and integrity that few bands achieve. Their legacy, although short, was greater than the sum of their recorded works, for they were true pioneers. Tony Hill would sum up the career of High Tide in these succinct terms: 'I was convinced that we could achieve musical success as a band, although attracting a large audience was an entirely different matter. We always moved audiences with our live performances and over the years our two albums have become well received and appreciated. It's just as well, as I think I would have lost the will to live had we not moved the listener to some degree.'

Both of High Tide albums recorded for Liberty Records were far ahead of their time in terms of creativity and are essential listening.

LOCOMOTIVE 'We Are Everything You See'

First released as Parlophone PCS7093 in February 1970
Highest UK chart position: N/A
Not currently available on CD

Overture
Mr Armageddon
Now is the End – The End Is When
Lay Me Down Gently
Nobody Asked You To Come
You Must Be Joking
A Day in Shining Armour
The Loves Of Augustus Abbey Part One
Rain
The Loves Of Augustus Abbey Part Two
Coming Down/Love Song For The Dead Ché
The Loves Of Augustus Abbey Part Three
Time of Light And Darkness

Norman Haines	**Lead Vocals, Piano, Organ, Mellotron, Harpsichord, Togetherness**
Mick Hincks	**Bass, Backing Vocals, Lead Vocal on 'Rain'**
Bob Lamb	**Drums, Percussion, Facial Expressions**
+ Their friends	
Bill Madge	**Tenor Saxophone**
Dick Heckstall-Smith	**Tenor Saxophone**
Chris Mercer	**Tenor Saxophone**
Lyn Dobson	**Tenor Saxophone**
Mick Taylor	**Trumpet**
Henry Lowther	**Trumpet**

Recorded at EMI Studios, Abbey Road, London in November 1968 and the spring and summer of 1969
Produced by Gus Dudgeon for Tuesday Productions in association with Tony Hall Enterprises
Executive producer Tony Hall
Engineered by Jeff Jarratt

The sole album recorded by Birmingham band Locomotive is one of the finest to be recorded by a British band in the late Sixties in the progressive genre. The fact it failed to make any impression commercially at the time of its release can be attributed to its delayed release, eventually appearing on EMI's Parlophone label in early 1970.

While most other EMI signings previously with Parlophone and Columbia such as Pink Floyd, Pete Brown and his Battered Ornaments, Barclay James Harvest and the Pretty Things were now on Harvest, enjoying increased attention and credibility as a result, Locomotive's only album was destined to languish among more mundane artists despite being better than some albums on EMI's progressive label.

The Locomotive story began in Birmingham in mid 1966 when trumpet-player Jim Simpson put the first of many incarnations of the band together. Many future greats passed through the ranks, including John Bonham (soon to join Led Zeppelin), Chris Wood (a founder member of Traffic) and Mike Kellie (later in Art and Spooky Tooth).

In January 1967, keyboard-player Norman Haines was recruited. He had previously played with Birmingham outfit the Brum Beats (not to be confused with the Brumbeats who had released one single on Decca in late 1964). Soon after Haines' arrival, Locomotive, with a line-up of Simpson, Jo Ellis on bass guitar, Bill Madge on saxophone and drummer Mooney Mazzone, entered the studio to record their first single. The A-side was a Haines composition, 'Broken Heart', which featured session drummer Clem Cattini deputising for Mazzone and later described by Haines as 'sounding like Joe Loss playing a cover of a soul number.'

Locomotive

The B-side was 'Rudi –A Message To You', the bluebeat classic that would be a hit 13 years later for the Specials). Haines' interest in ska began when he ran a record shop with his wife Elaine in the Smethwick area of Birmingham which catered mainly for the local West Indian community. 'The single was released as Direction 58-3814 in the spring of 1967 and, although it gained some airplay, failed to chart. Following its release Jim Simpson became Locomotive's full-time manager, going on to manage bands such as Black Sabbath, Bakerloo and Tea and Symphony. The single brought them wider attention which led to a deal with Parlophone Records in 1968 and their next release, another bluebeat-inspired release 'Rudi's In Love', penned by Haines.

This song would see Locomotive gain their only chart success when the single reached Number 25 in the UK in October 1968. By this time the band line-up h featured Norman Haines on vocals and keyboards, Mick Hincks on bass, Bob Lamb on drums, Bill Madge on saxophone and Mick Taylor on trumpet. But while 'Rudi's In Love' was in the charts, Locomotive were telling the music press their music was now heading in a more progressive direction.

In the autumn of 1968 the band entered Abbey Road studios with producer Gus Dudgeon to begin work on an album, augmented by the addition of Dick Heckstall-Smith (from Colosseum) and Chris Mercer on saxophones and Henry Lowther on trumpet. The first fruits of these sessions were released as the single 'Mr Armageddon' b/w 'There's Got To Be A Way' in January 1969.

This brilliant piece of dark, doom-laden psychedelia and its equally good flip-side received praise in underground quarters but failed to appeal to the pop audience who had bought Locomotive's previous vinyl outing. Underground DJ John Peel accurately commented that 'Mr Armageddon' was a great song, but Locomotive were saddled with a pop image thanks to the success of 'Rudi's In Love'.

The material recorded for the album was of a very high standard. 'Nobody Asked You to Come', 'Overture', 'A Day In Shining Armour', 'Rain' and 'The Loves Of Augustus Abbey' all saw Norman Haines collaborating with Nigel Phillips, a member of Harvest Records (and Jim Simpson) signing Tea and Symphony, on string arrangements.

The tracks were chosen to cross-fade into each other, causing 'Mr Armageddon' to lose the organ introduction present on the single. Additional highlights were the dark 'You Must Be Joking,' the uptempo 'A Day In Shining Armour' and the Mick Hincks composition 'Rain'. The band also covered 'Coming Down'/'Love Song For The Dead Ché' written and originally performed by US group the United States of America. Overall, the album had a consistency many debut albums lacked.

Prior to release, Parlophone selected 'You Must Be Joking' to back a cover of a Question Mark and the Mysterians' song 'Movin' Down the Line' for release as a single. Like its predecessor, it failed to chart despite good reviews and this led to the departure of Bill Madge and Mick Taylor soon afterwards. The summer of 1969 saw Jim Simpson secure a German TV spot appearing alongside Pink Floyd and performing five songs from their as yet unreleased album. Madge and Taylor were persuaded them to return for this one-off appearance. However, prior to leaving for Germany, Simpson rejected this idea and instead added his other signings Tea and Symphony to the Locomotive line-up.

For reasons no longer clear EMI, preoccupied with the launch of Harvest, continually pushed back the release date of Locomotive's album, much to the frustration of all concerned. This, together with Norman Haines feeling that Locomotive was no longer under his control, led to his departure to form the harder-edged Sacrifice, later known as Avalanche and then the Norman Haines Band.

Locomotive's 'We Are Everything You See' was finally released as Parlophone PCS7093 on 1 February 1970 to indifference from a music press whose taste had now moved on to music of a heavier nature. A last single – 'Roll Over Mary' b/w 'Movin' Down The Line', featuring a line-up of Bob Lamb and Mick Hincks joined by Keith Millar and John Casswell – was released by Parlophone in the spring of 1970, This quartet evolved into another legendary group, the Dog That Bit People, who recorded an album and single for Parlophone, both released in 1971.

Norman Haines had jammed with fellow Birmingham band Earth on keyboards while pursuing the formation of his new band. Some months later they changed their name to Black Sabbath and recorded a Haines composition, 'When I Come Down', during sessions for their first album. Unfortunately this recording failed to make the final tracklisting for 'Black Sabbath' and was consigned to the vaults.

Sacrifice recorded an equally impressive album for Parlophone in 1970 which appeared as 'Den Of Iniquity' the following year, credited to the Norman Haines Band, but failed to make any commercial impression. Over the years the reputation of Locomotive's 'We Are Everything You See' has increased, original copies changing hands for many hundreds of pounds.

LOVE SCULPTURE 'Forms And Feelings'

First released as Parlophone PCS7090 in February 1970
Highest UK chart position: N/A
Available on CD as Esoteric Recordings ECLEC2016

In The Land Of The Few
Seagull
Nobody's Talking
Why (How-Now)
Farandole (from L'Arlesienne)
You Can't Catch Me
People, People
Mars (on initial test pressings, US album and CD only)
Sabre Dance

Dave Edmunds	Vocals, Lead Guitar, Keyboards
John Williams	Bass, Keyboards, Vocals
Bob 'Congo' Jones	Drums

Recorded at Advision studios and Maximum Sound studios, London
Produced by Dave Edmunds, Mike Finesilver and Pete Ker
Engineered by Eddy Offord at Advision Studios and Dave Hadfield at Maximum Sound Studios

The late Sixties was an era when the major record companies in Britain were engaged in a mad scramble to find the 'next big thing' – a group or artist that would quickly scale the pop charts and bring in healthy returns for as little investment as possible. This attitude had prevailed following the success of British beat groups such as the Beatles and the Rolling Stones in the early/mid Sixties and once more when psychedelia became the watchword in the music press.

It was in this climate that EMI Records signed a trio of musicians from South Wales who would record two memorable albums in decidedly different styles and a clutch of singles for the Parlophone label that would later be regarded as fine examples of both blues-rock and psychedelia. Love Sculpture would forever be associated with their November 1968 hit 'Sabre Dance' and for being the springboard that would launch the career of the highly talented Dave Edmunds, whose incendiary guitar playing had made 'it such a hit. However, in hindsight, Love Sculpture produced music that was more than mere psychedelic meandering. The group featured highly gifted musicians who recorded music of quality and influence. The roots of Love Sculpture went back to the formation of the Image in Cardiff in the mid Sixties. Edmunds had been playing on the local circuit since 1961 in outfits such as the Raiders and the 99ers. By 1966 the Image had become a respected beat group in South Wales, comprising Edmunds on guitar and vocals, John Williams on bass and vocals and Tommy Riley on drums. The band came to the attention of brothers Kingsley and Charles Ward, proprietors of the recently opened Rockfield recording studios near Monmouth. It was thanks to the Ward brothers that the Image recorded a series of demos that sparked interest from EMI Records in London.

EMI's Columbia label released the single 'Morning Dew' b/w 'It's A Wonder' under a 'lease-tape' deal in July 1967, renaming the band the Human Beans in an attempt to make the record more attractive to the burgeoning underground audience. Despite the excellence of the A-side, an inspired cover of Tim Rose's classic, and airplay on pirate radio stations such as Radio London, the single failed to chart. Despite this, the Ward brothers expressed continued belief in the band who, by the end of the year, had changed their name to Love Sculpture. Further recording sessions took place at Rockfield which resulted in the single

'River To Another Day' b/w 'Brand New Woman' being released by Parlophone in February 1968. The single's A-side was written by the Ward brothers and once more received radio support, but also failed to make a chart impression. This lack of commercial success led to the departure of drummer Riley who was replaced by Bob 'Congo' Jones. Thanks to the continued enthusiasm of Kingsley Ward and the gifted young EMI A&R man Malcolm Jones, whose intention at that time was to make the Parlophone label EMI's underground imprint, the duo suggested Love Sculpture reinvent themselves as a blues-based rock band in an attempt to ride the second wave of the so-called British blues boom that saw acts such as Savoy Brown, Fleetwood Mac and Chicken Shack come to prominence.

'I didn't know anything about the blues,' Edmunds would later recall. 'EMI Records said that they wanted a blues band, just like all the other record companies at that time, and they asked us if we'd be it. They sent us down some tapes to listen to and gave us the chance to make an album. It was really our enthusiasm for making an album, not the blues, that led to the making of "Blues Helping". I listened to some BB King tapes and this and that, plus listening to John Mayall's "Bluesbreakers With Eric Clapton" album and nicked as many licks as I could.' Released in October 1968, 'Blues Helping' secured the band a session for the Radio 1 show Top Gear. Aside from performing some of the blues standards from their album, Love Sculpture also taped an interpretation of a classical piece by Russian composer Khatchaturian which had been adapted by Edmunds and had been a highlight of recent shows. The version of 'Sabre Dance' recorded was so striking that the BBC were inundated with requests to repeat the transmission.

Parlophone rush-released 'Sabre Dance' as a single, coupling it with Edmunds' own 'Think Of Love,' in the first week of November 1968. The same week DJ John Peel repeated the session and enthused greatly about the single, assuring it a Number 5 chart placing. This saw an upturn in the demand for the band on the concert stage, and for the remaining weeks of 1968 and the early months of 1969 Love Sculpture appeared at leading underground venues in London such as Implosion at the Roundhouse and Middle Earth.

Tiring of playing blues standards, Edmunds and company planned to record a follow-up directed more at the underground audience for whom their champion Peel was a respected figure. This change had been revealed in another BBC session the band recorded in January 1969, for which three new songs were recorded, 'The Inner Light', 'Evening' and a reworking of Bizet's 'Farandole' which involved more guitar pyrotechnics from Edmunds. Of these, only 'Farandole' would feature on a Love Sculpture record, becoming one of the first tracks to be recorded at Advision Studios in London, along with the emotive 'Seagull', a song about the damage to the environment caused by pollution. Released in February 1969 the single failed to make an impression on the UK charts, perhaps due to its similarity to 'Sabre Dance'. Love Sculpture continued playing live shows interspersed with

LOVE SCULPTURE GET
CRIES OF
FAKE

LOVE SCULPTURE

IT'S the fastest guitar feature in pop music in a long, long time . . . "Sabre Dance", by the Love Sculpture. But what do the three boys get? Cries of fake, fake, fake. "A studio job," say the cynics. "All faked".

Now hear the fastest vocal feature in defence of this theory. "Faked?" echoed Dave Edmunds, lead guitarist on the exercise. "Listen, if anyone thinks that, they have only to come and hear us play it on stage. On the record, there is a piano, playing away quietly in the background, but quite honestly we have played the number sometimes much better in person . . . on a live date."

Okay? We happen to know people who have heard the boys reproduce the record sound on stage in places like the Marquee, and there can't be much argument about how well they come up with the goods.

Even so, such a virtuoso performance on guitar makes one wonder how long the musician concerned has been playing. "I've been playing now for six years, seriously. But I was fooling around on guitar for two years before that. I'm com-

pletely self-taught . . . I remember starting on guitar at school on rock 'n' roll things."

Dave added: "I was very surprised when our record got so high in the charts. I thought it might make the lower thirties, but we really must thank people like John Peel for helping to get us across on radio so much."

The rest of Love Sculpture consists of John Williams on bass and a gent named Congo on drums. Why just Congo? "Well, he can't really remember how he got his name", said Dave in perplexed style. "Evidently it's a nickname which has hung over from his school days."

Dave also wished it to be known that the Love Sculpture is not a blues group. Neither are they an underground group. "That is specially something we don't want to be," he said. "If you classify a group, then there are always problems.

"We create our own market so we can please everyone. Before we became known in Cardiff, we used to play everything—ranging from pop to blues. Things like Beatles' numbers and real

blues material. Now we do a very wide range of material—R 'n' R, a few blues and instrumentals.

"I've always dreamed of having a record in the charts. Now this has happened I don't know what the next goal is for us. My main ambition is to own a recording studio. I've always been interested in recording and have been playing around with tape recorders for years."

How did Dave feel about groups using electronic effects for recordings and not being able to reproduce them on stage?

"I don't think it matters really. As long as the finished product turns out well I don't see why people should object. It certainly doesn't make any difference to out and out pop groups. Should they have a full orchestra on their recordings they still draw large crowds at dance halls and theatres. Groups like Casuals and Love Affair have proved this."

Get to see and hear Love Sculpture on stage if only to watch them perform "Sabre Dance".

IAN MIDDLETON

recording sessions for a new album at both Maximum Sound studios in London and Advision Studios. These sessions saw Edmunds assume a production role for the first time in his career alongside co-producers Mike Finesilver and Pete Ker (co-writers of the hit single 'Fire' by the Crazy World of Arthur Brown) and future Yes and Emerson Lake and Palmer engineer Eddy Offord. Finesilver and Ker contributed compositions of their own to the sessions, namely the wonderful 'In The Land Of The Few', the psychedelic 'Nobody's Talking', 'Why?' and the more gentle 'People People'. Sessions were interrupted by Love Sculpture's first American tour in the summer of 1969 which included a memorable series of concerts at the Fillmore West in San Francisco in July. By the time Love Sculpture returned to Britain, EMI had established the new Harvest imprint, moving artists from Parlophone and Columbia respectively to the new label. Love Sculpture was overlooked in this move, along with fellow labelmates Locomotive, and this may have had a restrictive effect on their future record sales. An association with Harvest, now regarded as a 'happening' label by both the UK music press and the underground audience, was a major asset in terms of both sales and reputation.

Sessions for the second album were completed at Advision Studios with the recording of a wonderfully frantic Chuck Berry cover, 'You Can't Catch Me' and an extended version of 'Sabre Dance.' Also recorded was an impressive, experimental arrangement of 'Mars' from Gustav Holst's 'The Planets Suite'. Featuring overdubbed and heavily flanged electric guitar, the piece was devised to segue into 'Sabre Dance' on the finished album. However, the Holst estate objected to this treatment of the work and the track was omitted from all European copies. Such legal wrangling delayed the release still further, the album finally appearing in February 1970 as 'Forms And Feelings'. In the US, the album appeared on the Parrot label, a subsidiary of Decca, and survived intact with 'Mars' opening the second side.

To coincide with the release of the album, Parlophone coupled 'In The Land Of The Few' with 'People People' for release as a single throughout Europe. Selling well in Germany, the single failed to chart in the UK. By the time both records were released Love Sculpture were enduring another personnel change and Edmunds was losing enthusiasm. Terry Williams, later to join Man, replaced Bob 'Congo' Jones on drums while second guitarist Mickey Gee was added. This line-up undertook further live concerts to honour outstanding commitments, but within months Love Sculpture had disbanded, leaving behind this wonderful album of psychedelic progressive rock.

On sale, Friday, week ending December 21, 1968 — NEW MUS.

LIFE·LINES of LOVE SCULPTURE

Up to No 8 this week

CONGO — JOHN WILLIAMS — DAVE EDMUNDS

	John Williams (CONGO)	Congo (JOHN WILLIAMS)	Dave Edmunds
Professional name:	John Williams	Congo	Dave Edmunds
Real name:	John David Williams	Rob Jones	Dave Edmunds
Birthdate:	19.1.46	13.8.46	15.4.44
Personal points:	5ft 11in, 10st, brown eyes, brown hair	5ft 7in, 10st, blue eyes, brown hair	5ft 10in, 10st 5lb, green-blue eyes, fair hair
Parents names:	Ivor, Mary	Dorothy	Mary Ann, Frederick James
Brothers and sisters names:	Julian, Judith, Richard	Marilyn, John	Geoffrey
Present home:	Cardiff	Barry	Cardiff
Instruments played:	Bass guitar	Drums	Guitar, piano.
Where educated:	Barry Grammar	Barry Grammar	Cardiff
Musical education:	4 years piano training	None	None
Age entered showbusiness:	17	20	18
First professional appearance:	The Pilot, Tiger Bay		—
Biggest break in career:	Being introduced to Dave Edmunds	John Peel	John Peel
Biggest disappointment in career:	"River To Another Day" not happening	—	Yet to come
Biggest influence on career:	Dave Edmunds	—	Rock and Roll
Former occupation:	Engineer	Engineer	Motor mechanic
Hobbies:	Ornithology	Records	—
Favourite colour:	Blue	Red	Black
Favourite food:	Steak	Anything good	Steak
Favourite drink:	Water	Milk	Milk
Favourite clothes:	Casual	Casual	Casual
Favourite singer:	Paul McCartney	Paul McCartney/Brian Wilson	—
Favourite actor/actress:	Jack Elam, Elizabeth Taylor	—	—
Favourite bands/instrumentalists:	Buddy Rich, Chet Atkins	Buddy Rich	—
Favourite composers:	Lennon and McCartney, Rachmaninov, Chopin	Lennon and McCartney	Lennon and McCartney
Favourite groups:	Beatles, Nice, Booker T, Beach Boys	Beatles, Beach Boys	Beatles, Booker T
Car:	Triumph Herald	—	Mini Cooper
Miscellaneous dislikes:	Fighting, drunks, insincerity	Drunks, violence	Drunks, being tired
Miscellaneous likes:	Love, animals, pianos	Cars, girls, sleep	Driving, clouds
Best friend:	Dave Edmunds	Jan	Nicky Beans and "Honka"
Most thrilling experience:	Meeting Dave Edmunds	Having "Sabre Dance" in Top Thirty	Yet to come
Tastes in music:	Most well-played music	Very wide	Anything from George Jones to the Swingle Singers, via Chuck Berry
Pets:	Alsatian "Sal"	Hamster "Timmy"	—
Personal ambition:	To live happily ever after	To be healthy and happy	To own recording studios
Professional ambition:	To have someone make a hit of one of my songs	To be successful and a good musician	—

COMMON TO ALL

TV debut: Colour Me Pop — Current hit: Sabre Dance — Disc label: Parlophone — Personal manager: Alan Field
Radio debut: Top Gear — Albums: Blues Helping — Recording manager: Us — Road manager: Choppo

McDONALD AND GILES 'McDonald And Giles'

First released as Island Records ILPS9126 in November 1970
Highest UK chart position: N/A
Currently available on CD as Virgin CDV2963

Suite In C:
including Turnham Green, Here I Am and others
Flight Of The Ibis
Is She Waiting?
Tomorrow's People – The Children of Today
Birdman:
involving
The Inventors Dream (OUAT)
The Workshop
Wishbone Ascension
Birdman Flies!
Wings In The Sunset
Birdman – The Reflection

Ian McDonald	Guitar, Piano, Organ, Saxes, Flute, Clarinet, Zither, Vocals and Sundries
Michael Giles	Drums, Percussion (including Milk Bottle, Handsaw, Lip Whistle and Nut Box), Vocals
Peter Giles	Bass guitar
Steve Winwood	Organ and Piano solo on 'Turnham Green'
Michael Blakesley	Trombone on 'Tomorrows People'

Strings and Brass on 'Birdman' and 'Suite in C' arranged and conducted by Mike Gray
Recorded at Island studios, London during May, June and July 1970
Produced by Ian McDonald and Michael Giles
Engineered by Brian Humphries

The huge impact of the album 'In The Court Of The Crimson King' had both a positive and unsettling effect on the members of King Crimson. The release of the album in the autumn of 1969 had been followed by critical praise and instant commercial success. Securing a Top 5 hit album also brought about a huge demand for the band to perform live, both in Europe and in America, where Atlantic Records had issued the album. Thus in November 1969 Robert Fripp, Greg Lake, Mike Giles, Ian McDonald and lyricist/lighting man Pete Sinfield embarked on a US tour. Tensions quickly developed within the ranks due to the fact that both Ian McDonald and Mike Giles had developed a distaste for life on the road.

Both also felt that the band's music was heading in a direction they felt unhappy with, McDonald in particular being keen to explore a lighter side to his musical character. By the time Crimson's US tour had reached California in December 1969, the drummer and woodwind player announced their intention to leave the group following the final show at the Fillmore West in San Francisco on 16 December 1969. McDonald and Giles' departure coincided with Greg Lake handing in his notice to form a new

outfit with Keith Emerson, leaving Robert Fripp to assemble a new line-up of King Crimson upon his return to Britain.

Ian McDonald had already begun writing new music with a view to recording a new musical project while on the road, and so in January 1970, EG Management approached Island Records with the idea of McDonald and Giles recording an album in their own right. With sessions funded by EG, the duo entered Island Studios in Basing Street, London, in May 1970 with Pete Giles on bass guitar to start work. Following the example of Steve Winwood, Jim Capaldi and Chris Wood of Traffic (who were working on their album 'John Barleycorn Must Die' at Island at the same time), McDonald and Giles employed the use of overdubbing rather than utilise many musicians. Ian McDonald played guitar, piano and organ alongside his more familiar saxophones, flutes and clarinets. Mike Giles attended to percussion duties and both provided vocals.

One of the first songs to be committed to tape was 'Suite In C' (including 'Turnham Green,' 'Here I Am' and others), an extensive work written by McDonald while on tour with Crimson and completed in early 1970. The 11-minute song cycle was also graced by the guest appearance of Steve Winwood on piano and organ on the 'Turnham Green' section. Of the remaining material, 'Is She Waiting?' was a McDonald tune written in the summer of 1969, originally offered to King Crimson, and the album's other lengthy work, 'Birdman', was a piece originally conceived by Crimson lyricist Pete Sinfield and set to music by McDonald that had evolved from as far back as December 1968. Mike Giles' 'Tomorrow's People – The Children of Today' had been initially written for the band Giles, Giles and Fripp in 1968 but had now been extended and reworked, featuring guest trombonist Michael Blakesley.

By June 1970, McDonald and Giles had produced 45 minutes of astounding, melodic music. Ranging from the Beatle-esque to jazz and rock idioms, the album 'McDonald And Giles' was greeted with much critical acclaim upon its release in the autumn of 1970. Sadly, this failed to result in a chart place in the UK.

With an unwillingness to tour the record, the duo inevitably went their separate ways at the beginning of 1971. Mike Giles became a respected session drummer, working with acts such as Jackson Heights, while Ian McDonald would enjoy vast success some years later as a member of the band Foreigner.

McDonald and Giles' sole eponymous offering remains a huge favourite among King Crimson faithful, although its music is quite different in feel. With a vinyl reissue in the late Seventies and a long-overdue CD release in 2002, it has enjoyed a greater success than it achieved upon initial release. Even more surprisingly, in 1998 Mike Giles' drum solo on 'The Children Of Today' was sampled by rappers the Beastie Boys and featured on their track 'Body Movin'', proving the continuing influence of the album on artists of many diverse musical genres.

Two of a mind

MIKE GILES AND IAN McDONALD (INSET)

. . . or how McDonald and Giles discovered what they didn't want to do. Rob Partridge reports

IAN McDonald and Michael Giles spent much of 1969 finding out what they didn't want to do. And much of 1970 finding themselves.

The two were original members of King Crimson, but the group's first American tour at the end of 1969 left McDonald and Giles with a very positive feeling that Crimso was not for them.

SPLIT

The split came. Crimso went one way; and McDonald and Giles decided to record an album together. The result, called simply "McDonald And Giles" was released a few weeks ago.

The whole style of the album is far away from Crimso; there are love songs, and altogether a much greater feeling of warmth and spontaneity than Crimso have so far displayed.

In fact, it sounds like the Beatles have been a greater influence on McDonald And Giles than Crimso.

Commented Mike: "Both Ian and I have a lot of regard for the Beatles and we are influenced by them, of course – not so much in the way they play their instruments, but rather in their musical thinking and attitude.

"It's important that their music has reached the majority of people without being shallow.

"We find that we have a similar attitude, and although we've got no desire to copy them we like the idea of using simplicity coupled with spontaneity and humour – and we found that Crimso wasn't capable of doing that sort of thing.

"Crimso might have love songs now – but then it had so many pressures that it couldn't break from its basic concept. Had we had a broader musical policy, then the original band might still be together."

So now Ian and Mike have had the opportunity to find their own musical identities. How did they go about writing the material?

"Well, we made no attempt to write together – we would have gotten in each others way, and, besides that would have interrupted each others thoughts – and the songs are dealing with personal subjects.

"Instead, we decided it was best to help each other by adding suggestions to each others basic ideas. In that way, for instance, Ian was able to give me an outside opinion on what I was doing – he could approach my material objectively.

"In a way, it's nice to be able to work on other people's songs without the responsibilities of having written it."

The connections with Crimso, however, are still there. Pete Sinfield, Crimso's lyricist wrote "Birdman" – the second side of the album.

Explained Mike: "Pete was very involved with Ian before we left the group – and that songs just one of the things they wrote. And Crimso never got round to recording it."

Another track uses the original melody Ian wrote for Crimso "Cadence And Cascade."

"When the group split we had the melody and Crimso had the words. So we found new words and they found a new melody line."

Mike Giles also played on "Wake Of Poseidon" album – as one of the musician friends Robert Fripp brought in to take the place of a fixed line-up Crimso.

Today, however, Mike Giles wants to move on. He hasn't played live for nearly a year.

"I have some broad plans at the moment – depending on the LP – of financing and forming my own band. It would be a loose structure – including occasionally Ian. I'd rather have a loose association rather than feel there's a permanent structure. That's too limiting.

"But at the moment both Ian and I are looking for session work – to broaden our musical outlook and, of course, to pay the rent.

"We've no other plans at the moment. Ian might do an album by himself – and, if there was a demand for our joint album, we'd consider doing another one.

"Ian and I have talked about it and we'd incorporate all the ideas we've found and avoid the mistakes we've made on the first one.

"My drumming hasn't devoped so much over the past year as it has over the previous year. I'd like to start again.

THE NICE 'Five Bridges'

First released as Charisma Records CAS1014 in May 1970
Highest UK chart position: Number 2
Available on CD as Charisma CASCDR1014

Fantasia: 1st Bridge/2nd Bridge
Chorale: 3rd Bridge
High Level Fugue: 4th Bridge
Finale: 5th Bridge
Intermezzo: 'Karelia Suite'
Pathétique (Sibelius' Symphony No 6, 3rd Movement)
Country Pie/Brandenburg Concerto No 6
One of Those People

Keith Emerson Keyboards
Lee Jackson   Bass and Vocals
Brian Davison   Drums and Percussion

The Sinfonia of London
Conductor Joseph Eger
Recorded at the Fairfield Halls, Croydon on October 17th 1969
'One Of Those People' recorded at Trident Studios, London in October 1969
Produced by the Nice
Engineered by Bob Auger
Mixed by Eddie Kramer and Malcolm Toft

In October 1969, a fascinating collaboration occurred between a symphony orchestra and Keith Emerson, Lee Jackson and Brian Davison of the Nice which successfully fused the hitherto disparate worlds of classical music and rock music. The Nice had explored classically influenced rock on their November 1968 album 'Ars Longa Vita Brevis' with the side-long title track and an interpretation of the Karelia Suite by Sibelius.

With an ever-increasing reputation as musicians of note, it came as no surprise when the band were finally invited to write a collaborative work with an orchestra for the 1969 Newcastle Arts Festival; bass guitarist and vocalist Lee Jackson was a native of the city. Working with noted conductor Joseph Eger, 'The Five Bridges Suite' would prove to be one of the highlights of the three-year career of the Nice.

Ironically, the commission to write the piece came at a time of turmoil for the group. Now managed by former sports journalist Tony Stratton-Smith, the Nice had embarked on a lengthy American tour in the spring of 1969, the highlight of which was a performance at the Fillmore East in New York recorded and released as the second side of 'The Nice' in September 1969. This album reached Number 3 in the UK, but was to be the band's last work for Immediate, which ceased operations soon after. Faced with such adversity, the commission by the Newcastle Arts Festival for the Nice to compose and perform a work for rock trio and orchestra proved a welcome respite from their misfortunes. 'The Five Bridges Suite' was premiered on 10 October 1969 and saw the Nice unite with an orchestra conducted by Joseph Eger. Inspired by the five bridges that spanned the River Tyne at that time, the work was presented in five short movements written by Emerson and Jackson and was well received. A performance of the work was arranged a week later on 17 October at the Fairfield Halls in Croydon. Performing to a capacity audience, the performance comprised a rendition of the suite along with superb interpretations of the Karelia Suite and Tchaikovsky's Pathétique (Symphony No 6, 3rd Movement).

The concert was enthusiastically received by the audience and was brought to a stirring conclusion with a unique medley of the Nice classic 'Rondo,' Bob Dylan's 'She Belongs To Me' and Prokofiev's 'Lieutenant Kije'. The proceedings were captured on tape by a mobile recording unit at the suggestion of Stratton-Smith, who by now was in the process of establishing Charisma Records, in part motivated by the lack of a new label for the Nice. The success of the 'Five Bridges' concerts was followed up with another American tour in December 1969, and it was during this tour that Emerson's dissatisfaction with the direction of the Nice came to the surface.

On a bill at the Fillmore West in San Francisco, the Nice shared a bill with another leading British band, King Crimson. It was here that Emerson met Greg Lake, also frustrated with his current musical path, and the pair resolved to form a new band once commitments with their current outfits allowed. Thus in January 1970 the Nice announced a final series of live concerts, completed work on the album of 'Five Bridges' and participated in the recording sessions for Roy Harper's 'Flat, Baroque And Berserk' album, performing on the closing track, 'Hell's Angels'. The band returned to the United States for a final series of live concerts and performed their last concert at the Sportpalast in Berlin on 30 March, their final engagement being a session for BBC Radio 1's Sounds Of The Seventies programme in April.

'Five Bridges' was released in May 1970 and would prove to be the most commercially successful album by the band to date. It featured highlights of the Fairfield Hall concert, alongside a recording of 'Country Pie'/'Brandenburg Concerto No 6' recorded at the Fillmore East in December 1970 and the studio track 'One Of Those People'. By the time of release Keith Emerson was engrossed in his new outfit Emerson, Lake and Palmer, while Brian Davison had formed Every Which Way with former Skip Bifferty vocalist Graham Bell and Lee Jackson was laying plans to form the first line-up of Jackson Heights.

During their relatively short life the Nice, one of the most innovative bands of their time, produced some truly enduring music. 'Five Bridges' is one of their most fully realised moments.

PRETTY THINGS 'Parachute'

First released as Harvest SHVL774 in June 1970
Highest UK chart position: Number 43
Available on CD as Snapper SMMCD566

Scene One
The Good Mr Square
She Was Tall, She Was High
In The Square
The Letter
Rain
Miss Fay Regrets
Cries From The Midnight Circus
Grass
Sickle Clowns
She's A Lover
What's The Use
Parachute

Phil May	**Lead Vocals**
Wally Allen	**Bass Guitar, Guitar, Vocals, Wind Instruments and Piano**
John Povey	**Organ, Sitar, Percussion and Vocals**
Victor Unitt	**Lead Guitar, Vocals**
Skip Alan	**Drums and Vocals**

Recorded at EMI Studios, Abbey Road, London
Produced by Norman Smith
Engineered by Tony Clark
Assistant Engineer Nick Webb

In December 1968 the Pretty Things' conceptual album 'SF Sorrow' was released to near-universal praise from critics and their musical peers. However, the atmosphere within the ranks was not as good as it could have been and 1969 began with the Pretty Things in search of new projects and a new direction.

Offered a part in the 'generation gap' comedy What's Good For The Goose starring comedian Norman Wisdom as a businessman who forms a relationship with young hippy Sally Geeson, the band wrote much of the incidental music and were seen performing material such as 'Alexander' and 'Eagle's Son' in the film. This not only brought some much-needed revenue but also led them to compose music for other soundtracks.

Guitarist Dick Taylor, a founder member of the band, had begun to tire of performing and working on the road. Having recently married, he decided to pursue a career in production and left the band soon after the making of What's Good For The Goose. Taylor was replaced by Victor Unitt, originally lead guitarist with the Edgar Broughton Band, his first recording sessions being a project the band had agreed to undertake for young French millionaire heir Philippe DeBarge.

DeBarge was a huge fan and had aspirations to record an album of his own as a vanity project. Inviting Phil May and Wally Waller to the south of France, he persuaded the pair to write some material for this album and for the Pretty Things to perform as his backing group. Travelling to London some months later, sessions were booked at Nova Studios and the Pretty Things recorded a series of May/Waller compositions with DeBarge overdubbing his vocals on top of guides laid down by Phil May. The material was mixed and pressed as a series of acetates but failed to see the light of day until the release of the album in 2008 from a cleaned-up acetate disc.

Soon after these sessions the atmosphere between Twink and Wally Waller had become fractious, and Skip Alan was back in the drum seat in time for the band to begin work on their next album for EMI Records. In June 1969 EMI had formed the progressive imprint Harvest and it was decided that all future Pretty Things material should be released on this new label. With Phil May and Wally Waller developing into a formidable writing team, the music for the album that would be the band's next masterpiece took shape.

'Wally and I were sharing a place on Westbourne Terrace in Bayswater,' May would later recall. 'It had a sort of communal atmosphere, with all sorts of creative people dropping in to have a chat, roll a joint and generally hang out. The pace of life was quite full on in those days, but it certainly spurred me on creatively. Wally and I had a Revox tape machine and we would make quite detailed demos, putting down guitars, bass, keyboards and vocal harmonies to play to the others in the band and to Norman Smith our producer.'

This approach to writing was to pay huge dividends when it came to recording the finished album at Abbey Road studios. The songs were devised to segue into one another around a loose concept of life in a city. Phil May later reflected; 'By 1969 the…dreams and hopes that had arisen a few years previously had all come to nothing. There seemed to be a sense of missed opportunity, with all expectations slowly being dashed and people becoming sucked back into "the system" once more.' It was this air of bleakness that pervaded the material.

The opening 'Scene One' had begun life as the track 'Graves Of Grey' recorded for the Philippe DeBarge sessions. A powerful introduction, this segued into the Beatle-esque 'The Good Mr Square', a fine example of their excellent harmonising ability which would later be released as the A-side of a single with the coda of 'She Was Tall, She Was High', a tale of a young woman fleeing the city to find herself in the countryside. 'In The Square', 'The Letter' and 'Rain' continued the tale with a splendid series of stylistic changes, while 'Miss Fay Regrets' was a bitter Phil May lyric about a fading movie starlet which led into the superb side closing track 'Cries From The Midnight Circus', recounting tales of the city underworld.

The album's second side would open with the majestic 'Grass', one of the finest pieces ever recorded by the band. Featuring a splendid instrumental backing of Mellotron and solo guitar, the tale of a search for a better life in the country was underpinned with some of the most impressive vocal harmonies the Pretty Things ever committed to tape. This pastoral beginning would give way to two rock tracks, 'Sickle Clowns' and 'She's A Lover.' The bitter 'What's The Use' was a tale of disenchantment with the dashed hopes of 1967, while melancholic album closer 'Parachute' was co-written by May and producer Smith.

Recorded in a series of sessions between the autumn of 1969 and the early months of 1970, the album 'Parachute' finally appeared in June 1970. Scraping into the lower reaches of the UK chart, the lack of commercial success for such of fine record is one of the great injustices of history. The record was hailed as 'Album of the Year' by Rolling Stone magazine on its US release on Motown's progressive Rare Earth label, but fell victim to a total lack of promotion to capitalise on such critical acclaim. A sense of disappointment fell over the band and Victor Unitt left to rejoin the Edgar Broughton Band. He was replaced by Pete Tolson, previously with Eire Apparent, and it was with Tolson as lead guitarist that the Pretty Things would end their tenure with EMI Harvest the following year.

Of all the incredible albums recorded by the Pretty Things, 'Parachute' is their greatest work and stands alongside 'SF Sorrow' — stylistically different, but outstanding nevertheless.

'Brilliant instrumental blending acoustic instruments with thundering beat and wild spacious harmonies. After six years with the group, Phil May is still in fine form on lead vocals and this is definitely the best they've ever done. Often Beach Boys like texture. The whole concept is clear and very attractive. L.G.

RECORD MIRROR 22/6/70

FREAK FALL FOR PRETTYS

THE PRETTY THINGS have a 'Parachute' to save them from their past.

The 'Parachute' in question is the name of their new album, and the past is, at least to lead singer, Phil May, an embarrassment.

'Parachute', which was released a few weeks ago, is a new direction for the Pretties — relying on strong songwriting rather than the freakiness, say, of their last album, 'S. F. Sorrow'.

And the past started with 'Rosalyn', their first single six years ago.

Phil May is the sole survivor from the original group.

He said: "I've been living the past down for the past five years. In a German club, recently, for instance, we were sitting in the corner when the dj put on 'Rosalyn'. Which was really embarrassing. The rest of the group weren't on the record so it had nothing to do with them.

"It's not the group's trip any more. None of us want that sort of scene again."

For the first two years the group were extremely popular. But then came the soul boom and the Pretties, churning out the old Chuck Berry, Jimmy Reed, Bo Diddley material, found things hard going.

"We used to go to gigs and find there was an audience of little mods who really wanted Geno Washington or someone. They certainly didn't want us."

At the same time, something was happening on the West Coast of America. It was the hippies, the flower children of the Love Generation. Their effectt was felt in Britain.

The Pretties changed their direction. They became part of the emerging Underground, and, once they had left their record company, Fontana Records, their new company, EMI, brought out their 'SF Sorrow'. A complete change of direction.

It was a conglomeration of sounds and effects. The new psychedelic music.

'SF Sorrow' used the lyrics as the vehicle for sound changes. But it's only just been released in the States and everyone's saying it's another copy of 'Tommy'.

"But really, of course, it was recorded months before 'Tommy'."

It has taken some time for the group's present album, 'Parachute' to reach the market. The delay has been because of changes inside the group. But they've used the breathing space well, writing their

Pretty good Things

PRETTY THINGS: PARACHUTE (Harvest SHVL 774 stereo; 45s.).

INTERESTING instrumental and choral experiment, backing up the frail voice of lead vocalist Phil May on the Good Mr. Square, which follows up Scene One, mostly an instrumental sound exercise in futuristics.

The Pretty Things have gone into the heavy class wholeheartedly. Veteran members **Phil May** and **Wally Allan** (Waller on the label) is behind the compositions, which vary from the quiet folksy sound, as in She Was Tall She Was High, with some good acoustic guitar by Wally, to the weirdo, smothered vocal of Cries From The Midnight Circus, with the accent on the macabre, going into a heavy rhythmic excitement with the guitar-organ strong.

Side two is about the country as compared with the city on side one. Grass has a beatles sound about it. Sickle Clowns seems to be about "Easy Rider" and protesting about how America killed all three leading characters in the film. Shortest track, What's The Use, has a peculiar charm, and the title tune has almost a church organ music sound about it, with some hard piano, and ending with the rush of wind getting faster and faster and dying to nothing. A most interesting album all through. Pity the sleeve, which has four sides to it, doesn't even name the players, although it gives the words of the songs.

The group is, however, **Phil May** (lead singer), **Wally Allan** (bass, vocals), **Skip Allan**, no relation (bass), **Pete Tolson** (lead guitar, but Vic Unitt is on LP), and **John Povey** (electric piano, organ, piano, vocals). And the reason why Waller is shown on composing credits with May, is that Wally Allan's real name is Allan Waller. **AE.**

Other titles: In The Square, The Letter, Rain, Miss Fay Regrets, She's A Lover.

a breath of fresh air

SOFT MACHINE 'Third'

First released as CBS Records 66246 in June 1970
Highest UK chart position: Number 18
Available on CD as Sony 8287687932

Facelift
Slightly All The Time
Moon In June
Out-Bloody-Rageous

Robert Wyatt	Drums and Vocal
Hugh Hopper	Bass Guitar
Mike Ratledge	Piano and Organ
With	
Elton Dean	Alto Saxophone
Jimmy Hastings	Flute and Bass Clarinet
Nick Evans	Trombone
Lyn Dobson	Flute and Soprano Saxophone
Rab Spall	Violin

Recorded at IBC studios, London April through May 1970
'Facelift' recorded at Fairfield Halls, Croydon on 4th January 1970 and at Mother's Club, Birmingham on 11th January 1970
Produced by Soft Machine
Engineered by Andy Knight

In August 1969 Kevin Ayers departed Soft Machine to pursue a career as a solo artist following an exhausting US tour. The vacuum was filled by Soft Machine roadie Hugh Hopper who agreed to assume the role of bassist. Immediately the band began rehearsals to write material for their second album.

Recorded at Olympic Studios in February and March 1969, the resulting 'Volume Two' was a major leap forward in terms of creativity. Heading in a more progressive direction, with pieces such as 'A Concise British Alphabet – Part One'/'Hibou Anemone And Bear'/'A Concise British Alphabet – Part Two' and the guesting of Brian Hopper (brother of Hugh and former Wilde Flowers member) on saxophone, the album demonstrated the band's increasingly jazz-influenced direction. The release of 'Volume Two' in September 1969 by the American ABC Probe label coincided with appearances at the Bilzen Jazz and Pop Festival in Belgium and at the Concertgebouw in Amsterdam, where Soft Machine's new compositions 'Facelift' and 'Moon In June' were given public airings.

By October 1969 the group had evolved into a very different and expanded musical unit with their musical emphasis on free and progressive jazz influences. Soft Machine had also expanded into a seven- piece unit with the inclusion of alto saxophonist Elton Dean, trumpet-player Marc Charig, trombonist Nick Evans and saxophonist/flautist Lyn Dobson into their ranks. The debut performance by this new line-up took place at Liverpool University prior to performing at the Amougies Festival in Belgium on 28 October. The end of November and most of December was spent touring France, with appearances on television helping build an increasingly large and enthusiastic following. British-based record companies finally paid attention, and 1969 ended with the group signing with CBS Records, the British division of American major label, Columbia. The year's end also saw the departure of both Charig and Evans from the line-up.

Of the few British concerts scheduled at the beginning of 1970, CBS Records elected to record performances at the Fairfield Hall in Croydon on 4 January and at Mothers Club, Birmingham a week later. These were destined to play a vital part in the creation of the track 'Facelift' that would appear on Soft Machine's forthcoming masterwork. The remainder of January was spent touring Germany and Holland, resulting in television appearances in both countries. Further extensive touring of France throughout February and March saw Soft Machine hone their craft to perfection and achieve critical acclaim. Such extensive touring brought further line-up changes with the departure of Lyn Dobson to the Keef Hartley Band at the end of March.

Soft Machine entered IBC Studios in London at the beginning of April to complete their third album, destined to be a highly ambitious work. The track 'Facelift' comprised sections of the piece recorded the previous January in Birmingham and Croydon joined together with an impressive use of 'cut and paste' editing techniques and tape loops. It also demonstrated Mike Ratledge's stunning improvisational ability, wringing incredible sounds from an electric organ, and was Soft Machine's most free-form work to date, the likes of which had never previously been heard from a British group.

Of the studio recordings, Mike Ratledge's 'Slightly All the Time' comprised parts of Hugh Hopper's 'Noisette' and featured the playing of Jimmy Hastings (elder brother of Caravan's Pye Hastings) on flute and bass clarinet. The composition finished with the marvellous 'Backwards', a melody later utilised to great effect in 1973 by Caravan as part of their 'L'Auberge Du Sanglier' suite.

Of all the music recorded, Robert Wyatt's 'Moon In June' was perhaps the most radically inventive. A nod to the style of the bands previous two albums, it was to be the last Soft Machine recording for an album to feature vocals of any kind. Essentially a solo effort from Wyatt, Ratledge and Hopper barely contributed to the recording, Elton Dean being entirely absent. Robert Wyatt had composed the various composite parts of the work as far back as 1967 and had demoed the whole piece in Los Angeles in 1968.

The startling work saw Wyatt overdub a majority of the organ and electric piano parts, while free jazz violinist Rab Spall guested effectively. In hindsight, the recording of 'Moon In June' and the absence of vocals from future Soft Machine recordings was the beginning of friction within the band's ranks, leading to the recording of Wyatt's first solo album, 'End Of An Ear', for CBS in the summer of 1970.

'Out-Bloody-Rageous' was another astonishing Ratledge composition which began with backwards tape loops of organ and electric piano, evoking comparisons to the work by Terry Riley on his albums 'In C' and 'A Rainbow In Curved Air.' The tape loops gave way to the main melody of the 18-minute piece which featured a guest appearance from Nick Evans. The looped keyboard phrases made occasional appearances in the piece before melding together to form the impressive coda to the work.

Final sessions for Soft Machine's third opus were completed in early May 1970. Considering the album had been recorded amid such a hectic live schedule, the completed recordings were all the more impressive. The fruits of such hard work were released on 6 June as the double album 'Third'. Of the concerts that followed, the most notable was an appearance at the Royal Albert Hall in London on 13 August 1970 as part of the season of Henry Wood Promenade classical concerts. The invitation was seen in some quarters as justification of the excellence and innovation of Soft Machine's work, while others found the appearance of an amplified group the ultimate insult to such a hallowed festival. Despite the controversy, Soft Machine delivered an inspired performance to a capacity audience which was broadcast live on BBC Radio 3, the national corporation's 'serious' music radio station.

For many aficionados, Soft Machine's 'Third' would be an achievement that would remain unequalled. The sheer inventiveness of the four works that comprised the album would inspire a host of imitators, few of whom would come close to their excellence.

Recording French radio session

T2 'It'll All Work Out In Boomland'

First released as Decca Records SKL5050 in July 1970
Highest UK chart position: N/A
Not currently available on CD

In Circles
JLT
No More White Horses
Morning

Keith Cross   **Guitars, Keyboard instruments, Harmony Vocals**
Peter Dunton   **Drums, Lead Vocals**
Bernard Jinks   **Bass Guitar, Harmony Vocals**

Recorded at Morgan Studios, Willesden, London
Produced by Peter Johnson and T2
Additional arrangements by Peter Johnson
Engineers: John Burns, Mike Butcher, Roger Quested and Robin Black

The late Sixties and early Seventies was an era when record companies, in an eager attempt to hit upon the next 'happening' act, released scores of albums by artists who were to fall by the wayside. In some cases, the quality of the material recorded justified the lack of sales, but in an age where the pace of popular music was moving at an alarming rate many worthy artists failed to enjoy the success they deserved.

T2 are arguably a prime example, their sole album being more widely known nearly 40 years on from its release by Decca Records in July 1970. The term 'lost classic' is often overused, but in the case of T2's 'It'll All Work Out On Boomland' it is no exaggeration.

T2 were a trio formed from the ashes of two late-Sixties British bands. Bernard Jinks (bass, vocals) had previously been in Bulldog Breed, a promising group who had recorded the album 'Made In England' for Deram's Nova imprint and had released the

single 'Portcullis Gate' b/w 'Halo In My Hair' before breaking up. Peter Dunton (drums, lead vocals), a highly talented musician, had served a short stint in the band Gun (fronted by brothers Adrian and Paul Gurvitz) who had enjoyed European success with the single 'Race With The Devil' in 1968, prior to that group dissolving.

The band's line-up was completed with the recruitment of the highly talented Keith Cross (guitar, keyboards, vocals). At just 17, Cross was a remarkable guitarist and his presence in the group raised the musical heights of the band considerably.

With just one week's rehearsal behind them where the new group crafted new material written by Peter Dunton, the newly formed band began to perform on the London club circuit under the name of Morning. By their third concert the reputation of the band as fine live act had spread by word of mouth to such an extent that A&R scouts from four major labels attended the next T2 concert with a view to signing the band. Decca succeeded in acquiring the band's services, in part desperate to fill a void at that time in a roster of groups that featured no hard-edged musicians. A residency at the Marquee Club did much to enhance Morning's reputation and the band soon entered Morgan Studios in Willesden to begin work on an album.

With producer Peter Johnson overseeing sessions, an album of excellent material was committed to tape in a matter of 10 days. 'In Circles' was a high-energy opening piece that also served as the first song of the band's live set. It immediately demonstrated the power of the band via Keith Cross' muscular guitar-playing. 'JLT' was lighter, but melancholic in mood, lifted musically by some excellent Mellotron from Cross and a horn arrangement by Peter Johnson. One of the album's highlights, 'No More White Horses' remains the song for which the band are best known. Initially a reflective work, it soon developed into a powerful progressive rock piece, building to a crescendo with a superb horn arrangement and a fine guitar solo from Cross.

The fourth track to be recorded would dominate the album's second side. The ambitious song cycle 'Morning' began with a melancholic acoustic guitar-dominated section before developing into a muscular work of intensity and power. Dominated by Cross' fine guitar-playing and the drumming of Peter Dunton, it closed an excellent album in fine style.

The group then had to undergo a change of identity due to a US outfit recording under the same name. Now known as T2, they embarked on a long series of concerts in colleges and leading underground clubs and venues up and down the British Isles.

Decca Records' faith in them was enough to ensure that the recently recorded album would be released on both sides of the Atlantic, Decca's London imprint handling the release in America, and in France and Germany. The album was also taken by Decca affiliates in South America and Japan. Hopes were high when 'It'll All Work Out In Boomland' was released in July 1970, gaining critical comparisons with other British acts such as Deep Purple, Free and Black Sabbath, but sales fell short of expectations.

US reaction had also been enthusiastic and a tour of America was planned to capitalise. It was while preparations were taking place that Keith Cross announced his departure, feeling under intense pressure from the gruelling gigging schedule undertaken by the band just to make ends meet. Seeking gentler musical pastures, he would team up with Peter Ross to form the duo Cross and Ross, recording the album 'Bored Civilians' for Decca in late 1971.

The blow of losing such a talented guitarist dashed any prospects of visiting the US and finding a suitable replacement appeared impossible. These events led to Bernard Jinks leaving T2 two months after Cross. Peter Dunton assembled a new line-up, but struggled to extricate himself from old management and agency contracts signed when T2 first began. This new line-up began performing live in July 1971 and continued to do so for the next two years, recording a series of demos but unable to secure a new recording contract thanks, in part, to ongoing management problems. T2 finally broke up in the autumn of 1972. Despite being their only album, T2's 'It'll All Work Out in Boomland' could not be a finer legacy.

WEB 'I Spider'

First released as Polydor 2383 024 in October 1970
Highest UK chart position: N/A
Available on CD as Esoteric Recordings ECLEC2027

Concerto For Bedsprings
Including:
a. I Can't Sleep
b. Sack Song
c. Peaceful Sleep
d. You Can Keep The Good Life
e. Loner
I Spider
Love You
Ymphasomniac
Always I Wait

Dave Lawson	**Organ, Piano, Harpsichord, Mellotron, Vocals**
Lennie Wright	**Drums, Vibraphone, Tympani, Congas, Guiro**
Kenny Beveridge	**Drums, Bongos, Woodblock, Jawbone**
Tom Harris	**Tenor Sax, Soprano Sax, Concert Flute, Alto Flute, Tambourine**
Tony Edwards	**Electric and Acoustic Guitars**
John Eaton	**Bass Guitar, Cabassa**

Recorded at Wessex Studios, London
Produced by Lennie Wright for GEM Productions

Released in 1970, the album 'I Spider' by Web has earned a deserved reputation as a groundbreaking progressive rock work. Featuring a line-up of Dave Lawson (keyboards, vocals), Tony Edwards (guitar), John Eaton (bass), Tom Harris (saxophones and flute), Lennie Wright (drums, vibraphone, percussion) and Kenny Beveridge (drums and percussion), Web successfully and radically broke away from their previous soul-influenced sound and fused the worlds of jazz and rock, their new direction the vision of former RAF band musician and keyboard-player Dave Lawson.

By the end of 1969 Lawson was a member of the band Episode Six, best known for having had vocalist Ian Gillan and bass player Roger Glover within their ranks. With Gillan and Glover recently departed to join Deep Purple, Episode Six recruited Lawson, drummer Alan Coulter and bass guitarist Tony Dangerfield. 'When we joined the image of band changed slightly, as Episode Six were primarily a pop covers band up to then,' Lawson would recall some years later. 'When we joined we began to introduce cover versions of material by bands such as Traffic. We became a band where hard rockers met soft rockers.

'Episode Six were booked to play a gig in the West Country and we shared the bill with a band called the Web who had a vocalist called John L Watson. They were basically a soul-influenced band, but they interested me because they had two drummers, Kenny Beveridge and Lennie Wright. Lennie also played vibraphone and percussion and gave the band a very different and contemporary sound, which was instantly attractive to me.

'I got talking to the guys after the show and they commented that they liked what I was playing on keyboards. They told me that John L Watson wanted pursue a solo career and the rest of the guys wanted to head in a different musical direction. I came on board and began to write material to suit the line-up. I hadn't been aware of Web's earlier material and I'm not sure how I became the main writer. I'm not a person who puts himself forward in those situations. I think it was mainly because we all agreed that we wanted to make music that was different, but I was the only member of the band who had written any material.'

With the Web out of contract with Deram Records, the time was right to change direction and compose new material. 'The musical fusion of jazz and rock came by accident,' later reflected. 'I'd had five and half years of service in the RAF as a musician and I'd had military music shoved down my throat for this time. I joined after I left school and I was exposed to classical music while I was there. Before I joined the RAF I was lucky enough to have piano lessons with Stan Tracey, now hailed as the godfather of British jazz. He was very good to me and would take me down to Ronnie Scott's club and I would see people like Roland Kirk and Johnny Griffin perform. When I left the air force I studied with Stan once more so the jazz influence wasn't conscious, it was just a part of me.

'I was also into some of the rock music of the time, so it all came together. Rock had an influence rhythmically speaking, but harmonically our music came from the jazz world.' Following rehearsals in a monastery and a nunnery, Polydor expressed an interest in signing the band. Given no more than five days in Wessex Studios to record a new album, the material laid down on tape was remarkable. Highlights such as 'I Spider', 'Love You' and the lengthy 'Concerto For Bedsprings' demonstrated both Lawson's ability as a composer and his unique vocal style. 'I tried to use my voice like an instrument and didn't use vibrato, which is very hard to do, but I didn't feel that I was given enough time to put vocals down to my satisfaction,' he later remembered.

As soon as 'I Spider' was released, Web took to the road to promote their new work. Scandinavia was particularly responsive to the newly incarnated band. 'A memorable gig was at the Festival of the Midnight Sun in Stockholm. The Swedes really seemed to like us. We flew to Sweden from Luton airport on a chartered aircraft and the concert was really good and gave us an introduction to a Swedish audience who were most receptive.'

Sadly, despite the amendment of the band's name and a clearly announced change of direction, Web were still occasionally billed as a soul- influenced group, a situation which did nothing to enhance their reputation. Dave Lawson would later comment: 'By this time we were considering changing our name because the other guys in the band got fed up with the name Web being mis-spelled. Sometimes we were billed as "Webb", other times "The Webb" and it was very frustrating.

'We were given a very meagre weekly wage by our management, but things got so bad that eventually Tom Harris had to leave because he had a wife and family to support and we weren't earning enough. There wasn't enough money to go around to pay for the number of musicians in the group. As a result we renamed ourselves Samurai and signed with Greenwich Gramophone, an independent label owned by songwriter Les Reed and recorded an album for the label which carried on stylistically from where "I Spider" left off.'

Now rightly lauded as a supreme achievement of early progressive rock, 'I Spider' receives constant praise in selective circles. Dave Lawson recently stated: 'I do find it strange that I still get a lot of emails from people who write to let me know how much the music of Web meant and still means to them.' A listen to 'I Spider' will explain why.

The Web

YES 'Time And A Word'

Released as Atlantic 2400 006 in July 1970
Highest UK chart position: Number 45
Currently available on CD as Rhino 8122-73787-2

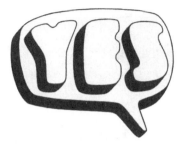

No Opportunity Necessary, No Experience Needed
Then
Everydays
Sweet Dreams
The Prophet
Clear Days
Astral Traveller
Time And A Word

Jon Anderson	**Vocals, Guitar**
Peter Banks	**Guitar**
Bill Bruford	**Drums, Percussion**
Tony Kaye	**Keyboards**
Chris Squire	**Bass, Vocals**

Orchestral arrangements by Tony Cox
Recorded at Advision Studios, London
Produced by Tony Colton
Engineered by Eddy Offord

The follow-up to Yes's deft and, considering their later flights of fancy, humble debut album was steeped in ambition. Again replete with a couple of almost completely overhauled covers mixed in with their own blossoming brand of grace and complexity, the album 'Time And A Word' was another step in the search for the Yes sound that the band would finally formulate on 'The Yes Album' the following year. Featuring the same line-up that had graced their eponymous debut, namely vocalist Jon Anderson, bassist Chris Squire, guitarist Peter Banks, keyboardist Tony Kaye and drummer Bill Bruford, the album was the first of a long line of their albums to feature the talents of engineer Eddy Offord.

In an attempt to move their progressive pop forward into the new territory that their debut had hinted at, the band here attempted to shed the 12-bar blues backdrop completely, opting for the kind of classically-inspired grandiosity that contemporaries like the Nice and Deep Purple were dabbling in. Symphonic grandeur was the result.

At the start of the Seventies, and after the praise given to them by every key journalist of the time, Yes found fulfilling their early promise troublesome. Entering Advision Studios in London to record a 'difficult second album' in November 1969, they were caught between the fragments of pop sensibility and the feeling that they were onto something unique and special. The album would be far from conventional, partly because the group refused to tone down but instead amplified their intricacy and prowess on their individual instruments.

Relying on highly-animated, bold performances from all the players, but in particular Kaye, Squire and Bruford, the recordings were the sound of a unit gelling in consistency and unifying in direction. Throughout the album, the music was presented with a taut, visceral excitement that came from the musicians revelling in each other's talents. 'No Opportunity Necessary, No Experience Needed' was a brave opening, a

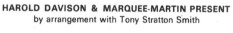

muscular adaptation of the Richie Havens song, melded with Jerome Moross' theme music from classic Western The Big Country. The rough formative edge on this track in particular, where the joins between their own playing and the rampant classicism they so admired are still visible, was as close as Yes ever got to punk.

The use of orchestration, written and conducted by Tony Cox, would dominate the album throughout. Of the other tracks recorded, the uptempo 'Then' kept the orchestral accompaniment to a minimum and allowed Kaye and Banks to stretch out. Jon Anderson's lyrics of 'Love is the only answer, hate is the root of cancer' arguably the first evidence of his spiritual awareness. 'Everydays' highlighted Anderson's voice as the bands most idiosyncratic weapon and also featured a convincing duet between the orchestra and Tony Kaye. A cover of Stephen Stills' masterpiece from the album 'Buffalo Springfield Again', it was one of the most satisfying tracks on the album and also one of the most imaginative in terms of its arrangement. 'Sweet Dreams' was one of two collaborations between Jon Anderson and David Foster, a former colleague in the band the Warriors. It was later selected for release as a single and was the most commercial offering ever recorded by Yes during their formative years.

Side two of the album featured a pair of tracks that were clear signposts to both Peter Banks' impending departure and the band's future musical direction. 'The Prophet' and 'Astral Traveller' were an indication of the sound of future Yes, albeit raw and embryonic, with tempo fluctuations and changes in key and time signature. 'The Prophet' began with a Hammond organ solo followed by strings, the building up and layering of the instruments an early indication of the 'group of individuals' or 'individuals in a group' dynamic that Yes adhered to forever after. During the instrumental passages of the piece, the variation in theme and tone was staggering. The album closed with 'Time And A Word', a melodic reflective piece that would retain a spot in live concerts for years to come.

The 'Time And A Word' album was the sound of a band seeking their musical destiny and demonstrated the instrumental dexterity of the group, in particular the contributions of Peter Banks and Tony Kaye. Released in July 1970 in the UK and in November the same year in the US (where it was adorned in a sleeve depicting Steve Howe in place of Banks), 'Time And A Word' was the last album to feature the band's first line-up. Before the album's release, Banks would depart, dismissed as a result of the bands changing musical sensibilities and direction soon after the album's completion. 'Time And A Word' reached Number 45 in the UK album charts, but surprisingly never charted in the US.

Perhaps because of the shift in direction, the album was not warmly welcomed by critics on release. However, over the years it has come to be seen as a vital and truly progressive part of the Yes oeuvre, a maturing blend of classical rock and pop that has become fondly remembered. In comparison to the musical excess of the band's work in the mid Seventies, 'Time And A Word' is Yes at their most elemental and stripped-down. Packed with a raw energy, naivety and intensity, it is both the sound of a band in flux and a masterpiece that still excites.

(with grateful thanks to Jon Wright)

YES, IT'S SUPERB!

YES: TIME AND A WORD (Atlantic stereo, 2400.006; 42s. 6d.). PERSONALLY speaking, this is by far the very best album that I've heard and completely enjoyed this year. And I feel that unless the Beatles decide to get back and produce yet another masterpiece, "Time And A Word" will be a very difficult collection to surpass during 1970.

By their very own admission this is already old material, only because they have rapidly accelerated their progress since the addition of guitarist **Steve Howe** to their present line-up.

However, to the listener it's refreshingly new and mentally exhilarating. Whereas, "Something's Coming" was the epic performance on their first album, **Richie Havens** "No Opportunity Necessary, No Experience Needed," is it's current counterpart. To this they have skilfully interwoven the proud and majestic theme from "The Big Country," which finally builds to a resounding crescendo.

Indeed, this opening track sets the mood and standard for the remaining seven cuts.

Whereas vocalist-composer **Jon Anderson** is one of pop's truely imaginative romantics, arranger **Tony Cox** acts as a most sympathetic foil for his consummate talents, recharting his ideas into very positive and highly decorative orchestral back-drops.

On **Steve Stills'** "Everyday," Mr. Cox adds alternating shimmering then pizzicato string passages, which tastefully grace the melody until the group explodes into a stop-time instrumental passage. This particular track is a fine example of Yes's ability to perform intricate and highly complex ensemble passages with meticulous dexterity and precision.

Much of the instrumental strength and excitement of the group comes from **Chris Squires'** full-toned bass playing, for Chris has become one of the very few rock bassists with a readily identifiable style. Matched to **Bill Bruford's** expertise drumming, they make a formidable rhythm team.

Throughout, organist **Tony Kaye** constantly adds to the overall originality of the group's sound, as does guitarist **Peter Banks**, who is now with Blodwyn Pig.

Other familiar Anderson songs include such in-person favourites as "Sweet Dreams," their own space odyssey "Astral Traveller," and the beautiful "Time And A Word."

In future, when groups are so bold as to proclaim that they are progressive let them first of all take heed of Yes, for they have much to offer. — **R.C.**

Other titles: Then, the Prophet, Clear Days.

YES: WORLD TREK— THEN BRITISH TOUR

YES is to undertake another British concert tour — its third this year — in mid-August. The group has already played a 1971 tour with Iron Butterfly and Dada, which was followed by a solo tour. Venues have not yet been lined up for its summer itinerary, but Yes plans to record a new album in early July for release at the time of the tour.

Prior to this, the outfit is set for extensive world travels. It commences a German tour next Thursday (15), which includes its Austrian debut in Vienna. A two-day trip to Italy on May 8 and 9 takes in concerts in Rome and Milan. Following a string of concerts in Mexico (May 31-June 5), Yes begins a four-week U.S. tour in Los Angeles on June 11. A nine-day visit to Australia starts on July 10, after which the group plays concerts in the Philippines and Japan.

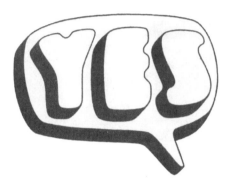

JON ANDERSON

CHRIS SQUIRE

TONY KAYE

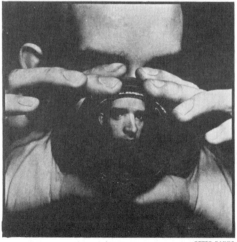

PETER BANKS

BILL BRUFORD

Yes

VAN DER GRAAF GENERATOR
The Least We Can Do Is Wave To Each Other
CAS 1007

GE[N]
Tre
CAS

TREVOR BILLMUSS
Family Apology
CAS 1017

HAPPY

RARE BIRD
CAS 1005

Manufac
B&C Records Lt

RARE BIRD
As Your Mind Flies By
CAS 1011

BRIAN DAVISON'S
Every Which Way
CAS 1021

JA

ICE
Bridges
1014

VAN DER GRAAF GENERATOR
H To He Who Am The Only One
CAS 1027

ARISMA

LINDISFARNE
Nicely Out Of Tune
CAS 1025

ributed by
uare, London W1.

CLASSICAL HEADS
CAS 1008

AUDIENCE
Friend's Friend's Friend
CAS 1012

GORDON TURNER
Meditation
CAS 1009

HTS

THIS GROUPS CERTAINLY NOT CHICKEN!

Atomic Rooster,

Vincent Crane, Carl Palmer, John Cann

RECORD MIRROR, May 2, 1970

THE ROOSTER has well and truly crowed, and with the sales of 'Atomic Rooster' up to 10,000 copies, appears to have made it's point.

There's some jazz phrasing of the old school from Carl Palmer, but it's the combination of the three musicians together which creates the new and vibrant sounds. Atomic Rooster are all or none, love or loathe, and the majority must surely love. They have their gimmicks, in a wild stage act, with Vincent Crane seated behind the skeleton of an organ, but the music is good. It's alive and pulsating.

John Cann has recently joined the group replacing Nick Graham, who first appeared with them at their London Speakeasy debut last September. Nick came from an unprofessional group, and found the pace which Rooster have been forced to keep up more than he had bargained for.

"This means that we don't use flute on stage any more," the long rangy Vincent Crane — explained. "But it's a bit impractical on stage anyway. It's very hard to hear properly through the PA, and very hard to pick up. This means that I can play bass on the organ through the cabinets, since we won't use bass guitar.

"Things are bound to change somewhat because John's writing influences us. We've already written five new numbers for a further album. No we won't be rushing one out, just because people feel you have to have another one. Then it becomes bad. I'm using a lot of sounds on the organ I didn't use before."

Atomic Rooster say they are an organ band, but the drumming of Carl Palmer, who was trained by Buddy Rich, plays an equally important part. Carl is a quiet, attractive and smiling character, who suddenly erupts into an explosion of sound, hair, arms, drum sticks, flailing legs, on stage. But when relaxing, he could almost be mistaken for a teeny-bopper entertainer.

"I think drummers have just got better in groups, that's why perhaps the sounds have been based on percussion more," he said. "A drummer's usually out on his own."

Atomic Rooster have found immense popularity on the Continent, and they are set for a French concert tour. In Britain they work on average four nights a week, and time between is filled with recording, writing, and with new member John, rehearsing.

Whether Atomic Rooster will play a return visit is debatable, but their popularity is certainly spreading!

VALERIE MABBS

'There's a Mockingbird singing songs in the trees...'

ATOMIC ROOSTER 'In Hearing Of...'

Originally released as Pegasus Records PEG1 in August 1971
Highest UK chart position: Number 18
Available on CD as Castle Music CMQCD926

Breakthrough
Break The Ice
Decision/Indecision
A Spoonful Of Bromide Helps The Medicine Go Down
Black Snake
Head In The Sky
The Rock
The Price

Vincent Crane	**Organ, Piano, Vocals**
Pete French	**Lead Vocals**
John Cann	**Guitars**
Paul Hammond	**Drums**

Produced by Vincent Crane and Atomic Rooster

By July 1971, Atomic Rooster appeared to be on the verge of huge success with a promising future and debut US tour ahead of them. The single 'Devil's Answer' had entered the UK singles chart and would reach Number 4, while their previous album, 'Death Walks Behind You' had been a chart success despite the band going through several painful line-up changes.

Atomic Rooster was founded by virtuoso organist and keyboard player, Vincent Crane, a fragile character who had been a founder and main writer in the Crazy World of Arthur Brown. When that band dissolved after a tempestuous American tour in 1969, Crane took young drummer Carl Palmer with him and formed his new outfit, expanding on the musical framework he had explored in Brown's group. With bass guitarist, vocalist and flautist Nick Graham, Atomic Rooster was born, with a sound that tried to fuse the excitement of soul music with the virtuosity and power of progressive rock with classical influences.

Debuting live in August 1969 the band secured a deal with B&C Records and recorded their self-titled debut album in December. 'Atomic Rooster' was released in February 1970 and flirted briefly with the UK album charts, but a month after its release Nick Graham departed and was replaced by lead guitarist and vocalist John Cann. Barely a month later, Carl Palmer announced his intention to join Greg Lake and Keith Emerson in a new trio, and Crane was forced to put Atomic Rooster on hold to search for a new drummer.

Recruiting Paul Hammond in Palmer's place, the new line-up recorded the album 'Death Walks Behind You' soon after formation. The album featured the track 'Tomorrow Night' which became their first UK hit when issued as a single in January 1971. This success in turn led to the album reaching Number 12 in the UK and saw the band break out of the club circuit into bigger league touring.

By now Crane was seeking a new refined sound to Atomic Rooster, and, unknown to his fellow band members, was considering making plans to make changes to the line-up. In April 1971 the band entered Trident studios to begin work on a new album. The first fruits of these sessions were impressive enough to be rush-released as a single. The Top 10 hit 'Devil's Answer' was a tremendous rock tour de force which appeared to bode well for the forthcoming album. It was at this moment that Crane's displeasure came to the fore.

Feeling that the material recorded to date wasn't suitable due to Cann's weak vocals, Crane announced that he had to find 'a real singer' and recruited vocalist Pete French, formerly with heavy rock outfit Leaf Hound. French was an accomplished vocalist and was invited by Crane to attend sessions at Trident Studios. He would later remember; 'When I arrived at the studio I realised

ATOMIC ROOSTER

that I was replacing all of John Cann's vocal parts and that some of his guitar parts were also being erased. It was a bit bizarre, to say the least.'

The material laid down prior to French's arrival was to comprise the finest and most commercially successful album Atomic Rooster would ever record. With his additional vocal ability French added much to the songs to make the music particularly special. The dark 'Breakthrough' was one of Rooster's finest moments and made for a fine opening track and was a great rock track. 'Break The Ice', 'Head In The Sky' and 'The Price' were also powerful songs. By contrast, the excellent 'Black Snake' and 'Decision/Indecision' were introspective in their feel and revealed the more delicate side of Crane's music. These were joined by two powerful instrumentals, 'A Spoonful Of Bromide Helps The Pulse Rate Go Down' and 'The Rock', both with a fine funk edge. Released in August 1971, 'In Hearing Of Atomic Rooster' was greeted with enthusiasm by fans and quickly reached Number 4 on the UK listings.

With usual poor timing, Vincent Crane chose this moment to dismiss John Cann as guitarist, Paul Hammond opting to follow him. With a hit album in the charts and a US tour looming he called upon drummer Ric Parnell and guitarist Steve Bolton to join the band. It was this line-up that toured America as opening act to bands such as Yes, Alice Cooper and Cactus with some success. Following a second US tour, Pete French departed the band to join Cactus, and Crane drafted in Chris Farlowe as replacement. While Atomic Rooster would record several albums for Pye Records' Dawn label, none would match 'In Hearing Of…', a blend of soul and progressive rock which captured the band at a true peak of their powers.

ROOSTER LEAP 11 PLACES

AFTER a few preliminary scratchings and changes in personnel the Atomic Rooster has finally crowed its way into the upper regions of the NME chart with "Tomorrow Night" — a record which was released as long ago as last September.

Hatched from the psychedelic remnants of the Crazy World of Arthur Brown, the Rooster features Vincent Crane, in his Phantom of the Opera guise, on organ; guitarist and lead vocalist John Cann and eighteen-year-old Paul Hammond who has the distinction of playing the biggest double bass drum kit yet made.

With their single now moving in an upward direction it seems quite possible that their current B and C album "Death Walks Behind You" will emulate the success of "Tomorrow Night."

ATOMIC ROOSTER (left to right) VINCE CRANE, PAUL HAMMOND and JOHN CANN

BARCLAY JAMES HARVEST 'Once Again'

Released as Harvest SHVL788 in February 1971
Highest UK chart position: N/A
Available on CD as EMI Harvest 07243 538406 2 4

She Said
Happy Old World
Song For Dying
Galadriel
Mockingbird
Vanessa Simmons
Ball And Chain
The Lady Loves

John Lees	**Vocals, Guitars, Recorder**
Stuart 'Woolly' Wolstenholme	**Vocals, Mellotron, Organ, Piano**
Les Holroyd	**Vocals, Bass**
Mel Pritchard	**Drums, Percussion**
Alan Parsons	**Jaw Harp on 'The Lady Loves'**

The Barclay James Harvest Symphony Orchestra
Conducted and arranged by Robert Godfrey
Produced by Norman Smith
Engineered by Peter Bown
Recorded at EMI Studios, Abbey Road, London

The roots of Barclay James Harvest lay in the mid-sixties R&B and soul scene of the northwest of England. John Lees and Woolly Wolstenholme had met while attending Oldham School of Art and had previously been in blues-based outfit the Sorcerers, which subsequently evolved into the Keepers. Les Holroyd and Mel Pritchard were in Heart and Soul and the Wickeds, a more soul-based group. In 1966 both camps fused to become the Blues Keepers.

This band gradually dwindled from an original six-piece line up to a stable four-piece that eventually adopted the identity of Barclay James Harvest by drawing names from a hat. After securing the financial patronage of Oldham boutique owner John Crowther, who first heard the band perform at a party he was attending, Barclay James Harvest soon found themselves ensconced in Preston House, formerly a 16th Century Inn, near the village of Diggle and set high on the Saddleworth moors.

The acquisition of a Mellotron, a keyboard instrument that reproduced orchestral or choral sounds recorded on a tape loop placed under and controlled by each individual key, led to the band adopting a highly individual symphonic style and gaining a reputation locally which culminated in Granada Television making a short film on the band in early 1968.

The interest generated by this television appearance led to Barclay James Harvest signing to EMI Records following the release of 'Early Morning' and 'Mr Sunshine' as a single, under a 'lease-tape' agreement as Parlophone R5693 in April 1968. Upon its release the record immediately gained airplay from leading underground DJ John Peel. Such support brought about a demand for Barclay James Harvest in the south of England with the band performing their first London concert on 13 September 1968 at the Roundhouse in Chalk Farm opening a bill for the Small Faces. A return trip to London to play a concert at All Saints Porchester Hall in November supporting Pink Floyd led to BJH linking up with Peter Jenner and Andrew King's Blackhill Agency.

A further concert supporting Gun at the Roundhouse in December led to a chance meeting with a student from the Royal College of Music, Robert Godfrey. 'Robert was a wunderkind from the Royal College,' Woolly Wolstenholme later explained. 'He

thought he could realise his ambition of arranging and conducting an orchestra through us and offered to write arrangements and to assemble the musicians for an orchestra. John Crowther employed him to act as our arranger and our dalliance with orchestras took off from there.' Soon after this chance meeting EMI made BJH one of the first signings to their newly formed underground label Harvest Records, leading to suggestions that the name was perhaps more than mere coincidence.

Following the release of the single 'Brother Thrush'/'Poor Wages' the band embarked on the recording of their eponymous debut album was released as Harvest SHVL770 in June 1970. To promote the album the band embarked on a short tour at the end of June with the Barclay James Harvest Symphony Orchestra (formerly the London Symphonia, an orchestra comprised of music students) with Robert Godfrey conducting. The fusion of orchestra and rock band in concert was a powerful and memorable experience for both performers and audience. 'I wasn't the instigator of heading in an orchestral direction,' Wolstenholme would reflect, 'but I did embrace it wholeheartedly. Rather than dabble in it, I was totally convinced by the possibilities of orchestrating our music and saw it as the way forward.'

John Lees remembers the tour as 'a tremendous logistical exercise. The further north we got, the smaller the orchestra became! Musically speaking, it wasn't as restrictive as you might think as there were spaces for solos. As long as you finished the solo when you were supposed to, there was room for improvisation.' The concerts at the Royal Albert Hall, Manchester Free Trade Hall, Birmingham Town Hall and the Usher Hall in Edinburgh were enthusiastically received.

Reflecting on this period of the Barclay James Harvest legacy, Wolstenholme would later admit, 'I felt that the first album wasn't as successful as it could have been. I thought it was rather overblown. Looking back now I think it could be seen as a kind of pre-emptive strike, a sort of rehearsal for the real thing.' Barclay James Harvest embarked on further dates in the North of England during September 1970 without an orchestra before journeying to London to commence work on their second album at Abbey Road Studios on the 9th October. Norman Smith assumed the role of producer once more and the selection of material chosen for the album was to be inspired.

'She Said' was a new composition comprising two songs written by Les Holroyd. The first song, 'Miss Bailey' comprised the main verses, while the other, 'And I Will Always Love Her' comprised the refrains. At the suggestion of Woolly Wolstenholme the two tunes were combined with an evocative Elizabethan recorder solo from John Lees to produce one of the most powerful opening songs for any album of the time. It was to remain a concert favourite for many years.

'Happy Old World' was a Wolstenholme song bemoaning environmental pollution, while Lees' 'Song for Dying' was a remarkably powerful anti-war piece with sensitive guitar solos.

The recording of 'Galadriel', a song with a title inspired by a character in Lord Of The Rings, was to provide an everlasting memory for Lees. John Lennon had been working at Abbey Road studios during the recording of 'Once Again' and his guitar, a blond Epiphone, was standing in the corner of Studio Two on the evening recording commenced. Lees used this guitar which

Lennon had used on the famous 'rooftop' session at the Apple headquarters in Savile Row and seen in the Let It Be film to record the memorable introduction to 'Galadriel'. It was a memory that would later inspire a song, 'John Lennon's Guitar'.

An equally memorable song was recorded that October. 'Mockingbird' was written by John Lees in 1968 upon first meeting his future wife. The song had evolved through many incarnations in both rehearsals at Preston House and at Abbey Road. Indeed, the song had first been attempted in May but the band and Norman Smith were dissatisfied with the results. A second version was attempted on 10 October, this time featuring an orchestral arrangement by Robert Godfrey which slowed the tempo slightly. The finished result was a majestic piece that was to become a major part of Barclay James Harvest folklore and would still feature in live sets 30 years later.

'Vanessa Simmons' was a soft, acoustic Lees ballad, while 'Ball And Chain' was a powerful Wolstenholme rock number which featured an apparently sophisticated special effect on the vocals obtained by singing into a paper cup. Closing track 'The Lady Loves', was notable for the appearance by young Abbey Road tape operator Alan Parsons who played the Jaw Harp

Such was the wealth of material offered for the album; it was almost inevitable that some material would be omitted. 'White Sails' was a Woolly Wolstenholme composition that had been arranged for orchestra by Robert Godfrey and was performed on the short orchestral tour in June. The arrangement had evolved and an orchestral track was recorded on 19 November. When a vocal track was attempted the orchestral backing was deemed unworkable and the recording consigned to the EMI vaults. The same fate befell 'Too Much On Your Plate', a Wolstenholme rocker, whose similarity to 'Ball And Chain' may have accounted for its omission.

The release of 'Once Again' in mid February 1971 was followed a few weeks later by the release of 'Mockingbird' b/w 'Vanessa Simmons' as a single. Barclay James Harvest's second album received generally good reviews in the music press. New Musical Express called them 'A gutsy musical group with plenty of drive and noise and a good lead vocalist in Stuart Wolstenholme.' Melody Maker called the album 'A swirling sea of delicious songs penned without complexity, with a simplicity that is above all delightfully musical. "Mockingbird" contains all that's needed in subtlety and instant colour.' The reviewer concluded that 'Once Again' was 'a fine album'.

This verdict, although not reflected by initial sales, was confirmed later in the decade when it secured gold status in several countries. 'Once Again' is Barclay James Harvest's finest hour for Harvest Records and one of the best albums of their entire career.

EDGAR BROUGHTON BAND 'Edgar Broughton Band'

First released as Harvest SHVL791 in May 1971
Highest UK chart position: Number 28
Available on CD as Harvest 07243 8 64134 2 0

Evening Over Rooftops
The Birth
Piece Of My Own
Poppy
I Don't Even Know Which Day It Is
House Of Turnabout
Madhatter
Getting Hard
What Is A Woman For?
Thinking Of You
For Doctor Spock Part One
For Doctor Spock Part Two

Rob 'Edgar' Broughton	Vocals, Guitars
Arthur Grant	Bass, Vocals
Victor Unitt	Guitar, Harmonica, Piano, Organ, Vocals
Steve Broughton	Drums, Vocals
With	
Mike Oldfield:	Mandolin on 'Thinking of You'
Johnny van Derek:	Violin on 'Piece Of My Own'
David Bedford:	Arrangement on 'Evening Over Rooftops' and 'What Is A Woman For?'

Produced by Peter Jenner for Blackhill Enterprises
Engineered by Peter Mew
Recorded at EMI Studios, Abbey Road, London

If one casts a furtive glance back at the British rock music scene of the late Sixties, the perceived image of this era is one of peace, love and gentle vibes. A deeper look would reveal that, underneath this veneer, a band existed that were rebellious, anarchic and serious about the social and political injustices of the day.

The Edgar Broughton Band were all these things and more and hit the music scene in June 1969 with the release of the first single on EMI's underground label Harvest ('Evil' b/w 'Death of an Electric Citizen') and a stunning debut album, 'Wasa Wasa'. The band's impact on an unsuspecting and emerging underground audience was immediate. Formed in the sleepy town of Warwick, Rob 'Edgar' Broughton (guitar, vocals), Rob's brother, Steve Broughton (drums) and Arthur Grant (bass, vocals) became flag wavers for any radical cause that needed their support. Along with cohorts Hawkwind and the Pink Fairies, the Broughton's were the first of the proto-punks, ploughing their furrow nearly a decade before Messrs Lydon and company burst forth.

The five albums the Edgar Broughton band recorded for Harvest between 1969 and 1973 were full-on sonic attacks that took no prisoners. They also contained some truly thoughtful and beautiful music of great originality. Originally a blues-based outfit inspired by an encounter with John Mayall's Bluesbreakers, they developed a small but loyal following in the Warwick area. The band had been expanded to a four-piece by the inclusion of Victor Unitt on guitar. Unitt later became frustrated by their abandoning their blues roots by embracing the emerging psychedelic influences and left.

In 1968 the band took the bold step of moving to London to play to a wider audience and secure a record contract. Basing themselves in Notting Hill Gate, they soon came to the attention of leading underground music managers Peter Jenner and Andrew King of Blackhill Enterprises, whose first foray into management had been with Pink Floyd.

Through Blackhill, the Edgar Broughton Band signed to EMI in December 1968 and embarked on a seemingly endless cycle of recording and touring. Their live schedule included many free open-air concerts performed on the back of trucks. The band had been champions of the free concert since their earliest days.

'One of the first we played was in Warwick,' Rob 'Edgar' Broughton later recalled. 'Our audience was comprised of a bunch of Hell's Angel's who had travelled up from London. They arrived at our house and left their weapons in my dad's shed before we all headed off to the local park to play. All the hairy people from the area turned up and soon the police arrived. We were told we would have to stop playing, but the Angels said to the police, "Sorry, you can't get onto the truck." And the police didn't do anything. That was a revelation to me because I realised that, if people took a united front, the police would stand back and wait for us to finish performing. After that, our stance was "We're the Broughtons, we're going to play, what are you going to do about it?" We were very much into playing the Free Festival circuit which really expanded with the Hyde Park concerts that Blackhill organised. Steve and I came from a political family and that was in our blood.'

The electricity of the Edgar Broughton Band in concert was never truly captured on record. An early attempt to do this in controlled conditions took place at Abbey Road Studio Two on 9 December 1969. A group of 150 fans and assorted hippies gathered in the studio to witness a live performance of the band's stage set and newly written material. The results were later consigned to the vaults aside from an edited version of 'Out, Demons Out!', a song which closed every Broughton Band show and became an anthem. With its release as a single, the Edgar Broughton Band found themselves unlikely chart stars, its Number 33 success enhancing the bands reputation still further.

The album 'Sing Brother Sing', released in June 1970, was a massive leap forward in creative terms from their first and contained some excellent material, reaching a UK chart peak of Number 18. Not content to rest on their laurels, they saw out the end of a momentous year by releasing another single destined for the UK charts. 'Apache Dropout' was a fusion of the classic 'Apache', written by Jerry Lordan and a huge hit for the Shadows in 1960, and Captain Beefheart's 'Dropout Boogie'.

Another Top 40 UK hit, its release was followed by the return of Victor Unitt, who had replaced Dick Taylor in the Pretty Things and played on their magnum opus 'Parachute'. 'Around the time Victor rejoined us,' Rob Broughton would later reflect, 'we were feeling the pressure to become better musicians and that was intensified by our experience of recording at Abbey Road studios. We strove to be more musical and I think by the time of the making of our third album this attitude had taken hold.' Certainly, the material was of the highest standard. 'Evening Over Rooftops' began as an acoustic song that was initially recorded without a band accompaniment. After much reworking, the song became a powerful and emotional Broughton classic, augmented by an excellent string arrangement by David Bedford. Rob recalls: 'The idea of bringing David in to write and conduct the strings on that album was Peter Jenner's. The nice thing about Blackhill was that there was this amazing pool of talent there to draw on. David had worked with Kevin Ayers, along with Mike Oldfield who featured on "Thinking of You". I think that "Evening Over Rooftops" is probably one of the most important Broughton Band tracks. The arrangement is stunning.'

Bedford's arrangements also graced 'What is a Woman For', a song that dated as far back as December 1969. Of the other material recorded, highlights included 'Don't Even Know Which Day It Is', a superb rock number, while 'Madhatter' was a comment on political and religious hypocrisy. The band dabbled in different styles, including country-rock on 'Piece Of My Own' (featuring Johnny van Derek on violin) and the closing track 'For Doctor Spock', a tribute to the noted American paediatrician and author whose views on the rearing of children had been praised and adopted by many free-thinking followers of underground culture.

'The Edgar Broughton Band' was released in May 1971 as Harvest SHVL791. It reached a height of Number 28 in June 1971 and was swiftly followed by the release of a double A-side single. 'Hotel Room' b/w 'Call Me A Liar' (Harvest HAR 5040) was the finest single released by the band. Although much of the Broughtons' EMI catalogue is of a high standard, 'The Edgar Broughton Band' remains their major achievement and remains one of the best albums issued by EMI's Harvest imprint.

Roll up Roll up — the Broughton circus is coming to town

FREDDIE and the Dreamers and groups of that ilk make a good living entertaining kiddies a lot of the time, while at the other end of the scale Frank Zappa's audience tends to consist of what are frequently termed "head." Edgar Broughton's followers most definitely fall into the latter category but this isn't going to deter him from having a crack at the former.

Not that this indicates a sell-out or an attempt to indoctrinate the next generation by any means. His plans, if they prove successful, stand a good chance of putting him in the "social worker" class. Which hardly sounds like Broughton.

To explain in detail what he has in mind, he met me in his publicist's London office fittingly located behind the Shaftesbury Theatre where "Hair" is playing. He presented a somewhat intimidating figure, his plump frame topped by a Struwelpeter coiffure, and chose to sit on the floor with his back resting against a wall and his plimsolled feet stretching across the carpet.

"I remember getting bored in the summer holidays and people in poorer areas must get even more bored as there's less to do," he began in his Warwick accent. "We plan to do some concerts for kids in those areas through the local authorities and play groups. We hope it will be different from a straight concert — games and that kind of thing. We can cope with any age group, we don't know if we'll appeal to them."

And at the same time that he's entertaining the younger set he plans to travel round the coast with his band on another venture.

"I've written to fifty towns right round the coast, except Scotland, and we hope to do ten concerts off the back of a lorry at the height of the season," he revealed. "We've already been offered a site in Morecambe, and Redcar has shown interest.

"Somebody phoned up our manager the other day and virtually said 'What's the catch?' but there is no catch, we're not into catches. The band wants to expand in every way and we thought it would be very nice to put into practice a lot of what we say.

Image

"It's not an attempt to change our image because we're not into images — you don't shout at kids 'Yankee bases out' or whatever it is these days."

The summer concerts will almost certainly turn out to be a lot more peaceful than many of the gigs the band has played, especially on the Continent where Broughton is thought of in some circles as the revolutionaries' Messiah. Tales of unrest and upheaval at his concerts are widespread and I asked him what were the drawbacks of such a reputation.

"The drawbacks are other people's inefficiency and inability to understand the roots of what we're trying to do," he replied simply. "We're not trying to convert people . . . I suppose you could describe us as the court jesters of the underground revolution or whatever. We're not a political party, we feel we have an insight into what's going to happen."

But what about the riots and people getting hurt? Doesn't he feel guilty?

"People have never got hurt at any of our concerts to my knowledge," he countered. "In Berlin once, though, the equipment was totally inadequate and we just couldn't use it and ours hadn't arrived so I had to go out and face the audience and tell them they'd have to wait. They just went outside and started fighting police and

EDGAR: SEASIDE CONCERTS SET

A SERIES of free concerts at seaside resorts this summer has now been arranged for the Edgar Broughton Band. This follows the NME report on May 8 that Broughton was planning a series of concerts on seaside beaches. In most cases, however, the outfit will be playing in promenade bandstands — probably the first time a pop group has ever been spotlighted in this manner! Towns to be visited are Morecambe (July 10), Redcar (18), Gravesend (31), Blackpool (August 1) and Worthing (7), with three more South Coast venues still to be confirmed.

Broughton is also to play free concerts at children's play centres at Lansdowne Drive, London, E.8 (July 29); Nelson Street, Manchester (August 2); Greenway School, South Mead, Bristol (5); Coram's Fields, London W.C.1 (10); and Queen's Drive Recreation Ground, Nottingham (16). Another charity concert in aid of the Bangla Desh victims is set for London's Alexandra Palace on July 24.

BROUGHTON GIVES UP!

EDGAR BROUGHTON has abandoned his plan to give a series of free concerts from the back of a lorry, following his two recent arrests which led to obstruction charges. His last appearance will be in Gravesend Music Bowl tomorrow (Saturday). A spokesman commented: "We had hoped that if all went well, we would continue — but one can only take so much!" However Broughton will continue with his concerts at children's play centres, and new additions to the list of venues include Birmingham Arena Theatre (August 15) and Newcastle Montague School (17).

POLICE HALT EDGAR'S SHOW & ARREST HIM!

THE four-man Edgar Broughton Band was arrested in Redcar at the weekend, while giving a free concert in a playing field against the local council's wishes. As previously reported in the NME, Edgar had planned to play up to 50 free concerts this summer, mainly in seaside resorts, and had acquired a mobile stage with this in view. But he met with resistance from several councils, who were worried about the prospects of rioting. Redcar was one of the towns which had banned the outfit from playing on the beach or promenade.

Broughton accordingly set up stage in a field one mile from the town centre, but the police intervened while the concert was in progress. The whole band was arrested, as well as six road managers and technicians, and several fans who became involved in skirmishes with the police. Edgar was remanded on £50 bail, and is due to appear in court next Tuesday accused of "obstructing the highway and obstructing the police in the execution of their duty."

Will Edgar continue to press on with his plans for more free concerts? He refused to common on Monday, but the following day he attempted to play another free concert — this time at Brighton — and was again arrested for his trouble! He was again charged with obstruction.

Edgar Broughton Band

CAN 'Tago Mago'

First released as United Artists UAS29211/12 in May 1971
Highest UK chart position: N/A
Available on CD as Spoon Records SPOONCD006/7

Paperhouse
Mushroom
Oh Yeah
Halleluhwah
Aumgn
Peking O
Bring Me Coffee Or Tea

Holger Czukay	**Bass**
Michael Karoli	**Guitar**
Jaki Liebezeit	**Drums**
Damo Suzuki	**Vocals**
Irmin Schmidt	**Keyboards**

Written and Produced by Can
Engineering and Editing by Holger Czukay
Recorded at Schloss Norvenich, near Cologne 1971

With the release of their debut album, 'Monster Movie' by United Artists in 1969, Can had established themselves as the most important German underground group. With this record Irmin Schmidt (keyboards), Michael Karoli (guitar), Holger Czukay (bass), Jaki Liebezeit (drums) and American vocalist Malcolm Mooney had made their mark with their unique brand of improvised music recorded in the surroundings of the Schloss Norvenich, a castle just outside Cologne.

The impact of their music had led to commissions to compose and record television and film soundtracks, alongside their stunning live performances. The subject of German media interest, Can's future seemed assured. It was at this point the band suffered the serious blow of losing vocalist Mooney, whose behaviour was becoming more and more erratic. At one notable concert he repeated the words 'upstairs, downstairs' for three hours, continuing this chant even after the band stopped playing. His mental health began to deteriorate and he became convinced the US Army was searching for him, as he inadvertently had become a Vietnam-era draft-dodger.

He had been visiting South America while the US draft board demanded he enroll for active military service in the Vietnam War, then at its height. His paranoia was fuelled when his picture appeared in German newspapers as a member of Can. Things came to a head when he locked himself in a wardrobe for four days. He was advised by a German psychiatrist to return to America for the sake of his mental health. This he did, and he subsequently became an art teacher.

Can now found themselves operating as a four-piece, pondering their future. In May 1970 they were booked to play four concerts at the Blow Up Club in Munich. Holger Czukay and Jaki Liebezeit were having a coffee at a Munich pavement cafe in the afternoon when their attention was drawn to a young Japanese busker. When asked by Czukay if he would like to perform with Can at that night's concert, Damo Suzuki accepted the offer to contribute to the entertainment.

The concert that night was eventful in the extreme. As Czukay later recounted, 'The venue was packed that evening and Damo started murmuring like a meditating monk. All of a sudden he turned into a fighting samurai; the audience was shocked and almost everybody left the hall. About 30 Americans were left and got totally excited about what they heard. Among them was Hollywood actor David Niven who probably thought he was attending some sort of nightmare happening. He stayed until the end.'

Following that chance meeting, Can embarked on their second phase, producing some of the best work of their career. Suzuki's impact was felt immediately on the 1970 album 'Soundtracks', a collection of their film and television music which also featured Malcolm Mooney. Containing the band's contributions to films such as Deadlock and Deep End, 'Soundtracks' was never intended to be regarded as an official Can studio album, yet it flowed incredibly well. Selling in larger numbers than their debut album, its success paved the way for Can's next work.

Still working from a simple eight-channel stereo mixing desk and two Revox two-track tape recorders, the sound achieved by Can's resident audio wizard Holger Czukay was astounding. The music that would comprise the first side of the ambitious double album was a stunning statement that has arguably never been bettered. The opening 'Paperhouse' began with an ethereal

Damo Suzuki vocal which built into a sinister crescendo of epic proportions. The tempo change on 'Paperhouse' in particular finely showcased the unique percussion playing of Jaki Liebezeit.

Cut into 'Mushroom', with its gentle whispering vocal introduction luring the listener into a false sense of serenity until Suzuki's voice reaches out shouting 'I'm gonna get my kicks there!', the rhythmic intensity would continue into 'Oh Yeah'. In those first 20 minutes the boundaries of rock music were pushed back to an extreme never before witnessed.

The ensuing side-long epics 'Halleluhwah' and 'Aumgn' (featuring Czukay's superb manipulation of tape recordings of radio atmospherics and session outtakes), along with the excellent 'Peking O' and 'Bring Me Coffee Or Tea' were perhaps the most consistent music Can would ever make. Long hours of recording in the surroundings of the Schloss Norvenich saw intense creativity, coupled with an equal amount of internal debate and conflict. 'Sure, we had a lot of conflict,' Schmidt would later recall. 'We were cruel in our criticisms of each other! That's just how we were, because coming from these different musical backgrounds we all still had our own different ideas. The differences between us made Can so rich and full of tension. That's what makes Can's music survive as a living organism; it's so mysterious because it unites things that don't appear to be able to go together.

'During those sessions we became a living organism, a sole being. The best concerts and recordings came from when we became a living thing, when we felt we weren't just playing our own instruments, when I didn't feel like Irmin Schmidt, but felt part of something bigger. Helping this musical organism live is an indescribable feeling. It's only when it happens and you are a witness to it and part of it that you can truly understand it.'

Upon completion, the members of Can felt their latest work should be divided and released as two distinctly different albums. However, thanks to the persuasion of manager Hildegard Schmidt, both Can and Siggi Loch of United Artists were talked into the idea of releasing the music as an ambitious double album. Released in 1971, 'Tago Mago' was universally praised and went on to become Can's biggest selling album. It was also perhaps their most influential. In the late Seventies both Pete Shelley of the Buzzcocks and former Sex Pistol and Public Image founder John Lydon championed the work, and in more recent times, alongside arch Krautrock fan Julian Cope and musicians such as Thom Yorke of Radiohead have hailed the magic of 'Tago Mago'. It remains a stunning musical statement and one which is progressive in the truest sense of the word.

When asked to sum up Can's musical achievement, Irmin Schmidt later remarked: 'Playing in the way we did meant giving everyone involved a whole lot of musical freedom, which created a lot of passion and a sort of musical anarchy, in a way. But in our case, that also generated a sense of passion with discipline and total professionalism. On the one side we were all free spirits, but on the other side we were four fucking serious musicians who were passionate and critically pitiless against ourselves as unit and each other individually. It was a pretty unique experience being part of it.'

Original German sleeve

Caravan

CARAVAN 'In The Land Of Grey and Pink'

First released as Deram SDL-R1 in April 1971
Highest UK chart position: N/A
Available on CD as Deram 882 9832

Golf Girl
Winter Wine
Love To Love You (And Tonight Pigs Will Fly)
In The Land Of Grey And Pink
Nine Feet Underground:
a. Nigel Blows A Tune
b. Love's A Friend
c. Make It 76
d. Dance Of The Seven Paper Hankies
e. Hold Grandad By The Nose
f. Honest I Did!
g. Disassociation
h. 100% Proof

Pye Hastings	Vocals, Guitars
Dave Sinclair	Organ, Piano, Mellotron
Richard Sinclair	Vocals, Bass, Acoustic Guitar
Richard Coughlan	Drums, Percussion
With	
Jimmy Hastings	Flute, Tenor Sax, Piccolo
Dave Grinstead	Cannon, Bell, Wind

Produced by David Hitchcock
Recorded at AIR Studios, London
Engineered by John Punter
'Nine Feet Underground' recorded at Decca Studios, West Hampstead, London
Engineered by Dave Grinstead and Derek Varnals
Re-mix engineers Dave Grinstead and Peter Rynston

When Caravan's first album for Decca Records, 'If I Could Do It All Over Again, I'd Do It All Over You', was released in September 1970 it was received with acclaim. Earlier that year, Caravan appeared at the Kraalingen Pop Festival at Kraalingse Bos, Rotterdam in Holland. The band found themselves on a bill that featured Pink Floyd, Jefferson Airplane, Flock, Frank Zappa, Santana, Quintessence, Skin Alley and many more. As Richard Sinclair later recalled, 'The festival was the biggest gig we did at that time. We played to an audience of about 250,000, only 10,000 of whom were awake because we were the first act on stage on the second day and it had been raining all night! Nevertheless, a lot of people got to see the band.'

This performance coupled with an appearance on 9 August at the 10th National Jazz, Pop, Ballad and Blues Festival at Plumpton (with Van der Graaf Generator, Yes, Colosseum and Juicy Lucy) and the release of 'If I Could Do It All Over Again...' enabled Caravan to develop their following still further. They had moved on leaps and bounds creatively and had overcome the trauma of their first record company, Verve, ceasing UK operations within months of the release of their debut album. Despite an unrelenting workload, Caravan began writing new material that would make up the bulk of their next vinyl outing, agreeing that this time they would hand over the production duties to an outside individual.

In the autumn of 1970 Caravan began sessions at both Decca Studios and Air Studios in London, with David Hitchcock in the producer's chair, for an album that would come to be regarded as one of their finest hours, 'In the Land of Grey And Pink.' It was Hitchcock's enthusiasm for Caravan that had led to the band signing with Decca. The aspiring young producer saw them perform at a midnight concert at London's Lyceum Theatre and next day approached his boss, Hugh Mendl, insisting that Decca Records sign them. Pye Hastings would later state; 'David was in the process of graduating from working in the art department to production. He really wanted to produce us, and I think that was his motivation. We were reluctant to have him produce our first album for Decca as we had never met him and he didn't have a track record, so we decided to produce the next album

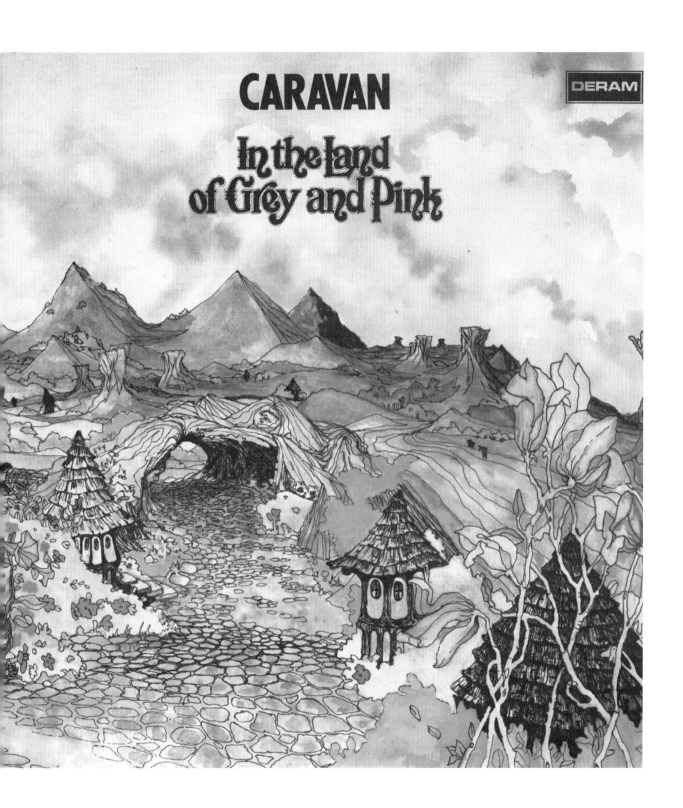

Caravan: another concert tour set

FOLLOWING the success of its recent British concert tour, Caravan is to continue promoting its new Decca album " In The Land Of Pink And Grey " by means of a second concert series in July. The tour opens at Oxford Town Hall on July 9, and other dates so far confirmed are Guilford Civic Hall (10), London Lyceum (11) and Liverpool Philharmonic Hall (17). It plays Stoke-on-Trent on July 18, though the venue has still to be confirmed, and other dates are still being set.

ourselves. After "If I Could Do It All Over Again…" came out we finally met David and got on really well. He came up with lots of interesting ideas, so we decided that he should produce our next album.'

Sessions for the album began at Decca Studios in Broadhurst Gardens, West Hampstead in September 1970. Initially Caravan worked on the first versions of what were to become legendary songs in their repertoire. On this occasion, Pye Hastings was only to offer 'Love To Love You' as his songwriting contribution. He would later explain his relative lack of material thus: 'For the first two albums I wrote most of the material, and Dave Sinclair also wrote a lot. When it came to '…Grey And Pink' the others had a big backlog of material. Dave especially was advancing way ahead of the rest of us in terms of musical development, so he had a lot of say on the album. Richard Sinclair also had a pile of good material. I only contributed one entire track, but offered bits to some others, which was only fair because I had written the bulk of the previous two albums. It made no difference to us because we shared our publishing credits.'

The first song to be recorded was Richard Sinclair's 'Group Girl', later to be known as 'Golf Girl'. 'Richard was, and remains, a very endearing writer,' Hastings later commented. 'He writes about things that are very close to him, like his friends and family and so on. When a song reached its final stage, he would change the lyrics to become less personal. The original version of 'Golf Girl' was a very personal song about him and Trisha, his wife to be. It was also about his son, Jason. All of that was happening in his life at the time. Of course Trisha became Pat and the rest is history!'

Another Richard Sinclair composition to grace the album was 'Winter Wine', a song of fairytales and dreams. Originally worked out in the studio during these initial sessions, this song went under the working title of 'It's Likely To Have A Name Next Week.' 'We tended to come up with the music first and the lyrics were usually the last thing to be finished', explained Pye. 'I think that "Winter Wine" is probably the finest song Richard has every written.' The remaining sessions in September were dedicated to a track provisionally entitled 'Dave's Thing', a major composition that would eventually take the name of 'Nine Feet Underground'. 'Dave had written four different pieces which were joined together by musical links the rest of us devised,' Hastings would later assert. 'One of the linking riffs was mine and Richard Coughlan came up with ideas too. We all helped by changing a few words here and there and suggesting different chord changes.'

The 22-minute opus was recorded in five distinct sections and skillfully edited by David Hitchcock and Decca engineer Dave Grinsted. Taking up a whole side of vinyl, the 'suite provided a worthy successor to 'For Richard', proving to be a concert favourite. The bizarre names given to each movement such as 'Dance Of The Seven Paper Hankies' and 'Hold Granddad By The Nose' added to the mystique. By December 1970 the band moved to the newly opened Air London studios in Oxford Street. These AIR sessions saw 'Golf Girl' re-recorded, with a superb piccolo solo from Pye's brother Jimmy. The work at Air London also produced two further Richard Sinclair compositions. 'In The Land Of Grey And Pink' featured some of Richard's most surreal lyrics and featured a bubble-blowing solo by its creator.

'In The Land Of Grey And Pink' was released to an unsuspecting world in April 1971, on Decca's progressive rock label Deram. The album packaging was the most lavish to grace a Caravan release to date, being the inaugural release in Deram's 'deluxe' series. Featuring a striking Tolkien-esque illustration by Anne-Marie Anderson, the gatefold revealed a silhouette of the band marching single file in a field. Overall both the music within and the album sleeve created a stunning impression. Despite failing to register on the official UK chart, 'In The Land of Grey And Pink' has remained on catalogue since its 1971 release and remains Caravan's biggest-selling album. Its fusion of folk, jazz and rock created an album that is still highly regarded.

Nearly four decades on from its original release, Pye Hastings would reflected; 'I think the reason "Grey And Pink" stands out is mainly due to the timing of everything. We began to peak in many ways at that time. Our production had peaked, thanks to David Hitchcock, and Dave Sinclair's writing and playing had begun to peak. We were playing very well as a band and things looked as though they were going to happen in a big way for us. Unfortunately we should have had increased attention from both management and record company at that point. For some reason it didn't happen, but we all knew that we had made a good album.'

The original liner note of 'In The Land Of Grey And Pink' declared: 'Here then is Caravan's third album: one side composed of four songs and the second side consisting of one track containing eight different sections but conceived as an entity. To describe the music would take up far more space than is available here but those of you who have heard Caravan live and on their previous records will know the quality to expect although you may not have heard all the numbers before. Those of you who haven't heard the group before are in for a very enjoyable initiation.'

Although Caravan would continue to record and perform full-time for the next six years, also enjoying a rejuvenated period of activity in the first four and half years of the new millennium with differing line-ups, 'In the Land Of Grey And Pink' remains their finest moment and the ideal introduction to the music of a wonderful band.

FAMILY 'Fearless'

First released as Reprise K54003 in November 1971
Highest UK chart position: Number 14
Available on CD as Mystic Records MYSCD172

Between Blue and Me
Sat'd'y Barfly
Larf And Sing
Spanish Tide
Save Some For Thee
Take Your Partners
Children
Crinkley Grin
Blind
Burning Bridges

Roger Chapman	**Vocals, Guitars and Percussion**
Charlie Whitney	**Guitars, Mandolin and Percussion**
Poli Palmer	**Keyboards, Vibes, Flute and Percussion**
John Wetton	**Guitars, Bass, Vocals, Contracts and Keyboards**
Rob Townsend	**Drums, Paiste Cymbals and Percussion**
Brass	**The Ladbroke Horns**

Produced by Family and George Chkiantz
Recorded at Olympic Studios, Barnes, London

By the beginning of 1971 Family had become associated with ever changing personnel line-ups. After enjoying a period commercial success and line-up stability on the albums 'Music in a Doll's House' and 'Family Entertainment', bass guitarist and violinist Ric Grech departed to join Eric Clapton, Ginger Baker and Steve Winwood in Blind Faith halfway through the band's first US tour. Grech was replaced by John Weider, previously with Eric Burdon and the Animals, on bass, guitar and violin and this line-up completed the series of US dates.

The band's American tour would prove eventful to say the least. At a show at the Fillmore East in New York City, Roger Chapman accidentally lost his grip of a microphone stand, hurling it towards Fillmore owner Bill Graham, stood at the side of the stage. Graham took the incident as a deliberate act and barred Family from appearing again at both Fillmore venues in America. Chapman responded to this incident by performing in a stilted manner on the remaining dates, leading to less than positive reviews and a failure to secure a return visit.

Back in the UK, Family toured continually throughout the remainder of 1969, pausing only to replace saxophonist Jim King (due to his increasingly erratic behaviour) with John 'Poli' Palmer, previously with Blossom Toes, on flute, vibraphone and piano. Palmer's arrival saw Chapman and Whitney re-think the direction of a future line-up of the band. The first album by this new line-up, 'A Song For Me', was a successful venture, reaching Number 4 in the

ALBUMS

'Fearless' Family —on target for a rock classic

FAMILY: FEARLESS (Reprise K54003; £2.49).

EVER since Doll's House and Entertainment, Family have been threatening to produce a classic rock album. I'm loathe to make snap judgements, and Fearless is a difficult product to assess because its immediate impact is one of surprise, but this could well be the nearest they've got yet to achieving that long-promised goal.

I should maybe first explain what I mean by surprise impact. Having lost the violin that had become a trademark of the band, Family have chosen not merely to attempt to replace it but have fearlessly and wisely chosen to expose whole new avenues that have opened up for them.

Thus, on Fearless, we find a brass section, copious use of harmonies—Roger Chapman assisted by new bassist John Wetton — and, more pointedly, we find them writing some of the best material of their career. There are several exceptional melodies here that will lodge themselves in your brain.

Yet many of the songs are so different—like Poli Palmer's spoof Larf And Sing, with Inkspots / Sing Something Simple vocals, and the acoustic, tenderly-lyrical Children— that the change requires a period of adaptation. It's rather like bracing yourself for having your brain punched in, and being handed a sweet instead. A good stereo — because there are some deft touches of production to relish — would be an advantage.

Taken as a whole then, Fearless is more an album of subtlety, possessing a strong streak of humour, the usual top class lyrics, yet still retaining sufficient of Family's characteristic restless aggression to counter any foppishness. They ain't poofs you know.

To this end you get cuts like Blind, Between Blue And Me and Take Your Partners contrasting their aggression against a lighter number like Children where, against a restrained boot-stomp rhythm, Wetton and Chapman harmonise a beautiful little song.

Again, now that the violin has gone, so has some of the schizoid pace. Between Blue and Partners are both more even-paced compared to past cuts like Weaver, with guitar breaks where Charlie Whitney allows himself the luxury of laying back on guitar, slicing with deliberated menace on the one track, mellow and stirring on the other.

The brass wheezes merrily a on the semi-novelty Sat'd'y Barfly, and again on the march-tempo Save Some For Thee. Both also use Poli Palmer's honky piano, and the latter a rousing military percussion. The fact that four in the band get credits for percussion on the sleeve is evidence of the attention given to that department.

Spanish Tide and Burning Bridges are other good strongly melodic examples of Family mixing roots and evolution. Tide is a cleverly constructed composition, using Palmer's vibes strongly, where subtle almost ballad-like qualities are contrasted with a characteristic Family staccato arrangement.

Bridges, the closing cut, again uses harmonics, and is a particular favourite for the way it seems, to my mind, to crystallise all the best elements of the first Doll's House album. That should give an indication that this is Family in the melting pot, and that Fearless is a deucedly fiendish stroke. — N.L.

GILLIAN McPHERSON: POETS AND PAINTERS AND PERFORMERS OF BLUES (RCA SF 8220; £2.09)

This is the first album from Gilly, who prefers to be regarded as a " contemporary giver " rather than a folk singer, and judging the material down I would say that was the only description. The numbers vary from easy paced to up-tempo, with the vocals coming over clearly and with charm all the time.

Certain tracks have a distinct jazz flavouring, which is down to two things: The producer was Danny Thompson, and because he had not seen her perform on stage, his own background obviously came through. Secondly because of the number of jazz orientated session men.

Gilly, I feel, can write some perceptive lyrics, though not all the songs are of an exceptional standard. And she also has this tendency to deliver some of the tunes without any conviction. Yet at other times she really gives herself completely.

On this set of eleven songs there is a definite indication her writing and singing style has not developed into something of her own. Noticeable on two tracks, I Am The Runner, and Lazy Dreamer, there was a certain Americanisation in the vocals. And the imagery in the words of Muff The Gong, certainly stemmed from the traditional folk music, with such lines as " He flew me above a black crowded grave/Poisoned ashes lay deep in the sun."

But she has quite a range in her singing, and keeps the voice well under control, such as on the title track. One of my favourites is " It's My Own Way " which is a truly beautiful song. I would like to

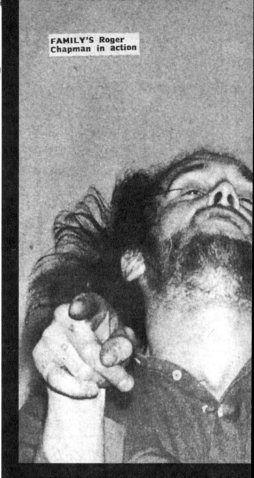

FAMILY — Fearless
This is Family's fifth album, and can in many ways be regarded as their best. The group has never been one to stand still, and the introduction of John Wetton on bass, and emergence of Poli Palmer as song-writer alongside Chapman and Whitney makes the progression in their music even more marked.

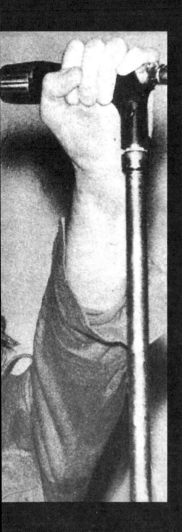

New member for Family

FAMILY this week signed their replacement for John Weider — Derbyshire-born John Wetton, 22, who will play bass guitar and piano and vocals

The search for a new member took six weeks. Wetton who is an experienced session musician (see also feature pages), makes his first live appearance with Family at Belgium's Bilzen festival to-day (Friday).

Wetton is also working with the group on its album being made at Olympic studios for October 15 release.

● Following their gig at London's Syon Park folk festival last weekend. Transatlantic recording artists Mr Fox are to lose drummer Alan Eden and bass player Barry Lyons. Leader Bob Peg feels the present instrumentation had not been ideally suited to the group's material.

FAMILY: the new line-up left to right is **ROB TOWNSEND, POLI PALMER, JOHN WHITNEY,** new member **JOHN WHETTON** and **ROGER CHAPMAN.**

'This is Family's fifth album and can in many ways be regarded as their best. The group has never been one to stand still, and the introduction of John Whetton on bass, and emergence of Poli Palmer as songwriter alongside Chapman and Whitney make the progression in their music even more marked.

RECORD MIRROR 30/10/71

UK in January 1970. By now Family were a major live and festival attraction in Europe and their next album, 'Anyway' (released in November 1970) featured material partially recorded live on its first side and new studio material overleaf. It was this new material that would demonstrate that Family were capable of delivering interesting music which drew from rock, jazz and folk influences.

In typical Family style, a further line-up change occurred in June 1971 when John Weider departed to join former Taste members in the band Stud. His replacement came in the form of John Wetton on double-neck bass and guitar. Previously with Mogul Thrash, Wetton was a more than competent vocalist in his own right and his arrival added a new impetus to Family. Chapman and Whitney had composed some of the strongest material to date, and with Wetton in the band this material was honed to perfection on the concert stage. By the time the band entered Olympic Studios to record their next album, Family's new music had a previously unheard polish and power.

Chapman and Whitney provided the lion's share of the material recorded. 'Between Blue And Me' did what Family did best, beginning in fairly relaxed manner before moving into a more strident direction. 'Sat'd'y Barfly' was a satirical piece that had roots in earlier Family albums, and featured Poli Palmer on Tuba. 'Spanish Tide' and 'Save Some for Thee' saw Chapman joined on vocals by John Wetton, with the former track being a highlight of the album along with the excellent 'Take Your Partners'.

The track 'Blind' featured the eerie sound of a tyre inner tube being whirled around to gain a bizarre 'whistling' effect which dominated the piece, while new time signatures and instrumentation were brought forth on the powerful 'Burning Bridges' which featured contributions from Poli Palmer on flute and bagpipes. He also wrote and sang the charming 'Larf And Sing', later released as a US single, while the tradition of including instrumental pieces on Family albums was continued with Palmer's 'Crinkly Grin.'

Released in October 1971, 'Fearless' didn't achieve the chart heights of Family's preceding albums but was welcomed by both dedicated fans and critics alike. The music was mature and diverse, displaying a subtlety previously unheard on the band's recorded work and this was possibly a factor in its disappointing chart position. Roger Chapman would later comment: 'There was never any big plan when Family came to make an album, it was just a matter of taking ideas and pursuing them to see where we would end up.' 'Fearless' was a culmination of those ideas and is perhaps one of the greatest records made by a truly unique and often overlooked band.

Roger Chapman

GENESIS 'Nursery Cryme'

First released as Charisma CAS1052 in November 1971
Highest UK chart position: Number 39
Available on CD as Charisma/Virgin 50999 519547 2 7

The Musical Box
For Absent Friends
The Return Of The Giant Hogweed
Seven Stones
Harold The Barrel
Harlequin
The Fountain Of Salmacis

Tony Banks	**Organ, Mellotron, Piano, Electric Piano, 12-string Guitar, Voices**
Michael Rutherford	**Bass, Bass Pedals, 12-string Guitar, Voices**
Peter Gabriel	**Lead Voice, Flute, Bass Drum, Tambourine**
Stephen Hackett	**Electric Guitar, 12-string Guitar**
Phil Collins	**Drums, Voices, Percussion**

Recorded at Trident Studios, London in August 1971
Produced by John Anthony
Assistant engineer David Hentschel
Tape Jockey Mike Stone

GENESIS — NURSERY CRYME —
CAS 1052
Genesis transfer their unique stage act on to record and comes off incredibly well. Tracks include Harold the Barrel, Musical Box and The Return of the Giant Hogweed. An excellent album that should enhance their growing reputation in universities, colleges and clubs.

The success of Genesis as leading lights of the progressive rock movement of the Seventies and evolving into major stars of the Eighties and Nineties often overshadows the group's beginnings. The Genesis story began at Charterhouse public school in 1967 when two members of school band the Anon, Anthony Philips (lead guitar) and Mike Rutherford (rhythm guitar), joined with Tony Banks (keyboards), Peter Gabriel (vocals) and Chris Stewart (drums) of rival school outfit the Garden Wall. This as yet un-named group recorded a demo tape featuring six songs recorded during free time after lessons. The tape soon found its way into the hands of Jonathan King, a former Charterhouse pupil who had recorded a number of singles and was now working for Sir Edward Lewis, head of Decca Records.

King had paid his former school a visit and was given a cassette by Peter Gabriel. Suitably impressed, King signed the young musicians to his production company (leased in turn to Decca) and organised recording sessions at Regent Sound Studios in London's Denmark street in December 1967 during the group's Christmas holidays. Given the name Genesis by King, the fruits of these sessions were issued as the single 'The Silent Sun' b/w 'That's Me' in February 1968. Although the single failed to chart, it did secure some airplay on Radio Luxembourg and response was encouraging enough to merit a further single release; 'A Winter's Tale' b/w 'One Eyed Hound' in May 1968.

In the summer of 1968 Genesis returned to Regent Sound to record their first album, with John Silver replacing Chris Stewart. An embryonic work, the songwriting reveals in hindsight the direction Genesis would take on their early albums for Charisma Records and would demonstrate the originality that was the hallmark of future Genesis work.

Released in March 1969 'From Genesis To Revelation' failed to achieve any commercial success, partly attributed by King to the fact that some record shops filed the album under 'Religious Music'. With King losing interest in the band, the members of Genesis retreated to a cottage in Surrey to write new material and rehearse a stage act that would see them break into the UK live circuit later that year. With John Mayhew taking the drum seat, Genesis signed with agent Marcus Bicknell and set out performing the British club circuit.

A concert with Charisma signings Rare Bird led the band to recommend the group to their producer John Anthony, who witnessed the band perform at Ronnie Scott's Club in March 1970 and suggested Charisma label boss Tony Stratton Smith should sign Genesis to the label. Within two weeks the band found themselves signed to a long-term contract. The album 'Trespass', released in October 1970 revealed that they had indeed found themselves musically. An impressive work, the album's highlight was the muscular piece 'The Knife', later to prove to be a particular live concert favourite, although the song was out of character with the more pastoral and ethereal feel of the rest of the album.

With an increasing live schedule, the pressure of performing proved to be too much for Anthony Phillips. He began to suffer stage fright and ill health which led to him announcing his in August 1970, prior to the release of 'Trespass.' Phillips' departure was a serious blow, particularly to Tony Banks and Mike Rutherford. However, encouraged by Tony Stratton-Smith, Banks, Gabriel and Rutherford sought a new guitarist and a new drummer to replace John Mayhew who also left at the news of Phillips' departure. Following an extensive series of auditions, the talented Phil Collins, former drummer with Flaming Youth, was recruited, alongside guitarist Mick Barnard. Barnard's tenure with Genesis was short-lived, the band dispensing with a guitarist for a period until they spotted an advertisement in Melody Maker by Steve Hackett. A period of live concerts and writing sessions followed with the former Quiet World guitarist, and in August 1971 Genesis returned to Trident studios to begin work on their third album.

It was obvious that Genesis had become a tight, well-honed musical unit. Their new material was their most proficient to date, and some songs would remain in the band's live set for years to come. With producer John Anthony supervising, Genesis were about to embark on the road to becoming progressive rock legends. The album would be dominated by the opening track, 'The Musical Box', which began life as far back as 1969, when the band had recorded music for a film about artist and painter Michael Jackson. It had evolved into a surreal Peter Gabriel lyrical tale of two Victorian children, Cynthia and Henry. While playing a game of croquet, Cynthia accidentally decapitates Henry with her croquet mallet.

After this tragic incident, Cynthia discovers Henry's musical box in their playroom. As she curiously opens the box, it begins to play 'Old King Cole'. As the music starts, the spirit of Henry enters the room and appears before Cynthia, gradually ageing before her eyes. As Henry ages, he vocally expresses a carnal desire for Cynthia. The noise is heard by Cynthia's nanny who hurls the musical box at the apparition, destroying both the box and the spirit. Accompanying this darkly humorous tale akin to the pages of Lewis Carroll, was a wonderful musical background in which Tony Banks utilised both organ and Mellotron perfectly.

'For Absent Friends' was an acoustic melodic piece with a uniquely English character, the first Genesis composition to have creative input from both Phil Collins and Steve Hackett. The song also featured a rare Collins lead vocal. 'The Return Of The Giant Hogweed' was the second Gabriel story set to music on the album, recounting the tale of a Victorian explorer who transported a giant hogweed from Russia to the Botanical Gardens at Kew. The plant becomes alive and spreads its seed at will throughout the land. Immune to any pesticide, it soon dominates the British Isles, victorious over mankind. Along with 'The Musical Box', this song would become a live favourite at Genesis concerts.

The majestic 'Seven Stones' opened the second side of the album. A superb epic tale of an old man recounting tales of wisdom and morality to younger men, it featured outstanding keyboard work from Tony Banks, taking inspiration from the church music he had heard in the chapel at Charterhouse. 'Harold The Barrel' was an amusing story of a restaurant owner in Bognor Regis who cut off his toes and served them in dishes to his clientele.

'Harlequin' was a short, gorgeous acoustic song featuring vocal contributions from all members of the band, while the album concluded with another lengthy piece, 'The Fountain Of Salmacis'. The song was based on a Greek mythological tale of the nymph Salmacis, a woman who forced her sexual favours on Hermaphroditus, an act which caused their bodies to be merged as one. With its majestic keyboard introduction, a lively middle section and innovative guitar from Steve Hackett, 'The Fountain Of Salmacis' would remain a part of Genesis' live act well after Peter Gabriel's departure.

Released in November 1971, 'Nursery Crime' was adorned with a Paul Whitehead sleeve depicting the tale of 'The Musical Box' and was enthusiastically greeted by critics; a Charisma Records ad featured a rave review from ELP's Keith Emerson. Although it failed to chart in the UK on release, the album was to enjoy huge success in Italy and on the continent. 'Nursery Crime' would bring the music of Genesis to a wider audience, the band soon attracting an extremely loyal core following. By 1974, Genesis would hit another level both commercially and creatively and this success would propel 'Nursery Crime' into the UK Top 40 over two years after release.

Genesis made many great albums, all of which merit lengthy prose. But it is with 'Nursery Crime', in later years one of their overlooked masterpieces, that they first took their initial steps on the road to glory.

GENESIS (l to r) PHIL COLLINS, STEVE HACKETT, MICK RUTHERFORD, TONY BANKS and PETER GABRIEL.

"COR, saw this ace band the other night," said a friend of mine during that sunny day that was the summer of 1971. "I've never seen anything quite like them."

The friend, known by many as Harry Laughing Trousers, went on to describe the band who turned out to be Genesis. I muttered something about never having the pleasure to have heard them and strolled off to the local for a few pints.

A few weeks later Genesis were in town so I thought I'd stroll along and find out what they were all about. It was a strange evening. It was a small gig and Genesis were regarded as a small time band, but their music was something else. Every song was a masterpiece.

I lovingly nurtured a high respect for the group as months rolled by and I lost track of them for a while. Were they dead, had they left the country? I had expected them to have become ginormous by this summer, but alas they were still doing those nervewracking little gigs and were still being treated as a small time band.

Then came Reading.

Genesis stole the show on the Friday and they were beginning to emerge.

Their bread and butter is still the club and college circuit and although they don't draw huge crowds every person that goes to see them knows what to expect and loves every minute.

Drummer Phil Collins and singer / flautist Peter Gabriel are probably the two men in the band whose personalities come over strongest on stage, and Gabriel is one of the strangest showmen on the scene right now.

While others have their hair done green, silver and other assorted colours, Peter has cut a wedge of hair from the front of his scalp.

"There are various reasons for having done this," said Peter in his usual wry way.

"The first is that it was done so that one can see the lights jumping from one side to another. Secondly it is a symbol of the desert that lies within, and finally it could also be translated by the fact that my razor slipped. "Who's a cheeky boy, then?

You can decide for yourself which version is true — if any are — but

GENESIS
OR
how Harry Laughing Trousers was proved right

by charles webster

the little tale gives one an insight into the serious yet humourous way Genesis look at life.

But is Peter just jumping on the glam rock bandwagon, after all you've got to be pretty strange to get attention these days. "I've been tarting myself up for years — since we first started in fact. It's all part of creating a fantasy for the audience to enjoy."

What makes Genesis different from most bands who are looking for their place alongside the big

guns in the business is their presentation, which is as entertaining as their music. In between numbers Gabriel enhances the fantasy by taking the audience on an excursion through a make believe world where people tend to get smashed to pieces in violent croquet matches.

One of my favourite Genesis horror tales tells of a lady dressed in a trousersuite who boards a tube train in London. Looking around at the blank faces in the carriage she decides to liven things up a bit and reach-

es to the top of her head where she finds a zip which runs around her body, cranium to crotch, and peels off her skin, her flesh falling to the floor of the carriage with a "plop."

"A few months ago I decided to cut my stories down a bit," said Peter. "We were playing a lot on the Continent and the audiences just couldn't understand what I was going on about. They just fell flat.

"I am going to work on my stories again, though, because the European

thing meant that I neglected them a little. I started telling them just to fill in in between numbers so that the rest of the band can swap instruments and get ready for the next song."

The new Genesis album, Foxtrot, is their fourth album, although their first LP, on Decca, is rarely talked about by the band or their followers. Since they joined Charisma Genesis have boldly tried to progress in their own field and have always gone where others may have feared to tread.

"This album will make or break us," said Phil, "but we say that whenever we bring out a new album. We always think the public will hate it and push us into oblivion. The first side of the new ablum is like four songs that have been arranged, but the second side really is a natural progression from what we were doing on Nursery Cryme."

"In the studio there is always the temptation to put a lot of extra instruments and sounds into the songs which we couldn't possibly hope to recreate on stage, but nevertheless we still take a lot of time getting an album together. Nursery Cryme took over 10 weeks to get together.

"We'd never do a live album because of this. There would be too much going on to make a good live recording."

Like many of today's musicians Peter admires the work of David Bowie who he thinks is one of the best lyricists around. "Bolan?" asked Peter, "He's blown it."

One can usually get close to what makes a band tick by finding out what their musical tastes are and it may not shock you to know that In The Court Of The Crimson King, the first King Crimson album, was one of the strongest influences on Genesis in the early days alongside some of Procol Harum's work, but both Phil and Peter are pop feaks on the quiet.

"There are plans for Phil and I to get some of our friends into a studio to cut a few pop-type singles," said Peter. "But I don't think we'd release them under our names."

What about those stories, would they be going on record. "Oh, no," said Peter. "The spoken word gets boring very quickly and people would get sick of them after a few plays."

GROUNDHOGS 'Split'

First released as Liberty LBS83401 in March 1971
Highest UK chart position: Number 5
Available on CD as Liberty 07243 584819 2 1

Split – Part One
Split – Part Two
Split – Part Three
Split – Part Four
Cherry Red
A Year In The Life
Junkman
Groundhog

Tony McPhee	**Vocals, Guitar, Organ**
Pete Cruickshank	**Bass**
Ken Pustelnik	**Drums**

Recorded at De Lane Lea studios, Holborn, London in November 1970
Produced by Tony (TS) McPhee for Zak Productions
Engineered by Martin Birch

By the autumn of 1970 the Groundhogs had successfully transformed from a good British blues band into an accomplished power trio showcasing the newly exposed songwriting talent of guitarist and founder Tony (TS) McPhee. The band's third album, 'Thank Christ For The Bomb' had demonstrated that McPhee was an accomplished writer, able to pen acerbic social commentary, entering the UK Top 10 and firmly establishing the group as a leading underground act. With critical praise being lavished on the trio, the Groundhogs' fourth album had much to live up to both critically and commercially. Indeed, although McPhee had many musical ideas, he was still struggling to find a lyrical subject to link his new music together when the band entered De Lane Lea in Holborn, (the location of their previous album's recording sessions), in November 1970 to begin work with engineer Martin Birch on their next LP.

'We recorded most of the instrumental backing tracks for the album before I had decided what the record was going to be about lyrically speaking,' Tony McPhee later recalled. 'It was when we came to listen to a playback of the backing tracks that I realised that the music reminded me of an experience I'd had back in May of that year. My first wife and I had taken our landlady's son out to Green Park in London for the day. It was very hot and I found it really difficult to sleep that night. Lying in bed, various thoughts came into my mind and I experienced a kind of terror attack where the various thoughts wouldn't leave my head. When I linked the music to that experience, I found it quite easy to write the lyrics. I spoke to Martin Birch about this and he told me that he had experienced something similar. I came up with the title "Split" for the four parts of music I had written, as the mental aberration I had suffered was almost like schizophrenia.'

The four parts of 'Split' were to dominate the album's first side, the power and intensity of the tracks making them the most electrifying and exciting yet recorded by the band. 'Split Part One' was a musical progression from the style of the Groundhogs' previous album, while 'Spilt Part Two' progressed from a suitably menacing wah-wah guitar introduction to a threatening guitar driven tale of mental terror. The next part of the song cycle was more subdued affair, featuring McPhee on organ as well as guitars at the songs introduction, before reaching to another fiery conclusion. The final part of 'Spilt' climaxed with a cacophony of electronic sounds wrung out of an assortment of specially built guitar effects pedals built by McPhee, a former Post Office telephone engineer.

The music on the album's second side comprised material that had been tried and tested on stage over the past six months. 'Cherry Red', the band's best-known song, was an incredible hard rocker that was a worthy successor to anything recorded by Hendrix. This piece also demonstrated McPhee's considerable prowess as a guitarist. 'Groundhog' was his tribute to blues musician John Lee Hooker, whom the band had backed on his British tour of 1964, and 'A Year In The Life' took its inspiration from the Beatles' song 'A Day In The Life.' The final track to be recorded in the sessions was the inspired 'Junkman', later described by McPhee thus; 'The song gave me the chance to air my opinions on how I felt food was increasingly over processed. It was strange as the term "junk food" hadn't been used at that point. I recorded the vocal track as I began to go down with flu. It was the final finishing touch of the album. We went straight from the session to United Artists' office in Mortimer Street and played the entire album to Andrew Lauder. I thought it sounded fantastic and forgot how ill I had been feeling.'

'Split' was released in March 1971 in a striking sleeve designed and photographed by Christopher Richardson depicting Tony McPhee on stage at the Yorkshire Jazz and Blues Festival in August 1970; the image was refracted in a broken mirror-like effect. Radio 1 DJ John Peel championed the Groundhogs' new work as he had done with 'Thank Christ For The Bomb', while Melody Maker declared; 'McPhee's guitar licks are slicker and more immediate than ever, and they throw their weight into simulating the mental conditions the album describes.'

'Spilt' would go on to be the most successful Groundhogs album, reaching Number 5 in the UK charts and becoming one of the biggest-selling home-grown rock albums in Britain that year. Considering the album was released in a year that saw major album releases by Black Sabbath, Led Zeppelin and Pink Floyd, it was a remarkable achievement. The album would later be hailed as an influence on musicians of the next generation such as punk pioneers the Damned and major parts of 'Spilt' continue to feature in the Groundhogs' live set. An often overlooked work, it remains an impressive, challenging and even unsettling listen.

PETE

KEN

TONY

GROUNDHOGS

OUT of the many gigs I've seen Groundhogs play, their concert at the Queen Elizabeth Hall on Saturday was easily one of the best. Perhaps the other times I saw them, the seating or standing arrangements were not quite conjusive to enjoying music.

After the Stones they seemed to be a lot tighter, a natural move to fit in a lot of material in a short time. But it's not like that now. Although Tony McPhee, Ken Pastelnik and Pete Cruickshank still follow and work in well with each other, the arrangements are again loose, and so include a lot more of Tony's guitar improvisation.

There is a difference though, he seems a lot more controlled than before the tour, and even his sound effects come through a lot better, with more relevance to the music.

Having seen them play at Lincoln, Derby and Birmingham, I was hoping that they would have introduced some new material, but alas no. Yes, they are a busy band, with little time for rehearsals, but surely the odd new number would create a lot more interest than their rearranged old ones. Even so, that is not a strong criticism.

As a festival group, Groundhogs are one of the best, having played the first Lincoln, Weeley, and last Friday Buxton. And it is no surprise that they are continually on call. Ken drives hard on his kit, with some complicated rhythm patterns, which often build the number up to a fever of excitement, blended with some persistent bass runs by Pete — holding the number together.

The blues still features prominently in their act, and naturally "Groundhog" received incredible applause. Other numbers included were "Mistreated," "Garden," "Still a Fool," "Split," "Eccentric Man," and the encore, "Cherry Red (after a great deal of shouting) combined with "Split" part two.

— **TONY STEWART.**

Chrysalis presents

GROUN

in concert with

6th November		North East Polytechnic, Barking	17th	"	Free
7th	"	The Pavilion, Hemel Hempstead	21st	"	Pala
8th	"	Colston Hall, Bristol	22nd	"	Guil
10th	"	Middlesex Polytechnic, Enfield	25th	"	Civi
11th	"	Victoria Hall, Hanley	27th	"	Tow
12th	"	St. Georges Hall, Liverpool	28th	"	Red
13th	"	Wintergardens, Weston-Super-Mare	29th	"	City
15th	"	Town Hall, Oxford	30th	"	St. (

DHOGS

& Quicksand

Manchester		1st December	City Hall, Newcastle
Westcliffe-on-Sea		3rd ''	St. Andrews Hall, Norwich
ampton		4th ''	Leeds University
lford		5th ''	Civic Hall, Wolverhampton
ingham		8th ''	Music Hall, Aberdeen
b, Coatham Hotel, Redcar		9th ''	Caird Hall, Dundee
eld		10th ''	Green's Playhouse, Glasgow
, Bradford		11th ''	Empire Theatre, Edinburgh

UNITED ARTISTS RECORDS

PETER HAMMILL 'Fool's Mate'

First released as Charisma CAS1037 in July 1971
Highest UK chart position: N/A
Available on CD as Charisma/Virgin CASCDR1037

Imperial Zeppelin
Candle
Happy
Solitude
Vision
Re-Awakening
Sunshine
Child
Summer Song In The Autumn
Viking
The Birds
I Once Wrote Some Poems

Peter Hammill	**All lead vocals, Acoustic Guitar, Piano**

Contributors

Guy Evans	**Drums, Percussion**
Martin Pottinger	**Drums**
Hugh Banton	**Piano, Organ**
Rod Clements	**Bass, Violin**
Nic Potter	**Bass**
Ray Jackson	**Harmonica, Mandolin**
David Jackson	**Alto and Tenor Saxophones**
Robert Fripp	**Electric Guitar**
Paul Whitehead	**Tam-Tam**

With The Fluctuating Chorale: Guy, Hugh, Dave, Ray, John, Norman, Alastair, John and Peter
Recorded at Trident Studios, Soho, London on 20th, 21st, 27th and 28th April 1971
Produced by John Anthony
Engineered by Robin Cable

July 1971 saw the release of one of the most interesting albums of the progressive genre to be issued that exciting year. 'Fool's Mate' by Peter Hammill was an intelligent, diverse and superbly crafted work. Enjoying a reputation as one of Britain's most exciting and innovative musicians as a focal member of Van der Graaf Generator, the album was received with enthusiasm by the British music press, but musically seemed completely out of character with the intense and experimental compositions most widely associated with Hammill's work with Van der Graaf. Considering his desire to push his compositional skills to the limit and his refusal to write and record anything that was 'expected' of him, the album 'Fool's Mate' should not have come as a surprise. By mid 1971 Van der Graaf Generator were being hailed in some quarters of the UK music press as one of the most creative and original bands on the British music scene. Their albums 'The Least We Can Do Is Wave To Each Other' and 'H To He Who Am The Only One', both issued by Charisma Records, had earned much well deserved praise for their innovation. January 1971 had seen the group embark on a series of UK dates in their own right before joining Genesis and Lindisfarne on the legendary 'Six Bob' tour of the UK. This was conceived by Charisma founder Tony Stratton-Smith as an ideal way to bring three of the leading acts on Charisma to a wider audience by presenting them on a package tour. With all tickets being sold for the low price of six shillings (30p), Stratton-Smith correctly assumed that audiences would be tempted to attend. Van der Graaf continued a hectic touring schedule throughout the first four months of 1971, performing an incredible 48 shows, interspersed only by a television appearance in Belgium during the first week of April. The only break in Van der Graaf's diary for the month, four free days in April, was destined to be filled by recording sessions at Trident Studios in Soho for Peter Hammill's first solo album. 'I chose to record material I had composed as far back as 1967 that had been performed by the earliest line-up of Van der Graaf

Generator,' he would later explain. 'I suppose the songs were a lot more lightweight than the material I was composing and recording with Van der Graaf at that time. It was perhaps the closest I had come to writing pop music.

'The songs recorded during those sessions were never going to be recorded by Van der Graaf Generator, although we had previously recorded live studio demos of them prior to me going into Trident to record the definitive versions, but I felt that all the songs had a certain validity. I recorded the album in a couple of days and the remaining time was spent mixing the material. I suppose it was a bit like a holiday project sandwiched between other commitments I had with Van der Graaf.' With John Anthony producing, Hammill enlisted the help of bandmates Hugh Banton, Guy Evans and David Jackson alongside ex-Van der Graaf bass player Nic Potter. Also present were Rod Clements and Ray Jackson of fellow Charisma act Lindisfarne and King Crimson guitarist Robert Fripp, all of whom made essential contributions. Of the material recorded, 'Candle' dated as far back as 1966, while the remaining material (including 'Imperial Zeppelin' and 'Viking', written with Van der Graaf co-founder Chris Judge Smith) had been conceived in 1967. The exception to this was the baroque 'Happy', written in 1969. Considering the songs had been written in his formative years, the maturity of Hammill's songwriting was exemplary, while the calibre of musicians contributing to the sessions also made a significant contribution. Banton, Evans and Jackson all shone on tracks such as 'Happy', 'Re-Awakening', 'Sunshine', 'The Birds', 'Summer Song In The Autumn' and 'Child.' Perhaps the most distinctive contributions were made by Ray Jackson and Rod Clements of Lindisfarne whose respective mandolin, harmonica and bass parts on 'Solitude' and 'Viking' were perhaps some of the most effective and atmospheric of all. Also unmistakable was the distinctive playing of Robert Fripp which graced 'Imperial Zeppelin', 'Sunshine', 'Child', 'Viking', 'The Birds' and 'I Once Wrote Some Poems.' The fruits of the Trident sessions were mixed and released with remarkable speed, 'Fool's Mate' appearing as Charisma CAS1037 in July 1971 in a sleeve designed by Paul Whitehead. The UK music press were generally enthusiastic, Melody Maker declaring it 'surely one of the albums of the year' and Sounds commenting 'Throughout, Hammill's work on piano is excellent and there are some nice contributions from Ray Jackson, David Jackson and Robert Fripp.'

With Van der Graaf Generator on the ascendant, the UK music press were also speculative as to the reasons for Hammill recording a solo album. In a contemporary interview he declared: 'The reason for me doing a solo album basically is that if I didn't do it now, I wouldn't be able to do it at all because most of the songs are three and four years old and I think that if I had left it any longer I wouldn't really be able to identify with them enough to want to record them.

'Lately I've found myself singing them to myself more and more and it seemed a shame just to let them go without giving them to anyone else to hear. It's a very heavy thing to do a solo album, because there is always the tendency for people to say "Ah! That's where he's really at." It's not where I'm at now, but part of me is there still, and in that way they are something that I have to exorcise. I had this feeling that I had to do them and that I wouldn't be able to rest easy until I did. Hammill's 'exorcism' of this earlier material from his creative psyche may have been a factor in the creation of one of Van der Graaf Generator's crowning glories, 'Pawn Hearts', work on which began the same moth as 'Fool's Mate' appeared. Regardless of the reasons for its creation, Peter Hammill's first solo album is an often overlooked gem, not only in his back catalogue but also in a wider appraisal of progressive rock. The feeling and emotion present on material such as 'Vision', 'The Birds' or 'Solitude', for instance, is evidence of the sheer genius present on 'Fool's Mate.'

Peter Hammill

ROY HARPER 'Stormcock'

First released as Harvest SHVL789 in April 1971
Highest UK chart position: N/A
Available on CD as Science Friction HUCD047

Hors D'Oeuvres
The Same Old Rock
One Man Rock And Roll Band
Me And My Woman

Roy Harper   **Vocals, Guitars, Piano**
S. Flavius Mercurius (Jimmy Page)
                 Guitar on 'The Same Old Rock'
David Bedford   **Arrangement on**
                 'Me And My Woman'

Produced by Peter Jenner for Blackhill Enterprises
Engineered by Philip MacDonald and Alan Parsons, Nick Webb, Peter Bown, John Leckie
Recorded at EMI Studios, Abbey Road, London between July and December 1970

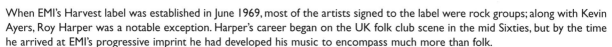

When EMI's Harvest label was established in June 1969, most of the artists signed to the label were rock groups; along with Kevin Ayers, Roy Harper was a notable exception. Harper's career began on the UK folk club scene in the mid Sixties, but by the time he arrived at EMI's progressive imprint he had developed his music to encompass much more than folk.

Born in Manchester in June 1944, Harper first took up the guitar during the Skiffle boom of the mid Fifties. He joined the RAF at 15 to escape an unhappy home life, but later grew unhappy in the services and sought to be discharged on the grounds of mental illness, a condition he faked. The feigned mental illness led to Harper being hospitalised and subjected to traumatic Electro Convulsive Therapy treatment, something he was later to write about. Discharged from hospital and the RAF, he spent a period drifting around Europe and North Africa, busking to earn money, but by 1965 ended up in London and was soon a regular face on the folk-club scene, sharing the stage at venues such as Les Cousins and Bunjies with musicians such as Al Stewart, John Renbourn and Paul Simon.

He made his recording debut with 'The Sophisticated Beggar', released on the independent Strike label in 1966. Although not selling in vast quantities, the album did bring him to the attention of a wider public, the track 'Circle', his first venture into long composition, already setting him aside from his folk-club contemporaries.

He moved to CBS Records in 1967 for whom he recorded the much improved 'Come Out Fighting Genghis Smith'. Roy performed at the first Hyde Park free concert in the summer of 1968, supporting Pink Floyd, and this performance led to a contract with Liberty Records. 1969's 'Folkjokeopus' was his most successful album to date and featured the epic song cycle 'McGoohan's Blues', a conceptual piece inspired by the surreal television series The Prisoner. The album had more in common with the progressive music that was emerging as a dominant force than folk. Harper would later express his dissatisfaction with the album, feeling he was denied enough studio time to bring his ideas to fruition.

With Peter Jenner of Blackhill Enterprises now Roy's manager, he signed to EMI Harvest in June 1969 and soon began work on his first album for the new label at Abbey Road. In January 1970 'Flat, Baroque And Berserk' appeared. The song 'Another Day' featured an orchestral arrangement by David Bedford, while 'Hell's Angels' featured the Nice as his backing group and was Roy's first venture into the world of rock. He found the experience liberating and this spurred him to write his next and what he himself regards as his finest album.

This was to consist of four lengthy pieces which utilised orchestration by David Bedford and saw him assisted by his friend and admirer Jimmy Page who, for contractual reasons, would be credited on the sleeve as S Flavius Mercurius. 'The Same Old Rock' was a majestic 12-minute opus which saw Harper play 12-string guitar and duet with Page on six-string acoustic. He also utilised the recording studio to perfection by double-tracking his vocals at the end of the song. The piece was arguably the most ambitious, in terms of technical production, undertaken by Harper up to that time.

'One Man Rock And Roll Band' was an acerbic attack of the Vietnam War, then at its height and was destined to become a concert favourite, the lyrics being applicable to any global conflict. The album's finest moment came in the shape of the beautiful 'Me And My Woman.' Featuring a fine string arrangement by David Bedford, it is the finest ode to love ever written by Harper, being both delicate and moving in terms of structure. 'Stormcock' was released in 1971 to considerable praise from some in UK music press, but greeted with indifference by others, perhaps in part due to Harper's open distain for some quarters of the music business. The title referred to the mistle thrush, noted for its pure song, which can be heard even in the stormiest of weather and as the album failed to chart a wider public was denied a sublime listening experience.

'Stormcock' sold well enough for EMI to retain faith in Roy Harper's abilities, and his stature among musicians such as Jimmy Page, Roger Waters, David Gilmour, Ian Anderson and Paul McCartney (to name but a few) was enough to ensure him a future with the label. He would record a succession of wonderful albums for EMI through the decade, but the majestic 'Stormcock', an album every music lover should own, was his crowning achievement. Even in these cynical times the album has its fans, with former Smiths guitarist Johnny Marr an advocate of its genius.

A FEAST OF GOODIES
ALL FOR A MERE £1·49.
TASTEFULLY WRAPPED
CONTAINING TWO RECORDS,
SPECIAL BAG - AND
FREE 12 PAGE BOOK.
HURRY ALONG TO YOUR
GRAMOPHONE RECORD
STORE AND ASK FOR DETAILS
OF THIS UNREPEATABLE
OFFER!

UDX 201/2

RECOMMENDED RETAIL PRICE *

BOOKLET AVAILABLE SEPERATELY, PRICE 10p

CANNED HEAT   MAN HELP YOURSELF   GYPSY
BLUNDER   ALLAN TAYLOR AMON DUUL II MORNING
OLIN SCOT COCHISE SUGARLOAF GROUNDHOGS
HN LEE HOOKER AND CANNED HEAT ERNIE GRAHAM
C BURDON AND WAR IF SWEET PAIN HAWKWIND
Y GRITTY DIRT BAND   REG KING   BRINSLEY SCHWARZ

HAWKWIND 'In Search Of Space'

First released as United Artists UAG29202 in October 1971
Highest UK chart position: Number 18
Available on CD as EMI 7243 8 37553 2 5

You Shouldn't Do That
You Know You're Only Dreaming
Master Of The Universe
We Took the Wrong Step Years Ago
Adjust Me
Children Of The Sun

Dave Brock	Vocals, Electric Guitar, 6 and 12-String Acoustic Guitars, Audio Generator
Nik Turner	Alto Saxophone, Flute, Audio Generator, Vocals
Dave Anderson	Bass Guitar, Electric and Acoustic 6-String Guitars
Del Dettmar	Synthesiser
Terry Ollis	Drums, Percussion
Dik Mik	Audio Generator
Stacia	Dances

Produced by Hawkwind and George Chkiantz
Engineered by George Chkiantz
Assistant Engineers Rod Thear, Phil Chapman and Rufus Cartwright
Recorded at Olympic Studios, Barnes, London

Formed in 1969 by ex-busker Dave Brock in the Ladbroke Grove area of London, Hawkwind originally came together following a mindblowing performance at All Saints Hall in Notting Hill. They appeared, billed as Group X, at an event staged by Clearwater Productions, a growing underground management and agency. The band soon came under the wing of manager Doug Smith, who managed to secure a contract with the UK office of Liberty Records, then undergoing a transition into an underground label thanks to the vision of A&R man Andrew Lauder.

Of the many bands that emerged from the Notting Hill/Ladbroke Grove scene at the very end of the Sixties, Quintessence, Skin Alley, High Tide and Cochise among them, it was Hawkwind that most transcended their beginnings. The image of the band standing outside the mainstream music business, supported by the exceptional visual imagery of artist Barney Bubbles and photographer Phil Franks and with the literary talent and vision of poet Robert Calvert alongside Britain's foremost science-fiction writer Michael Moorcock, is an enduring legend. Their psychedelic space-rock has been cited as a key influence across a swathe of the rock music world.

This original line-up was Brock (guitar, lead vocals), Nik Turner (saxophone, flute, vocals), John Harrison (bass), Terry Ollis (drums), Dik Mik (electronics and audio generator) and Mick Slattery (lead guitar). The careers of founder members Dave Brock and Mick Slattery had roots in the early Sixties, playing around Twickenham, Richmond, and Eel Pie Island. Brock mixed with the movers and shakers of the British blues revolution, notably Eric Clapton, and also sat in with US bluesmen such as Memphis Slim and Champion Jack Dupree.

Forming the Famous Cure, Brock gigged extensively in Holland, encountering the freewheeling Nik Turner at the rock'n'roll circus Tent '67. They'd meet up again when Brock and Slattery, with drummer Terry Ollis, electronics dabbler Dik Mik, and former Joe Loss bassist John Harrison were rehearsing a new group. Turner was enlisted as roadie and driver.

When Brock discovered Turner could 'honk a few noises that sounded quite good,' the stage was set for his membership. A handful of low-key gigs were played, then came their debut appearance at All Saints. John Peel, leaving the venue that night, advised Clearwater's impresario Doug Smith that they 'Sound like they're going to be good,' and was later instrumental in trimming the newly renamed Hawkwind Zoo to simply Hawkwind. Doug Smith would later describe them at this time as 'One phone and five people trying to answer it.'

Hawkwind's first, eponymous album, released in August 1970 and produced by Pretty Things' guitarist Dick Taylor), captured a dense and unsettling electronic cacophony, instrumentals with intoned background mantras that discordantly followed the opening 'Hurry On Sundown.'

'Hawkwind' sold encouragingly and gained the band many new followers. That same month the band performed for free at the Isle of Wight festival in a giant tent. At this event Huw Lloyd Langton was spiked with LSD, resulting in a traumatic trip that eventually led to him quitting the band.

By this time John Harrison had departed the band and former Skin Alley bass player Thomas Crimble filled his shoes. Crimble soon departed, along with Dik Mik, replacements being found in Dave Anderson (formerly with German band Amon Düül II) and roadie Del Dettmar.

This new line-up entered AIR Studios in late May 1971 to record their next album – and while Hawkwind's debut LP had been recorded in a very short space of time, the band were now granted room to experiment. With Brock being influenced by the music of German bands such as Can and Amon Düül II, the sound of Hawkwind would evolve into something special. After just a few days at AIR, the band were forced to move to Olympic Studios after some of their associates stole from the studio drinks cabinet and spiked engineers with LSD.

With a much tighter regime in place, the sessions at Olympic Studios would be produced by the band with assistance from engineer George Chkiantz. Of the material recorded, most pieces would go down in history as Hawkwind classics. First came the mighty 'You Shouldn't Do That', a lengthy track that had begun life as a jam session like much of Hawkwind's repertoire, and possessed not only a psychedelic improvisational feel but a sense of rhythm absent in other purveyors of the genre.

Dave Brock's 'You Know You're Only Dreaming' had first been recorded for a session for the BBC's Sounds Of The Seventies radio show and made an excellent closing track to the album's first side, the synthesiser noises etched into the runout groove in the final vinyl release. Side two opened with 'Master Of The Universe' written by Brock and Turner. 'We Took The Wrong Step Years Ago' was an acoustic track by Brock that was an apocalyptic tale that harked backed to his days as busker. 'Adjust Me' was a studio jam session that segued into the trippy 'Children Of The Sun' by Dave Anderson and Nik Turner, marking the first time Turner played flute on record. The finished album was released as 'In Search of Space' in October 1971 and rose to Number 18 on the UK album listings, as notorious for its elaborate packaging as the wonderful music within.

Designed by artist Barney Bubbles, the die-cut sleeve opened out to a 'T' shape and revealed photographs of Hawkwind performing a free concert under the Westway in London's Ladbroke Grove, including some of the local constabulary breaking up proceedings. At the last minute a photograph of Dik Mik had been incorporated in the cover, due to his rejoining the band immediately prior to release. Most significantly, the album also contained a 24-page book, The Hawkwind Log, written by Nik Turner's poet friend Robert Calvert who was soon to join the band in time for their next album, 'Space Ritual.'

Another new recruit was statuesque dancer Stacia Blake, whose penchant for removing all of her clothing while on stage reinforced Hawkwind's notoriety. Soon after the release of 'In Search of Space', Terry Ollis and Dave Anderson would be replaced by drummer Simon King and bass guitarist Ian 'Lemmy' Kilmister. 'In Search Of Space' was the band's first major musical statement and would be the launch-pad for the spaceship to blast off on a journey of cosmic greatness and infamy.

Whatever Turned Me On

A LOOK AT PAST INFLUENCES

HAWKWIND'S Dave Brock

VELVET UNDERGROUND I thought their first and second albums were particularly good. I like the band's basic simplicity. They almost stick to three chords — almost like us. Also, it's a very acid sort of music.

STEVE MILLER "Sailor": I liked this for the same reasons. When it came out I was hanging round the Gate, and it brings back memories. Again it's fairly simply structured music — '67 music, really, good old psychedelia which has just progressed a bit maybe. I think that all the Miller albums I've heard — up to number five — are really good.

THE WHO "Who's Next": This was really the first one of theirs that I liked. They use major chords in such a majestic way, and on this one they started to get into electronics. It's an inspiring album.

KRAFTWORK (a German band): I guess I'm more into music than lyrics. There's an album by this band that I particularly dig, because they've really got into electronic music. I think the album is about a year and a half old now, but along with Can they're pro-

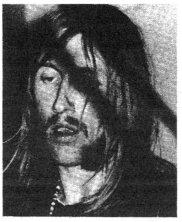

bably my favourite German band. They use electronics in the right way. Like, a lot of electronic records are f—— rubbish because things aren't in their right context. Like I thought the Pierre Henri/Spooky Tooth album was diabolical because it was just two tapes put on top of each other.

Kraftwork are doing things I'd like to see Hawkwind get into. At the moment we seem to be more of a rock band than anything. But I'd like to move more into electronics.

HERBIE HANCOCK "Crossings": This is one of the newer things I really dig.

It's hard to classify — I suppose a combination of electronics and avant garde jazz. Also, synthesizers are for once used to good effect.

SCRAPPER BLACKWELL, LEROY CARR, JELLY ROLL MORTON: I like a lot of the old blues things — I used to have a huge collection, of New Orleans stuff especially. Morton in particular was incredible . . . some of his chords were incredible. He was quite a revolutionary for his time.

I had to sell my whole blues collection at a time when I was hard up. I'd like to get some of those records back.

MOODY BLUES "Threshold Of A Dream": This meant a lot to me. I think the Moody Blues have gone off a bit now, but at one time you could be sure that their albums would be very good. I dig this one because I used to hear it while going round to people's houses and getting stoned, and once again it brings back memories. Actually I think that has a lot to do with why you like certain records because all the time you're changing, and it's nice to hear things that bring back certain experiences.

Meet the Band No 5

HAWKWIND (l to r) DIKMIK (electronics), TERRY OLLIS (drums), DAVE ANDERSON (bass), NICK TURNER (sax) and DAVE BROCK (guitar).

HAWKWIND – music more important than money

WITH one LP to their credit and a steadily increasing number of bookings each week, Hawkwind would seem to be doing quite well. But their general disregard for any kind of financial reward and a determination to avoid the hussling of the record industry means that they are often short of cash. It is on these occasions that singer, guitarist and composer Dave Brock is likely to be found busking in London's Portabello Road market.

But this breadline existence has not yet deflated their ideals or changed the groups direction. They play a continuous form of electronic music while socially they follow a life style similar to America's Grateful Dead or the German community band Amon Duul.

Wherever they play they bring along large numbers of friends, charge minimal prices for gigs and have probably played for free more times than any group in Britain.

Recent ventures have included almost spontaneous sets in the camping sites at the Isle of Wight and Bath festivals.

Basically they want to give their audiences something extra, adding new dimensions to live performances.

"We've played with so many groups who get payed phenomenal amounts of money but just play six numbers and go home that we want to try and give the audiences something more," explained easy-going Dave Brock.

"If we had a little more money I would like to turn the whole act into a kind of circus with a complete light show where we could give away papers and fruit, things like that.

"For instance if a monotonous sound like chanting goes on long enough it can really dull people's minds. It's all very interesting," he remarked.

"Originally we just wanted to freak people out but now we're just interested in sound. Very few people seem to realise what can be done.

"As it is we try to create an environment where people can lose their inhibitions. Sometimes it works, sometimes it doesn't.

"We also want to keep clear of the music business as much as possible. We want to just play for the people. It's like a ship that has to steer round rocks, we have to steer round the industry.

"But I'd like the group to go on Top Of The Pops. I mean, it's so ridiculous we could just go on and turn it into a party. Get everybody to join in and just never stop. They'd never be able to get us off."
— JAMES JOHNSON.

...and upheavals occur in Steamhammer Hawkwind

STEAMHAMMER's vocalist and guitarist Kieran White has left the group at the end of its first British tour with If. The split is described as amicable, and is due to the outfit developing into more complex musical forms, while White wants to concentrate on simple folk-based music. Martin Quitterton, who wrote "Maggie May" with Rod Stewart, is temporarily joining the band while it puts the finishing touches to its new album, but Steamhammer is now searching for a permanent fourth member.

Bass guitarist Dave Anderson has left Hawkwind due to a difference of musical outlook. He had been with the band for eight months, and is now forming a group named Amon Din in which he will be joined by Hugh Lloyd Langdon (who played on Hawkwind's first album) and ex-Jody Grind drummer John Lingwood. Hawkwind's new album "In Search Of Space" is issued by United Artists on October 8.

Hawkwind loss

HAWKWIND, who recently had a hit album with In Search Of Space, may have to disband as a direct result of the theft of their van and equipment.

The white Transit van and equipment, valued at a total of £10,000, were stolen from Russell Road, Palmers Green, London this week. There is a £500 reward for information leading to the recovery of the equipment, which is impossible to dispose of in its present state, as it is elaborately painted and stencilled with the group's name.

Already, the band has had to cancel a tour of Northern Ireland trouble spots as well as a number of capacity dates in Britain, and the only gig they can honour is the Bickershaw Festival on May 5, where they can use the Festival's system.

It is estimated that the group has donated about £4,000 to charity this year. They have supported a number of charities and political organisations, including Release, CND, and The Friends Of The Earth.

RM's clairvoyant staff peep into the crystal ball and predict 1972 stardom for some recent — and not so recent — arrivals on the scene

James Craig picks HAWKWIND

FOR me, the group to make it in 1972 must be Hawkwind. An ethereal search for cosmic consciousness — that is one way of putting where they're at. The medium of sci-fi musical projection being the message — that's another.

Their roots are in what the overground used to call the underground, but their common ideal based on a commune concept has been finding snowballing acceptance on the campus circuit. And it's about to break even bigger.

In some ways, they're just a band of roadies. Certainly toting gear has been a background common to saxman Nick Turner; to DikMik, who plays synthesizer; and Del Dettmar, who plays oscillators. And guitarist-singer Dave Brock, drummer Terry Olliss and bassist Lenny complete the present line-up.

My view is that without detracting from their individuality, Hawkwind's musical identity uses space and time as the backdrop for their odyssey.

What's more, they are unorthodox to the point of being unique. And the scope of their developments at musical level is free from pre-conceptions. Since their heads have already seen the turn of the next century, 1972 to them is just another year in the present past. Get the idea?

But for the rest of us, I reckon Hawkwind could well be the shape and sound of things to come.

PINK FAIRIES 'Never Never Land'

First released as Polydor 2383 045 in June 1971
Highest UK chart position: N/A
Currently available on CD as Polydor 589 550-2

Do It
Heavenly Man
Say You Love Me
War Girl
Never Never Land
Track One, Side Two
Thor
Teenage Rebel
Uncle Harry's Last Freakout
The Dream Is Just Beginning

Russell Hunter	**Drums**
Paul Rudolph	**Guitar, Vocals**
Duncan Sanderson	**Bass guitar, Vocals**
Twink	**Drums, Vocals**

Recorded at Command Studios, London
Produced by Pink Fairies, helped by Neil Slaven
Engineered by Andy Hendriksen and Gary Lyons

Rock history suggests that the concept of anarchic, loud protest music began around 1976 with the advent of the punk movement and the birth of acts such as the Sex Pistols and the Damned. However, it can strongly be argued that a band with its roots in London's Ladbroke Grove and the hippie counterculture of the late Sixties were godfathers to the generation of spiky hair, bondage trousers and anarchy signs.

Whatever attitude the punks had, the Pink Fairies had it years before, their loud political and social statements making up for whatever the band lacked in musical virtuosity and influencing a new generation of musical anarchists. Signing to Polydor in 1971, the Fairies released three seminal albums for the label. 'Never Never Land', 'What A Bunch Of Sweeties' and 'Kings Of Oblivion' were all heralded at the time by the underground press as milestones and are now regarded as classics of their genre. The roots of the Pink Fairies can be found in the Deviants, another legendary British underground act formed in late 1966 as the non-recording group the Social Deviants. Fronted by vocalist and self-appointed spokesman of the emerging counterculture Mick Farren, they featured a revolving line-up including bass-player Pete Munro and guitarist Clive Maldoon. Inspired by the recordings of the New York bohemian group the Fugs, the Social Deviants were poles apart from the laid-back hippy ethos, appealing to an audience of speedfreaks, drinkers and anarchists.

Drummer Russell Hunter soon joined the group who, within months, had become known as the Deviants and secured appearances at the legendary underground clubs UFO and Middle Earth. Farren's friendship with Barry Miles, founder of the underground paper International Times and John Dunbar, owner of the Indica bookshop, meant the Deviants were soon known in the select circle of London's counterculture elite. Through Barry Miles, Mick Farren was introduced to Nigel Samuel, 21 year-old nephew of Lord Goodman, a peer who owned significant property interests in London and had enthusiastically embraced all aspects of London's underground scene. The young heir agreed to invest £700 of his own money to allow the group to record their first album. Following two concerts in Holland, Pete Munro and Clive Maldoon departed the fold to be replaced by guitarist Sid Bishop and bass guitarist Cord Rees. It was this line-up that entered IBC Studios to commit the musical anarchy of the Deviants to tape. Mick Farren later commented; 'It was 1967, and all things seemed possible, we wanted the world and we wanted it now. Vietnam was getting ugly and LSD-25 was hitting the headlines.'

The influence of the Fugs and Frank Zappa and the Mothers of Invention was apparent, the finished album sounding like nothing ever attempted by any British rock band. The music was a radical departure from much of popular music and such a statement of the stance of the underground movement that the decision was made to press copies of 'Ptooff!' independently and sell the album through advertisements in International Times and fellow underground publication Oz.

Rees was replaced on bass guitar by Duncan Sanderson, a friend of Farren's who had made a vocal contribution to 'Ptooff!' The band evolved from being mainly a vehicle for Mick Farren's ideas to one of a collective creative. Newly established

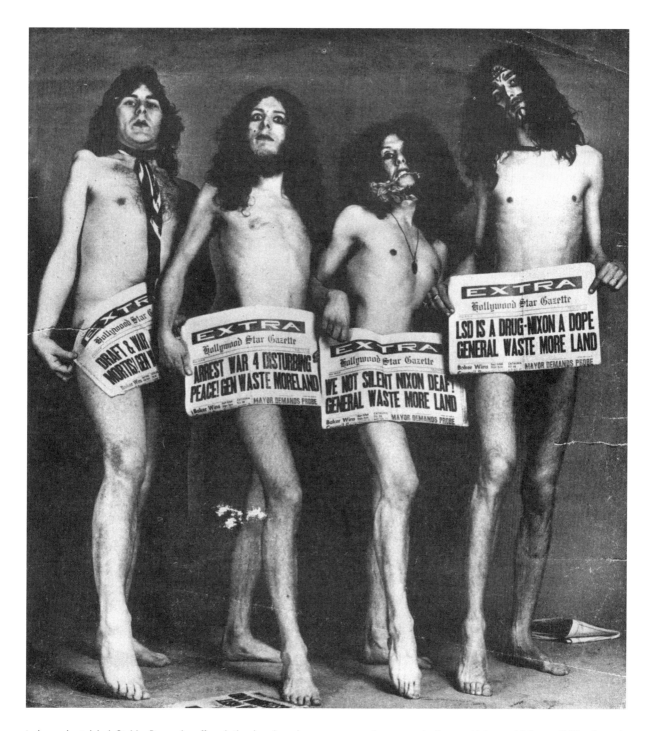

independent label Stable Records offered the band a chance to record a second album which would be available through conventional distribution rather than mail order only. 'Disposable' was more accomplished than 'Ptooff!' and gained much coverage in the UK underground press.

Stable Records then closed and guitarist Sid Bishop was replaced by Paul Rudolph, a guitarist friend of Canadian manager Jamie Mandelkau who would soon influence the direction of the band. As Mick Farren would later reflect, 'I had one idea and the rest of them wanted to be a Led Zeppelin-type guitar band.' Reaction to the new incarnation was favourable enough for Transatlantic Records to sign the group in the spring of 1969. After completing their third album the band performed at the Hyde Park Free Festival in July on a bill headlined by the Rolling Stones and featuring King Crimson. This would prove to be their final British concert.

Rudolph and Farren teamed up with notorious underground musician Twink to record a solo album for Seymour Stein's Sire label in the US. John 'Twink' Alder had previously played drums with psychedelic outfit Tomorrow (with Steve Howe, Keith West and John 'Junior' Wood) and the Pretty Things, performing on some tracks on their legendary 'SF Sorrow'. By the spring of 1969 Twink had been fired and had embarked on a solo career.

The resulting 'Think Pink' album featured many members of the Deviants entourage, such as Farren, Rudolph and roadie Dave 'Boss' Goodman plus John Povey and Wally Allen of the Pretty Things, Junior Wood, Steve Peregrin Took (of Tyrannosaurus Rex) and original Pretty Things drummer Vivian Prince. Also credited were 'Pink Fairies Motorcycle Club And All Star Rock And Roll Band', a loose collection of reprobates later described by Farren as a 'drinking club' that centred on the Speakeasy, a favourite haunt of late-Sixties musicians. The moniker was adopted by Farren, who had taken the name from a short story written by Jamie Mandelkau about his musician friends.

An invitation by a promoter in Vancouver, Canada led to the Deviants flying to the city to perform a series of shows, but when the promised work wasn't forthcoming Farren, already unhappy with the musical direction, returned to Britain. Reduced to a trio of Rudolph, Sanderson and Hunter, the Deviants secured some concerts in Seattle and finally travelled to San Francisco where they stayed in a squat in Haight Ashbury and performed at the Matrix Club.

Back in England, Farren had begun to perform with Twink and Steve Peregrin Took (who had by now left Tyrannosaurus Rex), and this loose trio adopted the moniker Pink Fairies for live work. But Farren decided to quit music to concentrate on writing, leaving Twink to call Messrs Hunter, Rudolph and Sanderson back to London and form a new Pink Fairies. The concept of two drummers was more by accident than design.

The first official Pink Fairies concert took place at the Roundhouse in London's Chalk Farm in the spring of 1970. The band soon became a regular fixture on bills with other leading underground acts of the day such as Hawkwind and the Edgar Broughton Band. The early sets comprised material such as Twink's '10,000 Words In A Cardboard Box' and cover versions such as Jefferson Airplane's '3/5 Of A Mile In Ten Seconds.'

That summer the Fairies performed at both the Isle of Wight and Bath festivals. Their appearance at both events, on the back of a flat-bed truck complete with a PA system powered by a generator, was a protest against ticket prices being charged. The Isle of Wight 'protest' gig also featured Hawkwind and gained some press coverage when Jimi Hendrix (performing his last UK show at the event), came to check out the music of both bands.

When Hawkwind signed to United Artists in 1970 Jamie Mandelkau, now in the role of manager, began touting the Pink Fairies around various record labels. After aborted discussions with Island, a deal was finally struck with Polydor. Prior to recording, Polydor licensed Twink's 'Think Pink' (the album which indirectly gave birth to the band) from Sire, releasing it in October 1970 as an introduction to their new signings.

A further tour of the Top Rank ballroom circuit and praise in the pages of Frendz, IT and Oz preceded the first Pink Fairies session for Polydor at Recorded Sound Studios in December 1970 to record a single. 'The Snake' evolved from a powerful Paul Randolph guitar riff and was chosen as the A-side of the release. The single's B-side, the infamous Twink composition, 'Do It! was inspired by Yippie radical Jerry Rubin's book of the same name, and became a concert anthem. The single was released in January 1971 (housed in a paper poster sleeve), an accompanying promotional film being shot at Shepperton Film Studios on the set of Carol Reed's film Oliver!.

Recording sessions for the Pink Fairies debut album began at Command Studios on 1 March 1971, producer Neil Slaven drafted in to supervise. Among the first songs attempted was 'Uncle Harry's Last Freakout', a jam based on a Rudolph guitar riff. Recording sessions continued for three weeks, during which time Pink Fairies had recorded some of the finest rock music committed to vinyl by a British band in the early Seventies. Highlight's included the trippy 'Heavenly Man' and 'War Girl' (proof that Pink Fairies could be subtle), a longer version of 'Do It!', 'Uncle Harry's Last Freakout', the aptly named 'Side Two, Track One' and 'Teenage Rebel.'

Released in June 1971 under the title 'Never Never Land', the first hundred pressings of the album were manufactured in pink vinyl, the printed inner sleeve depicting the band and roadie 'Boss' Goldman in Kew Gardens and its gatefold outer sleeve housed in a clear plastic cover. 'It was warmly received by an enthusiastic audience, the only criticism being that the band 'weren't loud enough' on record when compared to concert appearances!

Alas, the rare spirit of unity wasn't to last. Changes to the line-up would lead to the departure of Twink, the occasional appearance of ex-Move member Trevor Burton and several more line-up changes over the ensuing three years. Although the Pink Fairies would record two further excellent albums for Polydor, it is their debut that created a tremendous impact and would arguably pave the way for the new wave movement of the latter part of the decade, musicians such as Captain Sensible of the Damned being self-declared fans. 'Never Never Land' remains an essential part of the history of British underground rock music of the Seventies.

TANGERINE DREAM 'Alpha Centauri'

First released as Ohr Records OMM 556 012 in April 1971
Highest UK chart position: N/A
Available on CD as Castle Music CMRCD566

Sunrise In The Third System
Fly And Collision Of Comas Sola
Alpha Centauri

Edgar Froese	**Guitar, Bass, Organ, Voice**
Chris Franke	**VCS3 Synthesiser, Percussion, Flute, Zither, Pianoharp**
Steve Schroyder	**Organ, Voice, Electronics**
With	
Roland Paulyck:	**Synthesiser**
Udo Dennebourg	**Flute, Other Words**

Produced by Tangerine Dream
Engineered by Dieter Dierks
Recorded at Dierks Studio, Stommeln, Germany

Of the many German electronic groups to find favour with an audience outside their homeland, Tangerine Dream was the most successful and long-lasting. The band pioneered electronic music some time before their contemporaries Kraftwerk, and their earliest material stands as an equal to other mighty German acts such as Can and Amon Düül II.

Tangerine Dream came together in West Berlin in September 1967 as the vision of Edgar Froese, who had been a member of the German beat group the Ones since 1965 and played guitar for the band on live dates in Germany, France and Spain. In 1967, with the birth of psychedelia, Froese steered the Ones in this new direction, releasing the single 'Lady Greengrass' that year. However, a desire to explore new musical directions led to Edgar forming the first line-up of Tangerine Dream some months later. He had met surrealist artist Salvador Dali while in Spain and wanted to take music down a route similar to that in which Dali had taken his art. Influenced by bands such as Pink Floyd, early Tangerine Dream music was based on extended psychedelic improvisations backed by a liquid light show.

By 1969 the line-up of the group had stabilised to include Froese, Klaus Schulze on drums and Conrad Schnitzler on cello, electronics sounds and violin. After a notable performance at the 1969 Essen festival, the trio were taken under the wing of electronic music composer Thomas Kessler and were guided by his influence to head into a more avant-garde direction. Kessler assisted in arranging a recording session at Mixed Media studios in Berlin in October 1969 which produced the band's debut album 'Electronic Meditation.' The tapes came to the attention of Ralf Ulrich Kaiser, a devotee of all things 'cosmic' who was in the throes of launching an underground label, Ohr.

Impressed with what he had heard, Kaiser signed Tangerine Dream and released 'Electronic Meditation' in June 1970. A stunning collage of sound, the album defined the emerging German progressive rock movement and is now regarded as a classic of the Krautrock genre. Following the release of the album both Schnitzler and Schulze departed the band, leaving Froese to assemble a new line-up of Tangerine Dream with Chris Franke and Steve Schroyder.

Now almost entirely keyboard-based, the group developed an unique sound based on the use of synthesisers and the Farfisa organ. This different musical approach was captured on tape during sessions for Tangerine Dream's second album at Dieter Dierks' studio in Stommeln in January 1971. 'Sunrise In The Third System' set the cosmic atmosphere, with its building introduction of Farfisa organ and guitar building up to a crescendo of sound. This led into one of two lengthy tracks on the album, 'Fly And Collision Of Comas Sola', which was introduced by synthesiser noises before giving way to a musical sequence featuring flute by guest musician Udo Dennebourg. The real masterpiece was the 22-minute 'Alpha Centauri', named after a star, which featured all the hallmarks that made Tangerine Dream of this era a great band. A cosmic piece in the true sense of the word, Dennebourg's flute and electronically treated voice added to the sense of menace.

'Alpha Centauri' was released in Germany in March 1971. In Britain, DJ John Peel soon began to promote the band on his influential radio show and the album sold in healthy quantities as an imported title, particularly via an enlightened record mail order retailer by the name of Caroline Records, established by publisher of Student magazine, Richard Branson. Within three years Branson would establish Virgin Records and make Tangerine Dream one of his early signings. Beginning with 'Phaedra', Tangerine Dream would enjoy considerable chart success in Britain and Europe and make a significant breakthrough into the US market. Unreleased in Britain until a belated issue appeared on Polydor in 1975, 'Alpha Centauri' is one of Tangerine Dream's earliest masterworks and is a fine statement of their pioneering greatness.

Tangerine Dream

VAN DER GRAAF GENERATOR 'Pawn Hearts'

First released as Charisma CAS1051 in October 1971
Highest UK chart position: N/A
Available on CD as Virgin/Charisma CASCDR1051

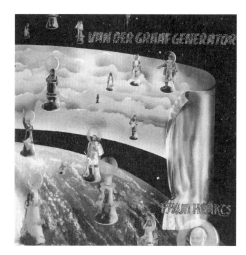

Lemmings (including Cog)
Man Erg
A Plague Of Lighthouse Keepers
a. Eyewitness
b. Pictures/Lighthouse
c. Eyewitness
d. SHM
e. Presence of the Night
f. Kosmos Tours
g. (Custard's) Last Stand
h. The Clot Thickens
i. Land's End (Sineline)
j. We Go Now

Peter Hammill	**Lead Vocals, Acoustic and Slide Guitar, Electric Piano, Piano**
Hugh Banton	**Hammond E & C, Farfisa Professional Organs, Piano, Mellotron, ARP Synthesiser, Bass Pedals, Bass Guitar, Psychedelic Razor, Vocals**
David Jackson	**Tenor, Alton and Soprano Saxophones and Devices, Flute, Vocals**
Guy Evans	**Drums, Tympani, Percussion, Piano**
With	
Robert Fripp	**Electric Guitar**

Produced by John Anthony
Engineered by Robin Cable, David Hentschel and Ken Scott
Recorded at Trident studios, London July through September 1971

Van der Graaf Generator was born in the heady atmosphere of Manchester University in the closing months of 1967 by student Peter Hammill and friend Chris Judge Smith had been performing in a blues and jazz based group. 'Judge discovered that I wrote tunes and I discovered that he wrote tunes and as we were getting fed up with playing other people's material we decided to form a band with Nick Pearne, who was an organist.' The trio adopted the Judge Smith-suggested moniker of Van der Graaf Generator, after Robert J Van der Graaf who had invented and named a device for creating static electricity.

This line-up of Hammill, Judge Smith and Pearne survived long enough to record a basic demo tape. 'We managed to acquire a manager in the form of a fellow student, Caleb Bradley who was convinced he could secure us a recording contract,' Hammill would recall.' In 1967 it wasn't clear that anyone could enter music as a full-time occupation. My intention was to complete my degree and then see what transpired but, as music was particularly exciting at that time, I decided to concentrate my energies in that direction.'

The 'recording time' promised by Bradley turned out to be a session recorded at his parents' house on the South Coast of England while they were away on holiday. 'The guitar amplifier I had been promised for the session turned out to be a television set which created such a ferocious buzz that I had to play in the garden to minimise the noise! Somehow Caleb managed to get a copy of the tape to Lou Reizner, head of Mercury Records in London, who saw something in the material and eventually offered a contract. Like any other 19 year-old I was keen to sign any contract that was waved under my nose, particularly without reading it!'

In terms of live performance, the three-piece incarnation of Van der Graaf Generator survived to play just one concert at a university rag ball in February 1968 before, as Hammill later put it, 'being bottled off stage by medical students.' He would add: 'Judge and I then reduced to a duo and we decided that we would seriously try to follow the yellow brick road to fame and fortune. Hugh was the brother of a friend of ours at the university and was the obvious choice for a keyboard player as he was an innovative musician.' Hammill, Smith and Banton spent the summer of 1968 rehearsing and writing before expanding to a five-

WEELEY FESTIVAL OF PROGRESSIVE MUSIC.

5p

piece and, importantly, securing full-time management. 'Hugh had placed an ad in International Times and somehow got to meet Tony Stratton-Smith, who was manager of a band called the Koobas. They had just split up and their bass player Keith Ellis was looking for a new band to play in. Guy Evans followed on drums soon after and Tony began to look after our management.'

Charisma stars for Marquee

CHARISMA is taking over London's famed Marquee Club from Monday to Friday next week, to present several of its top attractions in concert. Set to appear at this venue are Lindisfarne (Monday), Van Der Graaf Generator (Tuesday), Bell'n'Arc and Birth Control (Wednesday), Audience (Thursday) and Genesis (Friday).

Tony Stratton-Smith was a former sportswriter and horseracing enthusiast who had become involved in music management with the Nice and the Bonzo Dog Doo Dah Band. He was to guide the band through what was destined to become a turbulent year before eventually forming his own label, Charisma Records, in part to give Van der Graaf Generator's music the chance to reach a wider audience. In the autumn of 1968 the line-up of Hammill, Smith, Banton, Ellis and Evans recorded a series of aborted demos for Lou Reizner at Mercury before recording a single, 'People You Were Going To' b/w 'Firebrand' which appeared in January 1969 on Tetragrammaton Records in America and on Polydor in the UK. Within days the single had been withdrawn due to legal wrangling with Mercury, to whom Hammill was signed as an individual.

Legal arguments aside, Van der Graaf Generator were now slowly building up a live following thanks to increasing work on the UK university and college circuit which included support slots for such illustrious acts as Pink Floyd and the Moody Blues. Despite this, the band split up after an appearance at the Pop and Blues Festival in Nottingham on 10 May 1969.

'The reasons were many,' recalled Hammill. 'Essentially we didn't have any money, our equipment had been stolen along with our van in London and I had signed to Mercury as a solo act but my contract was so bad that the other members refused to sign it. Mercury refused to release me from my agreement with them and so Van der Graaf fell apart. We got the traditional "band get stuffed by music biz" thing over with within months of forming!'

After undertaking two solo support slots in shows at London's Lyceum in July 1969, Peter Hammill entered Trident Studios to record as a solo artist, engaging the assistance of Hugh Banton, Guy Evans and Keith Ellis as backing musicians for sessions that would result in the first Van der Graaf Generator album, 'Aerosol Grey Machine.' 'I had recorded the album using the members of Van der Graaf as musicians, but it was scheduled to come out under my name,' remembered Hammill. 'Tony Stratton-Smith did a deal whereby, if Mercury released the record under the name Van der Graaf Generator, they would release me from the awful deal I had signed.'

Due to various quirks of fate, the album appeared in September 1969 only in the US, although test pressings were made in the UK with a different sleeve. 'We then reformed at that point, but within a few weeks Keith Ellis decided to leave, Nic Potter replaced him and David Jackson joined too.'

With the recruitment of Potter and Jackson, Van der Graaf Generator were now a musical force to be reckoned with. In David Jackson they had a striking musician whose ability to play two saxophones at once would make a huge impact. A series of concerts at the London Lyceum and an appearance at Friars in Aylesbury led to an increased confidence. Tony Stratton-Smith's belief in Van der Graaf Generator was undiminished throughout the turmoil of their first year of existence. His frustration at failing to secure a more lucrative recording contract for the band resulted in him taking the bold step of forming Charisma Records as the answer. 'We were the first act to sign to Charisma and in a way were the reason for the label starting, mainly due to the fact that Tony couldn't interest any other label in signing us!' Hammill later reflected.

Wasting no time, Van der Graaf entered Trident Studios, then one of London's best recording facilities, on 11 December 11 1969 to record a second album. With John Anthony acting as producer once more, the ensuing four days would result in 'The Least We Can Do Is Wave To Each Other', a work of remarkable maturity released in February 1970.

In December 1970 the band's second Charisma album, 'H To He Who Am The Only One' was released to further praise and featured some fine moments, with songs from the album becoming staples of the band's live act at that time. January 1971 saw the group embark on a series of UK dates in their own right without Nic Potter, who had left the fold during sessions for 'H to He.' Van der Graaf then joined Genesis and Lindisfarne on the now famous 'Six Bob' Charisma package tour of the UK, conceived by Tony Stratton-Smith as an ideal way to bring three of the leading acts on Charisma to a wider audience by presenting on the same bill. With all tickets being sold for the low price of six shillings, Stratton-Smith correctly assumed that audiences would be tempted to speculatively attend the concerts.

The constant pace of performing had tightened the band's stage act immeasurably, making Van der Graaf Generator an increasingly hard act to follow on stage. Interviewed in Melody Maker at the time, Tony Stratton Smith declared that 'Van der Graaf Generator came of age on the six bob tour' and that the group had 'achieved a new peak of confidence and ability in front of larger audiences.' This experience was tested in Germany in May 1971 when the band participated in the Cosmos Tour with fellow Charisma acts Audience and Jackson Heights. Peter Hammill later reflected that 'We were playing great in Germany, but were going down crap. The audiences just didn't get us at all.' Despite enduring a hard tour, Van der Graaf Generator were firing on all cylinders. In-between soundchecks and travelling on a tour bus, embryonic compositional ideas were born for their next album.

In July 1971 they entered Trident with producer John Anthony once again to begin work on what would be their magnum opus. 'The original idea,' Peter Hammill would later explain, 'was to make a double album that would consist of the tracks that became "Pawn Hearts", but also include three individual instrumental tracks by Guy, Hugh and David. The other idea was to

VAN DER GRAAF
GENERATOR

record a few songs that had been live staples of the show for some time but were now getting a bit long in the tooth. We thought we could show what the live versions of that material had been like and so we recorded "Killer", "Darkness" and "Squid/Octopus" which had been played live as far back as the days when Keith Ellis was in the band. However, ultimately Charisma felt that it wasn't appropriate for us to release a double album and vetoed the live studio recordings and the solo tracks by Guy, David and Hugh.'

Sessions continued at Trident, with days off from live performance being dedicated to recording. Of the material that would appear over the coming months, 'Man-Erg' had been performed for the preceding few months on stage, but other compositions that began as embryonic ideas came to life in the studio. The superb 'Lemmings (including Cog)' was another song to be completed during this time. 'In those days we recorded over a long calendar period, but the actual sessions weren't long. We were on tight budgets and…would be allowed six hours in the middle of the night to record!'

An ambitious epic composition conceived by Hammill proved to be the most challenging of all the pieces recorded. 'All the parts of what became "A Plague Of Lighthouse Keepers" were conceived before we entered the studio,' Hammill would later comment. 'I have to say that these parts needed a great deal of writing manipulation and linking by the others in the group. It was recorded in small parts and we didn't know how the piece would turn out until we got down to mixing it. John Anthony later reflected that we pushed the facilities to the limit and had involved the use of every single tape machine in Trident at some stage!' David Jackson saw 'Lighthouse Keepers' as 'one of our crowning achievements. I recall that I wrote the "We Go Now", which I think was the spur of the piece. Peter wrote the lyrics and Hugh helped me sort out the harmonic progressions. The track was recorded in separate parts in the studio and we hadn't figured out how we would string the whole thing together; John Anthony came into his own as an engineer at that point. We were constantly asking, "Is this possible?" and seeking to achieve new sounds. 'John loved creating that piece with us in the studio. At one point we actually recorded a different Van der Graaf tune in mono on each separate track of the 16-track tape until we'd achieved the effect of having 16 different Van der Graaf Generators playing simultaneously. When we heard it played back it just sounded like total chaos, unsurprisingly. After all that effort we only used a small section of the cacophony near the line "maelstrom of my memory" and it hardly seemed worthwhile. But it shows how keen we were to push boundaries and experiment, even if we sometimes failed to achieve what we had hoped for!'

The final results of all this editing and complex mixing were nothing short of stunning and 'A Plague Of Lighthouse Keepers' is rightly cited as one of the band's most fully realised works, both musically and technically.

The album 'Pawn Hearts' appeared in October 1971, adorned in a striking sleeve designed by Paul Whitehead, but despite its quality failed to register on the UK charts. 'I think every Van der Graaf album was a crowning achievement.' Peter Hammill later reflected, 'because each one was produced, written and recorded to the best of our ability at that particular time. But "Pawn Hearts", although a fairly extreme musical statement, contains some of our most cohesive work.'

The reception in the UK music press was mixed. Melody Maker remained enthusiastic, but a reviewer in Record Mirror commented 'I have to confess complete ignorance of precisely what Van der Graaf Generator are trying to achieve.' The band continued a relentless and punishing schedule of live concerts throughout England which continued until December 1971. The new year began with news that 'Pawn Hearts' was enjoying remarkable success in Italy, eventually reaching the Number 1 spot.

An Italian tour was hastily arranged for February 1972 and the single 'Theme One' b/w 'W' was released throughout Europe to coincide with these dates. The first Italian tour was to prove momentous, as Peter Hammill later commented. 'The promotion of the new album and our concerts in Italy was excellent. By then we were at the top of our game when it came to playing live. In the early Seventies Italy was going through many changes and a whole new country was emerging. We had been adopted by some people in the country as being part of this new social movement.'

'From the minute we arrived at Rimini airport it went mad,' David Jackson would also reflect. 'There were all these people there to greet us as if we were superstars. Our promoter there had hyped the whole thing so much that we had to have the army at gigs with tear gas to keep the crowds in order! The Italians had a real passion for our music. We played bigger and bigger gigs which inevitably went to our heads when we were there. It was most bizarre to have crowds chanting "Jackson, Jackson" when you were on stage. But we worked our bollocks off on that tour!'

The ensuing four months would see the band tour Holland, Germany and Switzerland and make two further visits to Italy. By now the strain of this workload was beginning to have serious repercussions. 'By the end of the Italian tour in August '72 we were all going slightly mad with the intensity of it all,' Peter Hammill would later comment. 'David went in one vehicle, Guy travelled in the van and Hugh and I travelled in a separate car, it just got too much. Retrospectively, it appears that we were on the verge of a bigger breakthrough, although nobody told us so at the time! Cheques were being signed, but not in our direction and we were completely drained. When I got back to England I told the others that I wanted to embark on solo work and was determined to be more "literary" in my pursuits. I got an old friend, Gordian Troeller involved in my management and I told him that I wasn't prepared to go on the road, although that didn't last too long!'

Despite Peter Hammill pursuing a solo career, the apparent finality of events proved not to be permanent. Within two and a half years Van der Graaf Generator would be back, both wiser and stronger, with another stunning musical statement, 'Godbluff'. Of the first period of the band's existence, however, there is no doubt that 'Pawn Hearts' was the moment of glory.

YES 'The Yes Album'

First released as Atlantic 2400 101 in February 1971
Highest UK chart position: Number 4
Currently available on CD as Rhino 8122-73788-2

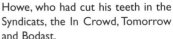

Yours is No Disgrace
The Clap
Starship Trooper
a. Life Seeker
b. Disillusion
c. Wurm
I've Seen All Good People
a. Your Move
b. All Good People
A Venture
Perpetual Change

Jon Anderson	**Vocals, Percussion**
Chris Squire	**Bass Guitar, Vocals**
Steve Howe	**Electric and Acoustic Guitars, Vachalia, Vocals**
Tony Kaye	**Piano, Organ, Moog Synthesiser**
Bill Bruford	**Drums & Percussion**
Colin Goldring	**Recorders on 'Your Move'**

Recorded at Advision studios, London
'The Clap' recorded at the Lyceum Theatre, London in July 1970
Produced by Yes and Eddy Offord
Engineered by Eddy Offord

While acknowledging the intelligent musical stepping stones of their first two albums, 'The Yes Album' was the record on which Yes formalised and cemented an entirely new syntax for rock music, one that methodically honed down a variety of musical constituents into an intelligent, lean sound that owed as much to the impressive individual talents of the members of the band as it did to the group as a whole.

It is perhaps simplistic to view this achievement as the result of a change of personnel, although that was certainly a factor in creating the music on the album. Guitarist Peter Banks, whose deft playing had done so much to formulate their early sonic dynamism of the band, was ousted just before the release of 'Time And A Word' and was replaced by the highly talented Steve Howe, who had cut his teeth in the Syndicats, the In Crowd, Tomorrow and Bodast.

Entering Advision studios in the autumn of 1970, Yes would co-produce their third album with engineer Eddy Offord, with whom they had worked since the recording of their eponymous debut album. Offord's input in a production role was to contribute much to the increased sophistication of Yes' studio sound. The sessions followed a period of writing in the rural retreat of a farmhouse in Devon. Of the music

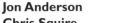

YES (l to r) STEVE HOWE, TONY KAYE, CHRIS SQUIRE, JON ANDERSON and BILL BRUFORD.

written for the album, two extended compositions dominated proceedings, with a series of shorter tracks sandwiched in-between the longer works.

'Yours Is No Disgrace' was an epic 10-minute opener, the most ambitious piece Yes had attempted to date and a tour de force of individual movements in which each musician showcased their talents. Opening with Steve Howe's jagged, unmistakable riff and continuing with Kaye's languid, warm organ tones and Squire's punching bassline, the track reached a crescendo with Anderson's fine acappella vocal. The song was also clear evidence of the democratic studio approach that underlined the 'individuals in a group' ethos that became the band's trademark.

Steve Howe's solo

YES PLEASE

YES guitarist Steve Howe: " We discuss every single mistake we make."

THE EXTENSIVE British tour which Yes have just completed must leave the band well pleased. Not only have they filled halls up and down the country but the reaction they've been getting has been giving an added boost to their egos. '71 must certainly go down as their year, and who knows, '72 might be better as Yes are constantly improving.

Two years ago, if I'm honest with myself, I wouldn't have gone out the back door to have seen this group. On the only occasion I'd seen them they'd struck me as just noisy. But times change, as do tastes — and after seeing them a few weeks back at Hemel Hempstead, Herts, I've nothing but praise.

Speaking to guitarist Steve Howe is easy because he's a good talker and he knows what he's on about. And even he admits Yes weren't too brilliant at the beginning.

"I don't think its true to say that we're like the saying 'when they are good they are very very good and when they are bad they are . . .' because I think we're a very consistent band. Before I joined I could see the group's potential, because they'd always been strictly musical. But at that time they hadn't enough warmth or emotion in their music. Now I feel there is a united musical feeling."

Bad gigs are rare for Yes — just one sticks out in Steve's mind.

"At one London Lyceum gig we played very badly. It's a baffling place to play — we couldn't get the right sound and we felt bad about it afterwards. If we play badly it's like our own punishment. But it must be difficult for the audience to accept that we had an off night. Normally the things that make a gig

not so good are if the stage is too small and we haven't enough space for the equipment."

Even though you may see a Yes gig and rate them highly, the band may not be satisfied. Steve explained:

"Generally speaking we discuss a gig after we've come off stage. Even the slightest error is brought up — who mised a cue, even feedback. It must be a little strange for the audience— some of them come back stage for autographs, and must be very disillusioned when we're discussing what went wrong.

"I think I'm the least critical about the show. I remember one of the first gigs Rick Wakeman did with us. When we came off stage he was just about to say how well it went, and then he stood open mouthed while we all pulled it to bits.

"Basically I think it's just because we are all perfectionists. Unless everything goes right then we're not happy."

Could Steve clear up the business about their new album being bootlegged?

"Yes, it's very simple really. We were all set to release 'Fragile' to coincide

with the British tour, but Atlantic wanted the album promoted in Britain and America. So if we'd released it here first there might be a danger of bootlegging, or they might be sold at high prices in America as 'imports.' We didn't want that to happen — so now it will be released simultaneously in America and Britain. What we've been doing is playing some of the numbers from the album on this tour — the advertising will come just before release date."

I asked how new member Rick Wakeman was fitting in.

"Oh yes — as I said

before there is a united musical feeling about the group. Although we respected Tony very much he didn't show the versatility Rick does. Rick can sit down and suggest ideas. He's also a nutcase — like Bill. Neither of them does anything by halves. They'd make a perfect Eric Morecambe and Ernie Wise — in fact I can see them doing that when they are about 40!"

Rick joined at a perfect time, really — he plays on the album. And with a group like Yes, needless to say there is no need for any session people to be used on the LP. But apart from the album the uppermost thought in their minds is the forthcoming American tour, which will be the group's second.

"We're playing second on the bill all the time — to people like Ten Years After and Beach Boys. I hope we get some reaction of interest shown over here this time we go. On the last tour no one in Britain realised how well we did.

"We were very disappointed that the press didn't keep track of our progress because at the risk of sounding big-headed we did do very well. Normally groups have to go to America about three times or more before American audiences know and accept them."

It's been a lucky year for the band. As Steve says: "It has definitely been our best yet. It's been a slow step up but we're very pleased it's happened now and not when we first started. The group would have probably fallen apart if we'd made it then. Only now I believe are we musically educated."

By JULIE WEBB

Yes are pleasing the fans and pleasing themselves. 1971 has been a good year — and 1972 should be even better!

contribution, 'The Clap', was inspired by the brilliant solo piece, 'Fingerbuster' by folk guitarist Davy Graham and written by Howe to celebrate his son Dylan's attempts to clap in his pram. A concert favourite, the piece had been recorded at Advision, but this version was later shelved in favour of a live recording made at a concert at the Lyceum Theatre in London on 17 July 1970. 'The Clap' would be a testament to the guitarist's prodigious and seminal style.

The first side of the album ended with 'Starship Trooper', another lengthy composition whose constituent parts of 'Life Seeker', 'Disillusion' and 'Würm' were written by Jon Anderson, Chris Squire and Jon Anderson and Steve Howe respectively, was another indication Yes had risen to a new level of musical excellence. The middle section, 'Disillusion', was directly adapted from an earlier Yes song, 'For Everyone', with Chris Squire singing the lead vocal. 'Würm' had also evolved from an early song called 'Nether Street' originally performed by Howe's earlier band Bodast. A continuous cadenza of chords played by electric guitar, then acoustic guitar, bass pedals, and drums, then organ and bass guitar climaxing with a guitar solo, it was a stunning climax to a fine new work.

The second side began with another lengthy epic, the superb 'I've Seen `All Good People' a two-part work that became a concert staple. The first part of the piece, 'Your Move', alluded to a game of chess, laced with Anderson's spiritual metaphors, while the closing section of 'All Good People' offered some vocal harmonies from Anderson and Squire. Following the short Anderson song 'A Venture', the album closed with the excellent 'Perpetual Change', showcasing the superb percussive skills of Bill Bruford.

Throughout the sessions, engineer Eddy Offord's painstaking and exacting work behind the mixing desk, using a new 16-track tape machine to cut and graft various individually recorded short segments into a cohesive whole, was also a significant part of the success of the record. He also had the sense not to interfere too much with the creative process from a production point of view, allowing the band members to find their own direction.

Few albums define and capture their moment in time, but 'The Yes Album' is unquestionably one of them. Unique, melodic, contrapuntal, absurd and in places staggeringly beautiful, the album possessed a sense of richness and depth that bears repeated listening and gave the music a timeless quality.

Released in February 1971 'The Yes Album' was the start of the second stage of Yes' career, climbing to Number 4 on the UK album listings and reaching Number 40 on the US Billboard chart upon its release a month later. Within six months Tony Kaye would move aside to make way for Rick Wakeman, whose professionalism moved them inexorably towards a more grandiose style. However, 'The Yes Album', a work that straddled the innocence of their early years and the virtuosity of their next two records, arguably remains the band's most dynamic and accessible work.

(with thanks to Jon Wright)

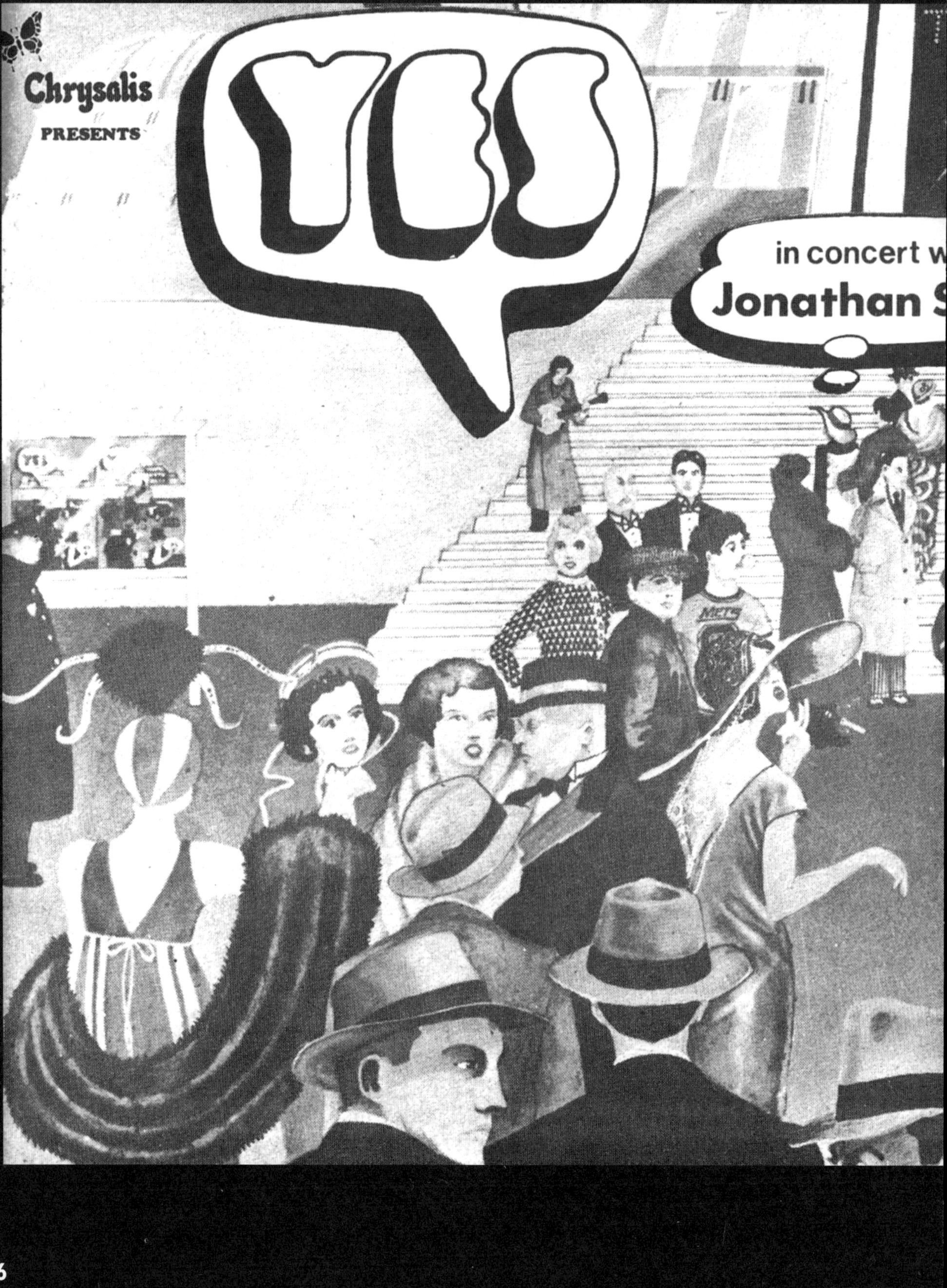
Chrysalis
PRESENTS
YES
in concert w
Jonathan S
YES

September 30th De Montford Hall LEICESTER

October Dates:

1st Free Trade Hall MANCHESTER
2nd St George's Hall BRADFORD
3rd Pavilion HEMEL HEMPSTEAD
4th Music Hall ABERDEEN
6th Greens Playhouse GLASGOW
8th Royal Festival Hall LONDON
9th Empire Theatre EDINBURGH
10th Caird Hall DUNDEE
11th Civic Hall WOLVERHAMPTON
12th Colston Hall BRISTOL

13th City Hall SHEFFIELD
15th A.B.C STOCKTON
16th City Hall NEWCASTLE
17th Trentham Gardens STOKE
18th Town Hall BIRMINGHAM
21st University WARWICK
22nd University LEEDS
25th Central Hall CHATHAM
26th Stadium LIVERPOOL
28th Guild Hall SOUTHAMPTON

TOP 30 LPs

(Week ending Wednesday, 11th August, 1971)

4	1	EVERY GOOD BOY DESERVES FAVOUR Moody Blues (Threshold)	3	1
1	2	BRIDGE OVER TROUBLED WATER....Simon & Garfunkel (CBS)	79	1
7	3	BLUE ....Joni Mitchell (Reprise)	4	3
2	4	RAM ....Paul McCartney (Apple)	12	1
3	5	MOTOWN CHARTBUSTERS VOL. 5 ....(Tamla Motown)	19	1
5	6	STICKY FINGERS......Rolling Stones (Rolling Stones Records)	16	1
8	7	TARKUS ....Emerson, Lake & Palmer (Island)	10	3
9	8	MUD SLIDE SLIM ....James Taylor (Warner Bros.)	12	5
11	9	EVERY PICTURE TELLS A STORY ....Rod Stewart (Philips)	4	9
10	10	LOVE STORY ....Andy Williams (CBS)	3	10
●	11	TAPESTRY ....Carole King (A & M)	2	11
●	12	HOT HITS SIX ....Various Artistes (M.F.P.)	1	12
●	13	STEPHEN STILLS 2 ....Stephen Stills (Atlantic)	1	13
●	14	MASTER OF REALITY ....Black Sabbath (Vertigo)	1	14
20	15	AFTER THE GOLD RUSH ....Neil Young (Reprise)	30	7
19	16	JIM REEVES GOLDEN RECORDS ....(RCA)	2	16
24	17	THE YES ALBUM ....Yes (Atlantic)	24	6
13	18	SWEET BABY JAMES ....James Taylor (Warner Bros.)	33	5
29	19	LED ZEPPELIN II ....(Atlantic)	91	1
●	20	HOME LOVIN' MAN ....Andy Williams (CBS)	22	1
12	21	LOVE LETTERS FROM ELVIS ....(RCA)	4	11
23	22	L.A. WOMAN ....Doors (Elecktra)	3	22
●	23	B, S. & T; 4 ....Blood, Sweat & Tears (CBS)	1	23
26	24	RELICS ....Pink Floyd (Starline)	11	16
16	25	SPLIT ....Groundhogs (Liberty)	17	5
15	26	MAGNIFICENT SEVEN Supremes & Four Tops (Tamla Motown)	9	8
17	27	ANDY WILLIAMS' GREATEST HITS ....(CBS)	65	1
21	28	C'MON EVERYBODY......................Elvis Presley (RCA)	2	21
22	29	PAINT YOUR WAGON ....Soundtrack (Paramount)	61	2
28	30	SONGS OF LOVE & HATE ....Leonard Cohen (CBS)	17	4

NME 14/8/71

'AND THEN THE LAMB OPENED THE FIRST SEAL...'

APHRODITE'S CHILD '666'

First released as Vertigo 6673 001 in June 1972
Available on CD as Vertigo 838 430-2

The System
Babylon
Loud, Loud, Loud
The Four Horsemen
The Lamb
The Seventh Seal
Aegean Sea
Seven Bowls
The Wakening Beast
Lament
The Marching Beast
The Battle of the Locusts
Do It
Tribulation
The Beast
Ofis
Seven Trumpets
Altamont
The Wedding Of The Lamb
The Capture Of The Beast
?Hic Et Nunc
All The Seats Were Occupied
Break

Vangelis Papathanassiou	Organ, Piano, Flute, Percussion, Vibes and Vocal Backing
Demis Roussos	Bass, Vocal Backings, Lead Vocal on 'The Four Horsemen', 'Babylon' and 'Hic et Nunc'
Lucas Sidera:	Drums, Vocal Backings, Lead Vocal on 'The Beast' and 'Break'
Silver Koulouri	Guitars and Percussion

Guests:
Harris Chalkitis	Bass, Tenor Sax, Conga Drums, Backing Vocals
Michel Ripoche:	Trombone, Tenor Sax on 'Babylon' and 'Hic et Nunc'
John Forst	Narration
Yannis Tsarouchi:	Greek Text
Irene Papas	Vocal on '??

Recorded at Europa Sonor Studios, Paris
Arranged and Produced by Vangelis Papathanassiou

Titled after the mythical number linked to the biblical book of Revelations, '666' is one of the most impressive creative achievements of the early Seventies. The double album continues to be a major influence on successive generations of musicians struck by the power of the record's apocalyptic concept juxtaposed with the sheer atmospheric beauty of much of the music.

The album was an early creative masterstroke by Vangelis, a composer who defies stylistic classification, but whose musical vision was, and remains, inspirational. Conceived and recorded at a crossroads in Vangelis' career, the album would prove to be a celebrated swansong for Aphrodite's Child, a band born out of the Greek beat group scene of the early Sixties.

Vangelis (born Evangelos O Papathanassiou) had an early taste of domestic success with the band Forminx, the most popular of the Greek beat groups, while Demis Roussos had come to prominence as vocalist and bass guitarist with the bands the Idols and We Five.

In the autumn of 1967 Vangelis, Roussos, drummer Lucas Sideras and guitarist Anargyros 'Silver' Koulouris came together to record the single 'Plastics Nevermore' b/w 'The Other People' under the moniker the Papathanassiou Set and presented the recordings to Philips Records in Greece. The recordings revealed that the musicians had absorbed a psychedelic influence from artists such as the Beatles, Procol Harum and others, but had retained a distinct Greek influence. Impressed with their work, A&R director Nikos Antipas recommended the band try their luck in England, passing the recordings on to Mercury Records' office in London. By this time Greece had undergone a military coup led by Colonel Papadopoulos, political and artistic freedom becoming severely limited. The chance to explore musical horizons in England appealed strongly to the four musicians and the decision was made to leave Greece.

However, prior to departure 'Silver' Koulouris received his military call-up papers and was forced to undertake national service. The remaining trio undertook the journey to Western Europe without a guitarist but were refused entry to the UK. They headed back to Paris where, upon the resolution of British work-permit problems, they found themselves stranded due to a nationwide transport strike, the first stirrings of the French industrial and student unrest of 1968. Making contact with Pierre Sberro, a senior A&R executive of Philips Records France, the members of the Papathanassiou Set signed to Philips' Mercury label, changing their name to Aphrodite's Child at the suggestion of European label head Lou Reizner, before commencing recording sessions.

The first release by the band was the single 'Rain And Tears' in May 1968, an instant hit throughout Europe. Buoyed by this success, in June 1968 Aphrodite's Child began work on their debut album, 'End Of The World, Rain And Tears.' Released in October 1968, it revealed the slightly schizophrenic musical nature of the band, experimental Mellotron-soaked psychedelic fables juxtaposed with the more obviously commercial title tracks. The album became a hit in France and Italy and by the end of 1968 Aphrodite's Child had become major stars in continental Europe.

1969 was to see even greater success with the release of more hit singles and the album 'It's Five O'Clock' (recorded at Trident Studios in London). As 1970 dawned, signs of Vangelis' growing frustration with the musical direction became apparent. Although he had achieved huge commercial success with the band, he remained unsatisfied creatively, later recounting: 'Right from the start I was only interested in playing my own music, not other people's. When I moved to Paris I worked my way up through the music industry to make enough money to open a studio of my own. We had one million-selling single after another. I hate it when a project I'm involved in, but don't particularly like, becomes

successful. I found myself doing things that I couldn't bear at the time, but I don't have any regrets as they were the means to an end.' This unease was demonstrated by Vangelis' absence on Aphrodite's Child's Italian and Spanish concerts that year, Greek musician Harris Chalkitis deputising on keyboards.

A meeting in Paris between Vangelis and another Greek exile would soon begin a creative journey that would last 18 months. Costas Ferris was one of the most promising young film directors in Greece and a leading light in the new wave of Greek cinema. He had first met Vangelis in 1966 while making a documentary on the band Formynx, but by the beginning of 1968 had relocated to Paris to escape the political climate.

Embracing the emerging counter-culture, Ferris began work on a radical film project that drew upon the social changes in Western Europe following the student uprising in Paris in 1968, the opposition to the war in Vietnam and the growing importance of rock music in the psyche of a generation just finding its collective voice. For such a project Costas Ferris sought a suitable musical collaborator, approaching Vangelis to compose a film score.

While the project failed to attract his interest, Vangelis was impressed enough with Ferris' ideas to ask the director to write a synopsis for a conceptual work which might serve as Aphrodite's Child's final album. The synopsis was inspired by the turbulent social and political climate of the times and involved the staging of a performance of the Apocalypse as related in the book of Revelations by a travelling circus. While the performance was being staged the actual Apocalypse commenced in the world outside, the performance and the genuine battle between good and evil becoming indistinguishable from one another.

Using Ferris' concept as a starting point, Vangelis began work on the music under the working title of 'Apocalypse'. The diversity of musical influences he drew upon was breathtaking, free jazz, rock, the avant garde and ethnic Hellenic music fusing effortlessly to create a unique body of work. Creative tensions between members were put to one side when Vangelis, Roussos and Sideras entered Europa Sonor studios in Paris to commence work on their final album, augmented once more by the presence of guitarist Anargyros 'Silver' Koulouris, who had completed his national service and whose unique style bridging the worlds of Greek and middle-eastern influences and western rock would become a notable feature.

The music recorded at Europa Sonor over the next few months could not have been further removed from any previous work by Aphrodite's Child. Pieces such as the opening chant of 'The System', the poetic 'Loud, Loud, Loud' and the marvellous 'The Four Horsemen' were progressive in the truest sense of the word, while the epic track '??' was a disturbing inversion of a phrase from the book of Revelations. Featuring extensive percussion by Vangelis and an ad-libbed vocal performance by acclaimed Greek actress Irene Papas, this section of the album would prove controversial due to Papas' repetitive, ecstatic and orgasmic cry of 'I am to come, I was.'

Perhaps the most outstanding work on the album was the 19-minute 'All The Seats Were Occupied', a sound collage which

overlaid a remarkably atmospheric instrumental work (enhanced by Vangelis' understated keyboard-playing which gave space for the other instrumentation to shine) with references to the previous music featured on the album before reaching a stunning apocalyptic climax. This intensity gave way to the simplicity and beauty of the album's closing piece, 'Break'.

When presented with final mixes, Mercury Records in France reacted in a less than favourable manner. Taking exception to the incorrectly perceived 'blasphemous' nature of the concept, and in particular Irene Papas' vocals on 'Infinity', Mercury applied considerable pressure for the work to be edited. As a result, the album sat in the vaults for a year while record company and artists refused to move from their respective positions.

The saga of '666' had been such an ongoing struggle that a party was thrown at Europa Sonor studios to mark the first anniversary of the non-appearance of the record, attended by the members of Aphrodite's Child, Costas Ferris, Irene Papas and assorted friends and partners of the musicians. The party was also graced by the notable presence of Salvador Dali. The gathering culminated with a playback of the entire album, following which Dali declared the album to be a work of greatness and suggested the staging of an event to launch the album of truly surrealist proportions which, in true Dali-esque manner, was too impractical to undertake.

Finally, due to overwhelming artistic and critical pressure, '666' appeared in France on the progressive Vertigo label at the end of 1971. The release was staggered across Europe, with the authorities in Spain (then under the rule of General Franco) banning the record. '666' finally secured British release in June 1972, where its influence was immediately felt. An early advocate of the album was Jon Anderson, vocalist with Yes, who hailed the record as one of the most influential albums of the year. (The pair would undertake a series of collaborative projects under the name Jon and Vangelis between 1979 and 1991.)

Vangelis' innovative approach to composition and recording was a world away from that of his fellow band members and by the time the album was released the group had ceased to exist. In 1973 he recorded the equally remarkable 'Earth' which followed on stylistically from '666' and was equally well acclaimed, setting him on the road to international recognition.

Of the other members of Aphrodite's Child, Demis Roussos became an international middle-of-the-road star by the mid Seventies, collaborating once more with Vangelis as of producer on 1977's 'Magic' and 1982's 'Demis.' Roussos would also add a stunningly effective vocal to the track 'Tales Of The Future', part of Vangelis' soundtrack to Ridley Scott's film Blade Runner. Silver Koulouris would collaborate once more with Vangelis 11 years later by playing guitar on the album 'See You Later'.

To state that the album '666' was ahead of its time is an understatement. Put simply, it is a masterpiece and a creative achievement that remains difficult to surpass.

KHAN 'Space Shanty'

First released as Deram SDL-R11 in June 1972
Highest UK chart position: N/A
Available on CD as Esoteric Recordings ECLEC2046

Space Shanty (including The Cobalt Sequence and March Of The Sine Squadrons)
Stranded (Effervescent Psychonovelty No 5)
Mixed Up Man Of The Mountains
Driving To Amsterdam
Stargazers
Hollow Stone (Escape Of The Space Pirates)

Steve Hillage	**Guitars, Vocals**
Nick Greenwood	**Bass, Vocals**
Eric Peachey	**Drums**
With	
Dave Stewart	**Organ, Piano, Skyceleste, Marimbas**

Produced by Neil Slaven for Gruggy Woof
Recorded at Command Studios, London
Engineer Pete Booth
Olympic Studios, Barnes, London
Engineer George Chkiantz
and Decca Studios, Tollington Park, London
Engineers Derek Varnals and Dave Grinstead

Khan was formed in April 1971 by guitarist Steve Hillage, a former student of the University of Kent in Canterbury. Born in London in August 1951, Hillage obtained his first guitar at the age of nine. His earliest influences included jazz genius John Coltrane and the supremely talented Jimi Hendrix, having witnessed one of the first London concerts by the guitar legend.

Hillage's first group, Uriel, formed while he was at his final year at the City of London School with fellow pupils Dave Stewart and Mont Campbell and drummer Clive Brooks (recruited via an ad in Melody Maker). Inspired by artists such as Cream and Hendrix, Uriel played a handful of local gigs with a repertoire consisting entirely of cover versions and a residency at the Ryde Castle Hotel on the Isle of Wight in the summer of 1968 before Hillage departed to attend university in Canterbury studying history and philosophy.

Whilst his former colleagues adopted the new moniker Egg and signed a record deal with Decca Records' new progressive label Nova in mid 1969, Steve Hillage became acquainted with local musicians such as Spirogyra (featuring singer Barbara Gaskin) and Caravan. His studies were interrupted in the summer of 1969 when his ex-Uriel colleagues approached him to play on sessions for an obscure low-budget psychedelic album that would emerge under the pseudonym Arzachel for the Zel label.

Following this distraction, Hillage returned to his studies. In April 1971 he left university and returned to London to form the first incarnation of Khan with Nick Greenwood on bass, Dick Henningham on keyboards and Pip Pyle on drums. Through his association and friendship with the members of Caravan, Hillage signed with their manager Terry King who, in turn, secured a one-off album deal with Decca's Deram label in December 1971. Prior to the commencing of recording sessions, Pyle departed the band to be replaced by Eric Peachey, closely followed by the departure of Henningham. With recording looming, Steve called upon his old friend and colleague Dave Stewart to guest on keyboards. Stewart would add some stunning work to an album of outstanding Hillage compositions.

The sessions took place at Decca's studios in Tollington Park, North London, with producer Neil Slaven supervising. The material committed to tape would be the embryonic blueprint of the space rock Hillage would later explore both in Gong and on his solo albums.

Opening track 'Space Shanty' was a clear indicator of the musical direction he was to take, the trademark delayed guitar solo apparent throughout.

With highlights including 'Driving To Amsterdam', 'Mixed Up Man Of The Mountains' and the wonderfully named 'Hollow Stone (Escape Of The Fire Pirates)', the album was an assured debut. Some years later, producer Neil Slaven would recall: 'The sessions were quite an experience for me. Steve would come into the studio with hand-drawn charts that were intended to convey the atmosphere he wanted to achieve on each song. I remember we had some problems trying to add some psychedelic phasing to the guitar parts on the album.

'As a result of this, the sessions overran and I was faced with another act who were waiting to use the studio. It happened that this act was the Bachelors, a clean-cut genteel Irish act who appealed to a more straight-laced audience. After a while they came into the control room to listen to what we were doing with Hillage's spacey, psychedelic masterpiece. One of them came up to me and said in a soft Irish accent; "Oh, this is great music." "Do you think so?" I replied, thinking he was just being polite and courteous. "Oh, yes," he replied. "We'd love to do this sort of stuff if we could get away with it!"'

In June 1972 Khan promoted the release of the album as support act for Caravan with Canadian Val Stevens on keyboards; Nick Greenwood departed to be replaced by Nigel Griggs while Steven' exit allowed the Dave Stewart to return. Despite new material being rehearsed (much of which would later surface on Hillage's 'Fish Rising' solo debut), Khan only played a handful of concerts before breaking up in October 1972 when Steve became a member of Kevin Ayers' band Decadence for a few months before joining Daevid Allen's Gong in 1973.

Despite the brevity of their career, Khan's sole album remains a classic of cosmic progressive rock.

MAN 'Be Good To Yourself At Least Once A Day'

First released as United Artists UAG29147 in November 1972
Highest UK chart position: N/A
Available on CD as Esoteric Recordings ECLEC2019

C'Mon
Keep On Crinting
Bananas
Life On The Road

Micky Jones	**Guitar, Vocals**
Clive John	**Guitar, Vocals**
Phil Ryan	**Keyboards, Vocals**
Will Youatt	**Bass, Vocals**
Terry Williams	**Drums**

Produced by Man with help from Dave Edmunds
Recorded at Rockfield Studios, Monmouth
Engineered by Kingsley Ward
Mixed at Trident Studios, London
Engineered by Roy Thomas Baker

By the beginning of 1972, the fortunes of the Man band were headed in a decidedly upwards direction after nearly four years of slogging the live circuit, mainly in Europe where their impressive talent had won an appreciative audience. Man had signed to United Artists in the summer of 1970 and now had a record label that understood their needs and gave them the creative room to develop in the direction they wanted.

The album '2 Ozs Of Plastic With A Hole In The Middle', (their last for Pye Records) was one of the first releases on Dawn, Pye's progressive label, in September 1969. Although failing to make an impact in the UK, the album brought Man to a wider audience in Europe, particularly Germany, where the group honed their craft via an intense gigging schedule.

Singer-guitarist Deke Leonard temporarily left immediately prior to the album's release and was replaced by Martin Ace. However, within months Leonard had returned to the fold and Ray Williams and Jeff Jones had been replaced by Ace (now playing bass) and Terry Williams respectively. Man quickly developed the fine art of extended jamming in concert, which began to pay dividends with the increasingly growing underground audience.

By January 1972 Man had two studio albums under their belt for Liberty/United Artists and were at last beginning to make some headway with UK audiences. The album 'Do You Like It Here Now, Are You Settling In?', released in November 1971, was greeted warmly by the music press. Man's popularity would be boosted by a performance on 13 February 1972 at the Greasy Trucker's Party, an event staged at the Roundhouse to benefit an organisation that staged free concerts for community-based causes. Man were the first band to perform on a bill which also featured Brinsley Schwarz and Hawkwind. Taking the stage as a four-piece due to the departure weeks before of keyboardist Clive John, Man gave a stunning 20-minute-plus version of their legendary instrumental 'Spunk Rock' which had originally appeared on their second album under the title 'Spunk Box'.

Man's inclusion on the resulting live album released in April 1972, won them many new admirers in Britain, their on-stage prowess demonstrated still further on the limited edition album 'Live At The Padget Rooms Penarth', recorded that same month. Conceived by Andrew Lauder as a limited-edition budget-priced album to entice new listeners to the talents of Man, the album quickly sold out, even reaching the top of the UK mid-price album chart upon release as United Artists USP100 in September 1972.

By that time, Man had been through yet more line-up changes. Martin Ace had departed to form the Flying Aces with his then wife, George, and Deke Leonard had been dismissed from the band and had begun to pursue a solo career, forming the band Iceberg. Replacements were found in the returning Clive John, now on guitar, and the addition of Phil Ryan (previously with Eyes of Blue, Pete Brown's Piblokto! and Big Sleep) on keyboards and Will Youatt, formerly of Quicksand, on bass. This line-up entered Rockfield Studios in August 1972 to record 'Be Good to Yourself At Least Once A Day'.

The sessions were co-produced by Dave Edmunds and saw the band fit recording time between a strenuous live schedule. Their increasing live popularity had resulted in the group suffering a creative block in terms of writing new material prior to entering the recording studio. As a result, they entered Rockfield with no new compositions and the minimum of new musical ideas. Prior to the sessions, Micky Jones had declared in an interview: 'We still haven't really got to grips with the recording studio. We'd always go in at first with the idea of trying to capture the "live" sound of the band, but I think we've come around to thinking that the two things are entirely different.'

The solution to the problem of finding new material suited to the studio environment appeared to come from the idea of recording a series of jams. 'We all felt we had to deliver a good album and that put quite a bit of pressure on us,' Clive John was later to reflect. 'Eventually we decided to adopt the attitude of forgetting we were making a record, just have an electric blow in the studio and see what might come out of it.'

Thankfully, the idea of recording jam sessions that would in turn give birth to new, lengthy material paid dividends. The instrumental 'Keep On Crinting' was born from such a jam and featured some wonderful synthesiser from Phil Ryan. The classic 'Bananas', a eulogy to the delights of smoking a certain hemp-derived herb, began life in the spring of 1972 at an earlier recording session at Rockfield that had been consigned to the shelf. Now revisited by Micky Jones, the music was reworked and became the epic number that would be a highlight of Man concerts for many years to come. Another classic track was the mighty 'C'Mon', a slice of musical bliss that would continue to undergo an evolution in terms of arrangement on the concert stage long after the version that would appear on their new album had been committed to tape. Finally, 'Life On The Road', with lyrics from Will Youatt (who remained uncredited due to a publishing deal), would serve as a fine testament to the lot of a hard-working musician on tour.

Released in November 1972 in an elaborate gatefold sleeve that folded out still further into a humorous map of Wales, the album narrowly failed to make an impression on the British album charts but was their best-selling release to date. It is now viewed by critics and fans alike as Man's finest hour in the recording studio, paving the way for the commercial success enjoyed by the albums 'Back Into The Future' And 'Rhinos, Winos And Lunatics'. For those who care to investigate further, 'Be Good To Yourself At Least Once A Day' is a true Welsh joy.

Man. Left: Live at The Oval

Above: At Rockfield

NEKTAR 'A Tab in The Ocean'

First released as Bacillus BLPS19118 in October 1972
Highest UK chart position: N/A
Currently unavailable on CD

A Tab In The Ocean
Desolation Valley/Waves
Crying In The Dark
King Of Twilight

Roye Albrighton	**Guitars, Lead Vocals**
Derek 'Mo' Moore	**Bass Guitar, Vocals**
Allan 'Taff' Freeman	**Keyboards, Vocals**
Ron Howden	**Drums, Percussion, Vocals**
Mick Brockett	**Lights**

Recorded at Dierks Studio, Stommeln, Germany
Produced by Peter Hauke and Nektar
Engineered by Dieter Dierks

Of all the British bands to emerge during the so-called progressive rock era of the late Sixties/early Seventies, Nektar were perhaps one of the most unique and followed the most unusual career path. The group would find fame and fortune in Germany, enjoying gold disc status on most of their album releases before even greater success in the US. Although the majority of their albums were released in Britain, Nektar had smaller but loyal following in their homeland. Roye Albrighton (guitar, lead vocals), Allan 'Taff' Freeman (keyboards, vocals), Derek 'Mo' Moore (bass guitar, vocals) and Ron Howden (drums and percussion) had been touring and recording solidly for four years, ably assisted by Mick Brockett's elaborate light show.

Often mistaken as a German band during their career, Nektar began life in Hamburg, Germany in 1969. Its musicians had all shared experiences performing around Europe throughout the Sixties. 'I began my musical career in the Sheffield area with local bands such as the Outlaws and Skyliners,' recalled Ron Howden. 'I then auditioned for a gig with a London-based band, the Rockin' Berries and left England to play on American bases in France. I lived in France for a while and met Mo, who was playing in a band called Judd's Mates and were in the process of changing their drummer. I loved the Chuck Berry style they played, so our bands swapped drummers and off we went.'

In 1967 a chance meeting with organist Taff Freeman in Ludwigsburg led to the formation of a new band, Prophecy. 'Our original guitarist was Colin Edwards,' explained Mo Moore. 'We met Roye Albrighton when we were playing the Star Club in Hamburg. When Colin left to go home, I sent Roye a telegram to join us. He came over, jammed the whole gig and it went down very well. Before that gig we had decided if the show went down badly we would call ourselves "Pollen". If it went down well we would call ourselves "Nektar". And so Nektar it was.'

Albrighton had been in a Coventry-based group when he got an offer to play in the house band for the rock musical Hair in London. After a few months he journeyed to Sweden where he jammed with Jimi Hendrix and Mitch Mitchell and earned a well-deserved reputation. Roye then journeyed to Hamburg, securing work at the Top 10 Club.

It was here that his path crossed with Freeman, Moore and Howden. 'Prophecy were playing down the road in the Star Club, where the Beatles had played. I used to call in there and jam with Ron Howden for something to do during the day. I told Ron that if ever Prophecy needed a guitarist I would like to join. I went back to London and soon got a call from Mo asking me to return to Hamburg. I went back immediately and Nektar was born.'

It was also in Hamburg that Nektar teamed up with lighting technician Mick Brockett, who had previously worked with Pink Floyd. Within months Nektar were known throughout Germany for their stunning live show, the combination of music and lights courtesy of Brockett and his assistant Keith Walters winning over audiences at every turn.

In the early months of 1970 Nektar were seen in Hamburg by American producer Charlie Dreyer, who owned a recording studio in Boston. 'Charlie saw us play at the PN Hit Club in Munich and offered to fly us over to the US to record,' recalled Albrighton. 'We thought he was joking at first, but we soon realised he wasn't. We flew to Boston and recorded some tracks at his studio. We used a Studer eight-track tape machine and the resulting sound was very thin.'

With the experience leading to nothing, Nektar found themselves back in Germany once more and embarked on yet more gigs to build their following. Their persistence paid off in early 1971 when the band came to the attention of producer Peter Hauke, who had established his own progressive label, Bacillus Records. 'Mo first met Peter in 1964 in Germany. We were invited to a battle of the bands which Peter was running for his new label with a record contract as the prize.' As Ron Howden later remembered, Nektar lost the contest 'but got the contract because of the capacity crowds we were pulling at our gigs!'

Hauke signed Nektar immediately prior to Bacillus being incorporated into the German company Bellaphon. Thus Nektar found themselves part of Bellaphon's roster, with Hauke as in-house producer and label manager. For their first album, Nektar had composed a conceptual work which was both outstanding and ambitious. Its concept was an elaborate science-fiction tale which expressed concerns about the nuclear arms race. 'Journey To The Centre Of The Eye' was recorded in August 1971 and released as Bacillus BLPS19049 in the first few months of 1972.

'We recorded "Journey" with Dieter Dierks, who owned his own eight-track studio in Stommeln. Although he was credited as producer on the album sleeve, Peter Hauke was never actually in the studio during the sessions,' recalled Mo Moore. The release of 'Journey' was backed up by an almost non-stop touring schedule of Germany and Switzerland.

By now Nektar had moved from their Hamburg base to Seedier, a town near Frankfurt. 'We were originally based in Hamburg when Nektar first got together,' recalls Mo Moore. 'Then Mick introduced us to a guy called Martin Scheimer, who was the owner of the Underground club in Darmstadt. Mick had played there with Fantasia Light Circus. Martin lived in Seeheim near Darmstadt and he invited us to live with him. Seeheim was where a lot of the Nektar music was written. We continued to be based in the area for the rest of our time in Germany.'

The initial time at OberBeerbacherstrasse 24 in Seeheim was spent rehearsing and writing together in the cellar of the house for the follow up album to 'Journey To The Centre Of The Eye.' 'We had a fish tank in there,' Roye Albrighton remembered, 'and one day we were all discussing a title for this new album while admiring the antics of our fish. Someone wondered out loud what would happen if a giant tab of acid was dropped in the sea. We found our title and concept for the new album!'

'The main riff of "Tab" gives a very nice feel of waves in rhythm.' Ron Howden recalled, 'and, if you add to this picture the state of mind of most of our audience, you can see where the inspiration came from! That cellar room pulsed with the music. The thick

stone walls kept the sound in very well and you could really feel it in your gut. I remember the birth of "Crying In The Dark" and "King Of Twilight" very well. I immediately knew we had something special.'

Sessions for 'A Tab In The Ocean' were recorded at Dieter Dierks studio in Stommeln once more. This time the band were able to take advantage of a refitted studio now equipped with 16-track facilities.

'We were all very influenced by the ambitious music bands like Yes were making at that time,' reflected Mo Moore. 'The title track on '"Tab" reflects this. I think we really stretched ourselves musically at that time which certainly paid dividends. Dieter Dierks' studio was one big room by then, with lots of little rooms for separation. For the recording sessions we were each in a separate room but could see each other for cues through the windows. The actual mixing studio was the same as before but on a different side along the longer wall. We had long, intense sessions with lots of experimentation.'

Indeed, the music recorded for 'Tab In The Ocean' was an immense leap forward in creative terms. It speaks volumes that Nektar performed most of the album in their live set throughout the Seventies and that every track featured in the stage set for their reunion shows in 2002.

The album's title track was a 16-minute musical tour de force that gave each member a chance to shine. From the strident open keyboard flourishes to the powerful bass introduction and the interplay between Albrighton and Howden, 'A Tab In The Ocean' immediately earned a place in the

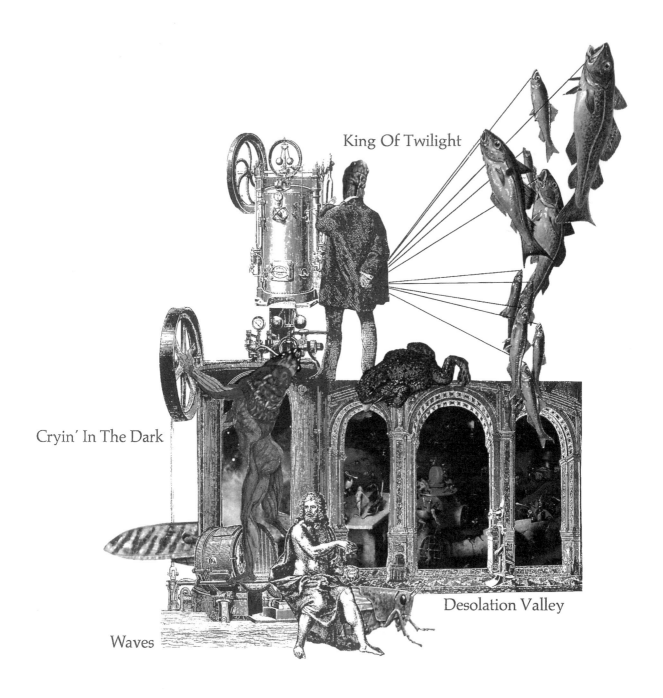

King Of Twilight

Cryin' In The Dark

Desolation Valley

Waves

hearts of all Nektar followers. The other tracks on the album revealed other sides of their musical character. 'Desolation Valley' was a superb jazz-influenced piece which turned into a powerful rock number. 'Crying In The Dark' and 'King Of Twilight' merged to form one of Nektar's most powerful rock numbers and one which would bring them to a wider rock audience (including Steve Harris of Iron Maiden, who would later persuade his band to cover 'King Of Twilight').

'A Tab In The Ocean' paved the way for Nektar's future success both inside and outside Germany. The album was also the first to be graced by the stunning artwork of German artist Helmut Wenske. The release of Nektar's second album would lead to the band securing a deal with British label United Artists and to the band being chosen by Frank Zappa as support act to his major European tour to promote the album 'Overnite Sensation'.

It took until 1976 for the album to find an American release on Passport Records. By this time Nektar had established themselves as a concert draw in the US and their albums 'Remember The Future' and 'Down To Earth' had been major successes. Sometimes overshadowed by 'Remember The Future' in critiques, 'A Tab In The Ocean' remains Nektar's most fully realised work.

STRAWBS 'Grave New World'

First released as A&M Records AMLH68078 in February 1972
Highest UK chart position: N/A
Currently available on CD as A&M Records 540 934-2

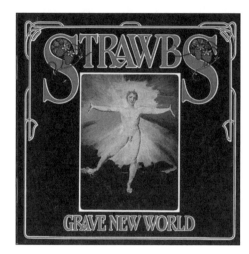

Benedictus
Hey, Little Man…Thursday's Child
Queen Of Dreams
Heavy Disguise
New World
Hey, Little Man…Wednesday's Child
The Flower And The Young Man
Tomorrow
On Growing Older
Ah Me, Ah My
Is it Today, Lord?
The Journey's End

Dave Cousins:	**Vocals, Electric and Acoustic Guitars, Dulcimer, Recorder**
Tony Hooper:	**Vocals, Acoustic Guitar**
John Ford:	**Vocals, Bass**
Richard Hudson:	**Vocals, Drums, Sitar, Tablas**
Blue Weaver:	**Organ, Piano, Mellotron, Clavioline, Harmonium**

Recorded at Morgan Studios and Island Studios, London in November 1971
Produced by Dave Cousins, Richard Hudson, John Ford, Blue Weaver and Tony Hooper
Engineered by Tom Allom
Assistant engineer Martin Levan
'Benedictus' produced by Tony Visconti
Arrangements by Tony Visconti and Robert Kirby

The autumn of 1971 saw the Strawbs at the crossroads of their career. In 1968 they had become the first British signings to the newly established A&M Records and already were drifting away from their early folk roots with the release of their first album in June 1969. Beginning life as the Strawberry Hill Boys, formed by Dave Cousins and Tony Hooper in 1963, the group had evolved into the Strawbs with such luminaries as Sandy Denny and Sonja Kristina passing through their ranks.

By the time of their first album, the band consisted of Cousins and Hooper on guitars and vocals and double bass player Ron Chesterman. The album 'Strawbs', was produced by Gus Dudgeon and featuring guest session players such as John Paul Jones (soon to join Led Zeppelin) on bass and Nicky Hopkins on piano. It was an impressive debut work and saw Dave Cousins begin to develop as a songwriter of varying style.

Prior to the release of the album 'Dragonfly' in February 1970, produced by Tony Visconti, the Strawbs had grown to a quartet, with cellist Claire Deniz joining their ranks. This line-up failed to last longer than the completed studio sessions with Deniz departing prior to the album's release. Ron Chesterman also departed the fold, feeling that Strawbs were heading too far from their folk roots with their recent work.

'Dragonfly' had been completed with the assistance of session musicians, one of whom was a highly talented Royal Academy of Music pupil by the name of Rick Wakeman. Impressed by Wakeman's keyboard-playing, Cousins gave him a credit on the sleeve. A grateful Wakeman wrote to Cousins to thank him for this act of generosity and found himself invited to join the Strawbs in April 1970. The line-up of Cousins, Hooper, Wakeman and cellist/string bass player Lindsay Cooper played for a week in the Rock'n'Roll Circus under a big-top in Paris before parting ways with Cooper in June 1970.

Taking stock, Hooper and Cousins felt that having veered so far from their original folk roots; they should go one stage further by bringing in a bass guitarist and drummer. On 11 July 1970 with ex-Velvet Opera members John Ford and Richard Hudson now in their ranks, the Strawbs played the Queen Elizabeth Hall in London to showcase this new line-up. Wakeman was hailed by Melody Maker as 'tomorrow's superstar' for his piano solo on 'Temperament Of Mind' and his stunning keyboard work on an expanded reworking of 'Where Is This Dream Of Your Youth'. The resulting live album was released as 'Just A Collection Of Antiques And Curios' in November 1970, becoming the first Strawbs album to chart at Number 27 in the UK.

In February 1971 the band recorded their first studio album with this expanded line-up. Working once again with Tony Visconti, 'From The Witchwood' was recorded at Air Studios and reached Number 39 in the UK album chart. The music press had predicted Wakeman would not stay long and this prediction came true in July 1971 when he replaced Tony Kaye in Yes. Wakeman's replacement was Blue Weaver, a highly talented player previously in Amen Corner and Andy Fairweather Low's progressive outfit Fairweather. Weaver would make his presence felt on the next Strawbs album, destined to become their masterwork.

Entering Morgan Studios in November 1971 with new material written by Dave Cousins in his Devon home, the band were to take full charge of production duties for the first time due to regular producer Visconti having other commitments with T-Rex. Of all the instruments utilised in the sessions, the major addition was Weaver's use of the Mellotron, which would add a dramatic power to the music.

This was immediately apparent in majestic album opener 'Benedictus', written by Cousins following Wakeman's departure from the band. 'Hey Little Man' would appear twice on the first side of the album as a refrain after several tracks while 'Queen Of Dreams', (written in Rimini, Italy), would also come to be regarded as a Strawbs classic.

Cousins' outstanding song was the bitter 'New World', arguably the most powerful the Strawbs had ever sounded on record and a comment on the futility of the conflict then raging in Northern Ireland between Protestant and Catholic militants. It remains one of the band's most progressive tracks and one of their finest moments.

Other members of the band would also contribute some fine material. John Ford's 'Heavy Disguise' was inspired by the Easter festivities in the town of Bacup in Lancashire, which involved traditional dancers moving through the town accompanied by a brass band. The finished piece had a marvellous brass arrangement by Robert Kirby (who had written arrangements for Nick Drake) and was a highlight. Richard Hudson's 'Is It Today' possessed a hymn-like quality which featured Indian musical influences and Hudson's own sitar accompaniment. The album was brought to a close with Dave Cousins' evocative 'The Journey's End'.

Released in February 1972, 'Grave New World' was issued in a highly elaborate double gatefold-sleeve with a 16-page booklet of lyrics and photographs. Praised in the music press, the album was the Strawbs most elaborate and accomplished musical statement to date and not only reached Number 11 in the UK but also became the first Strawbs album to enter the US album chart. A promotional film was shot to accompany the release of the record which toured UK cinemas as supporting feature to the film of Emerson, Lake and Palmer's 'Pictures At An Exhibition' concert film.

'We put a lot of hard work into making that album,' Dave Cousins would later reflect, 'taking time and care over what we recorded. The finished package with the elaborate sleeve was well over the top, but the combination of music, lyrics and artwork got us noticed. It did the Strawbs a tremendous amount of good and became our biggest-selling album in the UK.'

For those curious to investigate the sound of the progressive Strawbs, 'Grave New World' is an essential and awe inspiring place to start.

RICHARD HUDSON   TONY HOOPER   BLUE WEAVER   JOHN FORD   DAVID COUSINS

Film built round Strawbs' album

THE STRAWBS are to star in a 30-minute colour film built around the concept of their new album "Grave New World". The movie will have the same title as the LP, and is being produced by Des Cox for Crown International Productions. Director will be Steve Turner, formerly director of BBC-2's "Disco 2" series.

The picture, which will feature stereo sound, goes into production next week and shooting will take approximately a fortnight. Because of their filming commitments, the Strawbs have had to cancel their four March concerts in Ireland, although these will be re-scheduled for a later date.

General release of the picture is planned for April, and it is also being sold on the overseas market.

The outfit is currently in the final stages of a British concert tour, which has managed to avoid any problems with power cuts because the Strawbs are carrying their own generator with them.

STRAWBS TOUR DATES

FEBRUARY
11 SOUTHPORT FLORAL HALL
12 MANCHESTER FREE TRADE HALL
13 BARNSLEY CIVIC HALL
14 LONDON ROYAL FESTIVAL HALL
15 BIRMINGHAM TOWN HALL
17 QUEENS HALL BARNSTABLE
18 GUILDHALL PORTSMOUTH
19 WESTON–SUPER–MARE
   WINTER GARDENS

20 DARLINGTON CIVIC HALL
21 BRISTOL COLSTON HALL
22 SOUTHAMPTON GUILD HALL
23 NORWICH ST. ANDREWS HALL
24 NEWCASTLE-UPON-TYNE
   CITY HALL
25 HULL CITY HALL
27 SWINDON WYVERN
   THEATRE
29 OXFORD TOWN HALL

MARCH
3 LUTON COLLEGE OF TECH.
9 DUBLIN, EIRE TRINITY
   COLLEGE
10 DERRY, N. IRELAND MAGEE
   COLLEGE
11 COLERAINE NEW
   UNIVERSITY OF ULSTER
12 BELFAST QUEENS
   UNIVERSITY

The Moody Blues

Jethro Tull

The Nice

Supersister

THE MOODY BLUES
Days Of Future Passed

THE NICE
The Thoughts of Emerlist Davjack

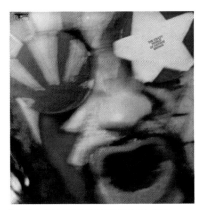

THE CRAZY WORLD OF ARTHUR BROWN
The Crazy World of Arthur Brown

CARAVAN
Caravan

CREAM
Wheels Of Fire

DEEP PURPLE
Shades of Deep Purple

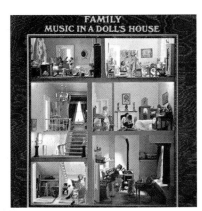

FAMILY
Music In A Dolls House

PRETTY THINGS
S.F. Sorrow

SOFT MACHINE
Volume One

KEVIN AYERS
Joy Of A Toy

JACK BRUCE
Songs For A Tailor

CAN
Monster Movie

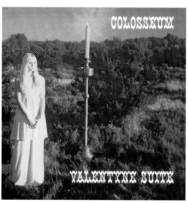

COLOSSEUM
Valentyne Suite

HIGH TIDE
Sea Shanties

JETHRO TULL
Stand Up

MAN
2 Oz's Of Plastic With A Hole In
The Middle

THE MOODY BLUES
To Our Children's Children's
Children

QUINTESSENCE
In Blissful Company

SPOOKY TOOTH
Spooky Two

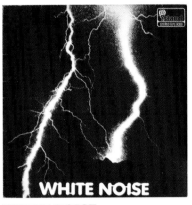

WHITE NOISE
An Electric Storm

ATOMIC ROOSTER
Death Walks Behind You

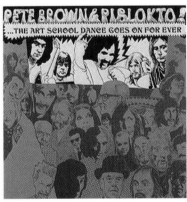

PETE BROWN & PIBLOKTO
Things May Come and Things May
Go, but the Art School Dance
Goes On Forever

EGG
Egg

**EMERSON, LAKE &
PALMER**
Emerson, Lake & Palmer

GROUNDHOGS
Thank Christ For The Bomb

BO HANSSON
Music Inspired By Lord Of
The Rings

HIGH TIDE
High Tide

LOCOMOTIVE
We Are Everything You See

LOVE SCULPTURE
Forms And Feelings

McDONALD & GILES
McDonald & Giles

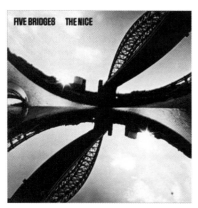

THE NICE
Five Bridges

PRETTY THINGS
Parachute

SOFT MACHINE
Third

T4
It'll All Work Out In Boomland

YES
Time And A Word

WEB
I Spider

ATOMIC ROOSTER
In Hearing Of...

BARCLAY JAMES HARVEST
Once Again

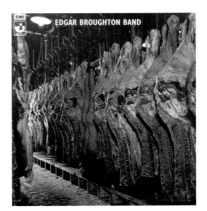

EDGAR BROUGHTON BAND
Edgar Broughton Band

CAN
Tago Mago

CARAVAN
In The Land Of Grey and Pink

FAMILY
Fearless

GROUNDHOGS
Split

PETER HAMMILL
Fool's Mate

ROY HARPER
Stormcock

HAWKWIND
X In Search Of Space

PINK FAIRIES
Never Neverland

TANGERINE DREAM
Alpha Centauri

**VAN DER GRAAF
GENERATOR**
Pawn Hearts

YES
The Yes Album

APHRODITE'S CHILD
666

KHAN
Space Shanty

MAN
Be Good To Yourself at Least
Once A Day

NEKTAR
A Tab In The Ocean

SUPERSISTER
Pudding En Gisteren

STRAWBS
Grave New World

WISHBONE ASH
Argus

**ARTHUR BROWN &
KINGDOM COME**
Journey

BADGER
One Live Badger

CARAVAN
For Girls Who Grow Plump
In The Night

**EMERSON, LAKE &
PALMER**
Brain Salad Surgery

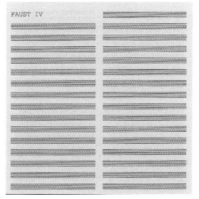

FAUST
Faust IV

MIKE OLDFIELD
Tubular Bells

PFM
Photos Of Ghosts

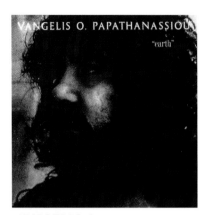

VANGELIS O. PAPATHANASSIOU
Earth

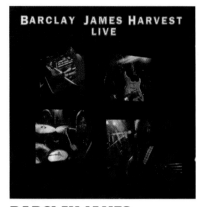

BARCLAY JAMES HARVEST
Live

BE-BOP DELUXE
Axe Victim

ROBERT CALVERT
Captain Lockheed and The Starfighters

CAMEL
Mirage

GONG
You

HATFIELD & THE NORTH
Hatfield & The North

CAMEL
Music Inspired by The Snow Goose

GENTLE GIANT
Free Hand

STEVE HACKETT
Voyage Of The Acolyte

STEVE HILLAGE
Fish Rising

HAWKWIND
Warrior On The Edge Of Time

NEKTAR
Recycled

**VAN DER GRAAF
GENERATOR**
Godbluff

AMON DUUL II
Phallus Dei

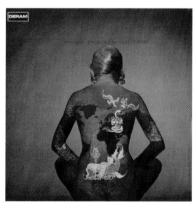

EAST OF EDEN
Mercator Projected

**MANFRED MANN
CHAPTER THREE**
Manfred Man Chapter Three

AFFINITY
Affinity

JODY GRIND
Far Canal

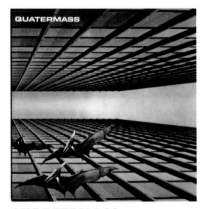

QUATERMASS
Quatermass

RARE BIRD
As Your Mind Flies By

SKIN ALLEY
Skin Alley

AUDIENCE
The House On The Hill

BEGGARS OPERA
Waters Of Change

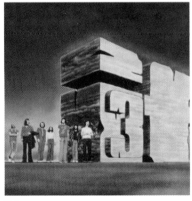

IF
If 3

SUPERSISTER
To The Highest Bidder

AGITATION FREE
Second

ROY HARPER
Life Mask

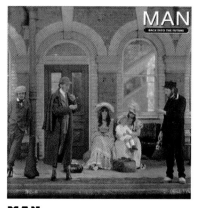

MAN
Back To The Future

NEKTAR
Remember The Future

STRING DRIVEN THING
The Machine That Cried

RENAISSANCE
Turn Of The Cards

DARRYL WAY's WOLF
Night Music

BE-BOP DELUXE
Futurama

CURVED AIR
Second Album

Arthur Brown

Love Sculpture

Piblokto

Traffic

Soft Machine

Ripening Strawbs

FOR SOME INEXPLICABLE reason the Strawbs have now been described as a rock band. A description I find puzzling. Perhaps it's because their album, "Grave New World" has established itself firmly in the charts.

To many the sound is completely new for the band, who have most certainly developed immeasurably in the past two years.

But is it a change of style, as some would claim? I think not. Rather a natural progression we were given notice of on "From The Witchwood". And in many ways links the Strawbs now, with the original trio, who used drums and bass extensively on the first two albums. The second, "Dragonfly", enhanced by a cellist.

Without a doubt, as a result of his playing and writing, keyboard man, Blue Weaver has contributed to the overall sound expansion. In many ways he has also given the group a wider spectrum of appreciative audiences.

"It's just that more people have liked us since Blue joined," admitted Richard Hudson.

"We want to be as successful as we can, and Blue's helping us do it. We're more of a group now than we were before Blue joined. We're doing more things together. And it must, I suppose, be coming over that way, one hopes."

But even with this former Amen Corner man, Hudson and bassist John Ford, believe they have retained their folk group reputation.

Said Hud, at their Marylebone flat: "Although it's not pure traditional folk, which the Strawbs never were — I think we've just added extra things to folky type songs, which we still write. Dave (Cousins) still writes basically folk songs. We're just using a different approach to them.

"I don't think we've gone completely away from the roots, it's still there. And the whole album ("Grave New World") is a concept of it.

"It's something that's natural. We didn't set out to do it deliberately, and we don't set out to go away from it.

"The things that are written and those we record, we just treat them the way we do. And they come out sort of folky. Because that's what they are more or less like.

"Instead of doing just songs, we've done songs with instrumental breaks in them.

"We might even do more eventually. The Strawbs albums have just been straightforward songs. Now we're doing the songs with instrumental breaks and passages. Just to make it more interesting for us to play as well. And there's parts where we can actually busk which is good for us."

Hud feels that from the "Witchwood" set to "Grave New World" has been a steady, thoughtful and creative improvement. Rather than a sudden hop, as some would have us believe.

"There was some stuff on 'Witchwood'," he explained, "where it was gradually coming up. 'Witchwood' isn't that much different from this one. It's only that we've added Blue, which probably has a lot to do with it.

"Blue's playing has made it sound more a heavier type thing that 'Witchwood' (recorded with Rick Wakeman) did. Although we had organ and mellotron on, perhaps we didn't use them to the extent we're using them now. And that's made it sound a bigger group.

"And using the drum kit is another thing. Again we started to use it on 'Witchwood', and it's more or less taken over as my instrument now. I've dropped the sitar for a while.

"I think this is something that's just come naturally. We used it, and now we find we can use it more. And so it will be used all the time. Until eventually we can go into a completely different direction. But I don't see that at the moment."

Using the drum kit to a fuller and more effective extent, even to the point of rendering congas impracticable, was first considered nearly two years ago. The rest of the group wanted it to happen, but Hudson had qualms. He believed it could be a detrimental utilisation, of being too aggressive, perhaps even brutal.

"I was saying," recalled Hud, "well, if we do it now, I think it will detract too much from the way we're going because at that time everything was feeling nice as it was, with congas and electric bass.

"I thought if we brought in the drums straight away, we might lose it. And I think leaving it that little bit longer, and bringing it in for that next album was a better thing to do."

And now it is used on most of the numbers. Basically because Hudson — who is as important in filling out the sound as Weaver — wanted more musical expression, which the kit can provide.

"Now it's just we're playing bigger venues, and the kit just helps to drive things along more than just the congas. And I want to play them more-anyway.

"But it's not really made it heavy the way I was thinking. Not that we're a rock band or anything like that. But I think it's made it just the right feel for the group. We're not a heavy band; it's just added to it."

Perhaps added a weeny bit too much? There has, with the drums and keyboards, been a considerable change in the Strawbs sound. Which I thought swamped and smothered much of the beauty and sincerity of the lyrical value of "Grave New World".

"I disagree," said Hud firmly, "because they're still there. It's just that the group's becoming more musical as well as the songs, and so it's giving us more opportunity to play.

"The songs before were just songs on the albums. I'm not saying that was a bad thing, but now it's giving everybody the chance to play. Musically as well; it's giving us organ and guitar breaks. Just to make it more interesting. But I don't think it takes away from the lyrics; because they're there."

Admittedly beneath, what I described as a "rock noise", there are some perceptive lyrics, especially on "New World". And also more co-operation between members. Making the group's contributions stronger, and acting as a contrast to Cousins' highly personal style.

"Precisely," agreed Hudson.

"The 'Grave New World' album is so varied really, because of all the different things on there. It makes it a much more interesting album.

"For everyone to put something into something, you must feel better about it. And it makes you play. Whereas before you can leave it to one person to do everything. That's OK, but you don't get as much satisfaction out of it.

"And I think that's why it's helped us. Like the number 'Tomorrow'. We all got together on that.

"I think it's a good thing, sure. But I'm not saying that everything should be written by the group.

"Now it's everybody putting in together. We've all thought of things; we've all produced it; and we've all written parts. That's why the effort came over stronger than on previous albums.

"It's given us something, musically, to do. Instead of just backing. Otherwise you might as well be paid as a backing musician and just play.

"Although it's good just to play, you can also contribute in your writing as well. When you get songs on an album, it does give you the incentive to write more. And the more you write, you'll only put out the ones which come out the best.

"If there's a lot of songs flying about from everybody, it gives you more of a chance to pick out the best ones from everything."

Commented John Ford, who has been quietly listening on the other side of the room, smoking a fat cigar: "When I first joined we didn't know the numbers and it was OK just to play along with them. But after you've been in the group for sometime you start to do things on your own."

Folk roots

Even so, it is not the group writing efforts that will dominate the Strawbs material. But still Cousins, because he composes in a style more fitting to the band. Another indication that the umbilical cord feeding from folk, has not been severed.

That could, though, prove frustrating to the others who write. So Hudson and Ford — both prolific in their own right, the latter composing "Heavy Disguise" — have found their own record ing outlet by releasing a couple of "discreet" singles.

And singles seem to be a new part of Strawbs. They've just released their first not taken from an album, "Here It Comes". Though Hudson does feel it's about time they got round to doing that, it is, to my mind, a commercial offering, with a repetitive riff, and Cousins being vocally too sweet.

But they admit they're aiming for that hit single.

"I wouldn't think it's a sell out," Hud qualified. "It's just something we played. We did that messing about on tour, just knocking about with the number. And it's something that came out, and we thought we'd release it."

By TONY STEWART

BLUE WEAVER: sound expansion

More people like the band since Blue came

SUPERSISTER 'Pudding En Gisteren'
('Pudding And Yesterday')

First released in the Netherlands as Polydor Records 2925 007 in April 1972
Highest UK chart position: N/A
Available on CD as Esoteric Recordings ECLEC2059

Radio
Supersisterretsisrepus
Psychopath
Judy Goes On Holiday
Pudding En Gisteren – Music For Ballet

Robert Jan Stips	**Keyboards, Vocals, Vibes, Mouth Organ**
Ron Van Eck:	**Four and Six String Bass Guitars, Guitar, Mouth Organ**
Sacha Van Geest	**Flute, Tenor Saxophone, Vocals**
Marco Vrolijk	**Drums, Congas, Percussion, Vocals**

Produced by Hans Van Oosterhout
Recorded at Phonogram Studios, Hilversum, Holland
Engineered by Jan Schurman

By the close of 1971, Supersister had reached a new height of popularity in their native Netherlands and the band was at a new peak of their creative powers. Released in the autumn of 1971, 'To The Highest Bidder', the band's second album, was a remarkable work that was a logical progression from their debut opus, 'Present From Nancy' and demonstrated an advanced musical maturity not present on their first album, thanks in part to Supersister having more time to realise their ideas and feeling more comfortable in the recording studio. 'To the Highest Bidder' was given a further major boost when British radio DJ John Peel released the record on his Dandelion label, at that time distributed and marketed by Polydor in the UK, adding their Dutch hit 'She Was Naked' to the tracklisting.

The band had come a long way since their formation in the Hague in 1967 with a line-up of Robert Jan Stips (keyboards, vocals), Sacha van Geest (flute, vocals), Ron van Eck (bass, guitar, vocals) and Marco Vrolijk (drums). Initially influenced by the likes of Soft Machine, Caravan and Pink Floyd and modern jazz, Supersister had successfully developed their own sound and style and by 1972 the critical acclaim for 'To The Highest Bidder' had led to a series of concerts in the Netherlands, followed by live work in France, Italy and England.

In October the band had the chance to work with an orchestra as part of a series of German concerts. The German TV channel NDR commissioned a performance with the Tanz und Unterhaltungsorchester des NDR, conducted by Alfred Hause. Ron van Eck and Robert-Jan Stips wrote and arranged some new pieces for this special occasion. Stips soon announced a collaboration between Supersister and the Nederlands Danstheater (the Dutch Dance Theatre company), a modern ballet with music written and played by Supersister.

Subsidised by a grant from the Dutch Department of Culture and choreographed by Frans Vervenne, the ballet, with a working title of 'Signalen' ('Signals'), was premiered on 3 March 1972 at the Circusgebouw, Scheveningen in the Hague. For the

performance of the ballet Supersister played live in the orchestra pit. By the time of the premiere, the name of the work had been changed to 'Pudding En Gisteren', names of characters in a Dutch comic. The ballet, which was directed by Walter Nobbe, was performed in a scenic backdrop of bright coloured lighting and visual projections on a huge screen at the back of the stage. The combination of ballet and rock music was very well received.

For the first performance the newly commissioned music was well performed, although the ballet dancers occasionally failed to synchronise entirely with the musicians. Despite this, the critical reception to the ballet was enthusiastic enough for the Nederlands Danstheater to take the ballet on tour, albeit without Supersister. Running parallel with preparations for the ballet, Supersister entered the Phonogram recording studios in Hilversum to begin work on their third album with Hans van Oosterhout assuming production duties once more.

The opening song, 'Radio', was a catchy, succinct melody, and was chosen to precede the album as the A-side of a single, coupled with the excellent instrumental 'Dead Dog'. Perhaps due to the title and commercial nature of the song, 'Radio' gained airplay and reached Number 21 in the Dutch singles charts. The first side of the album featured the darkly humorous 'Psychopath' with its musical introduction 'Supersisterretsisrepus', and ended with the remarkable 'Judy Goes On Holiday', a 12-minute opus that demonstrated all the finest facets of Supersister's music. Extended instrumental passages demonstrated the prowess of the quartet while, after a pause of 60 seconds, a hidden 'ghost' track, a pastiche of late-Fifties doowop concluded the proceedings. The inane lyrics 'I love you, baby' were repeated continuously, akin to Frank Zappa's musical experiments, becoming gradually faster until the track ended abruptly. On original vinyl pressings this section was pressed into the runout groove of the record. The album's second side was dominated by 'Pudding En Gisteren (Music For Ballet)' with time-signature changes, long flute solos and electronic sounds influenced by the work of Erik Satie. A superb exercise, 'Pudding En Gisteren' would be recognised as a major achievement.

Released in the early summer of 1972, the album was hailed by critics and followers as the finest by the band to date. Adorned in an elaborately designed gatefold by artist Wouter Stips, Robert-Jan's elder brother, the front had a small hole in which part of the comic-strip cartoon which comprised the inner gatefold could be seen. This comic strip related to the ballet but was also a satirical comment on the Dutch music industry at that time. As an added twist, a cryptic message gave instructions to cut

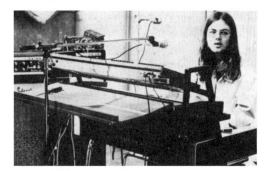

along the bottom of the glued sleeve to reveal pictures of the band and full credits printed on the inside.

Some weeks after the release of the album in the Netherlands, the record appeared in Germany and Britain under the translated title 'Pudding And Yesterday'. Once again Supersister were nominated for a prestigious Edison award (the Dutch equivalent of a Grammy) in the Best New Album category. Supersister appeared at the award ceremony, broadcast live on Dutch television and used the occasion to pass comment on the false nature of such ceremonies as they perceived it.

When accepting the award from the event's host, Robert-Jan Stips deliberately dropped the statuette and, instead of performing their hit single 'Radio', Supersister launched into a version of the 'ghost' track that had appeared after the track 'Judy Goes On Holiday', Stips miming on an organ made from a cardboard box. This gently anarchistic attitude was seen as an affront and gained the band further notoriety in the Netherlands. Soon after the event, Supersister declined offers to perform in Britain and the US, preferring to remain in their homeland.

By 1973 Robert-Jan Stips and Ron van Eck expressed a desire to take the band in a different direction, adopting more free jazz elements and instrumentation with more of an improvisational element. Marco Vrolijk and Sacha van Geest became increasingly opposed to this change of musical direction, preferring a more structured approach to performing and writing, and departed in August. Supersister's final album, 'Iskander', was recorded at the Manor Studios in Oxfordshire, England and was a significant change in style. Despite being augmented by such noted players as former Soft Machine saxophonist Elton Dean, Supersister disbanded by the end of 1974.

A series of reunion concerts in 2000 and planned further work was tragically cut short by the death of Sacha van Geest the following year. Of all of Supersister's many albums, 'Pudding En Gisteren' was arguably their most perfect moment, a sublime blend of progressive rock, jazz, pop and humour that still delights the ears over three decades later.

WISHBONE ASH 'Argus'

First released as MCA Records MDKS8006 in April 1972
Highest UK chart position: Number 3
Available on CD as MCA Records 984 9625/6

Time Was
Sometime World
Blowin' Free
The King Will Come
Leaf And Stream
Warrior
Throw Down The Sword

Andy Powell	**Vocals, Lead guitar on 'Time Was', 'Sometime World' (second passage), 'Blowin' Free', 'Leaf And Stream', 'Warrior' and 'Throw Down The Sword'**
Ted Turner	**Vocals, Lead guitar on 'Sometime World' (first passage), 'Blowin' Free' (quiet passage and slide guitar), 'The King Will Come' and 'Warrior'**
Martin Turner	**Vocals, Bass Guitar**
Steve Upton	**Drums and Percussion**
John Tout:	**Organ on 'Throw Down the Sword'**

Produced by Derek Lawrence
Engineered by Martin Birch
Recorded at De Lane Lea Studios, London

The mention of the name Wishbone Ash to any rock fan will probably result in a reply mentioning the album 'Argus'. Not only is the album one of the band's finest achievements, it is also considered to be one of the classic rock albums of the Seventies. Released in Britain on 28 April 1972, 'Argus' propelled Ash towards the major league of rock bands of the time – Deep Purple, Jethro Tull, Uriah Heep, Black Sabbath et al. The variety of styles covered in the accomplished compositions was the result of three years of sweat and toil on the concert stages of Europe and America, an unrelenting and extremely punishing schedule that saw them hone their craft both as songwriters and performers to perfection.

The roots of Wishbone Ash go back to the southwest of England and Torquay-based band the Torinoes, featuring local boys Martin Turner on bass guitar and vocals and his brother Glenn on guitar and vocals. Like many aspiring bands of the time, The Torinoes' set was drawn from such British groups as the Shadows and Johnny Kidd and the Pirates, alongside American R&B artists. The group performed throughout the west of England and grew in stature and confidence, eventually becoming known as the Empty Vessels in 1966.

In July of that year the fortunes of the Empty Vessels would change when, at a late-night roadside café in Exeter, Devon, Martin and Glenn Turner would meet Welsh-born drummer Steve Upton. Upton had already had begun a promising career as a professional musician, performing with several outfits and spending a three-month spell touring German clubs. Upon his return to England Steve had settled in Exeter and had scraped a living performing in various groups. It while Upton was considering his future that he met the brothers. He would later comment 'The Turners and I chatted the night away. Their drummer had just left their band and they wanted me to play with them. We rehearsed the following Wednesday and did our first gig together on the Saturday night, a week after meeting.'

For the next two years the Empty Vessels continued to play the west country circuit, building a dedicated local following and at the same time growing in confidence and ability. By May 1969 it had become apparent to the trio that, in order to secure a musical future and a recording contract, they would have to relocate to London. This saw the band change their name to Tanglewood and the next two months were spent living and working in the capital. Following a concert at the Country Club in Hampstead in July 1969, Glenn Turner returned home, tired of the pace of living and working as a musician in London. It was at this concert, with the knowledge that Tanglewood was going to lose their guitarist, that Steve Upton met future manager Miles Copeland, an American whose father was a CIA operative. Upton explained that both he and Martin Turner wanted to form a new group. Despite his lack of experience as a manager, Copeland signed them up and began the search for a new guitarist.

Among the applicants was Birmingham-based 19 year-old David 'Ted' Turner, no relation to Martin, who had previously played with blues band King Biscuit. The two musicians wanted to offer him the position of lead guitarist in their new band, but had also

ASH, FAIRPORT: CAMDEN EVENT

FAIRPORT CONVENTION and Dr. John the Night Tripper have been added to the line-up of this year's Camden Festival, to be staged at London's Chalk Farm Roundhouse from April 30 to May 6 inclusive. But America will not now be appearing due to heavy recording commitments, and Wishbone Ash have switched days. Pete Drummond will be compere for the week, except the Thursday (4) when Bob Harris takes over. Promoter Peter Bowyer has also set the supporting attractions, and the full running order now reads:

SUNDAY (30): WISHBONE ASH, Flash, Hookfoot, Linda Lewis and Cheech & Chong.
MONDAY (1): FAMILY, Sam Apple Pie and Byzantium.
TUESDAY (2): FAIRPORT CONVENTION, Quiver and Jonathan Kelly.
WEDNESDAY (3): DR JOHN the Night Tripper, Brinsley Schwarz and Stackridge.
THURSDAY (4): RORY GALLAGHER and the J. Geils Band.
FRIDAY (5): DONOVAN, the Sutherland Brothers and Duncan Browne.
SATURDAY (6): FACES and Nazareth.

been impressed by a guitarist from east London, Andy Powell. Unable to choose between the two, they decided to utilise the talents of both in a dual lead role. This innovative line-up of twin lead guitars, bass and drums would prove to be the new band's calling card.

By September 1969 the band had adopted the name of Wishbone Ash and began a period of writing and rehearsing. In November the band played their first concert at the Civic Hall in Dunstable as support act to the Aynsley Dunbar Retaliation. Over the coming months Wishbone Ash would perform frequently, both as headliners and as support act to a variety of bands including Taste, Mott the Hoople and Caravan.

As chance had it, a concert at the Civic Hall in Dunstable in May of that year as opening act for Deep Purple would provide the much sought-after change in fortune. Deep Purple's guitarist Ritchie Blackmore watched them perform and recommended them to producer Derek Lawrence, who had recently produced 'Deep Purple in Rock'). Lawrence was also in close contact with the London office of MCA Records and took Blackmore's recommendation seriously enough to contact Miles Copeland and witness the band in concert for himself.

On 20 August 1970, Wishbone Ash signed to MCA and within weeks they were in De Lane Lea Studios with Derek Lawrence acting as producer to record their debut album. 'Wishbone Ash' was released as MCA Records MKPS2014 on 4 December 1970. John Peel declared; 'I haven't been so impressed with a relatively new band for a long time. Their music is original, exciting and beautifully played.' This praise and support of Britain's leading underground radio DJ assisted in ensuring that 'Wishbone Ash' entered the British album charts to peak at a respectable Number 34.

MCA Records, an American company, were keen to break Wishbone Ash in the States, and before the band had the chance to promote their album with a full national UK tour they found themselves on their way to the US in February 1971 to begin a seven-week tour supporting such heavyweight acts as Elton John and the James Gang. Returning to the Britain with little time to draw breath, Wishbone Ash undertook a long series of British shows before returning to De Lane Lea in once more with producer Derek Lawrence to record 'Pilgrimage'. It was also during this time that Ted Turner guested on the track 'Crippled Inside' on John Lennon's 'Imagine' LP.

Released in 1971, 'Pilgrimage' was another fine work, building stylistically upon the music recorded for their first record and gaining even more ecstatic reviews in the UK music press. More importantly, Wishbone Ash had a built a large and loyal fan base which propelled 'it to Number 14 in the UK charts.

No sooner had recording sessions been completed than the band headed back to the US at the end of July for their second tour, lasting six weeks, where they again opened for major acts including the Who and Black Sabbath. Writing then began for a third album, while the demand for the group on the concert stage and in the music press remained unabated. In January 1972 they reunited with Derek Lawrence in the new state of the art De Lane Lea studio complex in Wembley, London.

Over the next month, the material committed to tape would, in the eyes of many fans, be the finest of their career. The music was considered, ambitious, thoughtful and in a word marvellous. From the album's opening track 'Time Was', all these qualities were evident. Beginning with a quiet vocal refrain, the song developed into a strident and assured rock number. 'Sometime World' was another song to highlight the musical diversity and capabilities of the band, while 'Blowin' Free', at once both driving and melodic, had evolved during the band's previous US tour and would become their signature tune.

The album's second side began with another finely crafted work, 'The King Will Come', lyrically influenced by passages of the Bible concerned with the second coming of the Messiah. The folk-influenced side of Wishbone Ash was revealed in 'Leaf And Stream', while the two segued closing pieces, 'Warrior' and 'Throw Down the Sword' (the latter enhanced by the keyboard-playing of guest musician John Tout of Renaissance, another Miles Copeland act) made for a superb climax to a faultless album.

'Argus' was released on 28 April 1972, named after the character in Greek mythology – a giant /monster with a hundred eyes that served as the ultimate guardian or watchman. The album, adorned in a striking sleeve designed by Storm Thorgerson of respected design team Hipgnosis (also noted for their sleeve designs for Pink Floyd), was universally praised, with Melody Maker writing an extensive feature of the band.

Reflecting on their latest work, Andy Powell declared: 'This time we've tried to loosen up in the studio. There is less guitar dominance and more subtle playing with a better balance between the instrumentals and vocals.' Martin Turner commented that 'Argus' was 'our favourite album so far and sums up Wishbone Ash very well. Our musical style has changed and during the last couple of years all our styles and influences have come together.'

Reaching Number 3 in the UK album chart, 'Argus' would be a tough act to follow for Wishbone Ash. Although it would earn the band a well-deserved place in rock history, it would forever overshadow the group and remains a milestone.

ARGUS
MDKS 8006
A NEW ALBUM BY WISHBONE ASH

FEATURED ON THIS ALBUM ARE
TIME WAS
SOMETIME WORLD
BLOWIN FREE
THE KING WILL COME
LEAF AND STREAM
WARRIOR
THROW DOWN THE SWORD

ANDY POWELL   MARTIN TURNER

STEVE UPTON   TED TURNER

Wishbone Ash

'Welcome back my friends, to the show that never ends...'

BADGER 'One Live Badger'
First released as Atlantic K40473 in March 1973
Highest UK chart position: N/A
Not currently available on CD

Wheel Of Fortune
Fountain
Wind Of Change
River
The Preacher
On The Way Home

Brian Parrish	**Vocals, Lead Guitar**
David Foster	**Vocals, Bass Guitar**
Tony Kaye	**Organ, Mellotron**
Roy Dyke	**Drums**

Recorded at the Rainbow Theatre, London on 15th & 16th December 1972
Mixed at Advision Studios, London
Produced by Geoffrey Haslam, Badger and Jon Anderson
Engineered by Geoffrey Haslam and Martin Rushent

When keyboard-player Tony Kaye departed Yes in 1971 due to friction with guitarist Steve Howe, he joined former Yes colleague Peter Banks to contribute to sessions for the eponymous debut album by Banks' new outfit, Flash. Although Flash remained relatively unknown in Britain, they enjoyed some degree of album-chart success in the US and were engaged on a long touring cycle which would eventually lead to their demise.

Although he performed on Flash's debut album, Tony Kaye did not go on the road with the band, opting instead to consider forming his own group with lyricist, vocalist and bass guitarist David Foster. Between them the pair sketched out ideas for new material. Foster also had a connection with Yes, being a member of Jon Anderson's pre-Yes group the Warriors and also co-writing some material on the album 'Time And A Word' with Anderson.

Kaye had initially worked on a planned Foster solo album which had later been shelved, but with this new outfit some of the ideas born out of that aborted project would be realised. Joined by drummer Roy Dyke (previously with the Remo Four in the Sixties and latterly part of Ashton, Gardner and Dyke) and guitarist and vocalist Brian Parrish (previously with Three Man Army), Badger was born.

Initial rehearsal sessions saw a series of wonderful songs emerge such as 'Wheel Of Fortune', 'Wind Of Change', 'On The Way Home' and 'River'. Each was an intriguing blend of progressive rock with a clear lineage to the stylistic approach of Yes on their first three albums, blended with more traditional rock and soul influences.

Having quickly established their own unique musical identity, Badger nevertheless secured the support slot on the Yes UK tour of December 1972, thanks to Jon Anderson's enthusiasm for his former colleague's band. The concerts at London's Rainbow Theatre on 15 and 16 December 1972 were recorded by Atlantic Records and

would become the live album 'Yessongs' when released in May 1973. With a mobile recording unit in place at the Rainbow to record Yes, Jon Anderson also arranged for Badger's live sets to be recorded. The band were warmly received as an opening act and their performances were well crafted. The set opened with 'Wheel Of Fortune', a progressive rock number with a soul edge hat featured outstanding guitar work from Parrish and excellent keyboard work from Kaye, who utilised Mellotron, Hammond organ and Moog synthesiser. Other highlights were the equally stunning 'Wind Of Change', which followed on stylistically from 'Wheel Of Fortune'. The more soulful side of the band was in evidence on pieces such as 'River', but the real kudos went to the set closer 'On The Way Home', with lyrical refrains more akin to gospel music underpinned by excellent Mellotron and organ work from Kaye and imaginative guitar from Parrish.

Aside from the enthusiastic response of the audience at the Rainbow Theatre, reaction from A&R staff of Atlantic Records was enthusiastic enough for the label to offer a contract to release the highlights of Badger's performances on album. Released in April 1973, 'One Live Badger' was adorned in a Roger Dean-designed gatefold sleeve that, when opened, revealed a pop-up badger. The album was greeted with enthusiasm by the Yes fan fraternity, but gained indifferent reviews in the British music press. Disc magazine declared; 'Badger have a sort of primitive Yes sound. Their playing is very tricky with lots of guitar and keyboard interplay. It's all very fine and the sort of music we all fell on our knees to five years ago, but it's a little basic now.' Perhaps because of such critical indifference 'One Live Badger' failed to enter the UK chart listings.

David Foster and Brian Parrish would soon depart the fold, leaving Kaye and Dyke to assemble a new line-up which included guitarist Paul Pilnick and bass guitarist Kim Gardner. In addition, former Apple signing Jackie Lomax was recruited as vocalist and took the band in a soul- influenced direction for the album 'White Lady' in 1974, bearing no relation in style to the group who had recorded that impressive live album two years earlier.

Despite the critical indifference to the record when it first appeared, 'One Live Badger' is an excellent snapshot of the embryonic band on stage and poses the listener to question what might have been had the original line-up recorded a studio album. It is a marvellous collection of highly original music.

Tony Kaye

Brian Parrish

Dave Foster

Roy Dyke

228

ARTHUR BROWN AND KINGDOM COME 'Journey'

First released as Polydor 2310 254 in February 1973
Highest UK chart position: N/A
Currently available on CD as Esoteric Recordings ECLEC2187

Time Captives
Triangles
Gypsy
Superficial Roadblocks:
a. Lost Time
b. Superficial Roadblocks
c. Corpora Supercelestia
Conception
Spirit Of Joy
Come Alive

Arthur Brown	**Bentley Drum Machine, Vocals**
Andy Dalby	**Electric Guitar, Vocals**
Phil Shutt	**Fender Bass, Vocals, Percussion**
Victor Periano	**Mellotron, Piano, Synthesiser, Theremin, Percussion**
Les Adey	**Lights**

Recorded at Rockfield studios, Monmouthshire in November and December 1972
Produced by Dave Edmunds except 'Spirit Of Joy' and 'Come Alive' produced by Dennis Taylor
Engineered by Ralph Down and Kingsley Ward
Mixed by Dave Edmunds

On disbanding the Crazy World of Arthur Brown in the spring of 1969, Arthur Brown set about redefining his musical future. Although his recent outfit had achieved immense commercial success, most of the funds generated by the international hit single 'Fire' and the band's eponymous hit album had failed to arrive in his hands. Teaming up with the first Crazy World drummer Drachen Theaker, dismissed at the insistence of keyboard player Vincent crane for being too, Brown assembled the band Puddletown Express, based in the Dorset village from which the group took their name. 'The group was really the polar opposite to Crazy World,' he would later recount. 'Whereas the latter was very much a formal affair, where we had a stage set and costumes, Puddletown Express was mainly improvised. Of course, I'd be naked onstage, and we'd hardly play "Fire" at gigs.'

This loose approach to making music satisfied Brown for a short time until the desire to form a more structured band took hold. 'I was working with Dennis Taylor, who'd started as a roadie with the Crazy World, and then became our lighting guy. He was involved in the Puddletown Express, and we went around looking for musicians to work with when it came to forming Kingdom Come. We underwent a few line-up changes during this process. Originally we had the drummer Rob Tait with us and he favoured one particular keyboard player we had auditioned, who was very jazz-oriented, whereas I wanted to work with another keyboardist, who was more neo-classical. So, Rob went. We then drafted in Andy Dalby on guitar and Martin Steer on drums who had been in the band Charge from Leicester.'

With Phil Curtis on bass guitar and Michael 'Goodge' Harris on keyboards, Kingdom Come secured the use of a former warehouse in London's Covent Garden to rehearse in, and also had the services of manger and lawyer Mark Radcliffe who secured a long-term worldwide contract with the German office of Polydor Records. The first fruits of Kingdom Come's writing and rehearsing sessions appeared in 1971 as the album 'Galactic Zoo Dossier'.

Brown's music had moved on hugely from the days of the Crazy World, as he would later reflect. 'Our first album was very adventurous, as I was keen to explore the use of the synthesiser as much as possible. I'd wanted to use one in the Crazy World, but Vincent Crane just wasn't interested in it at all.' The release of the album led to the band appearing at the Glastonbury Fayre in June 1971 and also in the film of the same name. 1972's follow-up 'Kingdom Come' was a further trip into the darkness and the bizarre, but it was the group's final album that would be Kingdom Come's finest hour.

This conceptual masterpiece of space rock was arguably the most unique sounding album of 1973, its sinister use of synthesiser and Mellotron, combined with one of the earliest uses of a drum machine on a rock record would all contribute to the brilliance of the record, a truly collaborative effort on the part of all the musicians of Kingdom Come. The development of the Bentley Rhythm Ace drum machine came at the point that the band had lost drummer Martin Steer and replacement Andy McCulloch in quick succession. With inspired writing sessions fuelled by the consumption of LSD, the music written in the autumn of 1972 was both experimental and imaginative.

The earliest material to be written by the band was the catchy, and at that time lengthy, 'Spirit Of Joy', the wonderful comment on the current music scene 'Slow Rock' and the odd instrumental 'Triangles'. This material was premiered on a BBC radio session for John Peel in September 1972, with a shortened 'Spirit Of Joy' being coupled with 'Slow Rock' for release as a single the same month.

Soon after its release, 'Goodge' Harris departed the band. 'While the rest of us had been taking acid,' Arthur later explained, 'Goodge had been on his own trip and felt it was time to leave. So, we got in Victor Peraino on keyboards. Goodge was very much into exploring classical music, that was his background, whereas Victor took our music in a different direction. He kept the classical format, but was also into sonic experimentation and the use of the synthesiser. Essentially we were attempting to do, in rock and electronic terms, the closest thing that we could get to a string quartet. So the parts for guitar, bass and keyboards were written with this in mind."

Prior to entering the recording studio to record their latest work, Kingdom Come debuted both their new line-up and new material at a concert at the London School of Economics. 'We went down extremely well, which was something we never expected. No-one had ever used a drum machine as a live instrument before, so this was going against what people knew and were familiar with.'

Entering Rockfield Studios in Monmouthshire in November 1972, the album sessions began with producer Dennis Taylor supervising proceedings, but after recording two songs he gave way to former Love Sculpture guitarist and now successful solo artist Dave Edmunds who, according to Brown, was more than keen to work on such an experimental project.'

Not many people realise that Dave was keen on experimentation in the recording studio. He was very sympathetic to our ideas and the results would speak for themselves.' Indeed, from the opening bars of the dramatic 'Time Captives' to the concluding 'Come Alive' (a reworking of the song 'Slow Rock'), the finished album took the listener on a captivating cosmic trip. Released in February 1973, 'Journey' (a title suggested by bassist Phil Shutt), was critically acclaimed but failed to sell in large quantities.

This lack of success and the pressure of keeping a band on the road eventually proved too much for Arthur Brown, who disbanded Kingdom Come later that year. He would later cite that he had tried to find spiritual enlightenment through writing and performing music, but that this no longer sustained him. Heading to a retreat in India, Arthur abandoned music for nearly two years, before returning to prominence in a different guise. Although best known for his groundbreaking work in his Crazy World, Arthur Brown arguably went one better with Kingdom Come's 'Journey'. A testament to the album's greatness is that, over three decades later, the album is cited by many younger musicians as an influence on their work.

Arthur Brown's Kingdom Come

Arthur B[r]

ARTHUR BROWN'S debut appearance as a vocalist came as a child, when he and his brother sang duets in church together. That was in the small fishing village of Whitby in Yorkshire, where he was born. But the Brown family shifted to Wales when he was 11 and he lost interest in music until his teens.

His interests were varied. He learned to play banjo, double bass and guitar. He played bass with Dave Morgan's trad band ("he had lethal hips," remembers Arthur), sang traditional folk, joined a modern jazz band and practised classical voice exercises for six months before forming an r-and-b band called Blues And Brown in 1964.

🔳🔳🔳

By this time, Arthur was well into singing and getting a much clearer idea of what he wanted to do. But the semi-pro outfits continued to come and go like tenants in a block of bedsitters. He teamed up with the Southwest Five, "which soon became the Arthur Brown Union due to my tremendous ego", he jests. They played the tunes of Bobby "Blue" Bland and James Brown.

After this band fell apart, he met the man who built the Marquee studios. He was on his way to start a tax exile in France and supposedly form an empire. He asked Arthur if perhaps he might like to go along and he jumped at the opportunity. The only thing was: Arthur needed a band. So, with a week to go before he was due to split for Paris, he began the Arthur Brown Set.

🔳🔳🔳

They only had three rehearsals before leaving, but they found themselves surrounded by a completely sympathetic atmosphere upon arrival, and stayed for six months. It was the beginning of the underground scene there and the group wound up with a residence at one of the more prominent

ballrooms.
make-up a

He'd co
with lighte
all of his
found this

🔳🔳

After th
went to S
pretty quie
money. He
his energie
World. W
played ke
took the d

At first,
booking.
and at oth
point, Art
"Baby No

Soon, t
round. Th
and the U
drew bette

🔳🔳

They si
Chris Sta
World of
career. O
nothing.
Vincent C
left Arthu
Atomic R
left a note

We want to bu

By DANNY HOLLOWAY

his time that Arthur first wore
...atrics from time to time.
...with a crown perched on his head
...and make up on his face, having
... except for one. The audience
...the least.

..., the band broke up and Arthur
... r-and-b band. That gig ended
...his way back to England with no
... a shoe shop previous to investing
...ble project to date — his Crazy
... came together, Vincent Crane
... pedals while Drachen Theaker

...where they could manage to get a
... contacts on the cabaret circuit
...ose as an r-and-b band. (At one
...oundations, but left just before
...d You" was recorded.)

...better gigs and the word spread
... Club which launched Hendrix
... audience was enthusiastic and

...o's managers, Kit Lambert and
...n their label, Track. The Crazy
...d a short and sweet recording
..."Fire", and an LP and then —
...hectic tours of the states before
...mer (who had replaced Theaker)
...d flew back to England to form
...d have been nice if they'd have
...ys Arthur.)

Now, he says of the Crazy World: "I found it very limited. We got to the stage where we couldn't do things musically and theatrically. Hopefully, there will be some tapes coming out of us with an amazing organist on Dandelion records." After he finally packed it in, he formed his present band, Kingdom Come, two years ago.

The atmosphere is now much more relaxed, even though his manager isn't experienced, at least he's not a spiv or a hustler. The career of Kingdom Come has been very erratic. Members have come and gone, but Arthur feels the band is finally settling down now. They've made two albums for Polydor and their weekly allowance has increased to £15 each. The rest of the loot is either re-channeled into the band (i.e. equipment) or spent on everyday living.

Kingdom Come consists of Andy Dalby on guitar, Phil Shep on bass, Goodge on VCS3, Dave Yoell, lights, and Arthur — vocals and drum machine. "The drum machine is like a thing called the Rhythm Ace. It's just a little box with controls which gives out various rhythms like tango, cymbals, snare, volume controls, speed controls. We're getting loads of things built into it like echoes, bells and gongs. It's changed the whole of our music, but the audience reaction has been very, very good.

"Even since this last album, we've changed. Now we don't have an organ, we just have a VCS3 (a form of synthesizer). The drum machine has changed the whole of our direction. Eventually, we're aiming to use the music and the lights in a very scientific way as opposed to just getting up and playing what we feel like. That's cool if you're a really great geezer and people like listening to you, or if you like getting into rock and roll, then anybody can listen to you.

"But we're trying to build up a parallel with magic. Not on any black magic or white magic scene. But in terms of scientific effects on people, where each sound has a colour value. (There are places all over England where you can go and be treated, if you've had a road accident and received a shock, you can be treated by colour. They'll start you off on a very ice blue and take you right through to red. The blue cools you out and the red brings you back to energy.) We want to build structures, musically, that will take people through some very nice trips.

"I'm sick of playing big time. It's a lot more organic being able to play and talk to the people afterwards, than when you have all that enormous publicity and tension behind you. Nobody needs that. If we'd have had a really big push when we started, we probably wouldn't be here today. We're into musical and entertainment quality. If that gets success, then great. Kingdom Come plays the best music that I've ever been associated with. It's what I've been aiming for for a long, long time."

Caravan

CARAVAN 'For Girls Who Grow Plump In The Night'

First released as Deram SDL-R12 in November 1973
Highest UK chart position: N/A
Currently available on CD as Deram 8829802

Memory Lain Hugh/Headloss
Hoedown
Surprise, Surprise
C'thlu Thlu
The Dog, The Dog, He's At It Again
Be Alright/Chance Of A Lifetime
L'Auberge Du Sanglier/A Hunting We Shall
Go/Pengola/Backwards/A Hunting We Shall Go (Reprise)

Richard Coughlan	Drums and Percussion
Pye Hastings	Guitar, Vocals
John G. Perry	Bass Guitar, Vocals, Percussion
Geoffrey Richardson	Electric Viola
Dave Sinclair	Organ, Piano, Electric Piano, Davoli Synthesiser & ARP Synthesiser
With	
Jimmy Hastings	Solo Flute
Tony Coe	Clarinet, Tenor Saxophone
Tommy Whittle	Clarinet, Tenor Saxophone
Harry Klein	Clarinet, Baritone Saxophone
Pete King	Flute, Alto Saxophone
Barry Robinson	Flute, Piccolo
Henry Lowther	Trumpet
Chris Pyne	Trumpet
Rupert Hine	ARP Synthesiser solo

on 'Memory Lain, Hugh'/'Headloss'
Woodwind and Brass arranged and conducted by Jimmy Hastings
Orchestra on 'L'Auberge Du Sanglier/A Hunting We Shall Go' arranged by Martyn Ford and John Bell
Conducted by Martyn Ford
Recorded at Chipping Norton Studios, Oxfordshire, Decca studios, Tollington Park, London and Decca Studios, West Hampstead, London
Mixed at AIR Studios, London
Produced by David Hitchcock
Engineered by Kevin Fuller, Derek Varnals, John Punter, Dave Grinstead and John Burns
Assistant engineers Sean Milligan, David Baker, Alan Leeming and Lindsay Kidd

The release of Caravan's fourth album, 'Waterloo Lily', in April 1972 revealed that the band had undergone a degree of musical transition. Dave Sinclair's departure the previous year saw ex-Delivery keyboard player Steve Miller join the ranks and the resulting album by this new line-up was a mixture of Pye Hastings' usual quirky songwriting and the jazz influences of keyboard player Steve Miller and Richard Sinclair.

It was Sinclair who had invited Miller to join the group following the departure of his cousin from the band in August 1971. 'Waterloo Lily' received a mixed reception from both critics and long-term fans alike. 'As far as our fans were concerned, it was a very different approach and a lot of them didn't like it very much,' Pye Hastings later commented. 'By attempting to break new ground and trying something different we attracted some new fans but also lost some too.'

The discussions about musical direction came to a head during a UK tour in June 1972, as Hastings would later remember: 'It became quite clear after a while that it wasn't working at all. I had a lot of conversations with Richard Sinclair about this, but he wanted us to become even more jazz-based in our approach. I wanted to go back into a rock direction and unfortunately we clashed.' Unable to resolve their differences the line-up of Coughlan, Hastings, Miller and Sinclair played their last concert on 25 July 1972 at Solihull Civic Hall, sharing the bill with Genesis.

for girls who grow

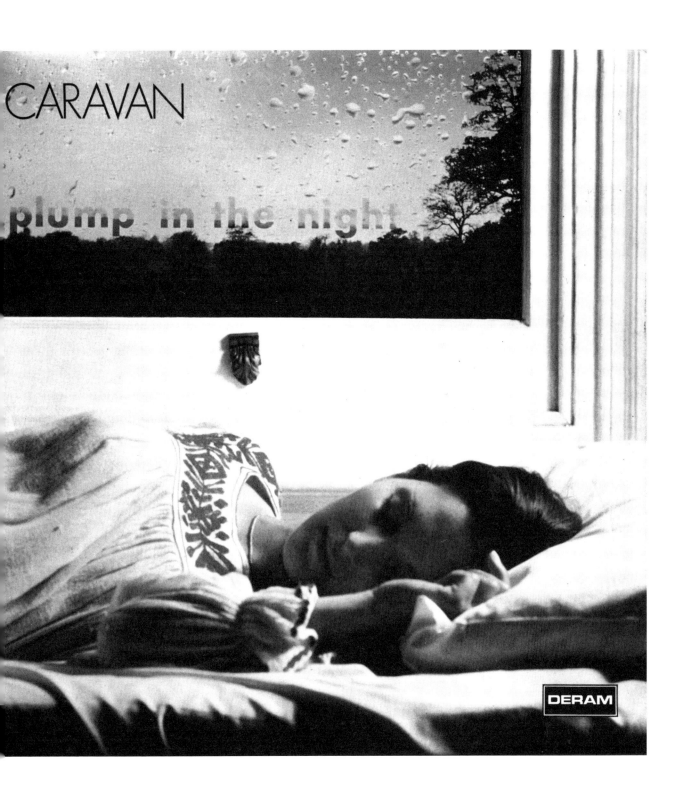

Miller left the band shortly after and within days Richard Sinclair also departed. Richard would later recall his reasons for leaving thus: 'It didn't quite work with Steve in the band, because the music started to go a bit too loose for the way that Pye and Richard Coughlan played. Whilst we were extending ourselves in a blues and jazz vein, I think Pye's idea was to be centred upon what our traditional following would like to hear. So things eventually split.'

Despite what some thought would be a fatal body blow, Hastings spoke to Richard Coughlan told him he was determined to continue. 'He agreed, so I went to Terry King, our manager to tell him of our intention to carry on. Terry organised auditions for a new keyboard player and bassist. I'd never done auditions before and it was quite a new experience to have complete strangers play in the band.'

From these auditions bassist Stuart Evans (ex-Thank You) on and keyboard player Derek Austin (ex-Keef Hartley Band) joined Caravan. Prior to finding these replacements Pye Hastings had been introduced to an outstanding young viola player by the name of Geoffrey Richardson. 'A friend of mine told me a friend of his had an ex-Winchester Art College student staying with him,' Hastings would later recount. 'Doug had heard him play and thought he was the best blues-influenced viola player he had ever heard.

'Geoff was staying with a chap called Steve Borrill who was bass player in a band called Spirogyra. When I originally auditioned for a bass player to replace Richard Sinclair I asked Steve to come along and suggested he bring Geoffrey as well. It was obvious that there was no chemistry between Steve and myself, but I was very impressed with Geoffrey and asked him to join straightaway.'

Richardson's viola immediately added a new dimension to Caravan's sound, extending their musical possibilities. Within two months this new incarnation of Hastings, Coughlan, Richardson, Austin and Evans was performing its first concert in Montbeliard, France on 10 September 1972. Initial audience reaction to Richardson was mixed but he persisted, allowing his virtuosity on both viola and flute to shine through. Within a year this initial resistance had waned and Richardson became an audience favourite and the main focal point on stage. Following a tour of Britain and France, which lasted on and off from October to December 1972, (during which the band had begun to work on writing new material during soundchecks), Caravan entered the recording studio for the first time in nearly nine months.

Producer David Hitchcock accompanied the band to Chipping Norton Studios in rural Oxfordshire for the week leading up to Christmas to begin work on their next album. These sessions were intended to commit Pye Hastings' instrumental ideas to tape. 'I always write lyrics at the last minute when it comes to recording,' he explained in a contemporary interview. 'I only come up with lyrics when it becomes time to record a vocal track. Before then I hum any old nonsense just to develop a vocal melody.'

The December sessions at Chipping Norton produced demos of new material with working titles such as the humorously named 'He Who Smelt It Dealt It' (later known as 'Memory Lain, Hugh'), 'Waffle' (later to become 'Chance Of A Lifetime'), 'No! – Part One' (known some months later as 'Be Alright'), 'C'Thlu Thlu' and 'Surprise, Surprise'. After a break for Christmas, the band returned in January to work on more new material, but at this point, further musical issues began to arise as Pye would later explain. 'Derek Austin's style was very much based around the Hammond organ and pedals. The problem was that it didn't sound like Caravan and so he began to clash musically with Richard, Geoffrey and myself.'

After a February 1973 tour of Australia with Slade, Lindisfarne and Status Quo Hastings decided another line-up change was called for. 'Before we got Stuart Evans in I had been in touch with a superb bass player called John Perry who was in a band called Spreadeagle. They were in the process of breaking up and he came to see us at the Marquee. He told me he would like to join but had other commitments at that time. When I came back from Australia he wrote to me saying that he would be free to join us from the beginning of March and so I asked him to come on board straight away.'

Evans and Austin duly departed, leaving Hastings, Coughlan, Richardson and Perry to welcome back Dave Sinclair. 'I had done a stint with Matching Mole and Hatfield and the North and Pye asked me if I would like to come back to the band for a forthcoming tour of France,' Sinclair later recalled. 'I agreed to do it for session fees as, at that point, I didn't want to become part of the band on a full-time basis again. I was happy to come back because I needed the money apart from anything else. After the French tour we went into the studio and I just sort of stayed in the band. The new band was incredibly tight. John Perry was such a good player; he drove the band along, making us all work hard as a unit.'

Encouraged by the success of their French excursion, Caravan entered Chipping Norton Studios once again in April 1973. 'Within a week the backing tracks were all done,' Pye explained, 'because we had rehearsed everything on the road. We recorded the whole thing live in the studio, near enough. We went back to correct any mistakes, but there weren't many as we had got things so tight by playing them live every night.' The band then undertook overdub sessions at Decca's Studios in West Hampstead and Tollington Park.

The opening track of the album, soon destined to serve as a Caravan live set opener, was the wonderful 'Memory Lain, Hugh', featuring a superb viola performance from Geoff Richardson and a woodwind and bass arrangement by Pye's brother, Jimmy Hastings, who also took the flute solo. Rupert Hine, a friend of John Perry's, played ARP synthesiser along with Dave Sinclair as the track neatly segued into 'Headloss'.

On the track 'C'thlu Thlu' Pye Hastings experimented with complex timings and riffs more associated with bands like King Crimson, while 'The Dog, The Dog, He's At It Again' was a humorous tale of lechery and was chosen by Decca to be the subject of a promotional film featuring the band performing the track in Decca's Broadhurst Gardens Studio. This even gained a screening on BBC2's influential Old Grey Whistle Test TV programme.

The album's closing track would demonstrate just how tight and inspired a musical unit Caravan was. 'A Hunting We Shall Go' was an instrumental track that had built up gradually over the last few months' live work. It was introduced by a section featuring acoustic guitar and viola called 'L'Auberge Du Sanglier', named after a guesthouse frequented by the band on their French visits. '…Hunting' was divided into further sections, namely 'Pengola', a short contribution from John Perry, and 'Backwards', a Soft Machine piece originally featured on the album 'Third' written by Mike Ratledge.

Pye would later explain: 'I wrote all of 'A Hunting We Shall Go' and got stuck when I reached the middle section. I had originally written another chord progression but I wasn't happy with it. Dave Sinclair was very fond of a melody written by Mike Ratledge and suggested we try that instead. It worked a treat.'

The track also featured a splendid orchestral arrangement by Martyn Ford and John Bell (who had previously worked with Barclay James Harvest). It provided a stunning climax to what many consider to be one of Caravan's finest albums. 'For Girls Who Grow Plump In The Night' was released on 5 October 1973, with the cover image featuring a slumbering, heavily pregnant woman designed by Mark Lawrence. The original plan was to depict a nude, pregnant lady on the gatefold sleeve, but Decca Records were less than enthusiastic and vetoed the idea.

Although failing to chart, the release of 'For Girls Who Grow Plump in the Night' was the beginning of Caravan's wider success. The consistency of Pye Hastings' songwriting combined with the outstanding instrumental prowess of the line-up of Coughlan, Hastings, Perry, Richardson and Sinclair explain why 'For Girls Who Grow Plump In The Night' remains one of the finest albums of Caravan's career.

EMERSON LAKE AND PALMER
'Brain Salad Surgery'

First released as Manticore K53501 in November 1973
Highest UK chart position: Number 2
Available on CD as Sanctuary 5308195

Jerusalem

Toccata

Still…You Turn Me On

Benny the Bouncer

Karn Evil 9 – 1st Impression – Part One

Karn Evil 9 – 1st Impression – Part Two

Karn Evil 9 – 2nd Impression

Karn Evil 9 – 3rd Impression

Keith Emerson   **Organ, Piano, Moog Synthesisers**
Greg Lake   **Vocals, Bass Guitar, Electric and Acoustic Guitars**
Carl Palmer   **Drums, Percussion, Electronic Percussion**

Produced by Greg Lake
Recorded at Olympic Studios, Barnes, London and at Advision Studios, London
Engineered by Chris Kimsey and Geoff Young

By the beginning of 1973, Emerson Lake and Palmer had established themselves part of rock's major league. The trio had been in existence for two years and in that time had delivered three stunning studio albums ('Emerson Lake And Palmer', 'Tarkus' and 'Trilogy') plus a live album featuring the band's interpretation of Mussorgsky's 'Pictures At An Exhibition'. The band had defined their sound by drawing on classical, jazz, folk and rock influences and creating a form of music all their own which put them at the forefront of the emerging progressive rock movement.

With the release of the album 'Trilogy' in August 1972, ELP embarked on a sell out arena tour of Europe and the US and proved they had reached the upper echelons of the rock hierarchy. Greg Lake would later explain; 'ELP was always trying to top anything we'd done before in those days, be it on stage or with our latest album. In my opinion the music recorded for "Trilogy" demonstrated that we were becoming more aware of the potential of the recording studio, particularly with the advent of 24-track recording.

'   On "Trilogy" we used overdubs to a greater degree and I think the album sounded wonderful as a result, but it was quite difficult to perform live. As a result of this, I think we all felt that when it came to making our next album, we should produce something that could be performed on stage and would work well as the focal point of a concert. I thought the next album should be more of a collaborative effort. In the past we all worked on our own to come up with ideas and they would then be presented in the recording studio. I really wanted our next album to be a true collaboration of ideas.'

To assist in this creative process, ELP had recently purchased a former cinema in Fulham, West London to act as their own rehearsal room and as a headquarters for the newly established Manticore Records. 'We set up Manticore,' Lake later recalled, 'to try and make the entire record process as good as it could be. We were also aware of a number of artists who we knew were having problems getting their music released and getting a record deal. We thought that we could control things a lot better and also help out some of the other artists we admired.

In a later interview Keith Emerson would add; 'We'd been looking for ages for somewhere to rehearse. We had previously rehearsed in Church Halls and were frequently upsetting the neighbours. On one occasion a man complained that when he took a bath the music we made was so loud that it caused waves in his water!'

The newly acquired Manticore building was duly converted into a sophisticated rehearsal facility, much in demand by other rock bands of the day, with the downstairs area of the building hired out to acts such as Led Zeppelin and Jethro Tull for production rehearsals. The building also had a own private workshop and rehearsal facility upstairs in a converted area that was formerly the balcony of the cinema, given over to the exclusive use of ELP. It was in this environment that Emerson Lake and Palmer would produce one of the finest albums of their career. The end of 1972 and the first month of 1973 saw two new compositions begin to take shape, one of which would dominate the forthcoming album and was one of their finest and most ambitious moments.

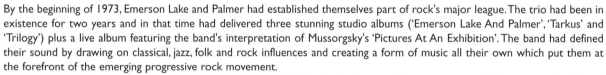

News Desk

That ELP single

EXCLUSIVE ALBUM CUTS ADDED

A BONUS selection of excerpts from ALL tracks on the upcoming Emerson, Lake and Palmer album has been added to the NME free single announced last week.

The single, "Brain Salad Surgery", was specially-recorded by ELP for NME readers during sessions on the band's new long-awaited album.

The album, too, is entitled "Brain Salad Surgery", although the special NME single — ELP's first — does not appear in the new set, nor will it appear in Britain in any other form except through the November 3 issue of New Musical Express.

Excerpts from all seven tracks on the album will be included on the ELP/NME single. These are "Jerusalem", an ELP arrangement of the traditional hymn, "Toccata", an adaptation of Alberto Ginastera's 1st Piano Concerto 4th Movement, "Still . . . You Turn Me On", "Benny The Bouncer" and "Karn Evil 9", which is divided into three impressions and takes up the whole of the second side.

The album is ELP's first for well over a year and the first on their own Manticore label — sleeve design is from original paintings commissioned from Swiss surrealist M. R. Giger.

THE NME FREE SINGLE WILL BE CONTAINED IN A MINIATURE FACSIMILE OF THE ACTUAL ALBUM COVER.

ELP are currently rehearsing for a major American tour, which opens on November 10. Their 35-day schedule includes concerts in 30 cities, climaxing at New York Madison Square Garden.

There are at present no plans for British dates, but a spokesman told NME that the band may play a few selected concerts here in the New Year.

● Carl Palmer is featured in London Weekend's "Aquarius" magazine programme which goes out to most ITV regions this Sunday (21). Various other regions see it either on Saturday or next week.

Palmer will be performing on all-steel drums, synthesised tom-toms, tympani, tubular bells and gongs — all set on a revolving Japanese pagoda.

● As stated last week, NME circulation will double for the November 3 issue scheduled to contain the ELP single.

Previous records in this NME reader-service series (Faces, Stones, Alice Cooper) have subsequently become much sought after collectors' pieces — to make sure you don't miss out, complete the order form on page 64 and deliver it to your local newsagent.

NME regrets that it is not possible to provide the free ELP single for overseas readers.

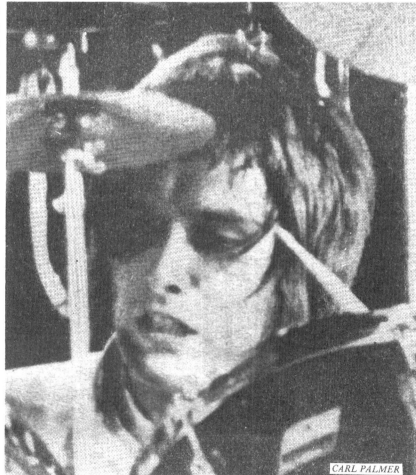

CARL PALMER

The first movement of the epic opus that became known as 'Karn Evil 9' began to take shape. Keith Emerson later explained; 'I suppose that track was the logical extension of the musical path we had taken with the piece "Tarkus". I decided that I wanted to write a musical exercise in counterpoint, but after the first movement had come together I gave up on the idea. The first time I played it to Greg and Carl they both agreed it was a very clever piece of music, but then commented "Can we get on with the song now?"! It's interesting because I think that sort of collective input helped to turn the germ of an idea into something very worthwhile.'

Carl Palmer adds: 'It's strange because we'd begun rehearsing the piece in our smaller rehearsal room which was upstairs in the Manticore building. We then decided to move to the big rehearsal room downstairs as no-one was renting it for a few weeks. It was when we moved into the bigger room that the piece took off.'

Greg Lake was to also add a special ingredient to the mixture that would produce an epic by enlisting a friend as lyricist he had worked with when in King Crimson. Pete Sinfield had been planning to record a solo album and had approached Greg with the idea. Lake had agreed that Manticore would back Sinfield's project and additionally suggested that he contribute lyrics to ELP's forthcoming work. 'I had begun as Ian McDonald's songwriting partner,' Sinfield would later reflect. 'When Ian joined King Crimson I hung around the rehearsal room to write lyrics, but also did their sound, sorted out lighting, etc. I was halfway through making a solo album when Greg called me to say that Manticore wanted to release it. The catch was that he wanted me to collaborate on lyrics for a long piece that had begun to take shape.'

'The title 'was Pete Sinfield's,' remembered Emerson. 'I had originally wanted to call the piece "Ganton 9", based on an idea I had about a fictitious planet. Pete thought the music I had written sounded like a carnival and so he came up with the new title." Sinfield, along with Lake would also develop the theme of the influence computers would have upon civilisation. 'I used to work with computers before I became a songwriter', he later commented. 'These were massive IBM machines that worked using reels of magnetic tape. I'd always been fascinated with the idea of artificial intelligence battling with natural intelligence. I came up with the idea of man being taken over by a machine he had invented, the computer.'

Another early piece to be ear marked for inclusion on the forthcoming album was a composition by the Argentinean composer Alberto Ginastera. 'Toccata' had been a piece Keith Emerson had wanted ELP to record as far back as the beginning of 1971. 'I first heard "Toccata'" when I was in the Nice. We were playing with an orchestra in Los Angeles,' Keith recalled. 'I was in my dressing room when I heard this incredible music being played on stage by a pianist. I went back onto the stage and asked the pianist what the piece was. It was Ginastera's piano concerto and I was struck with the music immediately. When I got back to England I bought the sheet music and went through it. I didn't think about ELP playing the piece until Carl suggested that he wanted to bring a drum solo into our repertoire that would be different from simply adding it to the end of another number.

'He wanted to make it a central part of the piece. I played "Toccata" to him and he thought it was fantastic. We then rehearsed as a group, though it was quite demanding. Greg didn't read music and Carl wasn't able to apply a score written for piano to the drums, so we learned the piece bar by bar. It was music by mathematics, but it was certainly a marvellous achievement.'

Indeed, a series of European concerts beginning at the end of March 1973 saw both 'Karn Evil 9 First Impression' and 'Toccata' appear as part of the band's set. Greg Lake would also unveil a new acoustic composition, 'Still…You Turn Me On' which was enthusiastically received by audiences. It was on this tour that ELP would cross paths with the Swiss artist HR Giger. It was while playing in Zurich that an associate of the group introduced Keith Emerson to the artist who took inspiration from the gruesome and macabre. 'Giger was obsessed with things like surgical procedures and skin diseases,' recalled Emerson. 'After I was introduced to him I went back to our hotel and suggested that Greg and Carl come and meet with him too. We all wanted to have an input into the artwork concept of the new album and I thought Giger was an ideal artist for us.'

Greg Lake remembered a visit to the artist's home: 'His house was like a horror movie. It was filled with his art depicting the grotesque. He had things like an electric chair in one room and a pair of arms coming out of a wall! He was actually quite a sweet character who really wanted us to use his work and we agreed that he could design the next album cover.'

Work began in earnest on the album in June 1973 at Olympic Studios in Barnes, South West London with the working title for the project being 'Whip Some Skull on Yer', an expression used by the manager of Manticore Records, Mario Medious, as a slang reference to the act of fellatio. The first sessions saw 'Karn Evil 9 – First Impression' committed to tape, along with 'Toccata'. After a further period of writing, sessions continued at Advision studios in August. It was here that the fourth ELP album would be completed after a series of long sessions. The lengthy 'Karn Evil 9' was completed in the first two weeks of August, with the final impression of the work being the first track to be recorded at Advision. Also recorded was ELP's arrangement of Ginastera's 'Toccata'. Although the track had been performed on ELP's European tour of March and April 1973, by the time the composition was committed to tape it had gained additional instrumentation in the form of electronic percussion designed by ELP technician Nick Rose, essentially the first percussion synthesizer.

Still requiring Ginastera's permission for their stunning reworking of his work, Emerson and manager Stewart Young travelled to his home in Geneva to play him their interpretation. Keith Emerson recalled; 'Ginastera listened to the tape and then declared "You've captured the essence of my music like no-one else has before." I was elated and he gave us permission to use the track on the album.'

The recording of the album continued apace with sessions that saw a studio version of Greg Lake's 'Still You Turn Me On' recorded, and a stunning adaptation of Hubert Parry's 'Jerusalem' (with the words of William Blake's poem set to it). This ELP interpretation was dramatic and effective, so much so that it was considered for release as a single in December 1973. However, the success of the single would be thwarted. 'We were so pleased with our recording that we figured it was worthy of releasing as a single,' Carl Palmer would later reflect. 'In Britain at that time they had this format where four or five people had the power of veto as far as airplay was concerned. I think there was some apprehension to our adaptation of a hymn, that in their opinion we had bastardised. As a result the BBC banned it.'

Greg Lake also felt the single would have had a future if the ban hadn't occurred; 'The BBC was very conservative in its outlook in those days. I think they felt our version of 'Jerusalem' was a bit of an affront to Britishness. It was totally unjustified and I think it could have been a hit had we gained some airplay.' Ironically, 'Jerusalem' was selected by the band for release as a single over a less controversial contender, Greg Lake's acoustic composition, 'Still…You Turn Me On'. The song had featured in the ELP set on their European tour in the spring and had gone down well with fans.

Lake's acoustic material had gained the band airplay, particularly in the US where songs such as 'Lucky Man' and 'From the Beginning' were hit singles. Lake explained; 'I think the reason that we overlooked 'Still…You Turn Me On' as a single was that we felt that the acoustic pieces, while they were more accessible from a radio standpoint and people could remember them, they weren't really typical of the band as a whole. We had released a couple of singles in acoustic vein and we felt that we didn't want people to think that ELP only issued acoustic singles".

One of the final songs to be recorded was the light-hearted 'Benny The Bouncer', a humorous tale of a doorman of a slightly less than salubrious establishment, followed on stylistically from tunes like 'Are You Ready Eddie?' on the album 'Tarkus' and 'The Sheriff' on 'Trilogy'. Pete Sinfield would later explain; 'That song was very much in the tradition of the British music hall. I think the song was almost an antidote to the bombastic approach on most of the album, alongside Greg's acoustic work.'

ELP WORLD TREK 'IN BIGGEST PRODUCTION EVER MOBILISED'

EMERSON, LAKE & PALMER have mobilised a massive musical caravan for their 1973 world tour, which opens in Germany at the end of this month and continues through the spring and most of the summer. Operating under the banner of "Get Me A Ladder", the production is described as "the most ambitious spectacular ever mobilised for a group."

The European segment of the tour covers 27 dates in 32 days, opening in Dusseldorf on March 31 and closing in Rome on May 2. Negotiations are now being finalised for subsequent tours of Japan, Australia and America. And it is envisaged that the world trek will culminate with one or two major appearances in this country.

The presentation will involve the transporting of 50 tour personnel and 20 tons of equipment valued at 750,000 dollars. Two 40 ft. articulated trucks will carry the specially designed and built proscenium — a Roman-style arch and stage, which will be erected at every performance. There are also over 100 spotlights and five sets of stage curtains.

A spokesman for the group commented: "Our aim is to create a sympathetic setting for ELP's new musical concept. It will be the largest mobile musical production ever seen."

Supporting act throughout the world tour will be new Anglo-American rock group Stray Dog, who were recently signed to ELP's own Manticore label.

GREG LAKE (with CARL PALMER in background)

In the first week of October 1973 the results of four months' work in the studio were finally mixed. An initial album master mix was rejected by the band and, as a result, most of the material was remixed once more to the satisfaction of Keith, Greg and Carl. The working title of 'Whip Some Skull On Yer' was shelved in favour of 'Brain Salad Surgery', a title that had the same meaning albeit slightly better disguised. The phrase was taken from the Doctor John song 'Right Place, Wrong Time' and met with everyone's approval. Indeed, Keith Emerson, Greg Lake and Pete Sinfield composed a song around the new title which had been recorded in September.

Alas, the same could not have been said of the artwork designed by HR Giger, as Keith Emerson explained: 'He really did deliver a striking sleeve design. The only problem was that under the chin of the image of a ghostly woman, actually Giger's wife or girlfriend, he had placed an erect penis. When we presented the artwork to Atlantic Records, who were marketing the Manticore label,

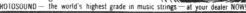

they went nuts! We were told that we had to remove the penis from the photograph to avoid being charged with pornography. At first Giger refused, but then he relented and we had the image of the penis airbrushed to turn it into a shaft of light. If you look closely at some versions of the album sleeve you can still just make out the original image of the helmet! Of course, a few years later Giger designed the monster and the sets for the movie Alien and his images became known to an even wider public.'

'Brain Salad Surgery' was released in Britain in November 1973. Its arrival was greeted by coverage in the New Musical Express music paper, which gave away a flexi-disc with each copy of the magazine featuring excerpts from the album, including the song 'Brain Salad Surgery' which wasn't released in full until it appeared as the B-side of the 'Fanfare For The Common Man' single in June 1977. The album reached Number 2 in the UK and, by the time the record was released, Emerson, Lake and Palmer were in the United States on their next tour of North America.

The concerts were the most lavish staged by the band to date, with a Quadraphonic sound system being utilised, a state of the art lighting rig and spectacular stage effects such as Emerson's use of a huge rig that elevated his grand piano into the air and spun it in a 360 degree circle. The American dates would be just the start of a massive world tour which saw ELP elevated to rock's aristocracy. These spectacular concerts also assisted in 'Brain Salad Surgery' reaching Number 11 on the US Billboard chart.

The album still courts critical controversy over 35 years from its release. Some cited 'Brain Salad Surgery' as a prime example of the overblown excesses now in evidence in the progressive rock bands and ELP unfairly became the target of the wrath of many critics, particularly in Britain. There is no doubt that the record is a tremendous achievement and one of the major releases from the heyday of progressive music. In 2006 Keith Emerson recalled; 'We were on a real creative roll when we wrote and recorded "Brain Salad Surgery". At that time we all worked very closely together. As a result we really did push boundaries forward and we came up with some amazing music. That album saw us push boundaries further than we'd ever done before and I listen to that music now and I wonder how we did it. I think it's because we had a happy team.

'It remains a time when ELP were most receptive to each other's ideas and a most creative period respecting each other's artistry and position. We'd actually settled down and were comfortable in each other's company; having achieved a degree of great success…success does provide, to a certain extent, some comfort. The idea of superseding our last album wasn't an issue, we'd always remained aware of, yet oblivious to, our contemporaries but now we gave them something to think about. We may have unintentionally worried a lot of people, but not in a supercilious fashion of indifference. We just did our own thing, oblivious to the rest of the music world… and it worked!'

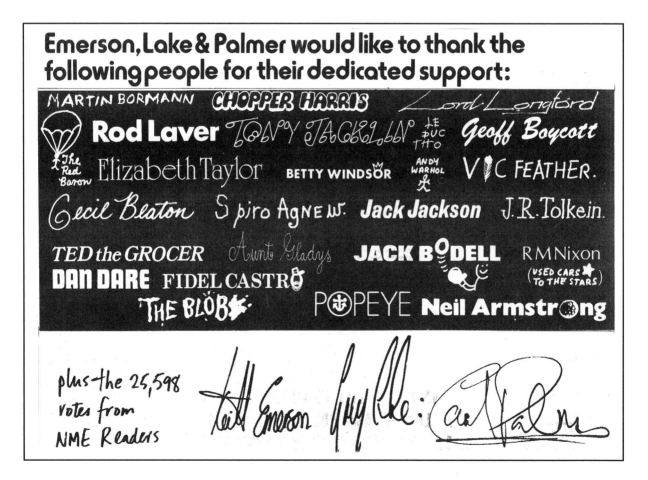

Emerson to test new Moog

KEITH EMERSON travels to America this week in order to test a new super-synthesiser at the Robert Moog factory, Buffalo, N.Y.

The synthesizer, rumoured to be polyphonic — which means it will play chords instead of just single notes — will be incorporated into ELP's stage act if Emerson is satisfied with the instrument's performance.

ELP's first single – free with NME

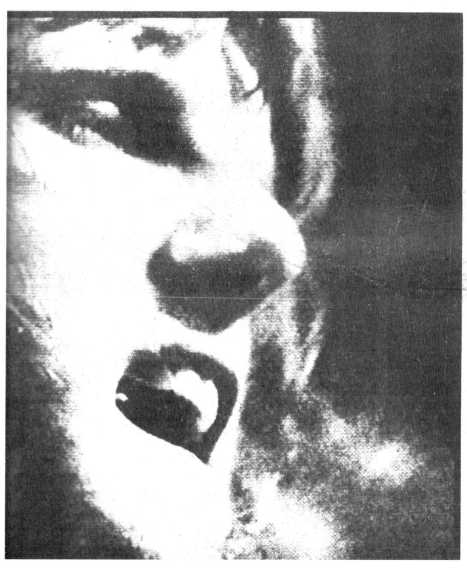

EMERSON, LAKE and Palmer have recorded their first ever single . . . to be given free exclusively with New Musical Express.

The single, "Brain Salad Surgery", is also the title of the band's new LP — but the specially-recorded track will not be appearing on the album, nor in fact will it appear in any form in Britain except through NME.

It therefore becomes another collectors item reader-service offer, following a line of NME free records from such illustrious names as Stones, Faces and Alice Cooper but breaking fresh ground with one innovative feature — the ELP disc will be contained in a colour cover, itself a miniature facsimile of the "Brain Salad Surgery" album sleeve.

Demand for the November 3 issue scheduled to contain the ELP single is certain to push NME circulation near the half million mark. In the past however, even this has not been enough to satisfy reader demand.

If you don't want to miss out on an exclusive chunk of rock history — colour cover and all — we suggest you strongarm your local newsagent immediately into placing you a regular order.

Emerson, Lake and Palmer meanwhile continue final work on the "Brain Salad Surgery" album — their first for well over a year. Release date is due early November.

■ *NME regrets that it is not possible to carry the free ELP single on export copies of the paper in Europe and elsewhere.*

FAUST 'Faust IV'

First released as Virgin V2004 in September 1973
Highest UK chart position: N/A
Available on CD as Virgin CDVR2004

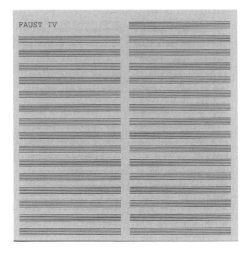

Krautrock
The Sad Skinhead
Jennifer
Just a Second (Starts Like That)/Picnic On A
Frozen River/Deuxieme Tableaux
Giggly Smile
Lauft…Heisst Das Es Lauft Oder Es Kommt Bald…Lauft

Hans Joachim Irmler	**Organ, Electronics**
Werner 'Zappi' Diermaier	**Drums, Percussion, Objects**
Jean-Herve Peron	**Bass, Vocals**
Rudolf Sosna	**Guitar, Vocals**
Gunther Wusthoff	**Saxophone and Synthesiser**

Produced by Uwe Nettlebeck
Recorded at the Manor Studios, Oxfordshire in June 1973

Faust stand alone in the maelstrom of creative chaos that was the emerging German rock scene of the early Seventies. As equally experimental as contemporaries such as Can, Faust also retained a sense of humour and an anarchistic approach to their music which other German experimentalists gradually lost. Their body of recorded work may have been small, but the excellence and lasting influence of the music created by Hans-Joachim Irmler (organ, electronics), Werner 'Zappi' Diermaier (drums), Jean-Herve Peron (bass), Rudolf Sosna (guitar and keyboards) and Gunter Wusthoff (saxophone and synthesiser) is undeniable.

Formed in the early months of 1970 in Hamburg, northern Germany, Faust came together out of two musical movements in the Hamburg area. Hans Joachim Irmler would later explain; 'I was in a band with Zappi, but the line-up was always changing. Then Zappi met a girl who knew some musicians in another loose band and we were introduced. We got together in an old underground air-raid shelter to rehearse. It was more like a damp, narrow and very long corridor. The corridor was so long we never went right to the end as we were frightened about what we might find there!'

Encouraged by their initial creative experiments, the as yet un-named band came up with an innovative strategy to fulfil their musical ambitions. 'We were all agreed that we didn't want to play in small clubs to indifferent audiences while finding our musical feet,' Irmler continues. 'We thought that it would be best to get together in the countryside, as it would force us all to work together to produce something interesting. Our main problem was that we had no money. Two of us had been students, one of us had been a teacher and the other two worked here and there. We needed someone to finance our ideas, but as we looked so way out at that time, we felt it better to find someone closer to the establishment in Germany who negotiate on our behalf. Through some friends of mine in the film industry we were introduced to Uwe Nettlebeck, a left-wing journalist, who offered to act in this role for us.'

Intrigued by the experimental nature of Faust's music, Nettlebeck undertook his role with relish and soon secured a contract for the band with Polydor in Hamburg. 'Polydor were known in Germany mainly for the many Schlager acts they had signed such as James Last and Bert Kampfaert, and certainly not many rock bands. Hendrix had recently died and Polydor were anxious to find the next big rock act. Uwe had managed to create such an aura around us that they signed us without even knowing what sort of music we would produce.'

Equally surprising was the size of the advance received by the band – a staggering £200,000, unheard-of in Germany for a previously unsigned act – and Polydor's agreement to provide the group with recording equipment, a recording engineer (Kurt Graupner) permanently at their disposal, accommodation in an old schoolhouse in the rural town of Wümme and enough money to live on for a year in order to produce their first album.

After many months of experimenting with 'cut and paste' editing techniques, location sound recordings of street protest marches, recordings of radio broadcasts and electronic music, Faust presented their finished album to their label. 'Polydor went crazy when they heard the tapes,' recalls Hans-Joachim. 'But they were contracted to release our albums and had little choice except to go along with the release.'

The stunning album 'Faust' appeared in September 1971, pressed in clear vinyl and housed in a transparent PVC sleeve with an X-ray of a fist the only image on the cover. Although initial reaction to the record was somewhat muted in Germany, reaction

Faust

to the record in Britain was much more encouraging. John Peel immediately championed the release on his BBC Radio 1 show. As a result of Peel's endorsement of the album, most of the initial 20,000 sales achieved were in the UK.

Faust continued their pattern of working in their schoolhouse, shunning live work in favour of further recording and releasing their second album, 'So Far', in 1972. By this time, relations between Polydor and the band had broken down. 'Polydor were not at all happy with us and they certainly weren't capable of understanding what Faust was about or what we were trying to achieve. There were one or two good people in the company, but they were in less senior positions and didn't have much influence,' explains Irmler.

'Just as relations began to sour between the German office and ourselves, we got a visit from Polydor's UK label manager. He came to see us at our studio in Wümme and brought with him a large bottle of very old Cognac. He was very interested in what we are doing. He told us our music was very much ahead of its time and that we were making music from the street, which gave us some encouragement that our music was understood outside Germany.'

Faust ended 1972 without a recording contract and, with the comments of Polydor's UK representative still fresh in their minds, looked to a British company to further their recording ambitions. After an initial approach to Chrysalis Records was rejected, the owner of a record shop and mail-order company came on the scene.

'We had exhausted every avenue in the UK when we discovered that Richard Branson, was going to set up his own label, Virgin Records' recalled Irmler. 'On hearing this we made contact with him and Branson came to Germany to see us, bringing Simon Draper, his A&R guy, with him. A friend of ours ran a small cinema and so Richard and Simon came there to meet us. They wanted to hear us play live and so we arranged a short performance. We must have been eager to impress them as I hated playing live at that time. I didn't enjoy the experience of being on stage, but in order get our desired contract I agreed to perform for Branson and Draper. Simon was a really great A&R man and in my opinion the success of Virgin Records was founded on Simon Draper's musical expertise.

'Simon always had an eye on the future and on what might become the next major musical trend. We signed to Virgin for a low advance when compared to our recent Polydor deal. With Polydor we had achieved a £200,000 advance, but Richard signed us for a tenth of that!' As part of their new-found contract with Virgin, Richard Branson promised Faust the full use of a recording studio at their disposal to record their first album for the label.

'We all left Wümme to relocate in England.' Irmler would later comment. On our way we agreed to perform some concerts. For me this was very hard as I had always objected to performing live. I was very shy. In those days the equipment wasn't good enough to reproduce the sort of sounds I wanted to achieve on stage. We were also a group of diverse influences, with some of the guys being heavily into Bob Dylan and writing songs, while I was more into experimenting with sounds, so any live performance could be uneven. However, the shows went better than I expected and we arrived in England well–rehearsed. We also decided that we would bring with us a gift for Virgin Records. We had compiled a series of recordings using cut and paste editing techniques and decided to let Virgin use it for our first release on our new label.'

The gift that Faust brought to Virgin Records was the legendary 'Faust Tapes', a record that would later be hailed as a major influence on British new-wave musicians of the late Seventies. 'The album had a definite concept behind its release,' Irmler adds. 'We decided to expose the fiction that was the British music charts. Our way of showing what a charade chart placements were was to sell "Faust Tapes" for next to nothing to see if the price would ensure the album charted. Simon Draper was very keen on the idea, but Richard Branson calculated the costs and told us that we couldn't do it. Our compromise was to sell the record for 49 pence, the price of a single at that time. We agreed that only 100,000 copies would be made and that after that the band would own the rights. Everything was done as cheaply as possible. Uwe Nettlebeck created the cover by typing the "reviews" that comprised the sleeve on his IBM typewriter!

'When we arrived at the Manor we found it full of equipment we had never used before. The studio was totally different and in the beginning it was quite hard to adjust to this and we took some time to settle in to the recording process. We had brought some recordings with us to those sessions and some parts of the album were not recorded at the Manor. Pieces such as "Picnic On A Frozen River", "Giggly Smile" and "It's A Bit Of A Pain" were begun at Wümme.'

As the album neared completion, tensions began to arise between Irmler and Nettlebeck. 'One day I came to the studio,' Irmler later explained, 'to find Uwe Nettlebeck and an engineer compiling the final album master without my knowledge. Our first rule in the formation of Faust had been that we should all be present when an album was compiled and mixed. Although Uwe was credited on our records as a producer, his job was really to sort our logistics for us and he had nothing to do with the creation of the music itself. It was totally against all the principles of the band and so I had a huge argument with him.'

This disagreement spilled over into Irmler's relationship with fellow band members and Richard Branson. 'I protested about the situation to Richard Branson and fought against other band members. As I was the youngest member of the group I was ignored, and my anger built up to the point where I had a meeting with Richard Branson during which he spoke in English and I only spoke in German! Richard wanted more of a say in the way Faust produced music, offering us a huge sum of money to remain with the label and wanting to send us to perform in America. At that point I decided it was time to call a halt to this. Within days of this I left the band and Rudolf left a few days after me.'

Zappi Diermaier, Jean-Herve Peron and Gunter Wusthoff opted to continue as Faust and recruited Peter Blegvad (of Slapp Happy) on bass and former Guru Guru member Uli Trepte on electronics. 'Faust IV' was released as Virgin V2004 on 21 September to a favourable critical reaction in the British music press. Although sessions had ended on a less than happy note and the music recorded was less avant-garde in nature than their preceding work, Faust had nevertheless created a masterpiece.

The release of the album coincided with an extensive British tour. Hans-Joachim Irmler would reunite with his erstwhile colleagues some weeks later. 'After I returned to Germany Zappi called me and begged Rudolf and me to come back. He must have been very persuasive because we rejoined Faust for their last couple of UK shows that year.' Despite the stunning concerts delivered, Faust ended their association with Virgin in acrimonious circumstances in the spring of 1974.

Hans-Joachim Irmler relocated to Southern Germany and invited the members of Faust to work on a new album. He explains; 'I rented a cottage outside of Munich and we worked on new music. I contacted producer and studio owner Giorgio Moroder and explained that we had no money, but asked if we could use his studio in "down time". He agreed. The music we made was during those sessions was far ahead of anything we had made before. The album never came out in its entirety, but some tracks later appeared on the '"Munich Tapes'" compilation. It was a taste of what might have been.'

Despite the untimely demise of Faust, the group resurfaced in 1996 with the album 'You Know Faust' and continues to perform and record in one guise or another. Faust's Polydor albums still retain the power to shock, but it is on 'Faust IV' that the fusion of all of the group's musical influences came together to produce a truly unique album.

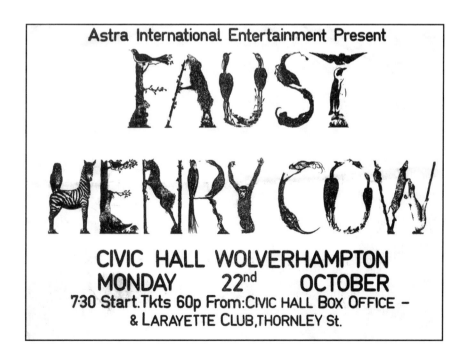

Astra International Entertainment Present

FAUST

HENRY COW

CIVIC HALL WOLVERHAMPTON
MONDAY   22nd   OCTOBER
7·30 Start. Tkts 60p From: CIVIC HALL BOX OFFICE –
& LARAYETTE CLUB, THORNLEY St.

MIKE OLDFIELD 'Tubular Bells'

First released as Virgin V2001 in May 1973
Highest UK chart position: Number 1
Available on CD as Mercury 0602527035055

Tubular Bells Part One
Tubular Bells Part Two

Mike Oldfield	**Grand Piano, Glockenspiel, Farfisa Organ, Bass Guitar, Electric Guitar, Speed Guitar, Taped Motor Drive Amplifier Organ, Mandolin-Like Guitar, Fuzz Guitars, Assorted Percussion, Acoustic Guitar, Flageolet, Honky Tonk, Lowry Organ, Concert Timpani, Guitars sounding like Bagpipes, Piltdown Man**
Steve Broughton:	**Drums on 'Tubular Bells Part Two'**
Jon Field:	**Flutes on 'Tubular Bells Part One'**
Viv Stanshall	**Master of Ceremonies on 'Tubular Bells Part One'**
Lindsay Cooper	**String Bass on 'Tubular Bells Part One'**
Girlie Chorus	**Sally Oldfield, Mundy Ellis**

Produced by Mike Oldfield, Tom Newman and Simon Heyworth
Recorded at the Manor, Oxfordshire, autumn 1972 and spring 1973
Engineered by Tom Newman and Simon Heyworth

In May 1973 an album was released that would change the perceptions of what was possible in the sphere of popular music. One of the most phenomenal albums ever issued, 'Tubular Bells' was an astounding achievement by a gifted musician who had only recently celebrated his twentieth birthday when the record was released. However, Mike Oldfield had sketched out his rudimentary ideas for the piece as far back as the autumn of 1971.

Despite being only 19 years old when he recorded this seminal work, Oldfield had in fact been a professional musician since the age of 15 when he performed with his sister Sally in the duo Sallyangie. He had performed in folk clubs in the Reading area, becoming an accomplished guitarist inspired by the music and playing of British folk legend John Renbourn alongside an appreciation of classical music and Flamenco guitar.

In 1969 Sallyangie signed to Nat Joseph's Transatlantic label, recording the album 'Children Of The Sun' and toured the colleges, universities and clubs of Britain for nearly a year, brother Terry acting as driver and road manager. When Transatlantic failed to take up the option of a follow-up album, Sallyangie disbanded. Sally Oldfield pursued a career as solo artist, while Mike formed the more rock-orientated Barefoot with his brother Terry.

Signing to NEMS, management was passed to Julia Creasy at the agency. Barefoot only performed a few concerts before ceasing. However, it was through Julia, who left NEMS to work at Blackhill Enterprises, that Mike secured his next professional role. Blackhill, the hippest agency in London at that time, was run by Peter Jenner and Andrew King, the first managers of Pink Floyd, and also represented former Soft Machine bass guitarist Kevin Ayers.

Ayers had struck out on a solo career and had recorded his debut album, 'Joy Of A Toy', for EMI's progressive label Harvest in 1969. He was now putting together a new backing group for live and recording work, and Julia Creasy brought Mike Oldfield to his attention. The young guitarist secured an audition as bass-player in Ayers' new band and, in March 1970, joined saxophonist Lol Coxhill, keyboard-player David Bedford and drummer Mick Fincher in the Whole World.

He would remain in Ayers' band for the next 14 months, recording and touring and striking up a friendship with David Bedford, who was also an orchestral arranger of note. Through Bedford, Oldfield was exposed to the composer's avant-garde works and his style of undertaking musical composition.

Soon after some concerts in Amsterdam in August 1970, Mike began to suffer from panic attacks and retreated to his parent's home in Harold Wood, Essex. Here he found solace in the music of classical composers from Beethoven and Bach to works by Sibelius, Bartok and Stravinsky. Teaching himself musical notation, Oldfield sketched out his musical ideas for piano and guitar in a notebook, devising his own form of musical notation in a chart-like form. Throughout this time he continued to perform as a member of the Whole World, but, by the spring of 1971, his anxiety attacks and a general dissatisfaction with performing in the band led to his departure following a session for Ayers' next album, 'Whatevershebringswesing'.

When Ayers dissolved the Whole World and assembled a new live band, Mike agreed to join on the condition that he had creative input into the arrangement of Ayers' material. With the new band came a new home in a house in Westbourne Gardens

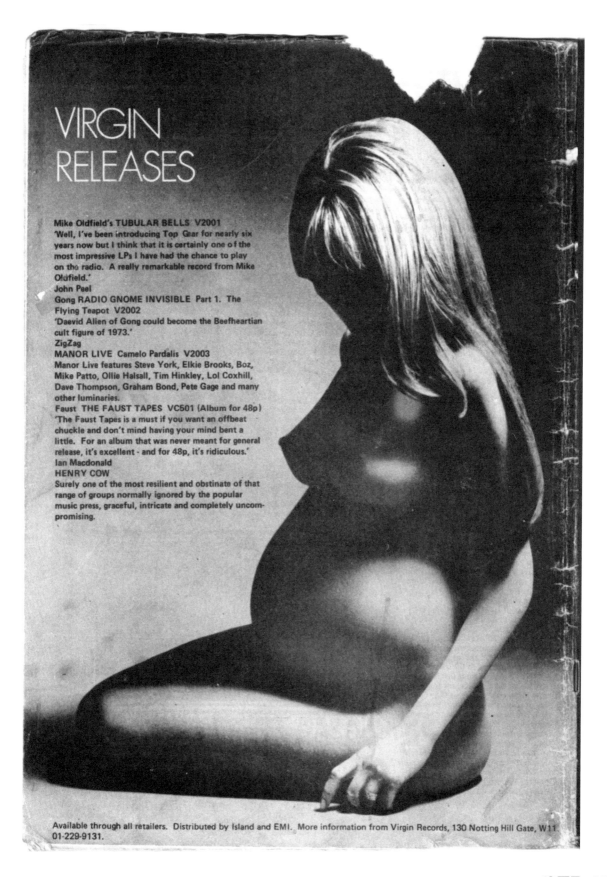

VIRGIN RELEASES

Mike Oldfield's TUBULAR BELLS V2001
'Well, I've been introducing Top Gear for nearly six
years now but I think that it is certainly one of the
most impressive LPs I have had the chance to play
on the radio. A really remarkable record from Mike
Oldfield.'
John Peel

Gong RADIO GNOME INVISIBLE Part 1. The
Flying Teapot V2002
'Daevid Allen of Gong could become the Beefheartian
cult figure of 1973.'
ZigZag

MANOR LIVE Camelo Pardalis V2003
Manor Live features Steve York, Elkie Brooks, Boz,
Mike Patto, Ollie Halsall, Tim Hinkley, Lol Coxhill,
Dave Thompson, Graham Bond, Pete Gage and many
other luminaries.

Faust THE FAUST TAPES VC501 (Album for 48p)
'The Faust Tapes is a must if you want an offbeat
chuckle and don't mind having your mind bent a
little. For an album that was never meant for general
release, it's excellent - and for 48p, it's ridiculous.'
Ian Macdonald

HENRY COW
Surely one of the most resilient and obstinate of that
range of groups normally ignored by the popular
music press, graceful, intricate and completely uncom-
promising.

Available through all retailers. Distributed by Island and EMI. More information from Virgin Records, 130 Notting Hill Gate, W11
01-229-9131.

MIKE OLDFIELD

Virgin Records
distributed by
Atlantic Recording Corp.

in Tottenham, rented by Ayers. However, this was destined to last only a few months. By July 1971 Ayers had tired of performing with his new group and accepted an invitation to tour with former Soft Machine bandmate Daevid Allen in his new group Gong.

Mike had tired of being a member of a backing group and was eager to pursue his own musical ideas. Influenced by the music of the large jazz-rock ensemble Centipede, formed by pianist Keith Tippett and featuring such luminaries as Julie Tippett (nee Driscoll), Robert Wyatt, Marc Charig, Ian Carr and Elton Dean, and the album 'A Rainbow in Curved Air' by minimalist American composer Terry Riley which featured a mesmerising repetitive keyboard sequence, Oldfield began to formulate ideas for a solo work he would later describe as being 'a way out of the mental anguish I was suffering at the time.'

Kevin Ayers offered Mike the use of his Bang and Olufsen Beocord quarter-inch tape machine upon which he could record demos of his new music. Thus in a bedroom overlooking the garden of a terraced house in North London, a musical phenomenon was sketched out and conceived. Oldfield devised an ingenious method of customising the tape recorder into a machine capable of basic multi-tracking. He discovered that, by some slight rewiring and the blocking of the machine's erase head with a piece of card, he could record an instrument on one track on the tape and 'bounce' the finished recording to the other while simultaneously recording a new instrument.

This allowed him to build up a piece of music layer upon layer by recording one individual instrument at a time. 'I loved the whole idea of a repetitive musical sequence,' Mike would later reflect. 'I thought that if I was to make up my own music I wanted to have a repetitive riff at the beginning. Using David Bedford's Farfisa organ I fiddled around with an idea for a few minutes and came up with a riff I liked. I thought of it as one bar in 7/8 time and one bar in 8/8 or 4/4 time.

'I found the record button on the Bang and Olufsen machine and played that riff for about five minutes or so. I listened back to it and the riff stuck.' Oldfield eventually produced a demo with seven overdubs that was approximately 20 minutes in length, a major achievement.

In January 1972 he participated in further sessions for Kevin Ayers' 'Whatevershebringswesing' at Abbey studios and took the opportunity to play his demo to the musicians. Aside from a favourable comment from David Bedford, the overall reaction was one of mystified silence. Undaunted Mike presented his demo to Nick Mobbs, A&R head of Harvest, but after some consideration the notion of signing Oldfield was rejected. Similar approaches were made to CBS and Pye, only to be met with the same indifference.

Still residing in a shared house in Tottenham and faced with the need to earn some money, Mike took the role of guitarist in the earliest incarnation of the Sensational Alex Harvey Band. Through the contact with Harvey Mike also joined the band of the stage musical Hair, of which the Scot was also a member. During this period he also formulated further ideas for his musical demo, known as 'Opus One'.

When the work in Hair came to an end, Mike was approached by Peter Jenner of Blackhill Enterprises with the offer of joining the backing group of Arthur Louis, a Jimi Hendrix-influenced signing to who was seeking a recording contract. As part of this process Louis had been booked into a new studio in a manor house in Shipton-on-Cherwell in Oxfordshire. The Manor was established by Richard Branson, who was then running Caroline Records, a mail order company that would tap into the musical tastes of the student fraternity. One of the earliest sessions booked at the Manor was Arthur Louis and his band.

It was while there that Mike Oldfield, hired as bass guitarist for the sessions, struck up a friendship with engineer Tom Newman. Discovering their mutual love of flying model aircraft, Oldfield and Newman struck up a rapport. 'I realised I might have the opportunity to play my demos to the people at the Manor,' Mike would later remember. 'Unfortunately I'd left the tapes at home. I mentioned this to Arthur Louis' roadie and he very kindly offered to drive me back to Essex to collect the tapes and then drive me back to Oxfordshire. It was about a three-hour drive. I can't remember his name, but I really do owe him everything; none of what came later would have happened if it weren't for him.'

Tom Newman offered to play the demos to Richard Branson and Simon Draper at Virgin; the idea of the company establishing a record label was still some months away. Mike returned to his parents' house in Harold Wood to work on further musical ideas and grew more despondent by the week. His mood was at its lowest when he was called by Simon Draper inviting him to join him and meet with Richard Branson.

Arranging to meet in the office above the Virgin record shop in Notting Hill Oldfield met with Simon Draper and was then taken to Richard Branson's house boat in Little Venice for dinner to discuss the possibility of turning Mike's demos into an album. At the end of the dinner Richard Branson agreed to grant a week of studio time in the Manor to record the first part of Mike Oldfield's 'Opus One'.

In November 1972 Mike returned to the Manor and found it a very different place to the studio he had visited some months earlier. By now it was equipped with the latest 16-track recording equipment and had

RECIPE for success: take one piano . . .

Tubular Bells

A new album by MIKE OLDFIELD which seems to be attracting a certain amount of interest.

V2001. Available at all retailers.

> Without borrowing anything from established classics or descending to the discords, squeals and burps of the determinedly avant-garde, Mike Oldfield has produced music which combines logic with surprise, sunshine with rain.

> It is one of the most mature, vital, rich and humorous pieces of music to have emerged from the pop idiom. One hearing should provide sufficient proof.

Al Clark—NME

> Whilst fully aware of the ineffability of absolutes, I can only say that this is the most phenomenally brilliant and frighteningly original music to have ever appeared as 'pop'. It moves me to the same immensity of feeling as Sibelius or Debussy. It is a major work, and an exquisite achievement.

TUBULAR BELLS IS A VAST WORK:
MIKE OLDFIELD:
Tubular Bells, (Virgin).

This is a completely different kettle of Oldfields and is no relation to ours. The Mike Oldfield under discussion here has recorded, virtually unaided, his own finely constructed composition. In doing so he has played a startling number of instruments, far too many to list here. Suffice it to say that if it can be plonked then Michael has plucked it, and if it can be plonked then he has plonked it, 'Tubular Bells' is a vast work, almost classical in its structure and in the way a theme is stated and deftly worked upon. Each part of the composition is allowed to 'grow' organically and if, as I suspect, the work is a fair reflection of Mr Oldfield himself, then he is a serene, calm and contemplative character. A happy, satisfied man with a feeling for the spiritual things in life, for he has a musical approach that hints at religiosity. His scope is, of course, broader than that would imply. There are moments of harshness. For instance, about half-way through the first side jagged electric guitars briefly cut into the relaxed mood. Mike has so carefully built. He's not without a sense of humour too, as in the accelerating 'Sailor's Hornpipe', which closes side two, and in the introduction of the incomparable Viv Stanshall as Master of Ceremonies. Vivian announces in serious, round, plum tones worthy of the Beeb the entrance of each instrument over the top of Oldfield's guitar riff. The mind flew back to 'Gorilla' and 'Intro And Outro'. As Viv introduces 'Tubular Bells' into the track side one climaxes and swiftly fades down to acoustic guitar. Side two is basically in the same mood. The light acoustic guitars giving a warm, sunny atmosphere - memories of basking on a Spanish beach. Later that same side, his use of guitar to get the skirl of bagpipes is fascinating. Again the uncomfortable middle section to this side (grunting in Piltdown Man style) has strength in its mood and simple riff. For that section, Mike has brought on Broughton (Steve, brother of Edgar) to help out on drums. An enjoyable, evocative album which bodes well for the future of both the country's newest label, and of Mike Oldfield.

Geoff Brown — MM

IT REALLY IS A REMARKABLE ALBUM
It is not often that you get in a batch of the first releases from a new record company and find among them an album that not only strikes you with its freshness of ideas and excellence of execution, but surpasses your expectations of the artist concerned. But Mike Oldfield's 'Tubular Bells' (Virgin V2001) does all that and more.

I was knocked sideways when I first heard it, went through a stage of not being sure what I thought of it, trying to examine it and pick holes in it, and ended up convinced that it really is a remarkable album—and that isn't an adjective I'm using lightly.

Unless you were a devotee of Kevin Ayers' Whole World or are a close scrutineer of session credits, Mike Oldfield may be an unfamiliar name, but having heard him with the Whole World and knowing that he was making a solo album. I was expecting to hear a good album that featured some outstanding guitar playing.

I was not expecting two uninterrupted sides of complex, interlocking carefully woven music that works its way through an enormous dynamic and emotional range, and gives me the same kind of feeling as I had when I first heard bands like Pink Floyd and Soft Machine. That is not to compare the structure of 'Tubular Bells' with those two bands, merely to say that what they were to their time, I believe Mike Oldfield's album will be to now.

I don't really want to attempt to describe the music, partly because I don't think I could and partly because I'd rather you approached it as unprepared as possible. But do approach it—I can't think of another album that I'd as unhesitatingly recommend to everyone who's likely to read this.

Steve Peacock, Sounds

PURE MUSIC
MIKE OLDFIELD
'Tubular Bells' (Virgin)

Formerly guitarist with the Kevin Ayers Circus, Mike Oldfield has been working on this music in varying forms and interpretations for almost three years. Now he is the first on the brand-new Virgin label, brainchild of Europe's Richard Branston.

Perhaps the original purpose of music was to create emotions, or express feelings, which could not be achieved by any other art form. Today that has certainly been lost. And this is why 'Tubular Bells' is so different. It is pure music, created by an absolute musician, and I can't see how anyone could listen to it unmoved. Whilst fully aware of the ineffability of absolutes, I can only say that this is the most phenomenally brilliant and frighteningly original music to have ever appeared as 'pop'. It moves me to the same immensity of feeling as Sibelius or Debussy. It is a major work, and an exquisite achievement. Even the sober and collected Mr John Peel described it as the most incredible music he had heard in all his four years as a disc jockey.

Mike Oldfield plays almost all the instruments, and there are many, ranging from tympani to flageolet and guitars sounding like bagpipes. Plus of course, tubular bells. And there is a brainwave of an appearance by Viv Stanshall, second only to the indescribable vocals of the Piltdown Man. This record indicates the emergence of a mammoth musical talent: there will be a huge reaction to it. And if you find this all too laudatory, then just listen to it. I do not think that words could ever do justice to this beautiful, beautiful music, nor praise it enough.

William A Murray
Time Out

A SUPERLATIVE RECORD
MIKE OLDFIELD:
'Tubular Bells' (Virgin).

Being familiar with Mike Oldfield only in the context of his playing on Kevin Ayers' records and having no further evidence of his abilities, it was not unreasonable to expect his first album to consist of, at best, one dexterously protracted guitar solo, or, at worst, a collection of songs delineating his juvenile fetishes.

'Tubular Bells' rapidly evaporates such notions. Although woven together by impeccable playing on numerous guitars, including some that sound like mandolins and others that sound like bagpipes, it is a continuous 50-minute general instrumental work for which—excepting the occasional flute, string bass or choral voice—Oldfield is entirely responsible.

This veritable orgy of overdubbing results in a remarkable piece of sustained music, never content with the purely facile yet equally disinclined towards confusing the listener. Oldfield is consistently inventive within established territory, so that, without departing from a framework familiar to rock-orientated ears, and without assuming the chilly austerity endemic among Teutonic explorers, he achieves a multilayered intricacy which is absorbing at every level.

HIS MUSICIANSHIP THROUGHOUT THE ALBUM IS FLAWLESS.
MIKE OLDFIELD
Tubular Bells, Virgin V2001. Producer: Mike Oldfield.

This album must rank as one of the best releases of the year and Oldfield seems set to convert the tremendous reputation he has as a session player into a sales bonanza. His musicianship throughout the album is flawless and Oldfield amazes the listener with the seemingly never-ending list of instruments he plays.

Music Week

THE FIRST BREAKTHROUGH INTO HISTORY THAT ANY MUSICIAN REGARDED PRIMARILY AS A ROCK MUSICIAN HAS MADE
On the all too frequent occasions when I'm told that a record by a contemporary rock musician is a work of 'lasting interest' I tend to reach for my hat and head for the wide open spaces. Tony Palmer's theories notwithstanding, rock music, even the very best of it, is essentially ephemeral. Even when it does survive over any period of time—and rock hasn't yet amassed 20 years over which to survive—it is, happily, the stuff which the experts dismiss out of hand that makes it across the Styx. In the fifties the pundits predicted that the Presley's, the Cochrans, the Little Richards and the Fats Dominos were merely transitory phenomena and would fade away with the first onrush of reality. The really durable music, they cried to a man, was the jazz and serious pop of the period. Well, forgive me, but I don't even remember the names of the people they praised for their quality and durability.

Today these same experts or their descendants would probably tell you that in 20 years' time collectors will still be enthusing over the records of such weighty bands as Yes and Emerson, Lake, Palmer. I'm ready to bet you a few shillings that Yes and ELP will have vanished from the memory of all but the most stubborn and that the Gary Glitters and Sweets of no lasting value and Top of the Pops will be regarded as representing the true sound of the Seventies.

Having said that, I'm going to tell you about a new recording that to me it represents the first breakthrough into history that any musician regarded as primarily a rock musician has made. Mike Oldfield even had the nerve to be something of a child prodigy, recording a pleasant, if somewhat sugary LP of dainty songs with his sister Sally at the age of 14. A year later he was working alongside such seasoned professionals as the itinerant sax hero Lol Coxhill and the composer David Bedford in Kevin Ayers' erratic but witty and articulate group, the Whole World.

In 1971 Mike Oldfield began work on a composition entitled 'Tubular Bells' and now, after 2,300 overdubs, 'Tubular Bells' is available on record as the first release from Virgin Records of Notting Hill Gate: Virgin V2001 (£2.19). Too often have we read of music that 'crossed the barriers between pop and the classics' when it manifestly did nothing of the sort. For too long also has the business of reviewing records and arranging them in attractive sequences. With 'Tubular Bells' we have a record that does quite genuinely cover new and uncharted territory. Without borrowing anything from established classics or descending to the discords, squeals and burps of the determinedly avant-garde, Mike Oldfield has produced music which combines logic with surprise, sunshine with rain. In the process of so doing he plays a bewildering range of musical instruments without ever playing merely for effect. Each device is there because that is where it should be. On the recording he has some assistance from other musicians, and it must be an indication of the scope of 'Tubular Bells' that the forthcoming live performance on 25 June at the Queen Elizabeth Hall in London will draw on the talents of Steve Winwood, the curious Viv Stanshall, Robert Wyatt (my own favourite drummer), the aforementioned David Bedford and Kevin Ayers, Frank Ricotti and members of Gong and the underrated Henry Cow. Sadly, I can't anticipate much interest from Radio 1, but perhaps it is not too late for Radio 3 at least to arrange for this first live performance of 'Tubular Bells' to be recorded.

John Peel, The Listener

. . . OVERDUB a mandolin. Seventy-five thousand times . . .

. . . And start worrying about the tax returns.

started taking bookings by established artists such as John Cale. The instruments Mike had requested were delivered and work began on turning demos into an album. The first instrument to be recorded was a Steinway grand piano. 'I began playing the opening riff without any backing,' Mike later recalled. 'I started adding a few things but my timing wasn't very good and it just wasn't working. The problem was resolved the next day by Simon Heyworth who suggested putting a metronome in another room next to a microphone and sending the click to me through my headphones.'

The sessions were added to by the presence of Jon Field of Jade Warrior who provided flute parts. Also invited was double bass player Lindsay Cooper (once cellist with the Strawbs) whose presence was also felt. Because the studio was also booked by the Bonzo Dog Band, who had reformed to record the album 'Let's Make Up and Be Friendly', recording time was extremely limited. With a day left the final repetitive section of the piece was recorded, a section that gradually increased in intensity featuring numerous guitar overdubs of the main riff. With Mike feeling the finale required the presence of another instrument thoughts turned to finding a suitable choice. Remembering that John Cale had used a set of tubular bells during his sessions, Oldfield suggested he use them.

'It was only because those bells were already in the studio that I decided to use them,' Oldfield later recalled. 'If they hadn't been there, the album may have turned out quite differently.' The last day of the sessions also produced the idea of introducing each instrument in turn in the finale of the piece. Mike remembered a Bonzo Dog Band track called 'The Intro And The Outro' in which band member Vivian Stanshall introduced members of a surreal band. With Stanshall having dinner in the room next to the studio Simon Heyworth asked him if he would act as master of ceremonies on the recording.

'Viv was a kind of superstar in those days,' Mike would remember three decades later. 'I couldn't believe he agreed to do it. Although he was a little worse off for drink he was charming and respectful. I wrote everything out for him and pointed to each line when it was time for him to introduce each instrument. He really got into the spirit of it and did it in one take. When he said "plus Tubular Bells!" it was just perfect.'

Impressed with the finished results, Draper and Branson consented to Mike recording a second part of the work at the Manor in 'down time' in the evening when other acts weren't using the studio. By now plans were hatched to launch Virgin as a record label. Much of the work on the second part of 'Opus One' was done at night with Simon Heyworth engineering. Vocal overdubs were undertaken with Sally Oldfield and Mundy Ellis to complete the closing section of the first part, recorded in the intense seven-day session. Also added was a beautiful acoustic guitar part which acted as a coda.

Some sections of the second part of Oldfield's work had begun life as ideas in 1971, such as the section known as 'Caveman'. For this section Steve Broughton, drummer with the Edgar Broughton Band, was called upon to contribute his percussive skills, Steve's drumming accompanying Oldfield's bass. When overdubbed with electric and acoustic guitars this section was one of the highlights of part two. Sessions were interrupted by the arrival of another band who had block-booked the Manor and, with the advent of Christmas, Oldfield would have to wait until February 1973 to complete work.

The final mixing of the album would prove to be an involved process. Long before the days of automated desks, the sessions involved the hands of Newman, Oldfield, Heyworth and two others. The slightest error by anyone meant that the entire process had to be re-started from the beginning. Another problem was that the multi-track tape had been passed over the heads of the tape machine so many times due the process of winding and rewinding that they had begun to wear out. Despite such adversity, mixing was finished and the album was completed in the early spring of 1973.

Richard Branson and Simon Draper took the album to the annual MIDEM music business conference in Cannes, where record companies from all over the world gathered to present their wares. Listeners to the recordings expressed doubt about the viability of such a record due to its instrumental nature. Branson even briefly considered adding lyrics and vocals but this idea was soon thankfully shelved. With work on the album completed and a release date set, thoughts now turned to giving a title to the recordings known to all who worked on them as 'Opus One'.

In search of a title, Richard Branson suggested 'Breakfast In Bed' and suggested using a picture he had of a boiled egg which appeared to have blood oozing out of it. In the end, photographer Trevor Key was engaged to design the iconic cover of the finished album, suggesting the image of a bell which had been destroyed in some way on the sleeve as a reference to Oldfield denting a bell during the recording sessions. It was at that stage that Mike Oldfield suggested the title 'Tubular Bells'.

GOLDFIELD: overdubbed his T-shirt 7,419 times   Pic: JOE STEVENS

Key travelled to the English south coast and photographed an image of some bones burning on a beach, then superimposed that photograph with an image of a model he had made of a twisted bell. A spot of humour was also added with a statement on the back of the album which declared: 'This stereo record cannot be played on old tin boxes no matter what they are fitted with. If you are in possession of such equipment please hand it into the nearest police station.'

Issued on 25 May 1973, 'Tubular Bells' began to take off when respected DJ John Peel, who was immensely impressed by the record, played both sides of the album on his BBC Radio 1 show. Peel also wrote a review of the album for The Listener magazine, stating; 'Without borrowing anything from established classics or descending into the discords, squeals and burps of the determinedly avant garde, Mike Oldfield has produced music which combines logic with surprise, sunshine with rain.'

Branson and Draper decided to organise a concert performance of the work at the Queen Elizabeth Hall in London. A reluctant Oldfield was finally persuaded to perform the work live when Branson offered to give him his old and much admired Bentley car. A cast of musicians including guitarists Mick Taylor of the Rolling Stones, Steve Hillage, Fred Frith of Henry Cow and Ted Speight plus Steve Broughton, David Bedford and Viv Stanshall gathered together at Shepperton film studios to rehearse.

Oldfield later reflected: 'I was stood backstage at the Queen Elizabeth Hall and was absolutely terrified. To me the music hadn't sounded good at the rehearsals and I was convinced it was going to go down badly. Mick Taylor brought Mick Jagger into my dressing room and he was very supportive. That gave me the confidence to at least walk on stage. When the concert was over I was stunned when the entire audience stood up and clapped. Once the concert was over I fled in Richard Branson's Bentley.' The critical reaction to the concert was overwhelming. On 14 July 1973 'Tubular Bells' entered the British album charts where it was to remain for 264 weeks .

The success of the album was boosted still further when director William Friedkin selected the opening theme of the first part of 'Tubular Bells' for inclusion in his film The Exorcist. Atlantic Records handled Virgin's releases in the US at that time and requested to release an excerpt as a single. Issued under the title 'Mike Oldfield's Theme to The Exorcist', this single edit was released in February 1974 and reached Number 7 on the US Billboard chart. Although the single was the contributing factor to the success of the album in America, the edit had not been approved by Oldfield who was most unhappy.

Now residing in the village of Kington in Herefordshire in a house called the Beacon, Oldfield shied away from the glaring light of publicity, installing recording equipment and beginning work on his next album, 'Hergest Ridge'. He would remain a studio-based musician for the next four years before finally agreeing to take to the road in 1979.

Of Mike Oldfield's impressive canon of work, 'Tubular Bells' is an iconic album that defied the established preconceptions of what was achievable with the studio technology of the time. The record's success was effectively the building block upon which Virgin became a household name and one of the most recognised brands in the world. This seminal work remains as fresh and as vital a piece of music as it was when it first appeared in May 1973.

PFM 'Photos Of Ghosts'

First released as Manticore K43502 in April 1973
Highest UK chart position: N/A
Available on CD as Manticore MANTCD1006

River Of Life
Celebration
Photos Of Ghosts
Old Rain
Il Banchetto
Mr 9 'Til 5
Promenade the Puzzle

Flavio Premoli	**Keyboards and Vocals**
Franco Mussida	**Guitars and Vocals**
Franz Di Cioccio	**Drums and Vocals**
Mauro Pagani	**Violin and Woodwind**
Giorgio Piazza	**Bass**

Premiata Forneria Marconi

Photos of Ghosts

Original Italian production by PFM and Claudio Fabi
Recorded at Fonorama Studios, Milan in October 1972
English album and vocals mixed and produced by Pete Sinfield
Recorded at Command Studios, London in February 1973

By 1973, progressive rock was the dominant force in the world of album-orientated music. Of all the European countries to embrace the genre, Italy was perhaps the first to open its arms to acts such as Audience, Genesis, Van der Graaf Generator and Emerson, Lake and Palmer. Of these acts, the first three enjoyed success in Italy in the early Seventies that they had yet to attain elsewhere, while Emerson, Lake and Palmer enjoyed huge success in the country prior to taking the world by storm.

The impact of progressive rock on the Italian album charts was to create a wave of highly creative Italian progressive rock bands emerged in this wake. Of all of these acts, PFM (Premiata Forneria Marconi) was, and still is, the most important, becoming the first Italian rock act to enjoy success in other European countries and the United States.

Born from the ashes of the Milan-based I Quelli, one of the best bands of the Italian beat scene of the late Sixties, PFM comprised Franco 'Yoghi' Mussida (guitar), Franz Di Cioccio (drums), Flavio Premoli (keyboards) and Giorgio 'Fico' Piazza (bass guitar). I Quelli had attained domestic success by recording Italian translations of famous British and American hits such as the Turtles' 'Happy Together' (recorded as 'Per Vivere Insieme') and Traffic's 'Hole In My Shoe' ('Tornare Bambino'). Absorbing the influence of underground rock from the UK and the US, I Quelli changed their name to I Krell and adopted a more serious approach. Writing original material, they were soon offered a contract with newly established Italian label Numero Uno, set up by songwriter Lucio Battisti. With the addition of talented multi-instrumentalist Mauro Pagani (formerly with the band Dalton) to their ranks in 1970, they became known as Premiata Forneria Marconi, taken from the name of a bakery where they rehearsed. Within a short time Premiata Forneria Marconi, (PFM) had signed to Italian agent Franco Mamone's roster and acted as support to visiting artists such as Procol Harum, Deep Purple and Yes. The chance to perform to large audiences led in turn to PFM quickly developing a loyal fanbase of their own. Strongly influenced by the music of Jethro Tull, King Crimson and Yes, Premiata Forneria Marconi also incorporated influences from the Italian romantic folk and classical traditions, resulting in a style that was easily identifiable as their own.

A stunning performance at the 'Festival di Avanguardia e Nuove Tendenze' (The Avant Garde and New Tendencies Festival) at the Pineta di Viareggio in 1971 earned them praise in the Italian music press and led to the release of debut single, 'Impressioni Di Settembre ' b/w ' La Carrozza Di Hans'. There followed the release of two excellent albums in relatively quick succession, 'Storia Di Un Minuto' and 'Per Un Amico', both significant Italian hits. During this period PFM had crossed paths with Emerson, Lake and Palmer on an Italian tour. Greg Lake was invited to the launch party of the 'Per Un Amico' album at the Pala Eur in Rome in December 1972 and was hugely impressed.

At this time ELP were in the early stages of establishing their own imprint, Manticore Records, to release their own music and to promote artists they felt were worthy of investigation. As a result, Lake invited PFM to London to perform to an invited audience of record-company executives and journalists. The visit led to PFM becoming the first signing to Manticore and, in

February 1973, they arrived at Command Studios in London to work with former King Crimson lyricist Pete Sinfield to record their first English-language album. The basis of the material came from their most recent Italian album, 'Per Un Amico', but for these new sessions Sinfield contributed new English lyrics and new overdubs and mixes were also undertaken. Familiar with the material, the musicians approached the new recordings with relish.

Of the material recorded, 'River Of Life' was both a gorgeous introduction to the album and a fine way of presenting PFM to an international audience. Beginning with a melodic flute and acoustic guitar introduction, the piece quickly built into a progressive tour de force. This was followed by the quirky 'Celebration' (later edited for release as a single). 'Photos Of Ghosts' was another fine melodic piece and was followed by the jazz-influenced instrumental 'Old Rain'.

While most of the material featured newly written English lyrics, one song, 'Il Banchetto' – one of the finest on the album – remained in Italian. The album was completed by 'Mr Nine 'Til Five' and 'Promenade The Puzzle', both with excellent Pete Sinfield lyrics, and the mixing process finished by the end of February.

PFM made their UK concert debut on 24 March 1973 with a concert at the ABC Theatre in Fulham, London. A Melody Maker writer wrote patronisingly: 'PFM are not bad musicians, the only problem is that they are Italians singing in English.' Despite this, a section of the UK rock audience took PFM to their hearts upon the release of 'Photos Of Ghosts' in the late spring. The association with Manticore and the UK rock scene would be crucial in establishing PFM's reputation as a globally recognised band. The single 'Celebration' obtained a significant degree of airplay on the BBC Radio 1 shows of DJs Bob Harris and John Peel which led to sharing the stage at the Reading Festival, with Genesis.

Drummer, spokesman and founder Franz Di Cioccio later explained the 'rebirth' of the band thus: 'Reaching the album charts in the UK and US meant that we could spearhead an appreciation of Italian musical talent.

'PFM never played a style of rock music that pretended to be Anglo-Saxon; we always defended our own style of music and our own roots. PFM's music was…a kind of progressive rock music that…also included our own musical personality: "Celebration"' was a kind of rock tarantella, and our live favourite "Dove E Quando" (originally from the first Italian album "Storia Di Un Minuto") was inspired by the madrigal tradition. These musical roots helped us create an original musical style in the sea of progressive music which was easily indentified as our own.

'It not only had an international feel which was recounted in the English language, but our music also had…an Italian feel and quality. Being an Italian group with success abroad was a great honour and achievement for us.'

While on tour in Britain, PFM received the news that 'Photos Of Ghosts' had entered the Billboard charts in America, a previously unheard-of achievement for an Italian rock band. The following year PFM would take their music to audiences to the US and secure a series of English-language albums for Manticore Records that would establish the band as the most successful act on the label outside of the ELP family.

(with thanks to Ernesto De Pascale and all at Il Popolo del Blues)

BAND

1 SLADE
2 EMERSON LAKE & PALMER
3 FACES
4 T. REX
5 Led Zeppelin
6 Lindisfarne
7 Rolling Stones
8 Moody Blues
9 Yes
10 New Seekers
11 Deep Purple
12 Wishbone Ash
13 Who
14 Pink Floyd
15 Roxy Music
16 Marvin, Welch, Farrar
17 Family
18 Jethro Tull
19 Hawkwind
20 Free

MOST PROMISING NEW NAME

1 ROXY MUSIC
2 PETER SKELLERN
3 LYNSEY de PAUL
4 GARY GLITTER
5 Home
6 Genesis
7 Colin Blunstone
8 Blackfoot Sue
9 Wizzard
10 Duncan Browne

FEMALE SINGER

1 MAGGIE BELL
2 OLIVIA NEWTON-JOHN
3 LYNSEY de PAUL
4 SONJA KRISTINA
5 Sandy Denny
6 Cilla Black
7 Shirley Bassey
8 Lulu
9 Lesley Duncan
10 Elkie Brooks

MALE SINGER

1 ROD STEWART
2 GILBERT O'SULLIVAN
3 DAVID BOWIE

---

5 Marc Bolan
6 Robert Plant
7 Elton John
8 Cat Stevens
9 John Lennon
10 Greg Lake
11 Jon Anderson
12 Paul Rodgers
13 Ian Gillan
14 Noddy Holder
15 Tom Jones
16 Mick Jagger
17 Brian Ferry
18 Roger Chapman
19 Peter Gabriel
20 Paul McCartney

LIVE BAND

1 SLADE
2 E.L.P.
3 FACES
4 HAWKWIND
5 Led Zeppelin
6 Who
7 T. Rex
8 Rolling Stones
9 Pink Floyd
10 Deep Purple

GUITARIST

1 ERIC CLAPTON
2 GEORGE HARRISON
3 JIMMY PAGE
4 HANK MARVIN
5 Rory Gallagher
6 Marc Bolan
7 Jeff Beck
8 Ritchie Blackmore
9 Pete Townshend
10 Dave Hill

BASS GUITARIST

1 PAUL McCARTNEY
2 JACK BRUCE
3 GREG LAKE
4 STEVE CURRIE
5 Chris Squire
6 Roger Glover
7 John Paul Jones
8 Jim Lea
9 Ronnie Lane
10 John Entwistle

KEYBOARDS

1 KEITH EMERSON
2 ELTON JOHN
3 RICK WAKEMAN
4 GILBERT

---

6 Ian MacLagan
7 Rod Argent
8 Nicky Hopkins
9 Eno
10 Ken Hensley

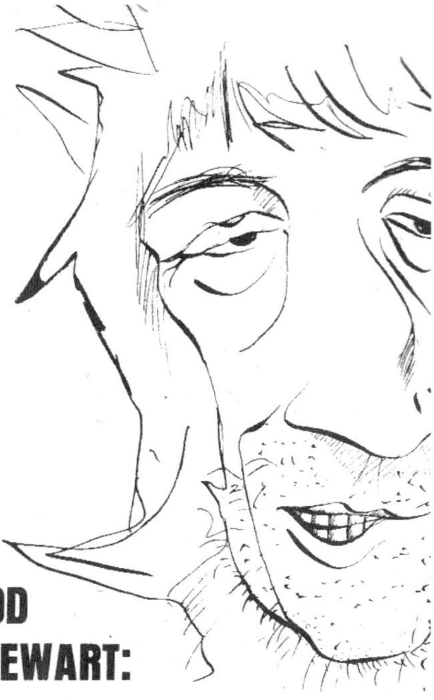

DRUMMER

1 CARL PALMER
2 RINGO STARR
3 KEITH MOON
4 JOHN BONHAM
5 Ian Paice
6 Kenny Jones
7 Bill Legend
8 Ginger Baker
9 Don Powell
10 Brian Bennett

MISC. INSTRUMENT

1 IAN ANDERSON
2 KEITH EMERSON
3 MICKEY FINN
4 RAY JACKSON
5 Darryl Way
6 Roy Wood
7 Elton John

ROD STEWART: Top singer

ALBUM

1 NEVER A DULL MOMENT
—Rod Stewart
2 TRILOGY
—ELP
3 ZIGGY STARDUST
—David Bowie
4 SLIDER
—T Rex
5 Argus—Wishbone Ash
6 Slade Alive
7 Machine Head
—Deep Purple
8 Close To The Edge—Yes
9 Led Zeppelin
10 Catch Bull At Four
—Cat Stevens

SINGLE

1 SILVER MACHINE
—Hawkwind
2 VIRGINIA PLAIN
—Roxy Music
3 YOU WEAR IT WELL
—Rod Stewart
4 LAYLA
—Derek and Dominoes
5 CLAIR
—Gilbert O'Sullivan
6 Mama Weer All Crazee Now—Slade
7 All The Young Dudes
—Mott The Hoople

VANGELIS O PAPATHANASSIOU 'Earth'

First released as Vertigo 6499 693 in October 1973
Highest UK chart position: N/A
Not currently available on CD

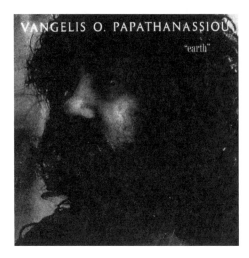

Come On
We Were All Uprooted
Sunny Earth
He-O
Ritual
Let it Happen
The City
My Face In The Rain
Watch Out
A Song

Vangelis O. Papathanassiou Flute, Background Vocals	**Keyboards, Percussion, Tablas,**
Argiris Koulouris	**Guitars, Flute, Background Vocals**
Robert Fitoussi	**Bass, Lead Vocals on 'Come On', 'He-O', 'Let it Happen', 'My Face in the Rain', Background Vocals**
Warren Shapovitch	**Narration on 'We Were All Uprooted' and 'A Song'**

Recorded at Europa Sonor studios, Paris
Produced and Arranged by Vangelis O Papathanassiou
Engineered by Roger Roche, Didier Pitois and Didier Perrier

One of the most interesting albums of progressive music released in 1973 was the first 'proper' solo album by Evangahlos O Papathanassiou (better known later as Vangelis), the keyboard-playing genius behind the successful Greek band Aphrodite's Child, whose stunning concept album '666' was one of the finest to be released in the so called progressive era.

The record was in fact the third album to be released by Vangelis in his own right. The first, the soundtrack to the French film Sex Power, was released in France on the Philips label in 1969 and was a jazz-based instrumental work later disowned by its creator. The success of Aphrodite's Child led to an increased demand for live appearances, much to the disdain of Vangelis, who wanted to explore the possibilities of experimentation in the recording studio and thoroughly disliked his status as a musical star. As his bandmates toured Europe with Harris Chakaltis deputising on keyboards, Vangelis worked on the soundtrack to Sex Power and began work on the epic album '666'. Taking some 14 months to complete, '666' was a clear indication of the musical differences within the ranks of the group and the inevitable break-up of Aphrodite's Child occurred. While Demis Roussos embarked on a successful solo career as a middle–of-the-road singer, Vangelis embarked on a pioneering solo career.

The first work issued by Vangelis was the unusual 'Fais Que Ton Rêve Soit Plus Long Que La Nuit' ('May Your Dreams Last Longer Than The Night'), released by Reprise in France only in early 1972. An esoteric work inspired by the student unrest in Paris in May 1968, the album was highly original but uncommercial. Taking inspiration from the critical acclaim of '666', Vangelis was approached by Vertigo to record a solo album and, in 1972, entered the studio to create another masterpiece, the conceptual album 'Earth'.

Engaging the services of Aphrodite's Child guitarist and lute player Anargyos 'Silver' Kouloris and Tunisian-born vocalist and bass player Robert Fitoussi, Vangelis played all the remaining instruments on an album which drew from rock and ethnic influences. The songs 'Let It Happen', 'He-O', 'Come On' and 'My Face In The Rain' featured lyrics from Richelle Dassin and were interspersed with the stunning instrumental pieces 'Sunny Earth', 'Ritual', 'The City' and 'Watch Out', much in the style of '666'. 'Earth' also followed that album by featuring two poems 'We Were All Uprooted' and 'A Song' both set to atmospheric musical soundscapes.

Other material created during these sessions went under working titles such as 'Friends', 'The River', 'Sunday In Central Park', 'Passer By' and 'The Witches Are Out', none of which would see the light of day. The concept of 'Earth' was an atmospheric musical journey through a day in the city and was highly regarded by critics upon its release in October 1973. The record was summed up by a liner note to the album that declared: 'In the present album, Vangelis is on his own. Fascinating, powerful and unpredictable. A remarkable interpreter, he explores the world of sounds, searching for the miraculous.'

Strangely, interest in territories outside of France was limited and Vertigo put little or no effort into its promotion in other countries. Indeed, the main promotional activity was undertaken in the form of two rare live performances at the Paris Olympia and at the Queen Elizabeth Hall in London (supporting Jon Hiseman's Tempest), during which the album was performed in its entirety. In France the reception was such that it gave Vangelis a suitable platform with which to build a solo career as a pioneer of electronic music and a composer of film soundtracks. Robert Fitoussi would later join the French rock band Les Variations before changing his name to FR David and enjoying success with the single 'Words' in 1982.

Vangelis' many solo albums and collaborations with Yes singer Jon Anderson have sold in excess of 35 million albums worldwide and he remains one of the world's most respected and influential musicians. His sole solo offering for the Vertigo label, 'Earth' remains a seminal work and frustratingly remains unavailable on CD outside of an official Greek release in 1996. Any serious fan of progressive music is strongly urged to track down a copy.

THE NME READERS'

DRUMMER

1 CARL PALMER
2 RINGO STARR
3 BUDDY RICH
4 GINGER BAKER
5 John Bonham
6 Keith Moon
7 Ronnie Tutt
8 Neill Smith
9 Bill Legend
10 Ian Paice

BASS GUITARIST

1 PAUL McCARTNEY
2 JACK BRUCE
3 GREG LAKE
4 STEVE CURRIE
5 John Paul Jones
6 Dennis Dunaway
7 Chris Squire
8 Klaus Voorman
9 John Entwistle
10 Roger Glover

PRODUCER

1 GREG LAKE
2 PHIL SPECTOR
3 TONY VISCONTI
4 JIMMY PAGE
5 Bob Ezrin
6 Bob Johnson

KEITH EMERSON: Top in three categories

7 David Bowie
8 Rod Stewart
9 Tony Clark
10 George Harrison

SINGLE

1 SCHOOL'S OUT
—Alice Cooper
2 BURNING LOVE
—Elvis Presley

3 ELECTED
—Alice Coop
4 AMERICAN I
—Don McLea
5 Without You—N
6 Layla—Derek an
Dominoes
7 You Wear It Wel
—Rod Stewart
8 My Ding-a-Ling
—Chuck Berry
9 Hocus Pocus—F
10 Virginia Plain
—Roxy Music

ARDS FROM OVER PAGE

CLAPTON: World and British top guitarist

ENTERPRISING LABEL

1   RCA
2   ISLAND
3   WARNER BROS.
4   ATLANTIC
5   Tamla Motown
=6   Apple
=6   Polydor
8   CBS
9   Charisma
10   Harvest

OVER-RATED HIT OF YEAR

1   PUPPY LOVE
—Donny Osmond
2   MY DING-A-LING
—Chuck Berry
3   MOULDY OLD DOUGH
—Lieutenant Pigeon
4   AMAZING GRACE
—Royal Scots Dragoons
5   Too Young
—Donny Osmond

ALBUM

1   NEVER A DULL MOMENT
—Rod Stewart
2   TRILOGY
—E.L.P.
3   ELVIS AT MAIDSON

SQUARE

4   SCHOOL'S OUT
—Alice Cooper
5   Led Zeppelin
6   Slider—T. Rex
7   Harvest—Neil Young
8   Simon & Garfunkel Greatest Hits
9   Caravanserai—Santana
10   Close To The Edge—Yes

Barclay James Harvest

'TIME KNOWS NO LIMITS ON DAYS SUCH AS THESE...'

BARCLAY JAMES HARVEST: 'Live'

First released as Polydor 2683052 in 1974
Highest UK chart position: Number 40
Available on CD as Esoteric Recordings ECLEC2122

Summer Soldier
Medicine Man
Crazy City
After The Day
The Great 1974 Mining Disaster
Galadriel
Negative Earth
She Said
Paper Wings
For No One
Mockingbird

John Lees	**Lead Guitar, Vocals, Recorder**
Les Holroyd	**Bass Guitar, Rhythm Guitar, Vocals**
Stuart 'Woolly' Wolstenholme	**Mellotron, Electric Piano, Moog Synthesiser, Vocals**
Mel Pritchard	**Drums**

Produced by Rodger Bain
Recorded at the Theatre Royal, Drury Lane, London and the Stadium, Liverpool by the Island Mobile Unit
Mixed at Island Studios, London
Engineer Brian Humphries

In the early Seventies Barclay James Harvest were one of the finest live acts on the concert circuit. They had delivered four albums of superbly crafted progressive rock to EMI's Harvest label, but by 1973 the future looked bleak.

Following the release of the single 'Rock And Roll Woman', recorded in an ill-advised attempt to break into the singles chart, the band were dropped from Harvest, in part due to a dispute between the band's management and EMI. Within months the band had dismissed their managers and found themselves without a record contract and hugely in debt due to the expense of touring with a symphony orchestra. It was to their credit that they would emerge from such adversity and deliver a live album that would turn their fortunes around.

The group would later admit that they would have split up in 1973 had they not owed so much money, but they still had belief in their own ability, a collection of fine new songs and enough dogged determination to continue. Through their friendship with Eric Stewart of 10CC, BJH secured a new management deal with Harvey Lisberg's Kennedy Street Enterprises. Lisberg successfully negotiated a complex new deal which involved transferring the band's financial obligations to their new label, Polydor. Part of this deal stipulated that, in return for clearing their debts, EMI would allow Polydor to release live versions of material originally recorded for Harvest, thus giving access to some classic songs.

The orchestra was now a thing of the past, but John Lees would attribute the band's later success to the problems they had at this time: 'The first fortunate thing that happened to us was the abysmal failure of the orchestral tour. It was fortunate we had to work to save the situation, to recoup the money and to recreate the sound of the orchestra that we no longer had. That produced the high standard of live shows that pulled us through.' The band's reputation as a live act was, indeed, growing steadily

by word of mouth, so Polydor decided that this would be a good time to exercise their option of issuing a live album encapsulating Barclay James Harvest's career to date. Plans were laid to record two concerts to promote new studio album 'Everyone Is Everybody Else', at the Liverpool Stadium and at London's Theatre Royal, Drury Lane, on 29 and 30 June 1974. As the band's road crew set up the stage for the Liverpool concert, they noticed a loud hum on the guitar amplifier. To their horror, they discovered the venue had no fuse boxes in the electric supply to the stage, making the situation too dangerous to continue. The concert was cancelled, leaving London, the last night of the tour, the only one which could be recorded. The performance was also to be filmed by Polydor to give them promotional footage of Barclay James Harvest and labelmates Rare Bird, who were supporting, so it was vital the London concert was a success. Although the performance at the Theatre Royal, Drury Lane was indeed a fine one, it was marred by a troublesome Mellotron changing pitch in the middle of songs and producing odd wailing sounds. The Liverpool Stadium concert was rescheduled for 31 August, but Polydor wanted the live album out before the end of 1974, leaving little time for post-production work on the second show. The decision was made to salvage everything possible from the Drury Lane tapes, mixing down the offending Mellotron as far as practicable, overdubbing a minimum of new parts with producer Rodger Bain and use the Liverpool tapes only for songs which could not be saved. The resulting album captured the live sound of the band perfectly and was more raw, impassioned and powerful than anything delivered in the studio.

The material recorded had undergone some reworking in terms of arrangement. 'Summer Soldier', a lengthy track on the band's 'Baby James Harvest' album, had been refined to become more dramatic while 'Medicine Man' had become a powerful rock number with solos from Lees, Wolstenholme and Holroyd respectively. Alongside familiar material, songs from 'Everyone Is Everybody Else' such as 'The Great 1974 Mining Disaster' were more convincing, and the stunning rendition of 'For No One' was definitive.

Climaxing with signature track 'Mockingbird', it was little wonder that upon release in November 1974, 'Barclay James Harvest Live' became the band's first ever chart album, reaching Number 40 in the UK. Its release did much to enhance their reputation as a live act and laid the groundwork for future success in the UK and in Europe. 'Barclay James Harvest Live' is still fondly remembered as one of their greatest works that saw John Lees, Woolly Wolstenholme, Les Holroyd and Mel Pritchard bring out the best in each other's performances, the whole being most definitely greater than the sum of the parts. It remains essential listening.

(with grateful thanks to Keith and Monika Domone)

ALBUMS

	Highest position reached	Weeks in Chart	TITLE	ARTIST	PRODUCER
			30 DECEMBER 1974 — 5 DECEMBER 1975		
1	1	37	THE BEST OF ★	Stylistics	Hugo / Luigi
2	1	33	ONCE UPON A STAR ★	Bay City Rollers	Phil Wainman
3	1	16	ATLANTIC CROSSING ★	Rod Stewart	Tom Dowd
4	1	23	HORIZON ●	Carpenters	Richard & Karen
5	1	13	40 GOLDEN GREATS ●	Jim Reeves	—
6	22	11	ELVIS PRESLEY'S 40 GREATEST HITS ★	Elvis Presley	—
7	2	50	TUBULAR BELLS ★	Mike Oldfield	Oldfield / Newman / Heg
8	1	46	ELTON JOHN'S GREATEST HITS ★	Elton John	Gus Dudgeon
9	1	23	VENUS AND MARS ●	Wings	Paul McCartney
10	3	50	THE SINGLES 1969 / 1973 ★	Carpenters	J. Daugherty / R& K.
11	1	7	40 GREATEST HITS ★	Perry Como	—
12	2	23	CAPTAIN FANTASTIC ●	Elton John	Gus Dudgeon
13	3	50	SIMON & GARFUNKEL'S GREATEST HITS	Simon & Garfunkel	Simon & Garfunkel
14	1	19	20 GREATEST HITS ●	Tom Jones	—
15	1	25	HIS GREATEST HITS ●	Engelbert Humperdinck	—
16	4	45	ROLLIN' ★	Bay City Rollers	Bill Martin / Phil Coulter
17	3	31	THE ORIGINAL SOUNDTRACK ●	10cc	10cc
18	2	11	FAVOURITES ●	Peters & Lee	John Franz
19	7	50	THE DARK SIDE OF THE MOON ★	Pink Floyd	Pink Floyd
20	1	14	GET DANCING	Various Artists	—
21	2	20	GREATEST HITS ●	Cat Stevens	—
22	1	12	WISH YOU WERE HERE ●	Pink Floyd	Pink Floyd
23	2	20	THE SHIRLEY BASSEY SINGLES ALBUM ●	Shirley Bassey	—
24	5	46	BAND ON THE RUN ★	Paul McCartney & Wings	Paul McCartney
25	21	18	LIVE AT TREORCHY ●	Max Boyce	Bob Barrett
26	1	27	PHYSICAL GRAFFITI	Led Zeppelin	Jimmy Page
27	1	15	SOULED OUT	Various	—
28	1	25	ON THE LEVEL ●	Status Quo	Status Quo
29	3	12	ALL THE FUN OF THE FAIR ●	David Essex	Jeff Wayne
30	5	15	THE VERY BEST OF ROGER WHITTAKER ●	Roger Whittaker	Denis Preston
31	1	7	WE ALL HAD DOCTORS PAPERS ●	Max Boyce	Bob Barratt
32	8	23	ONE OF THESE NIGHTS	Eagles	Bill Szymzyk
33	3	23	STRAIGHT SHOOTER ●	Bad Company	Bad Company
34			SAMPLE CHARLEY PRIDE	Charley Pride	—
35	2	25	THE MYTHS & LEGENDS OF KING ARTHUR ●	Rick Wakeman & The ERE	John Cleary
36	12	38	BRIDGE OVER TROUBLED WATER	Simon & Garfunkel	S& G / Halee
37	1	24	STARDUST	Soundtrack	—
38	4	16	CRIME OF THE CENTURY ●	Supertramp	Ken Scott
39	5	19	SHEER HEART ATTACK ●	Queen	Roy Thomas Baker / Quen
40	6	29	AND I LOVE YOU SO ●	Perry Como	Chet Atkins
41	12	37	HIS 12 GREATEST HITS ●	Neil Diamond	—
42	4	25	CAN'T GET ENOUGH ●	Barry White	Barry White
43	5	18	THANK YOU BABY ▬	Stylistics	Hugo / Luigi
44	16	27	THE BEST OF BREAD	Bread	—
45	4	16	BLUE JAYS ●	Justin Hayward & John Lodge	Tony Clarke
46	14	16	24 CARAT PURPLE ▬	Deep Purple	—
47	10	25	COP YER WHACK FOR THIS ●	Billy Connolly	Bill Martin / Phil Coulter
48	6	23	ROCK 'N' ROLL ▬	John Lennon	John Lennon / Phil Spect
49	4	16	BLOOD ON THE TRACKS ▬	Bob Dylan	—
50	4	21	THE BEST OF TAMMY WYNETTE ▬	Tammy Wynette	Billy Sherrill

★ PLATINUM LP   ● GOLD LP   ▬ SILVER LP

BE BOP DELUXE 'Axe Victim'

First released as Harvest SHVL 813 in June 1973
Highest UK chart position: N/A
Available on CD as Harvest CDP 7647262

Axe Victim
Love Is Swift Arrows
Jet Silver And The Dolls Of Venus
Third Floor Heaven
Night Creatures
Rocket Cathedrals
Adventures In A Yorkshire Landscape
Jets At Dawn
No Trains To Heaven
Darkness (L'Immoraliste)

Bill Nelson	**Lead Guitars, Lead Vocals, Acoustic Guitar and Piano**
Ian Parkin	**Rhythm and Acoustic Guitars, Organ on 'Rocket Cathedrals**
Robert Bryan	**Bass Guitar, Lead Vocal on 'Rocket Cathedrals'**
Nicholas Chatterton-Dew	**Drums and Percussion**

Orchestral arrangement on 'Darkness (L'Immoraliste)' by Andrew Powell
Recorded at AIR Studios, CBS Studios and Audio International Studios, London
Produced by Ian McLintock
Engineered by Steve Nye, Mike Ross, Pete Silver and Rod Harper
Mixing engineers John Leckie, Louie Austin and Mike Ross

Be Bop Deluxe were one of the most innovative acts to be signed to EMI's Harvest label at the tail-end of the progressive rock boom. The band was essentially the vision of guitarist and songwriter Bill Nelson. Born in the Yorkshire town of Wakefield, Nelson began to play guitar in his mid-teens and quickly developed an aptitude for the instrument for which he would be hailed as a master exponent in the Seventies. Initially influenced by guitarists such as Duane Eddy and Hank Marvin, he worked his way through Wakefield College of Art and soon became involved in the burgeoning local music scene.

Nelson first performed with the band Global Village who made some recordings for one of Britain's first small independent labels, Holyground. Participating in various other sessions at Holyground's rudimentary studio while working in the offices of the local council, he eventually recorded his first solo album, 'Northern Dream', in 1971. The recordings were financed by the owner of a local record shop, the Record Bar, and appeared on the Smile label with a limited pressing of 250 copies. One of these ended up in the hands of Radio 1 DJ John Peel, who championed the album on his radio show. This exposure soon led to Nelson coming to the attention of A&R staff at both EMI Records and Decca offshoot Deram.

By the time approaches were made by EMI, Nelson had formed Be Bop Deluxe in August 1972 featuring Rob

Bryan on bass, Ian Parkin on rhythm guitar and Nicholas Chatterton-Dew on drums, plus keyboard-player Richard Brown. By December Brown had departed the band, who had by now developed a local following. Their early shows incorporated elements of mime and theatre, all set to Nelson's innovative compositions. In April 1973 a limited edition independent single, Teenage Archangel' b/w 'Jets At Dawn', was released by Nelson's Smile label and again gained airplay support from John Peel. By October of that year the band had recorded a session for Peel's Radio 1 show, an impressive feat for an unsigned band, and recorded demos for EMI. With EMI procrastinating, a further demo session was recorded for Decca at their studios in December 1973. This spurred EMI to act and Be Bop Deluxe were signed in February 1974.

Almost immediately the band began work on their first album with producer Ian McLintock at AIR Studios in London, all the material written by Nelson with the exception of 'Rocket Cathedrals'. The magnificent 'Adventures In A Yorkshire Landscape' was full of lyrical imagery and featured one of the most beautiful guitar solos ever recorded. 'Jets At Dawn' was re-recorded in a much more relaxed style and songs such as 'Night Creatures', the autobiographical 'Axe Victim' and the classic 'Jet Silver And The Dolls of Venus' were all underpinned by Nelson's supreme playing and grasp of melody.

'Axe Victim' was released in July 1974 and, though it narrowly missed the UK charts, the support the record received from the UK music press ensured Be Bop Deluxe had a healthy future. In typical fashion, Nelson soon disbanded the first line-up of the band and worked with a variety of other musicians before settling on New Zealander Charlie Tumahai on bass and Simon Fox on drums. Following the recording of 'Futurama' in 1975, the band was expanded further with the inclusion of Andy Clarke on keyboards.

This quartet recorded a series of albums of stunning originality and quality over the next three years, beginning with 'Sunburst Finish', and enjoyed success on both the UK singles and album charts. However, in the period covered by the book, 'Axe Victim' was both the defining statement from Be Bop Deluxe and the launchpad for Bill Nelson's impressive solo career.

ROBERT CALVERT 'Captain Lockheed And The Starfighters'

First released as United Artists UAG29507 in August 1974
Highest UK chart position: N/A
Available on CD as Atomhenge ATOMCD1017

Franz Josef Strauss, Defence Minister, Reviews The Luftwaffe In 1958, Finding It Somewhat Lacking In Image Potential

The Aerospaceage Inferno

Aircraft Salesman (A Door In The Foot)

The Widow Maker

Two Test Pilots Discuss The Starfighter's Performance

The Right Stuff

Board Meeting (Seen Through A Contact Lens)

The Song Of The Gremlin (Part One)

Ground Crew (Last Minute Reassembly Before Take- Off)

Hero With A Wing

Ground Control To Pilot

Ejection

Interview

I Resign

The Song Of The Gremlin (Part Two)

Bier Garten

Catch A Falling Starfighter

Robert Calvert	Lead Vocals, Percussion, Acting
Paul Rudolph	Lead, Rhythm and Bass Guitars
Lemmy	Bass Guitar and Rhythm Guitar
Simon King	Drums
Brian Peter George St John Le Baptiste De La Salle (Brian Eno)	Synthesiser and Electronic Effects
Del Dettmar	Synthesiser
Nik Turner	Saxophones
Dave Brock	Lead Guitar on 'The Widow Maker'
Twink	Funeral Drum on 'Catch A Falling Starfighter'
Arthur Brown	Voice on 'Song Of The Gremlin'
Adrian Wagner	Keyboards and Series III Moog on 'Song Of The Gremlin'
The Ladbroke Grove Hermaphrodite Choir	Backing Vocals
Vivian Stanshall, Jim Capaldi, Tom Mittledorf and Richard Ealing	Actors

Produced by Roy Thomas Baker
Recorded at Island Studios, London, Olympic Studios, Barnes, London and Radio Luxembourg studios, London
Engineers Phil Brown, Frank Owen, Rufus Cartwright, Anton Matthews and Phil Chapman

Born in South Africa in 1945 and brought up in Margate, Kent, Robert Calvert is best known for his membership of the legendary Hawkwind. Calvert first came to the attention of the UK underground scene as a poet and short-story writer, contributing works to leading magazines such as International Times. His association with Hawkwind began in 1971 when he contributed prose to the Logbook which came with copies of the album 'In Search Of Space'. Childhood friend Nik Turner was a founder member of Hawkwind, and it was through Turner that he first moved to London, firstly contributing ideas to the band's presentation and eventually joining the outfit in early 1972 in time to appear at the legendary 'Greasy Truckers Party' at the Roundhouse in February and co-writing Hawkwind's hit single 'Silver Machine'.

Calvert's on-stage persona, reading stark poetry such as 'Sonic Attack', soon became a focal point of Hawkwind's stage show. He featured as lead vocalist on the single 'Urban Guerrilla', which he again co-wrote but which was withdrawn within two weeks

Robert Calvert

Robert Calvert

of release in July 1973 due to a series of terrorist bomb attacks by the IRA in London. Seeking pastures new, he departed Hawkwind soon after to work on his first solo project, the ambitious 'Captain Lockheed And The Starfighters'.

Nik Turner later explained the concept behind the work: 'Robert had always been obsessed with flying. As a boy, all he wanted was to be a fighter pilot. When he was old enough he attempted to join the RAF, but he failed the medical because of a perforated eardrum. Robert originally conceived "Captain Lockheed And The Starfighters" as a stage play that was based upon the sale of the American Lockheed Starfighter to the military of other countries. The Starfighter was a high-performance supersonic fighter that entered service with the US Air Force in the late Fifties but was phased out by 1967. Lockheed sold a lot of these aircraft abroad, particularly in the NATO countries such as Germany, but for applications for which they were completely unsuited. The aircraft, nicknamed the Widowmaker, had a bad reputation and track record for crashing. Robert took this story and wrote a satire around it.'

The album tells the story of the Starfighter in German Air Force service in terms of heavy rock music, sketches and dialogue. A concept album, made at a time when such things were respected, it was an acerbic comment on the American way of life and was a wonderful piece of English eccentricity, Bonzo Dog Band frontman Vivian Stanshall appearing as one of the actors. Above all, the album showed Robert Calvert for the lyrical genius he was. 'The album is Robert as a master poet, playwright, storyteller, lyricist and comedian at one and the same time,' Nik Turner would later add, 'all of which naturally fits in with Robert's own view of himself as writer first and musician second.'

The album was recorded between March 1973 and June 1974 and featured musical contributions from members of Hawkwind, the Pink Fairies, Brian Eno, Adrian Wagner and Arthur Brown. Songs such as 'Ejection', 'The Widowmaker', 'The Right Stuff' and 'Aerospace Age Inferno' were in the style typical of Hawkwind at that time and equal to anything by that band in terms of quality. 'Recording the album was immense fun,' Nik Turner would later remember. 'A certain air of danger, and the feeling that anything might happen pervaded the air. I was only involved in a couple of the studio sessions, but nevertheless experienced the full-frontal onslaught of all the zaniness.'

To complete the work, Calvert penned some hilarious dialogue and drafted in Jim Capaldi of Traffic and Vivian Stanshall to join him in acting out the parts he had written. Edited between the finished music, the finished work took on the form of a 45-minute musical story. The finished result was issued in August 1974 but failed to achieve the commercial success it deserved. It was also briefly presented as a live show.

'Unfortunately the stage production of "Captain Lockheed" was never realised to its full potential,' Nik Turner later reflected. It had a short run in a theatre club, but wasn't promoted to the full, partly because the players Robert wanted were not available for a long enough period of time and partly for other technical reasons. He was involved in many other projects and eventually the idea of staging the production became rather hard work and lost a lot of its steam. It was a great pity because, as a commentary, the album still very much stands up. I think it's is still as entertaining as ever.' Recording a further solo album, 'Lucky Leif And The Longships', produced by Brian Eno, Calvert rejoined Hawkwind in August 1975 and stayed with the band until the end of 1978.

His later tenure with Hawkwind would see him influence the band to produce arguably the most stylish and innovative music of their career. Although he would record further solo albums before his premature death from a heart attack in 1988, none would match the sheer originality and creative genius of 'Captain Lockheed And The Starfighters'.

CAMEL 'Mirage'

First released as Deram SML-R1107 in April 1974
Highest UK chart position: N/A
Available on CD as Deram 8829292

Freefall
Supertwister
Nimrodel/The Procession/The White Rider
Earthrise
Lady Fantasy:
a. Encounter
b. Smiles For You
c. Lady Fantasy

Peter Bardens	Organ, Piano, Mini Moog, Mellotron and Vocals
Andy Latimer	Guitars, Flute and Vocals
Doug Ferguson	Bass
Andy Ward	Drums and Percussion

Produced by David Hitchcock for Gruggy Woof
Recorded at Air Studios, London and Decca Studios, West Hampstead, London
Mixed at Island Studios, London
Engineered by John Punter, Bill Price, John Burns, Sean Milligan and Mike Jones

Camel's arrival at Decca Records as their new home in 1973 came after their self-titled debut album, released in February of that year, had been greeted with critical, if not commercial, success. Camel formed in 1971 when Surrey-based outfit the Brew (featuring Andy Latimer on guitar, flute and vocals), Doug Ferguson (bass) and Andy Ward (drums) recruited keyboard-player and Sixties blues-scene veteran Peter Bardens.

Prior to Bardens' arrival, the Brew had acted as backing band to singer-songwriter Philip Goodhand-Tait, performing on his album 'I Think I'll Write A Song', released in September 1971. It was unsuccessful and the Brew were dropped from DJM Records' roster, but the experience had opened their eyes to the possibilities offered by a keyboardist. Determined to secure a recording deal in their own right, they advertised in Melody Maker and the timespan between Bardens' chance spotting of the ad and his first concert with Latimer, Ferguson and Ward was only some three weeks. He had previous concert commitments in Ireland in October 1971 and fulfilled them with the Brew, billed as Peter Bardens' On.

The band changed their name to Camel and played their first concert under the new name supporting Wishbone Ash at Waltham Forest Technical College in December. Building a steady following on the live circuit, Camel came into contact with producer Mickie Most who signed Latimer to his RAK music publishing company and brought them to the attention of booking agent Geoff Jukes. Jukes, who had recently formed his own Gemini agency, was able to increase Camel's profile on the all-important live circuit and he eventually asked to manage the band. By August 1972, as a result of his efforts and impressive live reviews, Camel had signed a contract with MCA Records for one album with the option to record a second.

Although sales of Camel's first album had been respectable enough, MCA declined the option. Geoff Jukes maintained his confidence in Camel's future and, along with business partners Richard Thomas and Max Hole, signed the band to his newly formed Gama Records. Within weeks the band were ensconced at Island's Basing Street studios recording material for their second album with producer David Hitchcock who had established a reputation working with Caravan and Genesis. While these sessions were underway, Gama secured a long-term licensing deal with Decca Records.

The material recorded in November 1973 was Camel's strongest to date, with both Bardens' and Latimer's songwriting moving on in leaps and bounds. Much of the music recorded had been tried and tested in front of a live audience, and by the time the band had reached the studio any changes to arrangements had been done, making for an album that had both clarity and direction. However, not all the material recorded in those sessions would see the light of day.

From the urgency of 'Freefall', the albums opening track, the pace on 'Mirage' never waned. Bardens' 'Supertwister' led into Latimer's first long composition to feature on record, 'Nimrodel'/'The Procession'/'The White Rider'. This nine-minute opus was inspired by JRR Tolkien's Lord Of The Rings and demonstrated Latimer's ability as both a guitarist and (self-taught) flautist, providing a dramatic close to the albums first side. The second part of the album opened with a Bardens/Latimer composition, 'Earthrise', before giving way to what would become one of Camel's best-known pieces.

' Lady Fantasy' was a band composition that would close concerts from then on and, with its fusion of different musical moods, remains the quintessential Camel song. The finished selected results of the work at Basing Street studios were released on 1 March 1974 as 'Mirage' on Decca's Deram label, housed in a sleeve designed to be a pastiche of a packet of Camel brand cigarettes.

Although 'Mirage' was well received by the British music press, the album surprisingly failed to chart. 'You don't listen to a band like Camel for quick thrills.' Sounds music paper wrote. 'You really do have to hear them a few times before the music begins to register – all those long and delicately arranged instrumental passages burn slowly, but once the melodies are in your head they don't rub out easily.' Beat Instrumental magazine went one step further by declaring 'Mirage' album of the month: 'The musicianship throughout is excellent, and Camel seem to be one of the few bands who get the best out of each other and put it into strong and tight music.'

Camel spent April and May in Europe to promote Mirage', but while on tour the American division of Camel cigarettes became aware of the sleeve design and demanded the cover be withdrawn. In the US 'Mirage' had been licensed to Janus Records, who hastily redesigned the sleeve before release. The original design remained elsewhere after Camel's management came to an arrangement with the European division of Camel Cigarettes to produce small packs of five cigarettes with the Camel album artwork and tracklisting. These were given away free at concerts, where amplifiers covered with Camel skins and advertisements were the result of a sponsorship arrangement of which the band had no knowledge.

Despite the potential problems with the artwork, 'Mirage' entered the Billboard Top 200 album in late November 1973, reaching a height of 149. As a result, Camel were booked for a seven-week US tour supporting Wishbone Ash scheduled to finish in Miami in December 1974. The response was so great that the band stayed on in America, touring in their own right and performing to enthusiastic audiences. With barely any respite from a heavy workload, the band returned to Britain to record their second album for Decca Records and arguably the greatest of their career, 'Music Inspired By The Snow Goose'.

GONG 'You'

Released as Virgin V2019 in October 1974
Highest UK chart position: N/A
Available on CD as Virgin 866552 2

Thoughts For Naught
A PHP's Advice
Magick Mother Invocation
Master Builder
A Sprinkling Of Clouds
Perfect Mystery
Isle Of Everywhere
You Never Blow Yr Trip Forever

Daevid Allen	Vocals, Glissando Guitar
Gilli Smyth	Space Whisper, Poems
Mike Howlett	Bass Guitar
Pierre Moerlen	Percussion
Didier Malherbe	Wind instruments, Vocals
Steve Hillage	Lead Guitar
Tim Blake	Moog and EMS Synthesisers, Mellotron
Miquette Giraudy	Vocals
Mireille Bauer and	
Benoit Moerlen	Percussion

Recorded at the Manor, Oxfordshire in June and July 1974
Produced by Gong and Simon Heyworth
Engineered by Simon Heyworth

'You' constituted the final instalment of the Radio Gnome trilogy, following on from the unique albums 'The Flying Teapot' and 'Angel's Egg'. Over the course of the trilogy, Gong honed their jazz-influenced space-rock jams, gradually lessening their reliance on Daevid Allen's vocals to impart the narrative. The final result was what many regard as Gong's tightest and most unified album, a blend of jazz-rock, electronic music and the avant-garde.

Perhaps because of the relative lack of lyrics, 'You' was less eccentric than Gong's earlier work. The extraordinary musical interplay within the band made 'it a more serious record, and it would be the last of their albums to feature Allen until his return to reactivate Gong some years later. The sessions would prove to be their most consistently creative, leading for a short time to an air of calmness and harmony in the recording studio.

True to their communal democracy, the album was the result of a collaboration between the numerous band members who, by the early summer of 1974, were Daevid Allen (vocals, glissando guitar), Gilli Smyth (space whisper and poems), Mike Howlett (bass guitar), Pierre Moerlen (drums, percussion), Steve Hillage (lead guitar), Miquette Giraudy (vocals), Didier Malherbe (wind instruments and vocals), Tim Blake (Moog and EMS synthesisers and Mellotron), Benoit Moerlen and Mireille Bauer (percussion).

The recording session, were conducted in the midst of a week-long LSD adventure that was later fondly remembered by Daevid Allen thus: 'The creation of '"You"' was very different to '"Angel's Egg". We had come to the conclusion that, because had contributed a lot of the material to those albums, Gong was become too much of my creation. We all felt that it was time we created something completely new together, so we rented a cottage in Oxfordshire and lived there for a week. We saved up some wonderful acid and we took this acid together as a group. This was one occasion where there was no paranoia, it was just a wonderful, wonderful trip and we all played and played and played. We simply connected by improvising and recording it and then at the end of the day, we would listen to the recordings and take the pieces out that we wanted to learn.'

Aside from the music, the narrative threads of the previous two albums had also to be continued with Gong's new project. In this, the last instalment of the Radio Gnome trilogy, Zero the Hero returns from his trip to Planet Gong. On his return he asks Hiram, the Master Builder, to build his own invisible temple. He then sets off to organise the Great Melting Feast of Freeks on the Isle of Everywhere. At the feast, everyone has a great time, third eyes ablaze, except for Zero, who misses the party while eating fruitcake at the back. As a result, Zero misses having his third eye turned on and has to spend the rest of his life being continually reincarnated.

Gong returned to the Manor with co-producer and engineer Simon Heyworth to begin work on their new cosmic masterpiece. The album began with three short psychedelic tracks that would hint at what was to come. 'Master Builder' was a contender for being cited as the finest Gong tune. An intoxicating, trance-like rhythm with a punchy blues undercurrent, the track was a mini-manifesto of what Daevid Allen and Gong were all about, and would later influence the ambient and dance music scenes 20 years later. 'A Sprinkling Of Clouds' began as an ambient soundscape, and was an undoubted influence on Alex Paterson, whose outfit the Orb would acknowledge on their 1991 album 'Adventures Beyond The Ultraworld'. The album's final track, 'You Never Blow Yr Trip Forever', was another whirling, cosmic collage of sound that was both mesmerising and melancholic.

By the time 'You' was released in October 1974, Pierre Moerlen had been replaced on drums by Laurie Allan and Daevid Allen's interest in the band was beginning to wane. Most significantly of all, Hillage had embarked on the recording of his first solo album, 'Fish Rising'. By April 1975, Allen, Smyth and Blake had all departed and former Nice drummer Brian Davison had joined the band. Steve Hillage assumed the role of leader, but following sessions for the album 'Shamal' he too departed to pursue a successful solo career.

His departure saw Gong continue in various guises, getting deeper into jazz-rock territory, steered by a returning Pierre Moerlen. However, Gong's finest moments were undoubtedly found on the 'Radio Gnome' trilogy of albums that would also secure their place in rock history, with innovative musicianship, eccentricity and genuine innovation being their lasting legacy. Underneath the surface of Daevid Allen's wacky tales there is much fine music to be discovered.

'You' saw Gong hone all of these elements to perfection and is the finest example of why the band was such a huge influence on artists of later decades such as the Orb, who later worked extensively with Steve Hillage, and Ozric Tentacles. As the album artwork stated, 'Gong is one and one is you.' All should savour this cosmic trip.

(with thanks to Jon Wright)

HATFIELD AND THE NORTH 'Hatfield And The North'

First released as Virgin V2008 in March 1974
Highest UK chart position: N/A
Available on CD as Esoteric Recordings ECLEC2139

The Stubbs Effect
Big Jobs (Poo Poo Extract)
Going Up To People And Tinkling
Calyx
Son Of 'There's No Place Like Homerton'
Aigrette
Rifferama
Fol De Rol
Shaving Is Boring
Licks For The Ladies
Bossa Nochance
Big Jobs No 2 (By Poo And The Wee Wees)
Lobster In Cleavage Probe
Gigantic Land Crabs In Earth Take Over Bid
The Other Stubbs Effect

Richard Sinclair   **Bass and Singing**
Phil Miller   **Guitars**
Pip Pyle   **Drums**
Dave Stewart   **Organ, Piano and Tone Generator**
With assistance from:
THE NORTHETTES:
Amanda Parsons
Barbara Gaskin
Ann Rosenthal   **Singing**
Geoff Leigh   **Saxes and Flute**
Jeremy Baines   **Pixiephone**
Robert Wyatt   **Singing on 'Calyx'**

Recorded at the Manor studios, Oxfordshire
Produced by Tom Newman and the Hatfields
Engineered by Tom Newman

A great new British band and one of the latest releases from the excellent Virgin label. If I were a musician, then this would be my ideal album. Snorting saxes, tinkling pianos, rippling guitar chords, neat drum patters and just listen to the bass! Who could ask for more? It would be a great pity if this band didn't make it, as they have as much talent as any band you care to mention.

LET IT ROCK - May 1974

In the early Seventies the city of Canterbury had become synonymous with an imaginative, original and polished form of progressive rock with a jazz-influenced edge, tinged with a sense of humour. Thanks to the success of bands such as Soft Machine, Caravan and Gong (fronted by former Canterbury resident and ex-Soft Machine member Daevid Allen), the term 'Canterbury sound' was coined by the media to describe a particular style of music rather than a geographical reference.

Of all the Canterbury groups, Hatfield and the North were one of the more interesting. The band came together following the departure of bassist and vocalist Richard Sinclair and keyboard-player Steve Miller from Caravan following the release of the album 'Waterloo Lily'. Prior to joining Caravan, Miller had been a member of the blues and jazz-influenced Delivery, who had recorded the album 'Fool's Meeting' with vocalist Carol Grimes in 1971. Delivery had existed on and off since 1966, featuring Steve Miller's brother Phil on guitar and Pip Pyle on drums. By the summer of 1972, the Miller brothers and Richard Sinclair united with Pyle, who had recently enjoyed a stint in France with Gong, in a reformed Delivery.

With Phil Miller's departure from Robert Wyatt's band Matching Mole, Delivery performed sporadic concerts in the late summer of 1972. Steve Miller then departed to work with saxophonist Lol Coxhill, leaving the keyboard position vacant for another ex-Caravan member, Dave Sinclair. With Dave's arrival, the new line-up renamed themselves Hatfield and the North, taken from the directions on a road sign on the A1 trunk road heading out of London.

Following a short tour of France in January 1973 during which they appeared on French television with Robert Wyatt, Dave Sinclair left, eventually to rejoin Caravan. His replacement, Egg keyboard-player Dave Stewart, was an inspired choice whose arrival led to a new sense of musical direction. 'Dave really brought more classical influences into our sound,' Pyle would later recall. 'He was a big fan of Stravinsky and you could hear that in his writing,' while Stewart would remark: 'Joining Hatfield involved a steep learning curve, which was a good thing. They wanted me to play more like a jazz musician. That was where Pip and Phil had come from and jazz to me was more like alien territory and not something I'd paid much attention to.' This new confidence was apparent in live performance and led to the band being one of the early signings to the newly established Virgin Records label. Entering Virgin's Manor studios in November 1973, they began work on their debut album.

'The music evolved during those sessions,' said Pyle. 'On Dave's tune '"Son Of There's No Place Like Homerton" we used to bash various objects when we were playing it live. First it was plates and then gnomes. We were playing a tour in Holland and there were all these stoned Dutch boys down at the front, so we thought it would be a great way to wake them up! Some of the music we were presenting was pretty difficult so you had to draw them in and the on-stage humour was definitely part of our whole thing, often reflected in the titles. We tried to present that side of the band on our first album as it was an important part of our make-up.'

However, initial excitement about recording waned when technical issues arose. 'The Manor was a great place where you'd get waited upon hand and foot by pretty girls,' Pip would recall, 'but it was always breaking down. We used to hang about a lot waiting for the engineer, Tom Newman, to fix everything, forgetting that while waited, we were running up a huge bill – £20,000 or something, which was a lot of money back then.' Frustrations came to head still further when Newman accidentally erased the bass drum track from the master tape of 'Gigantic Land Crabs In Earth Take Over Bid'. 'It took me about two days to replace that part because the tempo was speeding up and slowing down all over the place' explained Pyle. 'I was so angry about having to replace that part that we credited Tom on the sleeve as Tom "Bulk Erase"' Newman.'

Despite this, the sessions also had their high points, particularly the guest appearance of Robert Wyatt on vocals on the track 'Calyx'. With a limited budget, the album was completed quickly utilising 'cut and paste' editing techniques to create a flowing cycle of music which enchanted the listener from the opening bars of 'The Stubbs Effect', through to the closing notes of 'The Other Stubbs Effect'.

Released on 1 March 1974, 'Hatfield And The North' had an enthusiastic critical reception, both in the music press and from BBC DJ John Peel. But live work became the band's only source of income due to them having to recoup the cost of recording at the Manor. In an attempt to lower costs they would utilise Saturn Sound in Worthing for their next album.

Although warmly received, both 'Hatfield And The North' and follow-up 'The Rotters' Club' failed to sell in vast numbers. 'I went to Virgin's offices,' Dave Stewart would later reflect, 'and told one of their staff: "Sadly, we seem to find ourselves in a position where we are short of money to such a degree that our bass player and his wife, who's just had a baby, has got nowhere to live. Do you think you could possibly advance us some money against sales of the next album?" I was told that that they couldn't help because our first album hadn't recouped yet. That was one of the reasons why the band split up – just soldiering on without any money. It affected everyone badly. Virgin were happy to see the band break up rather than pay us more money.'

Pip Pyle would later comment: 'If we'd stayed together we might have made one more record but a couple of years later when punk came in, all those original Virgin acts, apart from Mike Oldfield, were pretty much swept away and Simon Draper wasn't around any more so Virgin quickly turned into being just like every other record label.' The music on Hatfield and the North's eponymous debut remains special to all who understand the uniqueness of their music. It is a fitting tribute that author Jonathan Coe, an aficionado of the group, chose to name his sixth novel after second album 'The Rotters' Club'. But it is their wonderful debut that introduced this excellent group to a wider public.

Hatfield and the North

RICHARD SINCLAIR	Bass, Singing.
PHIL MILLER	Guitars.
PIP PYLE	Drums.
DAVE STEWART	Organ, Pianos and Tone Generator.

With assistance from:—

THE NORTHETTES Amanda Parsons Barbara Gaskin Ann Rosenthal	Singing.
Geoff Leigh (c/o HENRY COW)	Saxes and Flute.
Jeremy Baines	Pixiephone.
Robert Wyatt	Singing on "CALYX"

℗ & © VIRGIN RECORDS LTD.,
2/4 VERNON YARD,
119 PORTOBELLO ROAD,
LONDON W.11.

side c

THE STUBBS F
(
BIG JOBS (POO POO EX
(Richard
GOING UP TO PEOPLE AND TIN
(Dave

(Ph
SON OF "THERE'S NO PLACE LIKE HOME
(Dave
(Ph
AIG
RIFF
(Richard Sinclair, arr. Th

Also, Special Tha

Tom 'Bulk Erase' Newman . . . knob twirling and plenty laffs; Alistair and Ro
pleasant rehearsals in the congenial atmosphere of their public house
Lawson . . . contractual coherence; Bede . . . his coach and his subtle but
undermining of reality; John Peel . . . fave D.J.; Geoff Bevan . . . zoot horn eq
Steve Borrill . . . plectrum maintenance; Henk Weltevreden . . . Dutch
encouragement; Bob Hope,.. remarkable composure during the disruption
World' contest 1972; Clive Williamson . . . suggestive breathing on first te
Balchin . . . humpin and mixin; Dik . . . soul music, the very many pretty gals,
drinking; Fletcher and Munsen . . . for their effect; Benj and Tony . . . throwi
707's out of hotel windows, redecorating continents; Mont Campbe

and opening section of "HOME

ROL
(Sinclair)
G IS BORING

OR THE LADIES
(Sinclair)
NOCHANCE
(Sinclair)
S NO. 2 (by POO AND THE WEE WEES)
(Sinclair)
R IN CLEAVAGE PROBE
wart)
IC LAND-CRABS IN EARTH TAKEOVER BID
wart)
HER STUBBS EFFECT

at The Manor studios in 1973.   Engineered and Produced by Tom Newman and The Hatfields.   Cover Design and Photography by Laurie Lewis.

'Lives of great men all remind us we may make our lives sublime...'

CAMEL 'Music inspired By The Snow Goose'
First released as Decca SKL-R5027 in April 1975
Highest UK chart position: Number 22
Available on CD as Decca 531 4614

The Great Marsh
Rhayader
Rhayader Goes To Town
Sanctuary
Fritha
The Snow Goose
Friendship
Migration
Rhayader Alone
Flight Of The Snow Goose
Preparation
Dunkirk
Epitaph
Fritha Alone
La Princesse Perdue
The Great Marsh

Peter Bardens   **Organ, Piano, Mini Moog, Electric Piano, ARP Odyssey**
Andy Latimer   **Guitars, Flute**
Doug Ferguson   **Bass and Duffle Coat**
Andy Ward   **Drums, Vibes and Vari-Speed Percussion**

Produced by David Hitchcock for Gruggy Woof
Recorded at Island Studios, London
Engineered by Rhett Davies
Overdubs recorded at Decca Studios, West Hampstead, London
Engineered by John Burns, Graham Meek and Paul Cooper

The 1974 release of Camel's second album, 'Mirage', broke them to a wider audience and persuaded Decca Records that the group had a long future ahead of them. The extensive touring schedule that followed saw Camel establish themselves as one of the brightest hopes to emerge on the British music scene.

With their European tour completed, Camel returned to Britain and ensconced themselves in a rented cottage in Devon to commence work on their second album for Decca. Most of the material had already been sketched out and performed on the road. Indeed, work first began on a follow-up to 'Mirage' in June 1974. The suggestion to write an expanded work on a conceptual theme came at that time from Doug Ferguson, who felt the 'White Rider' suite on 'Mirage' to be a successful experiment. As all members of Camel were avid readers, each musician suggested a suitable novel on which to base their next album.

Peter Bardens suggested Herman Hesse's Siddhartha as a suitable subject to base a new concept upon and some songwriting was attempted around this theme. In June 1974 Camel entered Decca Studios to record an Andrew Latimer song intended to be the first. 'Riverman' was recorded as a potential single with David Hitchcock once again in the producer's chair, but failed to see the light of day when Camel abandoned the idea of using Hesse's novel. Peter Bardens suggested Steppenwolf, from the same author, as a suitable concept but this was deemed unworkable.

It was Doug Ferguson who suggested a short novel written in 1941 by American author Paul Gallico as a fitting inspiration for a concept album. The Snow Goose was a tale of the friendship between Fritha, a teenage girl, and reclusive disabled artist Philip Rhayader who lived in a disused lighthouse on the Essex marshes drawing the wildlife living on the marsh. The pair's friendship developed when caring for a snow goose wounded by a gunshot. The bird is nursed back to health and is seen following Rhayader to the beaches of Dunkirk where the artist had gone in his small boat to assist in the evacuation of British soldiers trapped by the advancing German army. Rhayader is killed during the evacuation and the snow goose returns to the Essex marshes to circle above Fritha, who sees this as symbolic of Rhayader's soul taking leave of the world.

With such incredible imagery as inspiration, Andrew Latimer and Peter Bardens worked solidly in their Devon retreat. The fruits of their labour would be performed live as early as October 1974, on a series of live dates in the UK. Before recording commenced Camel journeyed to America to support Wishbone Ash and elected to stay and tour clubs in their own right until the end of the year. In January 1975 work on 'Snow Goose' began at Island Studios in London, with David Hitchcock undertaking production duties once more.

Composer and conductor David Bedford, (who had acted as an acclaimed arranger for Roy Harper, Kevin Ayers and Mike Oldfield), was enlisted to write the evocative orchestral arrangements for Latimer and Bardens' creation. The instrumental album was intended to have a written narrative thread using extracts from the book on the sleeve to link each piece of music, but Gallico's publishers declined to grant permission as they had approved a project by composer Ed Welch who had written orchestral music to accompany narration by comedian and writer Spike Milligan for release on RCA Records.

In addition, Paul Gallico, a noted opponent of smoking, took exception to the title of his book being used by a band he believed to be connected with a well-known cigarette company. He threatened legal action unless the title was changed and so Camel's opus appeared under the title of 'Music Inspired By The Snow Goose' in April 1975, reaching Number 22 in the UK album chart in the summer of that year.

Considering the fluidity of the finished work, Andrew Latimer was later to recount that Camel had never performed the whole work in its entirety before recording commenced and therefore had no real idea about how the finished running order would sound. The release of the album led Melody Maker magazine to declare Camel Britain's Brightest Hope, an accolade which resulted in ever-increasing attendances at concerts.

The 'Snow Goose' proved to be one of the band's most commercially successful albums, securing silver status in the UK in 1981 and selling countless more copies since. It was a successful experiment in writing an instrumental concept, and remains the most enduring album of Camel's long and illustrious career.

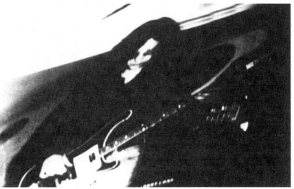

GENTLE GIANT
'Free Hand'

First released as Chrysalis Records CHR1093 in August 1975
Highest UK chart position: N/A
Available on CD as Alucard Records 804471000329

Just The Same
On Reflection
Free Hand
Time To Kill
His Last Voyage
Talybont
Mobile

Derek Schulman	**Lead vocals, Saxophone, Recorder, Keyboards, Bass, Percussion**
Ray Schulman	**Bass guitar, Vocals, Trumpet, Violin, Viola, Guitar, Recorder, Percussion**
Kerry Minnear	**Lead Vocals, Keyboards, Cello, Vibes, Guitar, Recorder, Percussion**
Gary Green	**Guitar, Mandolin, Vocals, Recorder, Bass, Percussion**
John Weathers	**Drums, Percussion, Vocals, Vibes, Guitar**

Recorded at Advision Studios, London in April 1975
Produced by Gentle Giant
Engineered by Gary Martin assisted by Paul Northfield

As 1975 began, Gentle Giant looked back on a traumatic and difficult year. The period of change that had affected the band began with the departure of Phil Shulman (saxophones, trumpet, vocals), a founder member of the band with his brothers Derek (lead vocals, saxophone) and Ray (bass, violin, guitar, vocals), Kerry Minnear (keyboards, vibes, cello, vocals) and Gary Green (guitar).

Phil Shulman's departure followed the extensive tour undertaken to promote the album 'Octopus', the band's fourth and last album for Vertigo Records in the UK. During their tenure with Vertigo they had enjoyed considerable acclaim with their demanding and complex music which had stunned audiences, drawing on influences ranging from rock, classical, folk, medieval and baroque music.

Gentle Giant was formed from the remnants of late-Sixties psychedelic beat group Simon Dupree and the Big Sound, who scored a 1967 UK Top 10 hit with the excellent 'Kites' single (which featured extensive use of Mellotron). Brothers Ray, Derek and Phil Shulman had recruited Minnear, a keyboard-playing graduate from the Royal College of Music, Green and drummer Martin Smith and spent several months, honing their craft in a cottage in Hampshire.

After signing a management contract with Gerry Bron they came to the attention of the newly formed Vertigo label, who saw the band as a potential rival to other major progressive acts of the day such as King Crimson. Certainly, Gentle Giant were as accomplished musically, and their 1970 Tony Visconti-produced debut album was suitably impressive, containing much fine material such as 'Funny Ways' and 'Nothing At All'. Although critical reaction was enthusiastic, sales in the UK failed to match such good reviews. In Europe however Giant found an eager and receptive audience which reflected in greater commercial success. 1971's 'Acquiring The Taste' was a major leap forward. The album liner notes stated that the record 'abandoned all thoughts of perceived commercialism,' which proved prophetic when the album failed to chart in the UK.

By the time of the release of 'Three Friends' in 1972 Martin Smith had been replaced by Malcolm Mortimore. The album was the band's first to be released in the US, which led to an American tour, during which Mortimore was seriously injured in a motorbike accident which led to many months' recuperation. To complete the tour, Mortimore was replaced by Welsh drummer John 'Pugwash' Weathers, previously with Pete Brown's Piblokto!, Graham Bond, Ancient Grease and Big Sleep. Truly progressive in every sense, 'Octopus', was Gentle Giant's final work for Vertigo, but the loss of Phil Shulman was a blow. His dissatisfaction with touring had possibly been brought to a head by the stressful tour to promote 'Octopus' which saw Gentle Giant open for Black Sabbath. In an interview many years later for the Sea Of Tranquillity website, brother Derek would later reflect: 'It was perhaps the most ludicrous pairing of acts in the history of showbusiness.'

The next Gentle Giant album, 'In A Glass House', released in September 1973, appeared on manager Patrick Meehan's WWA label and was a work of complex brilliance that was frustratingly denied a US release as the band's American label, Columbia, felt that it was too uncommercial. This was followed soon after by 'The Power And The Glory', issued in the US by Capitol. The quality of the music on both albums belied the fact that all was not well between band and management. After some months of wrangling, Gentle Giant managed to free themselves from a business arrangement they felt was stifling their musical freedom and found a supporter in the form of Terry Ellis, manager of Jethro Tull, who had founded Chrysalis Records with business partner Chris Wright.

'We really liked Jethro Tull and had supported them on tour some years before,' Kerry Minnear would later recall. 'They became just about the only friends we made on the road. It was through this relationship that we got to know Terry Ellis and brought about our change of labels.' Gentle Giant were finally given the opportunity to develop their style further with their next album.

Aware of their previous mixed commercial fortunes, the band resolved to present their music in a more polished, although still far from conventional, musical style. Entering Advision Studios in April 1975, much of the material recorded drew on the band's experiences with WWA Records and the vagaries of the music business. 'Just The Same' was an acerbic comment on the pretentiousness and ego displayed by some rock musicians, while 'Free Hand' described the break from WWA, commenting in its lyrics 'Now my hands are free from the ties. Now I look forward to the future where it lies.' 'Mobile' dealt with the stresses of touring, while 'On Reflection', on the surface a song about a failed personal relationship, could easily be interpreted as a comment on the band's business problems. 'Talybont' was a superb instrumental, while in 'His Last Voyage' Gentle Giant recorded one of the most finely crafted songs of their later period.

Released in August 1975, 'Free Hand' failed to chart in the UK, but reached Number 48 on the US Billboard chart, thanks in part to an extensive period of touring. 'Terry Ellis made us work hard on the road,' Derek Shulman would later state, 'and the buzz of playing live came back to us again. We began to have enthusiasm like we had before we made "Octopus".' Despite the 'simplification' of their music, Gentle Giant were to enjoy a period of chart success in America, but by 1978 they had undertaken a more drastic change in direction which would leave them a long way stylistically from their earlier albums and even 'Free Hand'.

Gentle Giant's first album for Chrysalis was not only their last great record, it remains the finest and the most accessible of their long career.

STEVE HACKETT
'Voyage Of The Acolyte'

First released as Charisma CAS1112 in November 1975
Highest UK chart position: Number 26
Available on CD as Charisma CDSCDR1111

Ace Of Wands
Hands Of The Priestess Part 1
A Tower Struck Down
Hands Of The Priestess Part 2
The Hermit
Star Of Sirius
The Lovers
Shadow Of The Hierophant

Steve Hacket:	**Electric and Acoustic Guitars, Mellotron, Harmonium, Bells, Autoharp, Vocals**
John Hackett	**Flute, ARP Synthesiser, Bells**
Mike Rutherford	**Bass Guitar, Bass Pedals, Fuzz 12-String Guitar**
Phil Collins	**Drums, Vibes, Percussion, Vocals**
John Acock:	**Elka Rhapsody, Mellotron, Harmonium, Piano**
Sally Oldfield	**Vocal**
Robin Miller	**Oboe, Cor Anglais**
Nigel Warren-Green	**Solo Cello**
John Gustafson	**Bass**
Percy Jones	**Extra Bass on 'A Tower Struck Down'**

Produced by Steve Hackett and John Acock
Recorded at Kingsway Recorders, London between June and July 1975
Engineer John Acock assisted by Paul Watkins and Rob Broglia

In 1975 Genesis suffered the apparent mortal blow of the departure of singer and frontman Peter Gabriel. A period of reflection followed, which the group would eventually resolve by having Phil Collins step from behind the kit. It was also a period during which the first solo album by any member of Genesis was released. Surprisingly, the record came not from Gabriel but from guitarist Steve Hackett. 'Voyage Of The Acolyte' was a fine work that featured contributions from cohorts Mike Rutherford and Phil Collins, but was no mere Genesis clone. The album gave Hackett his own distinct identity and would contribute to his eventual departure from the band in 1977.

He would later explain the circumstances of the creation of his first solo album thus: 'I suppose I got the chance to make a solo record thanks in part to Peter leaving Genesis. We all knew he was going to depart the band after we had finished touring our recent album, "The Lamb Lies Down On Broadway". I had mixed feelings about that record. I felt that while it was full of weird and wonderful sounds and ideas, it was not a typical Genesis album. Our music was essentially a bit more romantic than that.

'I longed to make a record that was more atmospheric and I was firmly committed to trying to make a group sound like an orchestra. Peter's departure had meant that the future of Genesis was by no means certain. He was already a star by the time he left the band and it seemed a bit like Mick Jagger leaving the Rolling Stones. Music journalists asked "Do Genesis have a future?" As a result a number of us got involved in solo projects as we really didn't know if things would continue to gel as Genesis after Peter's departure.'

Recording sessions began at Kingsway Recorders which was based in Aviation House on London's Kingsway. 'The building had a noise restriction placed upon it,' Steve later would recall, 'which meant that we couldn't play any music before 6pm, which suited me fine at the time. As the recording was done at night I think that coloured the whole feel of the album. As this was my first solo effort, I didn't know whether we would return home with a bunch of out-takes or a finished album.'

The concept was based around Tarot cards, each track being a reference to an individual card. Looking back on those sessions several decades later, Steve remembered: 'The track "Hands Of The Priestess" was the first to be attempted and by the

end of that first evening's recording it sounded so good that it gave me the confidence to attack all the other pieces I'd written, all of which had more ambitious arrangements. Phil Collins sang lead vocals on "Star Of Sirius" which in hindsight might be seen as perhaps paving the way for taking over as singer in Genesis.

'It was lovely to work with Phil and Mike outside the confines of the band. We worked in a very different way to Genesis on my album. I wrote "Shadow Of The Hierophant" with Mike Rutherford. There were moments in that piece when the track had drums and bass, but the very long verses featured acoustic instruments. Drums were only required during certain intervals, so we set up a click track to assist with timekeeping, the first time Phil had ever worked to one. The album was recorded in one month, during which time I got very little sleep and consumed a vast amount of cigarettes and chicken soup from a vending machine in the studio!'

Hackett duly delivered the album to Charisma Records, but the title 'Premonitions' was rejected by Tony Stratton-Smith. 'I accepted their suggestion of "Voyage Of The Acolyte",' said Hackett, 'and later found out that it was another artist's title of a proposed project for Charisma based on Tarot cards that had never got off the ground. When the album was released it was very well received and managed to get into the UK Top 30. As a result, all of us in Genesis felt that, if there was such an amount of interest in my solo career, then there would certainly be a large amount of interest in anything the four of us as Genesis could produce.

'It also became a little difficult within the band when I had a hit solo album as it didn't go down that well with the others, but I'd finally got to be the captain of my own ship, albeit briefly. On reflection I suppose there was no turning back after "Voyage Of The Acolyte". I stayed with Genesis for another couple of albums, but it was hard to go back to being a member of the crew. The idea of composition by committee had its drawbacks and limitations. The downside of being in a group is that all the material a band records has to have approval from the members, which I don't always think serves the best interests of the music. 'This feeling grew within me over the next two years until it reached the point where I felt I had no choice but to leave the band during the mixing of "Seconds Out" and embark on a solo career that began with "Please Don't Touch".

Steve Hackett continues to enjoy a successful solo career with many fine records to his credit, 'Voyage Of The Acolyte' remaining his supreme achievement.

Steve Hackett

HAWKWIND 'Warrior On The Edge of Time'

First released as United Artists UA 29766 in May 1975
Highest UK chart position: Number 13
Not currently available on CD

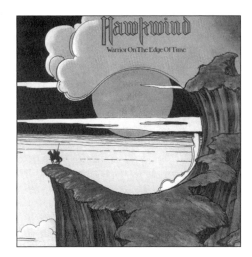

Assault And Battery
The Golden Void
The Wizard Blew His Horn
Opa-Loka
The Demented Man
Magnu
Standing At The Edge
Spiral Galaxy 28948
Warriors
Dying Seas
Kings Of Speed

Dave Brock	Guitar, Synthesiser, Bass on 'Opa-Loka', Vocals
Nik Turner	Tenor and Soprano Saxophone, Flute, Vocals
Lemmy	Bass Guitar
Simon House	Mellotron, Moog, Piano, Synthesiser and Violin
Simon King	Drums and Percussion
Alan Powell	Drums and Percussion
Michael Moorcock	Vocals on 'The Wizard Blew His Horn' and 'Warriors'

Produced by Hawkwind
Recorded at Rockfield Studios, Monmouthshire in March 1975
Engineered by Dave Charles
Mixed at Olympic Studios, Barnes, London in March 1975
Engineered by Phil Chapman and Steve Owen

As 1974 drew to a close, Hawkwind were riding high as British rock's most successful underground group. Retaining their connections to what remained of the British counterculture whence they had emerged in August 1969, Hawkwind had achieved the unthinkable feat of enjoying a string of UK Top 20 albums and a successful hit single 'Silver Machine' in 1972.

Following the release of 1971's 'In Search of Space', the band's line-up had gone through a more settled phase comprising Dave Brock (guitar, vocals, synthesiser), Nik Turner (saxophone, flutes, vocals), Lemmy Kilmister (bass, guitar, vocals), Simon King (drums), Del Dettmar (synthesiser), Dik Mik (audio generator) and augmented on stage by dancer Stacia. This line-up recorded the 1972 studio album 'Doremi Fasol Latido' before being joined by poet and vocalist Robert Calvert in time for Hawkwind's ambitious live project 'Space Ritual'.

The live album recorded on the 'Space Ritual' tour would prove to be Hawkwind's most commercially successful, reaching Number 9 in the UK charts. However, any sense of stability was destined not to last. Dik Mik departed the fold in 1973 and Robert Calvert also left to pursue a solo career. For 1974's excellent 'Hall Of The Mountain Grill', Hawkwind were joined by former High Tide and Third Ear Band violinist and keyboard player Simon House. This majestic album was a major step forward in creative terms for Hawkwind and was their most carefully crafted work to date.

House's use of Mellotron and violin made Hawkwind's sound much larger and more dynamic, as was evident on the band's 1974 European tour which followed the album's release in November 1974. Prior to the start of this series of live dates, Simon King broke his ribs during a game of football and former Vinegar Joe drummer Alan Powell was drafted in, initially as a temporary replacement. However, after the completion of concerts in Belgium and France the decision was made to retain Powell and continue with two drummers in the line-up. It was also at this point that long-time member Del Dettmar announced his departure, deciding to move to Canada. Thus Hawkwind's short UK tour of December 1974 heralded a new era. The new year began with a lengthy series of British dates which continued until the middle of February 1975. The tour was briefly interrupted by a recording session at Olympic Studios in London at the end of January to record a new song written and sung by Lemmy Kilmister; 'Motörhead' took its title from the slang term for an amphetamine user.

Once they were London's best-known freak band — now Stevie Wonder and Alice go to see them . . . .

Hawkwind— in search of new space

by Tony Jasper

"AMERICA was good with us," Simon King, Hawkwind's drummer, says with obvious relish at the thought, "some of our discs had been released there but sales hadn't exactly suggested we were sensational or anything yet in places like Chicago and Detroit, New York and L. A. the crowds were there."

Hawkwind have joined the current success roster of British groups in the States. "When we played Detroit the city had in the space of a few days ELP, The Who, Genesis and Humble Pie. Chicago is like a home town. It was a tremendous gig. In New York Alice Cooper and Stevie Wonder were in the audience.

"American kids may not have seen you in action before but they don't take long to get into it and we're not the easiest of groups to get to seeing we play a solid two hours without a break.

"We plugged our Space Ritual over there because that's how we were advertised, but we're more. The change should be seen on our current British tour."

That my friends is the important story for now. America is an important music public. It can make a group rich and certainly offers a richer monetary harvest in concert and record sales than here but if you're not American you obviously have to spend some time here and in any case most groups want appreciation from their own kin.

Hawkwind have gained legions of supporters with their Space Ritual. The group have produced a single destined to become with age a classic, Silver Machine. Simon King knows well that the interest created then has to be kept alive. He knows the group have to progress. America is past. The current tour is the vital event.

What has made it all the more important is the "Autumn Guerilla Happening".

Simon King explains: "At the time we were a bit divided about the whole thing. We wanted to have a single out to keep Hawkwind interest alive whilst we were on our American tour. Anyway we decided to make Urban Guerilla our release.

"Then came the various bombings and threats in London. The record wasn't about that and yet could be interpreted in such a way and we thought it best to withdraw the single. At the time it had just entered your single chart.

"To do this was to create a vacuum. We had a live album released early in '73 but once Urban Guerilla was removed from the scene we really had nothing."

So what then does the immediate future mean for Hawkwind? Simon King talks further, "We have been in the studio a few times but now we're touring and in fact within 48 hours of arriving back from the States we were off. When you play live it's a positive thing, you create interest in a large number of places. However then the record side does become a problem.

"I guess any new recording will have to be done bit by bit. I would like to see an album put out with two distinct parts. The first would be a recording of our new live material. The other side would be very much a studio job, something not really suited for stage. We would be able to utilise to the full synthesizers, tape and electronic devices.

"What helps us I think to keep there in the music public's mind is our uniqueness. I don't think there is anyone with our kind of scene. Our light show has really developed from say the kind of thing you might have seen during '67 psychedelia. We take round with us a special lighting crew under John Smitton with the name of Liquid Len and The Lensmen.

"Andy Dunkley, the dj, comes with us too and he's a great bloke and has always worked with us. He had the American audiences right there by doing a countdown on our act's beginning. You know he would say, "Ten minutes to Hawkwind" and then nine and so on.

"We couldn't think at first what to call our present tour and then we came up with The Ridiculous Road Show with the Silly Hawkwind Brothers. Anything ridiculous can go down well under that, anything in fact! The tour's beginning has been good. We still get people who come because we made the Top 20 but are winning back the hard-core, the faithful from underground days.

"Those days are still with us. It's impossible to exist playing for free. Our travelling expenses which includes crew, upkeep of equipment, transportation and so forth are enormous. However we still aim to play free gigs from time to time, particularly if it's for something within our thinking and needs money help.

"Some might say talk of the space image is a serious trip but we're really a fun BAND. we enjoy playing more than anything else. I mean we get some ridiculous happenings on stage. Our sax player went on well souped up one day. He begun to play a ridiculous sax solo and then fell flat! The strobe lights were busy and it was quite hilarious with him falling and three of us picking him up and carrying him away!

"Our gig musical programme always flexible though we always now have a standard number of pieces we know people want to hear. We jam quite a bit and when we tour next in America it looks as if Man will be with us. I tell you every show can't help but ending up with both of us there playing away, they're a great bunch pf people.

"We're still playing bits of our Space Ritual but rather mixed up amongst other music. What we need to find and get going is another theme, something we can develop and get out teeth into."

In a way Simon King is vague about Hawkwind's immediate future and yet in a positive way he's saying at the same time go and listen to the group's music and be part of the people getting into their scene.

In a musical sense the individual members have been progressing with their own respective music instruments and electronic techniques. Del and Dave have been getting more and more into the synthesizer's magic carpet whilst Dave Brock is becoming more versatile on guitar. Lemmy is making the bass talk and Simon? Modesty lets him say:

"Me? I tell you drum solos are a waste of time, unless excellent, nothing worse than a mediocre one, that's why I don't do one! now give me Baker for power, Keith Moon for tremendous energy but all in all Buddy Rich, he's governor."

Ask Simon for THE GROUP and he names The Who. Now Hawkwind obviously are not of The Who's stature but then few are. Hawkwind though are building a reputation both sides of the Atlantic. They're not small-timers, far from it. Ask Chicago music freaks. Ask any audience on Hawkwind's current British tour. They'll tell you Hawkwind are BIG.

At the beginning of March 1975, Hawkwind entered Rockfield Studios in Monmouthshire to begin work on their final album for United Artists records. With the reaction to 'Hall Of The Mountain Grill' fresh in their minds, they felt they had to go one better. At the suggestion of long-time collaborator and science-fantasy author Michael Moorcock, the loose concept of the album was based around Moorcock's Eternal Champion. Producing the sessions themselves, Hawkwind worked with resident Rockfield engineer Dave Charles.

Dave Brock's two-part opus 'Assault and Battery' and 'The Golden Void' was a superb work dominated by a dramatic bass line from Lemmy and Simon House's Mellotron. It remains a highpoint in the saga of Hawkwind. Brock would also contribute the atmospheric 'Demented Man' and the excellent rock number 'Magnu'. Michael Moorcock visited Rockfield for a day to offer three poems, 'The Wizard Blew His Horn', 'Standing At The Edge' and 'Warriors', all written in collaboration with Simon House, Alan Powell and Simon King. House would also offer his fine instrumental 'Spiral Galaxy 28948' (the number in the title derived from his date of birth). Nik Turner contributed 'Dying Seas', based upon a title offered by Moorcock. Proceedings were completed with 'Kings Of Speed', a track co-written by Brock and Moorcock, based upon an unreleased song recorded by Moorcock with his band Deep Fix.

The music recorded at Rockfield that March was undoubtedly Hawkwind's most accomplished to date. Following mixing sessions at Olympic in Barnes, London, the final touch came with the elaborate sleeve design conceived by designer Barney Bubbles and Michael Moorcock. On the inner side, the sleeve design folded out into a large shield, while the front design depicted a warrior on horseback standing at the edge of a high cliff face. 'Warrior On The Edge Of Time' was released in May 1975 and rose to Number 13 in the UK. By this time, Hawkwind had embarked on another US tour.

Following a concert at the Allen Theater in Cleveland, Ohio on 16 May, the band crossed the Canadian border to perform a concert in Toronto on 18 May. Unfortunately Lemmy was in possession of amphetamine sulphate given to him by a fan and, at the border crossing, he was arrested on suspicion of possessing cocaine. After a night in police cells, he rejoined the band to perform at the Convocation Hall, Toronto. Following the concert Lemmy was dismissed following a band vote at their hotel. With that event, an era ended for Hawkwind.

At short notice Canadian Paul Rudolph, former guitarist with the Deviants and the Pink Fairies, was drafted in as replacement bass player and the US tour was completed under a cloud. Following an extensive series of concerts in Europe and the UK, Stacia took her final bow following a headlining appearance at the Reading Festival that August. The set heralded the return of Robert Calvert to the band, a move to Charisma Records and a series of unique and creative albums beyond the time frame of this book.

If one album stands out among the vast Hawkwind discography, it is 'Warrior On The Edge Of Time'. It perfectly captured the essence of Hawkwind, while demonstrating a musical sensibility many detractors had doubted they possessed. Its lack of availability on CD remains frustrating, but the uninitiated are strongly urged to seek out an original copy and experience musical nirvana.

HAWKWIND'S XMAS DO

HAWKWIND ARE planning a "Christmas Party" tour and are being rejoined by former light show operator Jonathan Smeeton.

They will be playing 10 dates in the two weeks prior to Christmas, and all gigs, with the exception of Ipswich, will be without seating.

One of their London shows will be at the new rock venue in a large sports hall at Picketts Lock, Enfield, on December 20.

Other dates are: Blackburn, King George's Hall (December 10); Birmingham, Bingley Hall (12); Southend, Kursaal Ballroom (14); Reading, Top Rank (14); Cardiff, Top

Rank (16); Brunel University (17); Ipswich, Gaumont (18); Norwich, St. Andres Hall (19); Southampton, Top Rank (21).

During January and February they will be rehearsing a new stage show and finishing an album set for March release.

HAWKWIND / Hammersmith Odeon.
AS ALL keen astronomers will already know last Sunday evening witnessed the return to Earth of Ladbroke Grove's sole donation to the space race, spaced out race that is. Yes Hawkwind, the arch boggies of a generation, are back in town and terrorizing unsuspecting human beings again.

A stunning display of flashing lights soon had most of the earthlings hypnotised and completely at the mercy of lead guitarist Lemmy (Lemmy at Stacia) and his fellow astronauts. Whilst we're on the subject of mesmerisation I must warn you that robot dancer Stacia failed to display anything at all and was by all appearances making a large contribution to the finances of Playtex. She couldn't even dance properly. !

Weary Hawkwind ditch tour

HAWKWIND, who have cancelled eight of their remaining 10 dates claim they suffering from physical and nervous exhaustion.

They decided to cancel the dates after chaos broke out at the London Roundhouse gig on Monday.

About a thousand disappointed fans who were unable to get in to see the band attempted to burn down the side entrances and police had to be called.

Members of the band and road crew were prevented from getting back into the concert for more than an hour.

Nik Turner said later; "The hassles at the Roundhouse were the straw that broke the camel's back and we all realise that despite the disappointment it will cause there is no way the band can continue working any longer without time for a good rest."

The band have made two British and three American tours in 12 months, and release a new album, Kings Of Speed, on March 14.

The cancelled dates are: Folkestone (February 22); Gloucester (27); Yeovil (28); Dunstable (March 2); Aberystwyth (7); Swansea / Port Talbot (8); Preston (11) and Halifax (12). The dates kept in are Guildford Civic Hall (February 23) and Worthing Town Hall (24).

The regular 'Wind miracle

Hawkwind — class of '74.

New York pic: JOE STEVENS

NEW YORK just doesn't seem to be the place for Hawkwind.

After capacity crowds in Detroit, Chicago and clear across the Middle West, the two thirds full Academy of Music was something of a bringdown. An added difficulty was that the New York concert was the penultimate of a gruelling six weeks tour and some of the band were showing visible signs of exhaustion.

The night before the Academy show Simon King stood against the bar in Max's Kansas City, with a glazed expression, while the David Bowie look-alike competition wafted around him. Back at the hotel Lemmy refused, steadfastly, to emerge from his bed. Nick Turner and Dave Brock were reported to be missing. Hawkwind had generally reached a high point in their brink-of-disaster tour technique.

Saturday dawned bright and clear. New York was experiencing a spell of freak eighty degree sunshine and a bunch of the most intrepid Hawks stumbled blinking into the daylight for a last minute souvenir and gift buying excursion.

By sunset, the lobby of the Gramercy Park Hotel had turned into a Zappa style nightmare. The huge David Bowie show and road crew were booked into the hotel, and the ladies of the town thronged the foyer and camped on the pavement.

In fact, the star was across town in far plusher Regent; the presence of Hawkwind as a second option to a Bowie sideman caused emotional conflict and flurry of groupie status calculations.

Dave Brock seemed unaffected by the glitz madness in the lobby. He sat serenely in his sixteenth floor suite quietly passing out joints to a select group of friends, watching "Star Trek" and looking forward to being back at home. Lemmy still huddled in his cocoon of blankets and, despite all exhortations, refused to move unless some kind of artifical aid turned up. Showtime rolled closer and closer.

The Academy concert was scheduled to start at midnight, and at 11.45 p.m., the regular Hawkwind miracle happened.

Marshalled by Higgy, the implacable tour manager, who often seems to be playing the part of master sergeant in some bizarre movie version of Starship Troopers, the entire show is ready to go. The band have all shown up, looking together and relatively human. The stage is set up and all that remains is for the audience to file in before the whole thing can get under way.

The audience is something of a disappointment. They are older, less enthusiastic and far more solemn than the frenzied kids who flock to see Hawkwind at the Chicago Auditorium or the Detroit Palace. These New Yorkers are more like a Pink Floyd audience, staid veterans of the psychedelic generation who still like to watch a lightshow and hear the cosmic roar.

They're polite and appreciative, but they lack the zip of the Ripple wine and Quaaludes brigade. It really does seem as though the New York kids haven't grasped what Hawkwind are all about, or maybe, in New York, they are more interested in style and transsexuality than in the galactic outer limits.

The transformation in the band is incredible to behold. The shambling wrecks of a few hours earlier have turned into a tight, efficient unit.

There has always been debate about the validity of Hawkwind. Whether you like what they're doing is still a matter of taste. The thing they can no longer be faulted for is the way they do it.

Six hard weeks of the third US tour have welded the band together to an incredible degree. The most impressive change i the power of the rhythm section. The addition of Alan Powell as a second drummer has produced a percussion interplay that is a whole new source of interest and dynamics.

The transformation in Lemmy was also kind of amazing. The corpse of the early evening was romping, stomping and strutting out his Liverpool heritage, commanding the front of the stage and rocking with almost demonic energy. His bass line wove in and out of the double drum pattern like the star quarterback in the afternoon's TV ball game.

Not that the rhythm section had it all their own way. Dave Brock and Simon House have emerged as a melodic top line, far in advance of anything they have done previously. The clanks, honks and tweets of the early band have been resolved into sweeping harmonics that are reminiscent of the Floyd's careful-with-that-axe period.

Nick Turner's role in the band also seem to be changing. His reed playing is not longer so predominant. He sings more, and has started working increasingly with the statuesque Stacia in a series of strange Living Theatre pas de deux.

Despite the power of the performance, the audience were hardly tumultuous. The glazed tiredness quickly seemed to return, and was carried away to be slept off in the hotel, or worn out in the frantic craziness of New York's after hours bars.

Mick Farren

NIK TURNER

DAVE BROCK and (right) DEL DETTMAR

STEVE HILLAGE 'Fish Rising'

First released as Virgin V2031 in April 1975
Highest UK chart position: Number 33
Available on CD as Virgin CDVR2031

Solar Musick Suite:
a. Sun Song (I Love Its Holy Mystery)
b. Canterbury Sunrise
c. Hiram Afterglid Meets The Dervish
d. Sun Song (Reprise)
Fish
Meditation Of The Snake
The Salmon Song:
a. Salmon Song
b. Solomon's Atlantis Salmon
c. Swimming With The Salmon
d. King Of The Fishes
Aftaglid
A. Sun Moon Surfing
B. The Great Wave And The Boat Of Hermes
C. The Silver Ladder
D. Astral Meadows
E. The Lafta Yoga Song
F. Glidding
G. The Golden Vibe/Outglid

Steve Hillage	**Guitars, Vocals**
Pierre Moerlen	**Drums, Percussion, Marimba**
Dave Stewart	**Organ, Piano**
Mike Howlett	**Bass**
Lindsay Cooper	**Bassoon**
Tim Blake	**VCS 3 Synthesiser, Mini-Moog, Tambura**
Miquette Giraudy	**Vocals**

Produced by Steve Hillage and Simon Heyworth
Recorded at the Manor, Oxfordshire
Engineered by Simon Heyworth

By the summer of 1974 Steve Hillage had been a member of Gong for a year and a half. From the moment he joined in December 1972 his guitar-playing and compositional input had added extra texture and flair. However, Hillage was also beginning to feel a sense of frustration due to some of his material being rejected by band members.

'In addition to material I had written in a collaborative form for Gong, I had quite a lot of other material which was in a semi-completed state. In my off moments I carried on working on these ideas. I jammed some of the music with the members of Gong and it took on an extra quality through Gong's influence. Finally it reached a point where I felt that this music of mine just had to be recorded. I had already been approached by Virgin Records prior to me becoming a member of Gong about the possibility of me signing to them as a solo artist, and so they reacted favourably when I suggested recording a solo album.'

In August 1974, Hillage entered Virgin's Manor studio in Oxfordshire to commence work on his first solo album. 'On these initial sessions to record the backing tracks I went into the studio with bass player Mike Howlett and drummer Pierre Moerlen, who were members of Gong. They were familiar with some of the material because I'd been messing around with it during Gong rehearsals and it was obvious to me that they should play on the final album' he later remembered.

'Basically, the recordings of the backing tracks to the album were quite an event. Most of the music was played live in the studio with very few overdubs, which made for a simple and quite raw sound. That wasn't the sound I was going for on the final album, as I wanted a richer, psychedelic sound which is what I eventually got. But because the original backing-track mixes were quite different they acquired an air of notoriety. We recorded the basic backing tracks during a month-long gap in Gong's schedule, and as soon as they were completed I went on the road with Gong once more. Then in the early part of 1975 I was able to go back into the studio and finish. Dave Stewart, who had worked with me on the Khan album and was in Hatfield and the North at that time, came down and played on the sessions, as did Tim Blake from Gong, who overdubbed synthesiser.'

The sessions also featured contributions from Steve's partner, fellow Gong member Miquette Giraudy, saxophonist Didier Malherbe and bassoon-player Lindsay Cooper. The music recorded was of an incredibly high standard, thanks to the time Hillage had spent writing and arranging the music. Hillage later added: 'Basically, if I hadn't aborted the band, most of the music on "Fish Rising" would have appeared on a second Khan album. "The Salmon Song" dated from the Khan era, and "Pentagrammaspin" featured in some of Khan's live shows, as did "Solar Musick Suite", although that piece went under a different name and the lyrics were different. The one major piece that didn't date from my pre-Gong days was "Aftaglid" which was definitely influenced by Gong and even jammed by the group.'

'Fish Rising' was released on 11 April 1975, reaching Number 33 on the British album charts. 'I wasn't too surprised it did well,' he reflected three decades later, 'because I thought I'd made a great album and I was very happy with it. It was a baby that I had nurtured for three years and when it finally came to fruition I felt I'd made the right record at the right time.'

Ironically, the release coincided with serious upheaval within the ranks of Gong. 'The fact that I'd had a solo hit album didn't really produce too many problems. The so-called classic line-up of Gong had already imploded by that point,' Hillage remembered. 'The thing that became awkward and eventually intolerable for me was that in the absence of Daevid Allen, who founded the band, and Gilli Smyth and Tim Blake, who were also key members, Virgin tried to manipulate a situation that Gong would somehow morph into my backing band. The reason I had joined Gong and the reason I felt that it had enriched my musical and personal life was because the band was a community. The idea of me becoming a leader of the group and the publication of articles in Melody Maker describing me as "the leader of Gong" made my then long hair stand on end! For me, it meant that the only way I could move forward was to leave and pursue a solo career.'

For the remaining months of 1975, Hillage and Giraudy continued to perform with ever-fluctuating line-ups of Gong but left following a concert at the Roundhouse on 21 December, freeing him to concentrate on a solo career. While he recorded many fine sole albums throughout the remaining years of the decade and into the next, it is 'Fish Rising' that established Steve Hillage as a notable solo artist.

NEKTAR 'Recycled'

First released in Germany as Bellaphon BLPS19219 in October 1975
First released in Britain as Decca SKL-R5250 in January 1977
Highest UK chart position: N/A
Not currently available on CD

Recycle
Cybernetic Consumption
Recycle Countdown
Automoton Horrorscope
Recycling
Flight To Reality
Unendless Imaginations
Sao Paulo Sunrise
Costa Del Sol
Marvellous Moses
It's All Over

Roye Albrighton	**Guitars and Lead Vocals**
Taff Freeman	**Keyboards and Vocals**
Ron Howden	**Drums and Percussion**
Derek 'Mo' Moore	**Bass and Vocals**
Mick Brockett	**Visual Environment**
With	
Larry Fast	**Synthesisers and Moog orchestral arrangements**

The English Chorale, conducted by Robert Howes
Arranged by Karlheinz Schuster
Recorded at Chateau d'Herouville, France and AIR Studios, London (July and August 1975)
Produced by Peter Hauke and Nektar
Mixing engineered by Geoff Emerick, Steve Nye and Bill Price

By 1975 Nektar's star could not have shone brighter. Roye Albrighton (guitar, lead vocals), Allan 'Taff' Freeman (keyboards, vocals), Derek 'Mo' Moore (bass guitar, vocals) and Ron Howden (drums and percussion had found major success in Germany, enjoying gold status on most of their releases before finding even greater success in the US. Although the majority of their albums were released in Britain, Nektar remained a band with a small but loyal following in their homeland.

Forming in Hamburg in 1969, Nektar quickly established themselves as a major live attraction in Germany. Signing to Bacillus in 1970, the band had recorded the albums 'Journey To The Centre of the Eye' and 'A Tab In The Ocean' before securing release in the UK with United Artists. The first Nektar album to be released in Germany and Britain was 'live-in-the-studio' double set 'Sounds Like This'.

The follow-up album, 'Remember the Future', was their breakthrough album in the US, while its successor 'Down to Earth' was very much a departure from their trademark sound, featuring a horn section and guests such as PP Arnold on backing vocals.

Nektar toured the US in September 1974 with great success, playing a memorable concert at New York's Academy of Music which was broadcast on WNEW FM. Their set included a number of tunes which had yet to be recorded such as 'Marvellous Moses' and 'It's All Over'. Returning to Germany in triumph, Messrs Albrighton, Moore, Freeman and Howden pondered their next album.

The decision was made to record at the Chateau d'Herouville in France. 'When we arrived at the Chateau we only had one side of the album written', explains Mo Moore. 'Again we were in a "live-in" situation which worked so well as we were all drenched in the music. We wrote the remainder of the material in the studio.'

Nektar had a guest musician present on most of the sessions. Larry Fast had worked with synthesiser pioneer Robert Moog on the development of the polyphonic synthesiser, the first of the electronic keyboards that were capable of playing more than one note simultaneously. Fast had pioneered the art of synthesiser music and had been introduced to Mo Moore when the bass player had visited the US to plan a tour.

'Larry was at the Passport Records office in Plainfield, New Jersey, as he had just finished his new album "Synergy". I heard it and was blown away. We hit it off right away and became lifelong friends. We used Larry's music to open all of the Nektar shows on that first tour. We played the first track, with dry ice and intensely coloured light to get everyone's attention.' Moore subsequently invited Fast to participate in the sessions for the album.

Of the initial sessions in France, Ron Howden recalls; 'I remember us having to hoist the tympani up the outside walls of the Chateau because they wouldn't fit through the doors but they would fit through one of the upstairs windows! I seem to remember that the studio was in a permanent state of being refitted while we were there!'

Mo Moore continues: 'We had lots of music but very few lyrics, enough to make it work. "Marvellous Moses" was a great tune with lots of time changes. Larry put his synthesiser on at the end, overdubbing one note at a time as the polyphonic Moog was not yet available. Later on we became the first group in the world to use one, at a concert at the Beacon Theatre in New York. The song "Sao Paolo Sunrise" came about because his girlfriend at the time went to Sao Paolo in Brazil and spoke of the smog that hung over the city and obliterated the sun... "Costa Del So" ("Sun Coast" in Spanish) is a play on the words "Cost of the sun". We felt it fitted well into our concept.'

The concept of 'Recycled' was inspired by the first Nektar tour of the US. 'On that tour we noticed an abundance of disposable plastic cups, soda cans and paper cups which we had not seen before in Europe. We wondered what happened to all of this stuff when it was thrown away. We were all aware that the abuse of the planet couldn't go on.' This ecological concern became the basis of the extended work that would form the first side of the album.

The sessions at the Chateau were productive musically, but the strain of recording in a studio in a permanent state of flux began to show. 'The Chateau was dubbed "Chateau Horrorville" by us,' recalls Moore.' It was a very uncomfortable place to record. We got as far as recording some of Roye's vocals and some vocal harmonies. We bailed out and went to George Martin's AIR Studios in London to finish the overdubs. The bulk of the music was recorded in France.'

It was on arrival at AIR Studios that former Beatles engineer Geoff Emerick became involved, as Mo remembers. 'The Beatles were always Number 1 with us and Geoff was one of the resident engineers. He had some great ideas and added a lot to the sessions.'

Indeed, by July 1975 the sessions had reached the stage where Geoff Emerick mixed 'Recycled' and offered the mixes as a finished album.

'After some deliberation we decided that we were not altogether pleased with the mix. We all heard it differently and so I went back to Germany and convinced the head of Bellaphon Records to fund the recording of a choir, some overdubs and a remix. We went back to AIR and did a lot more work on the album,' recalls Moore. 'I remember George Martin coming into the studio when Larry was crafting the steel drum sound. I think there were about six overdubs to get the resonance and the out of tune tones to realise the sound of steel drums. Larry had it in his head and George was blown away.

'I remember Larry asked for a synthesiser and they dragged one in he had never used before. He worked for a few minutes and got a great sound. In the end we used two engineers, one for the first side of the album and another for the second side.'

It was also while in London that Mo Moore and Ron Howden caught up with an old musician friend they had met in Athens 10 years earlier, Vangelis. 'We first met Vangelis and Demis Roussos in Athens when Mo and I played in the Prophets' recalls Howden. 'Mo and I contacted Vangelis when we arrived in England and met at his London house. We then went to visit his studio which was a converted cinema just off Edgware Road. After that I remember that we travelled in his bright purple London taxicab (he always said he wanted to own one) to AIR Studios where we met up with Demis Roussos who was mixing a new album with George Martin.'

Mo Moore adds: 'We needed to borrow a small tape recorder to give

to our choral arranger, Kristian Kolonovits. He needed a tape recorder so he could score the choral parts in his hotel room. Vangelis let us borrow his personal tape recorder, a small hand one he kept by his bed for musical ideas in the night. He did not really want to part with it but we convinced him we really needed it! Kristian wrote the score that night from a playback of the Geoff Emerick mix for the session the next day. We cut it very close, but Kristian wrote a fantastic arrangement. He was a phenomenal musician.'

Finally, after a second mix of the album in September 1975, 'Recycled' was ready for release. It appeared in October 1975 and was toured extensively in Germany and Britain, although the album would not see a UK release until January 1977 when it was released by Decca Records. The album went gold once more in Germany and preparations were made for an extensive US tour in the early months of 1976, following which the album notched up a Billboard chart position.

By the end of 1975 Nektar had announced their intention to leave Germany. The year of the American bicentennial would see the band relocate to New Jersey and embark on their most intense touring to date, and would close with the departure of Roye Albrighton and the arrival of Dave Nelson into Nektar's ranks. Although the band would record the album 'Magic Is A Child' in 1977 with Nelson, Albrighton and Freeman cut the album 'Man In The Moon' as Nektar in 1981. The band would reform in 2002, continuing in some form or another to this day. 'Recycled' would remain their most ambitious release and crowning glory.

VAN DER GRAAF GENERATOR 'Godbluff'

First released as Charisma CAS1109 in October 1975
Highest UK chart position: N/A
Available on CD as Charisma CASCDR1109

The Undercover Man
Scorched Earth
Arrow
The Sleepwalkers

Peter Hammill Voice, Piano and Guitars
Hugh Banton   Organs and Basses
David Jackson   Saxophones and Flute
Guy Evans   Drums and Percussion

Produced by Van der Graaf Generator
Recorded and mixed at Rockfield studios, Monmouthshire
between 9th and 29th June 1975
Engineered by Pat Moran

Van der Graaf Generator took an extended break between 1972 and 1975. When asked three decades later to reveal the reasons, saxophonist David Jackson commented: 'I think our intense schedule was a major factor in us breaking up in 1972. Charisma Records sent us to Italy for a song in order to break us there, but when we found out that people were paying 10 times the amount we were actually receiving for the gigs it started to grate. We were expected to play these huge tours and then rush home to write and record a new album and it was too much pressure.

'We did three tours of Italy in 1972, which was crazy. It was a complex situation with our record company also being our management company. In the beginning we thought that earning £15 each a week was great to do what we did for a living, but it became like working in a factory and as a band we were still £35,000 in debt in 1972. By then we all had personal lives which were suffering hugely and it became too hard to balance everything. Peter Hammill was the first to say he wanted to concentrate on recording rather than touring. Even after we split up, we still got offers over the phone from Italy. Promoters called inviting us to tour there and I would explain that Peter wasn't working with us. They would respond by saying "Well, the three of you can play as Van der Graaf Generator!" It all demonstrated the size of the greed factor that had contributed to us breaking up.'

Peter Hammill embarked on a solo career that, over the next two years, would see the release of a series of excellent, innovative albums: 'Chameleon In The Shadow Of The Night', 'The Silent Corner And The Empty Stage', 'In Camera' and the radical 'Nadir's Big Chance'. All featured contributions from David Jackson, Guy Evans and Hugh Banton, although the last in this series – along with the appearance on stage by Banton and Jackson at two Peter Hammill concerts at the Commonwealth Institute, London on 27 and 28 November 1974 – was to prove a catalyst in the reformation of Van der Graaf Generator.

'We'd got together with Peter to help him with the recording of "Nadir's Big Chance",' David Jackson would later explain, 'and enjoyed it so much we wanted to continue to work together.' Hugh Banton concurred. 'The four of us never lost touch after we split. It was simply that we had all had enough. We often used to see each other and sometimes one or two of us would join Peter on stage at occasional solo concerts of his, so it was all pretty amicable. By the end of 1974 the time seemed right to give Van der Graaf Generator another try.'

Peter Hammill didn't believe that any one individual thing brought them back together. 'The possibility seemed to arise that we might be able to find the spirit to work together again as Van der Graaf Generator and the musical ideas I had were particularly suited to the band.' Thus in January 1975 Hammill, Banton, Evans and Jackson convened at an old Rectory in the village of Norton Canon in Herefordshire to rehearse and flesh out ideas for a new Van der Graaf album. Between January and April the group wrote, rehearsed and recorded demos. 'When we got back together, I thought it came really easily to us,' Hugh Banton later declared. 'We had all sorts of logistical problems, though. I'd started to build a new organ but I couldn't get it finished in time for us to rehearse and then to go on the road.'

Peter Hammill would later state: 'I wouldn't say the music came easily to us in those initial rehearsals because there was a conscious decision to move on stylistically from our earlier albums. "Pawn Hearts" was a product of creating in the studio, and as a result the material became studio focussed. With the material that eventually comprised "Godbluff" we were very aware of creating a new musical language between us that would work well on stage. We were not looking to make "Son Of Pawn Hearts". When we first played together, Hugh hadn't finished building his organ and was playing bass instead and I was playing electric guitar. All in all it was most interesting.'

'Charisma came up with a deal which was also a way of recouping our debt to them and we went for it,' David Jackson remembered. 'We had decided to manage ourselves as we didn't want to go back into the same mad situation a few years previously. We made a friend of Peter's, Gordian Troeller, an equal member of the band so that whatever happened to us happened to him. His role was to look after the business side of things.'

The band took the brave step of touring before any new product had been released. 'I suppose it was pig-headed to play what became the entire "Godbluff" album as our live set without anyone having heard it previously. We may even have played some of the "Still Life"' material on stage at that time too,' recalled Hammill. 'Our live act on that tour was predetermined to show a "new" Van der Graaf and the remaining material was drawn from my solo albums. It was important to the development of the group that we had road-tested the new material before recording began. I think we'd got over the thing of having to push studio technology to its limits. We were now seeking to push our musical abilities on stage to their limits and we certainly did that.'

The major change was the sight and sound of Peter Hammill playing electric guitar. 'I'm still basically a rhythm guitarist, but in the early days I was only competent enough to strum an acoustic. Somehow in the intervening period I had acquired enough technical competence to hold my own on electric guitar on stage and not feel too intimidated about having to compete with the others on an instrument with which I felt more comfortable.'

The first concert by the revitalised Van der Graaf Generator took place at Lampeter University on 9 May

Van Der Graaf Generator

VAN DER GRAAF GENERATOR

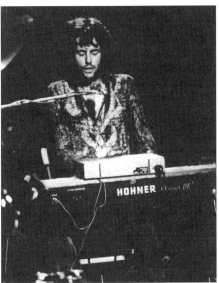

1975. Following a concert the next night in Bangor, the band embarked on an extensive tour of France and Belgium, returning to England during the first week of June. Without taking any time to recover from an exhaustive tour, the remainder of June was spent recording at Rockfield in Monmouthshire.

The material committed to tape was of an amazingly high standard and featured moments of vitality and confidence that were becoming increasingly rare in a slowly stagnating UK music scene. '"Godbluff" was a very strong record,' David Jackson later stated. 'We actually recorded more than enough material for one album and we were at our absolute creative peak. Any difficulties that we'd had in 1972 were now gone and as a result the music poured out. It was a magical time.'

Indeed, wonderful pieces such as 'Arrow' and 'Scorched Earth', powerful sonic assaults that featured imaginative twin saxophone solos from David Jackson, and 'The Undercover Man' and 'The Sleepwalkers', two darkly magnificent pieces of lyrical brilliance from Hammill, revealed the band operating at the height of their powers. The sound of the band on these pieces was different to the group who had recorded 'Pawn Hearts', with Peter Hammill turning his hand to playing electric guitar for the first time, arguably allowing more room for the song arrangements to make their powerful impact. The recording sessions went well enough to also produce recordings of two more songs, 'Pilgrims' and 'La Rossa', which would eventually see the light of day in April 1976 as part of 'Still Life'.

To Hammill, 'it was immediately obvious that the four songs that made up "Godbluff" were contenders to stand up as an album in their own right, even if they hadn't begun life like that. We had an awful lot of material from the outset and looking back I suppose it was a highly prolific time.'

On 27 July 1975, the group performed a triumphant concert at the Victoria Palace Theatre in London which received ecstatic reviews, Phil Bradbury of Record Mirror commenting 'Unless the house was packed with the VDGG fan club, the stomping and clapping for encores must indicate something of a sensational comeback.' August 1975 saw the band undertake a series of concerts in Italy, where they were greeted as heroes by their large and ever loyal Italian following. Returning to England, the group performed another sellout show in London at the New Victoria Theatre, before undertaking concerts in Holland and a full British tour that finished in November 1975.

The album 'had appeared in October to coincide with the UK tour and was greeted with acclaim. Melody Maker referred to the music as being 'in a very real sense, the sound of the mid-Seventies', while Sounds called it 'an essential buy.' 'Godbluff' was indeed a triumphant musical statement.

Harvest will be in
June this year —

Deep Purple
Pete Brown and His
Battered Ornaments
The Edgar
Broughton Band

E.M.I. Records (The Gramophone Co. Ltd.)
E.M.I. House, 20 Manchester Square, London W1A 1ES

TWENTY ADDITIONAL LESSER-KNOWN GREATS FOR YOUR COLLECTION

AMON DÜÜL II
'Phallus Dei'

Released as Liberty LBS83279 in October 1969

Kanaan
Dem Guten, Schonen, Wahren
Luzifer's Ghilom
Henriette Krotenschwanz
Phallus Dei

Amon Düül II represented one of the earliest groups to emerge on the embryonic German underground rock scene of the late Sixties. Founder member Chris Karrer (guitar, vocals) assembled the band from members of the Munich hippy commune of which he was a part. Following the turmoil in Europe created by the student uprising in Paris, the reaction to the Russian occupation of Prague and the tide of protest against the escalating Vietnam War, Amon Düül reflected the mood in their radical music.

The initial 11-piece line-up performed at the 1968 Songtagen festival in Essen before breaking apart. Karrer sought to form a more focused musical outfit, while the other faction adopted an even more radical agenda of musical street protest. By the autumn of 1968, Karrer had assembled a line-up of John Weinzierl (guitar), Renate Knaup (vocals), Falk-Ulrich Rogner (bass), Dieter Serfas (drums) and Christian Thierfeld (percussion). This line-up began to perform throughout West Germany, often performing benefit concerts for radical causes and generating a considerable following among the emerging German counterculture.

By the early spring of 1969 the German office of Liberty Records had signed the band and they entered the studio to record their first album, 'Phallus Dei'. By this time drummer Peter Leopold had replaced Serfas and English bassist Dave Anderson had filled the shoes of the departed Rogner. Produced by free jazz saxophonist Olaf Kubler, the album caused a sensation in Germany. The music of the album had a considerable effect upon many British musicians, the embryonic Hawkwind being influenced by the intense acid-rock improvisation of the 20-minute title track and the equally innovative album artwork.

Four decades later, 'Phallus Dei' remains an impressive debut, full of innovation and outrageous experimentation that was ahead of its time. Although Amon Düül II would record a series of wonderful albums such as the innovative 'Yeti', 'Dance Of The Lemmings' and 'Wolf City', the impact of their first album remains as intense as it did in 1969.

Names in the News

AMON DUUL II, the top German group which was due to commence a British tour this week, has cancelled its British visit. Main reason is that a fire at one of its concerts in Cologne recently destroyed virtually all its equipment. United Artists are now arranging another and more extensive tour for Amon, to take place in September.

EAST OF EDEN
'Mercator Projected'
Released as Deram SML1038 in April 1969
Highest UK chart position: N/A

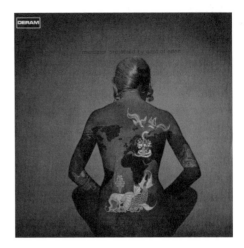

Northern Hemisphere
Isadora
Waterways
Centaur Woman
Bathers
Communion
Moth
In The Stable Of The Sphinx

Bristol's East of Eden, originally known as the Electric Light Orchestra and then Picture of Dorian Gray, was an early example of an outfit that fused the worlds of jazz, rock, classical and folk music to create an unique brand of progressive rock. Based around the talents of Dave Arbus (violin, flute, saxophones), Ron Caines (saxophones) and Geoff Nicholson (guitars, vocals), they recorded a solitary single for the UK division of Atlantic Records in 1968 before signing to Decca's Deram imprint.

'Mercator Projected' was their first album and featured Steve York on bass and Dave Dufort on drums. The ethnic psychedelia of 'Northern Hemisphere' and 'Bathers', together with the excellent 'In The Stable Of The Sphinx', makes 'Mercator Projected' an essential album for those who wish to delve deeper into British underground rock of the late Sixties.

This is East of Eden's first LP called Mercator Projected.
Take one electric violin which blows rock and Bartók, add one flute from the East,
mix in Sumerian saxophones, bass, drums, guitar and liquid word pictures - mark 'East of Eden'.

SHAKE YER BUMS ABOUT! TO AN IRISH JIG, WHAT?

ROBERT PARTRIDGE FINDS OUT ABOUT EAST OF EDEN

SHAKE YER BUMS ABOUT! It's rock 'n' roll music, any old way you choose it — even with Irish jigs. Irish jigs?

That's what East Of Eden are about. Enjoying. Having a good time. Bopping. and Irish jigs to make sure you really get into it all.

Ah onetwothreefour....

And it's right into some traditional Irish peasant number suitably electrified for contemporary consumption.....

The band was formed two years ago in Bristol by Ron Caines and Dave Arbus, two students long since fed up with the pretence of a good time offered my more polite music like most of the jazz prevalent in Britain during the 1960's.

Things have changed in jazz since then. People like John Surman, Keith Tippett and Mike Westbrook have put the guts back into the music. But then it was all very dignified and smooth — like after-shave TV ad music. And in rock everything making it. The Rolling Stones, the Beatles, the Who.....with the added ingredient guts. It was music you could move around to, music which involved all of you, not just the I-spy-a technical-feat-which -might-be-the-most boring-thing-since -instant-mash-but-at-least it's groovy-if-I-say-I-like it

syndrome.

Things might have changed since then, but at least it was the sort of scene which started East Of Eden. And East Of Eden are Ron Caines and Dave Arbus. From the first days they've had six drummers, two or three bass players, two guitarists......Said Dave: "We needed guys to help us to rock — not guys who thought we were freaks. We were very bored with jazz and, although we liked classical music we didn't like the narrow-minded people involved in that scene.

"What we wanted was something which was a reflection of our personalities. We wanted to weld together all the things we dug — such as avant-garde free jazz. We were nearer to rock, though, than to swing jazz.

"We wanted to achieve a basic rhythm. In fact we were very concerned to be rhythmic. We wanted the audience to be involved in the middle — so it would go in through the head and come out through the body. With rock it's not the whole thing to just stand and listen. That way people have missed out on something. We want to exhaust both ourselves and the audience. It's much more profound to dance. We played a gig in Bishop Auckland for instance, — that's not the sort

L to R: David Jacks: Ron Caines Andy Sneddon: Dave Arburs
SEATED: Jeff Allen

of most hip place in the country — and there everyone danced themselves into the ground.

"What we were reacting against when we formed the group was the Ronnie Scott sort of jazz. No-one wants to listen anymore."

Instead, people are beginning to bop again to East Of Eden. After the politeness of some sorts of trendy rock music, East Of Eden come as instant therapy— blasting away

at people's consciousness with a strange, and wholly individual fusion of rock music and jazz — with a final number of Irish jigs. Mad Dave swings like hell on his electric violin as all the band crash into a frantic stomp.

E.M.I. launch Harvest Record

UNDERGROU
GRO

LISSEN, man, those swingin' cats at EMI are really getting in the Underground groove, dig?

No, but seriously, folks, they have got it together, they know where it's at NOW and to prove it they've come up with a new label on which a number of artistes, new and well established, do their things.

The whole thing was launched at London's Roundhouse where some of the bands performed before an invited audience. It was a jolly occasion and I was hoping to collaborate with Ian Middleton on describing it but unfortunately Ian took a trip instead: right down the Roundhouse steps, putting himself in hospital for a few days. After that sad and bloody incident my memory of the music is a little hazy.

Happily, though, the label's first record releases give a fair indication of what we can expect. The singles by the Edgar Broughton Band and Michael Chapman, plus an LF by Chapman, are reviewed elsewhere in the RM. I've been listening to The Book Of Taliesyn by Deep Purple (Harvest stereo SHVL 751, A Meal You Can Shake Hands With In The Dark by Pete Brown And His Battered Ornaments (Harvest stereo SHVL 752), and Anthems In Eden by Shirley And Dolly Collins (Harvest stereo SHVL 754).

All the Harvest albums have double sleeves, which is a pleasant idea so long as some ideas have gone into the artwork. This bunch is disappointing: just some quite ordinary pictures of the group inside the Deep Purple foldout, a curiously corny set of cartoons inside the Pete Brown, and—rather attractive—Dorothy and Shirley are shown with a weirdo ram's head.

Less samey than usual . . . .

Musically, the Collins sisters turn in their usual expert work; exuberant, healthy open-air stuff, very folksy, nothing at all underground—except, possibly, the choice of olde instruments in the accompanying group. They're nearly all instruments that have fallen into deserved obscurity because they didn't measure up to subsequent inventions, but if you're curious to know what, say, the sackbut or the crumhorn sounds like, try Anthems In Eden.

Deep Purple's Harvest debut has some interesting musical ideas and is far less samey in sound than your average Underground outfit. But it is not an excitingly new production (it was made last year in fact) and while it is a great relief to hear a group that is not constantly striving for all-out freak effects and is trying instead for a little subtlety, maybe they ought to try a little more wildness, here and there, on their next LP.

DEEP PURPLE — a big
their third LP is issued

Pete Brown has some c
ambitious sounds. The ba
more serious, Bonzo Dog
—a few minutes worth li
the same old hoarse sho

5

SHIRLEY and DOROTHY COLLINS — pleasing folk sounds.

All goodish stuff yet I have to confess I'm eagerly awaiting the first release by The Third Ear Band (who, along with The Pink Floyd, Panama Limited Jug Band, Syd Barrett and The Pretty Things, have future Harvest offerings lined up). I mean, if this vague Underground tag is still haunting us then we might as well have portentous writing to match the mood. Here goes then with an EMI press release that could hardly be topped (maybe the music and the packaging and the concept of the Harvest label could use a touch more brilliance, but not the handout):

Reflection of the universe . . .

"The music of the Third Ear Band is a reflection of the universe as magic play illusion. At first hearing, it may seem a naive, meaningless dance of sound, but dig deeper, get your head into it, you'll hear alchemical repetition seeking the actual archetypal forms and rhythms that can change consciousness. Labels, even melodies, are left far behind, each piece is as alike or unalike as blades of grass or clouds. Under hypnotic repetition the listener's rational mind loses control, he is adrift in a strange Bosch-like musical landscape that changes endlessly. On very rare occasions, a vast door seems to open and band and audience find themselves in a new dimension transcending time and space. It is the music of the Druids, released from the unconscious by the alchemical process, orgasmic in its otherness, religious in its oneness. Communicating beauty and magic via abstract sound whilst playing without ego enables the musicians to reach a trance-like state, a 'high' in which the music produces itself. This is the aim of the Third Ear; to act as carriers of consciousness, and to play a music that, being non-conscious, is an organic synthesis of all musics."

A worthy aim indeed! And, since there's no Underground without smoke, I'll puff to that.

DAVID GRIFFITHS

with "Hush", now est

amusing ideas and some ounds like a roughed-up, the performances erratic , then a few minutes of pounding.

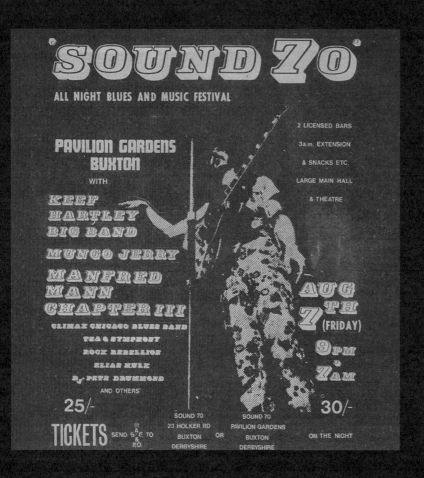

New Mann-Hugg Group

MANFRED MANN CHAPTER THREE (Vertigo, stereo VO 3; 37s 6d)

WAY-OUT musical patterns, sometimes sounding like outer space sounds and then with brass blaring at you, and then going jazzy. Vocals are mouthed so you can't quite hear them, and the cacophony is ragged and untidy, as if everyone is playing their bit regardless of the others or the whole.

Emanon— 'Something new' says Manfred

"WE are not splitting up," said a confident Manfred Mann, "we've been going for five or six years now and to break it up would be silly. The Manfreds will not go back on the road. As a group, we will exist just to record. For a long time now ever since we ceased to play live, the members of the group have been interested in their own ideas on the side. Tradition enslaved the Manfreds. People came expecting things and knowing what to expect. Musically, we were designed for a certain kind of thing and we played worse together than we could individually."

Emanon is the name of the section of Manfred Mann containing himself and drummer Mike Hugg. The group is the first solid hack-into-the-public-eye product to arise from the apparent tension within the Manfreds. What is the new line-up? What was the group created to do that isn't being done by the Manfreds themselves?

"As I said, the members of Manfred Mann seemed to play better outside, doing what they really wanted to do. Mike Hugg and myself were the only ones with similar ideas musically, so we remain together in Emanon. The Manfreds never took up too much time when we weren't doing live shows, so these new ideas began to develop. However, it is Emanon that is the sideline — not Manfred Mann.

"The new combination consists of Drummer Craig Collins from 'Procession', Steve York from 'East of Eden', Bernie on the sax, Mike Hugg doing a lot of singing, myself on the organ, plus a five piece brass section. I intend to play the organ in the context I want to, and this will give me the chance. Mike and myself will both be able to do what we've wanted as we will be in control. The group will play a mixture of jazz and pop, alternating most of the time. When people come to see us, they'll not be expecting any specific thing. We won't be playing the usual songs as we were in the Manfreds. It will be something new and likeable — we hope.

"All the others from Manfred Mann will be doing what they want to outside of recording under the old line-up. Mike, of course, started in 'Guliver's Travels' and should be doing well with that; Klaus has fixed himself a place in the BBC art department and Tom is continuing his writing. Meanwhile, Mike and myself will be playing the colleges and the clubs since live appearances is what we want to do once the whole thing really gets together."

MANFRED MANN CHAPTER THREE
'Manfred Mann Chapter Three'

Released as Vertigo VO3 in November 1969
Highest UK chart position: N/A

Travelling Lady
Snakeskin Garter
Konefuf
Sometimes
Devil Woman
Time
One Way Glass
Mister, You're A Better Man Than I
Ain't It Sad
A Study In Inaccuracy
Where Am I Going?

Manfred Mann, born Manfred Lubowitz in South Africa, had been a prominent feature of the UK music scene since he arrived in Britain in 1961, driven to the UK by a love of jazz music and a dislike for the apartheid system then in place in his homeland. In 1962 he formed the R&B outfit Mann-Hugg Blues Brothers who soon shortened their name to Manfred Mann after securing a contract with EMI's HMV label. Throughout the next six years Manfred Mann was to score 17 chart singles in the UK (including three Number 1 singles) for both HMV and latterly (from 1966 onwards) Fontana records.

Both Mann and keyboard-player Mike Hugg began to tire of performing unchallenging pop music and were also tired of the constant intrusions on their lives that were the result of being such major chart stars. To escape this tedium, they formed the short-lived jazz-rock band Emanon 'no name' backwards) and gigged around London. By the time the Manfred Mann group announced their dissolution, Mann and Hugg had formed Manfred Mann Chapter Three, featuring bass player Steve York (ex-East of Eden), drummer Craig Collinge and saxophonist Bernie Living. Still contracted to the Fontana/Philips stable, the band's eponymous debut album appeared as the third release on the newly formed Vertigo imprint in November 1969.

The tracks were essentially recorded live in Workhouse Studios in London's Old Kent Road and were a shock to any listener expecting to hear whimsical pop. Superb jazz-influenced workouts such as 'One Way Glass' and 'Travelling Lady' set the tone for an album which was uplifting and powerful, dark and menacing in equal measure. New Musical Express declared: 'If you like your music weirdo, then this album is for you.' In hindsight, the record is a work that heralded the progressive era and is highly recommended.

PHILIPS LAUNCH NEW LABEL

MANFRED MANN'S new group, Chapter Three, Colosseum and newcomer Juicy Lucy are among the artistes on a new progressive label from Philips called Ver which makes its bow on November 7.

At a meeting to launch the label, Philips' Olov Wyper, general marketing manager, introduced selections from the first three LP's. They are—Colosseum "Valentyne Suite", "Juicy Lucy" and "Manfred Mann—Chapter Three".

Manfred's album includes a track titled "One Way Glass" which features Manfred on lead vocal for the first time. Mike Hugg is also featured in the group.

Wyper said of Manfred's new group: "Britain has at last produced a big-band progressive group to rival anything coming out of America".

Vertigo has been conceived as a total packaging and musical entity, and Philips believe that in catering for the contemporary/progressive market, the sleeve is almost as important as the music itself: Philips intend to use young designers and art students to produce the right image for the sleeves.

A massive promotional campaign has been mounted for the new label, which will concentrate mainly on LP releases. Next big album release is scheduled for January with discs from Rod Stewart and Mother Earth.

The new group, "Juicy Lucy" is led by Glenn 'Fernando' Campbell, former leader of Misunderstood. R.C.

AFFINITY 'Affinity'
Released as Vertigo 6360 004 in May 1970
Highest UK chart position: N/A

I Am And So Are You
Night Flight
I Wonder If I Care As Much
Mr Joy
Three Sisters
Coconut Grove
All Along The Watchtower

Affinity began life at Sussex University when science students Lynton Naiff (piano), Grant Serpell (drums) and Nick Nicholas (double bass) formed the group US Jazz Trio. They were joined a year later by Mo Foster, who joined the band as a replacement for Serpell, who had graduated from university. US Jazz Trio continued to perform until its remaining members also graduated.

Naiff and Serpell reunited in short-lived pop outfit Ice before inviting Foster, now on bass, to join them in forming a new band with jazz influences. After holding auditions, guitarist Mike Jopp joined the line-up of Affinity, the name taken from an Oscar Peterson album. The group was completed in the summer of 1968 with the addition of Linda Hoyle, was a qualified English teacher and the possessor of a fine jazz/rock singing voice which drew comparisons to Julie Driscoll and Jefferson Airplane's Grace Slick.

Affinity came to wider attention through appearances at London's famous Ronnie Scott's jazz venue, where they shared bills with many legendary jazz musicians. They developed their musical style by incorporating contemporary rock influences alongside their jazz roots. Thanks to Scott's patronage, Affinity came to the attention of Vertigo Records, recording their sole album for the label in 1970.

Featuring such excellent material as 'Three Sisters', 'Night Flight' and an inspired 'All Along The Watchtower', the album was released to great acclaim and Affinity seemed on the verge of a breakthrough, with a US tour booked for 1971. At this point singer Linda Hoyle announced she was leaving the group. Having recorded a solo album for Vertigo ('Pieces Of Me', Vertigo 6360 060), she felt disillusionment with the music business and, after her marriage to Pete King, musical director to Ronnie Scott, she abandoned her career as a singer. Affinity attempted to record a follow-up album before being dropped by Vertigo, disbanding soon after. Their sole album, a fine legacy, is essential listening.

JODY GRIND
'Far Canal'

Released as Transatlantic TRA221 in July 1970
Highest UK chart position: N/A

We've Had It
Bath Sister
Jump Bed Jed
O Paradiso
Plastic Shit
Vegetable Oblivion
Red Worms And Lice
Ballad for Bridget

Formed in December 1968, Jody Grind were born out of Tim Hinkley's desire to showcase his considerable talent as a rock organist. Hinkley, a noted session player, first came to attention as a member of R&B outfit the Bo Street Runners in the mid-Sixties. By the spring of 1966 he had formed the outfit Patto's People with vocalist Mike Patto, also featuring ex-Pretty Things drummer Viv Prince, bass-player Louis Cennamo and trumpet-player Mike Felana.

They soon changed their name to the Chicago Line Blues Band, but by the beginning of 1967 Hinkley sought new musical horizons. After forming a backing group to singer Elkie Brooks, he finally struck out on his own with guitarist Ivan Zagni and drummer Martin Harriman to form Jody Grind, a powerful trio inspired by the Nice.

In June 1969 the band signed to Transatlantic Records, a UK independent folk label seeking to develop an underground roster, and recorded their debut album, 'One Step On', in July with drummer Barry Wilson replacing Harriman. Released in October 1969, it was well received by the UK music press but sadly failed to make any impression on the chart. Feeling that the current line-up of the band had reached its fullest potential, Hinkley recruited former Ferris Wheel guitarist and vocalist Bernie Holland and noted drummer Pete Gavin to form the band's most accomplished and cohesive line-up. From the beginning, this new trio delivered stunning live performances, writing material more direct in approach than that previously recorded.

'Far Canal' was cut in the early months of 1970, the quality of material such as 'We've Had It' (featuring lead vocals from both Holland and Hinkley), 'Jump Bed Jed' and 'Bath Sister' outstanding. As part of Tim Hinkley's desire to represent the band's live sound on record, a recording of the excellent Hammond organ-led environmental protest 'Plastic Shit' made at a memorable concert at the Roundhouse at the beginning of the year was one of the highlights. Augmented by other fine material such as 'Vegetable Oblivion', 'Red Worms And Lice' and 'Ballad For Bridget' (featuring Hinkley on vibraphone), the lack of greater commercial success for the album upon its release in July 1970 was puzzling.

Alas, with no significant upturn in their fortunes, the final incarnation of Jody Grind fell apart soon after the release. Hinkley would enjoy a long career as a celebrated session musician, and his contribution to early progressive rock on 'Far Canal' bears further investigation.

QUATERMASS 'Quatermass'

Released as Harvest SHVL 775 in May 1970
Highest UK chart position: N/A

Entropy
Black Sheep Of the Family
Post War Saturday Echo
Good Lord Knows
Up On The Ground
Gemini
Make Up Your Mind
Laughin' Tackle
Entropy (reprise)

Formed in September 1969, Quatermass were a fine power trio formed by musicians who had gained a reputation on the British rock circuit. John Gustafson (vocals, bass guitar) had enjoyed a distinguished career as a founder member of Liverpool-based groups such as Casey Jones and the Engineers, the Big Three, and the Merseybeats, while Mick Underwood (drums) had spent a number of years in the Outlaws with future Deep Purple guitarist Ritchie Blackmore before joining pop outfit the Herd. Prior to forming Quatermass he had played in the final incarnation of Episode Six alongside future Deep Purple members Roger Glover and Ian Gillan. Completing the line-up was Peter Robinson, a keyboard player previously with Chris Farlowe's Thunderbirds.

Quatermass came together as a result of the members meeting while contributing to an experimental sextet which never got off the ground. The band took inspiration from the Nice and Deep Purple and evolved into a powerful unit with classical overtones. A deal with George Martin's AIR Productions led to the recording of the band's sole, eponymous album in early 1970. A wonderful collection of powerful progressive rock, quasi-classical pieces and more sensitive compositions, 'Quatermass' was released in May to great critical acclaim and was predicted to fare well commercially. In Europe, the album was received well and sold in larger quantities than in Britain, where commercial success failed to materialise.

Following an American tour to promote the album's US release, the band broke apart. John Gustafson proved to be a much in demand musician, performing with Hard Stuff before joining Roxy Music in 1976. He also contributed to albums by artists such as Steve Hackett, Kevin Ayers and Bryan Ferry before joining Mick Underwood in Gillan in 1979. Peter Robinson also enjoyed a healthy session career, performing with Murray Head, Rupert Hine and Stealers Wheel among others. Leaving just one album as their recorded legacy, the music of Quatermass still retains the ability to excite.

SHVL 775

Agency Representation: A.H.A. 01-734 8902/4
Management: Gloria Bristow 01-828 8863
AN A.I.R. LONDON PRODUCTION
Produced by Anders Henriksson

RARE BIRD are a rare find — and very welcome. Inside a couple of months, they have come out of a front sitting-room in Battersea to standing ovations at the Marquee, Lyceum and such provincial "heavies" as the Van Dyke, Plymouth — and Mothers, Birmingham.

Charisma, the label owned by their co-manager Tony Stratton Smith, has rush-released the first album — and it moved some eight thousand copies in a few weeks. A prestigious American agent has picked them up for a seven-week Stateside tour, starting April 2.

That sitting-room was Graham Field's—organist, sometime session man, former student at Trinity College of Music. Graham had dreamed up an out-of-the-rut line-up . . . two keyboards (organ and electric piano), drums and bass. On piano, he had Dave Kaffinetti, who had previously been turning a few people on in a duo, Elio-Kaffinetti.

Big break came when Steve Gould joined on bass, "Steve", says the erudite T. Stratton Smith, "is a Stevie Winwood wearing Tom Jones' braces".

Completing the group was Turnstiles' former drummer Mark

Rare Bird start flying high!

Ashton, who dropped into the sitting-room for a blow one night and decided to stay for good.

Intensely musical, Rare Bird own vaguely to the influences of the Mothers of Invention, particularly the "Uncle Meat" album and to classical music. Be that as it may, they have certainly coined a scene of their own, original and refreshing.

Despite the reception for their first album, they tend to think they rushed into it too quickly. "Just wait for the next one", says Graham. With a rare grin.

RARE BIRD
'As Your Mind Flies By'

Released as Charisma CAS1011 in September 1970
Highest UK chart position: N/A

What You Want to Know
Down On The Floor
Hammerhead
I'm Thinking
Flight:
a. As Your Mind Flies By
ii. Vacuum
iii. New Yorker
iv. Central Park

Rare Bird was formed in London in 1969 by Scots-born drummer Mark Ashton. He had previously played with progressive pop outfit Turnstyle who released the single 'Riding A Wave' b/w 'Trot' on Pye Records in 1968 and gigged regularly supporting a number of acts, including the Nice, managed by future Charisma Records founder Tony Stratton-Smith.

Following the demise of Turnstyle, Ashton sought alternative musical employment. Keyboard-players Graham Field and Folkestone-born doctor's son David Kaffinetti had met through ads placed in the UK music press. Finding a common musical bond, further ads placed by Field found bass guitarist and vocalist Steve Gould and finally Mark Ashton.

The band spent time perfecting their dual keyboard-based sound, augmented by Gould's stunning vocals, and concentrated on writing original material while seeking both live work and a recording contract. Signing with Charisma in 1969, Rare Bird began their performing career with a concert at Birmingham's underground music club, Mothers. The band soon secured a residency at the Marquee Club and in October 1969 entered Trident Studios in Soho to record their debut album. A fine work, 'Rare Bird' included the huge European hit 'Sympathy'.

The album 'As Your Mind Flies By', released in September 1970, earned excellent reviews in the British music press and continental success followed once more. Another progressive work, the record would feature a song cycle that would dominate its second side and project Rare Bird into further continental success. Sessions were completed quickly, the standard of material recorded being even higher than Rare Bird's debut. Pieces such as 'What You Want To Know', 'Down On The Floor' and 'I'm Thinking' all developed the style pioneered on the band's first album, while the superb 'Hammerhead' and the song cycle known as 'Flight' which dominated the LP count as some of their best recorded music.

'As Your Mind Flies By' earned excellent reviews in the British music press but, despite being declared one of the Top 10 acts of the year by the US magazine Billboard, failed to impress on the American listings either. Graham Field then departed, along with Mark Ashton who later joined Headstone before embarking on a career as a solo performer and subsequently becoming an accomplished painter and artist. Graham subsequently formed the band Fields and secured a contract with CBS Records, releasing one album for the label. At this juncture Rare Bird effectively ceased to exist as Field had the rights to the name.

Gould and Kaffinetti asked that they be allowed to continue to use the name Rare Bird, to which Field consented. The new Rare Bird featured Steve Gould and David Kaffinetti along with drummer Fred Kelly, guitarist Andy 'Ced' Curtis and bass player Paul Karas but failed to match the excellence of the old band, suffering a series of line-up changes and finally disbanding in 1975.

ITALY'S No. 1 GROUP — RARE BIRD

RARE BIRD (l to r) DAVE KAFFINETTI, GRAHAM FIELD, MARK ASHTON and STEPHEN GOULD.

RARE BIRD have all the ingredients necessary to turn the group into another Nice and those qualities were never demonstrated better, in my view, than in a little progressive club on the outskirts of Milan on Sunday night. Rarely have I been so moved by an hour's music, music that was almost perfect in its construction and presentation.

Having reached No. 1 in the Italian chart with "Sympathy," Rare Bird embarked on a two and a half week tour on Saturday and I flew out to join them for two days at the weekend. Organist Graham Field was pondering Italian audiences whilst sitting in the hotel lounge but the other three tended not to worry too much.

Bit of a joke

As it turned out, they were right. The reaction on the opening night in Pontechino was extremely good to say the least. Going on after a dreadful group that slaughtered Led Zeppelin numbers but who the kids seemed to love was a bit of a joke, but Rare Bird coped and succeeded.

Because the huge club audience was a bit apathetic, the numbers that Rare Bird had planned to do were switched about and Graham even played a bit of "In The Summertime."

After the show, drummer Mark Ashton — who is lucky enough to be wed to one of those fantastic birds from "Up Pompeii" — explained: "We seem to be having a running battle with Mungo Jerry here and in France. One week we're number one, then they are, then we are again. We keep playing on the same gigs with them and we've never yet done well after them, I don't know why, their music is so simple it's easy but everyone seems to love it."

Manager Tony Stratton-Smith and guitarist and lead vocalist Steve Gould fought a losing battle with the world's largest moth in the bar where the promoter, who had earlier screamed his head off in Italian at the group and instantly been dubbed Tessie O'Shea, was buying us all champagne for some strange reason.

Electric pianist Dave Kaffinetti found the whole thing a huge joke and suddenly told me: "We weren't happy about the first album because it was released before we'd done any gigs. This next one, " As Your Mind Flies By," is a lot better." Odd thing to say under the circumstances.

The tour manager, a minute Italian who spoke no English and whose name was Nelli drove as only Italians can back to Milan the following day and it was here that Rare Bird came right on form.

Double play

The afternoon show was a bit of a shamoles with the organ packing up half way through, but the evening concert was beautiful. Opening with "Beautiful Scarlet," they silenced the talkative audience almost at once. Steve's voice is loud and rough and just what is needed these days — at times it bears a resemblance to Lee Jackson's but it's a lot stronger. Dave and Graham get an amazing bit of double play going between them and Mark's solos cannot be faulted even if his announcements can.

"New York Central Park After Dark" must be one of the best numbers I've heard and "I'm Thinking" isn't far behind, though it's totally different. The group is utterly professional and combines a certain degree of showmanship with outstanding musicianship.

Loads of fans — many of them boys — pushed and shoved after the show to get at Rare Bird and acquire an autograph and a rather attractive lass who responded to the title of Mavis From Avis seemed to

want rather more than that! Everybody was pleased with the results of that night's work.

Between gigs, Rare Bird spend ages discussing numbers and tampering with their instruments, trying to make sure that everything is just right for them and the kids. Steve

even kept me awake until 4 a.m. by playing his guitar in the room below mine — something I objected to, but could understand when I heard them play.

Rare Bird may not mean that much here at the moment, but on this showing they're bound to soon.

RARE BIRD (Charisma): Dave Caffinetti, Steve Gould, Mark Ashton and Graham Field.

RARE BIRD APPROACH GOLD DISC LANDMARK

WORLD sales of Rare Bird's " Sympathy " single now exceed 900,000 and are rapidly approaching the million mark. Although the disc only reached No. 24 in the NME Chart, it recently topped the French hit parade and is currently at No. 1 in Italy. It is also figuring in the charts of other countries, and the group is expected to qualify for a Gold Disc trophy before the end of the current month.

Rare Bird began a three-week Italian tour on Wednesday, and is due to pay a return visit to that country in November. A second American tour lasting six weeks is being negotiated for December by co-manager Terry King, who has also finalised a three-day visit to France and Belgium starting October 16.

Latest British dates for the group include Pontypridd College of Technology (October 8) and Devizes Corn Exchange (9). The following day, Rare Bird records a " Disco 2 " show for BBC-2, for transmission later that month.

Tomorrow's pop festival

Quintessence, Ian Anderson and Wayne Fontana have been added to this weekend's pop festival — headlined by the Kinks — being staged at the 110-acre Worthy Farm, Pilton, near Shepton Mallet in Somerset. It starts at 10 am tomorrow (Saturday) with records, and the first of the live performers is due on stage at mid-day. The festival continues non-stop until late Sunday.

SKIN ALLEY 'Skin Alley'

Released as CBS Records CBS63847 in March 1970
Highest UK chart position: N/A

Living In Sin
Tell Me
Mother, Please Help Your Child
Marsha
Country Aire
All Alone
Night Time
Concerto Grosso (Take Heed)
(Going Down The) Highway

Comprising Bob James (vocals, guitar, flute, saxophone, Mellotron), Thomas Crimble (vocals, bass), Krzysztof Henryk Juskiewicz (vocals, keyboards, Mellotron) and Alvin Pope (drums, percussion), Skin Alley was a hybrid of musical influences ranging from jazz to folk to blues. Formed in the autumn of 1968, the band had endured a series of line-up changes, with Max Taylor of leading London underground agency Clearwater Productions passing through their ranks. With his former involvement with the group, it was little wonder that Clearwater would sign Skin Alley upon their decision to turn professional in the spring of 1969.

By the summer of that year Skin Alley had secured a reputation as a people's band, and in August 1969 they appeared at a series of concerts staged over three consecutive weekends at All Saints Hall in Ladbroke Grove as a Clearwater Productions showcase. The final August concert proved to be particularly memorable, High Tide and Skin Alley being joined by the unknown Group X – soon to be known as Hawkwind.

After declining an approach from RCA, Skin Alley signed to CBS Records in October 1969 and immediately recorded their first album with Pretty Things guitarist Dick Taylor producing. The record was a confident debut, bridging the worlds of jazz-rock and progressive music with the selected tracks drawn from the highlights of Skin Alley's live set.

'Living In Sin' demonstrated the band's jazz sensibilities and also became perhaps their best-known piece thanks to its inclusion on the sampler album 'Fill Your Head With Rock' in 1970. 'Tell Me' was a more progressive work, featuring the use of a Mellotron and chronicling the tale of a doomed affair.

Other fine tracks included the stunningly dark 'All Alone', the lighter 'Country Aire' and the evocative 'Night Time'. 'Skin Alley' remains an impressive album that bears investigation.

ONE of the most intriguing qualities that Audience possess is the tortured shriek of Keith Gemmell's saxophone.

The group — Howard Werth (acoustic guitar, vocals), Tony Connor (drums) and Trevor Williams (bass guitar, vocals) are the other members — form an aggressive sound as it is. But the sax, like a wailing monstrosity from mythology, brandishes its throaty screams as a final argument for the music. Recently Keith talked about the group and his own part in it.

Keith's aggressive sound has little in common with most jazz sax players, but the fact is that many people cannot appreciate a sax in a group rather than jazz context.

"I've got a thing about that," Keith told me. "Most people seem to label any group with a sax player as a jazz group, which isn't so. I listen to more guitar players than saxes. I don't think the sax has ever been fully recognised. I'd like to see it more accepted in groups.

"There aren't many saxes taken seriously in groups. They are either taken in the Blood, Sweat and Tears or Chicago format or you get someone doing very heavy riffs over a rock backing.

"Most groups with saxes just sound very ordinary. I think there's a visual side to it too. I'm no great showman but I still try to get that across. I try to make it a bit violent. I play it quite aggressively and loudly."

How would he define his style of playing? "As far as that goes it's more related to the old rock and roll," he said.

"Also I try to do what a lead guitar player would do — like bending the notes. I think we get the best of both worlds with the sax, and I can always switch to flute."

"If you get set phrases where Howard's voice and the sax come together it really sounds like a brass section. The human voice is quite close in range to the tenor sax."

There was a time when Keith was considering using more electronic aids to extend his sound. He was probably the first in this country to use an echo device with his sax, and this is still the only device he uses.

"I didn't get a very good sound from bugs," he explained. "I suppose I just lost interest in the electronic side. Besides the echo I don't know what else you can do at the moment apart from wah-wah pedals."

Keith's echo has in itself made an important contribution to his sound. "It's quite a unique thing that echo," he agreed. "It makes the sax sound nothing like a sax at times. It sounds like an oscillator. I find myself doing things with the sax

AUDIENCE: aggressive sax

The scream of Audience

that aren't at all technical, just to get a nice sound out of it."

A maxi single called "Indian Summer" is being released in mid February. Keith was careful to explain that it had nothing to do with flower power. The title meant a flash of youth in old age. An album is also to be released soon, and I asked how it would differ from previous offerings.

"I think it will be more melodic," Keith replied. "It's a mixture really of our first and second albums. On the first the songs were good but the production wasn't so good. On the second it was the other way round. We're doing a longer version of "House On The Hill" as the title song. It was on the first album but it was such a weak version that we're doing it again. We've got to do all we can to make this one the one. It's got to make an impact."

"We used to have a medieval theme, but it's going away from that. The cover for this album is going to be based on a 1940's film set. It ties in with "The House On The Hill."

Did he have to adjust his style to fit in with the group's line-up. "Yes. I've had to alter my playing a lot since I joined Audience. I've had to change drastical-

ly really. Sometimes instead of playing something nice you have to play something to fill in. There's a gap in tone between the bass and guitar and you have to find something that will fit in. It's that which makes Audience's sound."

Another contribution to a good sound, on record at least, is a good producer. Were they happy with the production of their forthcoming album

"Gus Dudgeon is producing it, and we're completely happy with him," he replied. "He seems to be in sympathy with us. He let's us rehearse before recording. He was almost like a fifth member of the group when we did the single. It seems to me that there are not many good producers about, and we need someone like him because otherwise we get carried away. He also gets the best acoustic guitar sound that we've had."

Audience are going on tour next month. "There are a few things we have got to polish up on stage as far as communication with the audience goes," says Keith.

"Up to now Howard has done all the talking but we're going to let Trevor do some and with any luck there will be some repartée between the two of them."

— **ANDREW MEANS.**

330

AUDIENCE 'The House On The Hill'

Released as Charisma CAS1032 in May 1971
Highest UK chart position: N/A

Jackdaw
You're Not Smiling
I Had a Dream
Raviolé
Nancy
Eye To Eye
I Put A Spell On You
The House On The Hill
Indian Summer

Audience was one of the more original groups to emerge in the innovative year of 1969. Formed from the remnants of R&B outfit the Lloyd Alexander Blues Band, the London-based outfit comprised Howard Werth (guitar, lead vocals), Keith Gemmell (saxophones, flute, clarinet), Trevor Williams (bass, keyboards) and Tony Connor (drums). The band had no electric guitar in their line-up, Werth utilising a nylon-strung acoustic guitar with a contact microphone. This, together with his distinctive vocals and the band's unique use of saxophones and flute, helped make them a distinctive and a much-lauded live act.

Audience's debut at London's Marquee Club in February 1969 was a memorable affair, with such luminaries as Germaine Greer in attendance and artists Gilbert and George reciting monologues. Polydor Records offered Audience a one-off album deal soon afterwards.

Audience and Renaissance package venues finalised

VENUES have now been finalised for the package tour at the end of this month featuring Audience, Renaissance and Gordon Giltrap, plans for which were revealed in last week's NME. The schedule includes Southampton Guildhall (July 19), Oxford Town Hall (20), Guildford Civic Hall (21), Barry Memorial Hall (22), Manchester Free Trade Hall (23), Nottingham Albert Hall (26), Norwich St Andrew's Hall (27), Lincoln Drill Hall (28), Newcastle City Hall (29), Middlesbrough Town Hall (30) and Sheffield City Hall (31). Renaissance will not be appearing at Guildford, Middlesbrough and Sheffield, and a replacement band will be booked for these three venues. All concerts begin at 7.30pm and admission price is 40p.

Recorded at Morgan Studios, the eponymous album was a fine debut and featured the first version of 'The House On The Hill', a song re-recorded by the band two years later. Polydor released 'Audience' in the summer of 1969, by which time the band had concentrated on performing in Europe, gradually building a following in Italy which would bear fruit over the next 18 months. A concert at the Lyceum in October 1969 saw Audience open for Led Zeppelin, following which Tony Stratton-Smith, owner of the newly established Charisma Records, offered them a contract. A

Their debut album for the label was 'Friend's Friend's Friend' which, although failing to make an impression in the UK, was a success in Europe. The 1971 release 'The House On The Hill' was the band's finest effort and a European hit, reaching the Top 5 in Italy. Produced by Gus Dudgeon, the band's trademark blend of saxophone, nylon-strung acoustic guitar and powerful vocals were mixed perfectly to produce an album of true originality.

Aside from the frenetic reworking of the album's title track, another highlight was the excellent 'Jackdaw'. Although highly acclaimed, the album failed to make an impression on the UK album charts upon release. Indeed, it was the band's hardcore European following that sustained Audience for the remainder of their existence. A tour of the US and Canada supporting The Faces also established the group a loyal cult following in North America. Following the release of 'Lunch' (a Number 1 album in Italy), Audience disbanded, with Werth embarking on a solo career and drummer Tony Connor joining Hot Chocolate.

In 2004, to the surprise of many, Audience reformed with Werth, Gemmell and Williams being joined by new drummer John Fisher. The live album 'Alive And Kickin' And Screamin' And Shoutin'' was released in 2005 and was followed by Audience concerts in the UK, Germany and Canada, but the band withdrew from touring on Fisher's death. For those curious to sample the lesser-known delights of British rock music of the early Seventies, 'The House On The Hill' is a fine point to begin that journey.

The Brick Company and Pytheon Productions present

In Concert

AUDIENCE RENAISSANCE and Gordon Giltrap

On Tour in July — All seats 40p — All concerts begin at 7.30

Fri., 23: MANCHESTER Free Trade Hall   Thurs., 29 NEWCASTLE City Hall
Sun., 25: HULL City Hall   Fri., 30: MIDDLESBROUGH Town Hall
Tues., 27: NORWICH St. Andrew's Hall
Weds., 28: LINCOLN Drill Hall   Sat., 31: SHEFFIELD City Hall

(See local press for ticket agents)

BEGGAR'S OPERA
'Waters Of Change'
Released as Vertigo 6360 054 in November 1971
Highest UK chart position: N/A

Time Machine
Lament
I've No Idea
Nimbus
Festival
Silver Peacock Introduction
Silver Peacock
Impromptu
The Fox

Beggars Opera were formed in Glasgow in 1969 and featured Ricky Gardiner (guitar, vocals), Alan Park (keyboards), Marshall Erskine (bass guitar, flute), Martin Griffiths (vocals) and Raymond Wilson (drums). They came to the attention of Vertigo Records early in 1970 and became one of the first direct signings to the label. 'Act One' was their debut and featured many fine tracks which would point the way to the more grandiose follow-up, 'Waters Of Change', released in 1971.

     A huge step forward in terms of style and quality, the album was the band's finest hour thanks to fine material such as 'Time Machine', dominated by Gardiner's guitar-playing and Park's Mellotron work. During the recording of the album, Marshall Erskine was replaced by Gordon Sellar. 'Waters Of Change' helped Beggars Opera reach a wider audience, particularly in Germany and Holland where their music met with the most enthusiastic response.

     Two further albums followed: 'Pathfinder' was released in 1972 with an elaborate fold-out sleeve, while 1974's 'Get Your Dog Off Me', the band's final effort for Vertigo, was a less satisfying work. Beggars Opera continued to record and tour in Germany, releasing two albums in the mid/late Seventies. Ricky Gardiner concentrated on lucrative session work, beginning with guesting on David Bowie's 'Low' album in 1976. He met Iggy Pop and subsequently joined his band for 1977's tour promoting 'The Idiot'. Following this, Gardiner contributed to sessions for Iggy's 'Lust For Life', co-writing the legendary 'The Passenger', before returning to the UK to set up his own studio.

     Although their career produced music of varying consistency, in 'Waters Of Change' Beggar's Opera's made one of the most interesting albums to be released by the Vertigo label during its heyday.

IF 'If 3'

Released as United Artists UAG29158 in September 1971
Highest UK chart position: N/A

Fibonacci's Number
Forgotten Roads
Sweet January
Child Of The Storm
Far Beyond
Seldom Seen Sam
Upstairs
Here Comes Mister Time

Formed in 1969 by saxophonist Dick Morrissey and guitarist Terry Smith, If were one of the few British bands to successfully meld the styles of jazz and rock. Morrissey had already gained a reputation as one of the finest tenor players on the UK jazz scene and Smith had cut his teeth as both a jazz player and guitarist with Scott Walker's backing group.

After a brief incarnation comprising Darryl Runswick on bass, Spike Wells on drums and Lionel Grigson on keyboards, the line-up was completed by John Mealing on keyboards, Dave Quincy (another fine musician of some considerable pedigree) on alto sax, Jim Richardson (previously with backing bands for Lulu and Scott Walker) on bass, Dennis Elliott on drums and former Blue Flames vocalist JW Hodgkinson. Coming to the attention of American manager Lew Futterman, If spent their formative months touring the US and recording their eponymous debut album, released by Island in the spring of 1970.

After recording 'If 2' for Island later that year, they switched labels to United Artists and in 1971 recorded 'If 3', their finest moment. Such wonderful tracks as 'Here Comes Mister Time' and 'Child Of The Storm' met with great acclaim, particularly in Germany where If increasingly focused much of their attention. Following a final album for United Artists, an interesting experiment of recording live in the studio to an invited audience, the band endured a drastic line-up change with the departure of Elliot, Mealing, Hodgkinson and Richardson.

A new version of If put together by Dick Morrissey recorded three albums which saw European-only release. UK label Gull released the final two If albums in 1974 and 1975, after which the group disbanded. Of the original incarnation, Dennis Elliott would later find success as part of the US band Foreigner, JW Hodgkinson joined ex-Curved Air violinist Darryl Way in his band Wolf for their 1974 offering 'Night Music' and Dick Morrissey teamed up with guitarist Jim Mullen to record a series of highly innovative albums as Morrissey Mullen. Morrissey was also an in-demand session player, guesting on albums by musicians as diverse as Roy Harper, Vangelis and Bill Nelson. He died after a long illness in November 2000.

IF AND STEAMHAMMER PACKAGE TOUR VENUES

Plans for If to undertake a British concert tour in August, reported in the last two issues of NME, have now been finalised and dates set. It will be one of the attractions in a three-group package tour. The outfit will co-star with Steamhammer, and the support group will be Million — a new band making its debut appearance. The tour schedule opens with four dates in Scotland, then takes in 13 venues in England and one in Wales — including an Implosion show at London Roundhouse.

SUPERSISTER 'To The Highest Bidder'

Released in the Netherlands as Polydor 2925 002 in September 1971
Released in the UK as Dandelion 2310 146 in January 1973
Highest UK chart position: N/A

She Was Naked (On UK edition of the album only)
A Girl Named You
No Tree Will Grow (On Too High A Mountain)
Energy (Out Of Future)
Higher

By the beginning of 1971, Supersister were something of a Dutch musical phenomenon. Their debut album, 'Present From Nancy', released in 1970, had astounded many listeners with its musical dexterity, coupled with an acute sense of humour that made Supersister the equal of other whimsical progressive groups such as Caravan and Gong. The album also found its way into the hands of John Peel, who gave the band's Dutch hit single 'She Was Naked', a four-minute exercise in musical originality, exposure on his BBC Radio 1 show.

In the Netherlands, the band was under pressure from Polydor to come up with another hit single and, after some deliberation, 'A Girl Named You' b/w 'Missing Link' was released. Even when looked at in the light of these liberated times, both tracks were strange choices for release in the 45rpm format. However, with the release of the single, Supersister at last had the chance to concentrate on the recording of their second album.

This took shape during eight weeks in the summer of 1971 and would be a major milestone in the group's career. With Hans van Oosterhout producing once more, the album would feature four tracks of sophisticated originality. A 10-minute version of 'A Girl Named You' opened proceedings and immediately set the tone of the album. The trademark Supersister rhythmic dexterity introduced the piece, with an arrangement featuring solo flute, xylophone and harpsichord and subtle use of Mellotron in an effective ambient section of an otherwise jazz-influenced piece.

' No Tree Will Grow (On Too High A Mountain)' would be remembered as a highlight of the album, if not the entire Supersister repertoire. Beginning and ending with tape-looped electronic sounds, it was a work of dark musical genius. The lyrical pessimism of this track prevailed throughout the entire album. The second side began with the longest track on the record, 'Energy (Out Of Future)'. A typical Supersister piece, it opened with a complicated time signature giving way to an uptempo musical motif with darker lyrics. The track featured some superb fuzz-organ solo from Robert-Jan Stips and climaxed with electronic sounds before segueing into the lighter, more melodic 'Higher'.

Released in the autumn of 1971, 'To The Highest Bidder' demonstrated an advanced musical maturity not present on the band's first album thanks in part to having more time to realise their ideas and feeling more comfortable in the recording studio. The album, adorned in a striking gatefold sleeve depicting two eyes with Dutch coins in the pupils, was also released on John Peel's Dandelion label, at that time distributed and marketed by Polydor in the UK, adding 'She Was Naked' to the tracklisting.

To assist sales in the Netherlands Polydor released an edited 'No Tree Will Grow' along with 'The Groupies Of The Band' (a humorous insight into certain followers of Supersister) as a single. In Britain 'She was Naked' finally gained a release, coupled with the edited version of 'No Tree Will Grow'. Despite their excellence, neither made an impact on their respective chart listings.

Robert-Jan Stips later declared; 'We saw "Present From Nancy" as the closure of a period, a kind of document of our progression up to that point. "To The Highest Bidder" was more balanced, more serious, with less humour. Popular music is a reflection of society, maybe that's why that album sounded like it did.'

Whatever the reasons for its creation, 'To The Highest Bidder' was one of the finest albums to emerge from the Dutch progressive rock scene of the early Seventies.

Supersister

AGITATION FREE
'Second'
Released as Vertigo 6360 615 in October 1973
Highest UK chart position: N/A

First Communication
Dialogue and Random
Laila Part One
Laila Part Two
In the Silence of the Morning Sunrise
A Quiet Walk
a. Listening
b. Not Of The Same Kind
Haunted Island

Recorded in July 1973, the second long-playing opus by Berlin outfit Agitation Free was less 'ethnic' in feel to their innovative debut album 'Malesch', released the previous year. That highly original album was formed from ideas on recordings made as an 'audio diary' while on tour in the Middle East, sponsored by the Goethe cultural institute in Berlin. The line up of Lutz 'Luul' Ulbrich (guitar), Michael 'Fame' Gunther (bass), Jorg 'Joshi' Schwenke (guitar), Michael Hoenig (keyboards and electronics) and Burghard Rausch (drums) secured a contract with the European division of Vertigo soon after this visit.

Agitation Free had been in existence in some form or another since the end of 1967 when they became the first German band to perform with a backdrop of psychedelic projections, wax slides and lights to augment their psychedelic improvisations. Becoming the 'house band' of the legendary Zodiac Club, the hub of Berlin counterculture, the band had undergone various line-up changes, at one time or another incorporating guitarist Axel Genrich (later to join Guru Guru) and drummer Chris Franke (later to join Tangerine Dream) within their ranks. Studying under avant-garde composer Thomas Kessler had introduced the band to the possibilities of incorporating electronic sounds and the newly developed Moog and VCS3 synthesisers to their music.

In April 1973 Agitation Free expanded their line-up further with the addition of second drummer Dietmar Burmeister and embarked on a highly successful series of concerts in France, where the band enjoyed considerable popularity. By the summer of 1973 the band were rising stars of the German alternative rock scene and approached the recording of the second album with increased confidence, despite the departure of Schwenke. His replacement Stefan Diez brought more cohesion to the group, reflected in the excellence of the music committed to tape at Studio 70 in Munich.

The music recorded was of a more relaxed nature, the opening 'First Communication' setting the tone. The electronic sounds of 'Dialogue And Random' gave way to the infectious two-part instrumental 'Laila', while 'In The Silence Of The Morning Sunrise' was a jazz-influenced piece dominated by the subtle musicianship of Ulbrich and Hoenig. Equally impressive, although different in nature, was the avant garde 'A Quiet Walk', both sinister and pastoral in equal measure, featuring Ulbrich's excellent bouzouki-playing.

Arguably the highest spot of the proceedings came in the form of the Mellotron-dominated 'Haunted Island',

Burghard Rausch singing lyrics taken from Edgar Allan Poe's Dreamland. This psychedelic masterpiece was one of the finest works recorded by the band. Upon release in the autumn of 1973, Agitation Free's 'Second' became a best-selling album in France, prompting a further tour in January 1974, for which Stefan Diez was replaced by Gustav Lutjens.

Following a further series of concert in Germany in the summer of 1974, Agitation Free announced their intention to disband, performing a farewell concert in Berlin in November 1974. Sporadic reunions took place over ensuing decades, their most recent being a series of concerts in Japan in 2007. Of their impressive, often overlooked, catalogue, Agitation Free's 'Second' is one of the finest to emerge from the impressive ranks of Berlin experimental rock groups of the period.

Agitation Free

ROY HARPER
'Lifemask'

Released as Harvest SHVL808 in February 1973
Highest UK chart position: N/A

Highway Blues
All Ireland
Little Lady
Bank Of The Dead
South Africa
The Lord's Prayer
a. Front Song
b. Middle Song
c. End Song – Front Song Reprise
d.

With the critical success of his album 'Stormcock' in 1971, Roy Harper seemed assured of a commercial breakthrough. His reputation among fellow musicians was enhanced by the admiration of his work expressed by the members of Led Zeppelin and the contribution made by Jimmy Page to Harper's recent album.

Roy's notoriety was enhanced still further when he was approached by director John MacKenzie to play the part of singer Mike Preston in MacKenzie's film Made. A bitter slice of social commentary starring Carol White (an actress who had appeared in the controversial television play Cathy Come Home and the equally controversial film Poor Cow), the script recounted the story of a single mother living in a tower block in London who met with a singer-songwriter on a day trip to Brighton and their ensuing relationship.

An attack on religious and social hypocrisy, the role of Mike Preston seemed perfect for Harper, who beat Marc Bolan to the part. The film would feature performances by Harper of new work especially written for the movie, and would also feature music in the soundtrack.

Sessions began at Abbey Road studios soon after the completion of Made, with the songs 'Bank Of The Dead', (a reworking of 'The Social Casualty' from Made), 'Little Lady' and 'Highway Blues' featuring guests such as Jimmy Page and drummer Laurie Allan and being completed relatively quickly. Also added to the album was 'South Africa', a song recorded in October 1971 and originally entitled 'Living Here Alone' when it first appeared on the sampler 'The Harvest Bag' in November 1971. A tremendously evocative song that utilised numerous overdubbed vocal parts, it remains one of Harper's finest ever songs and a work of breathtaking originality.

During the embryonic sessions to lay down the basis of a song cycle that had begun life in the soundtrack music for Made, Roy was diagnosed with the blood disorder polycythemia, a barely understood and life-threatening condition. While hospitalised, Harper wrote the extensive lyrics for 'The Lord's Prayer', the epic poem he would later describe as his 'last will and testament' and which would dominate his new album's second side. He recovered from illness to return to Abbey Road studios, engaging the services of guest musicians Steve Broughton, Jimmy Page, Brian Hodges, Brain Davison and Ray Warleigh to complete the work.

The album proved to be a world away from the acoustic background from whence Harper came, a kind of progressive/folk fusion that was unique. Upon release in February 1973, 'Lifemask' (adorned in a stark fold-out cover depicting a 'death mask' of Harper) was enthusiastically received by fans but had a mixed critical reception, some reviews citing 'The Lord's Prayer' as pretentious. With the benefit of hindsight, both 'The Lord's Prayer' and 'Lifemask' as a whole can now be seen as trailblazing work, the product of a creative genius. For those seeking a different and enriching listening experience, the album reveals this most original of musicians at his inspired best.

MAN
'Back Into The Future'

Released as United Artists UAD60053/4 in September 1973
Highest UK chart position: Number 23

A Night In Dad's Bag
Just For You
Back Into The Future
Don't Go Away
Ain't Their Fight
Never Say Nups To Nepalese
Sospach Fach (live)
C'Mon (live)
Jam Up Jelly Tight/Oh No, Not Again
(Spunk Rock '73) (live)

By the end of 1972, legendary Welsh band Man had recorded and released one of their most fully realised albums, the imaginative 'Be Good To Yourself At Least Once A Day' and were at last making both artistic and commercial inroads in the UK. The album, issued in an elaborate foldout sleeve, narrowly failed to make an impression on the British album charts, but was their best-selling release to date.

The year closed with the staging of a legendary concert at the Patti Pavilion in Swansea in December 1972 which saw Man joined at their Christmas Party by friends such as the Flying Aces, Ducks Deluxe, the Jets, Plum Crazy and Help Yourself (featuring former Man guitarist Deke Leonard). The concert was recorded by United Artists and was released as a limited edition 10-inch double album 'Christmas At The Patti' in April 1973.

The album proved to be Clive John's last recorded appearance with the band as he quit soon after the Patti Pavilion concert, eventually recording the solo album 'You Always Know Where You Stand With A Buzzard' in 1975 with contributions from fellow Man members Martin Ace and Phil Ryan. Undeterred by John's departure, Man gathered at Clearwell Castle in Gloucestershire to rehearse and write for their next album and entered Rockfield studios later that month to begin work on their next opus.

Micky Jones (guitar, vocals), Terry Williams (drums), Phil Ryan (keyboards) and Will Youatt (bass) were joined by new guitarist Alan 'Tweke' Lewis, formerly with Jethro Tull spin-off Wild Turkey, and a series of highly productive writing sessions followed. On 24 June 1973, a special concert was staged at the Roundhouse in London which would see Man joined by the Gwalia Male Voice Choir for a memorable set. This idea, the suggestion of Andrew Lauder of United Artists, followed a successful performance with a choir the previous year at the Oval cricket ground, supporting Frank Zappa.

The highlight was a 17-minute version of 'C'Mon' which featured the Gwalia choir in its full glory. The concert was captured on tape by the Pye Mobile recording unit and would serve as the second album in a double set that would form Man's next release. Recording sessions of new material were completed at Chipping Norton Studios in Oxfordshire and Olympic in Barnes, London in July and the results were released as 'Back Into The Future' in September 1973. The

genius of such new material as the album's title track, 'A Night In Dad's Bag' and 'Don't Go Away', combined with the potency of the additional live recordings, made for an essential set.

As a result, 'Back Into The Future' became the first Man album to chart in the UK, reaching Number 23. Its success seemed set to open a new chapter for Man but, by the end of 1973, Ryan and Youatt had departed to form the Neutrons (who went on to record two albums for United Artists) and Deke Leonard returned to the fold, ousting Tweke Lewis. Malcolm Morley and Ken Whaley, both formerly of Help Yourself, replaced the pair and soon Man were preparing for their first American tour with Hawkwind. The most commercially successful era of Man's career would follow, all sparked by the originality of the excellent 'Back Into The Future'

Phil Ryan   Will Youatt   Terry Williams   Mick Jones   Tweke Lewis

NEKTAR
'Remember The Future'

Released as United Artists UAG29545 in November 1973
Highest UK chart position: N/A

Remember The Future Part One

a. Images Of The Past

b. Wheel Of Time

c. Remember The Future

d. Confusion

Remember The Future Part Two

a. Returning Light

b. Questions And Answers

c. Tomorrow Never Comes

d. Path Off Light

e. Recognition

f. Let It Grow

By January 1973 Nektar was one of the major acts in Germany, a major feat for a group of musicians who hailed from England. The albums 'Journey to the Centre Of The Eye', 'A Tab In The Ocean' and 'Sounds Like This' had been considerable hits in Nektar's adopted country, assisted by live shows accompanied by the imaginative lighting of fifth member Mick Brockett.

Nektar's reputation reached the ears of Andrew Lauder A&R head of United Artists in the UK, and a deal was struck with German label Bellaphon for UA to issue the band's next album in Britain. With this arrangement in place the decision was made to record Nektar's next album in England.

Based upon lyrics written by Mick Brockett, 'Remember The Future' was a conceptual piece, inspired by the blindness of Brockett's father, that had begun life during the sessions for their previous album. Essentially two long song cycles, the music had developed and expanded from two pieces 'Questions And Answers' and 'Let It Grow' which had been tried out on audiences throughout Europe while Nektar had undertaken a support slot for Frank Zappa. By the time 'Remember The Future' was completed, both these pieces had become sections of Part Two of the song cycle and the conceptual piece had been performed live many times.

The album was recorded at Chipping Norton in the Oxfordshire countryside in August 1973 and took just over one week to record. From the beginning the decision was made to mix the album for release in the SQ Quadraphonic sound system. At the end of August Roye Albrighton and Mo Moore took the completed multi-track tapes to CBS Studios in London for quadraphonic mixing. Unfortunately, upon arrival in Germany it was discovered that there was a technical problem with the mix which resulted in certain instruments being inaudible.

A further quadraphonic mix was undertaken at Dieter Deirks' studio in Stommeln, along with a stereo version in September 1973 to everyone's satisfaction and 'Remember The Future' was released in both the UK and Germany in November 1973. It failed to make an impression on the UK chart listings, despite a series of well received shows in England, including a performance at the Roundhouse in London. However, in Germany it became Nektar's biggest success to date, being voted album of the year by the magazine Musik Express. Importantly, the album enjoyed a US release by Passport Records and incredibly entered the US Billboard charts, breaking into the Top 20. A US tour quickly followed, leading to the growth of a loyal fan base in the United States which eventually led to the band relocating to the other side of Atlantic.

'Remember The Future' marks the point when Nektar's music at last caught the attention of a wider public and remains a satisfying album.

NEKTAR

NEKTAR — the English group which has become a top attraction in Germany — are to play a lengthy autumn tour of Britain. Dates so far set are Watford Town Hall (October 9), Sheffield Polytechnic (10), Bedford Corn Exchange (11), Norwich East Anglia University (12), Folkestone Leas Cliff Hall (13), Manchester Stoneground (17), London Central Polytechnic (19), St. Albans City

STRING DRIVEN THING
'The Machine That Cried'

Released as Charisma CAS1070 in August 1973
Highest UK chart position: N/A

Heartfeeder
To See You
Night Club
Sold Down The River
Two Timin' Rama
Travelling
People On The Street
The House
The Machine That Cried
River of Sleep

String Driven Thing were formed by husband and wife duo Chris and Pauline Adams in 1967 as a folk-influenced trio with guitarist John Mannion. They recorded a debut album for the small independent Concord label which is now a collector's item. Stylistically different from the music for which they later became wider known, the album did lead to the trio performing on the UK folk circuit and relocating to London from their native Scotland.

By 1971 the influence of progressive rock led to a restructuring of the band into a folk-rock outfit. Mannion departed and in came violinist Grahame Smith and bass guitarist Colin Wilson. They came to the attention of producer Shel Talmy who in turn recommended the group to Tony Stratton-Smith, leading to String Driven Thing signing to Charisma and releasing their second, eponymous album in October 1972. Greeted with enthusiasm by the music press, the band soon added drummer Billy Fairley to the line-up, touring both the UK and America and recording 'The Machine That Cried' for Charisma in 1973.

A much darker work, much of the music was written while Chris Adams had suffered health problems and this was reflected in such magnificent songs as 'Heartfeeder'. The album was a work of genius but fared poorly commercially speaking ,and the lack of success for such a finely crafted album led to the departure of Colin Wilson, who was replaced by Bill Hatje. Soon after Chris and Pauline Adams also left, handing over the name to Grahame Smith, who assembled an entirely new band with vocalist Kim Beacon, guitarist Alun Roberts, bassist James Exell and drummer Colin Fairley.

This line-up toured the US supporting Lou Reed and recorded the albums 'Please Mind Your Head' and 'Keep Your 'And On It' before disbanding in 1976. Chris and Pauline Adams would record two singles for Charisma and enjoy a boost to their fortunes when the Bay City Rollers covered 'It's A Game' (penned for and recorded by String Driven Thing) in 1977. Smith would join Van der Graaf Generator the same year and Kim Beacon would later sing lead vocals on Genesis keyboard-player Tony Banks' first solo album, 'A Curious Feeling' in 1979. In the new millennium Chris and Pauline Adams reformed String Driven Thing to tour and record.

For the uninitiated, 'The Machine That Cried' is an album that should be investigated without reservation.

6 Frankfurt am Main
Stiftstrasse 10
Telefon 0611 / 59 05 57

PRESENTS

MÄRZ / APRIL 1973

30./31. März 1973 1. April 1973	MC GUINNES FLINT
2./3./4./5./6. April 1973	S A M M Y
7./8. April 1973	O M E G A
10./11. April 1973	TIR NA NOG
12. April 1973	A T L A N T I S
13./14./15. April 1973	GNIDROLOG
18./20./21. April 1973	STRING DRIVEN THING
19. April 1973	EDGAR BROUGHTON BAND
	STRING DRIVEN THING
22. April 1973	ARMA GEDDON
23. April 1973	JACKSON HEIGHTS
24./25./26. April 1973	STACKRIDGE
27. April 1973	MANFRED MANN
28./29. April 1973	AGITATION FREE
30. April 1973	ARMA GEDDON

Mit einer Monatskarte ersparen Sie sich jeden Abend eine Eintrittskarte.
DM 30,– (Schüler und Studenten DM 25,–).
Visit the ZOOM with a monthly member card free entry.
DM 30,– (pupils and students DM 25,–).

Philharmonic Hall
LINCOLN CENTER

Wednesday Evening, December 13, 1972, at 8:00 and 11:00

WNEW-FM in association with
CHARISMA RECORDS

present

A CHRISTMAS CONCERT

for the benefit of the

CEREBRAL PALSY FOUNDATION

STARRING

Genesis

AND INTRODUCING

String Driven Thing

Sound by Bob Heill

Produced by Dominic Sicilia

Charisma Records is part of The Buddah Group

Thanks to Chris Hewitt Chris Hewitt / www.tractor-ozit.com these images

RENAISSANCE
TURN OF THE CARDS

All songs composed by Michael Dunford
and Betty Thatcher
published By Pytheon Music except*
*published by Turn of the Cards Music
Musical arrangements by Renaissance
Orchestral arrangements by Jimmy Horowitz
Produced by Renaissance, Dick Plant and Richard Gottehrer
Recorded at De Lane Lea Music Center, Wembley, Middlesex;
Engineer: Dick Plant; Assistant Engineers: Douglas Bogie
& Mike Pela and remixed at Media Sound, New York City;
Engineer: Jeffrey Lesser
Original cover design & photos by Hipgnosis. "Tarot Cards" by Joe Petagno
Many thanks to Miles Copeland, Julian, Shirley
Thanks to Albinoni for Cold is Being, and also thanks to
Jehan Alain for the opening piece of Running Hard
A British Talent Managers Production
by permission of Sovereign Records.

RENAISSANCE
'Turn Of The Cards'

Released in the US as Sire Records 7502 in September 1974
Released in the UK as BTM Records BTM1000 in March 1975
Highest UK chart position: N/A

Running Hard
I Think of You
Things I Don't Understand
Black Flame
Cold Is Being
Mother Russia

At the beginning of 1974, the line-up of Renaissance bore no similarities to that of the group formed by two former members of the Yardbirds who had recorded their eponymous debut album for Island in 1969. Keith Relf and Jim McCarty had departed the fold by 1971, their last involvement being as songwriters for material featured on the 1971 album 'Illusion'.

By the start of 1973 Renaissance were under the managerial guidance of Miles Copeland and were signed to EMI subsidiary label Sovereign. Their line-up (which had gone many changes over the previous months) had now settled to comprise Annie Haslam (lead vocals), Michael Dunford (acoustic guitar, vocals), Jon Camp (bass, vocals), John Tout (keyboards) and Terry Sullivan (drums). 'Ashes Are Burning' had been their finest album to date, featuring a classically influenced musical direction spearheaded by the compositions of Dunford and lyricist Betty Thatcher. The title track of the album would point the future musical path Renaissance would follow and featured an impressive guitar solo by Andy Powell of Wishbone Ash. Entering the US album charts upon release, 'Ashes Are Burning' led to the first US tour by Renaissance which included a concert with an orchestra at the Academy of Music in New York in May 1974.

Returning home to England, the band soon entered De Lane Lea studios in Wembley to start work on their first album for Miles Copeland's newly established BTM Label, working with arranger Jimmy Horowitz and co-producers Dick Plant and Richard Gottehrer to deliver one of the finest albums of their career. The blend of Annie Haslam's fine voice, Michael Dunford's acoustic guitar and impressive orchestration made for a majestic work. Highlights such as the epic 'Mother Russia' (inspired by the plight and works of Russian author Alexander Solzhenitsyn), 'Things I Don't Understand' and 'Black Flame' were all destined to become classics.

The album 'Turn of the Cards' was released in America in September 1974 on the Sire label, but for various reasons, including contractual difficulties with the now defunct Sovereign label, this excellent album failed to gain a UK release until March 1975. Breaking into the US Top 100, the album failed to gain a UK chart placing and the band thereafter concentrated on touring the US where they would enjoy increasing success. Although Renaissance would eventually strike gold at home with the album 'A Song For All Seasons' and single 'Northern Lights' in 1978, they never bettered the inspirational music featured on 'Turn Of The Cards'.

DARRYL WAY'S WOLF 'Night Music'

Released as Deram SML1116 in November 1974
Highest UK chart position: N/A
Available on CD as Esoteric Recordings ECLEC2064

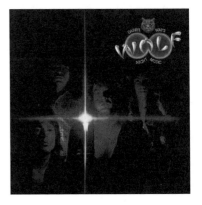

The Envoy
Black September
Flat 2/55
Anteros
We're Watching You
Steal The World
Comrade Of The Nine

One of the most talented of all the bands to sign to Deram during the later period of the label, Wolf was the musical vision of founding member of Curved Air, violinist Darryl Way. Formed in late 1972 following his departure from that successful outfit, the band featured John Etheridge on guitar, Canadian Dek Messecar on bass and Ian Mosley on drums. Wolf was primarily an instrumental band, showcasing the considerable electric violin, viola and keyboard-playing talents of Way.

Their debut album, 'Canis Lupus', featured former King Crimson saxophonist Ian McDonald in the role of both producer and guest musician and in places owed much to King Crimson in terms of influences. 'Saturation Point' followed in much the same vein, exploring instrumental rock with classical and jazz overtones and helping Wolf become a popular attraction on the college rock scene. Way then sought to expand their musical horizons still further by recruiting John Hodgkinson, formerly with jazz-rock outfit If, as lead vocalist.

With Hodgkinson in the group, the band took on a new lease of life as was evidenced both on stage and on the outstanding 'Night Music'. Hodgkinson's superb voice complemented their instrumental prowess, making the album Wolf's finest achievement. The stunning 'The Envoy' was a powerful jazz rock opener, with fine solos from Way, Messecar, Moseley and Etheridge, while the evocative 'Black September' was a melancholic introverted piece. The other highlights, 'Steal The World', 'Flat 2/55' and 'Comrade Of The Nine' made 'Night Music' arguably the finest and most fully realised rock album Darryl Way had yet recorded.

With such a fine record under their belt, it came as a surprise when Way announced that he was disbanding the group in late 1974 to join a reformed Curved Air, leaving a fourth album unfinished. Dek Messecar joined Caravan in 1976 while John Etheridge passed through the ranks of Soft Machine and embarked on a solo career. Ian Mosley became an in-demand session player and was an integral part of former Genesis guitarist Steve Hackett's band before joining Marillion, with whom he still performs.

IAN MOSLEY, drums   DEK MESSECAR, bass and vocals   DARRYL WAY, violin, viola and keyboards   JOHN ETHERIDGE, guitar

are

BE BOP DELUXE 'Futurama'

Released as Harvest SHSP4045 in May 1975
Highest UK chart position: N/A

Stage Whispers
Love With The Madman
Maid In Heaven
Sister Seagull
Sound Track
Music In Dreamland
Jean Cocteau
Between The Worlds
Swan Song

After the release of the album 'Axe Victim' in July 1974, Bill Nelson disbanded the first line-up of the band and assembled a short-lived Be Bop Deluxe featuring drummer Simon Fox and two former Cockney Rebels, keyboard-player Milton Reame-James and bassist Paul Jeffreys. By the end of September 1974 Nelson had settled on a three-piece incarnation featuring New Zealander Charlie Tumahai on bass and Simon Fox on drums. This incarnation undertook a series of UK dates in November 1974 before travelling to Rockfield in Monmouthshire to work with producer Roy Thomas Baker on a second album.

This new work would clearly show that the band had moved on in creative leaps and bounds. Nelson's writing was keenly sharp on wonderful three-minute workouts such as the excellent rock number 'Maid In Heaven' and the emotive 'Sister Seagull' in which his guitar soared to new heights. The opening piece 'Stage Whispers' was inspired, along with excellent 'Love With The Madman' and the gorgeous 'Sound Track'. 'Music In Dreamland' featured a beautiful brass band arrangement by Peter Oxendale, performed by the Grimethorpe Colliery Band, and 'Jean Cocteau' was a heartfelt tribute to the French artistic visionary so admired by Nelson. With the remaining tracks 'Between The Worlds' and 'Swan Song' also of a high standard, the quality was consistent.

By January 1975, the band was expanded further with the inclusion of Simon 'Andy' Clarke on keyboards. Amazingly, the album 'Futurama', named after the model of the first electric guitar owned by Nelson, failed to chart in the UK. However, the new quartet line-up would record a series albums of stunning originality and quality over the next three years, beginning with the wonderful 'Sunburst Finish' which enjoyed success in the UK album chart. Be Bop Deluxe continued to break new artistic ground, but by the time 'Drastic Plastic' was released in February 1978 Nelson had begun to tire of being labelled a guitar hero. The impact of the punk explosion and the subsequent birth of the British new wave inspired him to explore pastures new. In 1978 he disbanded Be Bop Deluxe to form the equally innovative Red Noise, retaining the services of Andy Clarke on keyboards. 'Futurama' features some of the finest songs written by Bill Nelson in his formative years.

A FURTHER TEN UK ALBUM-CHARTING GREATS THAT NEED LITTLE INTRODUCTION

ATOMIC ROOSTER 'Death Walks Behind You'

Released as B&C Records CAS1026 in December 1970
Highest UK chart position: Number 12

Death Walks Behind You
VUG
Tomorrow Night
Seven Streets
Sleeping For Years
I Can't Take No More
Nobody Else
Gershatzer

Atomic Rooster's second album is arguably their darkest, but also demonstrated a remarkable rejuvenation of the group following the departure of drummer Carl Palmer (to found ELP) and bassist, flautist and vocalist Nick Graham (to join Skin Alley) after the release of the band's eponymous debut. Keyboard-player and founder Vincent Crane changed the feel of the band entirely by dispensing with bass, recruiting guitarist and vocalist John Du Cann and drummer Paul Hammond. This new trio took a more muscular direction both on stage and in the recording studio. A

An album that features the dark title track, inspired by a short film made by Vincent Crane, is a worthy addition to any self-respecting record collection of the genres covered within these pages. Also featuring Atomic Rooster's first hit single, 'Tomorrow Night', and adorned with a striking Gothic painting by William Blake, little wonder 'Death Walks Behind You' was a successful chart album.

ATOMIC ROOSTER

ATOMIC ROOSTER (l to r) VINCENT CRANE, JOHN CANN and (back) PAUL HAMMOND.

By ROY CARR

Oⁿce a group becomes successful the most demanding pressures are quickly imposed. Seemingly, there is absolutely no let up in the all-important endeavour of trying to keep the customers satisfied. With the result that gigs, recording sessions and sleep are often plagued with the most unavoidable and irritating hang-ups.

Vincent Crane, Atomic Rooster's organist and mentor is by no means a newcomer to the bittersweet chart stakes; having first tasted the heady fruits as a founder member of Arthur Brown's psychedelic circus from which he managed to escape mentally and physically intact.

Since its inception, the Rooster have been fortunate in having a healthy date sheet, but since "Tomorrow Night" has settled at the No. 9 slot in this week's NME chart the phone hasn't stopped ringing.

The day I tracked the Rooster to earth, they were desperately trying to keep up with an almost impossible schedule. I caught them in between an interview with Radio Manx, a location photo-call and finally in a Taxi as we sped

through the congested traffic towards the BBC-TV centre at White City.

On arrival, we were greeted by a most amiable young lady wearing a pair of truly magnificent multi-coloured trousers who then escorted us through the labyrinth of corridors which comprises the building.

As we trundled along, Vince, who was wrapped in a large white Afghan coat, which was now beginning to show the first signs of wear, informed me: "We've only

just returned from a tour of Italy and at 10.30 tomorrow morning we've got to be in a German television studio.

"After that we have to fly to a gig in Ayr to begin a short Scottish tour the same evening."

His statement produced grimaces of agony from guitarist John Cann and drummer Paul Hammond.

Though many bands have been subjected to snobbery and adolescent criticism following an appearance on the national singles charts,

John admitted that funnily enough the Rooster had so far been exempt from this slur of having sold out.

On finally arriving at their allocated dressing room, there were raised eyebrows all round after reading a card which had the names, Gladys, Winifred and Ursula neatly typed on it.

"It should have said Winifred Atwell," John immediately joked as we entered and flopped down on the nearest chairs, while Paul disappeared in search of the studio so as to check over his mammoth drum kit.

"Prior to the single coming out, things were most definitely on the up for the band, in fact we had more than enough work. It's just that now the bread's better. But one thing is certain: we're not going to fall into the trap of out-pricing ourselves like so many bands," Vince explained as he brushed the long tangle of black hair out of his eyes.

Prestige

"Actually, I don't like writing with a single in mind," he continued, prior to admitting to the importance and prestige a hit single can give a band.

"If the album ('Death Walks Behind You') had reached the same placing as the single on the album charts it wouldn't have meant that much. For singles are a very valid thing in helping to establish a band on the inter-

SONJA KRISTINA

More performer than musician

By JULIE WEBB

windy. And my voice was too low compared with the rest of the school choir."

By the time she was thirteen, Sonja had switched to playing guitar — and her voice wasn't such an oddity!

"I was taught guitar by a nun. It was quite a new thing to learn — the guitar was very much in vogue at that time — it was about the same time Bert Weedon was around. My piano teacher was a bit upset that I gave up piano in favour of guitar."

Sonja picked up guitar so well that soon she was teaching other people, which at thirteen can't be bad! She also used to play at a folk club.

"I just used to sing a couple of songs — they paid my bus fare home — which was about five bob."

At fourteen she was playing regularly for another club on the same bill as people like The Karlins and Settlers. And her money had gone up by this time to £3/£5 a night.

"At school there was a certain amount of prestige attached to being a singer. No one was jealous I don't think."

Is Sonja a religious person? What influence did her convent education have on her?

"I'm religious in my own way — I could never really identify with a church service but I like churches as places to be alone. I don't think in terms of God and man but I think there is a better side to people that should be cultivated. I think my education did stimulate a religious side in me — I didn't rebel, because I never really conformed."

After school came drama college in Hampstead because Sonja decided she wanted to teach.

"I got a very academic background to drama although I only did one year of a three year course. I left because I wasn't giving enough to the academic side. I was becoming too involved with people in London and I was doing a residency at the Marquee."

After college Sonja got married and started rehearsing for "Hair." Happily "Hair" was successful for her — sadly her marriage wasn't. In fact, she says: "By the time I was pregnant the marriage had broken up."

Six weeks after her son was born, Sonja was back in "Hair," in fact the "Hair" cast were very good to her, but after two years of doing the show she left.

"Well it was two years of doing the same thing. You have to take a step forward. I was toying with the idea at the time of singing by myself but I couldn't have gone back to what I'd been doing before because my whole attitude towards music and working on stage had changed. I got an offer while I was with 'Hair' to do a solo album but I turned that down because I didn't have enough confidence in my own thing."

Why Curved Air then? Were you confident enough in them — surely it was a big risk?

"I had an idea of working with people who were first class and Curved Air are. I know now it's worked out. I am more of a performer than a musician I'll admit. I feel my way around music rather than know all the musical terms. Musically I'm lost at the moment — I write lyrics but not melodies, and the guitar as an instrument doesn't move me like it used to. In fact I've gone back now to playing piano because this may give me more of an insight."

Next month Sonja marries the group's personal manager Mal Ross but she insists this won't be the end of her career.

"I'm not intending to slow down and settle down. And as far as the group goes I'd like us to go on for ten years or more."

Are the group concerned that they may lose some of their following because they've got a single in the charts?

"No because we haven't 'sold out' — we haven't changed our music on the single radically, although it's true this number was written separately from an album. It was just something we wanted to put out in between albums."

And what of the future — have the group any plans for changing their stage act or music?

"Francis has been buying a lot of electrical equipment and we're working on two new songs. We don't have any new set ideas about the stage act — we just find with each number we do, something new is added to the act."

Is there any possibility that Sonja might at some stage do a solo act?

"No — because I like working for a nice crowd and I enjoy doing live gigs with them. And apart from that I wouldn't work on my own because I know my limits."

CURVED AIR (l to r) DARRYL WAY, FRANCIS MONKHAM, FLORIAN PICKLINGTON-MIKSA, IAN EYRE and SONJA.

CURVED AIR 'Second Album'

Released as Warner Bros. K49092 in September 1971
Highest UK chart position: Number 11

Young Mother
Back Street Luv
Jumbo
You Know
Puppets
Everdance
Bright Summers Day
Piece of Mind

Air's SONJA KRISTINA

Curved Air were formed in March 1970 when violinist and Royal College of Music student Darryl Way met guitarist and keyboard-player Francis Monkman. The first line-up was soon completed with the recruitment of singer Sonja Kristina (formerly a member of the London cast of stage musical Hair), bass player Robert Martin and drummer Florian Pilkington-Miksa.

Way and Monkman plotted a musical path that fused classical and rock music along with experimental electronic influences of American avant-garde musician Terry Riley, taking their name from his groundbreaking album 'A Rainbow In Curved Air'. Signing to manager Mark Hanau, who secured a contract with Warner Brothers' newly opened London office, the band issued 'Air Conditioning' the same year.

Notable for the use of electronics and synthesisers, combined with the classical influences of Way's violin-playing, the album had much fine material but was marred by poor production, not helped by the fact that the album had been pressed as a picture disc, resulting in poor sound quality. However, it enjoyed a Top 10 chart placing in the UK and earned them a following in Europe. By 'Second Album', bass player Martin had departed and was replaced by Ian Eyre. Now experienced in the recording studio, Curved Air's second opus benefited from exemplary material such as 'Young Mother' with its dramatic synthesiser introduction) 'Back Street Luv', 'Puppets' and 'Everdance', and was a Top 20 album. 'Back Street Luv' was issued as a single and gave the band their only UK hit single.

Two further albums, 'Phantasmagoria' and 'Air Cut', were recorded for Warners, but each saw further line-up changes. By 1973's 'Air Cut', both Way and Monkman had departed, leaving Kristina with keyboard player and violinist Eddie Jobson, bass guitarist and vocalist Mike Wedgwood (later to join Caravan), guitarist Kirby Gregory and drummer Jim Russell. In 1975 Way, Monkman, Kristina and Pilkington-Miksa reunited with Phil Kohn on bass to undertake a UK tour which was also captured on tape and subsequently released by Deram in 1975.

This line-up split and Way and Kristina, who had decided to continue as Curved Air, were left the task of putting a new band together. Leaving Deram, they recorded two albums for BTM, 'Midnight Wire' and 'Airborne', featuring Kristina's future husband Stewart Copeland on drums. In 1976 Curved Air disbanded and Copeland became a founder member of the Police. In 1990 the band reunited for a period and in 2008 Kristina, Way and Pilkington-Miksa assembled a new line-up Air, undertaking live concerts the UK, Europe and Japan. 'Second Album' remains the outstanding album in their impressive repertoire.

Curved Air, Harum for concert tour

CURVED AIR — which has just completed a concert tour with Black Sabbath — is lined up for another British concert tour in March. This time it will top the bill, with Procol Harum and Tir-Na-Nog as supporting attractions. And the maximum admission price throughout the tour will be 14s (70p). Curved Air is also set for a major tour of the United States, which begins on March 22 and lasts for six weeks.

Concert dates are as follows: Blackburn King's Hall (March 4), Wolverhampton Civic Hall (8), Plymouth Guildhall (9), Bournemouth Winter Gardens (10), Leicester De Montfort Hall (12), Guildford Civic Hall (15) and Nottingham Albert Hall (16).

Curved Air is also undertaking a solo one-nighter tour of concert halls, clubs and colleges during February.

Dates are Southampton Technical College (next Monday), Manchester Institute of Science and Technology (February 6), Dunstable Civic Hall (8), Tunbridge Wells Civic Hall (10), Bath University (12), Bradford University (13), Potters Bar Farx (17), Devizes Town Hall (19), Birmingham University (20), Manchester University (23), York University (26) and Nelson Imperial (27).

On sale Friday, week ending October 9, 1971   NEW MUSICAL EXPRESS

ALBUMS

Curved Air: No need for gimmicks

CURVED AIR on stage: DARRYL WAY and IAN EYRE.

CURVED AIR: SECOND ALBUM
(Warner Bros. K46092 £2.15)

AGAIN Curved Air will come under strong criticism for what could be described as another gimmicky album cover. This one is an elaborate affair with a bulls-eye type front which opens out. But there will still be the people who say the music is strong enough not to warrant gimmicks.

I've noticed in Air stage performances they are now going more into electronics and this album illustrates it. In fact there is a strong emphasis on the blended sound of the electric violin and various keyboard instruments. The result being that the guitar and bass rarely come through, and Sonja's voice is another instrument to fall in with this technique.

Most of the music is good, including some gentle emotive slow tempo pieces, with the medium paced ones and the odd rocker.

Over the time they have been together Air have developed well consistently. Everything is much together, and they now have a distinct sound, which would not only be hard, probably impossible, to imitate, but expensive because of the equipment they use.

The most obvious thing on this album is the difference between Darryl Way's writing style, and that of Francis Monkhan. The pieces Way is involved in seem to have a lot more depth than his colleague's, such as Jumbo, which is one of the most beautiful and emotive tracks on the album. But they lack force.

Monkhan likes to get the basic rock feel into most of his stuff, such as Everdance, and then uses the change of rhythm structure well. But at times his style seems a little stilted, such as on Bright Summer's Day '68 where Sonja Kristina's vocals don't blend.

Overall I liked the album, but the electronic devices are no substitute for good music, even if strictly within the context of the number. If it's the way the band is going, that's alright by me, as long as a tight balance is kept. T.S.

NEWS EXTRA

Rex, Crimson, Curved Air join Weeley bill

WITH the cancellation of the Canterbury Festival (reported last week) and no event taking place this year on the Isle of Wight, the Weeley Festival has the field to itself in the South of England this August Bank Holiday weekend. And several attractions which had been booked for Canterbury have now switched to Weeley instead. New bookings announced this week for Weeley, near Clacton in Essex, for the two-day event (August 28-29) include T. Rex, King Crimson, Curved Air, Status Quo and Paul Brett's Sage.

The arena at Weeley opens on the Friday (27) at 6pm, and entertainment will begin as soon as a crowd gathers. The camping site is open from the Monday before the festival (23). There is a hospital on the site, as well as an 11th Century church in which the Bishop of Colchester will conduct all-denominational services.

Acts already booked for Weeley include Faces, Mott The Hoople, Colosseum, Rory Gallagher the Grease Band, Groundhogs, Mungo Jerry, Barclay James Harvest, Quintessence, Edgar Broughton, Juicy Lucy, Stone The Crows, Lindisfarne, Caravan, Van Der Graaf Generator, Al Stewart, Argent, Bell & Arc, Gringo, Heads Hands & Feet and Tir Na Nog — plus 20 other groups!

ISLE OF WIGHT IS DEFINITELY OFF!

THERE will definitely be no pop festival on the Isle of Wight this August Bank Holiday, even though a Government ruling to prevent such an event will not become law until the end of the year. The decision came after a special meeting between police and councillors on the island. A statement said that "in the council's opinion, there is not sufficient time for the original promoter or any other person to make the detailed arrangements which would be necessary."

The Faulk brothers, who staged last year's event, had hoped to present a smaller scale festival this year. It would necessarily have been reduced in scope, because of the belated nature of the Government's ruling. But now the island's council has finally put paid to any such venture, although the Faulks have already said that they will fight for a festival next year. Meanwhile, rival promoter Richard Roscoe had already dropped out of the race — he stated two weeks ago that he had abandoned plans to present a festival on the island.

NEW TO SINGLES CHART

CURVED AIR

IN the words of Curved Air singer Sonja Kristina, "'Back Street Luv' was written with the public in mind." And to this end, it has made the No. 24 slot on this week's NME Singles Chart.

Thus this versatile group makes its singles chart debut after it has already been in the albums charts.

Conceived as a single and not as part of an album, Sonja admitted: "As our new album wasn't ready, we decided to put out a single in the meantime. Therefore, we made the best possible product at that particular time.

"Our second album is now mixed and completed, and as soon as the finishing touches are made to the sleeve design it will be in the shops. All being well it will be available around the first week in September." — ROY CARR.

The girl who puts the curves in Curved Air

GENESIS 'Selling England By The Pound'

Released as Charisma CAS1074 in October 1973
Highest UK chart position: Number3

Dancing With The Moonlit Knight
I Know What I Like (In Your Wardrobe)
Firth Of Fifth
More Fool Me
The Battle Of Epping Forest
After The Ordeal
Cinema Show
Aisle Of Plenty

Following the success of the excellent 'Foxtrot', featuring magnum opus 'Supper's Ready', Genesis went one better with their most cohesive and consistent album with Peter Gabriel as vocalist. From the opening 'Dancing With The Moonlit Knight' with its playful punning lyrics ('Knights of the Green Shield stamp and shout'), the tone was set for a masterful listening experience. 'I Know What I Like (In Your Wardrobe)' was the obvious contender for single success, while 'Firth Of Fifth' was the finest instrumental from both Steve Hackett and Tony Banks to date.

'More Fool Me', with vocal by Phil Collins, was a delicate acoustic ending to the album's first side, the pace being taken up once more with 'The Battle Of Epping Forest', a lyrically ambitious opening to side two. 'Cinema Show' would be destined to find a place in the hearts of the Genesis faithful with its bittersweet tone, climaxing in a superb instrumental coda that gave way to further delightful punning with the closing 'Aisle Of Plenty'. Sheer genius and essential.

Albums

The Pound recovers

Peter Gabriel of Genesis

GENESIS: — "Selling England By the Pound" (Charisma)

GENESIS FANS unite, stand proud and be counted; get ready to say 'I told you so' to all those people who have been doubting your praise of the band.

"Selling England By the Pound" is the band's best, most adventurous album to date.

There comes a time in every band's career when everything comes together, all the ideas, the playing, everything, the group has been trying to put across. And that's the case with this album.

There's not a half finished idea here, every track is worked out down to the last drum roll. There's so much subtlety that numerous listenings continue to reveal new found secrets.

"Dance With the Moonlight Night" begins the album as Peter Gabriel sings a folky lament acapella. A bit medieval, the piece features layed back guitar wandering and majestic melody lines.

Even on the first track, a difference is apparent. For starters, Tony Banks is playing more piano than organ; this is coupled with Gabriel's emotive singing. Steve Hackett's whining guitar and the all powerful rhythm section of Michael Rutherford and Phil Collins.

Yes, Genesis sound mightier than ever.

This band doesn't have to talk about dynamics, they're content to feature them constantly in the playing. They play harsh and rocky one mi-

nute and soft and gentle the next.

"I Know What I Like (In Your Wardrobe)" conjures up amazing visual possibilities with it's childlike quality of far away images. A flute comes in at the end, reminding one ever so slightly of early Traffic.

Classical themes are carefully mixed with rock, highlighted by Banks' grand master piano playing and Collins' orchestral percussion on tracks like "The Firth of Fifth" and "After the Ordeal".

"The Battle of Epping Forest" is the one that will no doubt be a grand stage production. One can easily envisage Gabriel playing the actor as his voice changes ranges and accents — while the piece builds to a fitting crescendo.

Never boring, never redundant, each piece is a minor tour de force, each played with the sensitivity and care all too often missing from popular music.

The lead guitar lines change

with each song, always blending in with the creative use of moogs, mellotrons and synthesizers.

Banks makes those instruments come alive. He never reverts to easy mechanical gimmickry like so many of his contemporaries.

So forget all those supergroups, all the super hype and all those mundane 'concept' albums. Disregard those mellotron based wonders that are almost always boring. Forget all those bands that sound the same. Genesis stand head and shoulders above all those so-called progressive groups.

Even the people upstairs like this one!

Barbara Charone

BLOOD, SWEAT AND TEARS: "No Sweat" (CBS)

IN MY YOUNGER days, friends and neighbours, would of times gather in an appointed district of the locality to play

360

The Ridiculous Roadshow

SIMON KING

ALIAS HAWKWIND ON TOUR: JAMES JOHNSON REPORTS

WITH JUST an off-hand laugh Dave Brock in Chicago put it like this: "We decided to call our next tour the Ridiculous Roadshow because all our tours are just so silly and disorganised."

Never a truer word was spoken. Hawkwind must win this year's Steve Took Award as the most hapless bunch of individuals ever to set foot on a stage.

They seem to exist in a state of gentle chaos for most of the time, things always seemingly on the edge of falling apart. The fact that in Chicago — probably the band's most important gig ever — the roadies showed up at the hall only around an hour before blast off is fairly standard procedure.

Nobody was too concerned. The band had set up their equipment themselves, so why worry?

Yet strangely, all this just adds to Hawkwind's charm. Nik Turner has always said that one reason why people get to Hawkwind gigs is that they like to see a bunch of folks, not necessarily very talented, who've just put some music together and made it work.

It helps to explain why Hawkwind, perhaps more than any other band, represent the gulf that often exists between critics and the public. Musically you could be mistaken for thinking the band have consciously adopted a policy of not improving — remaining a sort of musical dinosaur, that makes a new chord quite an event. Yet this group of one time buskers, roadies, Ladbroke Grove freaks now command a mighty following in Britain — they play an extra date at the Edmonton Sundown this week after the first was sold out — and have created a stir of interest in the States.

As might be expected, America didn't quite know how to react to Hawkwind. They were given horrendously bad reviews — one critic described Stacia as dancing like a stripper with tired blood — but as in Britain the grass roots crowd seemed to welcome the arrival of the sonic assassins, especially in Chicago.

Personally I've always felt travelling through space with Hawkwind would be rather like being stranded in the Sahara with a bunch of Eskimoes, but in Chicago they proved that their two-hour cosmic tour de force on stage does have a shattering effect, even if it's hard to tell sometimes whether it's for good or bad.

Even though the light show still does rely at times on vague, unrelated slides flowing across the screens, it's getting stronger, and the addition of effects like a police siren all adds to the confusion.

Hawkwind soldiered along with their customary heavy-handedness, running one number into another, reaching some neat climaxes at times and fouling themselves up at others.

Few other bands, one feels, sort themselves out of these situations with such calm and aplomb. Perhaps it's all a matter of what you're used to. Anyway it's the overall effect of their set that counts, not just the music, as the band will readily admit.

"I have been in more musical groups," says drummer Simon King, the only guy in the band to be a professional musician before Hawkwind and who joined them two years ago. "But when I joined Hawkwind and saw the atmosphere we were creating I thought the band had to have something.

"The point, is, people go to see a band like Yes for their music and they could just go and sit facing the wall for all they get out of it visually. But with us it's the event that counts, and the more effects we use the better."

So what does the future hold for this particular cosmic oddity? According to Nik Turner, none of them have a very set idea of the way Hawkwind should progress.

"All I can say is we're getting out of the space trip now — not concentrating so much on it — and we hope to diversity into other kinds of imagery. The space ritual project was a one-off idea and we'd like to use it now as a jumping off point for other ideas."

HAWKWIND CAUGHT IN TORNADO DRAMA

NIK TURNER

HAWKWIND, currently on tour in America, were caught up in the tornado which swept the mid-West last week. Their equipment sustained damage estimated at nearly £1,000 when the roof was ripped from the Nashville hotel in which they were staying. The band had to be evacuated from the hotel, but Nik Turner commented: "It was a terrifying experience, although fortunately we were warned in time and nobody was hurt."

The Hawks complete their U.S. tour on April 15, then return to Britain to complete their new album. Their concerts in Chicago and Detroit were recorded, but no decision has yet been made regarding a possible live album. The band are set for a European tour in May and June visiting Germany, Holland and Italy.

HAWKWIND
'Hall Of The Mountain Grill'
Released as United Artists UAG29672 in September 1974
Highest UK chart position: Number 16

The Psychedelic Warlords (Disappear in Smoke)
Wind Of Change
D-Rider
Web Weaver
You'd Better Believe It
Hall Of The Mountain Grill
Lost Johnny
Goat Willow
Paradox

The addition of keyboard-player/violinist Simon House into the ranks of Hawkwind in April 1974 would pay dividends on their fourth studio album. His presence brought a tighter, more cohesive direction to the music, felt almost immediately from the opening Dave Brock-penned 'Psychedelic Warlords (Disappear In Smoke)' and the instrumental 'Wind Of Change', dominated by House's violin and Mellotron, to Nik Turner's 'D Rider', it was clear Hawkwind were a musical force to be taken seriously.

The superb 'You'd Better Believe It' and 'Paradox' would be album highlights, taken from a concert at the Edmonton Sundown in January 1974 prior to House joining. With his keyboard overdubs, the songs became the stuff of Hawkwind legend. 'Lost Johnny', a collaboration between Lemmy and former Deviant Mick Farren, was also a fine rock workout. Graced with a cover design by Barney Bubbles, 'Hall Of The Mountain Grill' took its name from a greasy spoon hangout on Portobello Road beloved of the Ladbroke Grove underground scene; a photograph was included on the album's inner sleeve. This marvellous album would only be overshadowed by Hawkwind's even mightier 'Warrior On The Edge Of Time' the following year.

KING CRIMSON 'Larks' Tongues in Aspic'

Released as Island ILPS9230 in March 1973
Highest UK chart position: Number 20

Larks' Tongues In Aspic Part One
Book of Saturday
Exiles
Easy Money
The Talking Drum
Larks' Tongues In Aspic Part Two

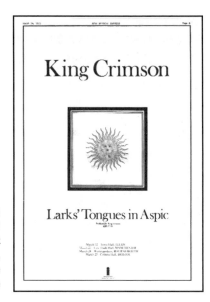

Heralding the accomplished third incarnation of King Crimson, 'Larks' Tongues In Aspic' is a highlight of the band's first spell between the years 1969 to 1974. It followed on the heels of the live album 'Earthbound' which had showcased the line-up of Robert Fripp (guitar, Mellotron), Boz Burrell (bass, vocals), Mel Collins (saxophones, flutes, Mellotron) and Ian Wallace (drums). The sound quality of the album left much to be desired, being taken from a stereo cassette recorded directly from the front-of-house mixing desk at various concerts between February and March 1972.

By the summer of that year Fripp had gathered bass player and vocalist John Wetton, eccentric percussionist Jamie Muir, violinist and Mellotron player David Cross, and had also lured drummer Bill Bruford away from Yes. Bruford's departure from such a successful band caused shockwaves in the music press on both sides of the Atlantic, but also promised much.

Recorded at Command Studios during the first two months of 1973 following a series of live dates, the material on 'Larks' Tongues In Aspic' was among the finest, and most extreme music ever recorded by the band. New lyricist Richard Palmer-James (replacing former incumbent Pete Sinfield who had now departed to work with Emerson, Lake and Palmer) perfectly complemented John Wetton's excellent vocals on 'Book Of Saturday', 'Exiles' and 'Easy Money', while Crimson's powerful dynamics were revealed in full glory on the stunning 'The Talking Drum' and both parts of the album's title track.

The full power and force of these compositions would be felt on subsequent live dates, a factor which assisted in the success of the album in both Britain and America. Jamie Muir would soon leave, to be followed by David Cross during sessions for the album 'Red', King Crimson's swansong in the Seventies and another mighty work.

KING CRIMSON'S JOHN WETTON (left) and BILL BRUFORD: working as a team this time

THE NEW King Crimson band's formation was, says former Yes drummer Bill Bruford, "a shot in the dark. We got to know each other and the equipment, after the beginning of the group.

"We'd both known Robert Fripp for a while but no-one knew anyone else," explains John Wetton, who is the group's vocalist and bass guitarist, well-known from Family. "It was sort of a bit like Robert's shopping expedition for musicians," Bill added. "He came round to my place and said 'Fancy a blow?' It wasn't until afterwards that I realised it had been a kind of audition. He'd done the same thing a few days before with Jamie Muir."

Jamie, Crimson's amazing percussion man, duly joined as well. Jamie's enormous collection of drums, gongs and pieces of metal, aren't what you would expect to find in the average rock band. In fact if there's one thing Crimson are not, it's that.

"Jamie had never played in a band with a drummer before; I'd never played in one with a percussionist like him," said Bill. "In fact, I'm not sure what Jamie was doing — I suspect it was a series of bizarre little concerts for rich Venetian ladies." John hadn't done much singing with Family, and became the main Crimson singer — not that singing is exactly at the heart of most of King Crimson's numbers. David Cross joined on violin. Bob Fripp has been Bob Fripp for quite some time, but is never a man to stand still anyway. It is one of the most experimental new bands for a long time.

Disparate

"The ingredients," as John put it "seem to be very disparate. If you come over with another King Crimson that's basically doing the same things as the last one, that smacks of another Temptations — it's only

LONG LIVE THE KING!

Many line-ups later ROB MACKIE finds that King Crimson goes soldiering on in brand new clothes, while below...

John Wetton: ex-Family man.

valid for us to be King Crimson if we're doing something entirely different."

It was sink or swim from the beginning and both the excitement of Bill and John about the group, and the date when I saw them at Great Malvern, strongly suggest they've done a

'Everyone should have to change their group once a year'

length or two already and are gathering steam for at the very least a Channel crossing.

"It's been a jolt for all of us," is how Bill put it. "And I know that's what I needed — someone to jar me. Jamie did that all right. He was the first person ever to tell me I was a shitty drummer." He looked far from hurt at the recollection. "Being in a successful band like Yes for four years and a month — it's a matter of so much pat-

ting on the back that you can lose sight of it all, get settled down.

"And that's all wrong for a musician. The idea that groups ought to stay together and the idea that they 'split up' all comes from the press. The reason most groups stay together is because of a welter of contracts

and leg-grasping, or else because it's easy — it's what people expect, and it's wrong, I think there should be a Musicians' Union ruling that everyone has to change their group every year — at least for the first five years. You can't hope to get all your musical experience you need with one group. I'm still unformed musically, and this is the ideal way to do it."

John was in general agreement: "Yes, a lot of people in bands must be very bored. The industry basically wants a successful band to stay together, so it's the easiest way to be — it's easy to say 'Life's good, why change it?' Through coming together in a band like this, you get to know more about yourself. Suddenly, you're on unsafe ground, territory you know nothing about. It's a kick up the arse. King Crimson is an adventure for all of us."

Bill: "The only way groups should stay together is if they're developing together. King Crimson are making an effort, taking risks. If it all ends in confusion then we'll have a laugh about

it. The public expects a certain standard from King Crimson, and I think we're living up to it. Nothing is impossible with this band.

"I tend not to think of us as a rock band" (John disagreed on that point) "but what's good about rock is that it expands to accommodate people who are doing something outside the accepted, to include people like Jamie. Fairport Convention, just to pick an example, were well outside of rock, and are now very much a part of it."

John: "With this band, I think it'll still be buoyant if it lasts five years. There's so much energy.

I don't mean that we all leap about on stage, but there's a lot of nervous hopping about before a gig — we might all be static on stage, but there's something coming out there, too. It comes out in a lot of ways — if you see Jamie eating a sandwich, he does that at 120 miles per hour. "

King Crimson wins my vote as the band that isn't going to get into a rut in 1973. It's not some weird, freaky band, as you might suppose from some of Bill and John's comments — just dedicatedly anti-formula. Which is of course what rock music started out as being by definition, and

which all too little of it has managed to keep faith with.

As yet, the band hasn't completed its first "cycle" (Bill's term for the round trip of rehearsing, playing, thinking and recording). The last is now pretty well completed, and as you might suppose, the "disparate ingredients" have come up with some unusual ideas. What's on it?

"Well," says Bill. "There's an industrial drum-kit". "Pardon!" It turns out that there isn't a definition for an industrial drum-kit, other than that. That was the idea of a sound they wanted, so that's what they did.

Formula

"There's no criteria for an industrial drum-kit," he explained. "It's not like going into a studio, and wanting 'a very good soul riff' — we know what that sounds like, and we could all do one."

Again, it's Crimson's refusal to fit to a formula — they are determined that not only should stage playing and recording be a breakaway from the accepted norm but that should be a breakaway from each other, too. With the album due out on March 16, and an English tour followed by "a continental whizz-round" followed in turn by an American tour in April, the enigmatic career of King Crimson looks set for another burst of colourful action.

The King is dead, long live the King. After all, nothing's impossible. Especially when a band's getting and giving as much of a kick out of what they're doing as King Crimson.

Bill Bruford: no more a Yes man.

...just around the korner! Where three other Kings went to!

TOGETHER with Danish singer Peter Thorup, Alexis Korner is a major crowd-puller on the Continent and the duo spend much of their time touring there. This month they are making a TV special in Germany and in March will be filming an hour-long special for "Hits A Go-Go" in Zurich.

This year Alexis celebrates 25 years in show-business and, reviewing his career, he discovered that 1972 was his most successful year ever. Having been recognised as a star internationally, he was much encouraged to finally achieve commercial and critical acclaim in his own country, England.

During '72 he saw his first hit album, CCS II, high in the British charts, and his fourth hit single in a row Brother. Two of CCS's hit singles, Brother and Tap Turns On The Water (performed last year for the Queen at the Royal Variety Performance), were co-written by Korner with CCS conductor-arranger John Cameron.

Alexis has long been recognised as "the father of British blues" and in '72 released a double-album called Bootleg Him which spanned his musical career from 1961 to 1971. He also received the first Gold Album of his career last June from Sweden for the first CCS album.

Each week "Top Of The Pops" opens its show with the CCS version of Whole Lotta Love and BBC Radio recently selected Brother to be the theme music for the new "Solid Gold 60" programme on Sunday afternoons.

In November, Mike Leckebush, Germany's famous producer of "Beat Club", pop

TV programme for 33 countries, launched a new series "Sounds 1972" with a special on Alexis and his Blues. Alexis also starred in two TV specials in Germany entitled "Sympathy For The Devil."

BBC Radio has tapped Korner to narrate the 13-hour radio special on The Rolling Stones scheduled for airing in the spring of 1973. Alexis was also tapped by David Frost's Paradine Productions to sing the title song in the forthcoming movie "Charlie One Eye", marking his film debut as a singer.

For the first six months of 1972, Alexis toured Europe and America with his co-star in CCS, Peter Thorup, as a duo. They had been invited to tour America as guests of Humble Pie and while there met up with King Crimson. Before long three members of Crimson joined the two singer guitarists and formed a new band of their own called Snape. They toured as top-of-the-bill attractions in Switzerland, Italy, Germany and England and completed an album Accidentally Borne In New Orleans.

Alexis is already in the homes of millions of Americans as a guest artist on two Humble Pie Gold albums and BB King's Live In London (on which King recorded a song written by Alexis called Alexis Boogie and they both play acoustic guitar together in a fantastic meeting of American and British blues). Warner Brothers Records have just given Alexis his first American recording contract and now he will be having a go at that huge country. 1973 promises to be an even bigger year for Alexis.

MOODY BLUES
'Seventh Sojourn'
Released as Threshold TH7 in November 1972
Highest UK chart position: Number 5

Lost In A Lost World
New Horizons
For My Lady
Isn't Life Strange
You And Me
The Land Of Make-Believe
When You're A Free Man
I'm Just A Singer (In A Rock And Roll Band)

In January 1972, following a period of near-constant touring and recording, the Moody Blues gathered once more to begin work on their seventh album. Justin Hayward, John Lodge, Mike Pinder, Ray Thomas and Graeme Edge all felt pressured to produce another album capable of equalling their previous achievements. As if in a desire to keep the outside world at bay, the band gathered at Beckthorns, the home of Mike Pinder, to begin work at his recently completed home studio.

'It was a ludicrous situation,' Hayward later reflected. 'We could afford to record anywhere in the world, and there we were in our keyboard-player's garage. We were so frightened of failure that we just tried to make ourselves smaller and smaller.' Thomas would also comment: 'By the time we began the sessions I think we needed a break from each other. Up to that time everywhere one of us went the others would be there too. All my experiences were their experiences.' Edge added: 'It was a strained and awkward period for us. Mike Pinder, particularly, found it difficult. We were all exhausted and had become prisoners of our own success.'

Despite an increasing sense of burnout, the Moody Blues were about to embark on recording one of their finest albums. The January recordings made at Pinder's home would become the bedrock of the new record. They would also be notable for the introduction of a new instrument by Pinder, as Hayward would later explain. 'We'd found a great replacement for the Mellotron, an American instrument called the Chamberlain. It worked on the same principle, but had much better quality sounds – great brass, strings and cello and so on. With a Mellotron you had to overdub and overlay it, adding echo to get it to sound nice. The Chamberlain was a louder instrument and had much better sound quality.'

The sessions included such wonderful compositions as John Lodge's 'Isn't Life Strange'. 'I was having dinner one night with some friends and heard the song in my head while I was eating,' he later recalled. 'I went straight to the piano and within fifteen minutes I'd got the outline of the song finished.' Also recorded in January were backing tracks for the optimistic Justin Hayward song 'You And Me' and Mike Pinder's stark 'Lost In A Lost World'. At the beginning of February work continued in the surroundings of Decca Studios in Tollington Park, London where the finishing touches were put to all three tracks. With barely time to draw breath the Moody Blues then embarked on yet another European and American tour.

Recording sessions resumed in May and would continue until the beginning of September. 'The album took a long time to make and I found it a painful experience,' Justin Hayward would later comment. 'It became obvious to me that the five of us wouldn't make another album. We didn't argue, it was just an unhappy time. No-one was really enjoying the creative process and it was a struggle to get things done.'

Despite this apathy within the band, the finished results were of an extremely high standard. Compositions such as Hayward's 'New Horizon's', Thomas' 'For My Lady', Pinder's 'When You're A Free Man' and John Lodge's 'I'm Just A Singer (In A Rock And Roll Band)' rank as some of the finest recorded by the Moody Blues.

Prior to the album's release in November 1972, the band undertook a further two-week tour of the US which assisted the album in reaching Number 1 on the Billboard chart. In the UK it rose to Number 5 and enjoyed 18 weeks on the charts. For a band seeking the solace of a break from each other, 'Seventh Sojourn' remains one of the Moody Blues' most enduring albums.

ALBUMS

Remarkable Moodies

MOODY BLUES: "The Moody Blues Seventh Sojourn" (Threshold). Anything the Moody Blues record is going to be musically good, with an incomparable production — as on this album. Naturally one cannot help but appreciate their studio performances. Whether you enjoy it is entirely a different thing.

After previous works, the Moodies have a lot to live up to regarding material and melodies. Once again they have taken their usual theme of social conscience, implying that we could make this world a lot better if we tried, and that there could be an atmosphere of universal love.

But the explanation of their themes through eight songs is different to their previous sets. So surely we can't discard their efforts as repetitive — after all, a relevant argument may be presented in many different ways.

Again, the musical presentation is interesting, sometimes crossing from ballads such as Ray Thomas's "For My Lady" and Mike Pinder's "When You're A Free Man", into good old rock and roll on "You And Me" and "I'm Just A Singer (In A Rock And Roll Band)".

Then there's the presentation of songs akin to Johnson's "Rasselas" in which the Moodies search through different aspects of society. They use the contrast of lonely travel over the sea ("For My Lady") and that of flight in "The Land Of Make-Believe".

Perhaps I'm looking a little too deeply into the meaning of this album, but I cannot help feeling that the "sojourn" mentioned in the album title

MIKE PINDER

comes with "New Horizons" and maybe "Isn't Life Strange", the latter a blissful love song with just a tinge of melancholy.

The starting point for the group's questioning does come from the philosophical Mike Pinder with "Lost In A Lost World", which states that the cruelty and injustices of the world are not moral as we all belong to the same family.

John Lodge follows this through with "I'm Just A

Singer", claiming that musicians are the bridge between discontented nations.

Of course there's absolutely no need to delve deeply into the Moodies music. It's just that some of us prefer to. As I was saying before, one has to decide whether it is good to listen to or not. I'll dawdle no longer — it is a remarkable album which will be seldom off my deck. —

Tony Stewart.

isn't life strange!

The new single from the Moody Blues.

 TH9

DECCA RECORDS SOUND · MONO & STEREO RECORDS · MONO/STEREO MUSICASSETTES · STEREO 8 CARTRIDGES
Threshold Records Decca House, Albert Embankment London SE1 7SW

LONDON WEMBLEY EMPIRE POOL SATURDAY

Moodies fly in U.S. crew and equipment for a sound spectacular

DESCRIBED BY promoters in America as the "Biggest British group in the world", the Moody Blues will take the stage at the Wembley Empire Pool on Saturday evening and perform as they do in America, with a complex sounds system on a scale grand enough to enable each note and chord to be heard by the ten thousand people who are likely to fill the mammoth arena.

It will be the first time ever the group has played outside the U.S. with equipment normally used only on American tours because

TEN UK ALBUM CHART GREATS THAT NEED LITTLE INTRODUCTION 367

MORE ALBUM REVIEWS

Floyd 'meddle' to good effect

PINK FLOYD: MEDDLE (Harvest SHVL 795; £2.40)

FLOYD have done it again; something I thought would be difficult after the brilliance they showed with the Atom Heart Mother Suite, a piece of musical mastery that took great courage to put on record, and even greater courage to perform live — which they did successfully. On the second side of this album we hear Echoes, which in many ways is more important than Atom Heart.

Side one is really three themes. One Of These Days and A Pillow Of Wind are linked to each other by the haunting wind (also a feature of Echoes, producing a continuing element), with gentle use of instruments including both acoustic and electric guitar, interplaying well. Days is more forceful, with Gilmour showing off his guitar techniques.

Fearless is on its own in many ways, with an almost countryish guitar and a variety of moods, with the football crowd chanting " You'll never walk alone " totally relevant to the theme of the lyrics. Then San Tropez and Seamus have a feel of blues mixed with jazz. The former track shows much of Wright's keyboard expertise and a more mellow Gilmour. The latter features howling dogs.

Now to Echoes — a zenith which Floyd have been striving for but only partly achieved last year. The introductory sound effects, giving the impression of a submarine underwater, provide a backcloth for the instrumentation — the effect then emerging and becoming wind. But it is more than that.

Before, I had regarded Nick Mason as a solid consistent drummer, but now he shows a lot more flair, and Gilmour, Wright and Waters all contribute strongly to the piece. The music is grand, a good example being the guitar bridge between th vocals, in what seems like a two part harmony, at the beginning. They use a similar technique in the arrangement to that used on Heart, building the music up, then easing it down, and never

letting the sound go empty, maintaining a compelling interest.

The middle part is a strong rock structure, with Gilmour cutting through hard, while Wright works around the theme. The effects, sometimes comparative to an electric cayotte, bring back the opening mood. It fades out at the end, rather than leaving you in limbo — which always makes me feel frustrated.

The important thing is that Floyd have created dramatic music without having to draw off the strength of full brass and a choir. The wind is used as the choir, and the effects of the organ soar and hold like an orchestra, with a deep bass synthesised sound like a viola.

Though this piece, Echoes, is not as adventurous in structure as Heart, I feel it is more significant because they've done it on their own. An exceptionally good album.

PINK FLOYD'S Roger Waters

THE GROUP THAT CAME IN FROM THE COLD

RICHARD WRIGHT of Pink Floyd

"YOU COULD SAY that we made it in spit of pop music," said Richard Wright, thoughtfully munching the last mouthful of eggs, bacon and tomato. He didn't mince words, though. He went on: "Our success is 99 per cent attributable to our music. It has nothing to do with images, hit singles or sex."

Nevertheless it was a long, hard grind: it took Pink Floyd almost four years to make it to the stage where they could play a seven week concert tour of America AND make money out of it.

And that ain't bad. For dozens of groups who slip across the Atlantic on the quiet, intent on making a quick killing, overlook the skyrocketing expense of it all.

At the end of two similar tours in '68 and '67 Floyd got back to England found that they had actually LOST money on the trips. Their third tour was closed, prematurely, in May.

Richard, organist and singer, explained: "We had all our equipment stolen in New Orleans, all £12,000 worth of it. We got on the radio and on television and the truck it was in was found abandoned with all our gear, except for three guitars, intact."

Too late for the final two concerts in Texas; not too soon

for Richard. He is 26, strikingly handsome, married to Juliette, a pretty dark haired girl, with a gug-gug-guggling baby daughter.

And it was a seven week tour, too long the Floyd have since decided. Next September the group goes on another USA tour, this time for three weeks.

"Seven weeks in just too long to be away from anyone you want to be with," he explained.

"It isn't just that though. In America today there is an almost frightening feeling of fear among people, particularly young people as we all know. But it is having some very strange effects.

"First of all it pushes young people and old people further and further apart, so that they are both suspicious of each other with no real reason. Then there is the incredible antagonism about long hair. They didn't bother about us . . . their attitude was 'you quaint olde English are always doing eccentric things' . . . it doesn't matter.

"But young Americans with long hair are regarded as dangerous. The whole hippie thing has turned a somersault, too. Now some of the people who were the leaders of the Love Generation have bought guns to protect themselves."

Surprisingly there was no violence during the group's

concerts, Richard said: "The audiences during our concerts were very good. The critics were magnificent . . . we didn't get one put-down during the whole tour."

It was a far cry from the days four years ago when the group each had about £5 per week to live on. "The times we thought about jacking it all in. I was living off Juliette and nothing seemed to work for the group."

He met the rest of the group through the London Polytechnic where he was studying architecture. He had previously studied music at the London College of Music for a year and a half and really got into pop music with an early Beatles number "Tomorrow Never Knows".

"There weren't any really formative things in music for me early on. I suppose if I was ever really influenced it was by people like Miles Davis."

For the next fortnight the group will be working on a new LP. One of the sides is to be orchestrated and the group hopes to take a choir on tour with them to perform. During July the group plays six major British festivals, then they holiday in August and set off for America again in September.

At last, it seems, Pink Floyd have come in from the cold.
DAVID SKAN

Pink Floyd

PINK FLOYD: Meddle (Harvest SJVL 795). Marvellous long-awaited album from a recluse group that maintains its high regard with every release. Typically professional use of studio effects, plus excellent musicianship. 'Fearless' is a superb track featuring electric guitar picking, steady drumming and an ascending base line. Terrific blend of acoustic guitar and electrics and added Liverpool football chanting to end it. Pastiche howlin' blues includes doggy wailing on 'Seamus'. The whole of side two is taken with the symphonic scale of 'Echoes'. From mood to mood, rhythm to rhythm, an expertly devised musical life-cycle that will take you down, back up, in, around, through and leave you on your way into outer space. Their best album yet.

PINK FLOYD 'Meddle'

Released as Harvest SHVL795 in October 1971
Highest UK chart position: Number 3

One Of These Days
A Pillow Of Winds
Fearless
San Tropez
Seamus
Echoes

As with so many great albums featured in this book, Pink Floyd's 'Meddle' was recorded following a period of re-evaluation. Work began in January 1971 following a lengthy tour of Europe and the USA to promote their previous album, 'Atom Heart Mother'. Although a chart-topper in the UK, the experimental nature of the album's side-long title track, co-written by avant-garde composer Ron Geesin and featuring a choir and orchestral brass ensemble, had divided opinions of fans and critics alike. Even within the ranks of Pink Floyd, doubts began to arise about the future direction of the group.

With embryonic musical ideas, sessions began at Abbey Road before moving to the more sophisticated environment of AIR Studios in London's Oxford Street to make use of newly installed 16-track recording facilities. It was here that experiments in sound utilising household objects and instruments fed through a rotating Leslie organ speaker gave birth to a series of demos entitled 'Nothings'. The most promising of these, 'Return Of The Son of Nothings', would evolve into the 22-minute 'Echoes' over the following four months.

A joint composition by David Gilmour, Nick Mason, Roger Waters and Richard Wright, this epic began with Wright's solitary piano note fed through a Leslie to emulate a sonar effect. 'Echoes' cross-faded into an eerie feedback effect overdubbed with the sound of crows cawing before returning into a mighty, spacey climax. This sublime work was joined by the excellent instrumental 'One Of These Days', the lazy 'A Pillow Of Winds' and 'San Tropez', both inspired by a group holiday with their wives to the south of France, the eccentric 'Fearless' with its coda utilising a recording of supporters of Liverpool football club chanting on the terraces on their home ground of Anfield and the bizarre blues parody 'Seamus', featuring the sound of a dog howling to Gilmour's harmonica.

This unlikely blending of styles created a masterpiece that remains inspirational, 'Echoes' being one of the finest progressive rock pieces ever written. 'Meddle's collaborative origins were far removed from the internal conflict that would mar Floyd's later years.

TRAFFIC 'John Barleycorn Must Die'
Released as Island ILPS 9116 in July 1970
Highest UK chart position: Number 11

Glad
Freedom Rider
Empty Pages
Stranger To Himself
John Barleycorn
Every Mother's Son

'John Barleycorn Must Die' began life as a solo project for Steve Winwood following his brief tenure with supergroup Blind Faith. When Traffic had broken up at the end of 1968, Winwood had been enticed by Eric Clapton to join him in a new group following the demise of Cream. Joined by fellow Cream member Ginger Baker and former Family bassist Ric Grech, Blind Faith came together in May 1969. In a matter of a few months the group had recorded a chart-topping album, performed a legendary free concert in Hyde Park, London and undertaken a lengthy US tour. By October 1969, Blind Faith was over and Winwood had retired to Olympic Studios with producer Guy Stevens to begin work on a solo album.

Recruiting former colleagues Chris Wood on flute and saxophone and Jim Capaldi on drums, it soon became obvious that the album should be the next work of a revitalised Traffic. The first two months of 1970 were spent with all three musicians working with Ginger Baker's supergroup Airforce, but by February 1970 work had begun in earnest on what would become Traffic's finest album. The jazz-influenced instrumental 'Glad' segued perfectly into 'Freedom Rider', a joyous piece jointly composed by Winwood and Capaldi. Joined by the excellent songs 'Stranger to Himself', 'Empty Pages' and 'Every Mother's Son', the album was of an outstanding consistency.

By far the most adventurous piece was Steve Winwood's arrangement of the English folk song 'John Barleycorn', initially attempted the previous year. The final version of this traditional work was evocative and sublime in its simplicity. Issued in July 1970, 'John Barleycorn Must Die' was a UK Top 40 album, but enjoyed even greater success in the US where it was a Top 5 hit. Although Traffic would deliver a stream of highly esteemed albums until their demise in 1974, 'John Barleycorn Must Die' would forever remain their creative high-water mark

June release for new Traffic LP

'JOHN BARLEYCORN', the new Traffic Album, will be released at the end of June — two weeks after its American release.

The reason for the early American release is to coincide with the beginning of Traffic's American tour, starting in New York on June 4.

The tour continues at Detroit, Boston, Philadelphia, New York's Fillmore East, Cleveland, Connecticut, St. Louis, Chicago, Minneapolis, Kansas, Fort Worth, San Antonio and Houston. There is also the possibility of some west coast dates which have still to be arranged.

Meanwhile, Dave Mason, one of the original members of Traffic, is due to have a solo album released in the autumn.

Scott dies in crash

TWENTY-SEVEN-YEAR-OLD vocalist with the Windmill group, Dick Scott, died at the weekend following a road accident. His wife was also killed when the car in which the couple were travelling went off the road. They were travelling to West Berlin at the time for a concert appearance. Dick Scott was taken to a hospital in Magdeberg, East Germany, following the incident. He died on Sunday.

With albums like this, it's getting difficult to criticise Island for anything. This is the best LP Traffic have done and it proves that nothing was lost during their nomadic wanderings. The gap left by Dave Mason has been neatly filled by Winwood's excellent acoustic guitar work. Six tracks of solid, inspired and melodic tunes in a nice combination of rock and traditional flavouring. I hated everything they did except their LP 'Traffic', which was superb. This, however, tops that. The title track is glorious. I hope Winwood gets some lead in his feet and stays put for a while. L.G.

RECORD MIRROR 25/7/70

TRAFFIC RARIN' TO GROW

TRAFFIC'S STEVE WINWOOD: Feeling strain as a trio.

WHATEVER analytical terms are used by people in attempting to define Traffic's music, however many superlatives are attached to the group and among the hundreds of thousands of words written about the members individually and collectively, the word "confusing" never seems to crop up.

But it is just such a word that is most easily and acurately applied to Traffic whose chequered career since its inception three years ago has been a constant source of perplexity.

Dave Mason's on-off flirtation with the group, the success and comparative failure of singles, the mysterious goings-on in a Berkshire cottage and, finally we all thought, the untimely split last year.

Throughout all this chaos and the occasional periods of calm, the one solid thing that has remained without any doubt has been the talent and power of Steve Winwood. Now that Traffic is together again — albeit in a different shape basically — he confesses to a slight uncertainty as to where things are going to head.

"Rick Grech is joining and we're getting a French horn and keyboard player," Steve revealed at the end of the week. "We should all be doing a lot less. Three nights in the same place is okay, but when you fly in to a place, play for an hour and then fly off to somewhere else it's cold and takes a lot of getting together."

Expanding

Steve puts the cause of the strain down to the fact that Traffic is a trio and this is why he is increasing the size. He is still uncertain, however, exactly how long it will take to develop a new sound or even if the change will be that noticable.

"We could notice it affecting the music," he admitted. "We've known it ever since we started as a trio that there's lots of things we can't do. We get lots of people coming up saying 'Listen, man, I want to join your group,' so obviously they notice it as well.

"We can't play a lot of the old songs for people because we're a trio. America made us take the decision to expand and doing the gig. We had the same problem before when we were a trio . . . it makes it more mobile, elusive, compact, but we should all be doing a lot less."

Steve describes 1967 as "our freak-out year" but adds "we all felt when we broke up just before Blind Faith that we'd never come together again."

Twirling round on a swivel chair in Island Records offices and smoking heavily, he enlarged: "We all did very different things and played with different people and learned about things. It's all so complex — there's a way that musicians have difficulty communicating ideas to each other since people stopped writing things down. It's getting very difficult just playing with people like that."

What of Blind Faith and the reasons for the split?

"It was caused by a combination of everything," Steve told me. "It wasn't so much untogether as sold out. As soon as we thought of the name it was out of our hands, we had no control about where we were going to play.

"Consequently everything was rushed, the album and everything. It tended to be four people playing their own thing, there were various attempts to get it together but it always turned out to be four individual people.

"Everyone decided that when they got back from America they were all going to do something different. I'd had enough of the whole thing and the way it was going. There was a lot of conceit coming from the supergroup tag and the way we travelled and the hotels we stayed in and the food we ate and all the things. It was 1950's Hollywood chaos!"

When all that ended Steve was "trying to make music on my own with tape machines, over-dubbing and stuff. It's a good way of writing but it's very weird. The whole thing of music is people."

He says: "I was getting to the point where I needed to play with people. Jim had come back from the States and he was just hanging about doing nothing and we just played

and there was a nice feeling. At the time we got it together with Chris, Dave Mason had just done a thing in Hollywood and he seemed to be pretty successful, though there was talk about him re-joining at one stage. He's pretty independent, though."

Steve talks about Traffic's future thus: "What we're all into is music; Jim's into his words and I'll be writing a few words. Basically we want to play more pure music, but there's always that thing that art for art's sake isn't enough. There are lots of things that need to be done."

Power

"People associate a lot of power with so-called rock stars, but it's very difficult to marry it with music. The words are just with the music, not really part of it. We want to get into a sort of travelling music-making unit.

"I suppose the album is the first step in that direction because it's a relation to folk music which is basically what I think all writers are trying to do. Pure excitement isn't really enough, it has to be channelled. People accept folk music without being ready to accept it.

"Rock music has got to come to terms with classical music, there's a lot of good things in classical music, pure musical effects. Rock musicians never write anything down, except maybe Zappa.

"John Lord's idea was great but it's still the end result that counts. Spirit did some good things with the classics. The sentiment and the end result are what counts. After it's all over, all you're left with is the sound."

The "John Barleycorn" album was to have been a solo effort by Steve as part fulfilment of a contract with United Artists. Then it turned out that Jim Capaldi and Chris Wood were in town so they were drafted in to the sessions.

"Most of it we didn't even dub on it, there's just the three of us," Steve pointed out. "It was very easy to do, we began recording just before Christmas. There's still one album to do under the contract and we'll be doing it after we've been to Moraceo next month.

"No, I'm not completely satisfied with the album, I never have been. That's what makes you want to do another one. There's lots of things I'd like to change on it, but . . ."

While Steve still isn't quite clear about Traffic's music and the way it'll turn out, he says: "Because we're not really into any theatre as such, we've got room to try other things. I've been interested for a long time in doing visuals, movie scores and a good light show."

It is generally agreed that what Traffic do now is among the best something better must be worth hearing. Let's only hope they get it all sorted out before too long this time.

With track-by-track of their new LP

TRAFFIC: JOHN BARLEYCORN MUST DIE (Island stereo ILPS 9116; 39s 11d).

THE first Traffic album for far too long consists of a mere six tracks. This is not a bad thing though because each one is fairly lengthy and given enough space in which to develop and draw to a natural conclusion.

GLAD is the first track, a STEVE WINWOOD composition. Incidentally, Steve has a hand in all six numbers, four with JIM CAPALDI. The piano is dominant with CHRIS WOOD'S sax occasionally taking the lead and the flute going off on short flights. It's a bit voodoo-ish in its concept with Jim's drums going ten to the dozen and all three members on percussion. A quieter passage towards the end introduces echo in an ethereal atmosphere that contrasts with the preceeding rhythmns.

FREEDOM RIDER runs straight on from the previous instrumental track. Steve's vocals are interspersed with sax and flute passages and, again, the organ and piano play over one another. The tempo is kept down deliberately and Chris's flute solo is excellent in its construction. A bit of a roar-up gradually develops only to end suddenly in a piano chord.

EMPTY PAGES is one of those typical Traffic numbers that allow Steve's voice to lead the way. The drumming is spot-on whether light and skipping or heavy. Both Steve and Chris play organ and the former also takes over bass guitar and electric piano, playing some remarkably well-designed riffs.

STRANGER TO HIMSELF is just about Steve's very own track — he plays all the instruments himself and is only assisted by Jim on vocal harmonies! It's a showcase for his amazing talent and underlines how vital a force he is in contemporary music. Muted lead guitar passages step in among a frenzy of drums, piano and organ.

JOHN BARLEYCORN is Steve's arrangement of a traditional song about the effect on people of drinking alcohol distilled from barley. It's light and has the feeling of the era (15th century) — acoustic guitar, piano, tambourine and flute being used to good effect. This number was a highlight of Traffic's Hollywood Festival appearance and comes over well here also.

EVERY MOTHERS SON. There's no sign of Chris on this track which is another Steve Winwood special. Apart from Jim on drums, Steve takes care of all else again. The lead guitar has most of the attention, throwing in whining passages against a lighter backing of drums and piano. When Steve's voice rises in pitch, the music goes with it to create a full sound. There's a nice section where the organ and drums take precedence over the proceedings and lead into a furious finale with all sorts of activity going on.

Caught in the shower — TRAFFIC (l to r) CHRIS WOOD, STEVIE WINWOOD and JIM CAPALDI, who have recently got together again.

Traffic: Outtakes from John Barleycorn photo shoot

YES 'Close To The Edge'
Released as Atlantic K50012 in September 1972
Highest UK chart position: Number 4

Close To The Edge
And You And I
Siberian Khatru

If any album could be said to define the music of Yes at the height of their popularity, 'Close To The Edge' would be that artefact. Featuring just three tracks, the album would reach Number 3 on the US Billboard charts and Number 4 on the UK listings, ensuring Yes a place in rock's hierarchy. The album had followed the success of 'Fragile', the group's fourth album and their first to feature Rick Wakeman on keyboards.

Entering Advision Studios in April 1972, the pivotal song was the lengthy suite 'Close To The Edge', an epic work comprising four movements composed by Jon Anderson, Steve Howe and Chris Squire. Anderson would later comment that the lyrical inspiration for the piece had been Herman Hesse's classic novel Siddhartha, a tale of spiritual rebirth and awakening. This 18-minute epic would be joined by the classic 'And You And I', with its memorable acoustic guitar introduction and superb keyboard from Rick Wakeman. Both melodic and complex, the song was destined to become a live favourite. The closing track, 'Siberian Khatru', had begun life as a demo known as 'Siberia' and offered a remarkably complex countermelody on keyboards and guitar to Jon Anderson's memorable vocal refrain.

Thanks to the skills of engineer and co-producer Eddy Offord, 'Close To The Edge' was the most technically accomplished albums by Yes to date, in addition to being the most musically sophisticated.

Soon after the album's completion in June 1972, drummer Bill Bruford announced his shock decision to leave the group of which he had been a co-founder to join a new incarnation of King Crimson. The move from a hugely successful group to one with more esoteric appeal baffled many critics, but Bruford cited the need to develop as a musician as one his reasons for departing. With Alan White as his replacement, Yes toured their new album to great acclaim upon its release in September 1972. But with Bruford's departure, an element of the creative spark that had made albums essential listening up to that point also disappeared.

Yes would continue to record music of an accomplished nature, but no future album would recapture the magic present on both sides of 'Close To The Edge'.

A NEW ALBUM FROM

"CLOSE TO THE EDGE"
ON ATLANTIC RECORDS AND TAPES

VANGELIS 'Heaven And Hell'

Released as RCA Victor RS1025 in December 1975
Highest UK chart position: Number 31

Heaven And Hell Part One

a. Bacchanale
b. Symphony To The Powers B
c. Movement Three
d. So Long Ago, So Clear

Heaven And Hell Part Two

a. Intestinal Bat
b. Needles And Bones
c. Twelve O'clock
d. Aries
e. A Way

Following the recording of the magnificent 'Earth' in 1973, Vangelis undertook two live concerts in Paris and London to promote his latest work. While in London he made the decision to relocate to the city from Paris, his home since arriving in France with Aphrodite's Child in 1968. He eventually made the move in July 1974, building a studio in a building that had previously housed a school just off the Edgware Road.

His arrival in England had led to an invitation by Jon Anderson for Vangelis to join Yes to fill the place left by Rick Wakeman. Anderson had been an admirer of the Aphrodite's Child album '666' and considered Vangelis to be an ideal replacement. However, following three weeks of rehearsals, Vangelis decided to pursue his career as a solo artist. The construction of his new Nemo studio in London necessitated him undertaking commissions to write a series of film soundtracks, and work preparing the studio continued at a slow pace.

By the beginning of 1975 synthesiser technology had moved ahead considerably with advent of the first polyphonic synthesisers, enabling more than a single note to played on a keyboard at a time. With the prospect of being able to play chords without having to build them up through a process of time-consuming overdubbing, Vangelis utilised the instrument as a more spontaneous means of writing. Signing a contract with RCA Records in the UK, Vangelis began his next album in September 1975 at Nemo. Composing music on the themes of heaven and hell, Vangelis created one of the masterpieces of electronic music.

'That period was not an easy time for me,' he would later reflect. 'I was recording 'while construction was still taking place in my studio. There was unmixed concrete everywhere and builders all over the place making a lot of noise while I was working.' Considering the chaos of the surroundings, the quality of the music that would comprise his next album would be even more remarkable. The first part of the work was divided into three movements and was dominated by dramatic synthesiser work and a choral arrangement featuring the English Chamber Choir conducted by Guy Protheroe that gave way to a reflective delicate piece 'So Long Ago, So Clear', featuring a vocal by Jon Anderson. The second part of the piece had five shorter movements but was equally impressive.

Released in December 1975, 'Heaven And Hell' introduced Vangelis' music to a wider public and was greeted with acclaim by critics. Reaching a height of Number 31 in the UK charts, 'Heaven And Hell' would become even more enduring when a movement from the first part of the piece was selected as soundtrack music for the television series Cosmos, written by Carl Sagan, two years later. The start of a series of stunning albums by Vangelis, 'Heaven And Hell' remains a breathtaking work.

TEN GREAT PROGRESSIVE AND UNDERGROUND ROCK SINGLES

1967

FAMILY 'Scene Through The Eye Of A Lens' b/w 'Gypsy Woman'
Released as Liberty LBF15031 in October 1967

This exciting slab of vinyl introduced the wonderful band from Leicester to the wider world. Praised by contemporaries such as John Lennon, Family's debut release was produced by Jimmy Miller, noted for his production work with Traffic, Spooky Tooth and, later, the Rolling Stones. With guest appearances by Dave Mason and Jim Capaldi from Traffic, this is one of the great singles of 1967. Family would go on to achieve greatness and chart success with a succession of imaginative albums, beginning with 'Music In A Doll's House', produced by Dave Mason. 'Scene Through The Eye Of A Lens' was an impressive beginning to their story.

THE FAMILY: Scene Through The Eye Of A Lens; Gypsy Woman (Liberty LBF 15031). Lots of promise in this group. A cleverly commercial top deck and imaginative Jimmy Miller production. Almost eerie in parts. Do hear it. ★ ★ ★ ★

Record Mirror 14/10/67

PRETTY THINGS 'Defecting Grey' b/w 'Walking Through My Dreams'
Released as Columbia DB8300 in November 1967

Recorded at Abbey Road while Pink Floyd were working on their first album and the Beatles were completing 'Sgt Pepper', this psychedelic masterpiece was the Pretty Things' first release for EMI's Columbia label. 'Defecting Grey' was the product of many hours of studio experimentation with producer Norman Smith. Opening with a whimsical psychedelic story, the song dramatically lurched into powerful rock before crashing back to earth with a phased organ swirl. Originally nearly ten minutes long, the track was edited to more manageable length and released as the A-side of a single. Simply unique and utterly awe-inspiring.

1968

LOVE SCULPTURE 'Sabre Dance' b/w 'Think Of Love'
Released as Parlophone R5744 in October 1968
Highest UK chart position: Number 5

Love Sculpture's third single was released by EMI's Parlophone imprint following the release of the album 'Blues Helping' on which Dave Edmunds, John Williams and Bob 'Congo' Jones had performed an admirable array of blues standards. Keen to branch out from this direction (Edmunds would later comment 'We were never a blues band'), the release of a blistering guitar-dominated interpretation of Khachaturian's classical 'Sabre Dance' followed a performance of this live favourite for John Peel's Radio 1 show Top Gear, after which he was inundated by demands to repeat the session.

Parlophone rush-released the single in late October 1968 and it reached the UK Top 10 the following month. Its success proved to be both a blessing and curse for the band, but 'Sabre Dance' remains one of the finest rock singles of 1968.

DEFECTING GREY
Mr. EVASION
The Pretty Things

SABRE DANCE
LOVE SCULPTURE

1969

PETE BROWN'S BATTERED ORNAMENTS
'The Week Looked Good On Paper' b/w 'Morning Call'
Released as Parlophone R5767 in March 1969

Pete Brown had several abortive attempts at establishing himself as a bandleader in his own right prior to the formation of the Battered Ornaments in 1969. As a poet, lyricist and writing partner of Jack Bruce, Pete had proved himself to be the supreme wordsmith of the psychedelic and emerging progressive eras.

He formed the Battered Ornaments in late 1968 with musicians Rob Tait (drums), Chris Spedding (guitar), George Khan (sax) and Roger Potter (bass), signing to EMI Records in January 1969 and recording this superb single for the Parlophone imprint soon after. Featuring guest Dick Heckstall Smith on saxophone alongside Khan, the A-side was a fine psych/jazz crossover track with wonderful Brown lyrics. 'Morning Call' was equally fine, a more uptempo affair that heralded the excellence of the group.

Brown's tenure with the band was to be short-lived. Following the release of the album 'A Meal You Can Shake Hands With In The Dark' for EMI's Harvest label, he was dismissed from the band on the eve of their performance opening for the Rolling Stones in Hyde Park. Undeterred, Brown formed the even better Piblokto! and recorded two albums and a clutch of excellent singles.

1970

RARE BIRD 'Sympathy'
b/w 'Devil's High Concern'
Released as Charisma CB120 in January 1970
Highest UK chart position: Number 27

The second single to be issued by Charisma Records would also give the label their first significant international hit. This group-composed effort was a worthy successor to Procol Harum's 'A Whiter Shade of Pale', utilising a classically influenced organ motif alongside a superb vocal from Steve Gould. 'Sympathy' reached Number 27 on the UK chart and became a Number 1 single in several European countries, achieving Top 10 status in most others.

In all, over two million copies of the single were sold and 'Sympathy' went on to become the top publishing hit of 1970, to date inspiring over 200 separate cover versions. Equally impressive was the B-side, 'Devil's High Concern', a muscular progressive rock track surprisingly omitted from a future album release and a plausible contender for a single A-side in its own right.

1971

ATOMIC ROOSTER 'Devil's Answer' b/w 'The Rock'
Released as B&C Records CB157 in June 1971
Highest UK chart position: Number 4

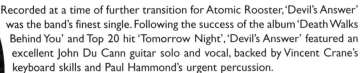

Recorded at a time of further transition for Atomic Rooster, 'Devil's Answer' was the band's finest single. Following the success of the album 'Death Walks Behind You' and Top 20 hit 'Tomorrow Night', 'Devil's Answer' featured an excellent John Du Cann guitar solo and vocal, backed by Vincent Crane's keyboard skills and Paul Hammond's urgent percussion.

All of these elements assisted in the single reaching Number 4 in the UK chars and attaining similar heights throughout Europe. Soon after its release, former Leafhound vocalist Pete French joined the group to begin work on the album 'In Hearing of Atomic Rooster'. In the US, Elektra selected 'Devil's Answer' for single release, intending it to promote the band prior to their first Stateside tour. At their insistence John Du Cann's vocals were replaced by Pete French, making the US release a much sought-after rarity. However, it is the UK version of 'Devil's Answer' that remains Atomic Rooster's most essential single.

EDGAR BROUGHTON BAND 'Hotel Room' b/w 'Call Me A Liar'
Released as Harvest HAR5040 in 1971 in June 1971

At first glance, the Edgar Broughton Band were unlikely contenders for chart success, but prior to the release of this, their finest single, the Broughtons had already enjoyed two Top 40 UK hits with 'Out Demons, Out' and 'Apache Dropout'. With 'Hotel Room' and 'Call Me A Liar', the band really excelled themselves. 'Hotel Room' was a Rob (Edgar) Broughton-penned piece that evoked shades of Morricone's spaghetti western soundtracks, while 'Call Me A Liar' was an uptempo anti-establishment rocker of the highest calibre.

Issued as a double A-sided single, both sides of the disc were played on daytime radio, much to the surprise of Broughton. 'I woke up one morning to a phonecall from a friend who told me that Tony Blackburn had played "Hotel Room" on his show and that it was going to be his record of the week. Blackburn actually stated that he hated everything we stood for, but that the single was the best thing he had heard that year. It was bizarre that by not playing the game we had been able to secure airplay on mainstream radio regardless.'

Despite such unlikely support, the single failed to register as a result of a national postal strike making compilation of charts in the UK impossible. A classic 45, It is a great injustice that such a wonderful record failed to earn its just reward.

1972

JONESY 'Ricochet' b/w 'Every Day's The Same'
Released as Dawn DNS1030 in October 1972

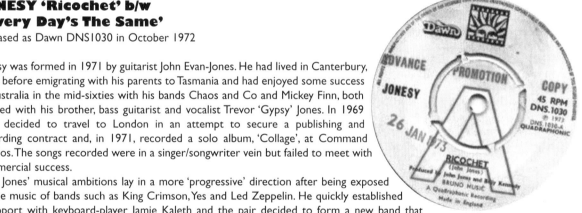

Jonesy was formed in 1971 by guitarist John Evan-Jones. He had lived in Canterbury, Kent before emigrating with his parents to Tasmania and had enjoyed some success in Australia in the mid-sixties with his bands Chaos and Co and Mickey Finn, both formed with his brother, bass guitarist and vocalist Trevor 'Gypsy' Jones. In 1969 John decided to travel to London in an attempt to secure a publishing and recording contract and, in 1971, recorded a solo album, 'Collage', at Command Studios. The songs recorded were in a singer/songwriter vein but failed to meet with commercial success.

Jones' musical ambitions lay in a more 'progressive' direction after being exposed to the music of bands such as King Crimson, Yes and Led Zeppelin. He quickly established a rapport with keyboard-player Jamie Kaleth and the pair decided to form a new band that would explore a different musical path. After a number of auditions were undertaken the first line-up of Jonesy came together, with Evan-Jones and Kaleth joined by David Paull on bass guitar and Jim Payne on drums. Through Bruno Management the band secured a contract with Dawn Records at the end of 1971 and Jonesy's debut album, 'No Alternative', was released in October 1972.

The title track drew comparisons with King Crimson and the album would feature extensive use of the Mellotron, the instrument featuring heavily for the remainder of Jonesy's recording career. The excellent single 'Ricochet' b/w 'Every Day's The Same', released prior to the appearance of the 'No Alternative' album, had the distinction of being the first 45rpm disc (and one of only a few) to be released in quadraphonic. 'Ricochet' was a strong single, but despite an infectious hook the record failed to chart.

Two further excellent albums would follow for Dawn Records before Jonesy disbanded, and trumpet-player Alan Bown would also grace their ranks. The three albums and one single Jonesy made for Pye's Dawn label in 1972 and 1973 featured some of the most imaginative music of the progressive era and some of the finest issued by the label. Of this, 'Ricochet' is their most outstanding.

VAN DER GRAAF GENERATOR 'Theme One' b/w 'W'
Released as Charisma CB175 in February 1972

The last vinyl offering from Van der Graaf Generator before the band took a two-and-a-half-year hiatus is a marvellous coupling. 'Theme One' was an interpretation of the George Martin composition written by the famous producer as incidental music to open and close the transmissions of BBC Radio 1 in its early days. Subject to an imaginative rearrangement dominated by Hugh Banton's Gothic organ work and David Jackson's supreme saxophone-playing, this instrumental track had all the hallmarks of a potential hit single, but failed to hit the UK listings. In Italy, it provided the band with another chart appearance following the Top 5 success of the album 'Pawn Hearts'.

The single's B-side, 'W', was a Peter Hammill composition recorded during sessions for their recent album. 'When we recorded "W",' he would later recall, 'we had driven all the way from Newcastle directly to Trident Studios in Soho. We tumbled out of the van, went into the studio, recorded the track and finally were able to go home, such was the pace of life for us in those days!' It was a pace of life that would lead to Hammill opting to take time out from touring to develop his career as a solo artist. Van der Graaf's interpretation of 'Theme One' featured as the theme to BBC Radio 1's Friday Rock Show for many years, ensuring its place in the hearts of all progressive rock fans.

1973

HAWKWIND 'Urban Guerrilla' b/w 'Brainbox Pollution'
Released as United Artists UP35566 in August 1973
Highest UK chart position: Number 39

Following their tremendous success with both the 'Silver Machine' single and the impressive 'Space Ritual' tour, this Dave Brock and Robert Calvert opus was an obvious contender for release as a single in an attempt to emulate the success of Hawkwind's previous seven-inch outing. Satirising the various terrorist groups that had emerged throughout Europe with the biting Calvert lyric 'Let's not talk of love and flowers and things that don't explode', the single had the misfortune to be released at the same point as the IRA embarked on a campaign of terrorist bombings on the UK mainland.

The single had entered the UK singles chart at Number 39 in the week of its release, but progress was halted when United Artists, in consultation with the band, decided to withdraw it from release, feeling its subject-matter could be misinterpreted by the British media. This denied much of the Hawkwind faithful the chance to hear the equally excellent flipside, a tale of drug-induced psychosis that fused a traditional rock'n'roll riff with Hawkwind's unique brand of acid rock. Despite this setback, Hawkwind continued to move on to greater creative heights with their next two studio albums for United Artists. 'Urban Guerrilla' is an oft-overlooked gem in Hawkwind's extensive repertoire, and arguably their finest single issued during the period covered by this book.

HAWKWIND WITHDRAW 'GUERILLA'

HAWKWIND'S new single "Urban Guerilla" has been withdrawn form the market with immediate effect by United Artists, at the special request of the group themselves — despite the fact that the Hawks are currently undertaking a tour to promote the record, which is on the verge of Chart entry. Reason for the withdrawal is the current spate of bombings in Central London.

A spokesman for the group commented: "Although the record was selling very well, we didn't want to feel that any sales might be gained by association with recent events — even though the song was written by Bob Calvert two years ago as a satirical comment, and was recorded three months ago."

At the group's suggestion, United Artists now plan to release the "B" side of "Urban Guerilla" as a new single. It is "Brainbox Pollution" and will be out as soon as possible.

Hawkwind's LEMMY — with his best friend.

MANCHESTER

Sunday 11th February. Tickets £1.00, 80p

| JEFF | TIM | CARMINE |

BECK, BOGERT, APPICE

Thursday 22nd February Tickets 75p. 50p

FAIRPORT CONVENTION

Tuesday 27th February. Tickets: £1.50, £1.25

SLADE

Tickets available from:
HARDROCK BOX OFFICE, ONE STOP RECORDS
PAPER CHASE, HIME & ADDISON

The Hardrock Concert Theatre, Greatsone Road
Stretford, Manchester. Tel. 061-865 6023/4

SALFORD UNIVERSITY Students' Union

Friday, 9th February, 8 p.m.-12.30 a.m.
MAIN HALL
JULIE FELIX
THE YETTIES
MIKE MARAN
60p advance, 65p on door.
Non-Students welcome

UNIVERSITY OF LANCASTER SOCIAL COMMITTEE

Friday, 9th February

SHARKS
MIKE ABSALOM
JO-ANNE KELLY'S SPARE RIB
Tickets 60p

Wednesday, 14th February

GRIMMS
Tickets 60p

Friday, 23rd February

GENESIS
+ STRING DRIVEN THING
Tickets 70p

COUNTY ROCK NORTHAMPTON C.C.C. WANTAGE ROAD

Saturday, 10th February

VINEGAR JOE
+ MOJO HANNAH

Lights   Doors Open 8 p.m.   Bar

Leeds Polytechnic Union Calverley Street Leeds 1   Telephone 0532 30171

IN CONJUNCTION WITH LEEDS ARTS FESTIVAL

Thursday Feb. 8th   30p & 40p
At Leeds Town Hall
STOMU YAMASH'TA

Friday, Feb. 9th   50p
At The Polytechnic
GRIMMS

Saturday, Feb. 10th   60p
At The University
BECK, BOGERT, APPICE
+ FLASH

Monday Feb. 12th   30p
At The Irish Centre
PLANXTY

S.A.E. for tickets. Doors open 8 p.m. Starts 8.30 p.m.
LIGHTS BY DAFYDD

GLEN BALLROOM, LLANELLI
Saturday, 10th February
Tony Kaye's
BADGER
+ FRUUPP
Next Week: **STEALER'S WHEEL**

CHAMPION PROMOTIONS
presents
LOCARNO STEVENAGE
This Sunday February 11th at 7.30 p.m.

FAMILY
+ SUPPORT

Advance Tickets 90p (Tel. Stevenage 2833) £1 on door

Next Sun. Feb. 13
VINEGAR JOE

THE REGENCY DISCO Ilkeston Derby Tel: 4155

THE FRIDAY ROCK SCENE

Feb. 9th **CLIMAX CHICAGO**
Feb. 16th **MAN**
Feb. 23rd **STACKRIDGE**
7.30 - 11 p.m. Adm. 60p BAR

THE LONDONER
2 East India Dock Road, London, E.14
Every Sunday at 8 p.m.

THE DYNAMIC
TERRY SEYMOUR BIG BAND

*12 top-class studio musicians combine to present their
exciting music to you, the public, for the price of a pint.
Enjoy a meal in our excellent restaurant.*

384

The Catalogue...

ESOTERIC:

ECLEC2001	Rare Bird	Rare Bird
ECLEC2002	Rare Bird	As Your Mind Flies
ECLEC2003	Egg	The Civil Surface
ECLEC2004	Daevid Allen	Good Morning!
ECLEC2005	Paladin	Paladin
ECLEC2006	Paladin	Charge!
ECLEC2007	Marsupilami	Arena
ECLEC2008	Big Sleep	Bluebell Wood
ECLEC2009	Jonesy	Masquerade - The Dawn Anthology
ECLEC2010	Barclay James Harvest	Legacy
ECLEC2011	Space Ritual	Otherworld
ECLEC2012	Man	Man
ECLEC2013	Man	Do You Like It Here Now, Are...
ECLEC2014	Man	Live At The Pagents Room
ECLEC2015	Love Sculpture	Blues Helping
ECLEC2016	Love Sculpture	Forms And Feelings
ECLEC2017	Maestoso	Caterwauling
ECLEC2018	Man	Christmas At The Patti
ECLEC2019	Man	Be Good To Yourself At Least
ECLEC2020	Man	Rhinos, Winos And Lunatics
ECLEC2024	Claire Hamill	The Minor Fall, The Major Lift
ECLEC2025	Samurai	Samurai
ECLEC2026	Michael Moorcock & Deep Fix	New World's Fair
ECLEC2027	Web	I Spider
ECLEC2028	Fair Weather	Beginning From An End
ECLEC2029	Gary Farr	Strange Fruit
ECLEC2030	Heaven	Brass Rock 1
ECLEC2031	Claire Hamill	One House Left Standing
ECLEC2032	Claire Hamill	October
ECLEC2033	East Of Eden	Mercator Projected
ECLEC2034	East Of Eden	Snafu
ECLEC2035	Egg	Egg
ECLEC2036	Egg	The Polite Force
ECLEC2037	Bill Fay	Bill Fay
ECLEC2038	Bill Fay	Time Of The Last Persecution
ECLEC2039	Julian's Treatment	A Time Before This
ECLEC2040	Julian Jay Savarin	Waiter's On The Dance
ECLEC2041	John G. Perry	Sunset Wading
ECLEC2042	Bond And Brown	Two Heads Are Better Than One
ECLEC2043	Room	Pre-Flight
ECLEC2044	Mellow Candle	Swaddling Songs
ECLEC2045	Denny Gerrard	Sinister Morning
ECLEC2046	Khan	Space Shanty
ECLEC2047	Keef Hartley Band	The Time Is Near
ECLEC2048	Keef Hartley Band	Overdog
ECLEC2049	Giles Giles And Fripp	Cheerful Insanity Of....
ECLEC2050	Keef Hartley Band	Halfbreed
ECLEC2051	Keef Hartley Band	Little Big Band
ECLEC2052	Keef Hartley Band	Battle Pf North West Six
ECLEC2053	Stud	Stud
ECLEC2055	Web	Theraphosa Blondi
ECLEC2056	Supersister	Present From Nancy
ECLEC2057	Supersister	To The Highest Bidder
ECLEC2058	Supersister	Iskander
ECLEC2059	Supersister	Pudding En Gistern
ECLEC2060	Man	Back Into The Future
ECLEC2061	Man	Maximum Darkness
ECLEC2062	Man	Slow Motion
ECLEC2063	Jan Schelhaas	Dark Ships
ECLEC2064	Darryl Way's Wolf	Night Music
ECLEC2065	Darryl Way's Wolf	Canis Lupus
ECLEC2066	Darryl Way's Wolf	Saturation Point
ECLEC2067	Curved Air	Live
ECLEC2068	Claire Hamill	Voices
ECLEC2069	Satisfaction	Satisfaction
ECLEC2070	Claire Hamill	Love In The Afternoon
ECLEC2071	Walrus	Walrus
ECLEC2072	West, Bruce And Laing	Live 'N' Kickin'
ECLEC2073	Jack Bruce And Friends	I've Always Wanted To Do This
ECLEC2074	National Head Band	Albert 1
ECLEC2075	West, Bruce And Laing	Whatever Turns You On
ECLEC2076	Quintessence	Self
ECLEC2077	Claire Hamill	Touchpaper
ECLEC2078	Ashley Hutchings	My Land Is Your Land
ECLEC2079	Chris Wood	Vulcan
ECLEC2080	Web, The	Fully Interlocking
ECLEC2081	Stomu Yamashta	Go
ECLEC2082	Stomu Yamashta	The Man From The East
ECLEC2083	Stomu Yamashta	One By One (East Wind)
ECLEC2084	Stomu Yamashta	Floating Music
ECLEC2085	Stomu Yamashta	Raindog
ECLEC2086	Stomu Yamashta	Go Live In Paris
ECLEC2087	Stomu Yamashta	Freedom Is Frightening
ECLEC2088	Trader Horne	Morning Way
ECLEC2089	Quintessence	Indweller
ECLEC2090	Hardin And York	The World's Smallest Big Band
ECLEC2091	Rare Bird	Somebody's Watching
ECLEC2092	Rare Bird	Born Again
ECLEC2093	Cmu	Open Spaces
ECLEC2094	Cmu	Space Cabaret
ECLEC2095	Marsupilami	Marsupilami
ECLEC2096	Neil Ardley	Harmony Of The Spheres
ECLEC2097	Arc	Arc...At This
ECLEC2098	Galliard	Strange Pleasure
ECLEC2099	Galliard	New Dawn
ECLEC2100	Keef Hartley Band	Seventy Second Brave
ECLEC2101	Keef Hartley	Lancashire Hustler
ECLEC2102	Fruupp	Seven Secrets
ECLEC2103	Fruupp	The Prince Of Heaven's Eyes
ECLEC2104	Fruupp	Future Legends
ECLEC2105	Fruupp	Modern Masquerades
ECLEC2106	Jimmy Campbell	Son Of Anastasia
ECLEC2107	Jimmy Campbell	Half Baked
ECLEC2108	Jimmy Campbell	Jimmy Campbell's Album
ECLEC2109	Tom Newman	Faerie Symphony
ECLEC2110	Jackie Mcauley	Jackie Mcauley
ECLEC2111	Demon Fuzz	Afreaka!
ECLEC2112	Paul Brett Sage	Paul Brett Sage
ECLEC2113	Paul Brett Sage	Jubilation Foundry
ECLEC2114	Paul Brett Sage	Schizophrenia
ECLEC2115	William R. Strickland	...Is Only The Name
ECLEC2116	Jack Bruce	Automatic
ECLEC2117	Fire	The Magic Shoemaker
ECLEC2118	Deviants, The	Ptooff!
ECLEC2119	Deviants, The	Disposable
ECLEC2120	Deviants, The	Deviants Three
ECLEC2121	Mick Farren	Mona - The Carnivorour Circus
ECLEC2122	Barclay James Harvest	Live
ECLEC2125	Daevid Allen	Now Is The Happiest Time Of...
ECLEC2126	Gilgamesh	Another Fine Tune You've Got Me
ECLEC2127	Man	Revelation
ECLEC2128	Man	2 Oz's Of Plastic With A Hole
ECLEC2129	National Health	National Health
ECLEC2130	National Health	Of Queues And Cures
ECLEC2131	Soft Heap	Soft Heap
ECLEC2133	Spooky Tooth W/ Pierre Henry	Ceremony
ECLEC2134	Fat Mattress	Fat Mattress
ECLEC2135	Fat Mattress	Fat Mattress II
ECLEC2136	Circus	Circus
ECLEC2137	Dick Heckstall-Smith	A Story Ended
ECLEC2139	Hatfield And The North	Hatfield And The North
ECLEC2140	Hatfield And The North	The Rotters' Club
ECLEC2141	Eric Burdon	Mirage
ECLEC2142	Graeme Edge Band	Kick Off Your Muddy Boots
ECLEC2143	Graeme Edge Band	Paradise Ballroom
ECLEC2144	Alquin	Marks
ECLEC2145	Alquin	The Mountain Queen
ECLEC2146	Earth And Fire	Earth And Fire
ECLEC2147	Earth And Fire	Song Of The Marching Children
ECLEC2148	Earth And Fire	Atlantis
ECLEC2149	Thunderclap Newman	Hollywood Dream
ECLEC2150	Armageddon	Armageddon
ECLEC2151	Stomu Yamashta	Go Too
ECLEC2152	Morgan	Nova Solis

ECLEC2154	Camel	Stationary Traveller
ECLEC2155	Camel	Breathless
ECLEC2156	Camel	Single Factor
ECLEC2158	Camel	I Can See Your House From Here
ECLEC2159	Camel	Nude (Expanded Edition)
ECLEC2160	Tony Banks	A Curious Feeling
ECLEC2163	Steve Swindells	Messages (Expanded Edition)
ECLEC2164	Igginbottom	Igginbottom's Wrench
ECLEC2165	Peter Banks	Two Sides Of Peter Banks
ECLEC2166	Flash	Flash
ECLEC2167	Darryl Way	Concerto For Electric Violin
ECLEC2168	Sweet Okay Supersister	Spiral Staircase
ECLEC2169	Made In Sweden	Made In England
ECLEC2170	Jackson Heights	The Fifth Avenue Bus
ECLEC2171	Jackson Heights	Ragamuffins Fool
ECLEC2172	Jackson Heights	Bump N Grind
ECLEC2174	Wigwam	Nuclear Nightclub
ECLEC2175	Wigwam	The Lucky Golden Stripes And Straprose
ECLEC2176	Pekka Pohjola	B The Magpie
ECLEC2177	Pekka Pohjola	The Mathematicians Air Display
ECLEC2179	Arthur Brown & Kingdom Come	Galactic Zoo Dossier
ECLEC2180	Ken Hensley	Proud Words On A Dusty Shelf
ECLEC2181	Ken Hensley	Eager To Please
ECLEC2182	Wigwam	Fairyport
ECLEC2183	Wigwam	Being
ECLEC2184	Ramases	Glass Top Coffin
ECLEC2185	Wigwam	Live Music From The Twilight Zone
ECLEC2186	Arthur Brown & Kingdom Come	Kingdom Come
ECLEC2187	Arthur Brown & Kingdom Come	Journey
ECLEC2188	Bob Downes	Electric City
ECLEC2189	Bob Downes	Open Music
ECLEC2190	Alan Bown	The Alan Bown
ECLEC2191	Home	The Alchemist
ECLEC2192	Parlour Band, The	Is A Friend
ECLEC2193	Alan Bown	Listen
ECLEC2194	Alan Bown	Stretching Out
ECLEC2196	Soft Machine	Bundles
ECLEC2197	Sam Gopal	Escalator
ECLEC2198	Jade Warrior	Way Of The Sun
ECLEC2199	Jade Warrior	Kites
ECLEC2200	Flash	Out Of Our Hands
ECLEC2201	Flash	In The Can
ECLEC2202	Soft Machine	Softs
ECLEC2203	High Tide	High Tide
ECLEC2204	High Tide	Sea Shanties
ECLEC2205	Aphrodites Child	End Of The World
ECLEC2206	Aphrodites Child	Its Five O'clock
ECLEC2207	Fields	Fields
ECLEC2208	Soft Machine	Land Of Cockayne
ECLEC2209	Asgard	In The Realms Of Asgard
ECLEC2210	Jade Warrior	Floating World
ECLEC2211	Jade Warrior	Waves
ECLEC2212	Trifle	First Meeting
ECLEC2213	Cafe Jacques	Round The Block
ECLEC2214	Cafe Jacques	International
ECLEC2215	Juicy Lucy	Juicy Lucy
ECLEC2216	Juicy Lucy	Lie Back And Enjoy It
ECLEC2217	Barclay James Harvest	A Concert For The People (Berlin)
ECLEC2218	Blonde On Blonde	Contrasts
ECLEC2220	Peter Bardens	Peter Bardens
ECLEC2221	Peter Bardens	The Answer
ECLEC2222	Here & Now	Give And Take
ECLEC2223	Here & Now	All Over The Show
ECLEC2224	Machiavel	Jester
ECLEC2225	Machiavel	Mechanical Moonbeams
ECLEC2226	Titus Groan	Titus Groan
ECLEC2227	Randy California	Kapt. Kopter And The (Fabulous) Twirly Birds
ECLEC2228	Locomotive	We Are Everything You See
ECLEC2229	The Dog That Bit People	The Dog That Bit People
ECLEC2231	Renaissance	Renaissance
ECLEC2232	Renaissance	Illusion
ECLEC2235	Pierre Moerlen's Gong	Downwind
ECLEC2236	Pierre Moerlen's Gong	Time Is The Key
ECLEC32157	Barclay James Harvest	Sea Of Tranquility
ECLEC22123	Barclay James Harvest	Live Tapes (Expanded)
ECLEC22124	Woolly Wolstenholme & Maestoso	Uneasy Listening
ECLEC22132	Spooky Tooth	Lost In My Dream
ECLEC22138	Liverpool Scene, The	The Amazing Adventures Of...
ECLEC22161	Tony Banks	A Curious Feeling (Cd+Dvd)
ECLEC22162	Camel	Pressure Points ~ Live In Concert
ECLEC22178	Arthur Brown	The Crazy World Of Arthur Brown
ECLEC22195	Clark-Hutchinson	Free To Be Stoned - The Complete
ECLEC22230	Mountain	Crossroader ~ An Anthology 1970-74
ECLEC22233	John Lees	A Major Fancy
ECLEC22234	Soft Machine	Alive And Well Recorded In Paris
ECLEC32173	Various Artists	Cave Of Clear Light - Pye Anth. (3cd)
ECLEC42219	Ray Thomas	From Mighty Oaks...(4cd Box)
ECLECBOX1	Jack Bruce	Can You Follow At Six (6cd Set)

ATOMHENGE:

ATOMCD1001	Robert Calvert	Freq
ATOMCD1005	Hawkwind	Astounding Sounds Amazing...
ATOMCD1008	Hawkwind	Electric Teepee
ATOMCD1010	Hawkwind	Pxr 5
ATOMCD1011	Hawkwind	Live Seventy Nine
ATOMCD1012	Hawkwind	Chronicle Of The Black Sword
ATOMCD1014	Hawklords	Live '78
ATOMCD1015	Steve Swindells	Fresh Blood
ATOMCD1017	Robert Calvert	Captain Lockheed And The Starfighters
ATOMCD1018	Hawkwind	Alien 4
ATOMCD1020	Harvey Bainbridge	Dreams Omens & Strange
ATOMCD1021	Hawkwind	Church Of Hawkwind
ATOMCD1022	Hawkwind	The Xenon Codex
ATOMCD1023	Psychedelic Warriors	White Zone
ATOMCD1024	Lloyd Langston Group	Night Air
ATOMCD1025	Hawkwind	Space Bandits
ATOMCD2006	Hawklords	25 Years On
ATOMCD2007	Hawkwind	Live Chronicles
ATOMCD2009	Hawkwind	Quark, Strangeness And Charm
ATOMCD2013	Hawkwind	Love In Space
ATOMCD2019	Hawkwind	Sonic Attack
ATOMCD2026	Hawkwind	Choose Your Masques
ATOMCD3016	Hawkwind	Levitation (Expanded Edition)
ATOMBOX3002	Hawkwind	Spirit Of The Age: 1976-84
ATOMBOX3003	Hawkwind	The Dream Goes On: 1985 - 1997

REACTIVE:

EREACD1001	Schike Fuhrs & Frohling	Symphonic Pictures
EREACD1002	Schike Fuhrs & Frohling	Sunburts
EREACD1003	Fuhrs & Frohling	Ammerland
EREACD1004	Schike Fuhrs & Frohling	Ticket To Everywhere
EREACD1005	Brainticket	Psychonaut
EREACD1006	Brainticket	Celestial Ocean
EREACD1007	Eela Craig	One Niter
EREACD1008	Deuter	D
EREACD1009	Deuter	Aum
EREACD1010	Out Of Focus	Wake Up
EREACD1012	Out Of Focus	Out Of Focus
EREACD21011	Out Of Focus	Four Letter Monday Afternoon

MANTICORE:

MANTCD1001	Stray Dog	Stray Dog (Expanded edition)
MANTCD1002	Stray Dog	While You're Down There
MANTCD21003	Pete Sinfield	Still (Expanded Edition)
MANTCD21004	P F M	River Of Life - The Manticore Years
MANTCD1005	P F M	The World Became The World
MANTCD1006	P F M	Photos Of Ghosts
MANTCD1007	P F M	Jet Lag
MANTCD2008	P F M	Chocolate Kings
MANTCD1009	Banco	Banco
MANTCD1010	Banco	As In A Last Supper
MANTCD3011	P F M	Cook
MANTCD31011	P F M	Cook (3CD)
MANTCD21012	Keith Christmas	Tomorrow Never Ends

Other titles available from Cherry Red Books:

You're Wondering Now - The Specials from Conception to Reunion
Paul Williams

Celebration Day – A Led Zeppelin Encyclopedia
Malcolm Dome and Jerry Ewing

All The Young Dudes: Mott The Hoople & Ian Hunter
Campbell Devine

Good Times Bad Times - The Rolling Stones 1960-69
Terry Rawlings and Keith Badman

The Rolling Stones: Complete Recording Sessions 1962-2002
Martin Elliott

Embryo - A Pink Floyd Chronology 1966-1971
Nick Hodges And Ian Priston

Those Were The Days - The Beatles' Apple Organization
Stefan Grenados

The Legendary Joe Meek - The Telstar Man
John Repsch

Truth... Rod Steward, Ron Wood And The Jeff Beck Group
Dave Thompson

Our Music Is Red - With Purple Flashes: The Story Of The Creation
Sean Egan

Quite Naturally - The Small Faces
Keith Badman and Terry Rawlings

Irish Folk, Trad And Blues: A Secret History
Colin Harper and Trevor Hodgett

Number One Songs In Heaven - The Sparks Story
Dave Thompson

A Plugged In State Of Mind – The History Of Electronic Music
Dave Henderson

Kiss Me Neck – The Lee 'Scratch' Perry Story in Words, Pictures and Records
Jeremy Collingwood

Random Precision - Recording The Music Of Syd Barrett 1965-1974
David Parker

Bittersweet: The Clifford T Ward Story
David Cartwright

Children of the Revolution – Glam Rock 1970-75
Dave Thompson

PWL: From The Factory Floor
Phil Harding

Goodnight Jim Bob - On The Road With Carter Usm
Jim Bob

Tamla Motown - The Stories Behind The Singles
Terry Wilson

Block Buster! – The True Story of The Sweet
Dave Thompson

Independence Days - The Story Of UK Independent Record Labels
Alex Ogg

Indie Hits 1980 – 1989
Barry Lazell

No More Heroes: A Complete History Of UK Punk From 1976 To 1980
Alex Ogg

Rockdetector: A To Zs of '80s Rock / Black Metal / Death Metal /Doom, Gothic & Stoner Metal / Power Metal
Garry Sharpe-Young

Rockdetector: Black Sabbath - Never Say Die
Garry Sharpe-Young

Rockdetector: Ozzy Osbourne
Garry Sharpe-Young

The Motorhead Collector's Guide
Mick Stevenson

Fucked By Rock (Revised and Expanded)/ I Have The Greatest Respect For You, George
Mark Manning

The Day The Country Died: A History Of Anarcho Punk 1980 To 1984
Ian Glasper

Burning Britain - A History Of UK Punk 1980 To 1984
Ian Glasper

Trapped In A Scene - UK Hardcore 1985-89
Ian Glasper

The Secret Life Of A Teenage Punk Rocker: The Andy Blade Chronicles
Andy Blade

Best Seat In The House – A Cock Sparrer Story
Steve Bruce

Death To Trad Rock – The Post-Punk fanzine scene 1982-87
John Robb

Johnny Thunders - In Cold Blood
Nina Antonia

Deathrow: The Chronicles Of Psychobilly
Alan Wilson

Hells Bent On Rockin: A History Of Psychobilly
Craig Brackenbridge

Music To Die For – The International Guide To Goth, Goth Metal, Horror Punk, Psychobilly Etc
Mick Mercer

Please visit www.cherryredbooks.co.uk for further info and mail order

CHERRY RED BOOKS

Here at Cherry Red Books we're always interested to hear of interesting titles looking for a publisher. Whether it's a new manuscript or an out of print or deleted title, please feel free to get in touch if you have something you think we should know about.

books@cherryred.co.uk

www.cherryredbooks.co.uk
www.cherryred.co.uk

CHERRY RED BOOKS
A division of Cherry Red Records Ltd,
Power Road Studios
114 Power Road
London
W4 5PY

THE AUTHOR

Mark has been a consultant to major UK record labels on Progressive, Psychedelic and Classic Rock reissues since the late 1990s, working extensively with major record companies such as Universal Music, EMI Records and Sony Music Entertainment on over two hundred projects.

He has worked with Barclay James Harvest, Jack Bruce, Caravan, Emerson Lake and Palmer, Peter Hammill, The Moody Blues, Mike Oldfield and Van Der Graaf Generator among others, and has also been label manager of Esoteric Recordings and Atomhenge since 2007.

Mark has also worked on tours and concerts throughout the world with acts such as John Lees' Barclay James Harvest, Caravan, Curved Air and Nektar, and has featured as a contributor and consultant to radio and TV shows such as "Freak Zone" (BBC 6 Music) and the documentary "Prog Britannia" (BBC TV). As a freelance feature writer he has interviewed many internationally acclaimed musicians and written numerous reviews for a variety of publications.

He is married with one son; his family continuing to endure the strange and esoteric sounds that emanate from his office on a daily basis.